D1592023

ADVANCED TOPICS IN FORENSIC DNA TYPING

This work was funded in part by the National Institute of Justice (NIJ) through an interagency agreement with the NIST Law Enforcement Standards Office. Points of view in this document are those of the author and do not necessarily represent the official position or policies of the U.S. Department of Justice or the National Institute of Standards and Technology. Certain commercial equipment, instruments, and materials are identified in order to specify experimental procedures as completely as possible. In no case does such identification imply a recommendation or endorsement by the National Institute of Standards and Technology, nor does it imply that any of the materials, instruments, or equipment identified are necessarily the best available for the purpose.

ADVANCED TOPICS IN FORENSIC DNA TYPING: INTERPRETATION

JOHN M. BUTLER

National Institute of Standards and Technology
Gaithersburg, Maryland, USA

AMSTERDAM • BOSTON • HEIDELBERG • LONDON • NEW YORK
OXFORD • PARIS • SAN DIEGO • SAN FRANCISCO
SINGAPORE • SYDNEY • TOKYO
Academic Press is an imprint of Elsevier

Academic Press is an imprint of Elsevier
The Boulevard, Langford Lane, Kidlington, Oxford, OX5 1GB
525 B Street, Suite 1800, San Diego, CA 92101-4495, USA

Contribution of the National Institute of Standards and Technology 2015 Published by Elsevier Inc.

Notices
Knowledge and best practice in this field are constantly changing. As new research and experience broaden our understanding, changes in research methods, professional practices, or medical treatment may become necessary.

Practitioners and researchers must always rely on their own experience and knowledge in evaluating and using any information, methods, compounds, or experiments described herein. In using such information or methods they should be mindful of their own safety and the safety of others, including parties for whom they have a professional responsibility.

To the fullest extent of the law, neither the Publisher nor the authors, contributors, or editors, assume any liability for any injury and/or damage to persons or property as a matter of products liability, negligence or otherwise, or from any use or operation of any methods, products, instructions, or ideas contained in the material herein.

British Library Cataloguing in Publication Data
A catalogue record for this book is available from the British Library

Library of Congress Cataloging-in-Publication Data
A catalog record for this book is available from the Library of Congress

ISBN: 978-0-12-405213-0

For information on all Academic Press publications
visit our website at store.elsevier.com

Printed in the United States of America
Last digit is the print number: 10 9 8 7 6 5 4 3 2

Working together
to grow libraries in
developing countries

ELSEVIER   Book Aid International

www.elsevier.com • www.bookaid.org

Dedication

To my parents Doug and Marsha Butler
who instilled in me an important worldview of education and service
by which I interpret everything around me
and to Bruce Budowle
who helped me to become a better writer when I was a graduate student
and since then has challenged me to become a better scientist and a better man.

Contents

I

DATA INTERPRETATION

II

STATISTICAL INTERPRETATION

Foreword

Another book from the prolific writings of John Butler that keeps pace with the rapidly changing world of DNA profiling in forensic science — it reminds me of the "Red Queen's Race" in Lewis Carroll's *Alice Through the Looking-Glass*: "...it takes all the running you can do, to keep in the same place. If you want to get somewhere else, you must run at least twice as fast as that!" Over the past few years there have been major changes in DNA profiling technology and interpretation. The introduction of more sensitive instrumentation, coupled with the introduction of modern multiplexed loci from the manufacturers that employ up to 24 loci with new biochemistry and detection platforms, also realizes the dream of approaching the ultimate in sensitivity — it is almost a matter of routine to detect DNA profiles from a handful of cells. Such advances are not without significant challenges, particularly in the area of interpretation of the evidence. Fortunately there have been significant advances in this area too, although the complete adoption by the community is yet to be realized.

The book is divided into 16 chapters and 4 appendices that describe the "state of the art" and beyond. Starting with an overview of data interpretation, subsequent chapters lead onto a discussion of the characterization of DNA profiles in terms of heterozygote balance, stutter, artifacts, and mutation and stochastic effects. There is an introduction to the phenomenon of allele drop-out, a characteristic of low-template DNA that results in "false homozygotes." To interpret DNA profiles, a system of thresholds (e.g. stochastic threshold, stutter threshold, limit of detection) has evolved. However, there are limitations and risks to consider. There is an extensive discussion on the deliberation of the scientific societies that is linked to an outline of the steps to interpret mixtures, before moving onto challenging "complex DNA profiles," i.e. those profiles that are mixtures of two or more contributors, where allele drop-out, secondary transfer, and contamination are additional complications. There has been a fundamental shift by the forensic community towards the analysis of these kinds of profiles. In one laboratory we are informed that the proportion of submissions of samples with <100 pg DNA has increased from 19% in 2004 to 45% in 2008. Chapters 9—13 are devoted to the interpretation of evidence complemented by Appendix 1, which has a complete list of STR loci used in the U.S. and their respective allele frequencies. There is a comprehensive review of statistical theory and methods — this leads to a complete description of various programmed solutions that have recently evolved to interpret "complex DNA profiles." Appendix 4 has a worked example, concisely written by Mike Coble, that further explains the rationale, theory, and benefits of the practical use of probabilistic methods. The reader is able to use the book as a handy one-stop guide to everything that is currently available (and where to find out more information).

Chapter 14 turns to relationship testing, providing an outline of the theory, a summary of recommendations from the scientific societies, a list of available software, along with an outline of the use of high-density SNP arrays to identify distant relationships. The penultimate Chapter 15 deals with lineage markers, including mitochondrial DNA, and Y-chromosomal and X-chromosomal DNA.

These markers are useful in missing persons, disaster victim identification, and other complex inquires.

Finally, Chapter 16 explores the most contentious area in forensic science, namely, the interpretation of the evidence. It isn't just the fact of the DNA profile to consider. With the introduction of methods that are ever more sensitive, the focus turns to *how* and *when* the DNA profile was transferred. Is it possible that a contamination event, or secondary transfer is possible? How can cognitive (psychological) bias be avoided in reporting? A useful way to think about evidence is described by the "hierarchy of propositions" — can we ascribe a "source," such as blood, or an "activity," such as stabbing, to the DNA profiling evidence? To prepare this chapter, John Butler has consulted widely with practitioners, gathering their views, cross-referenced to historical and recent deliberations of the scientific societies and advisory boards (Appendices 2 and 3), distilling the information into a treatise on how to write a report for the court.

This book complements John Butler's previous works with the most comprehensive and up-to-date text of its kind. As such, it will readily be adopted by the forensic community as the definitive guide to the galaxy of forensic DNA-typing technologies.

Peter Gill, Ph.D.
April 2014

Introduction

The third edition of *Forensic DNA Typing* has been divided up into three volumes: a basic volume for students and beginners in the field and two advanced volumes for professionals/ practitioners who may be interested in more detail. The basic volume was released in September 2009 (with a publication date of 2010) and is entitled *Fundamentals of Forensic DNA Typing*. The first advanced volume, *Advanced Topics in Forensic DNA Typing: Methodology*, was released in August 2011 (with a 2012 publication date). The present book, *Advanced Topics in Forensic DNA Typing: Interpretation*, is intended as volume 3 of the third edition, with a focus on data interpretation and statistical analysis.

Several reasons exist for dividing the material. First and foremost, people use books more frequently if they are less bulky. I have heard from more than one colleague at conferences that they prefer to carry the smaller first edition with them to court or other teaching situations. Second, by having multiple books, each volume can be focused on its intended audience rather than trying to be all things to all readers. Third, the books will enable both undergraduate and graduate studies, with each building upon the previous volumes.

There is only minor overlap in subject matter among the various volumes. The basic *Fundamentals* volume contains the simpler "starter" information, while most of the "updates" to the field are found in the *Advanced Topics* volumes. It is my intention that the three volumes together provide a comprehensive view of the current state of forensic DNA analysis. With a field advancing as rapidly as forensic DNA typing is, this is a challenge.

The present book has been divided into two primary sections: data interpretation (Chapters 1–8) and statistical interpretation and reporting (Chapters 9–16). The first part covers data analysis and factors impacting a DNA profile, while the second part examines evidence evaluation and interpretation – essentially what information exists in a DNA profile and what does this information mean in the context of variability expected from the DNA results obtained. In this edition, I again utilize **D**ata, **N**otes, and **A**pplications (D.N.A.) Boxes to cover specific topics of general interest, to review example calculations, or to cover a topic that serves to highlight information needed by a DNA analyst.

NEW MATERIAL IN THIS VOLUME

Advanced Topics in Forensic DNA Typing: Interpretation is substantially enhanced with additional information beyond what was available in the second edition of *Forensic DNA Typing*, which was completed in June 2004. Much has happened to advance our understanding of DNA evidence interpretation in the past decade.

I am grateful to have had three years between writing the *Methodology* and this *Interpretation* volume. During this additional time, I have learned a great deal as I have responded to numerous questions from forensic scientists around the world via email or in person. I have also had the privilege of preparing and presenting hundreds of slides on DNA mixture interpretation. Materials from these training workshops are available at the NIST website (NIST 2014a). In addition, recent publications have provided new research and perspectives on DNA interpretation. For example, the International Society for Forensic Genetics DNA Commission published recommendations on DNA mixtures and probabilistic approaches in the December 2012 issue of *Forensic Science International: Genetics*.

As with previous books, a fairly comprehensive list of references is included at the end of each chapter that serves as a foundation for citations in the chapter as well as a launching point where interested readers can go for additional information. More than 2,000 references are provided, enabling readers to expand their study beyond the information contained between the covers of this book. References to journal articles include titles to enhance value.

More than 80% of this book is completely new. Figures, tables, and D.N.A. Boxes have been created (>200 in total) to help illustrate the principles being taught. Since I do not now write or review laboratory reports, I sought and received valuable input from more than a dozen laboratory analysts, laboratory directors, police investigators, lawyers (prosecution and defense), and private consultants who regularly review laboratory reports. Their collective wisdom and insights are captured in Chapter 16. Numerous others have contributed to information contained in this volume, and their input is gratefully appreciated and acknowledged.

Throughout this book I have prepared teaching examples with the STR locus D18S51, which is one of the original U.S. core markers and also is used in Europe, China, Australia, and elsewhere around the world. I have endeavored to mind my Ps and Qs in using a consistent allele nomenclature in statistical equations. In some areas, material in this book may not be as advanced as readers might like. There is, however, enough information to help provide a bridge to more detailed work already available or soon to be available from authors like John Buckleton and Peter Gill.

At points throughout the text, I quote from the 2010 SWGDAM Interpretation Guidelines for Autosomal STR Typing by Forensic DNA Testing Laboratories. Although I chaired the group that prepared these guidelines, the opinions expressed in this book are mine alone and in no way should be thought of as the official opinion of SWGDAM or the SWGDAM Autosomal STR Interpretation Committee.

OVERVIEW OF BOOK CHAPTERS

Chapters 1 to 8 cover data interpretation. Chapter 1 provides an overview and perspective on principles, protocols, and practice in an effort to understand the "why," "what," and "how" of forensic DNA typing. Autosomal and Y-chromosome STR loci and kits are reviewed. Chapter 2 describes data generation by the Applied Biosystems Genetic Analyzers as well as introducing the role of statistical models in setting thresholds such as the analytical threshold. Chapter 3 covers issues surrounding measurement of STR alleles and distinguishing alleles from artifacts such as stutter products. Chapter 4 reviews peak height ratios (heterozygote balance) and null alleles that can impact STR genotypes. Stochastic thresholds and allele drop-out are introduced. Chapter 5 focuses on evaluation of multi-locus STR profiles, tri-allelic patterns, and issues with amelogenin as a sex-typing marker. Chapter 6 considers DNA mixtures and steps for interpreting them, including determining the number of contributors. Chapter 7 explores complex DNA mixture issues, including allele sharing and allele drop-out due to low-level DNA contributors. Chapter 8 seeks to inform readers regarding principles and processes involved with capillary electrophoresis so that high-quality data may be obtained and common problems avoided. It discusses how troubleshooting improves as close attention is paid to details in the laboratory data produced.

Chapters 9 to 16 involve statistical interpretation and reporting. Chapter 9 introduces the role of statistics in forensic DNA analysis with a review of the individuals who have influenced the field. The laws of probability are introduced along with likelihood ratios and Bayesian versus frequentist approaches to statistics. Chapter 10 describes principles of population genetics and how population data are used to estimate STR profile frequencies. Chapter 11 covers approaches and assumptions made with generating STR profile frequency estimates. Chapter 12 involves DNA mixture statistics and contrasts combined probability of inclusion methods with likelihood ratio calculations. Chapter 13 deals with situations where allele drop-out from stochastic effects with low-level DNA present challenges in comparing evidentiary profiles to reference profiles. Chapter 14 reviews kinship analysis used in relationship testing. Paternity testing, mutations, and disaster victim identification are among the topics discussed. Chapter 15 addresses Y-chromosome, X-chromosome, and mitochondrial DNA lineage markers and how their different genetic transmission influences statistical interpretation of results. Finally, Chapter 16 covers laboratory reports and the importance of effectively communicating results and conclusions. Input from more than a dozen laboratory report providers and users enhanced this material.

Appendices

There are four appendices at the back of the book that provide helpful supplemental material:

- Appendix 1 provides U.S. population data in the form of STR allele frequencies based on studies performed at NIST. This information is utilized in worked examples throughout the book.
- Appendix 2 lists the recommendations made by both National Research Council reports (NRC I and NRC II) in their 1992 and 1996 publications entitled "DNA Technology in Forensic Science" and "The Evaluation of Forensic DNA Evidence."
- Appendix 3 contains the FBI's DNA Advisory Board recommendations on statistics that were released in February 2000 to provide a historical perspective.
- Appendix 4 is a DNA mixture example prepared by Dr. Mike Coble, a valued colleague within the Applied Genetics Group at the National Institute of Standards and Technology.

A brief "cross-walk" of major topics covered across the various editions of *Forensic DNA Typing* is shown in Table I.1 with chapters (Ch.) and appendices (App.) indicated. In a few cases, information was limited to a single D.N.A. Box.

In my *Interpretation* book, I have included information from the latest articles as well as insights I have gained over the past two decades of working in the field. Writing these books on forensic DNA typing has been richly rewarding as I must carefully think through each issue and decide how to best address it. As David McCullough points out in the quote at the beginning of this

TABLE I.1 "Cross-Walk" of Major Topics

Topic	1st edition (2001)	2nd edition (2005)	3rd edition, volume 1 *Fundamentals* (2010)	3rd edition, volume 2 Advanced Topics: *Methodology* (2012)	3rd edition, volume 3 Advanced Topics: *Interpretation* (2015)
Amelogenin	Ch. 5	Ch. 5	Ch. 8	Ch. 5	Ch. 5
Capillary electrophoresis	Ch. 9 & 11	Ch. 12 & 14	Ch. 9	Ch. 6	Ch. 8
Data interpretation	Ch. 6 & 13	Ch. 6 & 15	Ch. 10	–	Ch.1–8
Disaster victim identification	Ch. 17	Ch. 24	Ch. 17	Ch. 9	Ch. 14
DNA basics	Ch. 2	Ch. 2	Ch. 2	–	–
DNA databases	Ch. 16	Ch. 18	Ch. 12	Ch. 8	–
DNA extraction	Ch. 3	Ch. 3	Ch. 5	Ch. 2	–
DNA quantitation	Ch. 3	Ch. 3	Ch. 6	Ch. 3	–
Expert witness testimony	–	–	–	Ch. 18, App. 4	–
Familial searching	–	–	Ch. 12 (p. 282)	App. 2	D.N.A. Box 14.9
FBI Quality Assurance Standards	App. 3 (1998/99)	App. 4 (1998/99)	–	–	–
FMBIO gel imaging system	Ch. 12	Ch. 14	D.N.A. Box 9.2	–	–
Glossary	–	–	App. 1	–	–
History of DNA	Ch. 1	Ch. 1	Ch. 1 & 3	–	–
Kinship analysis	–	Ch. 23	Ch. 17	–	Ch. 14
Low copy number DNA testing	–	Ch. 7	Ch. 14	Ch. 11	Ch. 7
Match probability calculations	–	Ch. 21	Ch. 11	–	Ch. 11
Mixtures	Ch. 7	Ch. 7	Ch. 14	–	Ch. 6 & 7, App. 4
Mixture statistics	–	Ch. 22	D.N.A. Box 14.2	–	Ch. 12 & 13
Mitochondrial DNA	Ch. 8	Ch. 10	Ch. 16	Ch. 14	Ch. 15
New technologies	Ch. 15	Ch. 17	Ch. 18	Ch. 17	–
Non-human DNA	Ch. 8	Ch. 11	Ch. 15	Ch. 16	–
Null alleles	Ch. 6	Ch. 6	D.N.A. Box 10.3	Ch. 5	Ch. 4
PCR	Ch. 4	Ch. 4	Ch. 7	Ch. 4	–

TABLE I.1 "Cross-Walk" of Major Topics (cont'd)

Topic	1st edition (2001)	2nd edition (2005)	3rd edition, volume 1 _Fundamentals_ (2010)	3rd edition, volume 2 **Advanced Topics:** _Methodology_ (2012)	3rd edition, volume 3 **Advanced Topics:** _Interpretation_ (2015)
Population data	—	Ch. 20	Ch. 11	—	Ch. 10
Report writing	—	—	—	—	Ch. 16
Sample collection	Ch. 3	Ch. 3	Ch. 4	Ch. 1	—
SNP testing	Ch. 8	Ch. 8	Ch. 15	Ch. 12	—
Statistics & probability	—	Ch. 19	App. 3	—	Ch. 9
STR alleles	App. 1	App. 1	—	App. 1	Ch. 3
STR kits	Ch. 5	Ch. 5	Ch. 8	Ch. 5	Ch. 1
STR markers	Ch. 5	Ch. 5	Ch. 8	Ch. 5	Ch. 1
Stutter products	Ch. 6	Ch. 6	Ch. 10	—	Ch. 3
Thresholds	—	—	Ch. 10	—	Ch. 2
Tri-allelic patterns	Ch. 6	Ch. 6	D.N.A. Box 10.2	—	Ch. 5
Validation	Ch. 14	Ch. 16	Ch. 13	Ch. 7	Ch. 5
Variant alleles	Ch. 6	Ch. 6	D.N.A. Box 10.1	App. 1	Ch. 3
X-STRs	—	—	—	Ch. 15	Ch. 15
Y-STRs	Ch. 8	Ch. 9	Ch. 16	Ch. 13	Ch. 15

Introduction, writing is hard work. This hard work has been beneficial to my personal learning but comes at the price of significant time away from my family and other responsibilities. I am grateful for the support of others, especially my wife, who have permitted me the time needed to complete this book.

My father, Doug Butler, has written about a dozen textbooks and spent his career teaching and helping to shape his profession. He is an amazing teacher because of his dedication to learning and excelling at the highest level. Recently when I told him some of the things I was learning while working on this book and other presentations that I was giving to the forensic DNA community, he shared an important lesson: "You never really learn anything until you have to teach it to someone else." While I hope the information in this book helps the field, I know that I have been the main beneficiary of this effort in terms of what I have learned during the process of trying to teach the concepts to others.

The pressure to carefully craft each phrase so that my words are less likely to be misunderstood has increased with the widespread use of my books, particularly in courts of law. I do not take lightly the opportunity to share my thoughts and perspective in this book. While I have benefited from discussions and input from many people, I alone am responsible for the content. My goal in preparing training materials on the topic of forensic DNA has always been to be on the side of good science that is well-documented and appropriately applied to benefit the forensic science community. I hope that this book contributes to that goal.

References

National Endowment for the Arts (NEA). Awards & Honors, 2003 Jefferson Lecturer. http://www.neh.gov/about/awards/jefferson-lecture/david-mccullough-interview. Accessed Apirl 2, 2014.

NIST (2014a). *DNA Mixture Interpretation.* http://www.cstl.nist.gov/strbase/mixture.htm. Accessed Apirl 2, 2014.

Acknowledgments

I express a special thanks to colleagues and fellow researchers who kindly provided important information and supplied some of the figures for this book or previous editions of *Forensic DNA Typing*. The list continues to grow. These individuals include Ricky Ansell, Michael Baird, Susan Ballou, Brad Bannon, Leslie Biesecker, Martin Bill, Erica Butts, Lisa Calandro, Theresa Caragine, George Carmody, Ranajit Chakraborty, Tim Clayton, Mike Coble, Robin Cotton, Cecelia Crouse, Amy Decker, Christopher Duby, David Duewer, Dan Ehrlich, Nicky Fildes, Lisa Forman, Ron Fourney, Lee Fraser, Dave Gillespie, Catherine Grgicak, Richard Guerrieri, Ravi Gupta, Chip Harding, Doug Hares, Bruce Heidebrecht, Mary Herdman, Becky Hill, Debbie Hobson, Bill Hudlow, Ted Hunt, Alice Isenberg, Dennis Kilcoyne, Margaret Kline, Sonja Klein, Ken Konzak, Carll Ladd, Steve Lee, Dina Mattes, Bruce McCord, Terry Melton, Ruth Montgomery, Niels Morling, Steven Myers, Steve Niezgoda, Kristen Lewis O'Connor, Antonio Possolo, Mecki Prinz, George Riley, Norah Rudin, Jeff Sailus, Thomas Schnibbe, Richard Schoske, Jim Schumm, Scott Scoville (and the Orange County DA's DNA Unit), Bob Shaler, Michelle Shepherd, Gary Sims, Melissa Smrz, Amanda Sozer, Jill Spriggs, Mark Stolorow, Kevin Sullivan, Lois Tully, Pete Vallone, Ray Wickenheiser, and Charlotte Word.

I am indebted to the dedicated human identity project team members, past and present, who have worked with me at the National Institute of Standards and Technology: Jill Appleby, Erica Butts, Mike Coble, Amy Decker, David Duewer, Becky Hill, Kevin Kiesler, Margaret Kline, Kristen Lewis O'Connor, Jan Redman, Dennis Reeder, Patti Rohmiller, Christian Ruitberg, Richard Schoske, and Pete Vallone. It has been a pleasure to work with such supportive and hard-working scientists. Since I moved into a new role at NIST in April 2013, I miss the daily interaction with the Applied Genetics Group.

Several other people deserve specific recognition for their support of this endeavor. The information reported in this book was in large measure made possible by a comprehensive collection of references on the STR markers used in forensic DNA typing. For this collection, now numbering more than 3,500 references, I am indebted to the initial work of Christian Ruitberg for tirelessly collecting and cataloging these papers and the steady efforts first of Jan Redman and then Patti Rohmiller to regularly update this STR reference database. A complete listing of these references may be found at the NIST website (NIST 2014b).

My wife Terilynne, who carefully reviewed the manuscript and made helpful suggestions, was always a constant support in the many hours that this project took away from our family. As the initial editor of all my written materials, Terilynne helped make the book more coherent and readable. In addition, David Duewer and Katherine Sharpless provided a fine technical review of my two previous books as well as this one. The support of NIST management, especially Laurie Locascio, Mike Tarlov, Richard Cavanagh, and Willie May, made completion of this book possible.

Reference

NIST (2014b). *STRs and DNA Typing.* http://www.cstl.nist.gov/strbase/str_ref.htm. Accessed April 2, 2014.

About the Author

John Marshall Butler grew up in the U.S. Midwest and, enjoying science and law, decided to pursue a career in forensic science at an early age. After completing an undergraduate education at Brigham Young University in chemistry, he moved east to pursue graduate studies at the University of Virginia. While a graduate student, he enjoyed the unique opportunity of serving as an FBI Honors Intern and guest researcher for more than two years in the FBI Laboratory's Forensic Science Research Unit. His Ph.D. dissertation research, which was conducted at the FBI Academy in Quantico, Virginia, involved pioneering work in applying capillary electrophoresis to STR typing. After completing his Ph.D. in 1995, Dr. Butler obtained a prestigious National Research Council post-doctoral fellowship to the National Institute of Standards and Technology (NIST). While a postdoc at NIST, he designed and built STRBase, the widely used Short Tandem Repeat Internet Database (STRBase 2014) that contains a wealth of standardized information on STRs used in human identity applications. He worked for several years as a staff scientist and project leader at a California startup company named GeneTrace System developing rapid DNA analysis technologies involving time-of-flight mass spectrometry. In the fall of 1999, he returned to NIST to lead their efforts in human identity testing with funding from the National Institute of Justice. He served as leader of the Applied Genetics Group from 2008 to 2013.

Dr. Butler is a NIST Fellow and Special Assistant to the Director for Forensic Science. He is a regular invited guest of the FBI's Scientific Working Group on DNA Analysis Methods (SWGDAM) and served for many years on the Department of Defense Quality Assurance Oversight Committee for DNA Analysis. Following the terrorist attacks of 11 September 2001, he aided the DNA identification efforts and served as part of the distinguished World Trade Center Kinship and Data Analysis Panel (WTC KADAP). He is a member of the International Society of Forensic Genetics and the American Academy of Forensic Sciences. Dr. Butler serves as an Associate Editor for *Forensic Science International: Genetics* and is on the editorial board for the *Journal of Forensic Sciences*.

Dr. Butler has received numerous awards, including the Presidential Early Career Award for Scientists and Engineers (2002), the Department of Commerce Silver Medal (2002) and Gold Medal (2008), the Arthur S. Flemming Award (2007), the Edward Uhler Condon Award (2010), Brigham Young University's College of Physical and Mathematical Sciences Honored Alumnus (2005), and the Scientific Prize of the International Society of Forensic Genetics (2003).

He has more than 150 publications describing aspects of forensic DNA testing and is one of the most prolific active authors in the field, with articles appearing regularly in every major forensic science journal. In 2011, *ScienceWatch*, which monitors the number of citations by other scientists that authors receive for their research work, reported that Dr. Butler was the #1 world-wide high-impact author in legal medicine and forensic science over the decade of 2001–2011.

Dr. Butler has been an invited speaker to numerous national and international forensic DNA meetings and in the past few years has spoken in Argentina, Australia, Austria, Belgium, Brazil, Canada,

China, Cyprus, Denmark, England, France, Germany, Israel, Japan, Korea, Mexico, The Netherlands, Poland, Portugal, Sweden, and Taiwan. Much of the content in this book has come from the NIST Applied Group's research efforts over the past two decades. In addition to his busy scientific career, he and his wife serve in their community and church and are the proud parents of six children, all of whom have been proven to be theirs through the power of DNA typing.

Reference

STRBase (2014). http://www.cstl.nist.gov/strbase. Accessed April 2, 2014.

DATA INTERPRETATION

CHAPTER

1

Data Interpretation Overview

"We see the world, not as it is, but as we are — or, as we are conditioned to see it."
Stephen R. Covey (The 7 Habits of Highly Effective People, p. 28)

PURPOSE OF THIS BOOK

This book is primarily intended for DNA analysts or those trying to understand what a DNA analyst does in his or her review of forensic DNA data that was obtained by polymerase chain reaction (PCR) amplification and short tandem repeat (STR) typing via capillary electrophoresis (CE). A DNA analyst, according to the FBI Quality Assurance Standards (QAS) that govern U.S. laboratories, is an individual who "conducts and/or directs the analysis of forensic samples, interprets data and reaches conclusions" (QAS 2011, definitions). Many laboratories employ technicians to perform the analytical techniques required to obtain a DNA profile from a biological sample — typically under the supervision of a trained and qualified analyst. However, as noted by the QAS, "technicians do not interpret data, reach conclusions on typing results, or prepare final reports" (QAS 2011, definitions). Thus, there is an expectation that DNA analyst training involves developing an understanding and mastery of data interpretation as well as report writing and statistical analysis used in reaching conclusions on typing results.

The general steps and workflow involved in forensic DNA typing are illustrated in Figure 1.1. The companion volume to this book entitled *Advanced Topics in Forensic DNA Typing: Methodology*

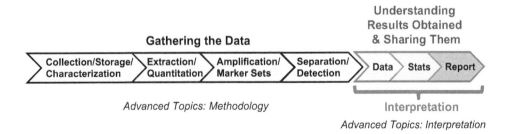

FIGURE 1.1 Steps involved in the overall process of forensic DNA typing. This book focuses on understanding the data through data interpretation and statistical interpretation.

Advanced Topics in Forensic DNA Typing: Interpretation
http://dx.doi.org/10.1016/B978-0-12-405213-0.00001-4

(Butler 2012) covered many aspects of gathering the data used in DNA testing. Picking up where that book left off, the purpose of this book, *Advanced Topics in Forensic DNA Typing: Interpretation*, is to help readers understand data obtained from the STR typing process, with a focus on interpreting and reporting results. Data interpretation is covered in Chapters 1 through 8 where we address the question, "What are the data obtained from a set of samples?" Statistical interpretation is reviewed in Chapters 9 through 15 to help discuss, "How significant are the data?" Chapter 16 focuses on drawing conclusions and report writing to assess, "What do the data mean when comparisons are made between evidentiary and reference sample results?"

Everyone may think that their way of DNA analysis is correct. However, misinterpretations of some fundamental principles have given rise to a variety of approaches being undertaken in labs today, some of which are not optimal, or even border on being incorrect for certain scenarios of use. Unfortunately, often times the approaches taken for interpretation are subjective, and therefore become the weakest part of the overall DNA typing process. I have written this book because I believe that a better understanding of fundamental principles will aid consistency and quality of work being performed in forensic DNA laboratories around the world.

In February 2009, the U.S. National Academy of Sciences released a report entitled "Strengthening Forensic Science in the United States" (NAS 2009). The report emphasized that good (forensic) science includes: (1) valid and reliable methodologies, and (2) practices that minimize the threat of bias in data interpretation. My *Methodology* volume demonstrates that valid and reliable methodologies can be achieved with forensic DNA typing. This *Interpretation* volume seeks to help minimize the threat of bias in data interpretation.

Good science takes time and effort to do well. It is worth noting that some measurements and interpretations are more reliable than others. Hence, uncertainty in measurements and interpretation should be reflected in the reports generated in a forensic case investigation. As will be described throughout this book, it is important that assumptions made during the interpretation process be documented and conveyed as clearly as possible. This documentation will aid those individuals reviewing the lab report to appropriately assess the results obtained and the conclusions drawn. It is important for analysts to offer what they know from the data obtained in a case in a fashion that is as clear and unbiased as possible.

That being said, I recognize that there are two areas of forensic DNA interpretations that are particularly challenging: (1) low-level DNA samples where *sensitivity* is an issue, and (2) complex mixtures where *specificity* is an issue. In other words, how much DNA is needed to obtain a reliable result and how well can the number of contributors to a sample be estimated to limit the uncertainty or ambiguity in the conclusions drawn. Chapters 7 and 13 will discuss some potential approaches to handling difficult interpretations. Unfortunately, in many situations involving complex results where uncertainty in the interpretation is large, the only scientifically responsible conclusion is "inconclusive" to avoid the chance of inappropriately including or excluding a potential contributor from an evidentiary result.

THE INTERPRETATION PROCESS

If the companion volume entitled *Advanced Topics in Forensic DNA Typing: Methodology* begins with an evidentiary biological sample from a crime scene, then this book begins with a computer file. This computer file contains data points corresponding to time and fluorescence intensity at various wavelengths of light that represent the digital signature of a DNA profile. When these data points are plotted with time on the x-axis and fluorescence intensity on the y-axis, an electropherogram is created. This electropherogram, sometimes referred to as an EPG or e-gram, is then evaluated using STR genotyping software to produce a final results table representing the biological sample's DNA profile.

An overview of the components and processes involved in data interpretation are illustrated in Figure 1.2. A sample data file contains time and fluorescence information for a PCR-amplified sample along with an internal size standard. The sample data file, which has a file extension of .fsa or .hid, is loaded into genotyping software along with an allelic ladder data file containing the same internal size standard to enable the sample and allelic ladder results to be correlated. Along with the allelic ladder sample, STR kit manufacturers provide a computer file specific for each STR kit containing *bins* (that define the allele repeat number for each STR locus) and *panels* (that define the STR loci present in the kit). When combined with the allelic ladder data file, bins and panels provide genotyping software with the capability to transform DNA size information into an STR allele repeat number for each observed peak.

Laboratory Protocols to Aid Interpretation

Laboratory protocols, which are often referred to as standard operating procedures (SOPs), are step-by-step instructions used to provide a consistent framework to gather and interpret information from analyzed samples. As part of a quality assurance system, accredited forensic laboratories will have written SOPs. Laboratory personnel are trained to understand and follow their laboratory-specific SOPs.

As will be described in more detail in Chapter 2, laboratories define parameters as part of their SOPs that act as thresholds within the genotyping software to filter information and aid analyst decisions that are made in determining the final sample DNA profile. These SOPs should be created based on validation data and then verified to work properly with control samples before being put into routine use.

A primary purpose of SOPs is to provide consistent results across DNA analysts within a laboratory as well as across cases analyzed by the same DNA analyst. The hope is that by following well-defined directions in a laboratory's SOP, the same result can be obtained on a particular DNA sample by *any* qualified analyst or data reviewer.

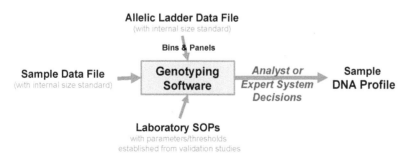

FIGURE 1.2 Overview of DNA interpretation process illustrating that sample data files, at least one allelic ladder data file, and information from laboratory SOPs are entered into genotyping software. Analysts (or expert system software) review the information from the software to produce the final sample DNA profile.

Decisions during Data Interpretation

An analyst must make decisions about whether electrophoretic data from an evidentiary or a reference sample represent peaks or noise, whether peaks are alleles or artifacts, whether alleles can be confidently paired to form genotypes, whether genotypes from individual loci can be combined to create a contributor profile, whether the data are too weak or too complex to be reliably interpreted, and if overall data quality is appropriate for obtaining reliable results. Table 1.1 correlates the discussion of further details on these decisions with the various chapters in the first half of this book.

A DNA profile produced from the evidentiary sample, often referred to as the question (Q) sample, is then compared to a reference, or known (K) sample, which must also undergo data analysis and the same interpretation decision process. Reference samples may come directly from a suspect or indirectly from a DNA database search of previous offenders. Fortunately, expert system software programs have been validated and implemented in many labs to help rapidly evaluate single-source samples (see Butler 2012, Table 8.4).

Following comparison of the Q and K sample profile results, conclusions are drawn regarding a potential match or not, and a report is written (see Chapter 16). If there is deemed to be a match (or some kind of kinship association) between the Q and K samples, then statistical interpretation is performed to estimate the weight-of-evidence. Chapters 9 through 15 describe approaches for statistical interpretation and issues involved. A summary of the steps and decisions in STR data interpretation are illustrated in Figure 1.3.

The DNA Profile Computer File

The computer file extension for a DNA result produced by an Applied Biosystems Genetic Analyzer will be either .fsa or .hid depending on the instrument used to collect data from separated components of PCR-amplified STR markers. The .fsa (fragment size analysis) files are produced with ABI 310, 3100, 3130, 3700, and 3730 series CE instruments, while the .hid (human identity) files are produced with ABI 3500 series CE systems.

TABLE 1.1   Information Flow in the Data Interpretation Process Correlated with Chapters in This Book

Chapter	Input Information	Decision to be made	How decision is made
2	Data file	Peak or Noise	Analytical threshold
3	Peak	Allele or Artifact	Stutter threshold; precision sizing bin
4	Allele	Heterozygote or Homozygote or Allele(s) missing	Peak heights and peak height ratios; stochastic threshold
5	Genotype/full profile	Single-source or Mixture	Numbers of peaks per locus
6	Mixture	Deconvolution or not	Major/minor mixture ratio
7	Low level DNA	Interpret or not	Complexity/uncertainty threshold
8	Poor quality data	Replace CE components (buffer, polymer, array) or call service engineer	Review size standard data quality with understanding of CE principles

Steps in DNA Interpretation

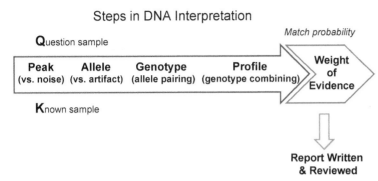

FIGURE 1.3 Steps in DNA interpretation. The evidentiary (Q) sample and reference (K) sample are processed from peaks to profile and then compared. If Q and K match, then a match probability is computed to assess the weight of this evidence. Finally, a report is written describing the results obtained. A separate technical review by another analyst in the originating laboratory is performed prior to the casework report being finalized and released by the laboratory.

As described in D.N.A. Box 1.1, the .fsa files are in a binary file format known as ABIF (Applied Biosystems, Inc. Format) and are similar to Tag Image File Format (TIFF), which has been used for graphics files (Applied Biosystems Genetic Analysis Data File Format 2009). Although we will focus on the electronic information used to create a DNA profile, it is worth noting that other diagnostic information, such as laser power and run current, is also stored in the computer file during data collection; this information can be helpful in troubleshooting efforts described in Chapter 8.

During the process of data analysis and genotyping, information from the .fsa or .hid data file is converted from time (scan) points to DNA size relative to an internal size standard and then to an STR allele call relative to STR typing kit-specific bins and panels and allelic ladders.

Software for Analysis of DNA Profile Computer Files

Sophisticated software has been developed to take sample electrophoretic data rapidly through the STR genotyping process (Ziegle et al. 1992). Life Technologies/Applied Biosystems (Foster City, CA), which manufactures the Genetic Analyzer CE instruments used in forensic DNA laboratories, supplies software for processing the .fsa or .hid files generated by their CE instruments. This software enables peaks to be defined and STR alleles designated using kit-specific allelic ladders and bins and panels. GeneScan and Genotyper software programs were used originally with early Mac and NT versions of data collection from the ABI 310 and 3100 series instruments. In more recent years, GeneMapper*ID* v3.2 and GeneMapper*ID-X* v1.1 or 1.2 have replaced GeneScan/Genotyper functions (in 2012, GeneMapper*ID-X* v1.4 expanded data analysis capabilities to 6-dyes).

GeneMarkerHID software (Holland & Parson 2011) from Soft Genetics (State College, PA) can also process .fsa and .hid files directly as can Cybergenetics' TrueAllele (Pittsburgh, PA; see also Kadash 2004) and Qualitype's GenoProof (Dresden, Germany). In addition, the National Center for Biotechnology Information (NCBI) has produced an open-source STR genotyping software program (Goor et al. 2011) called OSIRIS, which stands for Open Source Independent Review and Interpretation System (OSIRIS 2014).

D.N.A. BOX 1.1

WHAT INFORMATION IS STORED IN THE .FSA AND .HID DNA PROFILE COMPUTER FILE?

ABI 310, 3100, 3100-*Avant*, 3130, 3130xl, and 3730 Genetic Analyzer instruments (Life Technologies/Applied Biosystems, Foster City, CA) produce .fsa files during capillary electrophoresis data collection. ABI 3500 and 3500xl instruments produce .hid files for human identity applications and .fsa files for other applications. During analysis with the Applied Biosystems software GeneMapper*ID* and GeneMapper*ID-X* programs, the .fsa or .hid sample files are imported into an Oracle database along with allelic ladders and other controls for further analysis (Applied Biosystems 2003, 2004). These Gene-Mapper projects can be then be exported as .ser files (Java serialized file) for storage. While .fsa files can be read by all versions of GeneMapper*ID* and *ID-X*, the .hid files can only be read by GeneMapper*ID-X* v1.2 or above.

The .fsa files are written in a binary file format known as ABIF (Applied Biosystems, Inc. Format) and are similar to the TIFF files (Tag Image File Format) that are sometimes used for graphics files. Applied Biosystems has published various versions of their .fsa file format schema, most recently in September 2009, to enable other software developers to create products that can utilize Genetic Analyzer data. Unfortunately, the full details of their .hid file format have not yet been publicly released.

However, both .fsa and .hid files appear to consist of the same basic structure: (1) a header that points to (2) a directory of tags which then points via a file offset to (3) electrophoretic data. The electrophoretic data are collected by scan number (time) and fluorescence signal in specified dye-channels. In the developer toolkit on the Applied Biosystems website, a detailed description of the file tags are provided for (a) ABI 3100 and 3100-*Avant*, (b) ABI 3130 and 3130xl, (c) ABI 3500 and 3500xl, and (d) ABI 3730 and 3730xl

instruments. It appears that the .fsa data file structure has storage room for up to 99 different fluorescent dyes, so there is room to grow beyond the four, five, or even six dyes that STR kit chemistry currently provide! The .fsa file format has two sets of tags that point to the same electropherogram data, while the .hid format consists of four sets of tags − three essentially in .fsa format containing the same data, and a fourth set of tags that are proprietary to Applied Biosystems software for use in signal normalization. The fluorescence signal collected by the charged-coupled device (CCD) camera is stored in a 2-byte format-enabling signal to be collected between +32,767 and −32,767. Spectral calibration, known as "multi-componenting," is applied to enable color correction with a mathematical matrix involving the fluorescent dyes used.

With the introduction of the ABI 3500 and 3500xl Genetic Analyzers in 2010, the .fsa file format was replaced by .hid files. Initially these files could only be read by Applied Biosystems software GeneMapper*ID-X* v1.2 or higher. Now alternative genotyping software programs such as GeneMarkerHID (SoftGenetics, State College, PA), GenoProof (QualiType, Dresden, Germany), TrueAllele (Cybergenetics, Pittsburgh, PA), and OSIRIS (National Center for Biotechnology Information, Bethesda, MD) can process .hid file formats. The new .hid file format captures additional information in the sample file including the 3500 radio frequency identification (RFID) information used for instrument consumables, such as the polymer and buffer lot numbers. In addition, normalization capabilities exist with ABI 3500 .hid files. Normalization, which enables signal to be equalized between different ABI 3500 or 3500xl instruments, is performed by multiplying the data points by a factor calculated from the intensity of some of the internal size standard

---

peaks in the LIZ600v2 size standard. This feature is only available with ABI STR kits. With ABI 3500 .hid files, GeneMapper*ID-X* and other non-Applied Biosystems software programs show similar-sized peaks for data displayed without the 3500 normalization feature turned on. However, minor differences in relative fluorescence unit (RFU) peak heights may exist depending on

how programs perform baseline subtraction and other forms of signal processing.

Source: Applied Biosystems Genetic Analysis Data File Format, *Sept 2009 (available at http://www.appliedbiosystems. com/absite/us/en/home/support/software-community/tools-for-accessing-files.html); information shared by George Riley, Douglas Hoffman, and Robert Goor from OSIRIS development (see http:// www.ncbi.nlm.nih.gov/projects/SNP/osiris/)*

Data Processing and Analysis

Following the steps of DNA extraction, DNA quantitation, PCR amplification, and CE separation and detection of the STR alleles, a computer file becomes the electronic representation of the DNA information obtained from a crime scene (Q — question) or reference (K — known) biological sample. As noted previously, a trained DNA analyst using compatible software or a validated expert system software program then reviews the results following laboratory-established parameters (see Chapter 2).

The data collected and stored in the sample .fsa or .hid file is transformed from time and fluorescence intensity at specific wavelengths to size and peak height by dye color to STR allele and peak height by locus information (Figure 1.4). This information is then compiled for each individual locus

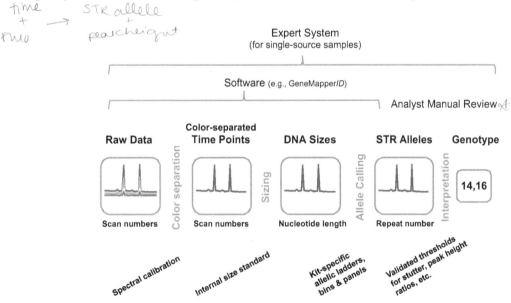

FIGURE 1.4 An example of the transformation of sample information that occurs at a single STR locus during the course of data interpretation. This same transformation occurs with all other STR loci that are PCR-amplified in a multiplex kit. Additional information (indicated across the bottom) helps convert the initial data through steps of color separation, sizing, and allele calling. An analyst must review the initial software results as part of the interpretation process. Expert system software can take a sample from raw data to genotype for high-quality, single-source samples.

to determine the overall STR profile representative of the original DNA template. Understanding each step facilitates the troubleshooting efforts that reviewed in Chapter 8.

Through calibration to an internal size standard run with every sample, data points measured in time (scan number) on the x-axis are converted to a relative size typically expressed to the one-hundredth of a nucleotide. While we may sometimes refer to the DNA size of a PCR product in base pairs (bp), in the denaturing environment of the capillary electrophoresis instrument we are actually examining single-stranded DNA so nucleotides (nt) is a more correct unit of size. Thus, example DNA size results might be 107.23 nt or 315.02 nt.

Different sizing algorithms are available in the GeneMapper*ID* software, with the default method being local Southern sizing (Elder & Southern 1983, Mayrand et al. 1992). Local Southern involves determining the size of a DNA fragment by utilizing two peaks from the size standard larger and two peaks smaller than the DNA fragment being sized.

Validation Studies

The purpose of validation studies is to observe, document, and understand variation in the data generated under specific laboratory conditions. Validation helps define the scope or range of conditions under which reliable results may be obtained. Throughout this book, suggestions are made for validation studies that can be performed and the means for translating this information into parameters and thresholds used to assess and interpret data. By operating within validated ranges, uncertainty in measurements made on evidentiary samples with the technique can be accurately conveyed in laboratory reports.

CHARACTERISTICS OF IDEAL DATA

In physics and physical chemistry, important concepts are often introduced with ideal situations (e.g. a perfect sphere) that are easier to model than the real world with all of its complexity and uncertainty. In this manner, theoretical principles can be taught more effectively.

The same is true for DNA analysis. By starting with an example of ideal data, we can more effectively see throughout this book why and to what extent data is non-ideal in the real-world, particularly the poor quality DNA templates containing mixtures of multiple contributors often examined in forensic casework. Starting with the ideal enables examination of the primary principles in data interpretation and statistical analysis. Throughout this book we will see the challenges, difficulties, and uncertainties that exist when working with and attempting to interpret non-ideal, real-world data.

Figure 1.5 illustrates what an ideal DNA profile might look like for four loci from a single dye channel of an STR electropherogram. In this artificial example, each allele possesses a signal of 1,000 relative fluorescence units (RFUs). At this signal level, the tops of peaks are well above the background noise and analytical threshold (see Chapter 2), but not too high where we might have to worry about off-scale data and bleedthrough into adjacent color channels. Note that all four loci have nice, well-defined peaks, and that all peaks size within the shaded bins defined by the allelic ladder alleles enabling definitive allele calls to be made. The two alleles present in Locus 1, Locus 2, and Locus 4 are identical in height. In other words, these heterozygotes all have a 100% peak height ratio (PHR). No difference exists with the intralocus PHR depending on the heterozygous allele spread — all are 100% regardless if the difference is one repeat (Locus 1), two repeats (Locus 2), or

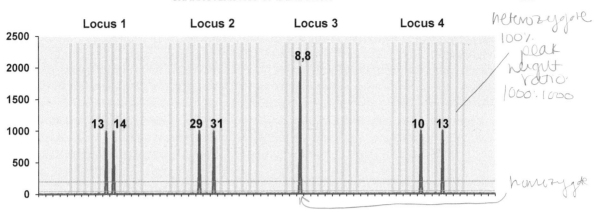

handwritten annotations: heterozygote 100% peak height ratio. 1000:1000 — homozygote

FIGURE 1.5 An artificial electropherogram with ideal STR typing data demonstrating perfect intra-locus (100% peak height ratios) and perfect inter-locus balance (heterozygous alleles from different loci are the exact same height). With this electropherogram, homozygous alleles in Locus 3 stack to produce a peak height exactly twice that of heterozygous alleles in other loci. Shaded vertical bins reflect potential alleles defined by a previously run allelic ladder. Horizontal dashed lines represent potential stochastic and analytical thresholds. Numbers above the peaks represent STR allele calls. The y-axis is in relative fluorescence units (RFUs). Hypothetical data image created with EPG Maker (SPM v3) kindly provided by Steven Myers.

three repeats (Locus 4). The homozygous alleles in Locus 3 (each possessing 8 repeats and a signal of 1,000 RFU) stack to produce a signal of 2,000 RFU.

In this example, there is 100% interlocus balance between all four loci. Peak heights of the alleles present in the three heterozygous loci are all 1,000 RFU. Within each locus, the sum of alleles present is 2,000 RFU. This perfect interlocus balance enables the double signal from stacked homozygous alleles to be easily recognized. Furthermore, no observable stutter artifacts interfere with the ability to decipher whether a minor component from a second contributor might be present in this sample result. In fact, the absence of any other detectable alleles provides great confidence in assuming that this sample originates from a single source.

A major benefit of ideal data without artifacts such as stutter products would be the ability to detect and decipher mixtures more readily and at lower contributor amounts. With all observed data on-scale (i.e. well below typical signal saturation levels), no signal bleedthrough peaks (commonly referred to as pull-up artifacts) are expected in the dye channels that are not shown.

In an ideal world, we might have genetic markers that are so polymorphic that all DNA profiles are fully heterozygous with distinguishable alleles to better enable mixture detection and interpretation when multiple contributors are present in a mixed sample. However, with such highly variable markers, the mutation rate would likely be high for each locus, making it difficult to establish links across generations in kinship testing. The reality is that some loci contain relatively few common alleles, and thus more homozygotes are present in the general population (e.g. the 8,8 result at Locus 3 in Figure 1.5).

Completely repeatable peak heights from injection to injection on the same or other CE instruments in the lab or other labs would enable greater confidence in correlating DNA amounts to the observed fluorescence signal. If all CE instruments and PCR amplifications within a laboratory or between different laboratories produced the same 1,000 RFU peaks and clean DNA profile allele calls on this same sample, then comparisons between evidentiary and reference samples would be trivial whether performed within a single laboratory or with database results generated from different laboratories. Unfortunately, with real-world data, the situation is more complex and interpretation is more challenging.

Real-World Challenges

Stochastic (random) variation in sampling each allele at a locus during PCR amplification leads to variation in peak heights and peak height ratios for heterozygous samples (see Chapter 4). DNA quality and quantity play a major factor in the degree of stochastic variation. Degraded DNA templates may make some STR allele targets unavailable. Alleles may fail to amplify if a sequence difference exists (due to mutation relative to the standard template sequence) in a PCR primer binding region. These alleles, which are present in the original sample but fail to amplify, are termed "silent" or "null" (see Chapter 4). PCR inhibitors present in forensic evidentiary samples may reduce efficiency in amplifying some loci and/or alleles resulting in an imbalance in the signal obtained across the DNA profile. The PCR process is also highly dependent on DNA sample quantity; this can lead to great variability in amplifying individual alleles (if retesting the identical DNA extract) when amplifying smaller amounts of DNA.

The existence of PCR amplification artifacts, such as stutter products or STR alleles that are not fully adenylated and possess −A peaks (see Chapter 3), complicates interpretation, particularly when a mixture of DNA templates from more than one individual may be present. The possibility of tri-allelic patterns (see Chapter 5) can further complicate the ability to recognize and discern whether a DNA profile originates from more than one individual.

Technological artifacts can arise due to fluorescent dye impurities in the primer synthesis (dye blobs), failure of the spectral calibration due to signal saturation (pull-up or bleedthrough between dye channels), and other anomalies such as electrophoretic spikes. See Chapter 8 for more information on these artifacts.

To complicate factors even more, variability exists between CE instruments due to the individual instruments' optics used to detect the fluorescence signal arising from the dye-labeled PCR products.

GUIDANCE FOR DNA INTERPRETATION

With a technique as powerful as forensic DNA testing to help establish guilt or innocence in the context of criminal investigations, it is imperative that measures are in place to create confidence in the results obtained. Around the world a number of organizations exist that work on a local, national, or international level to aid quality assurance and to promote accurate forensic DNA testing. These organizations are primarily made up of select working scientists who coordinate their efforts to benefit the DNA typing community as a whole.

One of the primary groups that the forensic DNA community looks to for guidance regarding topics such as validation and data interpretation is the Scientific Working Group on DNA Analysis Methods, or SWGDAM (D.N.A. Box 1.2).

In 1994, the United States Congress established a DNA Advisory Board (DAB) that operated for five years, from 1995 to 2000, to develop the initial Quality Assurance Standards (QAS) used in the U.S. Since 2000, SWGDAM has inherited the role of the DAB, and during its semiannual meetings

---

D.N.A. BOX 1.2

WHAT ROLE DOES SWGDAM HAVE IN PRODUCING GUIDANCE DOCUMENTS?

The *Technical Working Group on DNA Analysis Methods* (TWGDAM) was established in November 1988 under FBI Laboratory sponsorship to aid forensic DNA scientists in North America. After its first decade of existence, TWGDAM's name was changed in 1998 to SWGDAM, which stands for the *Scientific Working Group on DNA Analysis Methods*.

SWGDAM is a group of approximately 50 scientists representing federal, state, and local forensic DNA laboratories in the United States and Canada. A representative of the European Network of Forensic Science Institutes (ENFSI) DNA Working Group often attends as well. Meetings are held twice a year, usually in January and July. For several years, public SWGDAM meetings were held in conjunction with the International Symposium on Human Identification, sponsored each fall by the Promega Corporation. Since 2006, the public SWGDAM meeting has been held as part of the FBI-sponsored National CODIS Conference (FBI 2012).

Over the years, a number of TWGDAM or SWGDAM Committees have operated to bring recommendations before the entire group. These Committees have included (at different times) the following topics: restriction fragment length polymorphism (RFLP), polymerase chain reaction (PCR), Combined DNA Index System (CODIS), mitochondrial DNA, short tandem repeat (STR) interpretation, training, validation, Y-chromosome, expert systems, quality assurance, missing persons/mass disasters, mixture interpretation, mass spectrometry, enhanced method detection and interpretation, and rapid DNA analysis. TWGDAM issued guidelines for quality assurance in DNA analysis in 1989, 1991, and 1995. Revised SWGDAM validation guidelines were published in 2004, and 2012 and interpretation guidelines for autosomal short tandem repeat (STR) typing were released in 2010. Several *ad hoc* working groups have produced recommendations on such topics as the review of outsourced data and partial matches. SWGDAM documents were originally made available through *Forensic Science Communications*, an on-line journal sponsored by the FBI Laboratory. More recently, a SWGDAM website enables the community to access SWGDAM work products and resources.

Source: SWGDAM, *http://www.swgdam.org*; Butler, J.M. *(2013). Forensic DNA advisory groups: DAB, SWGDAM, ENFSI, and BSAG.* Encyclopedia of Forensic Sciences, 2nd Edition. *Elsevier Academic Press: New York.*

---

discusses methods and produces guidance documents to aid the forensic DNA community (including revisions to the QAS). A helpful guidance document is the 2010 SWGDAM Interpretation Guidelines for Autosomal STR Typing by Forensic DNA Testing Laboratories (SWGDAM 2010). The September 2011 Quality Assurance Standards for Forensic DNA Laboratories are available online (QAS 2011).

Other groups around the world that play a similar role as SWGDAM include the DNA Commission of the International Society for Forensic Genetics, the European Network of Forensic Science Institute's (ENFSI 2014) DNA Working Group, and the Australia/New Zealand Biology Specialist Advisory Group (BSAG).

NRC I and NRC II Recommendations

The U.S. National Academy of Science's National Research Council (NRC) issued two reports during the 1990s commonly referred to as NRC I and NRC II that provide guidance on quality assurance and recommendations for appropriate statistical methods in DNA analysis. Appendix 2 lists the memberships and recommendations of NRC I and NRC II, as well as a number of references that provide background and criticism of the reports.

The FBI Quality Assurance Standards

Several sections of the FBI Quality Assurance Standards for Forensic DNA Testing Laboratories focus on the importance of interpretation. For example, U.S. forensic DNA laboratories are required to have and follow written guidelines for interpretation of data (QAS 9.6), to verify that control results meet the laboratory guidelines for all reported results (QAS 9.6.1), to use internal validation experiments to help define laboratory interpretation guidelines including approaches for mixture interpretation (QAS 8.3.2), and to perform validation prior to implementation and when changes are made to collection or analysis software that may impact data interpretation (QAS 8.7).

The QAS also require U.S. forensic DNA laboratories to have and follow a documented procedure for mixture interpretation that addresses major and minor contributors, inclusions and exclusions, and policies for the reporting of results and statistics (QAS 9.6.4), and to follow NRC II recommendations (see Appendix 2) with statistical analysis of autosomal STR data using a documented population database appropriate for the calculation (QAS 9.6.2). Furthermore, laboratories are required to "retain, in hard or electronic format, sufficient documentation for each technical analysis to support the report conclusions such that another qualified individual could evaluate and interpret the data" (QAS 11.1).

DNA Commission of the International Society for Forensic Genetics

The International Society for Forensic Genetics (ISFG) is an organization of over 1,100 scientists from more than 60 countries promoting scientific knowledge in the field of genetic markers as applied to forensic science. Since 1989, the ISFG has issued recommendations on a variety of important topics in forensic DNA analysis through a DNA Commission. These recommendations have included naming of STR variant alleles and STR repeat nomenclature, mitochondrial DNA and Y-STR issues, DNA mixture interpretation, paternity testing biostatistics, disaster victim identification, use of animal DNA in forensic genetic investigations, and coping with potential allele drop-out and drop-in through probabilistic genotyping. For more information on the ISFG DNA Commission, see their website (ISFG 2014).

SWGDAM Interpretation Guidelines

While the QAS provide requirements (the "what"), in many cases they do not provide many details that might enable further guidance (the "how"). SWGDAM guidelines offer guidance on important topics related to validation and interpretation. While the QAS provide policies, SWGDAM guidelines focus more on principles that impact lab protocols and how analysts put SOPs into practice (D.N.A. Box 1.3).

D.N.A. BOX 1.3

PRESCRIPTIONS AND PERSPECTIVES ON HOW PRINCIPLES, PROTOCOLS, AND PRACTICE IMPACT PERSONAL PERFORMANCE WITH INTERPRETING DNA DATA

Our perspective impacts how well we see everything around us. Since I wear eyeglasses and cannot see well without them, I understand what it is like going from not having my glasses on (or having ones with the wrong prescription) to putting on glasses with the right prescription. About age 10, when I first obtained a pair of eyeglasses containing the correct prescription to focus light appropriately into my near-sighted eyes, I suddenly become aware of what I was not seeing previously. Hazy objects come into focus. This was especially evident at night when the fuzzy blurs of streetlights in the distance became discrete pinpoints of light with corrected eyesight. Eyeglasses help me see better, which in turn has helped improve my understanding of the world around me.

Similarly, an appropriate "prescription" to aid understanding of basic principles underlying forensic DNA concepts can help an analyst better "see" how to interpret and report data. A primary purpose of SWGDAM guidelines (**D.N.A. Box 1.2**) is to provide principles and best practices to enable a framework of good science. Following the precepts of these principles, laboratories then develop written *protocols* − or standard operating procedures (SOPs) − based on experience gained from their internal validation studies. Finally, analysts put these SOPs into *practice* on individual cases based on their training and experience. Within the United States, laboratories and analysts are audited according to their performance against specific *policies* established by the FBI Quality Assurance Standards (QAS). Thus, as noted in the table below, a pattern of policy, principles, protocols, and practice exists and impacts how forensic DNA analysis and interpretation is performed. Ideally, analysts with appropriate training within a laboratory and across the community will interpret forensic DNA cases in a consistent and high-quality manner.

	Example	Who is impacted	Based on
Policies	QAS	Community	Decisions from organizations like SWGDAM
Principles	SWGDAM Guidelines	Community	(hopefully) Good science
Protocols	Lab SOPs	Laboratory	Validation experiments
Practice	Casework in a specific case	Individual analysts	Training & experience

Throughout this book, we try to identify a D.N.A. pattern where the "D" of dogma or a fundamental law of biology, chemistry, or physics addresses answers to "why" questions, the "N" of notable principles covers answers to "what" questions, and the "A" of application within a specific laboratory environment deals with the "how" questions. For example, peak height ratio measurements with heterozygous alleles (the "how") permit assessment of potential allele pairing into genotypes (the "what") because offspring receive one allele from each parent in normal diploid individuals (the "why").

The hope of this approach is that by understanding the "why" better, the "what" and "how" will come into an improved focus. Analysts armed with a better "prescription" can then "see" more clearly an appropriate scientific solution as they interpret their DNA profiles, develop conclusions, and write reports.

Source: Rudin, N., & Inman, K. (2012). *The discomfort of thought: a discussion with John Butler*. The CAC News, 1st Quarter 2012, pp. 8−11. Available at http://www.cacnews.org/news/1stq12.pdf.

In early 2010, SWGDAM approved and released "SWGDAM Interpretation Guidelines for Autosomal STR Typing by Forensic DNA Testing Laboratories." With the availability of these interpretation guidelines, laboratories were "encouraged to review their standard operating procedures and validation data and to update their procedures as needed" (SWGDAM 2010).

As will be emphasized throughout this book, a forensic DNA laboratory should develop STR interpretation guidelines based upon its own validation studies. Information from STR kit and instrument manufacturers and results reported in the literature can be helpful. Practical experience with instrumentation and results from performing casework are also important factors in developing an interpretation strategy.

A MATCH OR NOT A MATCH: THAT IS THE QUESTION...

Generally, the process of comparing two or more samples is limited to one of three possible outcomes that are submitted in a case report (see Chapter 16):

1. **Inclusion** (Match) — Peaks between the compared STR profiles have the same genotypes, and no unexplained differences exist between the samples. Statistical evaluation of the significance of the match is usually cited in the match report. Alternatives for presentation of a match range from statements of identity, to computations of the likelihood ratio for the hypothesis that the defendant is the source, to descriptions of random-match probabilities in various populations.
2. **Exclusion** (Non-match) — The genotype comparison shows profile differences that can only be explained by the two samples originating from different sources.
3. **Inconclusive** — The data does not support a conclusion whether the profiles match. This finding might be reported if two analysts remain in disagreement after review and discussion of the data and it is felt that insufficient information exists to support any conclusion. Poor quality evidentiary samples or lack of a reference sample for comparison purposes can be other reasons for an inconclusive result.

As noted in the 2010 SWGDAM STR Interpretation Guideline 4.1, "the laboratory must perform statistical analysis in support of any inclusion that is determined to be relevant in the context of a case, irrespective of the number of alleles detected and the quantitative value of the statistical analysis" (SWGDAM 2010). Providing an appropriate weight to the evidence provides an opportunity to reflect the uncertainty in the result obtained — particularly with partial profiles where more ambiguity may exist.

If a match is observed between a suspect (known sample "K") and crime-scene evidence (question sample "Q"), then three possibilities exist: (1) the suspect deposited the sample, (2) the suspect did not provide the sample but has the profile by chance, and (3) the suspect did not provide the sample and the matching result is a false positive due to a sample switch or some other kind of error.

The first explanation is the basis behind the use of DNA testing in the criminal justice system. The second possibility depends on population genetics principles, covered in the second half of this book, specifically Chapter 10, from which the probability of a random match is determined. The third explanation of why a match might occur concerns the possibility of laboratory mistakes. Chapter 7 in *Advanced Topics: Methodology* (Butler 2012) discusses quality assurance measures that are in place to prevent or reduce the possibility of error in performing DNA testing. Generally speaking, a great deal of effort goes into ensuring reliable forensic DNA testing.

TABLE 1.2 Characteristics of Autosomal STR Loci Present in 31 Commercially Available STR Kits

Autosomal STR Loci / Autosomal STR Kits

Chr	STR Locus	Repeat	Allele Range (Butler et al. 2012)	CODIS 13 (US 1997-present)	CODIS 20 (US future)	ESS 12 (EU 2009-present)	PowerPlex 16 (HS)	PowerPlex 18D	PowerPlex ESI 16	PowerPlex ESX 16	PowerPlex ESI 17 Pro	PowerPlex ESX 17	PowerPlex 21	PowerPlex CS7	PowerPlex S5	PowerPlex Fusion	Profiler Plus	COfiler	Profiler	SGM Plus	SEfiler Plus	SinoFiler	MiniFiler	Identifiler (Direct, Plus)	VeriFiler	NGM	NGM SElect	GlobalFiler	ESSplex	ESSplex SE	Hexaplex ESS	Nonaplex ESS	Decaplex SE	IDplex
				required							Promega STR kits								Life Technologies (ABI) STR kits										Qiagen STR kits					
1q31	F13B	AAAT	6 to 11											2																				
1q42	D1S1656	TAGA	10 to 19.3			■			3	2	3	2	3			3										3	3	2	2	2	3	2	
2p25.3	TPOX	AATG	5 to 13	■			4	4					6			6	3	3					3				5						1
2p14	D2S441	TCWA	8 to 17		■				5		5				4							1			1	1	1	1		
2q35	D2S1338	TKCC	15 to 27		■		2		3	3	3	3	3			3				4	4	5	2	5	2	4	4	4	5	5			4	5
3p21.31	D3S1358	TCTR	11 to 20	■		■	1	1	2	2	2	2	2			2	1	1	1	1	1	1		1	1	1	1	1	3	3		3	3	3
4q31.3	FGA	YTYY	16.2 to 43.2	■		■	5	5	4	4	4	4	2	4	3		3	3	3	3	3	3	4	4	4	4		4	2	4
5q23.2	D5S818	AGAT	7 to 15	■			1	1				5			5	1		1		2	2		2	2				4
5q33.1	CSF1PO	AGAT	7 to 15	■			5	5			4			4	4	4		4	4		4				2
6p24	F13A01	AAAG	3.2 to 17										4																			
6q14	SE33	AAAG	6.3 to 36						2	4										3			5	5		4	3	1
6q15	D6S1043	AGAY	8 to 26										4																	
7q21.11	D7S820	GATA	6 to 14	■			3	3				4			4	3	1	3		3	2	3					2
8p22	LPL	AAAT	7 to 15									1															
8q24.13	D8S1179	TCTR	8 to 18	■		■	3	3	1	3	1	3			3	2		2	2	1		2	2	3	4	4		3	2
9p13	Penta C	AAAAC	5 to 16									1																	
10q26.3	D10S1248	GGAA	8 to 19		■				4	1	4	1	5							1	1	1	1	1	1	2	1	
11p15.5	TH01	TCAT	5 to 11	■		■	2	1	1	3	1	1	1	2	2	2	2	2	3	3	3	3	2	1	2	2	2
12p13.31	vWA	TCTR	11 to 21	■		■	2	2	2	2	2	2	2	2	2	2	2	2	2	4	4	4	4	4
12p13.2	D12S391	AGAY	14 to 27		■	■			4	4		2	3	4	4	3	3	3	2	3
13q31.1	D13S317	TATC	8 to 15	■			2	2			6		6	2	2	3	3	3		3
15q25	FESFPS	ATTT	5 to 14																			
15q26.2	Penta E	AAAGA	5 to 25				5				6	1	7							
16q24.1	D16S539	GATA	5 to 15	■			4	4	1	4	1	4	1	1	4	1	4	3	3	1	1	1	1
18q21.33	D18S51	AGAA	9 to 28	■		■	4	2	2	5	2	2	4	4	2	4	4	4	5	2	1
19q12	D19S433	WAGG	9 to 18.2		■			3	1	1	1	1	2	2	2	2	3	3	2	3
21q21.1	D21S11	TCTR	24.2 to 39	■		■	3	3	3	4	3	3	3	3	3	2	3	3	4	5	5	5	5
21q22.3	Penta D	AAAGA	2.2 to 17				6	6			5		5							
22q12.3	D22S1045	ATT	8 to 19		■			1	5	1	6			1	1	1	1	2	2	2
Xp, Yp	Amelogenin	--	--	■			1	1	1	1	1	1	1	1	1	1	1	1	1	1	1	1	1	1	2	1	1	1	1	1
Yq11.21	DYS391	TCTA	7 to 13									7							6
Yq11.221	Yindel	TTCTC/-	"1" or "2"									1							1
	autosomal STRs amplified						15	17	15	15	16	16	20	7	4	22	9	6	9	10	11	15	8	15	9	15	16	22	15	16	6	13	11	15

Allele range is from the NIST 1036 data set (D.N.A. Box 1.4). Numbers inside the colored boxes indicate relative size position for that locus within a dye channel for the specific STR kit.

When utilizing data comparisons with DNA databases that may have data coming from many sources, it is important to recognize that different PCR primer sets may detect or not detect an allele (allele dropout) due to primer binding site mutations (see Chapter 4).

In forensic DNA Q-K comparisons (as currently practiced in many parts of the world), if any STR locus fails to match when comparing the genotypes between two or more samples, then the comparison of profiles between the questioned and reference sample is usually declared a non-match,

TABLE 1.3   Characteristics of Y-STR Loci and Y-Chromosome Sex-Typing Markers in Commercial Kits[a]

ChrY Position (Mb)	Y-STR Marker	Repeat Motif	Allele Range[b]	Present in Y-STR Kit
3.13	**DYS393**	AGAT	7 to 18	PPY, Yfiler, PPY23, Yfiler Plus
4.27	DYS456	AGAT	11 to 23	Yfiler, PPY23, Yfiler Plus
6.74	*AMEL Y*	+AAAGTG		*Fusion, GlobalFiler,[d] etc.*
6.86	DYS570	TTTC	10 to 25	PPY23, Yfiler Plus
7.05	DYS576	AAAG	11 to 23	PPY23, Yfiler Plus
7.87	DYS458	GAAA	10 to 24	Yfiler, PPY23, Yfiler Plus
8.22	DYS449	TTTC	22 to 40[c]	Yfiler Plus
8.43	DYS481	CTT	17 to 32	PPY23, Yfiler Plus
8.65	DYS627	AAAG	11 to 27[c]	Yfiler Plus
9.52	**DYS19**	TAGA	9 to 19	PPY, Yfiler, PPY23, Yfiler Plus
14.10	**DYS391**	TCTA	5 to 16	PPY, Yfiler, PPY23, Yfiler Plus, *Fusion, GlobalFiler*
14.38	DYS635	TSTA	15 to 28	Yfiler, PPY23, Yfiler Plus
14.47	DYS437	TCTR	11 to 18	PPY, Yfiler, PPY23, Yfiler Plus
14.51	**DYS439**	AGAT	6 to 17	PPY, Yfiler, PPY23, Yfiler Plus
14.61	**DYS389 I/II**	TCTR	9 to 17/ 24 to 35	PPY, Yfiler, PPY23, Yfiler Plus
14.94	**DYS438**	TTTTC	6 to 16	PPY, Yfiler, PPY23, Yfiler Plus
15.51	*M175*	[TTCTC/−]	"1" or "2"	*GlobalFiler[d] Y-InDel (Y±)*
17.27	**DYS390**	TCTR	17 to 29	PPY, Yfiler, PPY23, Yfiler Plus
17.32	DYS518	AAAG	32 to 49[c]	Yfiler Plus
17.43	DYS643	CTTTT	6 to 17	PPY23
18.39	DYS533	ATCT	7 to 17	PPY23, Yfiler Plus
18.74	GATA-H4	TAGA	8 to 18	Yfiler, PPY23, Yfiler Plus
20.80, 20.84	**DYS385 a/b**	GAAA	7 to 28	PPY, Yfiler, PPY23, Yfiler Plus
21.05	DYS460	ATAG	7 to 14[c]	Yfiler Plus
21.52	DYS549	GATA	7 to 17	PPY23
22.63	**DYS392**	TAT	4 to 20	PPY, Yfiler, PPY23, Yfiler Plus
24.36	DYS448	AGAGAT	14 to 24	Yfiler, PPY23, Yfiler Plus
25.93, 28.03	DYF387S1 a/b	RAAG	30 to 44[c]	Yfiler Plus

[a] *See Figure 1.8 for loci layouts in Y-STR kits. Markers in bold font are the 11 recommended by SWGDAM and are present in all kits. Shaded markers are present in some newer autosomal STR kits. The Y-chromosome positions were determined using the February 2009 human reference sequence and BLAT (2014)*
[b] *Allele range listed is for PowerPlex Y23 allelic ladders (Promega 2012)*
[c] *Range of Yfiler Plus allelic ladder alleles*
[d] *GlobalFiler (2014).*

D.N.A. BOX 1.4

NIST 1036 DATA SET

Since 2002, the Applied Genetics Group at the National Institute of Standards and Technology (NIST) has worked with a set of U.S. population DNA samples for purposes of understanding genetic marker variability and performance. These samples have been extensively studied with numerous autosomal and Y-chromosome STR commercial kits and assays developed at NIST. Although more than 1,450 samples have been studied in some cases, the full set of samples includes related individuals such as fathers and sons. In 2012, a set of 1,036 unrelated individuals, termed the NIST 1036 data set (Butler et al. 2012), was established that includes 1,032 males and four females examined with 29 autosomal STR loci (Hill et al. 2013) and 23 Y-STR loci (Coble et al. 2013).

Throughout this book, allele frequencies used in examples will come from information derived from the NIST 1036 data set. The full set of allele frequencies is found in Appendix 1. Information and data on these DNA samples are available from the NIST Population Data section of STRBase (NIST Population Data 2014). An extensive description of the results from the NIST 1036 data set is found in *Profiles in DNA* (Butler et al. 2012), which is freely available on the Promega website.

Sources: Butler, J.M., et al. (2012). Variability of new STR loci and kits in U.S. population groups. Profiles in DNA. *Available at http://www.promega.com/resources/articles/profiles-in-dna/2012/variability-of-new-str-loci-and-kits-in-us-population-groups/; Coble, M.D., et al. (2013). Haplotype data for 23 Y-chromosome markers in four U.S. population groups. Forensic Science International: Genetics, 7, e66–e68.; Hill, C.R., et al. (2013). U.S. population data for 29 autosomal STR loci. Forensic Science International: Genetics, 7, e82–e83.*

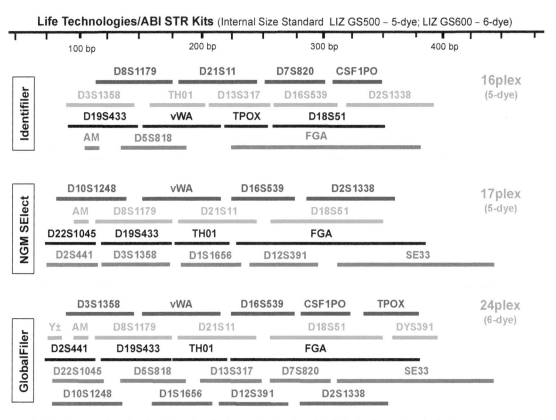

FIGURE 1.6 Layout of loci by dye channel and relative size in selected Life Technologies (Applied Biosystems, ABI) STR kits.

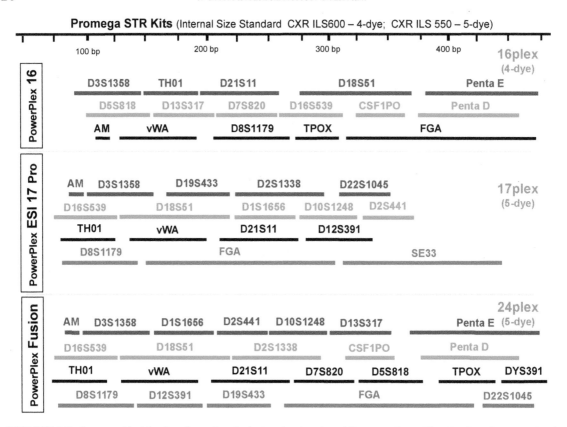

FIGURE 1.7 Layout of loci by dye channel and relative size in selected Promega PowerPlex STR kits (Promega 2012).

regardless of how many other loci match. This binary (match/no-match) approach becomes problematic with low-level evidentiary DNA samples where stocastic allele dropout is likely. Probabilistic approaches are under development to help with these difficult situations (Gill et al. 2012).

As noted in Chapter 14, paternity testing is an exception to this "single mismatch leads to exclusion" rule because of the possibility of mutational events. When analyzing and reporting the results of parentage cases, an allowance for one or even two possible mutations is often made. In other words, if 13 loci are used and the questioned parentage is included for all but one locus, the data from the non-inclusive allele is usually attributed to a possible mutation.

In the end, interpretation of results in forensic casework is a matter of professional judgment and expertise. Interpretation of results within the context of a case is the responsibility of the case analyst with supervisors or technical leaders conducting a follow-up verification of the analyst's interpretation of the data as part of the technical and administrative review process (see Chapter 16). When coming to a final conclusion regarding a match or exclusion between two or more DNA profiles, laboratory interpretation guidelines should be adhered to by both the case analyst and the supervisor. However, as experience using various analytical procedures grows, interpretation guidelines will evolve and improve. These guidelines should always be based on the proper use of controls and validated methods.

STR LOCI, KITS, AND POPULATION DATA

At the time this book is being written, three commercial manufacturers provide more than two dozen different STR kits. These kits examine subsets of markers from a total of 29 autosomal STR loci, a sex-typing marker named amelogenin, and a Y-STR marker DYS391. Table 1.2 lists the characteristics of these STRs, including their chromosomal location, primary repeat motif, and allele range. For Y-chromosome analysis, up to 29 Y-STR loci can be examined with commercial kits available as of early 2014 (Table 1.3).

U.S. population data from 1,036 individuals has been collected on these 29 autosomal STR loci and 23 Y-STR loci (D.N.A. Box 1.4). Data generated from these DNA samples will be used throughout the book.

The STR locus dye color and size range for several commonly used STR kits are laid out in Figure 1.6 for Life Technologies kits (Life Technologies 2012), Figure 1.7 for Promega kits (Promega 2012), and Figure 1.8 for Y-STR kits from Life Technologies and Promega. As these STR kits will be referred to in many of the following chapters, we include them here as a helpful reference.

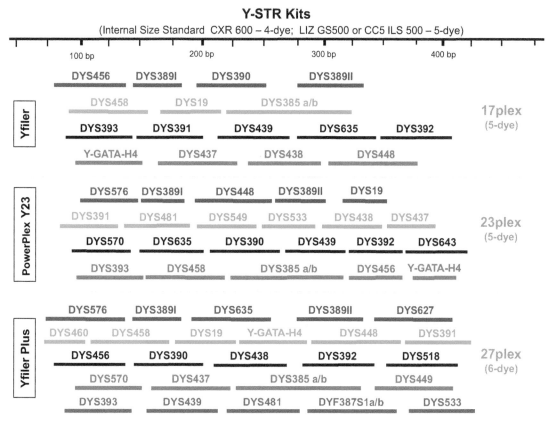

FIGURE 1.8 Layout of loci by dye channel and relative size in Y-chromosome STR kits from Life Technologies and Promega.

SUMMARY

DNA interpretation with STR markers involves utilizing genotyping software and laboratory SOPs to evaluate CE data. Peaks in multi-colored CE electropherograms generated as CE mobility time points are translated into DNA size information and then to allele repeat number for each STR locus. In both evidentiary and reference samples, decisions are made for each peak above an analytical threshold regarding whether or not the peak is an allele or an artifact, whether or not alleles at an STR locus can be paired to form a genotype, whether it is possible for some alleles to be missing from the data, and whether or not the sample originated from a single-source or a mixture of multiple contributors. Validation studies are essential for setting parameters used in a laboratory's SOPs to make these decisions. Guidance on validation studies and data interpretation has been provided from organizations such as SWGDAM and the ENFSI.

Reading List and Internet Resources

Purpose of This Book

Butler, J. M. (2012). *Advanced Topics in Forensic DNA Typing: Methodology*. New York: Elsevier Academic Press.

National Academies of Science. (2009). *Strengthening Forensic Science in the United States: A Path Forward*. Washington, D.C: The National Academies Press.

QAS. (2011). *Quality Assurance Standards for Forensic DNA Testing Laboratories effective 9-1-2011*. See http://www.fbi.gov/about-us/lab/codis/qas-standards-for-forensic-dna-testing-laboratories-effective-9-1-2011. Accessed March 18, 2014.

The Interpretation Process

STR Data Analysis and Interpretation (on-line training): http://www.dna.gov/training/strdata/

Computer Files and Genotyping Software

Applied Biosystems. (2003). *GeneMapper ID Software Version 3.1 Human Identification Analysis User Guide*. Foster City, California.

Applied Biosystems. (2004). *GeneMapperID Software Version 3.2: Human Identification Analysis Tutorial*. Foster City, California.

Applied Biosystems. (2009). *Genetic Analysis Data File Format, Sept 2009*. Available at http://www.appliedbiosystems.com/absite/us/en/home/support/software-community/tools-for-accessing-files.html. Accessed March 18, 2014.

BatchExtract. ftp://ftp.ncbi.nih.gov/pub/forensics/BATCHEXTRACT. Accessed March 18, 2014.

GeneMapperID-X (from Applied Biosystems): http://www.lifetechnologies.com/us/en/home/technical-resources/software-downloads/genemapper-id-x-software.html. Accessed March 18, 2014.

GeneMarker HID (from Soft Genetics): http://www.softgenetics.com/GeneMarkerHID.html. Accessed March 18, 2014.

GenoProof (from Qualitype AG): http://www.genoproof.de/en/. Accessed March 18, 2014.

Goor, R. M., et al. (2011). A mathematical approach to the analysis of multiplex DNA profiles. *Bulletin of Mathematical Biology*, 73(8), 1909−1931.

Holland, M. M., & Parson, W. (2011). GeneMarker® HID: a reliable software tool for the analysis of forensic STR data. *Journal of Forensic Sciences*, 56(1), 29−35.

Kadash, K., et al. (2004). Validation study of the TrueAllele automated data review system. *Journal of Forensic Sciences*, 49, 660−667.

OSIRIS (Open Source Independent Review and Interpretation System). http://www.ncbi.nlm.nih.gov/projects/SNP/osiris/. Accessed March 18, 2014.

TrueAllele (from Cybergenetics). http://www.cybgen.com. Accessed March 18, 2014.

DNA Sizing

Elder, J. K., & Southern, E. M. (1983). Measurement of DNA length by gel electrophoresis II: comparison of methods for relating mobility to fragment length. *Analytical Biochemistry, 128*, 227–231.

Mayrand, P. E., et al. (1992). The use of fluorescence detection and internal lane standards to size PCR products automatically. *Applied and Theoretical Electrophoresis, 3*(1), 1–11.

Rosenblum, B. B., et al. (1997). Improved single-strand DNA sizing accuracy in capillary electrophoresis. *Nucleic Acids Research, 25*, 3925–3929.

Ziegle, J. S., et al. (1992). Application of automated DNA sizing technology for genotyping microsatellite loci. *Genomics, 14*(4), 1026–1031.

Guidance for DNA Interpretation

Butler, J. M. (2013). *Forensic DNA advisory groups: DAB, SWGDAM, ENFSI, and BSAG. Encyclopedia of Forensic Sciences* (2nd ed.). New York: Elsevier Academic Press.

DNA Commission of the ISFG (2014). http://www.isfg.org/Publications/DNA+Commission. Accessed March 18, 2014.

European Network of Forensic Science Institutes (ENFSI) DNA Working Group (2014): http://www.enfsi.eu/page.php?uid=98. Accessed March 18, 2014.

Gill, P., et al. (2012). *The interpretation of DNA evidence (including low-template DNA)*. Available at http://www.homeoffice.gov.uk/publications/agencies-public-bodies/fsr/interpretation-of-dna-evidence. Accessed March 18, 2014.

Gill, P., et al. (2012). DNA commission of the International Society of Forensic Genetics: recommendations on the evaluation of STR typing results that may include drop-out and/or drop-in using probabilistic methods. *Forensic Science International: Genetics, 6*, 679–688.

Hobson, D., et al. (1999). STR analysis by capillary electrophoresis: development of interpretation guidelines for the Profiler Plus and COfiler systems for use in forensic science. *Proceedings of the 10th International Symposium on Human Identification*. Available at http://www.promega.com/products/pm/genetic-identity/ishi-conference-proceedings/10th-ishi-oral-presentations/. Accessed March 18, 2014.

International Society of Forensic Genetics (ISFG): http://www.isfg.org/. Accessed March 18, 2014.

Puch-Solis, R., et al. (2012). Assessing the probative value of DNA evidence: guidance for judges, lawyers, forensic scientists and expert witnesses. Practitioner Guide No. 2. Prepared under the auspices of the Royal Statistical Society's Working Group on Statistics and the Law (Chairman: Colin Aitken). Available at http://www.rss.org.uk/uploadedfiles/userfiles/files/Practitioner-Guide-2-WEB.pdf. Accessed March 18, 2014.

Quality Assurance Standards (QAS) for Forensic DNA Laboratories. September 2011. Available online at http://www.fbi.gov/about-us/lab/biometric-analysis/codis. Accessed March 18, 2014.

Rudin, N., & Inman, K. (2012). The discomfort of thought: a discussion with John Butler. *The CAC News, 1st Quarter, 2012*. pp. 8–11. Available at http://www.cacnews.org/news/1stq12.pdf. Accessed March 18, 2014.

SWGDAM website: http://www.swgdam.org. Accessed March 18, 2014.

SWGDAM. (2010). *SWGDAM Interpretation Guidelines for Autosomal STR Typing by Forensic DNA Testing Laboratories*. Available at http://www.swgdam.org/Interpretation_Guidelines_January_2010.pdf. Accessed March 18, 2014.

A Match or Not a Match: That is the Question...

Gill, P., et al. (2012). DNA commission of the International Society of Forensic Genetics: recommendations on the evaluation of STR typing results that may include drop-out and/or drop-in using probabilistic methods. *Forensic Science International: Genetics, 6*, 679–688.

STR Kits, Loci, and Population Data

BLAT Search Genome: http://genome.ucsc.edu/cgi-bin/hgBlat. Accessed March 18, 2014.

Budowle, B., et al. (1998). *CODIS and PCR-based short tandem repeat loci: law enforcement tools. Proceedings of the Second European Symposium on Human Identification*. pp. 73–88. Madison, Wisconsin: Promega Corporation. Available at http://www.promega.com/products/pm/genetic-identity/ishi-conference-proceedings/2nd-eshi-oral-presentations/. Accessed March 18, 2014.

Butler, J. M. (2006). Genetics and genomics of core short tandem repeat loci used in human identity testing. *Journal of Forensic Sciences, 51*, 253–265.

Butler, J. M., & Hill, C. R. (2012). Biology and genetics of new autosomal STR loci useful for forensic DNA analysis. *Forensic Science Review, 24*(1), 15–26.

FBI. (2012). *Planned process and timeline for implementation of additional CODIS core loci.* Available at http://www.fbi.gov/about − us/lab/codis/planned − process − and − timeline − for − implementation − of − additional − codis − core − loci.

Gill, P., et al. (2006a). The evolution of DNA databases − Recommendations for new European STR loci. *Forensic Science International, 156*, 242–244.

Gill, P., et al. (2006b). New multiplexes for Europe − amendments and clarification of strategic development. *Forensic Science International, 163*, 155–157.

Hares, D. R. (2012a). Expanding the CODIS core loci in the United States. *Forensic Science International: Genetics, 6*(1), e52–e54.

Hares, D. R. (2012b). Addendum to expanding the CODIS core loci in the United States. *Forensic Science International: Genetics, 6*(5), e135.

Life Technologies (2012). http://www.invitrogen.com/site/us/en/home/Products-and-Services/Applications/Human-Identification/globalfiler_str_kit.html. Accessed March 18, 2014.

GlobalFiler information (2014). http://www.invitrogen.com/site/us/en/home/Products-and-Services/Applications/Human-Identification/globalfiler_str_kit/resources.html. Accessed March 18, 2014.

Mulero, J. J., & Hennessy, L. K. (2012). Next-generation STR genotyping kits for forensic applications. *Forensic Science Review, 24*(1), 1–13.

Promega. (2012). *PowerPlex Fusion System.* http://www.promega.com/products/pm/genetic-identity/powerplex-fusion. Accessed March 18, 2014.

Ruitberg, C. M., et al. (2001). STRBase: a short tandem repeat DNA database for the human identity testing community. *Nucleic Acids Res., 29*, 320–322.

STRBase: http://www.cstl.nist.gov/strbase. Accessed March 18, 2014.

Population Data on NIST U.S. Samples

Butler, J. M., et al. (2012). *Variability of new STR loci and kits in U.S. population groups. Profiles in DNA.* Available at http://www.promega.comz/resources/articles/profiles-in-dna/2012/variability-of-new-str-loci-and-kits-in-us-population-groups. Accessed March 18, 2014.

Coble, M. D., et al. (2013). Haplotype data for 23 Y-chromosome markers in four U.S. population groups. *Forensic Science International: Genetics, 7*, e66–e68.

Diegoli, T. M., et al. (2011). Allele frequency distribution of twelve X-chromosomal short tandem repeat markers in four U.S. population groups. *Forensic Science International: Genetics Supplement Series, 3*, e481–e483.

Hill, C. R., et al. (2013). U.S. population data for 29 autosomal STR loci. *Forensic Science International: Genetics, 7*, e82–e83.

NIST Population Data (2014). http://www.cstl.nist.gov/strbase/NISTpop.htm. Accessed March 18, 2014.

Data, Models, Thresholds

"All models are wrong — but some are useful."

George Box (Box 1979)

DATA COLLECTION IN ABI GENETIC ANALYZERS[1]

Data used for short tandem repeat (STR) analysis comes from Genetic Analyzers, which are laser-induced fluorescence (LIF) capillary electrophoresis (CE) instruments, produced by Applied Biosystems (now known as Life Technologies a premier brand of Thermo Fisher Scientific, see D.N.A. Box 2.1). These instruments are typically referred to as ABI Genetic Analyzers along with their model numbers, which relate to the number of capillaries available. The term "ABI" is an abbreviation of Applied Biosystems Incorporated, the company's name at the time it developed the early DNA sequencers. A summary of Genetic Analyzer instrument descriptions and history may be found in Table 6.1 of the accompanying volume Advanced *Topics in Forensic DNA Typing: Methodology* (Butler 2012).

Much of the data collection process in ABI Genetic Analyzers is considered proprietary by the manufacturer. Thus, while it would be beneficial to more fully understand what is going on inside the gray box when STR electropherograms are produced, we will unfortunately not be able to get into the complete nitty-gritty of how signal is produced to create DNA profiles. In preparing this chapter, questions were directed to Life Technologies scientists and they kindly shared information that was not considered proprietary. After this chapter section was completed, Life Technology scientists were given an opportunity to review the accuracy of what was written.

As stated in the footnote to this section, the National Institute of Standards and Technology (NIST) does not endorse or recommend commercial products. Information is included on these Genetic Analyzers because they are the sole instruments currently used by the forensic DNA community for STR analysis.

---

[1] Certain commercial equipment, instruments, and materials are identified in order to specify experimental procedures as completely as possible. In no case does such identification imply a recommendation or endorsement by the National Institute of Standards and Technology, nor does it imply that any of the materials, instruments, or equipment identified are necessarily the best available for the purpose.

D.N.A. BOX 2.1

A BRIEF HISTORY OF NAME CHANGES
FOR APPLIED BIOSYSTEMS

Applied Biosystems, Inc. (ABI) has dominated the genetic instrument business for the past three decades. What began as a small biotechnology company in 1981 named GeneCo, for Genetic Systems Company, has grown through mergers and acquisitions over the years. Along with this growth has come a number of name changes, as noted in the table below. In February 2014, Life Technologies became a premier brand of Thermo Fisher Scientific.

Year	Company Name
1981	Genetic Systems Company (GeneCo)
1982	Applied Biosystems, Inc. (ABI)
1993	Applied Biosystems Division of Perkin-Elmer
1996	PE Applied Biosystems

Year	Company Name
1998	PE Biosystems
1999	PE Biosystems Group of PE Corporation
2000	Applied Biosystems Group of Applera Corporation
2002	Applied Biosystems (AB)
2008	Life Technologies (after Applied Biosystems merged with Invitrogen)
2014	Thermo Fisher Scientific (Life Technologies is a premier brand)

Sources: http://www.lifetechnologies.com/us/en/home/about-us/news-gallery/company-fact-sheet/company-history.html; http://en.wikipedia.org/wiki/Applied_Biosystems; author's personal experience over the past 20 years.

A key component of the data detection process is the charge-coupled device, or CCD, camera, which is an electronic detector with thousands-to-millions of little square pixels. Each of these pixels is photosensitive so that a photon of light is converted into an electron when it strikes the CCD pixel. The CCD was invented in 1969 at AT&T Bell Labs by Willard Boyle and George Smith, who shared the 2009 Nobel Prize in Physics for their discovery and its impact on science and society (Nobel Prize 2009). CCDs are used in digital cameras. The more pixels, the higher the resolution or ability to resolve closely spaced photon strikes. Cameras with megapixel (millions of pixels) CCD imagers are commonplace today.

A CCD camera in an ABI Genetic Analyzer collects visible light in a rainbow of colors ranging from 520 nm to 690 nm (Sailus et al. 2012). The visible light detected comes from laser-induced fluorescence of the dyes attached during the polymerase chain reaction (PCR) process that copies STR markers. As the dye-labeled STR PCR products are separated by mobility (approximately by size) via capillary electrophoresis, they pass a detection window where the fluorescent dyes are excited by a laser. The primary excitation wavelengths of the laser are 488 nm for 310, 3100, and 3130 series instruments and 505 nm for 3500 series instruments. A shutter on the laser, similar to a camera shutter, opens and closes rapidly to permit short pulses of light to excite the fluorescent dyes over a short period of time (a "frame"). Each frame is similar to a single image collected from a series of video images.

Emitted light from the laser-excited fluorescent dyes passes through filters, mirrors, and lenses before it strikes a diffraction grating, which separates the light into a spectrum of colors similar to that produced by a prism. The color-distributed "rainbow" of light illuminates the CCD detector, and the intensity of light is recorded for each pixel by the data collection software.

Figure 2.1(a) depicts the spatial and spectral separation of signal on a CCD detector for a single frame. Note that one axis (the y-axis in the figure) of the CCD image captures the full range of wavelengths of light and the other axis (the x-axis in the figure) reflects the activity within each capillary at that moment in time. The relative signal intensity on the CCD camera (the z-axis, which would be perpendicular to the page) is converted to relative fluorescence unit (RFU) values through proprietary software algorithms (Sailus et al. 2012). With each opening of the laser shutter, a new frame is created. And with each frame, data are collected on the CCD camera that correspond to each capillary and the range of color wavelengths.

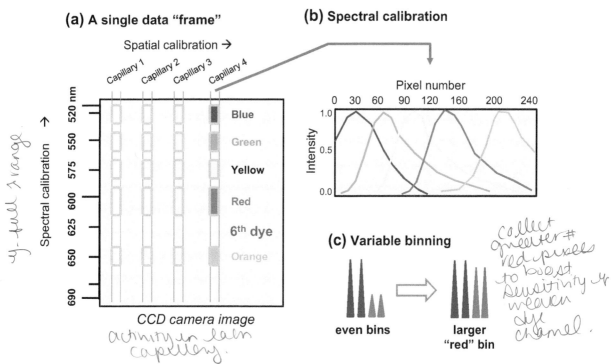

FIGURE 2.1 (a) Depiction of a CCD camera image from a multi-capillary electrophoresis system that collects fluorescence signal over a short period of time (a "frame"). Spatial calibration defines the position of capillaries along the x-axis of the CCD camera image. Spectral calibration with virtual filters (open boxes) assign y-axis positions to dye colors. A sixth dye position, which can be activated in ABI 3500 series instruments, is available between the red and orange dye channels. (b) Illustration of overlapping dye emission spectra requiring spectral deconvolution by the data collection software. Spectral calibration helps define, for example, how much "green" dye signal is in the "blue" region (colored box), in order to reduce or eliminate pull-up (bleedthrough) between the dye colors depicted in the sample electropherogram. (c) Variable binning of the red channel involves collecting more signal along the y-axis of the CCD camera image to even signal peak balance between red dye-labeled and other STR kit amplicons. See also Figure 2.2.

I. DATA INTERPRETATION

When a new capillary or capillary array is placed on an instrument, a spatial calibration must be performed to help define which pixels on the CCD camera correspond to each capillary. Likewise, a spectral calibration is run with a specific set of fluorescent reference dyes in order to calibrate the contribution of each dye to the fluorescence observed at specific wavelengths (Figure 2.1(b)). The reference dyes must match the fluorescent dyes used in an STR kit to label PCR products in order to achieve an appropriate color separation among allelic peaks. This spectral calibration, also known as a matrix correction, enables the analysis software to distinguish the different color dyes from one another.

For weaker fluorescent dyes, such as those used to produce the "red" channel, a greater number of pixels may be collected to boost sensitivity relative to other dye channels. This process is referred to as "variable binning" (Figure 2.1(c)). Chapter 8 on troubleshooting data collection provides additional details on spatial and spectral calibration.

Figure 2.2 depicts the collection of multiple CCD camera image frames and their conversion into a sample electropherogram. The sample electropherogram for each capillary and dye channel is created by the data collection software through linking a series of data points captured in succession, which is depicted in Figure 2.2(a) as "Frame 1," "Frame 2," etc. It is important to remember that both Figure 2.1 and Figure 2.2 provide a high-level representation and simplification of what is actually a complex process, most of which is proprietary to the data collection software used by Life Technologies.

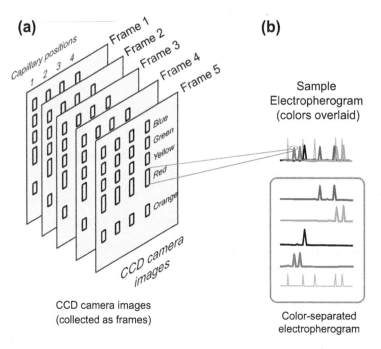

FIGURE 2.2   (a) A series of CCD camera images (see also Figure 2.1) are used to create a sample electropherogram through signal collection at virtual filter points defined on the CCD camera image with spatial and spectral calibration. (b) Data points in sample electropherogram come from combining signal from multiple pixels within the virtual filter window. Typically around 8,000 frames are collected in a 30 to 40 minute CE run.

Essentially there are four dimensions of data collected on a CCD detector when DNA samples are injected into a Genetic Analyzer: (1) capillary position (x-axis), (2) wavelength of light across the visible spectrum (y-axis), (3) intensity of light at specific wavelengths that is translated into CCD electrical signals (z-axis), and (4) the time period during which each frame is collected (t-axis), defined by the opening and closing of the laser shutter. Thus, the CCD detector in Genetic Analyzer instruments is similar to a digital video camera capturing fluorescent signal from multiple capillaries across the visible spectrum while dye-labeled PCR products are being separated through polymer-filled capillaries in terms of their relative mobility and size. By connecting the data in the thousands of CCD signal frames collected over the course of a DNA separation run, the analysis software synthesizes an electropherogram of the STR PCR products from a biological sample (Figure 2.2(b)).

While the data collection software parses information obtained from the CCD camera into individual sample electropherograms, it is the analysis software, such as GeneMapper*ID-X* from Life Technologies or GeneMarkerHID from Soft Genetics, that displays the color-separated peaks used in DNA interpretation.

Noise exists in all measuring systems. As stated in the June 2011 User Bulletin on the ABI 3500/3500xL Genetic Analyzer: "Noise in a CE system can be generated inherently from the hardware components or as a result of the introduction of chemicals or dye-labeled fragments into the system. Background capillary electrophoresis instrument signal may be attributed to electrical noise from the instrument electronics or background Raman signal from the water in the polymer. Because of these factors, it is impossible to eliminate all the baseline noise in a detection system" (Applied Biosystems 2011).

Some additional artifacts as they relate to CCD detectors used with telescopes include saturation trails, diffraction features, dust on a filter or on the window of the CCD camera, and bad columns of pixels (CCD Artifacts 2014). Ideally any significant artifacts from a bad CCD camera will be identified and eliminated during initial instrument set-up and evaluation by an ABI Genetic Analyzer service engineer.

Signal Processing

Data viewed as an electropherogram has been "cleaned up" through a series of signal processing steps including baselining, multi-componenting, and data smoothing. While a user has some control over data smoothing and baseline subtraction, most of the signal processing occurs automatically in the data collection software. The software creates an electropherogram file as a graph representing relative dye concentration (typically plotted separately for each dye channel) against time, which is adjusted into DNA size using an internal size standard.

Baselining adjusts the baselines of all detected dye colors to the same level for a better comparison of relative signal intensity. Baselining occurs after the application of the spectral calibration and therefore also represents the state of the data after virtual binning has occurred (Sailus et al. 2012).

Multi-componenting involves separating color contributions of light emitted by the various fluorescent dyes using parameters established from spectral calibration (Applied Biosystems 2001). This correction for spectral overlap between the dye colors is applied during data collection on the ABI 3100 and 3500 series instruments.

Smoothing connects discrete points in the electropherogram in a "smooth" or continuous fashion (Sailus et al. 2012). An electropherogram peak represents a series of discrete data points, composed of many frames (see Figure 2.2) each collected with a single opening of the laser shutter. The data collection software links the data points in a logical fashion and presents the information as a peak in an electropherogram that is then used for data interpretation.

GeneScan, GeneMapper*ID*, and GeneMapper*ID-X* analysis software provides the user with three options for data smoothing: none, light, or heavy. The smoothing process averages information from neighboring data points to connect two points in a seamless pattern. Light smoothing provides four passes of a binomial smoothing algorithm over the data and heavy smoothing represents 16 passes (Sailus et al. 2012). Smoothing removes some electronic jitter noise from the signal.

Smoothing affects peak height slightly such that the more the data are smoothed, the more a peak's height is reduced. Different versions of analysis software using different signal processing algorithms have also resulted in variation of peak heights from the same DNA profile depending on how the data were processed (e.g. Gilder et al. 2004). Typically the "light smoothing" option provides an appropriate balance to maintain most of the signal peak height and provide approximate Gaussian type peak morphology (Sailus et al. 2012).

A proprietary algorithm is used by the manufacturer to determine the height and area of each peak in an electropherogram. While peak area was originally preferred with gel-based systems, such as the ABI 377 that exhibited peak tailing, peak height is more commonly used with capillary systems where the peaks are more symmetrical.

Differences between Instruments

Each Genetic Analyzer CE instrument has a unique laser, CCD detector, and optical alignment. Thus, signal differences are expected and certainly observed between different CE systems. While forensic DNA laboratories often have multiple instruments to cope with their volume of work, differences among the instrument detection sensitivities are typically ignored so that a single interpretation protocol is in use across the laboratory.

In an ideal world, the capability would exist for obtaining identical signal between two or more instruments in the same laboratory. Unfortunately, this is not possible due to the many components leading to the electropherogram signal being produced. This is one reason the RFU signal strength is defined as "relative" fluorescence units rather than "absolute."

The inclusion of a solid-state laser with the ABI 3500 Genetic Analyzer has reduced instrument-to-instrument variability (Sailus et al. 2012). A Genetic Analyzer service engineer can vary the power output on the ABI 3500 solid-state laser within a specified range and obtain a more consistent fluorescence excitation level. Argon ion gas lasers, which are used in the ABI 310, 3100, and 3130 series instruments, have a wider range of power output variability.

Laser beam alignment relative to the detection window on the capillary or capillary array impacts instrument sensitivity differences. This is the primary reason why spatial calibration should be performed with each capillary array change in order to maintain optimal performance.

Upper and Lower Limits for Reliable Data

Data collection with any instrument has upper and lower limits for reliable data. ABI Genetic Analyzers likewise have regions of signal intensity that correspond to appropriate "on-scale" data. Figure 2.3 illustrates general patterns in analytical instrument response. Most analytical instruments

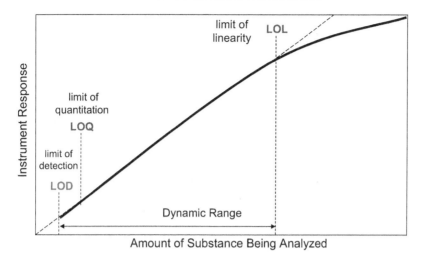

FIGURE 2.3 Graphical representation of signal range and limitations when determining instrument response to amount of substance being analyzed. Signal saturation often prevents a linear response at the upper end of a reliable dynamic range. Staying above the limit of quantitation and limit of detection ensures sufficient signal exists to reliably distinguish instrument signal from background noise.

have a range where a linear relationship can be expected between the quantity being analyzed and the instrument response, which is typically the amount of signal produced.

This "dynamic range" usually extends from the limit of detection (LOD) or the limit of quantitation (LOQ) to the limit of linearity (LOL). Above the limit of linearity, instrument response may not reliably reflect the analyte amount due to signal saturation. An example of signal saturation is what occurs when someone takes a picture of a bright light with a digital camera. In this situation, the camera detector is overwhelmed by the amount of light received, and thus essentially a blank image is stored by the camera detector. The best results with any detector are those "on-scale" — that is, the data are above the LOQ and below the LOL.

A close examination of tops of tall peaks in an electropherogram reveals that these "off-scale" peaks are flat-topped. A theoretical upper limit can exist with peak heights due to data storage limits of the detection system (D.N.A. Box 2.2).

Using on-scale data is essential when calculating information that is impacted by peak height, such as stutter percentages and peak height ratios. If, for example, a stutter percentage (see Chapter 3) was being calculated from the peak shown in D.N.A. Box 2.2(b), then the true top of the peak is above the maximum and the calculated stutter value would be inflated. A primary problem of off-scale data is pull-up or bleedthrough of one dye color into an adjacent dye channel.

Low levels of true signal from PCR products need to be distinguished from background noise. Background CE instrument signal is due to electrical noise in the instrument electronics as well as the introduction of chemicals and fluorescent dyes into the system. Residual Raman scattering from the water in the polymer is also a source of low-level background noise although some of this can be reduced or removed during the baselining process (Applied Biosystems 2011, Sailus et al. 2012).

Since it is impossible to completely eliminate baseline noise, analytical chemists have devised methods to assess the LOD and the LOQ of true signal. Either the LOD or the LOQ may be considered an analytical threshold (AT), although reliable *quantitative* information is by definition obtained above the LOQ.

D.N.A. BOX 2.2

WHY AN UPPER LIMIT FOR DATA STORAGE LEADS TO FLAT-TOPPED PEAKS IN AN ELECTROPHEROGRAM

The CCD detector and computer software in the ABI Genetic Analyzers use a 2-byte system for data storage, which enables fluorescence values to be encoded with 16 bits (each bit holding a value of 0 or 1). This 2-byte storage format enables the data collection software to provide a range of 0 to 65,535 in decimal (base-10) digits, or 0000000000000000 to 1111111111111111 in binary (base-2) digits. If both positive and negative values are permitted, then the maxima of a 2-byte storage system are +32,767 and −32,767. Opening the "raw data" view on GeneMapper*ID* or Genemapper*ID-X* for a sample run on an ABI 3500 will show that all off-scale peaks are flat-topped at +32,767. With ABI 3100 or 3130 series instruments, signals are divided by four making their maximum 8,192 relative fluorescence units (RFUs).

While the ABI 310 had a static maximum of 8,192 RFUs, multi-capillary systems employ better methods for determining saturation within the CCD camera. For example, when the CCD camera electronics detect a saturating signal on the ABI 3500, a message is sent to the instrument firmware and transferred to the data collection file. This message is used by the downstream data analysis software in the form of an Off-Scale flag in GeneMapper*ID-X* v1.2 or later (Sailus et al. 2012).

Peaks having a maximum true signal of 32,767 or less will have a "normal" shape as illustrated in (a) in the figure below. Theoretically speaking, peaks with true signal above 32,767 will be flat-topped due to a data storage saturation limit as illustrated in (b). If the off-scale data could be measured beyond this data storage saturation limit, then the peak would not be flat-topped. Quite often with off-scale data, there will be a dip that occurs in the middle of a flat-topped peak as illustrated in (c). This dip is due to the spectral subtraction (multi-componenting) being applied to the data based on the mathematical matrix established via spectral calibration to account for dye overlap (i.e. the amount of green color in the blue signal, etc.). Numerous off-scale peaks can typically be seen in the primer region spanning a range of approximately 20 nucleotides to 40 nucleotides in an electropherogram.

Sources: *http://computer.howstuffworks.com/bytes1.htm; Sailus, J., et al. (2012). Written response to author's questions regarding the function of the 3500 Genetic Analyzer and GeneMapper ID-X software v1.3. Received via email June 22, 2012.*

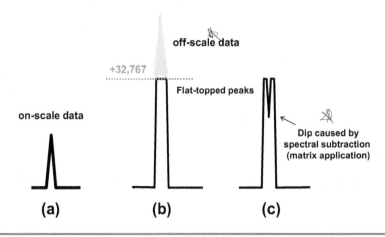

D.N.A. BOX 2.3

CALCULATING A LIMIT OF DETECTION AND A LIMIT OF QUANTITATION

Methods for distinguishing true signal from background noise have been studied for years by analytical chemists (e.g. Rubinson & Rubinson 2000). These methods have been rediscovered and applied to STR data (Gilder et al. 2007). The limit of detection (LOD) reflects a point at which signal in the form of data peaks can be reliably distinguished from noise. LOD thresholds are typically established based on the average noise level and then adding three times the standard deviation (SD) of the noise variation as illustrated in the figure below. The limit of quantitation (LOQ) reflects a point at which signal can be reliably quantified. LOQ thresholds are commonly determined by adding ten times the standard deviation of the noise variation to the average noise signal. Thus, peak 1 is above the LOD and considered a true peak, but only peak 2 can be used for quantitative evaluation since it is above the LOQ.

A peak with a height just above the LOD has a 95% or 99.7% chance of not being noise depending on how the LOD is set. However, from an analytical perspective, because a signal just above the LOD is likely contaminated with some noise, it should not be used in quantitative comparisons until peak heights are at least above the LOQ. Since quantitative decisions are typically being made in STR typing in terms of relative ratios of peak heights, the LOQ is most likely to be considered equivalent to the analytical threshold used in STR data interpretation. While getting at the actual noise level in an electropherogram on a routine basis can be challenging, analytical threshold validation studies can be performed by collecting and analyzing all of the peaks above 1 RFU (relative fluorescence units) in areas of the electropherogram where true peaks are not present.

Sources: Rubinson, K.A., & Rubinson, J.F. (2000). Sample size and major, minor, trace, and ultratrace components. Contemporary Instrumental Analysis. *Upper Saddle River: Prentice Hall, pp. 150–158; Gilder, J.R., et al. (2007). Run-specific limits of detection and quantitation for STR-based DNA testing.* Journal of Forensic Sciences, 52, 97–101.

D.N.A. Box 2.3 illustrates the calculation of LOD and LOQ. An analytical threshold is effectively a gatekeeper for allowing peaks with sufficient signal to be deemed "reliable" to pass into consideration for further processing. Additional details on setting and using an analytical threshold are described later in this chapter.

Summary of ABI Genetic Analyzer Signal

Data collected on an ABI Genetic Analyzer goes through multiple levels of signal processing with most of the details unavailable to users since signal collection specifics are considered proprietary by the manufacturer. However, consistent treatment of data signal processing should enable relative peak heights to be meaningful in terms of relative amounts of DNA detected. Data quality metrics aid interpretation. Modern data analysis software includes the ability to alert analysts to off-scale data where caution is warranted for specific data use.

Due to the many variables that go into the data collection process, peak height variation occurs from run to run even if the same DNA samples are processed multiple times. In addition, different Genetic Analyzer instruments will exhibit variation. Most laboratories, however, utilize fixed analytical thresholds across multiple instruments for convenience.

MODELS

In an effort to explain real-world data, scientists develop mathematical models and examine how well these models fit what is observed. For example, is a linear relationship correct in describing the relationship between two variables? Or does an exponential curve provide a better description? If a model does not adequately fit observed data, then the model may be refined until it does — or discarded and replaced with a better one. However, as chemical engineer and statistician George Box famously noted, "Essentially all models are wrong — but some are useful" (Box 1979).

All models are shaped by assumptions. And all interpretation of data — including STR DNA profiles — depends on data models. With any data collected, decisions have to be made regarding reliability of the information obtained.

Georg Rasch, a Danish mathematician, wrote: "That the model is not true is certainly correct, no models are — not even the Newtonian laws. When you construct a model you leave out all the details which you, with the knowledge at your disposal, consider inessential...Models should not be true, but it is important that they are *applicable* [italicized in the original], and whether they are applicable for any given purpose must of course be investigated. This also means that a model is never accepted finally, [but is] only on trial. In the case which we discuss, we may tentatively accept the model described, investigate how far our data agree with it, and perhaps find discrepancies which may lead us to certain revisions of the model" (Rasch 1960).

Validation data, which are collected as part of establishing the reliability and the limitations of a technique, help inform or refine data interpretation models and assumptions behind those models. To perform validation studies, known samples are examined, often through replicate analyses. These sample replicates help define performance characteristics and the expected range of results.

Gaussian Distributions

One of the most commonly used models to describe collections of independent values (data sets) obtained from measurements on a defined population of samples is the normal or Gaussian distribution. Gaussian curves, sometimes referred to as bell-shaped curves, can be described in terms of the mean (average) value along with a standard deviation to reflect the variance observed about the average.

If data can be modeled with a Gaussian distribution, then levels of confidence can be associated with the results based on the average value and distance from it using standard deviation values. By convention, a 95% confidence interval is commonly applied to data to reflect a range around the average value of plus or minus two times the standard deviation (D.N.A. Box 2.4).

D.N.A. BOX 2.4

NORMAL OR "GAUSSIAN" DISTRIBUTIONS

Carl Friedrich Gauss, a German mathematican who lived from 1777 to 1855, has lent his name to a probability distribution involving the following equation:

$$f(x) = \frac{1}{\sigma\sqrt{2\pi}} e^{-\frac{(x-\mu)^2}{2\sigma^2}}$$

where μ is the mean (average) and σ is the standard deviation. Gaussian distributions are also known as normal distributions. A "standard normal distribution" is where $\mu = 0$ and $\sigma = 1$.

As can be seen in a figure of the normal distribution, which is often called by social scientists a "bell curve," about 99.7% of random, independent values drawn from a given Guassian distribution are expected to fall within the interval $\mu - 3\sigma$ to $\mu + 3\sigma$. About 95% of such values are expected to fall within the interval $\mu - 2\sigma$ to $\mu + 2\sigma$. This $\mu \pm 2\sigma$ region is referred to as a 95% confidence interval.

Sources: http://mathworld.wolfram.com/NormalDistribution. html; http://en.wikipedia.org/wiki/Normal_distribution; figure adapted from Wikipedia (based an original graph by Jeremy Kemp).

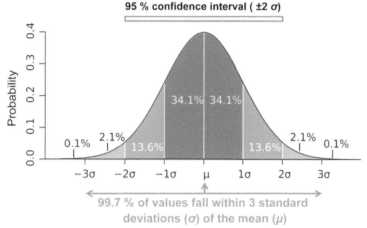

A normal (Gaussian) distribution or area under the "bell curve" showing that 99.7% of random, independent values fall within 3 standard deviations (σ) of the mean (μ). A 95% confidence interval reflects data within about 2 standards deviations of the mean. Figure from Wikipedia (based an original graph by Jeremy Kemp) About 68.27% of the values lie within 1 standard deviation of the mean. Similarly, about 95.45% of the values lie within 2 standard deviations of the mean. Nearly all (99.73%) of the values lie within 3 standard deviations of the mean.

http://upload.wikimedia.org/wikipedia/commons/thumb/8/8c/Standard_deviation_diagram.svg/2000px-Standard_deviation_diagram.svg.png

As will be discussed in the next section, threshold values are often established based on an average plus two or three times the standard deviation. The value used reflects the expected level of coverage of data using the set threshold. For example, about 99.7% of data that follows a Gaussian distribution is expected to fall within three standard deviations of the mean. When the possibility exists for distributions to be skewed or outliers are observed, there are established statistical and data analysis techniques to handle more complex situations.

THRESHOLDS USED IN STR TYPING

While data come in a continuum of values, thresholds are often placed on data in an attempt to reflect the reliability of results obtained in different regions of that continuum. Typically these thresholds are used to represent or define reasonable limits to data based on prior observations. In other words, the performance of validation data sets helps inform users that data should conform to certain expectations.

For example, imagine a data set with values ranging from 0 to 100 differing by single integers. If a greater confidence in data reliability comes with a higher numerical value, then a threshold might be set at 5 so that the numbers 0, 1, 2, 3, or 4 would not be used for further analysis (due to their unreliability) while 5, 6, 7, 8, and so on would be used. It is helpful to appreciate that in this example a value of 6, while above the defined detection threshold, has more uncertainty associated with it compared to a higher value such as 96. In this example, the selection of a threshold of "5" may have been arbitrary. However, in forensic DNA analysis, laboratories ideally set detection thresholds and other interpretation parameters with empirical data obtained from validation studies of known samples.

Purpose and Limitations of Thresholds

The primary purpose of a threshold is to exclude unreliable data from further consideration and base that further analysis only on reliable data. The hard part is often setting a meaningful threshold. Thresholds are essentially a risk assessment applied to the reliability of data.

Students can relate to thresholds in terms of how letter grades in school classes are determined. For example, a test score of 90 may result in an "A" grade while a score of 89 is rated a "B," even though the two scores are only one point apart. Likewise, category thresholds can be used to bin values together such that test scores from 90 to 100 are an "A," 80 to 89 are a "B," 70 to 79 are a "C," and so forth. These test score thresholds may only have meaning in the context of a specific class with values that have been predetermined by the teacher.

If detection thresholds are appropriately determined and run conditions remain sufficiently stable over time in order to meaningfully compare results obtained at different times, then threshold values can be used to assess the reliability of new results. A good example of a threshold is the value used by the data analysis software to return the peak height for a signal in an electropherogram. Many users of ABI 310 or 3130xl Genetic Analyzers use a peak detection threshold of 50 relative fluorescence units (RFUs) because this is the manufacturer's default value.

While thresholds are used for practical purposes, it is important to recognize that data exist in a continuum rather than a binary "step function" of pass or fail in terms of data quality in assessment of reliability. Thus, in the simple example just described of a series of numbers from 0 to 100, a value of "4" is deemed unreliable because it is below the set threshold of "5," yet it only differs from 5 by a single digit. Similarly with CE data, a peak at 49 RFUs is just below a 50 RFU analytical threshold, yet the 49 RFU peak is not deemed reliable while the 50 RFU peaks is. As will be discussed later in the book, probabilistic approaches are being developed to address the limitations of fixed thresholds (Gill & Buckleton 2010a and 2010b, Taylor et al. 2013).

The use of a particular RFU analytical detection threshold (e.g. 50 RFU) represents a model for data behavior from a specific instrument (e.g. 3130xl) under specific conditions (e.g. injection parameters, range of DNA template, STR kit, etc.). Thresholds represent an effort to reflect data quality and to define the limits of reliability. Detection thresholds and other thresholds are based on specific assumptions relating to consistency of data collection over time. Different instruments may have different noise levels. However, from a practical standpoint with data interpretation, a DNA technical leader may decide to select a universal analytical threshold to apply across CE instruments in their laboratory.

As a 2012 report on interpretation of DNA evidence notes, "thresholds are difficult to apply in a meaningful way, for example, in a sample that comprises DNA from two or more individuals, the total quantifiable [DNA] does not reflect the individual contributions" (Gill et al. 2012; p. 7). Keep in mind that there are assumptions and limitations behind any model or approach: "All models are wrong — but some are useful" (Box 1979).

Thresholds are typically used in a binary fashion (i.e. effectively treated as a "0" or a "1"). Data on one side of a threshold may be deemed okay (i.e. given a probability value of "1") while data on the other side of the threshold are considered unreliable (i.e. given a probability value of "0"). Using a threshold approach, data observed at the boundary of a threshold and beyond are treated as fully reliable. However, it is important to recognize that more uncertainty in the actual data value exists near a threshold boundary than further from it.

Consider an example such as the amount of stutter product produced during the PCR amplification of an STR allele (see Chapter 3). If our stutter ratio threshold is set in data analysis software at 15%, then a peak in a stutter position detected at 14% of the STR allele can be designated as a stutter product and will be filtered out by the data analysis software. Alternatively, if a peak that is 16% of the STR allele occurs in a stutter position, then it will be labeled by the software. However, this does not necessarily mean that this peak that exceeded the threshold is necessarily a true allele. It could be a true stutter product that happens to possess more stutter than expected. Sometimes outlier data exist that do not fit well with the concept of a single symmetric population.

A DNA analyst reviewing this potential stutter data will need to make an interpretation decision. Is this peak, which occurs just above the 15% defined-stutter threshold, a true stutter product that exceeded expectations and the established software filtering threshold? Or, could a mixture possibly be present with the 16% peak representing part of a minor contributor to a DNA mixture? In truth, either one of these scenarios is possible (see D.N.A. Box 5.3). Thus, analysts have to look at the big picture of a profile — and not focus on a single locus — when trying to make interpretation decisions.

Table 2.1 lists thresholds commonly used in STR data interpretation along with principles behind the meaning of these thresholds. Understanding the typical variation that is expected in a DNA profile is important to making meaningful interpretation decisions. Thus, validation studies are vital in both setting thresholds used by interpretation software *and understanding the limitations of these thresholds*. Table 2.2 reviews decisions to be made with various thresholds and potential validation data to inform these decisions.

TABLE 2.1   Principles Behind the Various Thresholds Used in Forensic DNA Analysis

Thresholds (example values)	Principles Behind (if properly set based on lab- & kit-specific empirical data)
Analytical Threshold (e.g. 50 RFU)	Below this value, observed peaks cannot be reliably distinguished from instrument noise (baseline signal).
Limit of Linearity (e.g. 5000 RFU)	Above this value, the CCD camera can become saturated and peaks may not accurately reflect relative signal quantities (e.g. flat-topped peaks) and lead to pull-up/bleed-through between dye color channels.
Stochastic Threshold (e.g. 250 RFU)	Above this peak height value, it is reasonable to assume that allelic dropout of a sister allele of a heterozygote has not occurred at that locus; single alleles above this value in single-source samples are assumed to be homozygous.
Stutter Threshold (e.g. 15%)	Below this value, a peak in the reverse (or forward) stutter position can be designated as a stutter artifact with single-source samples or some mixtures (often higher with lower DNA amounts).
Peak Height Ratio (e.g. 60%)	Above this value, two heterozygous alleles can be grouped as a possible genotype (often lower with lower DNA amounts).
Major/Minor Ratio (e.g. 4:1)	When the ratio of contributors is closer than this value in a two-person mixture, it becomes challenging and often impossible to correctly associate genotype combinations to either the major or minor contributor.

TABLE 2.2   Threshold Decisions and Potentially Useful Validation Data

Thresholds to Determine	Decisions to Make (lab- & kit-specific)	Useful Validation Data
Analytical = ____ RFU	Will a single overall value or color specific values be used?	Noise levels in negative controls or non-peak areas of positive controls.
Stochastic = ____ RFU	Will a minimum peak height value or alternative criteria such as a quantitation value be used? Or will a probabilitistic genotype approach be used?	Level where dropout occurs in low-level single-source heterozygous samples under conditions used (e.g. different injection times, post-PCR cleanup).
Stutter filter = ___%	Will profile-wide, locus-specific, or allele-specific stutter filters be applied?	Stutter in single-source samples (helpful if examined at multiple DNA quantities).
Peak Height Ratio = ___%	Will profile-wide, locus-specific, or signal height (quantity) specific PHRs be applied?	Heterozygote peak height ratios in single-source samples (helpful if examined at multiple DNA quantities).
Major/Minor Ratio = ____	At what mixture ratio will an attempt be made to separate components of a two-person mixture into major and minor contributors for profile deductions?	Defined mixture ratios (e.g. 1:1, 1:3, 1:9) with known samples to observe consistency across loci and to assess ability to deduce correct contributor profiles.

Limitations of "Binary" Thresholds in a Continuous World

The treatment of data on one side of a threshold value differently than data on the other side is sometimes referred to as a "binary" threshold approach, where information is effectively being treated as either a zero (0) or a one (1). Any data above the threshold value are deemed reliable and treated as useful. From a probabilistic standpoint, it is given a value of one, and the result is treated as though it is 100% reliable (i.e. no uncertainty). Any data below an established threshold value is deemed unreliable and therefore not used. Results below a threshold are essentially given a probability of zero (Figure 2.4).

An analogy involving light (Bednar 2011) may be useful in helping readers understand the difference between binary (0 or 1) and continuous systems. When an individual walks into a dark room with no windows and turns on a light switch, electricity flows rapidly to a light bulb and light fills the room almost instanteously. This situation could be termed a binary system – the room is either dark (0) or the room is light (1). The transition between these two states is almost instantaneous. A threshold is crossed as the switch is turned on and the room becomes light.

Contrast this binary off/on situation with the morning light coming after a dark night through a gradual introduction of light. When exactly does the morning begin? The dawn's first light is certainly present before the sun crosses the horizon and can be fully seen by an observer. Defining a specific "threshold" of light is more challenging with the dawn because it is gradual. However, for practical reasons thresholds are used even in this example of a sunrise. Astronomers define the specific threshold of morning's first light as the moment the top edge of the sun rises above the horizon (Rise, Set, and Twilight Definitions 2014).

A major challenge with using a binary approach is how to reliably assign or establish appropriate threshold values. Validation data are typically collected in an attempt to derive a threshold value, such as the analytical threshold. However, different sets of validation data may result in different apparent thresholds. Which one(s) are correct? It is important that run conditions are sufficiently stable over time so that determinations made with validation data will be meaningful when sample data are collected.

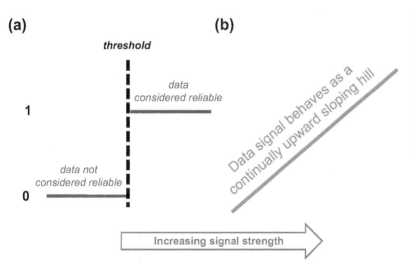

(a)

threshold

(b)

1

data
considered reliable

Data signal behaves as a
continually upward sloping hill

data not
considered reliable

0

Increasing signal strength

FIGURE 2.4 Illustration of the step-like function of (a) a binary threshold-based approach where data are considered unreliable (probability of 0) below a threshold and considered reliable (probability of 1) above the threshold in spite of the fact that increasing data signal behaves as (b) a continuum similar to a continually upward sloping hill.

Commenting on the issue of thresholds, New Zealand researchers state in a 2010 publication: "The use of bounds applied to data that show continuous variation is common in forensic science and is often a pragmatic decision. However it should be borne in mind that applying such bounds has arbitrary elements to it and that *there will be cases where the data lie outside these bounds*" (Bright et al. 2010; emphasis added). Therefore, another deficiency of a binary approach is that information content is lost whenever a threshold is established. In other words, some data will always lie outside the bounds set with a chosen threshold.

In speaking at an April 2012 conference regarding challenges surrounding low-level DNA, Professor David Balding (University College London) commented: "In ideal analysis, we would never use thresholds, but in practice they are useful. I do not think we have sophisticated enough models in many situations to understand all of the details of the data. Thresholds provide a simplification. That is reasonable as long as they are backed up by calibration evidence" (Rome meeting 2012). Also speaking at this same conference, Professor Peter Gill (University of Olso) remarked: "If you are going to have a threshold, at least try to associate it with a level of risk. You can have a threshold anywhere you like but the lower the [stochastic] threshold, the greater the risk is of wrongful designation [of genotypes]. The higher the threshold, the more likely you will have an inconclusive result" (Rome meeting 2012).

Advantages and Challenges of a Probabilistic Approach

Probabilistic genotyping methods have been advocated to replace threshold methods (Gill & Buckleton 2010a and 2010b, Taylor et al. 2013). Probabilistic approaches enable calculations to be performed to assess the chance of missing a particular allele in the evidence profile when the question profile does not perfectly match the known profile. This approach is particularly helpful when assessing low-level DNA that may be present in complex mixtures. Further information on probabilistic genotyping will be covered in Chapter 7 and Chapter 13 of this book.

A purely probabilistic approach does not use a stochastic threshold in the sense that will be described in Chapter 4 to assess the likelihood of missing an allele with low-level DNA data. Calculating the various possible genotypes to explain observed DNA mixture data can be challenging if not impossible to do manually in a timely fashion. Therefore, computer software programs have been developed to perform these calculations (see Chapter 13). It is important to keep in mind that probabilistic models assume that PCR and CE run conditions are not significantly changing over time so that when parameters are initially modeled during validation studies the same probability distributions will hold when samples are tested. An important advantage of probabilistic methods is that the results reflect interpretation uncertainty.

SETTING AND USING ANALYTICAL THRESHOLDS

Data produced in any analytical instrument will contain baseline "noise" like static on a radio. In the case of a radio signal, the message cannot be clearly understood unless it is louder than the static. In forensic DNA, the signal observed must be "loud" enough (have sufficient sensitivity to be detected) and "clear" enough (have sufficient specificity when deciphering mixture components) in order to reliably reflect the DNA molecules present in the sample being tested.

Peak detection thresholds are set on capillary electrophoresis instruments at a level so that if "peaks" are observed below this level these "peaks" are considered indistinguishable from the baseline noise. A common peak detection threshold on the ABI 310 or 3130 series instruments is 50 RFUs. Only peaks above this user-defined *analytical threshold* are considered a reliable analytical signal and thus recorded by the data analysis software.

Current software only permits a single threshold to be applied across the entire electropherogram. Sensitivity and baseline noise levels can vary between instruments and even dye channels within an individual electropherogram (D.N.A. Box 2.5). Different amounts of input DNA can impact the relative baseline noise levels (Figure 2.5), and baseline noise levels can vary across an electropherogram. Thus, laboratories should conduct validation studies with low amounts of DNA to assess appropriate detection levels on their instruments and establish an analytical threshold based on signal-to-noise analyses of internally derived empirical data (SWGDAM 2010). Although individual dye channels can be set to have individual analytical (detection) thresholds, this is rarely done as it makes data interpretation more complex.

Run-specific LOD and LOQ calculations have been proposed (Gilder et al. 2007) but have not been adopted in large measure due to practical issues and limitations with current analysis software. Thus, most forensic DNA laboratories will use a single analytical threshold across all dye channels of 50 RFU or 75 RFU for ABI 3130 instruments. Analytical thresholds for 3500 series instruments are likely to be higher due to different dynamic ranges of signal and noise (see D.N.A. Box 2.5).

In the example of setting an analytical threshold for CE peak detection, if the threshold is set too high, then useful data may be lost and lead the analyst to draw false negative conclusions. On the other hand, if the analytical threshold is placed too low, then baseline noise artifacts may be interpreted as alleles giving rise to false positive conclusions (Figure 2.6, Table 2.3).

As noted in the 2010 SWGDAM STR Interpretation Guidelines (Guideline 3.1.1.2), the analytical threshold should be established based on signal-to-noise considerations in order to appropriately distinguish potential allelic peaks from baseline noise (SWGDAM 2010). The analytical threshold should not be set artificially high in order to avoid labeling potential artifacts (e.g. pull-up peaks) because if it is too high, then true allelic information may be lost, as illustrated in Figure 2.6.

A commonly asked question that has been posed to the author is, "should data visually observed below a set analytical threshold, such as 50 RFUs, be considered for interpretation purposes?" My first response is usually something like, "if you think you have legitimate data below your established analytical threshold, then perhaps your threshold is set too high!" The point is that a properly set analytical threshold (if it is set according to the baseline noise observed on an instrument) by definition means that any peaks observed below this threshold are not appropriate for further consideration as reliable peaks. In other words, do not even bother looking for useful information below the analytical threshold.

The concern about potential "real" peaks below an analytical threshold arises because many analytical thresholds are set well above the LOQ. Thus, the analytical threshold in use for a laboratory's interpretation protocol may not be directly linked to the baseline noise of the instrument in use.

I will point out though that seeing low-level peaks that are below the analytical threshold does reflect on the overall quality of the profile. However, in my opinion, these sub-threshold peaks should not be used to make *quantitative* decisions. If the laboratory's analytical threshold is significantly different than a calculated LOQ, then it would probably be worth reassessing the analytical threshold and how it is being used by the laboratory. Allele and locus drop-out rates are impacted by adjusting the analytical threshold (Rakay et al. 2012). A number of different methods for carefully calculating analytical thresholds have been described (Bregu 2011, Bregu et al. 2013).

D.N.A. BOX 2.5

BASELINE NOISE LEVELS VARY BASED ON INSTRUMENT AND DYE CHANNEL

ABI 3500 relative fluorescence unit (RFU) signal is approximately four times that of the ABI 3130 signal. As illustrated below, ABI 3500 noise levels may also be re-scaled giving rise to the visual appearance of noisier baselines. Generally speaking though, the signal-to-noise ratios are unchanged.

Likewise, noise levels vary across dye channels, with blue and green channels exhibiting less noise than the yellow and red channels, as can be visually seen from the figure below.

Sources: Top figure based on information from Life Technologies personal communication with the author; bottom figure is a negative control with the ABI 3130 and Identifiler courtesy of Catherine Grgicak (Boston University).

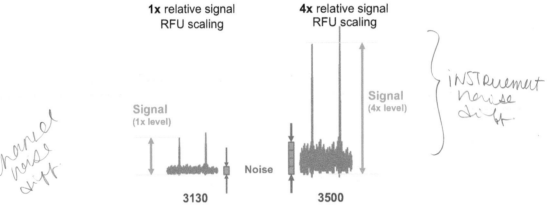

ABI 3500 signal is approximately 4-fold relative to the ABI 3130 signal. This theoretically means that noise levels may be higher on the ABI 3500.

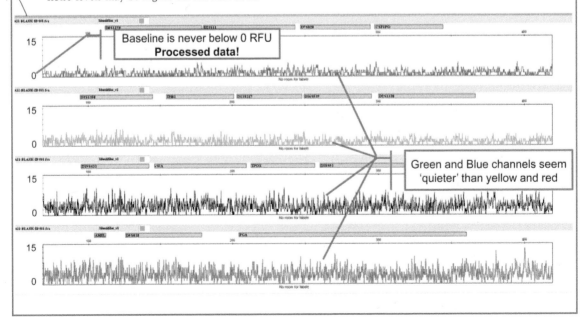

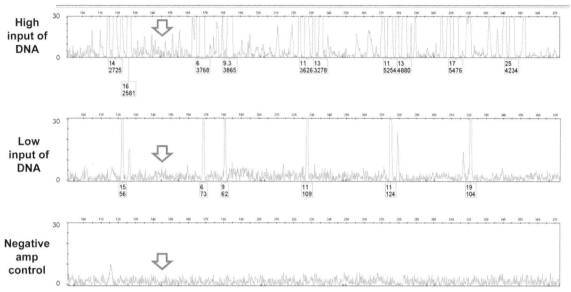

FIGURE 2.5 Baseline noise levels can vary by amount of DNA template. With a high input of DNA (top panel), the baseline between alleles (indicated by arrow) exhibits more variation. A low input of DNA (middle panel) possesses baseline noise levels on the order of a negative control (bottom panel). Figure adapted from Bregu et al. (2013) courtesy of Catherine Grgicak (Boston University).

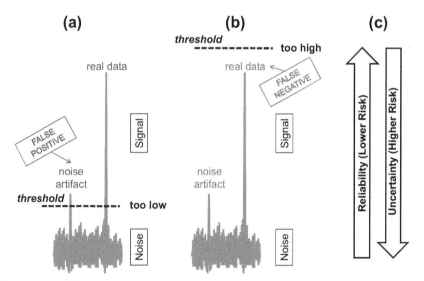

FIGURE 2.6 Relationship of thresholds (dashed horizontal line) with detected data. (a) If a detection (analytical) threshold is set too low, then noise artifacts can be classified with real data. (b) If a detection (analytical) threshold is set too high, then real data is falsely excluded along with noise artifacts. (c) Reliability of data increases with signal strength essentially lowering the risk of falsely designating signal as noise or noise as signal. Conversely, data uncertainty increases with lower signal strength, which increases the risk of confusing signal and noise designations.

TABLE 2.3   Impact of Setting Threshold too High or too Low

If	Then
Threshold is set too high…	Analysis may miss low-level legitimate peaks **(false negative conclusions produced)**
Threshold is set too low…	Analysis will take longer as artifacts and baseline noise must be removed from consideration as true peaks during data review **(false positive conclusions produced)**

By definition, any peak data observed below the LOQ (and analytical threshold if they are equivalent) cannot be used to make quantitative decisions. With commonly used DNA analysis software (e.g. GeneMapper*ID*), peaks below the analytical threshold are not labeled, and therefore are not processed further as the electropherogram is examined. Thus, setting and applying an appropriate analytical threshold is crucial to the rest of the DNA interpretation process.

There has to a balance between what can be practically determined and used versus what may be theoretically possible. The idea of run-specific thresholds (Gilder et al. 2007) is an admirable one, but not practical given the software available to forensic analysts and the time constraints of casework. Every sample cannot become a research project. Thus, fixed analytical thresholds are set (ideally with underpinning validation data to support the value used) in an effort to reflect reliability in determining legitimate instrument signal versus baseline noise.

Keep in mind that if threshold values (e.g. expected stutter percentages or an analytical threshold) are meant to reflect a change in how data are treated, then remember that uncertainty increases when approaching the set threshold. For example, the quantitative characteristics of a peak displaying 51 RFU that is just over an analytical threshold of 50 RFU should not be thought of with as much confidence as a peak that possesses a signal of 1000 RFU or more.

In some ways, setting a threshold establishes an acceptable level of risk. However, with any threshold it is not possible to fully separate unreliable data from reliable data 100% of the time. For example, the limit-of-detection threshold, which is established using a model of the average baseline noise levels plus three standard deviations (see D.N.A. Box 2.3), reflects only 99.7% of the noise variation if it is following a normal probability distribution (see D.N.A. Box 2.4). Thus, if an analytical threshold was set as low as the calculated LOD value, then approximately 0.3% of the time a noise peak could be falsely designated as a true signal peak.

When driving a car on a mountain road, it is generally wise to stay as far away from the edge of the cliff as possible. Likewise, using STR data with signal high above an established analytical threshold "cliff" is much wiser than working routinely near the edge of the cliff. Hence, the use of analytical thresholds that are farther away from the LOD and LOQ than might be theoretically desirable helps reduce the likelihood of falsely including baseline noise as a true signal for further assessment in the STR typing process that is described further in the next few chapters.

Reading List and Internet Resources

Data Collection in ABI Genetic Analyzers

Applied Biosystems. (2001). *ABI Prism 3100 Genetic Analyzer User's Manual*. Electronic copy available at http://bti.cornell.edu/manuals/Sequencer_Manual.pdf (see particularly pp. 314–318).

Applied Biosystems. (2011). *User Bulletin: Applied Biosystems 3500/3500xL Genetic Analyzer*. Available at http://www3. appliedbiosystems.com/cms/groups/applied_markets_marketing/documents/generaldocuments/cms_096535.pdf. Accessed March 21, 2014.

Butler, J. M. (2012). *Capillary electrophoresis: principles and instrumentation. Chapter 6 in Advanced Topics in Forensic DNA Typing: Methodology*. San Diego: Elsevier Academic Press. pp. 141−165.

CCD Artifacts (2014). Available at http://www.eso.org/∼ohainaut/ccd/CCD_artifacts.html. Accessed March 21, 2014.

Gilder, J. R., et al. (2004). Systematic differences in electropherogram peak heights reported by different versions of the GeneScan software. *Journal of Forensic Sciences, 49*, 92−95.

Nobel Prize (2009): http://www.nobelprize.org/nobel_prizes/physics/laureates/2009/. Accessed March 21, 2014.

Sailus, J., et al. (2012). *Written response to author's questions regarding the function of the 3500 Genetic Analyzer and GeneMapper ID-X software v1.3*. Received via email June 22, 2012.

Models

Box, G. (1979). Robustness in the strategy of scientific model building. In R. L. Launer, & G. N. Wilkinson (Eds.), *Robustness in Statistics* (p. 202). San Diego: Academic Press.

Rasch, G. (1960). Probabilistic models for some intelligence and attainment tests (reprint, with Foreword and Afterword by B. D. Wright, Chicago: University of Chicago Press, 1980). Copenhagen, Denmark: Danmarks Paedogogiske Institut., pp. 37−38. See http://en.wikiquote.org/wiki/Talk:George_E._P._Box. Accessed March 21, 2014.

Thresholds Used in STR Typing

Bednar, D. A. (2011). *The spirit of revelation*. Available at http://www.lds.org/general-conference/2011/04/the-spirit-of-revelation?lang=eng. Accessed March 21, 2014.

Bright, J.-A., et al. (2010). Examination of the variability in mixed DNA profile parameters for the Identifiler™ multiplex. *Forensic Science International Genetics, 4*, 111−114.

Cupples, C. M., et al. (2009). STR profiles from DNA samples with "undetected" or low Quantifiler results. *Journal of Forensic Sciences, 54*, 103−107.

Gill, P., & Buckleton, J. (2010a). Commentary on: Budowle B, Onorato AJ, Callaghan TF, Della Manna A, Gross AM, Guerrieri RA, Luttman JC, McClure DL. Mixture interpretation: defining the relevant features for guidelines for the assessment of mixed DNA profiles in forensic casework. J Forensic Sci 2009;54(4):810−21. *Journal of Forensic Sciences, 55*(1), 265−268. author reply 269−272.

Gill, P., & Buckleton, J. (2010b). A universal strategy to interpret DNA profiles that does not require a definition of low-copy-number. *Forensic Science International Genetics, 4*(4), 221−227.

Gill, P., et al. (2012). *The interpretation of DNA evidence (including low-template DNA)*. Available at http://www.homeoffice.gov. uk/publications/agencies-public-bodies/fsr/interpretation-of-dna-evidence. Accessed March 21, 2014.

Goor, R. M., et al. (2011). A mathematical approach to the analysis of multiplex DNA profiles. *Bulletin Mathematical Biology, 73*, 1909−1931.

Kirkham, A., et al. (2013). High-throughput analysis using AmpFlSTR Identifiler with the Applied Biosystems 3500xl Genetic Analyzer. *Forensic Science International Genetics, 7*, 92−97.

Pascali, V., & Prinz, M. (2012). Highlights of the conference 'The hidden side of DNA profiles: artifacts, errors and uncertain evidence'. *Forensic Science International Genetics, 6*, 775−777.

Puch-Solis, R., et al. (2011). Practical determination of the low template DNA threshold. *Forensic Science International Genetics, 5*(5), 422−427.

Rakay, C. A., et al. (2012). Maximizing allele detection: effects of analytical threshold and DNA levels on rates of allele and locus drop-out. *Forensic Science International Genetics, 6*, 723−728.

Rise, Set, and Twilight Definitions. Available at http://aa.usno.navy.mil/faq/docs/RST_defs.php. Accessed March 21, 2014.

Rome meeting. (2012). *Video of conference entitled "The hidden side of DNA profiles: artifacts, errors and uncertain evidence" kindly provided by Vince Pascali to Author following the April 27−28, 2012 meeting.*

Taylor, D., et al. (2013). The interpretation of single source and mixed DNA profiles. *Forensic Science International Genetics, 7*(5), 516−528.

Westen, A. A., et al. (2009). Higher capillary electrophoresis injection settings as an efficient approach to increase the sensitivity of STR typing. *Journal Forensic Sciences, 54*, 591−598.

Setting and Using Analytical Thresholds

Bregu, J. (2011). *Investigation of baseline noise: establishing an RFU threshold for forensic DNA analysis.* Master of Science thesis for Boston University School of Medicine. Available at http://www.bumc.bu.edu/gms/files/2013/03/Joli-Bregu-Thesis-2011.pdf. Accessed March 21, 2014.

Bregu, J., et al. (2013). Analytical thresholds and sensitivity: establishing RFU thresholds for forensic DNA analysis. *Journal Forensic Sciences, 58,* 120–129.

Gilder, J. R., et al. (2007). Run-specific limits of detection and quantitation for STR-based DNA testing. *Journal Forensic Sciences, 52,* 97–101.

Rakay, C. A., et al. (2012). Maximizing allele detection: Effects of analytical threshold and DNA levels on rates of allele and locus drop-out. *Forensic Science International: Genetics, 6,* 723–728.

SWGDAM. (2010). *SWGDAM Interpretation Guidelines for Autosomal STR Typing by Forensic DNA Testing Laboratories.* Available at http://www.fbi.gov/about-us/lab/biometric-analysis/codis/swgdam-interpretation-guidelines. Accessed March 21, 2014.

Methods for Determining Limit of Detection Values

Currie, L. (1999). Detection and quantification limits: origin and historical overview. *Analytica Chimica Acta, 391,* 127–134.

Kaiser, H. (1970). Report for analytical chemists: part II. Quantitation in elemental analysis. *Analytical Chemistry, 42,* 26A–59A.

Long, G. L., & Winefordner, J. D. (1983). Limit of detection: a closer look at the IUPAC definition. *Analytical Chemistry, 55,* 712A–724A.

Miller, J. C., & Miller, J. N. (2005). Errors in instrumental analysis; regression and correlation in *Statistics Analytical Chemistry. Ellis Horwood and Prentice Hall,* 101–137.

Mocak, J., Bond, A. M., Mitchell, S., & Scollary, G. (1997). A statistical overview of standard (IUPAC and ACS) and new procedures for determining the limits of detection and quantification: application to voltammetric and stripping techniques. *Pure Applied Chemistry, 69,* 297–328.

Rubinson, K. A., & Rubinson, J. F. (2000). Sample size and major, minor, trace, and ultratrace components. *Contemporary Instrumental Analysis.* Upper Saddle River: Prentice Hall, pp. 150–158.

Skoog, D. A. (1985). *Principles of Instrumental Analysis* (3rd ed.). Philadelphia: Sanders College Publishing.

Tools and information available from Boston University's Biomedical Forensic Sciences program. Available at http://www.bumc.bu.edu/gms/biomedforensic/faculty-and-staff/faculty/grgicak/tools/. Accessed March 21, 2014.

CHAPTER

3

STR Alleles and Amplification Artifacts

"The science of deduction and analysis is one which can only be acquired by long and patient study."
Sherlock Holmes (A Study in Scarlet)

INTRODUCTION

Having established an analytical threshold (see Chapter 2) that enables differentiation between signal and noise in a sample electropherogram, an analyst with the aid of a computer program is now ready to decipher whether detected peaks are alleles or artifacts (see Figure 1.3). The polymerase chain reaction (PCR) process used to generate copies of the short tandem repeat (STR) alleles that make up a DNA profile may create additional detectable PCR products. Impurities from the fluorescent dyes used to detect the PCR products can be injected into the capillary electrophoresis (CE) system and give rise to artifactual peaks in the sample electropherogram. This chapter reviews issues surrounding STR allele measurements during data interpretation.

On the topic of distinguishing alleles from artifacts, the SWGDAM, 2010 Interpretation Guidelines state (SWGDAM 2010):

> *3.1 Non-Allelic Peaks. Because forensic DNA typing characterizes STR loci using PCR and electrophoretic technologies, some data that result from this analytical scheme may not represent actual alleles that originate in the sample. It is therefore necessary, before the STR typing results can be used for comparison purposes, to identify any potential non-allelic peaks. Non-allelic peaks may be PCR products (e.g. stutter, non-template dependent nucleotide addition, and non-specific amplification product), analytical artifacts (e.g. spikes and raised baseline), instrumental limitations (e.g. incomplete spectral separation resulting in pull-up or bleed-through), or may be introduced into the process (e.g. disassociated primer dye). Generally, non-allelic data such as stutter, non-template dependent nucleotide addition, disassociated dye, and incomplete spectral separation are reproducible; spikes and raised baseline are generally non-reproducible.*

It is important to keep in mind that obtaining results from different STR kits may reflect a specific perspective on the sample tested. Thus, even though the same STR locus is being examined with two different kits — and perhaps even the same PCR primer sequences are being used — the amplification environment can be different if a different PCR buffer is used or mobility modifiers have been added to the primer sequence or there are different loci co-amplified in the multiplex PCR reaction. In addition, each lot of the STR kit may contain different amounts of disassociated primer dye (often called dye blobs), and inter-locus balance may differ slightly with minor variation in the relative amount of primers present. Therefore, some artifacts may be specific to the kit and even the kit lot being examined.

OVERVIEW OF THE STR TYPING PROCESS

A high-level overview of the overall STR typing process is illustrated in Figure 3.1. This process involves using PCR primers that are specific to the flanking regions of the STR locus of interest in order to generate copies of this marker during PCR amplification from the biological sample being tested. A fluorescent dye is attached to one of the PCR primers in order to effectively label the PCR products for detection purposes. The resulting DNA molecules are then separated and sorted by relative size (from smallest to largest) with capillary electrophoresis (CE). The color of the fluorescent dye labeling each PCR product is detected by the CE instrument and differentiated from other colors permitting multiple loci with overlapping size ranges to be analyzed simultaneously, a "multiplex."

An internal size standard is run concurrently with the PCR products in order to size all of the DNA fragments like an internal "ruler" or measuring stick. The DNA sizes for each PCR product are then

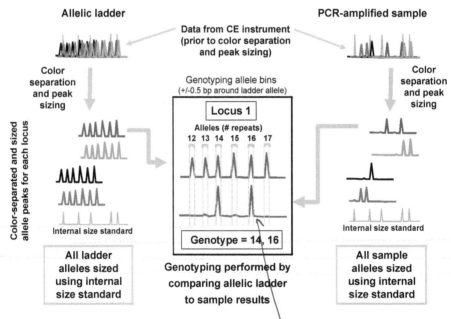

FIGURE 3.1 Genotyping is performed through a comparison of sized peaks from PCR-amplified samples to allele size bins. These allele bins are defined with the genotyping software using size information from an allelic ladder run with each batch of samples. Any peak falling in a particular dye color and allele bin size range is designated as an allele for that locus. Peaks in both the allelic ladder and the PCR-amplified samples are sized using the same internal size standard so that they may be compared to one another.

$\pm 0.5 bp$

converted to allele designations through a comparison to allelic ladders containing known common alleles for each locus. The allelic ladders are run in an adjacent capillary at the same time (on multi-capillary instruments), or in the same capillary at a different time (on single-capillary instruments) as the samples. Provided that consistent environmental and electrophoretic conditions exist between the sample and the allelic ladder — and the same internal size standard and sizing algorithm are used — allelic ladder sizes can be directly compared to sample sizes in order to make an allele designation. This size-to-allele conversion is performed by genotyping software[1], such as GeneMapper*ID* from Life Technologies (South San Francisco, California, USA) or GeneMarkerHID from Soft Genetics (State College, Pennsylvania, USA).

Uncertainty in STR Interpretation

As with any measurement process, uncertainty exists in the STR typing process, and subsequent interpretation efforts due to natural genetic variation in alleles and the complexity of the biological samples being examined. For example, the potential of DNA mixtures (i.e. samples containing DNA from more than one contributor) can lead to uncertainty in the STR interpretation process. This uncertainty can lower the level of confidence in the determination of possible genotypes for each contributor.

Interpretation uncertainty and difficulties may result from (1) variant alleles with DNA sizes that differ from the expected STR sequence motif, (2) internal sequence differences where the overall allele size is the same but variation occurs in the types of sequence motifs present, (3) non-template addition where an extra peak could be a variant allele from another contributor, (4) stutter product that could be an allele from a minor amount of another contributor, and (5) a null or silent allele where the allele is truly present but fails to be amplified and detected due to a primer binding site mutation. Each of these topics will be briefly covered in this chapter.

So-called variant alleles exist in the human population that do not match the expected variation in the core repeat motif (e.g. allele 8.1 instead of 8 or 9). Genotyping software may label these variant alleles as "off-ladder." However, the observation of an "off-ladder" allele could also be due to poor measurement precision and sizing "slippage" or "drift" between the allelic ladder calibration size and the measured allele. Thus, demonstrating tight sizing precision is important during internal validation experiments. These experiments are often performed by re-injecting an allelic ladder multiple times and observing the mean values and standard deviations for each allele (see D.N.A. Box 8.2).

Measurement uncertainty (variability) in an electropherogram exists along the x-axis of size due to run-to-run sizing precision, which is impacted by the internal size standard peak spacing, sizing algorithm used, and potential temperature variation due to laboratory environmental conditions.

Along the y-axis of peak height in an electropherogram, measurement uncertainty exists due to amplification varability. The uncertainty of genotype determination (appropriate allele pairing) increases when amplifying low-levels of DNA template (see Chapter 7) and is exhibited in

---

[1] Certain commercial equipment, instruments, and materials are identified in order to specify experimental procedures as completely as possible. In no case does such identification imply a recommendation or endorsement by the National Institute of Standards and Technology (NIST), nor does it imply that any of the materials, instruments, or equipment identified are necessarily the best available for the purpose.

single-source samples by heterozygote imbalance. In addition, when working with DNA mixtures (see Chapter 6), potential allele sharing and stacking between contributor genotypes as well as stutter products can make it difficult to confidently assess the number of contributors or their mixture ratios present in the collected forensic sample.

Software Used and Parameters Set

Fairly sophisticated software has been developed to take sample electrophoretic data rapidly through the genotyping process illustrated in Figure 3.1. When the ABI 310 instrument was first released in the mid-1990s, sample processing was performed in two steps by two different software programs: GeneScan and Genotyper. The GeneScan software was used to spectrally resolve the dye colors for each peak, to label peaks above a minimum analytical threshold, and to size the DNA fragments in each sample. The resulting electropherograms were then imported into a second software program where genotyping was performed. The Genotyper program determined each sample's genotype by comparing the sizes of alleles observed in a standard allelic ladder sample to those obtained at each locus tested in the DNA sample. The user could select allele-calling ranges utilizing the allelic ladder allele DNA size information based on the specific STR kit in use.

These older programs have now been replaced by a software package called GeneMapper*ID*, and more recently by *GeneMapperID-X* that combines the functions of GeneScan and Genotyper with additional quality scores for the data. "Bins" and "panels" are created by the user or provided by the STR kit manufacturer that enable the electrophoretic peaks to be designed as STR alleles for each tested locus depending on the DNA size and dye color channel of the detected peak.

After the data has been processed, the analyst examines the peaks that have been called, and based on experience and laboratory protocol may or may not edit the calls made by the software. Decisions to edit a software-designated peak come from an understanding of biological or instrumental artifacts that will be discussed later in this chapter. Any editing of the data is usually documented either in an analyst's case notes or in comments made in the electronic or paper printouts of the STR data. An allele table may then be created from the edited allele calls. Prior to finalizing the DNA profile results, a second reviewer performs a confirmatory review to verify all results as part of the quality assurance process.

The allele calls produced by the GeneScan/Genotyper or GeneMapper*ID* software may be exported to a spreadsheet program for further data analysis. Data uploaded into a DNA database are converted to a common format to be compatible with previously uploaded DNA typing information.

Bins are specific regions in the electrophoretic space (dye color and DNA fragment size) that define the expected sizes for each known allele from an STR locus. Panels define what combination of STR loci are present in a specific assay or kit. Physical bins correspond to alleles present in an allelic ladder, while virtual bins may be designated in the genotyping software based on extrapolated sizes from alleles in the allelic ladder (Figure 3.2). Default bin widths are ±0.5 nucleotides (nt), but could be increased or decreased depending on precision study results during validation.

In the Figure 3.2 example, alleles 10, 11, 12, 13, and 14 are present in the allelic ladder. Virtual bins have been defined for alleles 9 and 15, which are one repeat smaller or larger than the physical bins defined by allelic ladder alleles, and for alleles 10.2 and 13.2, which occur between ladder alleles. Intra-allelic virtual bins, such as 10.2 and 13.2, are typically included because they have been observed previously and were deemed by the kit manufacturer as being common enough to be

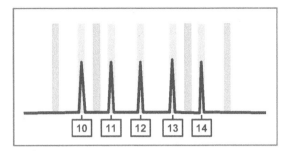

Physical bins: 10, 11, 12, 13, 14
Virtual bins: 9, 10.2, 13.2, 15

FIGURE 3.2 Illustration of allelic ladder data overlaid on physical and virtual bins. Any peak falling outside a bin window is labeled "off-ladder" and would need to be reviewed for consideration as a potential variant allele or an artifact.

registered in the established set of possible size bins. If an allele was observed in the putative allele 12.2 position, it would be labeled an "off-ladder" allele by the genotyping software and require analyst review and assessment. If allele 12.2 was commonly observed in the course of their work, then a laboratory would add the variant allele to the list of virtual bins to avoid having to regularly remove the "off-ladder" designation.

Some of the newer STR kits have hundreds of allele bins. For example with GlobalFiler allelic ladders and the physical and virtual bins available, 589 distinct alleles can be assigned automatically using GeneMapper *ID-X* v1.4 software (GlobalFiler 2014).

Parameters can be set within the GeneMapper*ID* Analysis Method Editor for dye-specific analytical thresholds, locus-specific stutter values, size calling method, level of baselining and data smoothing, and levels of heterozygote peak balance. These values are typically based on internal validation studies performed in a forensic laboratory.

STR Kits

An STR typing kit typically comes with some physical material (an allelic ladder, size standard, PCR primers, PCR buffer, and DNA polymerase) and some electronic information (a user manual and bins and panels). Chapter 1 describes various STR kits available for human identity testing from Promega Corporation (Madison, Wisconsin, USA), Life Technologies (South San Francisco, California, USA), and Qiagen (Hilden, Germany).

STR ALLELES AND THEIR MEASUREMENT

An Example Locus: D18S51

For purposes of teaching various points about STR markers throughout this book, the locus D18S51 will be used as an example. D18S51 is a core STR marker for the U.S. and the European Standard Set, and is thus present in almost all commercial STR kits used around the world. It is a tetranucleotide marker located on the long arm of chromosome 18 with known alleles ranging from 6 to 40 AGAA repeats. While a worldwide survey found 73 alleles for D18S51 (see Butler 2012, Appendix 1), a U.S. population study observed 22 alleles and 93 genotypes for this locus (Butler et al. 2012).

Figure 3.3 shows a portion of the DNA sequence around the STR repeat for D18S51. This particular allele contains 18 AGAA repeats, which are emphasized through using lowercase font and forward slashes between each repeat unit. PCR primers have been developed by the STR kit providers to anneal to portions of the sequence on either side of the repeat region. In this manner, the length variation that occurs between different alleles (e.g. 14 AGAA repeats or 16 AGAA repeats instead of the 18 AGAA repeat units shown) will be captured by the overall size of the PCR product. Alleles differing by a single AGAA repeat unit will be approximately 4 nucleotides apart when separated by size using capillary electrophoresis. *[handwritten: →17 OR 19]*

In Figure 3.3, primer-binding regions for the PowerPlex 16 primers, which have been published by Promega Corporation (Krenke et al. 2002), are underlined. Keep in mind that the reverse primer is represented on the complementary strand of the DNA, which is not shown. The D18S51-forward primer, 5′-TTCTTGAGCCCAGAAGGTTA-3′, is labeled with the "blue" dye fluorescein (FL) in the PowerPlex 16 kit. The gray shaded portion of the sequence in Figure 3.3 shows the nucleotides that will be amplified using the PowerPlex 16 primers (remember that only the top strand of DNA sequence is represented in this figure). With these primers and 18 repeat units, there are 330 bp copied

[handwritten left margin: 18x AGAA]   *[handwritten: 5′]*   *[handwritten: PRIMER]*

```
TACAAAAAAATACAAAAATTAGTTGGGCATGGTGGCACGTGCCTGTAGTCTCAGCTACT
TGCAGGGCTGAGGCAGGAGGAG TTCTTGAGCCCAGAA [G→A] GTTA AGGCTGCAGTGAG
CCATGTTCATGCCACTGCACTTCACTCTGAGTGACAAATTGAGACCTTGTCTC/agaa/
agaa/agaa/agaa/agaa/agaa/agaa/agaa/agaa/agaa/agaa/agaa/agaa
/agaa/agaa/agaa/agaa/agaa/ [AAAGAGAGA] GGAAAGAAAGAGAAAAAGAAAA
GAAATAGTAGCAACTGTTATTGTAAGACATCTCCACACACCAGAGAAGTTAATTTTAAT
TTTAACATGTTAAGAACAGAGAGAAGCCAACATGTCCACCTTAGGCTGACGGTTT GTTT
ATTTGTGTTGTTGCTGGTAG TC [G→A] GGTTTGTTATTTTTAAAGTAGCTTATCCAAT
ACTTCATTAACAATTTCAGTAAGTTATTTCATCTTTCAACATAAATACGCACAAGGATT
TCTTCTGGTCAAGACCAAACTAATATTAGTCCATAGTAG
```

[handwritten: 3′]

FIGURE 3.3 DNA sequence of a D18S51 allele containing 18 AGAA repeats. The STR repeat sequence is included in lowercase font with breaks between each repeat unit for emphasis. This top strand of the reference sequence is the reverse complement of GenBank entry AP001534 available from STRBase (STR Markers 2014). The green underlined regions indicate PowerPlex 16 primer binding sites (Krenke et al. 2002) with the shaded portion showing the PCR product. This 18 AGAA repeat allele has 86 bases in the 5′-flanking region ("upstream"), 72 bases (18 × 4) in the repeat region, and 169 bases in the 3′-flanking region ("downstream"). At the asterisk point there are an additional three nucleotides created in the PCR product because Promega includes an ATT sequence at the 5′ end of their reverse primer to aid full adenylation. Thus, when amplified with PowerPlex 16 primers a 330 bp (86 + 72 + 169 + 3) PCR product is created.

Other known flanking region variations that can impact allele sizes or amplification with certain STR kits are also illustrated. The blue underlined AAAG sequence that is immediately 3′ of the repeat region is replaced with AG[AGAG] for x.2 alleles and A[AAAG] for x.1 alleles (Dauber et al. 2009). The bracketed nine nucleotides [AAAGAGAGA] are deleted to create a "5.3" allele from one that contains 8 AGAA repeats (Kline et al. 2011). A G→A mutation, shown in red font, 71 nucleotides upstream of the repeat (Vanderheyden et al. 2007), creates a primer binding site mutation in the PowerPlex 16 forward primer, while a G→A mutation 172 bases downstream of the repeat region (Kline et al. 2011) causes allele dropout in Applied Biosystems kits such as SGM Plus (Clayton et al. 2004).

[handwritten: + 3 bases b/c promega adds an ATT to aid adenylation]

I. DATA INTERPRETATION

from the D18S51 locus. Thus, because allele 18 is 330 bp with the Promega primers, allele 17 will be 326 bp (4 bp smaller), allele 19 will be 334 bp (4 bp larger), and so forth.

Sizing Precision

STR genotyping is performed by comparison of the size of a sample's alleles to size of alleles in allelic ladders for the same loci being tested in the sample (see Figure 3.1). A high degree of precision is needed between multiple runs in order to make an accurate comparison of data from two runs, where one run is the allelic ladder standard and the other run is the questioned sample. The precision for a measurement system is determined by analyzing replicate samples or allelic ladders under normal operating conditions (see D.N.A. Box 8.2).

Precision for the separation and detection platform must be less than ±0.5 nt to accurately distinguish between microvariant (partial repeat) alleles and complete repeat alleles that differ by a single nucleotide. For single-capillary CE instruments, there is a reliance on a high degree of precision for run-to-run comparisons since a number of samples are run in a sequential fashion through the capillary between each injection of the allelic ladder. This same principle applies for multi-capillary array systems.

The DNA sizing precision on CE instruments is typically better than 0.1 nt. However, a laboratory temperature variation of as little as 2°C or 3°C over the course of a number of runs can cause allele peaks to migrate slightly differently from the internal sizing standard and therefore size differently over time. To alleviate this problem, the allelic ladder may be run more frequently (e.g. every 10 injections instead of every 20 injections), and the samples can be typed to the allelic ladder sample that was injected nearest in time to them. Many protocols with multi-capillary instruments inject an allelic ladder with each set of samples to maintain appropriate size-to-allele calibration.

Sizing Algorithm and Internal Standards

The sizing of DNA fragments with internal standards is performed as illustrated in D.N.A. Box 3.1. The Local Southern method works very well for accurate sizing of DNA fragments over the 100-bp to 450-bp size range necessary for STR alleles — primarily because in this size range DNA molecules migrate during electrophoresis with an approximately linear relationship between size and separation time.

However, there are some caveats that should be kept in mind that depend upon the internal size standard used. Within the GS500-ROX and GS500-LIZ size standard, the 250-bp peak (and sometimes the 340-bp peak as well) does not size reproducibly, especially when there are temperature fluctuations across or between runs. Therefore, the 250-bp peak is typically left out of analyses by not designating it as a standard peak.

It is important to realize that unknown DNA fragment peaks that are larger than the peaks present (or designated by the software) in the internal sizing standard cannot be accurately determined. Peaks that fall near the edge of the region defined by the internal sizing standard are less accurately sized since only one size standard DNA fragment is available. The Local Southern sizing algorithm requires two peaks from the size standard on either side of the unknown peak.

Therefore, with the GS500-ROX internal standard commonly used in conjunction with the AmpFlSTR kits, any unknown peaks falling above 490 bp or below 50 bp will not be sized with the Local Southern method. Likewise, if the signal intensity for any of the calibration peaks in the

D.N.A. BOX 3.1

LOCAL SOUTHERN SIZING ALGORITHM

The most common algorithm used for determining the DNA fragment size is known as the Local Southern method (Elder & Southern 1983). The "Southern" portion of the technique's name refers to Ed Southern, the same English scientist who developed the Southern blotting technique for restriction fragment length polymorphism protocols used in the early days of forensic DNA testing. The Local Southern method uses the size of two peaks on either side of the unknown one being measured in order to make the calculations in nucleotides (nt). In the figure, the "165.05-nt" peak size is determined with Local Southern sizing by the position of the 150-nt and 160-nt peaks on the lower side and the position of the 200-nt and 250-nt peaks on the upper side (Mayrand et al. 1992).

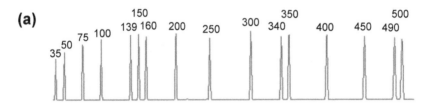

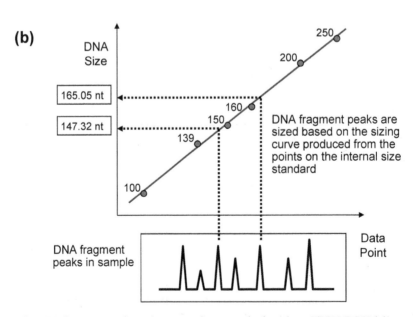

Peak sizing with DNA fragment analysis. An internal size standard, such as GS500-ROX (a), is analyzed along with the DNA sample and used to calibrate the peak data points to their DNA size (b). This standard is labeled with a different color fluorescent dye, in this case ROX (detected as red), so that it can be spectrally distinguished from the STR alleles which are labeled in other colors.

Several studies have found that a different sizing algorithm called the Global Southern method works well and maintains a better precision than Local Southern sizing in situations where temperature fluctuations can occur (Hartzell et al. 2003, Klein et al. 2003). Global Southern involves fitting a larger number of the peaks in the size standard to form a best-fit size calibration line rather than just using the two peaks above and below the peak of interest as is done with Local Southern. Regardless of which method is used, it must be consistently applied to both the allelic ladders and samples being typed so that equivalent size comparisons may be made.

Sources: Elder, J.K., & Southern, E.M. (1983). Measurement of DNA length by gel electrophoresis II: comparison of methods for relating mobility to fragment length. Analytical Biochemistry, *128, 227–231; Mayrand, P.E., et al. (1992). The use of fluorescence detection and internal lane standards to size PCR products automatically.* Applied and Theoretical Electrophoresis, 3(1), *1-11; Hartzell, B., et al. (2003). Response of short tandem repeat systems to temperature and sizing methods.* Forensic Science International, *133, 228-234; Klein, S.B., et al. (2003). Addressing ambient temperature variant effects on sizing precision of AmpFlSTR Profiler Plus alleles detected on the ABI Prism 310 Genetic Analyzer.* Forensic Science Communications, *5(1). Available at http://www.fbi.gov/about-us/lab/forensic-science-communications/.*

internal sizing standard is too weak, then unknown peaks in that region will not be sized accurately. For this reason it is important to check that all peaks in the internal sizing standard are above the relative fluorescence threshold to be called as peaks and that these peaks are accurately designated by the software.

Applied Biosystems has developed a GS600-LIZ size standard that contains 36 DNA fragments ranging in size from 20 bp to 600 bp (Figure 3.4(a)). The presence of additional internal size standard peaks can lead to more precise sizing when environmental temperatures (and hence CE instrument temperatures) are not optimally consistent. For PowerPlex kit users, the internal lane standard ILS-600 is commonly employed. This size standard contains 22 DNA fragments, ranging in size from 60 bp to 600 bp, that have been labeled with the red fluorescent dye CXR. More recently, Promega developed the ILS-500, which (relative to ILS-600) adds a 65-bp fragment at the low end and removes the 550-bp and 600-bp DNA fragments at the high end and maintains the 20-bp and 25-bp even spacing between the internal size standard peaks (Figure 3.4(b)). Qiagen has developed a 550 BTO size standard with 26 DNA fragments for use with its kits (Figure 3.4(a)).

Allelic Ladders

Following the sizing of all peaks above the analytical threshold, the peaks in each sample are converted from DNA size to STR allele through use of allelic ladders (see Figure 3.1). An allelic ladder is an artificial mixture of the common alleles present in the human population for a particular STR marker (Sajantila et al. 1992). Allelic ladders are generated with the same primers as tested samples and thus provide a reference DNA size for each allele included in the ladder.

Allelic ladders have been shown to be important for accurate genotype determinations (Smith 1995, Kline et al. 1997). These allelic ladders serve as a standard like a measuring stick for each STR locus. They are necessary to adjust for different sizing measurements obtained from different instruments and conditions used by various laboratories.

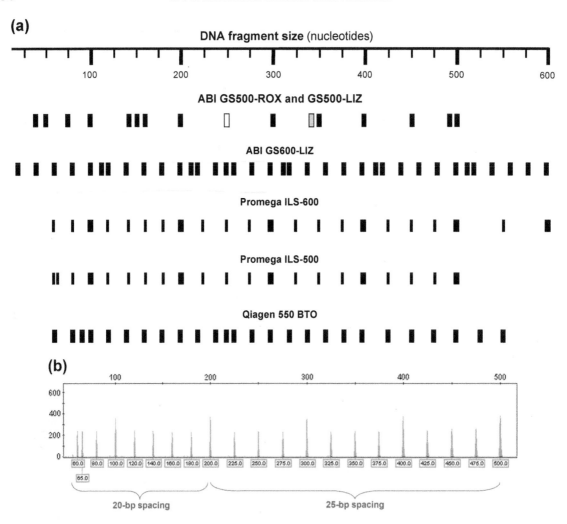

FIGURE 3.4 (a) DNA fragment sizes for different internal size standards. Each rectangle represents a specific DNA fragment size. Sizing precision improves with additional peaks. Note that the ABI GS500-ROX and -LIZ line has an open rectangle for the 250-nucleotide (nt) fragment since its electrophoretic behavior is atypical and is generally not used for size determinations. The electrophoretic behavior of the 340-nt fragment shown with gray shading can also be anomalous. (b) Example result with ILS-500 size standard (Promega Corporation, Madison, WI) that contains 21 fragments labeled with orange dye (for a 5-dye detection system) and evenly spaced DNA fragments enabling Local Southern sizing between 66 nucleotides and 474 nucleotides.

Commercial manufacturers provide allelic ladders in their STR typing kits so that individual laboratories do not have to produce their own. Although a research laboratory could prepare its own ladder by gathering alleles from a diverse set of samples, operational forensic laboratories benefit from having common allelic ladders for comparison purposes. However, kits from the various manufacturers may contain different alleles in their allelic ladders for the same STR locus although many of the STR loci allele ranges are similar across kits.

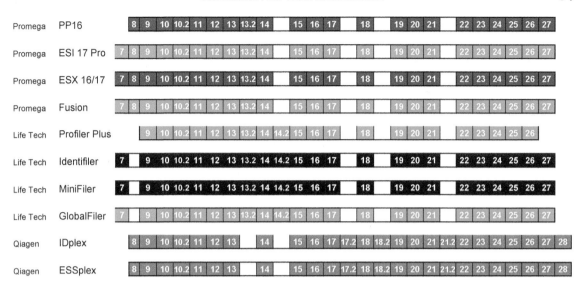

FIGURE 3.5 Comparison of alleles present in D18S51 allelic ladders for various commercial STR kits. Dye-label colors are indicated as well as the specific alleles present.

Figure 3.5 illustrates the alleles present in D18S51 allelic ladders for 10 different kits from three manufacturers. For example, comparing the GlobalFiler kit to the PowerPlex Fusion kit reveals that both allelic ladders cover the range of 7 repeats to 27 repeats. However, the GlobalFiler D18S51 allelic ladder lacks an allele 8 while the PowerPlex Fusion D18S51 allelic ladder lacks allele 14.2.

An examination of Figure 3.5 shows that most alleles present in kit allelic ladders are the same across kits from the same manufacturer, although occasionally new alleles are added, usually to one or both ends of the allele range, with more kits. For example, alleles 7 and 27 were included in the Identifiler D18S51 allelic ladder, whereas alleles 9 and 26 were the extreme alleles in the earlier Profiler Plus kit. Alleles are typically included based on their availability at the time the allelic ladder was created.

The ladders are prepared with commonly observed STR alleles usually spaced a single repeat unit apart from one another. The ladder alleles are PCR-amplified with the same primers as provided in the STR typing kit for testing unknown samples. Thus, samples amplified with a kit will produce alleles that are the same size as an allele in the allelic ladder.

Each allele or "rung" of an allelic ladder has been characterized in terms of the number of repeats it contains through DNA sequencing. The STR kit manufacturer supplies information to the users regarding the allele nomenclature and number of repeats present in each allele in the ladder. The data analysis software enables a conversion of all peaks in samples being processed from DNA size (relative to a common internal size standard) to repeat number. The DNA sizes of the allelic ladder alleles are used to calibrate size ranges for allele classification. A common size range for the genotyping allele bins is ±0.5 nucleotides around each allele. This size range enables PCR products that are one nucleotide different from one another to be differentiated. Due to slight changes in instrument environmental conditions over time, allelic ladders are run regularly (typically with every batch of samples) in order to keep the size-to-allele conversion process well calibrated.

Variant alleles occurring in the middle of a repeat array (e.g. 14.2) may not have a physical allele in the ladder, but may still be reliably called by genotyping software through use of virtual bins (see Figure 3.2).

STR Allele Nomenclature

To aid in inter-laboratory reproducibility and comparisons of data, a common nomenclature has been developed in the forensic DNA community. As described in Chapter 5 of *Advanced Topics in Forensic DNA Typing: Methodology* (Butler 2012), a DNA Commission of the International Society of Forensic Genetics (ISFG) has provided guidance on STR repeat nomenclature (Bär et al. 1994, Bär et al. 1997, Gill et al. 2001, Gusmão et al. 2006).

Briefly, the repeat sequence motif is typically defined so that the first 5′-nucleotides (from the protein coding strand or first GenBank entry) that can define a repeat motif are used (Bär et al. 1997). A 1994 International Society of Forensic Genetics (ISFG) DNA Commission publication addressed designations of alleles containing partial repeat sequences: "When an allele does not conform to the standard repeat motif of the system in question it should be designated by the number of complete repeat units and the number of base pairs of the partial repeat. These two values should be separated by a decimal point" (Bär et al. 1994). For example, an allele with [AATG]$_5$ ATG [AATG]$_4$ is designated as a "9.3" since it contains nine full AATG repeats plus three additional nucleotides. Thus, tetranucleotide repeats (i.e. those containing four nucleotides in the repeat motif) could have x.1, x.2, and x.3 variant alleles that exhibit one, two, or three additional nucleotides beyond the number of complete repeat units found in the allele. Note that it is not possible to have a x.4 variant for a tetranucleotide repeat as four additional nucleotides would appear as an incremental increase of a full repeat unit.

Today most forensic DNA scientists do not worry about STR allele nomenclature because STR typing is almost universally performed with commercially available kits containing allelic ladders prepared with alleles designated according to the ISFG rules by the manufacturer. However, occasionally there are differences in nomenclature that need to be spelled out to avoid confusion, such as with the Y-STR locus GATA-H4 contained in the Yfiler kit (Mulero et al. 2006). The use of certified reference materials and common positive controls with known genotypes also further guarantees consistency across laboratories in terms of STR allele designation.

The vast majority of the time, measured alleles will correlate to the alleles present in the STR kit allelic ladders and be appropriately designated as "on-ladder" alleles using genotyping software. However, "off-ladder" alleles are being discovered as more DNA samples are examined around the world. In addition, sometimes more than two alleles can be inherited or exhibited as such with the so-called triallelic patterns. Trialleles are addressed in Chapter 5. Finally, due to variation in the STR flanking regions, some PCR primers may fail to amplify a particular allele — a situation known as allele drop-out due to a silent or "null" allele.

VARIANT AND "OFF-LADDER" ALLELES

Rare alleles are encountered in the human population that may differ from common allele variants at tested DNA markers by one or more base pairs. Sequence variation between STR alleles can take the form of insertions, deletions, or nucleotide changes. Alleles containing some form of sequence variation compared to more commonly observed alleles are often referred to as *variant alleles* or *microvariants* because they are only slightly different from full repeat alleles. Because microvariant alleles often do not size the same as the commonly observed consensus alleles present in the reference allelic ladder, they can be referred to as "off-ladder" alleles (D.N.A. Box 3.2).

If an allele peak falls in between the nominal alleles present in the allelic ladder, the sample may be designated by the allele number followed by a ".x" (Crouse et al. 1999). For example, the larger FGA allele shown in D.N.A. Box 3.2 would be designated as a "28.x" allele. However, it is more common to label variant alleles by their calculated repeat content (e.g. 28.1). If an allele migrates above or below the defined allelic ladder, the allele is described as "<" or ">" than the nearest allele (Crouse et al. 1999).

One example of a common microvariant is allele 9.3 at the STR locus TH01. The repeat region of TH01 allele 9.3 contains nine full repeats (AATG) and a partial repeat of three bases (ATG). The 9.3 allele differs from the 10 allele by a single base deletion of adenine in the seventh repeat (Puers et al. 1993).

Microvariants exist for most STR loci and are being identified in greater numbers as more samples are being examined around the world. For example, in one study, 42 apparent microvariants were seen in over 10,000 samples examined at the CSF1PO, TPOX, and TH01 loci (Crouse et al. 1999). Microvariants are most commonly found in more polymorphic STR loci, such as FGA, D21S11, and D18S51, that possess the largest and most complex repeat structures compared to simple repeat loci, such as TPOX and CSF1PO (see Butler 2012 Appendix 1).

Studies with large numbers of samples are more likely to turn up variant alleles. An examination of 32,429 individuals with Profiler Plus and COfiler kits found 515 off-ladder variant alleles, some of which were observed multiple times (Allor et al. 2005). Of the 85 distinct variants, 52 were flanked by ladder alleles (i.e. they were within the ladder range and sizes could be interpolated) and 33 were outside the kit allelic ladder ranges (i.e. sizes had to be extrapolated, and thus allele designations may not be as accurate). The variants occurred in 12 of the 13 CODIS STR loci with only D16S539 exhibiting no off-ladder alleles in this study (Allor et al. 2005). With data from 13 loci across 32,429 individuals, there are 421,577 genotypes or 843,154 possible alleles. Thus, 515 variant alleles represents 0.061% of the total possible alleles. Sequence information for 12 of the 85 distinct alleles was also obtained during this study.

Two other large-scale studies also reported finding a number of variant alleles. A set of 32,800 Bosnian and Serbian samples yielded a total of 275 off-ladder alleles — of which 31 were distinct — from 10 of the 15 loci amplified with PowerPlex 16 (Huel et al. 2007). From 11,565 Koreans examined with Profiler Plus, 25 off-ladder alleles were observed (Cho et al. 2011).

Appendix 1 in *Advanced Topics in Forensic DNA Typing: Methodology* (Butler 2012) contains a listing of all known normal and variant alleles that have been observed by forensic DNA laboratories around the world to the point in time when the information was compiled. These have either been published in the literature and/or cataloged on the NIST STRBase website. As of January 2014, there were 415 variant alleles cataloged from the original 13 CODIS core loci. An up-to-date listing of cataloged variant STR alleles is available on the NIST Variant Allele Reports web page (STRBase Variant Allele Reports 2014). Table 3.1 includes a listing of variant alleles catalogued for the D18S51 locus.

The NIST Applied Genetics Group has provided free variant allele sequencing to laboratories around the world for a number of years. The NIST STR allele sequencing primers and methods have been published (Kline et al. 2011).

I. DATA INTERPRETATION

D.N.A. BOX 3.2

VARIANT ALLELE SIZE CALCULATIONS

Suspected microvariants can be fairly easily seen in heterozygous samples where one allele lines up with the fragment sizes in the allelic ladder and one does not. In the example shown here, the sample contains a peak that lines up with allele 25 from the FGA allelic ladder and a second peak that is labeled as an "off-ladder allele" and lines up between the 28 and 28.2 shaded virtual bins created by the ladder. Each peak is labeled with its calculated size in nucleotides (nt) determined by reference to the internal GS500 sizing standard. The relative size difference between the questioned sample and an allelic ladder marker run under the same electrophoretic conditions is then used to determine if the allele is truly a microvariant (Gill et al. 1996).

The size difference between the sample allele 25 and the ladder allele 25 is -0.12 nt (δ_1), while the "off-ladder allele" differs from the ladder allele 28 by $+0.87$ nt (δ_2). The relative peak shift between the two alleles in this heterozygous sample is 0.99 bp ($|\delta_1 - \delta_2|$), and therefore the "off-ladder" allele is 1 nucleotide larger than allele 28, making it a true 28.1 microvariant at the FGA locus.

The presence of a STR microvariant at a particular locus usually becomes evident

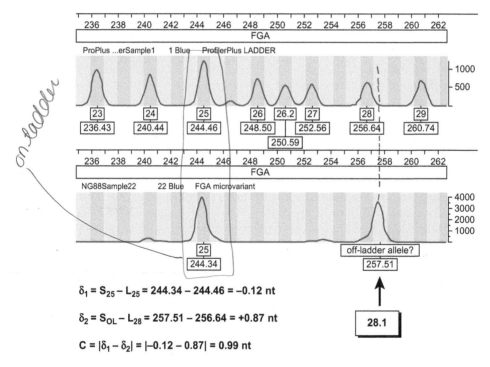

$$\delta_1 = S_{25} - L_{25} = 244.34 - 244.46 = -0.12 \text{ nt}$$

$$\delta_2 = S_{OL} - L_{28} = 257.51 - 256.64 = +0.87 \text{ nt}$$

$$C = |\delta_1 - \delta_2| = |-0.12 - 0.87| = 0.99 \text{ nt}$$

Detection of a microvariant allele at the STR locus FGA. The sample in the bottom panel is compared to the allelic ladder shown in the top panel using Genotyper 2.5 software. Peaks are labeled with the allele category and the calculated fragment sizes using the internal sizing standard GS500-ROX.

following a comparison to an allelic ladder made up of characterized alleles for that locus. However, not all alleles (particularly rare microvariant alleles) can be incorporated into the standard allelic ladder used for genotyping STR markers. Therefore, interpolation of data from peaks that migrate between two characterized alleles or limited extrapolation of data from peaks that fall outside the expected allele range may be performed.

Sources: Gill, P., et al. (1996). A new method of STR interpretation using inferential logic — development of a criminal intelligence database. International Journal of Legal Medicine, 109, 14–22.

Flanking Region Variation

Flanking region variation can also give rise to apparent "off-ladder" alleles. One of the best examples of this phenomenon is found in the STR locus D7S820. There are a number of x.1 and x.3 alleles (e.g. alleles 10.1 and 9.3) for D7S820. Sequence analysis of some of these variants has shown a difference in the number of consecutive T nucleotides in a poly(T) stretch that is 13 bases downstream of the GATA repeat region (Egyed et al. 2000). "On-ladder" alleles contain nine T's while the x.3 alleles have 8 T's and the x.1 alleles contain 10 T's.

While insertions and deletions (indels) in the flanking region can create discernable differences in migration time of variant alleles, such as the D7S820 examples just provided, single nucleotide polymorphisms (SNPs) can also exist in alleles that may not be detected without sequence analysis or a base composition analysis using mass spectrometry (Hall & Hofstadler 2012). These flanking region SNPs are most often detected during concordance studies when different primer sets are compared for amplification of the same STR loci.

Mobility Altering Sequence Variation

The STR locus SE33, also known as ACTBP2, is highly complex, extremely polymorphic, and exhibits extensive sequence variation within the repeat region as well as in the flanking region (Hering et al. 2002). A recent review of the SE33 literature found 178 alleles when internal sequence rearrangements are considered (Butler 2012). In addition, SE33 flanking region sequence variation has been shown to cause STR allele discordance with different PCR primer positions due to electrophoretic mobility shifts in some STR amplicons (Butler et al. 2011, Wang et al. 2012, Davis et al. 2012).

Figure 3.6 provides an example of the impact of the mobility shift for a SE33 allele possessing 16.2 repeats and a G→A mutation 68 bp downstream of the repeat region (Butler et al. 2011) that is designated as "16.3" when amplified with PowerPlex ESI 17 kit primers. Other STR kits including PowerPlex ESX 17 and AmpFlSTR NGM SElect correctly designate this allele 16.2 because their reverse PCR primer is internal to the G→A mutation, which causes disruption of a hairpin structure and impacts the relative mobility during the CE DNA separation process (Wang et al. 2012).

To avoid this secondary structure mobility issue with SE33, scientists at Promega Corporation redesigned the position of the SE33 reverse PCR primer for their PowerPlex ESI 17 kit and have released a new kit named PowerPlex ESI 17 Pro (McLaren et al. 2013).

This situation with SE33 is a reminder that DNA "sizing" of STR alleles is actually a measure of relative electrophoretic mobility of amplified PCR products compared to an internal size standard and not strictly a measure of the overall amplicon length. While flanking region variation may impact

TABLE 3.1 D18S51 Variant Alleles Reported on the NIST STRBase Website or in the Literature

Variant allele	# on STRBase	Literature sequence	Variant allele	# on STRBase	Literature sequence
5.3	—	Kline et al. (2011)	19.2	2	Gill et al. (1996)
6	2		20.1	1	Dauber et al. (2009)
7	3		20.2	11	
8	3	Griffiths et al. (1998)	20.3	1	
9	1	Barber & Parkin (1996)	21.1	2	
9.2	1		21.2	13	
11.1	1		22.1	1	
11.2	8	Dauber et al. (2008)	22.2	4	
11.3	1		23.2	1	
12.2	10		24.2	2	
12.3	4		27	1	Barber & Parkin (1996)
13.1	4	Phillips et al. (2011)	28	2	Morales-Valverde et al. (2009)
13.2	1	Barber & Parkin (1996)	28.1	1	
13.3	6	Allor et al. (2005)	28.3	4	
14.1	1		29	—	Morales-Valverde et al. (2009)
14.2	3	Barber & Parkin (1996)	29.3	1	
15.1	1		30	—	Morales-Valverde et al. (2009)
15.2	22	Barber & Parkin (1996)	31	—	Morales-Valverde et al. (2009)
15.3	3		32	—	Morales-Valverde et al. (2009)
16.1	5	Allor et al. (2005)	33	—	Morales-Valverde et al. (2009)
16.2	9	Dauber et al. (2009)	34	2	Morales-Valverde et al. (2009)
16.3	3		35	—	Morales-Valverde et al. (2009)
17.1	1		36	—	Morales-Valverde et al. (2009)
17.2	4	Gill et al. (1996)	37	—	Morales-Valverde et al. (2009)
17.3	3		38	—	Morales-Valverde et al. (2009)
18.1	8		40	1	Morales-Valverde et al. (2009)
18.2	4				
18.3	1				
19.1	2				

The number of variants listed on STRBase ("# on STRBase") are from January 2014.

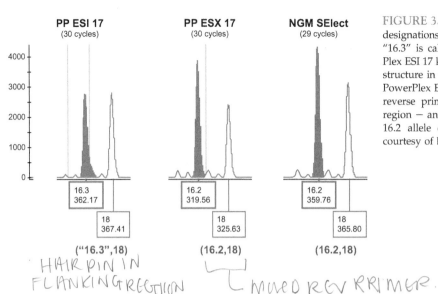

FIGURE 3.6 Comparison of SE33 designations with various STR ki "16.3" is called with the original Po Plex ESI 17 kit that encompassed a hairpin structure in the SE33 flanking region. The PowerPlex ESI 17 Pro kit moved the SE33 reverse primer to avoid amplifying this region – and now provides a concordant 16.2 allele call (data not shown). Data courtesy of Becky Hill, NIST.

local secondary structure in a PCR product and influence how an amplicon migrates during capillary electrophoresis, the primary challenge will be in comparing STR results among different kits. Because sample allele "sizes" are compared to sequenced allelic ladder allele "sizes" using the same PCR primers for genotyping purposes, potential electrophoretic mobility variation impacting STR genotype calls will only be a problem across STR kits that utilize different PCR primer positions.

Alleles Outside the Allelic Ladder Range

Occasionally new rare alleles may fall outside the allele range spanned by the locus allelic ladder. If these peaks fall between two STR loci in a multiplex set, they can be challenging to assign to a particular locus unless testing is performed with individual locus-specific primer sets or a different multiplex. These extreme "off-ladder" alleles can be confirmed with singleplex amplification of the two loci that bracketed the new allele in the multiplex.

Alternatively, the sample could be amplified again using a separate multiplex where the loci are present in a different order. For example, if a PCR product was observed between the typical vWA and D16S539 allele ranges when using the SGM Plus kit, then it could be either a large vWA allele or a small D16S539 allele, which is doubtful because allele 5 is the smallest rung on the D16S539 ladder. A different kit, such as PowerPlex 16, could be used on this same sample to help address the source of the new allele since the loci are put together in a different combination. With PowerPlex 16 a large vWA allele would appear between the vWA and D8S1179 expected allele ranges, but a small D16S539 allele would fall between D7S820 and D16S539 (see Figure 1.7).

Extrapolating extensively beyond the allele range of the allelic ladder can, in some cases, lead to false variant alleles. A study characterizing 12 large D18S51 alleles found that allelic designation by extrapolation from the largest allelic ladder allele (allele 27) was only correct for the two immediately adjacent alleles 28 and 29 (Morales-Valverde et al. 2009). A sequenced 30 allele appeared as a "29.3" (off by 1 nucleotide or 0.25 tetranucleotide repeats) while a AGAA-40 repeat appeared as "39.2" (off by 2 nucleotides or 0.5 tetranucleotide repeats).

The Israel Police DNA database laboratory observed a large allele at D3S1358 that was designated as an "off-ladder" allele within the vWA marker range in the SGM Plus kit, the TH01 marker range with the PowerPlex ESX 17 kit, and the D19S433 marker range with the PowerPlex ESI 17 kit (Raziel et al. 2012). With the NGM kit this same large D3S1358 allele was designated as an "allele 9" within the D1S1656 locus (Figure 3.7). Sequence analysis revealed that the D3S1358 allele contained 22 repeats with a structure of TCTA(TCTG)$_3$(TCTA)$_4$TCTG(TCTA)$_{13}$ (Raziel et al. 2012).

This study also noted the problem of estimating allele repeat number by extrapolating the size from the nearest allelic ladder allele, which in the case of the SGM Plus kit and D3S1358 ladder is allele 19. With the closest D3S1358 allelic ladder allele being more than three repeat units away (OL$_{sample}$ − allele 19$_{ladder}$ = 153.30 nt − 139.81 nt = 13.49 nt or 3.37 tetranucleotide repeats), such an analysis would suggest that the mystery peak contains 22.1 repeats (+3.25 tetranucleotide repeats) or 22.2 repeats (+3.50 tetranucleotide repeats). Furthermore, with the SGM Plus kit, the apparent repeat size difference between the 127.28-nt D3S1358 allele 16 and the 153.30-nt mystery peak is 26.02 nt or 6.5 tetranucleotide repeats.

A difference of 6.5 tetranucleotide repeats would suggest that the large D3S1358 allele is 22.2 repeats. However, allele sequence analysis indicated that the mystery peak was 22 repeats (Raziel et al. 2012), not 22.1 or 22.2, as size extrapolation from the largest allelic ladder allele or the peak spacing from the sample allele 16 suggested.

These results suggest that it is unwise to draw a strong conclusion (such as 22.1 or 22.2 compared to 22) when over one repeat beyond the kit allelic ladder. Indeed, this poor size extrapolation issue is the reason that many laboratories will simply designate an allele outside the allelic ladder range as greater than (or less than) the largest (or smallest) allelic ladder allele. In this example, ">19" rather than trying to place it into a specific allele bin of 22, 22.1, or 22.2.

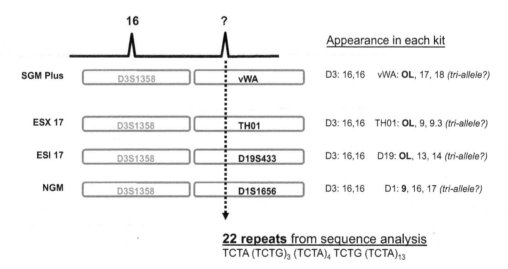

22 repeats from sequence analysis
TCTA (TCTG)$_3$ (TCTA)$_4$ TCTG (TCTA)$_{13}$

FIGURE 3.7 Summary of results from Raziel et al. (2012) with a large D3S1358 allele. The largest D3S1358 allele in most STR kit allelic ladders contains either 19 or 20 repeats. Use of different STR kits including PowerPlex ESX 17, PowerPlex ESI 17, and AmpFlSTR NGM, which have different loci adjacent to D3S1358, helped verify that the mystery allele was associated with a large D3S1358 allele because apparent tri-alleles changed with each STR kit result. Subsequent sequence analysis confirmed a 22-repeat D3S1358 allele.

In another situation, small D2S1338 alleles in the Identifiler STR kit have given the appearance of microvariants in the adjacent D16S539 region. For example, a D2S1338 11 allele was initially typed as a D16S539 "14.2" (Onofri et al. 2008). Sequence analysis of the D2S1338 allele and analysis with a second STR kit confirmed that the correct genotypes for this sample were D16S539 11,11 and D2S1338 11,19 (Onofri et al. 2008).

Characterizing "Off-Ladder" Alleles Occurring between Loci

As noted previously in a review article on STR loci (Butler 2006), there are several points of consideration that can be made in order to help ascertain to which locus an extremely off-ladder and inter-locus allele belongs. An inter-locus allele is defined here as an allele that occurs between the defined ranges of two adjacent STR loci and could therefore be assigned to either locus. If one of the STR marker ranges contains two alleles and the other one only one allele within the common allele range, then it is likely that the inter-locus allele belongs to the apparent homozygote. It is also worth checking to see whether any variant alleles have been reported previously by other labs (e.g. examining cataloged variant alleles on STRBase, such as seen in Table 3.1).

Heterozygosities of the two loci in question can be considered to predict which locus is more likely to be a heterozygote and possess two different alleles. For example, if a green-colored peak occurs between D16S539 and D2S1338 in the Identifiler kit and only a single allele is observed in each of the D16S539 and D2S1338 normal allele ranges, then the inter-locus allele more likely belongs to D2S1338 because D2S1338 has a higher heterozygosity. Also, examination of the genotype frequencies can be informative. In an Identifiler genotype database, such as found on STRBase (STRBase Identifiler Genotype Database 2014), it is noted that a D16S539 11,11 homozygote occurs 10.7% of the time while a D2S1338 20,20 homozygote occurs only 0.92% of the time. Thus, it is more likely that the inter-locus allele is a D2S1338 allele 13 rather than a D16S539 allele 17. While these considerations can help instruct an analyst on the best way to proceed with associating inter-locus off-ladder alleles, it is recommended that final confirmation be performed with single locus amplification for each of the two adjacent STR loci.

Variant Alleles Can Create False Tri-Allelic Patterns

It is important to keep in mind the possibility of an extremely off-ladder allele from an adjacent locus creating an apparent tri-allelic pattern. True tri-alleles will be covered in Chapter 5. Typically singleplex testing or use of another kit with a different configuration of PCR products is necessary to detect this situation, but paying attention to stutter amounts and peak height ratios may alert a careful analyst that he/she needs to investigate further. An example of a false tri-allele pattern was seen in the D8S1179 locus of the Serac genRES MPX-2 kit due to an extremely off-ladder D21S11 allele later found to contain 43.2 repeats, whereas the typical limit of the D21S11 allele range is 38 repeats (Grubwieser et al. 2005).

Likewise, with an Identifiler PCR amplification at NIST, an apparent tri-allelic pattern was seen at D21S11 with alleles 25, 29, and 30 (Figure 3.8(a)). Follow-up with PowerPlex 16 HS PCR amplification showed only a 29,30 at D21S11, but an apparent "8.1" allele was now observed in TPOX. By noting that D8S1179 is the locus just below the STR marker with the apparent tri-allele or supposed variant allele, it was surmised that a large D8S1179 allele was present in the sample. Testing with other STR

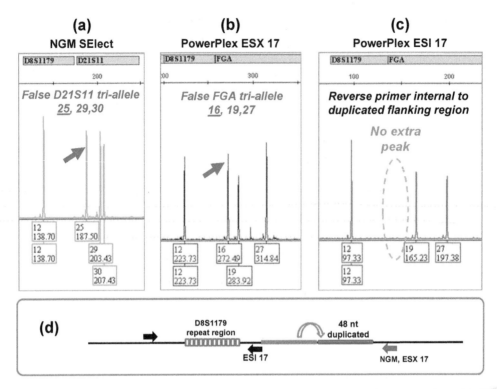

FIGURE 3.8   Impact of large D8S1179 allele on different STR kits. This large D8S1179 allele appeared as a D21S11 allele 25 with (a) AmpFISTR NGM SElect and as FGA allele 16 with (b) PowerPlex ESX 17. No large D8S1179 allele was observed with (c) PowerPlex ESI 17 because this kit's reverse primer is internal to a duplicated flanking region as illustrated in (d). The large D8S1179 allele contains only 12 tetranucleotide repeats but has a 48-nucleotide (nt) duplication downstream of the repeat region. Data courtesy of Erica Butts, Becky Hill, and Margaret Kline, NIST.

kits resulted in a false tri-allele at the FGA locus (Figure 3.8(b)) or loss of the extra peak when amplified with PowerPlex ESI 17 (Figure 3.8(c)). Subsequent singleplex PCR testing found that indeed an unusually large D8S1179 allele appearing to contain 24 repeats had been detected. Sequence analysis of this allele revealed a 48-nucleotide insertion next to 12 TCTA repeats (Figure 3.8(d)). Hence, sometimes STR alleles are more complicated than might be initially expected.

Amplification artifacts, such as stutter and non-template addition, can actually be used to help detect extreme off-ladder alleles. The amount of stutter present for an STR allele follows locus-specific and allele-specific patterns. For example, if attempting to discern to which locus an inter-locus allele belongs, looking at the relative height of the stutter product can be informative. Since a longer run of STR repeat units typically produces higher stutter, a high stutter product compared to what is observed from an allele from the lower relative molecular mass locus could suggest that the inter-locus allele belongs to the smaller locus. Finally, certain loci are more likely, based on the 5′-end of the reverse PCR primer, to have non-template addition issues. Thus, lack of full adenylation may be helpful in some situations (see below).

Isoalleles: Same Length but Different Internal Sequence

Complex repeat sequences, such as those found in D21S11, can contain variable repeat blocks in which the order is switched around for alleles that are the same length. For example, the STR locus D21S11 has four alleles that are all 210 bp when amplified with the Identifiler kit (Butler 2012). While these alleles would be sized based on overall length to be "allele 30," they contain repeat blocks of 4-6-CR-12, 5-6-CR-11, 6-5-CR-11, and 6-6-CR-10 for the pattern [TCTA]-[TCTG]-constant region (CR)-[TCTA]. In such cases, variant alleles will only be detectable with complete sequence analysis (Rockenbauer et al. 2014). Another example is two isoalleles reported for DYS635 allele 17: [(TCTA)$_4$(TGTA)$_2$(TCTA)$_2$(TGTA)$_3$(TCTA)$_6$ and (TCTA)$_4$(TGTA)$_2$(TCTA)$_2$(TGTA)$_2$(TCTA)$_7$] (Omran et al. 2008).

From an operational point-of-view, internal allele variation is not significant. In the end, a match is being made against many loci, not just one, such as D21S11, with possible internal sequence variation. Most of the STR loci used in human identity testing have not so far been reported to exhibit internal sequence variations (see Butler 2012), particularly so with the simple repeat loci TPOX, CSF1PO, D5S818, D16S539, TH01, D18S51, and D7S820. Remember that STR typing using CE analysis essentially bins alleles based on measured size. Sequence analysis of individual alleles has traditionally been too time consuming and would, in most cases, rarely reveal additional information because STR variation is primarily size-based. However, recent work with base composition analysis by mass spectrometry and next-generation sequencing (NGS) has expanded the ability to more readily assess internal variation in STR allele sequence.

Over the past several years, work with mass spectrometry has demonstrated that same-size STR alleles with different internal sequences, or alleles with sequence variation in the flanking region, can be resolved from one another using a base composition approach (Oberacher et al. 2008, Pitterl et al. 2008, 2010, Planz et al. 2009). This sequence variation is sometimes referred to as a SNPSTR, where single nucleotide variation is coupled with STR allele identification (Mountain et al. 2002). Certain STR loci are more prone to internal sequence variation, especially some of the new core loci such as D12S391 (Dalsgaard et al. 2014).

A comparison of the variation observed in 11 STRs – the 10 SGM Plus loci and SE33 – on 94 Yakut and 108 Khoisan was performed using conventional STR analysis, mass spectrometric STR analysis, and direct sequencing (Pitterl et al. 2010). The mass spectrometry approach that enabled both sequence and length variation to be detected clearly expanded the number of detectable alleles (Duncan et al. 2011, Planz & Hall 2012, Planz et al. 2012). However, with some of the more complex loci like SE33, allele sequencing is necessary to recover the complete power of discrimination at the STR locus.

STR allele sequencing with a conventional Sanger sequencing approach (e.g. Kline et al. 2011) works well, but is not something that is routinely used since it is slow and labor-intensive. So-called NGS approaches utilize millions of parallel reactions to rapidly generate DNA sequences that can then be aligned bioinformatically to a reference sequence. In one study involving D21S11, an NGS approach was used to demonstrate that four apparent homozygotes with CE methods were in fact heterozygous due to different sequence isoalleles (Rockenbauer et al. 2014). Likewise, many novel D12S391 variants were discovered including three 20.3 isoalleles when these alleles were fully sequenced (Dalsgaard et al. 2014).

Alleles of the same length but of different internal sequence can be used in research to track mutations if the sequences can be differentiated from one another. A C→T polymorphism was discovered 13 nucleotides upstream of the D5S818 repeat region (Edwards & Allen 2004). A restriction enzyme cutting site is created when the T is present that enables differentiation of samples with and without the polymorphism. Use of this SNPSTR assay permitted evaluation of mutations that were observed, of which 34 out of 40 were paternal in origin and 23 of 26 (where the repeat change could be determined) were single repeat unit shifts. This study also found that while alleles 13 and 14 were prone to mutation, allele 11 was not — suggesting that not all alleles have equal frequencies of mutation (Edwards & Allen 2004). In fact, several of the annual reports on relationship testing laboratories from the American Association of Blood Banks (AABB) have reported allele-specific mutation events (see Chapter 14).

ARTIFACTS OF STR ALLELE AMPLIFICATION

During PCR amplification of STR alleles, a number of artifacts can arise that may interfere with the clear interpretation and genotyping of the alleles present in the DNA template. The concluding portion of the chapter focuses on those PCR products that give rise to additional peaks besides the true, major allele peak(s). These artifacts include non-template nucleotide addition, stutter products, and null alleles.

Artifacts matter because as methods are pushed to detect lower levels of DNA, interpretation reliability can be strained when attempting to differentiate between true alleles and amplification artifacts. For example, poor electrophoretic resolution can lead to failure to resolve full-length PCR products from their adenylated form (see below), resulting in wider peaks that may be inaccurately sized. Stutter products make mixture interpretation more challenging because it is difficult to clearly decipher minor component genotypes. Finally, primer binding site mutations may lead to loss of allelic amplification rather than allele drop-out due to stochastic effects.

NON-TEMPLATE ADDITION

DNA polymerases, particularly the *Taq* polymerase used in PCR, often add an extra nucleotide to the 3′-end of a PCR product as they are copying the template strand (Clark 1988, Magnuson et al. 1996). This non-template addition is most often adenosine, and is therefore sometimes referred to as "adenylation" or the "+A" form of the amplicon. Non-template addition results in a PCR product that is one base pair longer than the actual target sequence.

Addition of the 3′ A nucleotide can be favored by adding a final incubation step at 60°C or 72°C after the temperature cycling steps in PCR (Clark 1988, Kimpton et al. 1993). However, the degree of adenylation is dependent on the sequence of the template strand, which in the case of PCR results from the 5′-end of the reverse primer (Figure 3.9). If the forward primer is labeled with a fluorescent dye to amplify the STR allele, then only the top strand is detected by the fluorescent measurement. Since the sequence at the 3′-end of the top (labeled) strand serves as a template for polymerase extension, the terminal nucleotide of the labeled strand is determined by the 5′-end of the reverse primer used in generating the complementary unlabeled strand (Magnuson et al. 1996). One study found that if the 5′-terminus of the primer is a guanosine, then a complete addition is favored by the polymerase (Brownstein et al. 1996). Thus, every locus will have slightly different adenylation properties because the primer sequences differ.

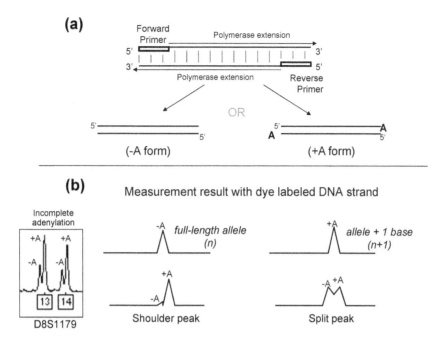

FIGURE 3.9 Schematic of non-template nucleotide addition shown (a) with illustrated measurement result (b). DNA polymerases add an extra nucleotide beyond the 3′-end of the target sequence extension product. The amount of non-template addition is dependent on the sequence of the 5′-end of the opposing primer. In the case of dye-labeled PCR products where the fluorescent dye is on the forward primer, the reverse primer sequence is the critical one.

Why is all of this important? From a measurement standpoint, it is better to have all of the molecules as similar as possible for a particular allele. Partial adenylation, where some of the PCR products do not have the extra adenine (i.e. −A peaks) and some do (i.e. +A peaks), can contribute to peak broadness if the separation system's resolution is poor. Sharper peaks improve the likelihood that a system's genotyping software can make accurate calls.

In addition, variation in the adenylation status of an allele across multiple samples can have an impact on accurate sizing and genotyping potential microvariants. For example, a non-adenylated TH01 10 allele would be the same size as a fully adenylated TH01 9.3 allele because they contain an identical number of base pairs. Therefore, it is beneficial if all PCR products for a particular amplification are either −A or +A rather than a mixture of +/−A products. Table 3.2 lists some of the methods that have been used to convert PCR products into either the −A or +A form.

During PCR amplification, most STR protocols include a final extension step to give the DNA polymerase extra time to completely adenylate all double-stranded PCR products. For example, the standard AmpFlSTR Identifiler kit amplification parameters include a final extension at 60°C for 60 minutes at the end of thermal cycling (Applied Biosystems 2001). In order to make correct genotype calls, it is important that the allelic ladder and the sample have the same adenylation status for a particular STR locus. For all commercially available STR kits, this means that the STR alleles are all in the +A form.

TABLE 3.2   Ways to Convert STR Allele Peaks to Either −A or +A Forms

Method	Result	Reference
CONVERSION TO FULLY ADENYLATED PRODUCTS (+A FORM)		
Final extension at 60°C or 72°C for 30 minutes to 60 minutes	Promotes full adenylation of all PCR products	Kimpton *et al.* (1993), Applied Biosystems (1999)
Addition of single G or the sequence GTTTCTT on the 5′-end of reverse primers ("PIG-tailing")	Promotes nearly 100% adenylation of the 3′ forward strand	Brownstein *et al.* (1996)
CONVERSION TO BLUNT-ENDED PRODUCTS (−A FORM)		
Restriction enzyme site built into reverse primer	Makes blunt end fragments following restriction enzyme digestion	Edwards *et al.* (1991)
Enzymatic removal of one base overhang	Exonuclease activity of *Pfu* or T4 DNA polymerase removes +A	Ginot *et al.* (1996)
Use of modified polymerase without terminal transferase activity	Polymerase does not add 3′ A nucleotide	Butler & Becker (2001)

Amplifying higher quantities of DNA than the optimal amount suggested by the manufacturer's protocols can result in incomplete 3′ A nucleotide addition and therefore split peaks. Thus, quantifying the amount of DNA prior to PCR and adhering to the manufacturer's protocols will produce improved STR typing results when using commercial STR kits.

STUTTER PRODUCTS

An examination of electropherograms containing STR data typically reveals the presence of small peaks several bases shorter than each STR allele peak. These "stutter product" peaks result from the PCR process when STR loci are copied by a DNA polymerase. In the literature, this stutter product has also been referred to as a shadow band or a DNA polymerase slippage product (Hauge & Litt 1993).

The amount of stutter product can be characterized in terms of stutter ratios or stutter proportions (Gill et al. 2000, Brookes et al. 2012). Calculations of stutter ratios involve dividing the height of a stutter peak by the height of its corresponding allele. Stutter proportions, which are not used as frequently, reflect the height of a stutter peak divided by the height of the total allelic product. The total allelic product is the sum of an allele and its stutter product(s) peak heights. Although peak heights are mentioned here, peak areas may also be used in calculations, although this is rarely done with capillary electrophoresis data.

Figure 3.10 shows multiple stutter products around a DYS481 allele containing 27 CTT repeats. This example is used here because it has an unusually high degree of stutter due to its shorter repeat

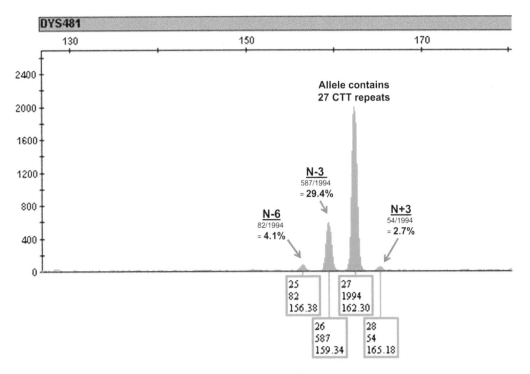

FIGURE 3.10 Stutter products observed at the trinucleotide Y-STR marker DYS481 from a single-source male DNA sample when amplified with the PowerPlex Y23 kit. Calculations of stutter percentages were performed using peak heights (no stutter filter was applied). Figure courtesy of Mike Coble, NIST.

motif (trinucleotide instead of the more commonly used tetranucleotide) and its large number of uninterrupted repeat units (in this case 27 CTT repeats). Also, as a single-copy Y-chromosome STR, there should be only a single allele with DYS481 in single-source samples.

Note that additional peaks occur on both sides of the allele 27 primary peak. The "N−3" (allele minus three nucleotides) and "N−6" (allele minus six nucleotides) peaks contain one and two repeat units less, respectively, than the full-length allele. These peaks are sometimes referred to as "negative stutter," "back stutter," or "reverse stutter." The "N+3" (allele plus three nucleotides) peak contains one additional repeat unit and has been termed "positive stutter" or "forward stutter" (Gibb et al. 2009).

The level of stutter decreases when moving away from the primary allele, such that for the reverse stutter products the N−3 peak height is 29.4% of the allele peak height and the N−6 peak height is 4.1% (82 relative fluorescence units (RFU) compared to 1994 RFU for the allele peak). Forward stutter is always lower than reverse stutter (2.7% vs. 29.4%), and many times with tetranucleotide repeats may not be observed at all.

One detailed study by the Royal Canadian Mounted Police provided stutter percentages in terms of peak heights and peak areas for 325 casework samples and 754 database samples (Leclair et al. 2004). For D18S51 peak height stutter values, this study noted a median plus three standard deviation of 16.2% stutter in database samples and 15.6% stutter in casework samples.

Stutter Filters

Validation studies conducted in a laboratory help define maximum percent stutter for each locus. However, if the target allele peak is off-scale, then the stutter product can appear larger than it really is in relationship to the corresponding allele peak (Moretti et al. 2001).

For data interpretation, an upper-limit stutter percentage interpretational threshold is often set for each locus as three standard deviations above the average stutter percentage normally observed at that locus, although a variety of approaches have been used. Alternatively, some laboratories prefer to apply a universal stutter filter, usually in the range of 10% to 20%. A genotyping software-implemented stutter filter then automatically removes the peak labels on any peaks found within the designated size range (e.g. 4 bp ± 0.25 bp) and relative height (e.g. 10% to 20%) of the STR allele peaks.

Genotyping software utilizes stutter filters to remove the allele designations from potential stutter products. Thresholds set for these stutter filters can vary based on the validation data used as well as the method (statistical model) used to establish them. Table 3.3 lists some of the manufacturer-recommended stutter filter values specified for D18S51 in various STR kits. These stutter filter values range from "12.89%" with the Identifiler Direct kit to "18%" with MiniFiler. Note that in some instances with the kits listed in Table 3.3 the kit manufacturer decided to use the highest observed stutter to set the stutter filter value, while in other instances the average stutter plus three times the standard deviation was used.

Allele-Specific Stutter

Stutter product amounts increase with the length of the allele. Table 3.4 shows stutter product percentages with D18S51 alleles ranging in length from 12 to 20 AGAA repeats based on results

TABLE 3.3   Stutter Filters Used for D18S51 with Various Applied Biosystems STR Kits

STR Kit	D18S51 Stutter filter value	How filter values were calculated
Identifiler Direct	12.89	mean stutter + 3 SD (N = 669)
Profiler Plus	< 13	highest observed stutter
Identifiler Plus	13.6799	mean stutter + 3 SD (N = 500)
NGM SElect Express	13.78	mean stutter + 3 SD (N = 668)
NGM SElect	13.81	mean stutter + 3 SD (N = 1080)
NGM	13.89	mean stutter + 3 SD (N = 996)
SGM Plus	16	+3 SD above highest stutter
SEfiler Plus	16.43	highest observed stutter
Identifiler	17.0	highest observed stutter
MiniFiler	18	mean stutter + 3 SD (N = 668)

Significant figures and how values were calculated are as reported in the various kit user manuals.

TABLE 3.4 Stutter Data from a Set of 345 D18S51 Alleles Measured at NIST Using the PowerPlex 16 Kit

Allele	Allele size (nucleotides)	# Measured	Median (%)	Standard deviation
12	296.9	43	4.8	0.4
13	300.7	27	5.7	0.5
14	304.6	35	6.2	0.5
15	308.5	55	6.9	0.6
16	312.4	46	7.7	0.5
17	316.2	47	8.3	0.4
18	320.2	38	9.0	0.9
19	324.0	30	9.6	0.9
20	328.0	24	10.6	0.8
		345	Average 7.7 ± 1.9	

Results were generated using the STR_StutterFreq program available at http://www.cstl.nist.gov/strbase/software.htm. Data courtesy of Becky Hill, NIST.

generated at the National Institute of Standards and Technology (NIST) with Promega's PowerPlex 16 kit. Note the steady increase in the median stutter percentage with repeat length. Whereas allele 12 has a 4.8% median stutter, allele 20 has a 10.6% median stutter. With an overall locus average stutter percentage of 7.7 (± 1.9)%, an average value plus three standard deviations would be 13.4%, which is close to the Identifiler Plus recommended D18S51 stutter filter of 13.7% that was calculated in a similar manner (Table 3.3).

Forward Stutter

Stutter products that are larger in size by one repeat unit than the corresponding alleles are only rarely observed in commonly used tetranucleotide repeat STR loci. However, occasionally this so-called "forward" or "N+4" stutter has been reported in the 1% to 3% range of the associated tetranucleotide STR allele (Gibb et al. 2009).

Trinucleotide loci exhibit a higher amount of forward slippage (N+3 stutter) as observed with the locus DYS392 (Mulero et al. 2006) and the DYS481 examples shown in Figure 3.10. The autosomal STR trinucleotide locus D22S1045, which is part of the expanded European core loci (Gill et al. 2006a, 2006b), can display forward N+3 stutter at the 5% level or higher. One group set their N+3 stutter threshold for D22S1045 at 7.27% based on 2,153 data points in reference DNA profiles (Westen et al. 2012). The individual locus stutter characteristics need to be kept in mind when performing DNA mixture interpretation. Sometimes pull-up from a high peak in an adjacent color channel may lead to the appearance of forward stutter that is not real.

A comparison of stutter percentages with Identifiler versus Identifiler Direct and Identifiler Plus kit found slightly higher values of forward stutter with the new kits (Sailus et al. 2012). These new kits, Identifiler Direct and Identifiler Plus, possess higher magnesium concentrations in their PCR buffer to help overcome PCR inhibitors. The Applied Biosystems research team hypothesized that these higher levels of magnesium can lower binding stringency and therefore permit more efficient extension of misaligned DNA strands after strand slippage events (see next section). This phenomenon would lead to higher stutter products. In an Identifiler Plus stutter study of 1,621 peaks in the N+4 position, 24 observations were made with N+4 stutter exceeding 2% (Sailus et al. 2012). Of the 15 tetranucleotide repeat loci amplified with Identifiler Plus, D19S433 had the highest average N+4 forward stutter (1.25%) and TH01 the lowest (0.44%).

It is important to keep in mind that with a parent allele peak possessing a height of 5000 RFU, a N+4 stutter peak of 2% would only be 100 RFU in height. Depending on the analytical threshold used, many forward stutter peaks may not be detected with alleles below the 1000 RFU to 2000 RFU range unless stochastic effects elevate the levels of stutter observed. Thus, forward stutter is not likely to be a significant issue with data analysis and interpretation in most cases. Nevertheless, the variations in stutter levels that are possible with new STR kits necessitate internal validation studies with specific conditions in use in a laboratory.

Possible Mechanism for Stutter Product Formation

Stutter products have been reported in the literature since STRs (microsatellites) were first described. The primary mechanism that has been proposed to explain the existence of stutter products is slipped-strand mispairing (Levinson & Gutman 1987, Hauge & Litt 1993, Walsh et al. 1996). In the slipped-strand mispairing model, a region of primer—template complex becomes unpaired during primer extension, allowing slippage of either primer or template strand such that one repeat forms a non-base-paired loop (Hauge & Litt 1993). The consequence of this one repeat loop is a shortened PCR product that is less than the primary amplicon (STR allele) by a single repeat unit (Figure 3.11). Sequence analysis of stutter products from the tetranucleotide repeat locus vWA found that they contain one repeat unit less than the corresponding main allele peak (Walsh et al. 1996).

In the examples illustrated so far, both D18S51 and DYS481 contain simple repeat units. Thus, the allele number also reflects the total number of repeats. However, this is not always the case with many complex STR loci, such as D21S11, where the total allele length may contain different internal sequences. Such loci may possess alleles with different lengths of uninterrupted stretches of repeats. If an allele contains multiple repeat sections interrupted by a non-consensus repeat unit or a conserved sequence, then stutter levels will typically be lower.

For example, TH01 allele 9.3 possesses five [TCAT] repeats, a CAT partial repeat, and then four [TCAT] repeats (or six [AATG], an ATG partial repeat, and three [AATG] repeats, depending on which strand is examined). The stutter percent characteristics of a TH01 9.3 allele are closer to an allele 5 than an allele 9 or allele 10.

A type of correlation of the length of uninterrupted portions of the STR repeat region to amount of stutter was noted in several studies (Walsh et al. 1996, Lazaruk et al. 2001, Klintschar & Wiegand 2003). However, it was not until 2012 when the term "longest uninterrupted stretch" (LUS) was introduced to describe the behavior of stutter product formation (Brookes et al. 2012). LUS is defined as the longest stretch of basic repeat motifs within an allele. Thus, in the TH01 example below, allele 9.3, which has five [TCAT] and four [TCAT], would have a LUS equal to five. This type of LUS correlation fits well across STR loci. LUS correlates better to stutter ratio than the allele designation based on the total number of repeat units (Figure 3.12).

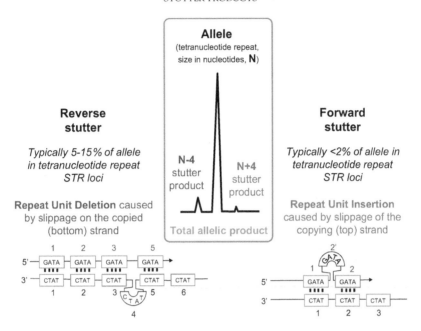

FIGURE 3.11 Illustration of stutter product formation due to repeat unit bulges when strand breathing occurs during replication. During replication the two DNA strands can easily come apart in the repeat region, and since each repeat unit is the same, the two strands can re-anneal out of register such that the two strands are off-set by a single repeat unit. If the repeat unit bulge occurs in the template strand, then the resulting synthesized strand is one repeat unit shorter than the full length STR allele and "reverse stutter" (N−4 stutter product) occurs. If a repeat unit bulges out on the new synthesized strand during extension, then an insertion results in the next round of amplification and "forward stutter" (N+4 stutter product) results.

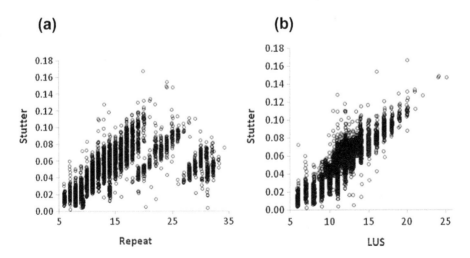

FIGURE 3.12 A comparison of stutter ratio vs. (a) repeat allele designation and (b) longest uninterrupted stretch (LUS) of repeats for STR loci containing repeat units with the same A-T base content. This Identifiler data includes peak area information from 30 replicates each of FGA, vWA, D3S1358, D16S539, D18S51, D21S11, D8S1179, CSF1PO, D13S317, D5S818, D7S820, and TPOX. Reproduced with permission from Brookes et al. (2012).

I. DATA INTERPRETATION

Many of the LUS studies to date have utilized average LUS values based on information available on STRBase or Appendix 1 of *Advanced Topics in Forensic DNA Typing: Methodology* (Butler 2012). More accurate LUS characterization requires sequencing of individual STR alleles, which is time-consuming with traditional sequencing methods.

Impact of Stutter Products on Data Interpretation

Stutter products impact interpretation of DNA profiles, especially in cases where two or more individuals may have contributed to the DNA sample (see Chapter 6). Because stutter products are the same length as actual allele PCR products, it can be challenging to determine whether a small peak is a real allele from a minor contributor of the original sample or a stutter product of an adjacent allele created during the PCR amplification process.

Mixture interpretation requires a good understanding of the behavior of stutter products in single-source samples (SWGDAM 2010). Internal validation studies quantify the percentage of stutter product peak heights compared to their corresponding allele peak heights. The percentage of stutter product formation for an allele is determined simply by dividing the stutter peak height by the corresponding allele peak height as performed with the DYS481 example in Figure 3.10.

Although stutter is generally considered an undesirable aspect of STR typing, the existence of stutter products can actually aid data interpretation in some situations. Data collection artifacts, such as spikes and pull-up peaks from off-scale data in another dye channel, can be distinguished from the fluorescent signal of true STR alleles because spikes and pull-up peaks will not have any stutter products associated with them.

Therefore, the presence of stutter peaks, while not desirable in terms of clean mixture interpretation, actually aid with confirming true STR alleles. Of course, signal for the true allele has to be high enough to detect stutter. Thus, if a stutter product is expected at around 10% of a true allele, then the allele will need to have a peak height of at least 500 RFU to detect a stutter product when an analytical threshold of 50 RFU is in place.

Modeling and Predicting Stutter

Using a fixed stutter threshold (e.g. 12%) does not reflect the locus- and allele-specific nature of stutter product formation. To improve the capabilities of probabilistic genotyping methods, efforts are underway to model stutter for the purposes of predicting potential stutter levels as effectively as possible (Bright et al. 2013a, 2013b, 2014, Brookes et al. 2012, Puch-Solis et al. 2013).

STR repeat units with a higher A-T content produce greater amounts of stutter likely due to weaker hydrogen bonding between A and T nucleotides, which have two hydrogen bonds compared to the three hydrogen bonds between G-C base pairs (Schlötterer & Tautz 1992, Brookes et al. 2012). In addition, the use of the total allelic product, which is the sum of the true allele plus all observable stutter products, has been shown to be effective in modeling the amount of stutter (Bright et al. 2013a). As discussed previously, the most important factor for correlating stutter percentage appears to be the LUS value (Figure 3.12).

A linear regression model was developed to predict Y-STR stutter heights using allele and parental peak height as explanatory variables (Andersen et al. 2011). The authors of this study concluded that the use of a single stutter threshold per locus is not optimal because stutter rates are allele-specific and differ based on the amount of template DNA. If high stutter values are used for software filters, then in many cases usable data is thrown away during DNA mixture interpretation.

Efforts to Reduce Stutter Product Formation

The amount of stutter product formation may be reduced when using STR markers with longer repeat units (e.g. pentanucleotide repeats rather than trinucleotide repeats), STR alleles with imperfect repeat units, PCR additives such as sorbitol or betaine, and possibly with DNA polymerases possessing faster processivity.

In the late 1990s, several pentanucleotide repeat loci were developed by Promega Corporation in an effort to produce STR markers that exhibit low amounts of stutter products to aid in mixture interpretation (Bacher & Schumm 1998). The first seven loci discovered were labeled Penta A through Penta G. Penta E was incorporated into the PowerPlex 2.1 system, and early work demonstrated an average stutter percentage of less than 1% with Penta E (Bacher et al. 1999). Penta D and Penta E became part of the PowerPlex 16 kit (Krenke et al. 2002) and a number of subsequent Promega kits including PowerPlex Fusion.

Alleles for an STR locus with a somewhat variable repeat motif exhibit a smaller amount of stutter product formation. This can be explained by the longest uninterrupted stretch information discussed earlier in this chapter. For example, the common repeat motif for the STR marker TH01 is AATG. However, with allele 9.3, there is an ATG nucleotide sequence present in the middle of the repeat region (Puers et al. 1993). When the core repeat sequence has been interrupted, stutter product formation is reduced compared to alleles that are similar in length but possess uninterrupted core repeat sequences. This fact has been demonstrated with sequencing results from several vWA alleles (Walsh et al. 1996).

Applied Biosystems filed several patents on "Methods for the reduction of stutter in microsatellite amplification" (Coticone & Bloch 2004, 2005, 2007). These patents include the addition of sorbitol to the PCR reaction to reduce D2S1338 stutter from 6.7% to 4.5% (Coticone & Bloch 2004). Some of the other patents mention addition of betaine as well to aid stutter reduction.

Typically stutter product formation increases when amplifying low levels of DNA template with elevated PCR cycle numbers due to stochastic effects (e.g. Butler 2012, Figure 11.2 therein). Lowering the annealing/extension temperature during PCR was found to reduce the stutter ratios when amplifying low-template DNA samples (Seo et al. 2014).

The amount of stutter may be related to the DNA polymerase processivity, or how rapidly it copies the template strand. Stutter products have been shown to increase relative to their corresponding alleles with a slower polymerase (Walsh et al. 1996). A faster polymerase may be able to copy the two DNA strands before they could come apart and re-anneal out of register during primer extension. However, recent work with rapid PCR amplification of STR loci with new rapid DNA polymerases has not significantly reduced stutter product formation observed with the 50 to 60 base processivity of *Taq* DNA polymerase (Laurin & Frégeau 2012).

Stutter Trends and Principles

An overlay of information from multiple STR loci reveals variation in the percentage of stutter for each locus and allele (Figure 3.13). Again, as in Figure 3.10, Y-STR alleles are used to simplify the problem of having to separate adjacent heterozygous alleles with autosomal STR loci. In other words,

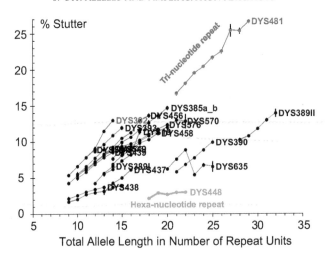

FIGURE 3.13 Stutter trends for Y-STR loci in PowerPlex Y23 shown on a repeat scale (using STR_StutterFreq program created by Dave Duewer, NIST). Note that loci with shorter repeat units, such as DYS392 and DYS481, which are tri-nucleotides, have a steeper growth in percent stutter with longer alleles than DYS448, which is a hexa-nucleotide repeat. Figure courtesy of Mike Coble, NIST.

stutter is not masked by a sister allele in Y-STRs since there is only a single allele amplified, with the exception of most samples amplified with the multi-copy Y-STR locus DYS385a/b.

Figure 3.13 illustrates several important principles by overlaying the stutter % (y-axis) on the allele number (x-axis), which represents a putative number of STR repeat units. Figure 3.13 only displays the reverse stutter observed with these Y-STR alleles.

First, each locus has a different amount of stutter product formation. Tetranucleotide repeats with the same number of repeats group well together in the lower left of the graph.

Second, longer alleles for an STR locus exhibit a greater degree of stutter than smaller alleles for the same locus. For example, DYS390 alleles ranging from 21 to 25 repeats steadily increase from about 6% stutter to 10% stutter.

Third, slopes of lines connecting measured stutter for the alleles at each STR locus show a nice correlation between the increasing number of repeats and the core repeat motif of each locus. Thus, the slope for DYS448 alleles, which possesses a hexanucleotide repeat motif, is almost horizontal between the observed DYS448 alleles containing 18 to 22 repeats (middle bottom part of the graph) while the slope of the stutter for DYS481 alleles, which is a trinucleotide repeat, is much steeper with its 21 to 29 repeat alleles (top part of graph).

Fourth, in some cases a dip in the percent stutter is observed with increasing allele length within a locus. The most obvious in Figure 3.13 is allele 23 in DYS635, which drops to about 5% stutter, compared to allele 22 that is closer to 9% stutter. This is likely due to a change in the DYS635 longest uninterrupted stretch of repeats as noted by researchers in Copenhagen (Olofsson et al. 2012). This Danish group noted in their data set that when a DYS635 allele "23" had a LUS of 9, then the median stutter rate was 5.1%, while for the same overall length allele that possessed a LUS of 13, then the median stutter rate was increased to 8.8% (Olofsson et al. 2012).

Locus DYS389II, which has the longest alleles in Figure 3.13 (further to the right on the graph), is really two separate sections, and thus the LUS is about half of the total allele length. A tetranucleotide repeat STR locus with LUS alleles ranging from 28 to 32 repeats would be expected to have a higher % stutter.

The fifth and final principle to glean from Figure 3.13 is that the stutter percentage with the tetra-nucleotide repeat loci is less than 15% under standard amplification conditions. Thus, as with the autosomal STR loci, 15% serves as a fairly effective stutter filter.

A summary of stutter product formation is listed below:

- Primarily one repeat unit smaller than corresponding main allele peak;
- Typically less than 15% of corresponding allele peak height;
- Quantity of stutter depends on locus as well as PCR conditions and polymerase used;
- Propensity for stutter decreases with longer repeat units (pentanucleotide repeats < tetra- < tri- < dinucleotides);
- Longest uninterrupted stretch of repeats impacts stutter product formation;
- Quantity of stutter is greater for longer alleles within a locus;
- Quantity of stutter is less if the sequence of core repeats is interrupted (e.g. compound repeat);
- Stutter amount increases when amplifying low levels of DNA template due to stochastic effects.

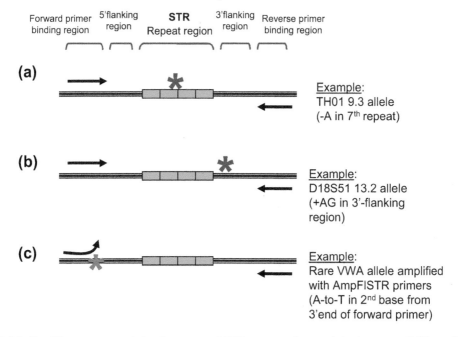

FIGURE 3.14 Possible sequence variation in or around STR repeat regions and the impact on PCR amplification. The asterisk symbolizes a DNA difference (base change, insertion or deletion of a nucleotide) from a typical allele for a STR locus. In situation (a), the variation occurs within the repeat region and should have no impact on the primer binding and the subsequent PCR amplification (although the overall amplicon size may vary slightly). In situation (b), the sequence variation occurs just outside the repeat in the flanking region but interior to the primer annealing sites. Again, PCR should not be affected, although the size of the PCR product may vary slightly. However, in situation (c) the PCR can fail due to a disruption in the annealing of a primer because the primer no longer perfectly matches the DNA template sequence.

I. DATA INTERPRETATION

NULL (SILENT) ALLELES

When amplifying DNA fragments that contain STR repeat regions, it is possible to have a phenomenon known as *allele drop-out*. Sequence polymorphisms are known to occur within or around STR repeat regions. These variations can occur in three locations (relative to the primer binding sites): within the repeat region, in the flanking region, or in the primer-binding region (Figure 3.14).

If a base pair change occurs in the DNA template at the PCR primer-binding region, the hybridization of the primer can be disrupted, resulting in a failure to amplify, and therefore failure to detect an allele that exists in the template DNA. More simply, the DNA template exists for a particular allele but fails to amplify during PCR due to primer hybridization problems. This phenomenon results in what is known as a *null allele*. Fortunately null alleles are rather rare because the flanking sequence around STR repeats is fairly stable and consistent between samples. Null alleles are typically uncovered through concordance studies using PCR primers that anneal to different portions of the flanking region for the same locus. STR kit concordance studies will be covered in the next chapter.

Reading List and Internet Resources

General Information

Butler, J. M. (2012). *Advanced Topics in Forensic DNA Typing: Methodology*. San Diego: Elsevier Academic Press.

Collins, P. J., et al. (2004). Developmental validation of a single-tube amplification of the 13 CODIS STR loci, D2S1338, D19S433, and amelogenin: the AmpFlSTR Identifiler PCR Amplification Kit. *Journal Forensic Sciences, 49*, 1265–1277.

Cotton, E. A., et al. (2000). Validation of the AmpFlSTR SGM Plus system for use in forensic casework. *Forensic Science International, 112*, 151–161.

Ellegren, H. (2004). Microsatellites: simple sequences with complex evolution. *Nature Reviews Genetics, 5*, 435–445.

Gill, P., et al. (2006a). The evolution of DNA databases — Recommendations for new European STR loci. *Forensic Science International, 156*, 242–244.

Gill, P., et al. (2006b). New multiplexes for Europe — amendments and clarification of strategic development. *Forensic Science International, 163*, 155–157.

SWGDAM Interpretation Guidelines (2010). http://swgdam.org/Interpretation_Guidelines_January_2010.pdf. Accessed March 18, 2014.

STR Alleles and their Measurement

Gill, P., et al. (1995). Automated short tandem repeat (STR) analysis in forensic casework — a strategy for the future. *Electrophoresis, 16*, 1543–1552.

Gill, P., et al. (1996). A new method of STR interpretation using inferential logic — development of a criminal intelligence database. *International Journal Legal Medicine, 109*, 14–22.

GlobalFiler (2014). http://tools.invitrogen.com/downloads/GlobalFiler-FAQs.pdf. Accessed March 18, 2014.

Krenke, B. E., et al. (2002). Validation of a 16-locus fluorescent multiplex system. *Journal Forensic Sciences, 47*, 773–785.

Lazaruk, K., et al. (1998). Genotyping of forensic short tandem repeat (STR) systems based on sizing precision in a capillary electrophoresis instrument. *Electrophoresis, 19*, 86–93.

DNA Sizing

Elder, J. K., & Southern, E. M. (1983). Measurement of DNA length by gel electrophoresis II: comparison of methods for relating mobility to fragment length. *Analytical Biochemistry, 128*, 227–231.

Hartzell, B., et al. (2003). Response of short tandem repeat systems to temperature and sizing methods. *Forensic Science International, 133*, 228–234.

Klein, S. B., et al. (2003). Addressing ambient temperature variant effects on sizing precision of AmpFlSTR Profiler Plus alleles detected on the ABI Prism 310 Genetic Analyzer. *Forensic Science Communications, 5*(1). Available at http://www.fbi.gov/about-us/lab/forensic-science-communications/. Accessed March 19, 2014.

Mayrand, P. E., et al. (1992). The use of fluorescence detection and internal lane standards to size PCR products automatically. *Applied Theoretical Electrophoresis, 3*(1), 1–11.

Rosenblum, B. B., et al. (1997). Improved single-strand DNA sizing accuracy in capillary electrophoresis. *Nucleic Acids Research, 25*, 3925–3929.

Ziegle, J. S., et al. (1992). Application of automated DNA sizing technology for genotyping microsatellite loci. *Genomics, 14*(4), 1026–1031.

Allelic Ladders

Baechtel, F. S., et al. (1993). Multigenerational amplification of a reference ladder for alleles at locus D1S80. *Journal Forensic Sciences, 38*, 1176–1182.

Griffiths, R. A., et al. (1998). New reference allelic ladders to improve allelic designation in a multiplex STR system. *International Journal Legal Medicine, 111*, 267–272.

Kline, M. C., et al. (1997). Interlaboratory evaluation of short tandem repeat triplex CTT. *Journal Forensic Sciences, 42*, 897–906.

Puers, C., et al. (1993). Identification of repeat sequence heterogeneity at the polymorphic short tandem repeat locus HUMTH01 [AATG]n and reassignment of alleles in population analysis by using a locus-specific allelic ladder. *American Journal Human Genetics, 53*, 953–958.

Sajantila, A., et al. (1992). Amplification of reproducible allele markers for amplified fragment length polymorphism analysis. *Biotechniques, 12*, 16–22.

Smith, R. N. (1995). Accurate size comparison of short tandem repeat alleles amplified by PCR. *Biotechniques, 18*, 122–128.

STR Allele Nomenclature

Bär, W., et al. (1994). DNA recommendations – 1994 report concerning further recommendations of the DNA Commission of the ISFH regarding PCR-based polymorphisms in STR (short tandem repeat) systems. *International Journal Legal Medicine, 107*, 159–160.

Bär, W., et al. (1997). DNA recommendations – further report of the DNA Commission of the ISFH regarding the use of short tandem repeat systems. *International Journal Legal Medicine, 110*, 175–176.

Barber, M. D., et al. (1996). Structural variation in the alleles of a short tandem repeat system at the human alpha fibrinogen locus. *International Journal Legal Medicine, 108*, 180–185.

Barber, M. D., & Parkin, B. H. (1996). Sequence analysis and allelic designation of the two short tandem repeat loci D18S51 and D8S1179. *International Journal Legal Medicine, 109*, 62–65.

Butler, J. M., et al. (2008). Addressing Y-chromosome short tandem repeat (Y-STR) allele nomenclature. *Journal Genetic Genealogy, 4*(2), 125–148.

Gill, P., et al. (1997a). Considerations from the European DNA profiling group (EDNAP) concerning STR nomenclature. *Forensic Science International, 87*, 185–192.

Gill, P., et al. (1997b). Development of guidelines to designate alleles using an STR multiplex system. *Forensic Science International, 89*, 185–197.

Gill, P., et al. (2001). DNA Commission of the International Society of Forensic Genetics: Recommendations on forensic analysis using Y-chromosome STRs. *Forensic Science International, 124*, 5–10.

Gusmão, L., et al. (2006). DNA Commission of the International Society of Forensic Genetics (ISFG): an update of the recommendations on the use of Y-STRs in forensic analysis. *Forensic Science International, 157*, 187–197.

Mulero, J. J., et al. (2006). Letter to the Editor — Nomenclature and allele repeat structure update for the Y-STR locus GATA-H4. *Journal Forensic Sciences, 51*, 694.

Urquhart, A., et al. (1994). Variation in short tandem repeat sequences — a survey of twelve microsatellite loci for use as forensic identification markers. *International Journal Legal Medicine, 107*, 13–20.

Variant Alleles

Allor, C., et al. (2005). Identification and characterization of variant alleles at CODIS STR loci. *Journal Forensic Sciences, 50*, 1128–1133.

Bhoopat, T., et al. (2003). Identification of DYS385 allele variants by using shorter amplicons and Northern Thai haplotype data. *Journal Forensic Sciences, 48*, 1108–1112.

Butler, J. M. (2006). Genetics and genomics of core STR loci used in human identity testing. *Journal of Forensic Sciences, 51*, 253–265.

I. DATA INTERPRETATION

Cho, E. H., et al. (2011). Variant alleles detected in a large Korean population using AmpFlSTR Profiler Plus. *Forensic Science International Genetics, 5*(5), 552–554.

Clayton, T. M., et al. (2004). Primer binding site mutations affecting the typing of STR loci contained within the AMPFlSTR SGM Plus kit. *Forensic Science International, 139*, 255–259.

Crouse, C. A., et al. (1999). Analysis and interpretation of short tandem repeat microvariants and three banded patterns using multiple allele detection systems. *Journal Forensic Sciences, 44*, 87–94.

Dauber, E. M., et al. (2008). Unusual FGA and D19S433 off-ladder alleles and other allelic variants at the STR loci D8S1132, vWA, D18S51 and ACTBP2 (SE33). *Forensic Science International Genetics Supplement Series, 1*, 109–111.

Dauber, E. M., et al. (2009). Further allelic variation at the STR-loci ACTBP2 (SE33), D3S1358, D8S1132, D18S51 and D21S11. *Forensic Science International Genetics Supplement Series, 2*, 41–42.

Egyed, B., et al. (2000). Analysis of eight STR loci in two Hungarian populations. *International Journal of Legal Medicine, 113*, 272–275.

Grubwieser, P., et al. (2005). Unusual variant alleles in commonly used short tandem repeat loci. *International Journal Legal Medicine, 119*, 164–166.

Heinrich, M., et al. (2005). Characterisation of variant alleles in the STR systems D2S1338, D3S1358 and D19S433. *International Journal Legal Medicine, 119*, 310–313.

Huel, R., et al. (2007). Variant alleles, triallelic patterns, and point mutations observed in nuclear short tandem repeat typing of populations in Bosnia and Serbia. *Croatian Medical Journal, 48*(4), 494–502.

Klein, R., et al. (2003). A very long ACTBP2 (SE33) allele. *International Journal Legal Medicine, 117*, 235–236.

Kline, M. C., et al. (2011). STR sequence analysis for characterizing normal, variant, and null alleles. *Forensic Science International: Genetics, 5*(4), 329–332.

Lareu, M. V., et al. (1996). Sequence variation of a hypervariable short tandem repeat at the D12S391 locus. *Gene, 182*, 151–153.

Lareu, M. V., et al. (1998). Sequence variation of a hypervariable short tandem repeat at the D1S1656 locus. *International Journal Legal Medicine, 111*, 244–247.

Lederer, T., et al. (2008). Characterization of two unusual allele variants at the STR locus ACTBP2 (SE33). *Forensic Science Medicine Pathology, 4*, 164–166.

Margolis-Nunno, H., et al. (2001). A new allele of the short tandem repeat (STR) locus, CSF1PO. *Journal Forensic Sciences, 46*, 1480–1483.

Miozzo, M. C., et al. (2007). Characterization of the variant allele 9.2 of Penta D locus. *Journal Forensic Sciences, 52*, 1073–1076.

Mizuno, N., et al. (2003). Variant alleles on the Penta E locus in the PowerPlex 16 kit. *Journal Forensic Sciences, 48*, 358–361.

Möller, A., et al. (1994). Different types of structural variation in STRs: HumFES/FPS, HumVWA, and HumD21S11. *International Journal Legal Medicine, 106*, 319–323.

Morales-Valverde, A., et al. (2009). Characterisation of 12 new alleles in the STR system D18S51. *Forensic Science International Genetics Supplement Series, 2*, 43–44.

Mornhinweg, E., et al. (1998). D3S1358: Sequence analysis and gene frequency in a German population. *Forensic Science International, 95*, 173–178.

Onofri, V., et al. (2008). D16S539 microvariant or D2S1338 off-ladder allele? A case report about a range overlapping between two loci. *Forensic Science International Genetics Supplement Series, 1*, 123–124.

Phillips, C. P., et al. (1998). Band shift analysis of three base-pair repeat alleles in the short tandem repeat locus D12S391. *Forensic Science International, 93*, 79–88.

Phillips, C., et al. (2011). Analysis of global variability in 15 established and 5 new European Standard Set (ESS) STRs using the CEPH human genome diversity panel. *Forensic Science International Genetics, 5*(3), 155–169.

Puers, C., et al. (1993). Identification of repeat sequence heterogeneity at the polymorphic short tandem repeat locus HUMTH01 [AATG]n and reassignment of alleles in population analysis by using a locus-specific allelic ladder. *American Journal Human Genetics, 53*, 953–958.

Raziel, A., et al. (2012). Discordance at D3S1358 locus involving SGM Plus and the European new generation multiplex kits. *Forensic Science International Genetics, 6*, 108–112.

Rockenbauer, E., et al. (2011). Sequences of microvariant/"off-ladder" STR alleles. *Forensic Science International Genetics Supplement Series, 3*, e204–e205.

STRBase Identifiler Genotype Database (2014): http://www.cstl.nist.gov/strbase/NISTpopdata/JFS2003IDresults.xls. Accessed March 19, 2014.

STRBase Variant Allele Reports (2014): http://www.cstl.nist.gov/strbase/var_tab.htm. Accessed March 19, 2014.

STR Markers (2014): http://www.cstl.nist.gov/strbase/seq_ref.htm. Accessed March 19, 2014.

Tsuji, A., et al. (2006). The structure of a variant allele which is considered to be 30.3 in the STR locus D21S11. *Legal Medicine, 8,* 182—183.

Vanderheyden, N., et al. (2007). Identification and sequence analysis of discordant phenotypes between AmpFlSTR SGM Plus and PowerPlex 16. *International Journal of Legal Medicine, 121,* 297—301.

Walsh, S. J., et al. (2003). Characterisation of variant alleles at the HumD21S11 locus implies unique Australasian genotypes and re-classification of nomenclature guidelines. *Forensic Science International, 135,* 35—41.

SE33 Flanking Region Variation

Butler, J. M., et al. (2011). SE33 variant alleles: sequences and implications. *Forensic Science International Genetics Supplement Series, 3,* e502—e503.

Butler, J. M. (2012). *Appendix 1 in Advanced Topics in Forensic DNA Typing: Methodology.* San Diego: Elsevier Academic Press. pp. 549—602.

Davis, C., et al. (2012). Variants observed for STR locus SE33: a concordance study. *Forensic Science International Genetics, 6*(4), 494—497.

Hering, S., et al. (2002). Sequence variations in the primer binding regions of the highly polymorphic STR system SE33. *International Journal Legal Medicine, 116,* 365—367.

McLaren, R. S., et al. (2013). Developmental validation of the PowerPlex® ESI 17 Pro System. *Forensic Science International: Genetics, 7*(3), e69—e73.

Wang, D. Y., et al. (2012). Identification and secondary structure analysis of a region affecting electrophoretic mobility of the STR locus SE33. *Forensic Science International Genetics, 6*(3), 310—316.

ISOAlleles: Same Length, Different Sequence STR Alleles

Bornman, D. M., et al. (2012). Short-read, high-throughput sequencing technology for STR genotyping. *Biotechniques Rapid Dispatches,* 1—6.

Brinkmann, B., et al. (1996). Complex mutational events at the HumD21S11 locus. *Human Genetics, 98,* 60—64.

Dalsgaard, S., et al. (2014). Non-uniform phenotyping of D12S391 resolved by second generation sequencing. *Forensic Science International Genetics, 8,* 195—199.

Duncan, D. D., et al. (2011). Development of a genotyping assay for the UK, European, and CODIS core STR loci identifying length and sequence variation in the target loci. *Forensic Science International Genetics Supplement Series, 3,* e267—e268.

Edwards, M., & Allen, R. W. (2004). Characteristics of mutations at the D5S818 locus studied with a tightly linked marker. *Transfusion, 44,* 83—90.

Hall, T., & Hofstadler, S. A. (2012). *High throughput mass spectrometry to exploit genetic differences in same-length STR alleles. Final report from NIJ grant 2008-DN-BX-K304 submitted to the National Institute of Justice.* Available at https://www.ncjrs.gov/pdffiles1/nij/grants/239302.pdf. Accessed March 19, 2014.

Hofstadler, S. A., et al. (2009). Analysis of DNA forensic markers using high throughput mass spectrometry. *Forensic Science International Genetics Supplement Series, 2,* 524—526.

Hsieh, H.-M., et al. (2002). Sequence analysis of STR polymorphisms at locus ACTBP2 in the Taiwanese population. *Forensic Science International, 130,* 112—121.

Möller, A., & Brinkmann, B. (1994). Locus ACTBP2 (SE33): Sequencing data reveal considerable polymorphism. *International Journal Legal Medicine, 106,* 262—267.

Mountain, J. L., et al. (2002). SNPSTRs: empirically derived, rapidly typed, autosomal haplotypes for inference of population history and mutational processes. *Genome Research, 12*(11), 1766—1772.

Oberacher, H., et al. (2008). Increased forensic efficiency of DNA fingerprints through simultaneous resolution of length and nucleotide variability by high-performance mass spectrometry. *Human Mutation, 29*(3), 427—432.

Oberacher, H., & Parson, W. (2007). Forensic DNA fingerprinting by liquid chromatography-electrospray ionization mass spectrometry. *Biotechniques, 43*(4). vii—xiii.

Omran, G. A., et al. (2008). Diversity of 17-locus Y-STR haplotypes in Upper (Southern) Egyptians. *Forensic Science International Genetics Supplement Series, 1,* 230—232.

Pitterl, F., et al. (2008). The next generation of DNA profiling — STR typing by multiplexed PCR-ion-pair RP LC-ESI time-of-flight MS. *Electrophoresis, 29,* 4739—4750.

Pitterl, F., et al. (2010). Increasing the discrimination power of forensic STR testing by employing high-performance mass spectrometry, as illustrated in indigenous South African and Central Asian populations. *International Journal Legal Medicine, 124,* 551—558.

I. DATA INTERPRETATION

Planz, J. V., et al. (2009). Enhancing resolution and statistical power by utilizing mass spectrometry for detection of SNPs within the short tandem repeats. *Forensic Science International Genetics Supplement Series, 2*, 529–531.

Planz, J. V., & Hall, T. A. (2012). Hidden variation in microsatellite loci: utility and implications for forensic DNA analysis. *Forensic Science Review, 24*(1), 27–42.

Planz, J. V., et al. (2012). Automated analysis of sequence polymorphism in STR alleles by PCR and direct electrospray ionization mass spectrometry. *Forensic Science International Genetics, 6*, 594–606.

Rockenbauer, E., et al. (2014). Characterization of mutations and sequence variants in the D21S11 locus by next generation sequencing. *Forensic Science International Genetics, 8*, 68–72.

Rolf, B., et al. (1997). Sequence polymorphism at the tetranucleotide repeat of the human beta-actin related pseudogene H-beta-Ac-psi-2 (ACTBP2) locus. *International Journal Legal Medicine, 110*, 69–72.

Scheible, M., et al. (2011). Short tandem repeat sequencing on the 454 platform. *Forensic Science International Genetics Supplement Series, 3*, e357–e358.

Urquhart, A., et al. (1993). Sequence variability of the tetranucleotide repeat of the human beta-actin related pseudogene H-beta-Ac-psi-2 (ACTBP2) locus. *Human Genetics, 92*, 637–638.

Non-Template Addition

Butler, J. M., & Becker, C. H. (2001). *Improved analysis of DNA short tandem repeats with time-of-flight mass spectrometry. Final Report for NIJ Grant 97-LB-VX-0003 Office of Justice Programs National Institute of Justice 75 published pages.* Available at http://www.nij.gov/pubs-sum/188292.htm. Accessed March 19, 2014.

Brownstein, M. J., et al. (1996). Modulation of non-templated nucleotide addition by Taq DNA polymerase: primer modifications that facilitate genotyping. *Biotechniques, 20*, 1004–1010.

Clark, J. M. (1988). Novel non-templated nucleotide addition reactions catalyzed by prokaryotic and eukaryotic DNA polymerases. *Nucleic Acid Research, 16*, 9677–9686.

Edwards, A., et al. (1991). DNA typing and genetic mapping with trimeric and tetrameric tandem repeats. *American Journal Human Genetics, 49*, 746–756.

Ginot, F., et al. (1996). Correction of some genotyping errors in automated fluorescent microsatellite analysis by enzymatic removal of one base overhangs. *Nucleic Acids Research, 24*, 540–541.

Kimpton, C. P., et al. (1993). Automated DNA profiling employing multiplex amplification of short tandem repeat loci. *PCR Methods Applications, 3*, 13–22.

Magnuson, V. L., et al. (1996). Substrate nucleotide-determined non-templated addition of adenine by Taq DNA polymerase: implications for PCR-based genotyping and cloning. *Biotechniques, 21*, 700–709.

Stutter Products

Andersen, M. M., et al. (2011). Estimating stutter rates for Y-STR alleles. *Forensic Science International Genetics Supplement Series, 3*, e192–e193.

Applied Biosystems. (1998). *AmpFlSTR COfiler PCR Amplification Kit User's Bulletin.* Foster City, California: Applied Biosystems.

Applied Biosystems. (1998). *AmpFlSTR Profiler Plus PCR Amplification Kit User's Manual.* Foster City, California: Applied Biosystems.

Applied Biosystems. (1999). *AmpFlSTR SGM Plus PCR Amplification Kit User's Manual.* Foster City, California: Applied Biosystems.

Applied Biosystems. (2001). *AmpFlSTR Identifiler PCR Amplification Kit User's Manual.* Foster City, CA.

Blackmore, V. L., et al. (2000). Preferential amplification and stutter observed in population database samples using the AmpFlSTR Profiler multiplex system. *Canadian Society Forensic Sciences Journal, 33*, 23–32.

Bright, J.-A., et al. (2013a). Developing allelic and stutter peak height models for a continuous method of DNA interpretation. *Forensic Science International Genetics, 7*(2), 296–304.

Bright, J.-A., et al. (2013b). Investigation into the performance of different models for predicting stutter. *Forensic Science International Genetics, 7*(4), 422–427.

Bright, J.-A., et al. (2014). Characterising the STR locus D6S1043 and examination of its effect on stutter rates. *Forensic Science International Genetics, 8*(1), 20–23.

Brookes, C., et al. (2012). Characterising stutter in forensic STR multiplexes. *Forensic Science International Genetics, 6*, 58–63.

Gill, P., et al. (1997). Development of guidelines to designate alleles using an STR multiplex system. *Forensic Science International, 89*, 185−197.

Gill, P., et al. (2000). Report of the European Network of Forensic Science Institutes (ENFSI): formulation and testing of principles to evaluate STR multiplexes. *Forensic Science International, 108*, 1−29.

Hauge, X. Y., & Litt, M. (1993). A study of the origin of 'shadow bands' seen when typing dinucleotide repeat polymorphisms by the PCR. *Human Molecular Genetics, 2*, 411−415.

Klintschar, M., & Wiegand, P. (2003). Polymerase slippage in relation to the uniformity of tetrameric repeat stretches. *Forensic Science International, 135*(2), 163−166.

Laurin, N., & Frégeau, C. (2012). Optimization and validation of a fast amplification protocol for AmpFlSTR Profiler Plus for rapid forensic human identification. *Forensic Science International Genetics, 6*, 47−57.

Lazaruk, K., et al. (2001). Sequence variation in humans and other primates at six short tandem repeat loci used in forensic identity testing. *Forensic Science International, 119*, 1−10.

Leclair, B., et al. (2004). Systematic analysis of stutter percentages and allele peak height and peak area ratios at heterozygous STR loci for forensic casework and database samples. *Journal Forensic Sciences, 49*, 968−980.

Levinson, G., & Gutman, G. A. (1987). Slipped-strand mispairing: a major mechanism for DNA sequence evolution. *Molecular Biology Evolution, 4*(3), 203−221.

Meldgaard, M., & Morling, N. (1997). Detection and quantitative characterization of artificial extra peaks following polymerase chain reaction amplification of 14 short tandem repeat systems used in forensic investigations. *Electrophoresis, 18*(11), 1928−1935.

Moretti, T. R., et al. (2001). Validation of STR typing by capillary electrophoresis. *Journal of Forensic Sciences, 46*, 661−676.

Olofsson, J., et al. (2012). Sequence variants of allele 22 and 23 of DYS635 causing different stutter rates. *Forensic Science International Genetics, 6*, e161−e162.

Puch-Solis, R., et al. (2013). Evaluating forensic DNA profiles using peak heights, allowing for multiple donors, allelic dropout and stutters. *Forensic Science International Genetics, 7*, 555−563.

Pumpernik, D., et al. (2008). Replication slippage versus point mutation rates in short tandem repeats of the human genome. *Molecular Genetics Genomics, 279*, 53−61.

Schlötterer, C., & Tautz, D. (1992). Slippage synthesis of simple sequence DNA. *Nucleic Acids Research, 20*, 211−215.

Sparkes, R., et al. (1996). The validation of a 7-locus multiplex STR test for use in forensic casework. (II): artefacts, casework studies and success rates. *International Journal Legal Medicine, 109*(4), 195−204.

Walsh, P. S., et al. (1996). Sequence analysis and characterization of stutter products at the tetranucleotide repeat locus vWA. *Nucleic Acids Research, 24*, 2807−2812.

Wang, Y., et al. (2004). A novel strategy to engineer DNA polymerases for enhanced processivity and improved performance in vitro. *Nucleic Acids Research, 32*, 1197−1207.

Forward Stutter

Gibb, A. J., et al. (2009). Characterization of forward stutter in the AmpFlSTR SGM Plus PCR. *Science Justice, 49*, 24−31.

Mulero, J. J., et al. (2006). Characterization of the N+3 stutter product in the trinucleotide repeat locus DYS392. *Journal Forensic Sciences, 51*, 1069−1073.

Sailus, J., et al. (2012). Considerations for the evaluation of plus stutter for AmpFlSTR PCR amplification kits in human identification laboratories. *Forensic News.* Available at http://www3.appliedbiosystems.com/cms/groups/applied_markets_marketing/documents/generaldocuments/cms_102368.pdf. Accessed March 19, 2014.

Westen, A. A., et al. (2012). Assessment of the stochastic threshold, back- and forward stutter filters and low template techniques for NGM. *Forensic Science International Genetics, 6*(6), 708−715.

Stutter Reduction

Bacher, J. W., & Schumm, J. W. (1998). Development of highly polymorphic pentanucleotide tandem repeat loci with low stutter. *Profiles DNA, 2*(2), 3−6. Available at http://www.promega.com/resources/profiles-in-dna/1998/development-of-highly-polymorphic-pentanucleotide-tandem-repeat-loci-with-low-stutter/. Accessed March 19, 2014.

Bacher, J. W., et al. (1999). Pentanucleotide repeats: highly polymorphic genetic markers displaying minimal stutter artifact. *Proceedings 9th International Symposium Human Identification*, 24−37. Available at http://www.promega.com/products/pm/genetic-identity/ishi-conference-proceedings/9th-ishi-oral-presentations/. Accessed March 19, 2014.

Coticone, S. R., & Bloch, W. (2004). *Methods for the reduction of stutter in microsatellite amplification.* US Patent 6,780,588.

Coticone, S. R., & Bloch, W. (2005). *Methods for the reduction of stutter in microsatellite amplification.* US Patent 6,841,349.

Coticone, S. R., & Bloch, W. (2007). *Methods for the reduction of stutter in microsatellite amplification.* US Patent 7,211,385.

Krenke, B. E., et al. (2002). Validation of a 16-locus fluorescent multiplex system. *Journal Forensic Sciences, 47*, 773–785.

Seo, S. B., et al. (2014). Reduction of stutter ratios in short tandem repeat loci typing of low copy number DNA samples. *Forensic Science International Genetics, 8*, 213–218.

4

STR Genotypes

Heterozygote Balance, Stochastic Thresholds, Allele, and Concordance Studies

"It has long been an axiom of mine that the little things are infinitely the most important."

Sherlock Holmes (A Case of Identity)

IMPORTANCE OF GENOTYPES VS. ALLELES

Individual alleles are amplified using the polymerase chain reaction (PCR) and measured following capillary electrophoresis (CE) separation and detection. However, because humans are diploid, with one allele coming from an individual's mother and one allele coming from an individual's father, it is the genotype — the specific allele pair — that matters in human DNA profiles at each short tandem repeat (STR) locus tested. To determine whether two measured alleles can be associated into a genotype, validation data are collected from single-source samples to determine expected heterozygote peak height balance ranges. This information can then inform DNA mixture interpretation efforts (see Chapter 6).

PEAK HEIGHT RATIOS

Generally, an individual will be homozygous or heterozygous at each genetic location tested. Homozygous loci possess alleles that are electrophoretically indistinguishable, and therefore only a single CE peak will be detected. In an electropherogram with well-balanced loci (e.g. Figure 1.5), it may be possible to infer that two same-size copies of an allele are present at a locus by comparing the overall peak heights of the single observed allele to the result from a neighboring heterozygous locus.

Heterozygous STR loci possess two alleles that are different in overall amplicon size. The heights of these two "sister" alleles can be compared in single-source samples to enable genotype assumptions in samples containing more than one contributor. This comparison of sister allele peak heights is commonly called a peak height ratio (PHR) or heterozygote balance (Hb) calculation. Different nomenclatures and different methods have been used for examining peak height ratios (D.N.A. Box 4.1).

D.N.A. BOX 4.1

NOMENCLATURE FOR HETEROZYGOTE BALANCE

Within the United States, the term peak height ratio (PHR) is commonly applied to the relative amount of two alleles at a heterozygous STR locus. In Europe and other parts of the world, it is more common to see heterozygote balance (Hb, Hb′, H_b, or H'_b) used to describe the relative peak heights of heterozygous alleles. In early articles from Peter Gill when he was at the UK Forensic Science Service (Gill et al. 1997), and more recent ones from John Buckleton's group at New Zealand's Environmental Science & Research (Kelly et al. 2012), it is common to see the Greek letter phi used to reflect the peak height or area in a theoretical description of heterozygote balance. Both capital phi (Φ) and lowercase phi (φ) have been used in various articles.

Hb′ (H'_b) = φ_a / φ_b where φ_a is the peak height (or area) of the shorter allele and φ_b is the peak height (or area) of the taller allele so that the ratio will always be less than 1.0 and can be viewed as a percentage (e.g. H'_b = 0.6 or 60% PHR). This is method #1 in Figure 4.1 and is more commonly used in the U.S. Hb (Hb) involves dividing the longer-size (higher relative molecular mass) allele by the shorter-size (lower relative molecular mass) allele. This is method #2 in Figure 4.1. These two methods were studied extensively where it was noted that Method #1 provides a more even weight for every ratio increment (Leclair et al. 2004). Recent New Zealand work (e.g. Kelly et al. 2012) prefers Method #2 as it retains more information about the direction of heterozygote imbalance.

Sources: Gill, P., et al. (1997). Development of guidelines to designate alleles using an STR multiplex system. Forensic Science International, 89, 185–197; Kelly, H., et al. (2012). Modeling heterozygote balance in forensic DNA profiles. Forensic Science International: Genetics, 6, 729–734; Leclair, B., et al. (2004). Systematic analysis of stutter percentages and allele peak height and peak area ratios at heterozygous STR loci for forensic casework and database samples. Journal of Forensic Sciences, 49, 968–980.

Method in Figure 4.1	Equation	Definition of terms	Reference
Method #1	$Hb' = h^{(2)} = \dfrac{\emptyset_{smaller}}{\emptyset_{larger}}$	*smaller* = smaller peak height *larger* = larger peak height	Leclair et al. 2004 Kelly et al. 2012
Method #2	$Hb = h = \dfrac{\emptyset_{HMW}}{\emptyset_{LMW}}$	h = heterozygote balance $\emptyset$ = peak height HMW = higher molecular weight allele LMW = lower molecular weight allele	Leclair et al. 2004 Kelly et al. 2012

Often smaller-size alleles amplify slightly better than larger-size alleles. This is known as *preferential amplification*, which is the unequal sampling of the two alleles present in a heterozygous locus. PCR amplification variability occurs particularly with lower amounts of DNA template. Even though two alleles are present at an STR locus in equal amounts in the DNA template, stochastic (meaning random) variation can occur in the early rounds of PCR and lead to selectively amplifying one allele over the other. Thus, peak height ratios for heterozygotes will rarely be 100% where both alleles are quantitatively equal in detected peak height signal.

The peak height ratio in single-source heterozygous loci is a measure of the recovery of both alleles in the tested sample. PHR can vary by locus, allele size separation, and DNA template amount. PHR calculations can be performed two different ways: (1) dividing the weaker intensity allele peak height by the stronger intensity allele peak height, or (2) dividing the longer-size allele peak height by the shorter-size allele peak height (Leclair et al. 2004).

Figure 4.1 examines two situations for heterozygous allele pairs. The smaller-size allele in a heterozygous genotype can either be taller (Situation #1) or shorter (Situation #2) than its sister allele. Depending on the method used to calculate the heterozygote balance, different results can be obtained. Note that under Situation #1, both Method #1 and Method #2 generated the same results. However, when the larger-size allele is also the taller peak, then the two methods will generate different results. If the Hb calculation is greater than one with Method #2, this indicates that the larger-size allele is the taller one.

During the course of studying STR kit metrics such as peak height ratios (Hill et al. 2011), several software programs were developed by David Duewer at the National Institute of Standards and

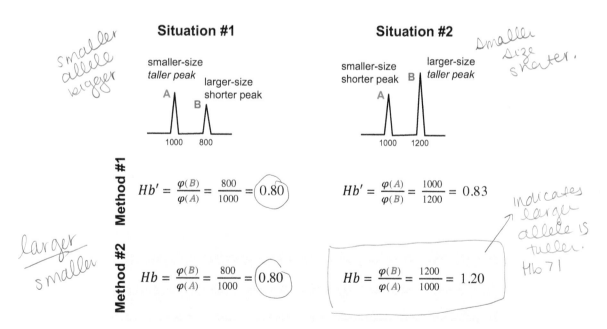

FIGURE 4.1   Two situations compared with two methods for calculating heterozygote balance (Hb). Method #2 retains more information as it reflects the position of the taller peak. When Hb is >1, then the taller peak is the larger-size allele. When the smaller-size allele is the tallest peak in the heterozygote, then Method #1 and Method #2 arrive at the same value.

Technology. These programs are freely available on the NIST STRBase website (NIST 2014). STR_ AlleleFreq is an Excel-based program that helps characterize peak height ratios and STR allele frequencies. Other programs enable stutter percentage calculations and population genetics metrics to be performed.

Plots can be made with the heterozygote balance (larger size allele divided by the smaller size allele) versus the average peak height (Bright et al. 2010). Alternatively, the Hb can be plotted against the taller STR allele (Manabe et al. 2013). It is often easier to think of PHRs in terms of percentages, although as is noted in D.N.A. Box 4.1, this approach loses the directionality of the peak imbalance. Thus, Hb′ is easier to conceptualize but Hb retains more information.

An examination of D18S51 data from the PowerPlex 16HS kit run with 30 cycles and targeting 1 ng of template DNA found that most data was greater than 70% PHR (Figure 4.2). Note that only one sample (0.41%) had a <50% PHR. This sample had allele peak heights that were 94 RFU and 196 RFU. Four samples fell in the 50% to 60% PHR range, and 15 samples had PHRs between 60% and 70%. Thus, 20 total samples out of 242 (8.3%) exhibited <70% PHR and five samples (2.1%) were <60%. Note that all of the lower PHR data points correspond to alleles possessing reduced peak heights. Thus, with the low amounts of DNA template being amplified, stochastic effects impact the variability in the heterozygote balance observed.

Assuming that the PHR data follow a normal distribution across the 242 heterozygous samples, a locus-specific PHR threshold can be set using the average minus three times the standard deviation. A threshold set at this value would be expected to cover 99.7% of the observed data (see D.N.A. Box 2.4). With an average PHR of 0.852 and a standard deviation of 0.103, the D18S51 PHR threshold

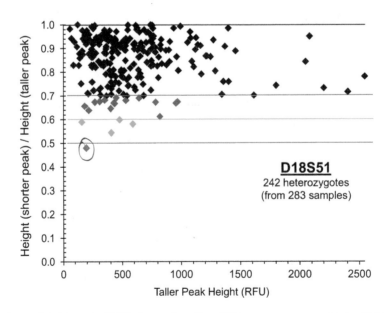

FIGURE 4.2 D18S51 peak height ratio (PHR) observations from 242 heterozygotes examined with PowerPlex 16HS using 30 cycles and a 1 ng target DNA template amount. Fifteen samples (blue diamonds) fell between 60% and 70% PHR, four samples (green diamonds) were in the range of 50% to 60% PHR, and one sample (red diamond) fell below 50% PHR. Data courtesy of Becky Hill, NIST. Plot generated with STR_AlleleFreq available at http://www.cstl.nist.gov/strbase/software.htm.

would be 0.543. A review of the data displayed in Figure 4.2 reveals that two data points possess a PHR at or below 0.543. Two out of 242 represents 0.7% of the data. Thus, a fixed threshold model of the average minus three times the standard deviation fits the data fairly well since 99.3% of the observed D18S51 peak height ratios in this PowerPlex 16HS data set are above this threshold. Looking at this situation from another point-of-view, when a DNA sample possesses two peaks whose peak height ratios are above this threshold (e.g. 0.543), then the individual alleles in this single-source sample may be correctly associated into genotypes.

Size spacing between the heterozygous sister alleles can sometimes influence the degree of peak imbalance. Table 4.1 displays PHR information by allele spread providing metrics for each defined distance in allele spacing. Even with an allele spread of 44 base pairs (alleles 12 and 23; alleles 10 and 21), the PHR was 83% (600 RFU and 500 RFU) and 78% (404 RFU and 317 RFU).

TABLE 4.1 D18S51 Peak Height Ratios from a Portion of the 283 Samples Run with PowerPlex 16HS

(a)

Δbp	#	Mean X	Mean s(X)	Median X	Median s(X)	Min	2.5%	10%	25%	75%	90%	97.5%	Max
4	63	0.876	0.103	0.888	0.095	0.667	0.705	0.770	0.829	0.936	0.974	0.988	0.993
8	51	0.855	0.108	0.889	0.103	0.480	0.672	0.724	0.795	0.932	0.965	0.994	0.999
12	45	0.856	0.110	0.886	0.103	0.589	0.657	0.684	0.758	0.946	0.976	0.986	0.998
16	27	0.882	0.110	0.906	0.107	0.639	0.658	0.729	0.837	0.942	0.986	0.998	1.000
20	22	0.827	0.107	0.877	0.139	0.543	0.620	0.700	0.718	0.920	0.935	0.969	0.997
28	10	0.827	0.102	0.849	0.109	0.646	0.658	0.695	0.752	0.917	0.933	0.940	0.942

(b)

Δbp	#	Mean X	Mean s(X)	Median X	Median s(X)	Min	2.5%	10%	25%	75%	90%	97.5%	Max
4	63	0.860	0.106	0.878	0.111	0.551	0.623	0.697	0.825	0.940	0.977	0.991	1.000
8	51	0.838	0.105	0.845	0.107	0.562	0.630	0.705	0.769	0.914	0.986	0.996	0.998
12	45	0.853	0.105	0.858	0.109	0.601	0.653	0.699	0.790	0.928	0.984	0.994	0.997
16	27	0.834	0.105	0.846	0.120	0.623	0.634	0.709	0.752	0.924	0.967	0.979	0.994
20	22	0.829	0.106	0.851	0.112	0.595	0.625	0.677	0.754	0.924	0.979	0.987	0.990
28	10	0.811	0.111	0.813	0.070	0.577	0.607	0.699	0.751	0.896	0.941	0.955	0.960

(a) 30 cycles with 1 ng DNA template or (b) 32 cycles with 0.5 ng DNA template. The first data row lists summary statistics for the peak height ratios of the 63 allele pairs that were spaced 4 bp apart. These statistics are: mean and standard deviation, their robust analogs median and adjusted median absolute difference from the median (MADe), and the ratio values at eight percentiles. The minimum and maximum values are the 0% and 100% percentiles; median is the 50% percentile. The interval between the 2.5% and 97.5% percentiles contains 95% of the ratios. Data courtesy of Becky Hill, NIST. Output from STR_AlleleFreq available at http://www.cstl.nist.gov/strbase/software.htm.

I. DATA INTERPRETATION

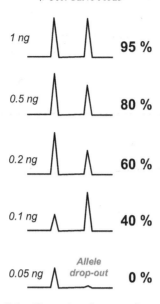

FIGURE 4.3 Hypothetical heterozygous alleles illustrating the general trend that heterozygote balance decreases with DNA template levels until one of the alleles fails to be amplified. When allele drop-out occurs (shown here at the 0.05 ng DNA template level), then a false homozygote is observed. Here the PHR values are shown as a percentage of the shorter height allele to the taller height allele (see Method #1 in Figure 4.1).

Generally, PHR values will decrease with lower quantities of DNA template being tested until allele drop-out occurs (Figure 4.3). Allele drop-out is an extension of the amplification disparity that is observed when heterozygous peak heights are unequal. Faced with the observation of a single allele and the possibility of allele drop-out, an analyst cannot always distinguish whether or not this is a true heterozygote that is masquerading as a homozgote. For this reason, stochastic thresholds can be established to provide a degree of comfort regarding what is a true homozygote versus a heterozygote missing an allele due to drop-out (either by stochastic effects or a primer binding site mutation).

An early validation study involving Profiler Plus and COfiler STR kits noted PHR dependence on relative height. Whereas heterozygotes with an average peak height of >3500 RFU possessed a median PHR of 0.94 (±0.06), data with an average peak height of <500 RFU had a lower median PHR of 0.87 (±0.13) (Buse et al. 2003). Note that at lower RFU values, there is a slightly lower PHR and a slightly higher standard deviation supporting the principle that with lower amounts of DNA more stochastic variation occurs.

A study of 1,763 heterozygous allele pairs concluded that peak height imbalance in heterozygotes varies with the magnitude of the peaks being evaluated at a locus (Gilder et al. 2011). Thus, a sliding scale can be used to reflect an expected lower PHR with lower peak heights. Unpublished studies by Todd Bille and colleagues at the Alcohol, Tobacco, Firearms and Explosives (ATF) Laboratory agree with these findings. The GeneMapper*ID*-X software permits use of multiple PHRs based on heights of observed peaks. Thus, a PHR threshold could be set at 0.70 for peaks whose heights are above 1000 RFU, 0.60 for peak heights in the 500 RFU to 1000 RFU range, and 0.50 for peaks below 500 RFU in height.

It is important to keep in mind that PHRs actually exhibit locus-specific (e.g. Debernardi et al. 2011) and peak height/DNA quantity-specific (e.g. Buse et al. 2003) variability. However, for ease of use, a flat PHR threshold of 50% or 60% is typically used in many protocols to associate and pair alleles into genotypes.

STOCHASTIC THRESHOLDS AND ALLELE DROP-OUT

Peak heights are proxies reflecting the amount of DNA present in a tested sample. When lower amounts of DNA are amplified during the PCR reaction, whether due to PCR inhibitors being present or smaller than expected amounts of DNA being included in the PCR reaction (e.g. from minor components of a mixture), a higher variation in peak height fluctuation is expected due to stochastic effects during PCR.

A useful way to assess the level of variation is to conduct replicate amplifications of the same dilute DNA extract and then examine the resulting peak height ratios (Manabe et al. 2013). Appropriately pairing sets of alleles at each STR locus to form putative genotypes is especially important and challenging with mixtures comprised of DNA from two or more individuals.

Purpose, Use, and Limitations of a Stochastic Threshold

An effective risk assessment of the chance of allele drop-out can be performed through development of a logistic regression curve that plots the height of a surviving allele against the drop-out probability of its sister allele (Gill et al. 2009). Figure 4.4 shows such a plot. Note that on this plot at 200 RFU the drop-out probability is very close to zero. Thus, under these PCR and CE conditions, it would be appropriate to set the stochastic threshold at 200 RFU because single peaks above this level can reasonably be assumed to be homozygous since drop-out of a sister allele is expected to be rare.

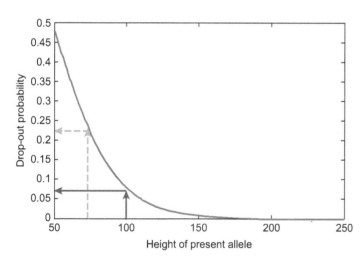

FIGURE 4.4 Probability of allele drop-out as a function of the surviving sister allele peak height. With a single detected peak at 100 RFU (blue arrows), there is approximately a 7% chance of a sister heterozygous allele having dropped out (i.e. being below the analytical threshold). Likewise with a single peak at 75 RFU (green dotted arrows), there is approximately a 22% chance of a sister heterozygous allele having dropped out. Adapted from Gill et al. 2009.

Several articles have described methods for creating this probability of drop-out logistic regression curve (Tvedebrink et al. 2009, Puch-Solis et al. 2011, Tvedebrink et al. 2012). It is worth noting that the position and shape of this curve may change based on altering parameters that impact peak detection, such as CE injection time, PCR cycle number, and post-PCR cleanup.

As discussed in Chapter 2, models depend on and are shaped by assumptions. Any threshold set will be based on a specific set of data and assumptions. With a stochastic threshold, it is worth regularly confirming the arbitrary limits to the model applied by checking known data where allele drop-out is expected to be observed.

The stochastic threshold and the analytical threshold are associated with one another as illustrated in Figure 4.5. The lowest expected peak height ratio connects these two thresholds. For example, using the data from Figure 4.2, where the lowest PHR was just under 0.50, an appropriate stochastic threshold from the studied STR kit and PCR and CE conditions might be 100 RFU if the analytical threshold was 50 RFU.

As more sensitive STR kits are being exploited to attempt analysis of low-level DNA samples, peak height ratios can decline in heterozygotes (see Figure 4.3). In addition, replicate amplification of the same sample will likely become more erratic due to stochastic effects. This variability with low-template DNA samples translates into greater uncertainty with associating genotyping of contributors in mixtures (or in some cases even accurately determining that a sample is from a mixture of two or more contributors).

A stochastic threshold may be established for a specific set of conditions to reflect possibility of allele drop-out. The stochastic threshold should be re-examined with different conditions and may need to be changed when using a higher CE injection, sample desalting, or an increase in the number of PCR cycles. The stochastic threshold will be dependent on the analytical threshold set with a method. The stochastic threshold and analytical threshold are connected through peak height ratio. Due to the potential for allele stacking in DNA mixtures (see Chapters 6 and 7), an assumption as to the number of contributors is important to correct application of a stochastic threshold. The concept

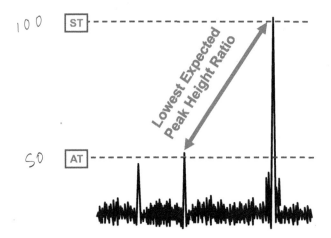

FIGURE 4.5   The stochastic threshold (ST) is fundamentally connected to the analytical threshold (AT) through the lowest expected peak height ratio. The peak on the left below the AT has effectively "dropped out" because it is not designated as a real peak.

of a stochastic threshold can become meaningless in complex mixtures due to the potential for allele stacking.

Approaches to Setting a Stochastic Threshold

Stochastic thresholds are typically set by examining peak height data from a number of dilute samples and noting where allele drop-out occurs. It is important to use known heterozygous samples at low DNA quantities to see the point at which false homozygotes arise. Setting the specific stochastic threshold will depend on the statistical model or approach used to assess the data obtained.

Sonja Klein, a research scientist at the California Department of Justice DNA Laboratory, examined three different DNA samples amplified with the Identifiler Plus STR kit. For her ABI 3500 validation, she studied multiple replicates of the three samples at each DNA amount of 1 ng, 0.5 ng, 0.25 ng, 0.125 ng, 0.062 ng, 0.031 ng, and 0.016 ng (Table 4.2). The 3130 validation data set contained replicates of two samples from 0.5 ng down to 0.031 ng. Then using different approaches that had been published in the literature or presented at scientific conferences, stochastic thresholds were estimated. On the ABI 3130 values ranged from 160 RFU to 341 RFU.

TABLE 4.2 Estimated Stochastic Thresholds Using the Same Set of Identifiler Plus Data Examined with Different Approaches

Designation	Description	Estimated ABI 3130 Stochastic Threshold	Estimated ABI 3500 Stochastic Threshold
Method 1	Tallest false homozygote	198 RFU	502 RFU
Method 2a	False homozygote average +3 standard deviations (using most relevant input amounts)	256 RFU	516 RFU
Method 2b	False homozygote average +3 standard deviations (using all observed false homozygotes)	202 RFU	456 RFU
Method 3	Average peak heights for heterozygotes +3 standard deviations	306 RFU	1119 RFU
Method 4	Average peak height ratio −3 standard deviations vs. signal	341 RFU	785 RFU
Method 5	Analytical threshold divided by minimum observed peak height ratio	172 RFU	682 RFU
Method 6	Partial profile at ∼150 pg and 3 times the analytical threshold	160 RFU	1200 RFU
Method 7	Where majority of peak height ratios start to fall below 60%	190 RFU	980 RFU

Studies involved multiple amplifications of two or three DNA samples with serial dilutions representing 1 nanogram (ng), 0.5 ng, 0.25 ng, 0.125 ng, 0.062 ng, 0.031 ng, and 0.016 ng. Data courtesy of Sonja Klein, California Department of Justice. Originally from a presentation given at the California Association of Criminalistics meeting (Sacramento, CA) on October 25, 2011 entitled "Approaches to estimating a stochastic threshold."

Method 1 in Table 4.2 involves looking across a data set of known heterozygotes and determining the tallest false homozygote. In other words, what is the highest height of the surviving sister allele when an allele of a known heterozygote fails to be amplified and/or detected above the analytical threshold. Other methods in Table 4.2 involve different ways of trying to assess the chance of missing an allele in a true heterozygote.

CONCORDANCE STUDIES AND NULL ALLELES

Sequence polymorphisms are known to occur within or around STR repeat regions (Figure 4.6). These variations can occur in three locations (relative to the primer binding sites): within the repeat region, in the flanking region, or in the primer binding region (see Figure 3.14). Sequence changes that occur outside of the primer binding regions will not impact a specific pair of primers — but could lead to discordance with a different primer set.

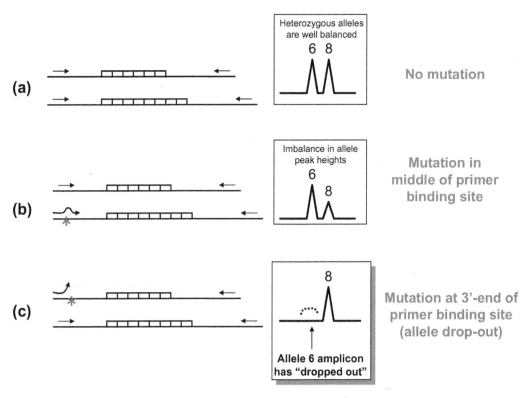

FIGURE 4.6   Impact of a sequence polymorphism in the primer binding site illustrated with a hypothetical heterozygous individual. Heterozygous allele peaks may be (a) well-balanced, (b) slightly imbalanced due to some primer binding disruption, or (c) exhibit allele drop-out because a mutation near the 3'-end of the primer binding site fully disrupts appropriate primer annealing during the PCR amplification.

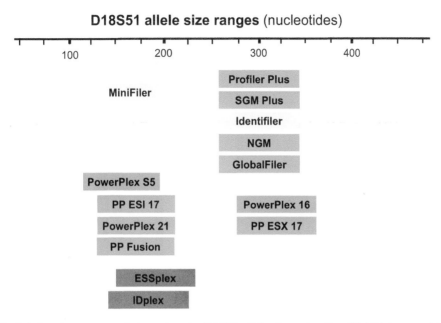

D18S51 allele size ranges (nucleotides)

FIGURE 4.7   Relative size ranges and dye colors for D18S51 alleles (spanning 7 to 27 AGAA repeats) in 14 different STR kits.

If a nucleotide change occurs in the DNA template at the PCR primer binding region (relative to the sequence to which the primers were originally designed), the hybridization of the primer can be disrupted (Figure 4.6). This failure to properly anneal to the DNA template results in a failure to copy the target region, and therefore failure to detect an allele that exists in the template DNA. Put simply, the DNA template exists for a particular allele, but fails to amplify during PCR due to primer hybridization problems. This phenomenon results in what is known as a silent or *null allele*. Fortunately null alleles are rather rare because the flanking sequence around STR repeats is fairly stable and consistent between samples.

Different STR kits generate different size PCR products when amplifying the same STR locus. For example, with D18S51 about half of the STR kits generate PCR products in the 125 bp to 225 bp range while the rest fall in the 265 bp to 365 bp region (Figure 4.7). Depending on the STR kit configuration, different dye labels may be used among the various kits from the same manufacturer to amplify a specific STR locus.

Concordance Studies Aid Discovery of Null Alleles

Null alleles have been "discovered" by the observation of different typing results when utilizing independent STR primer sets. During a comparison of STR typing results on 600 population samples at the vWA locus, one sample typed 16,19 with Promega's PowerPlex kit and 16,16 with Applied Biosystem's AmpFlSTR Blue kit (Kline et al. 1998). In this case, the vWA allele 19 dropped out with the AmpFlSTR vWA primer set due to a sequence polymorphism near the 3'-end of the forward primer (Walsh 1998).

Allele dropout may occur due to mutations (variants) at or near the 3′-end of a primer. However, depending on the surrounding sequence and annealing temperature used, even incomplete hybridization near the 5′-end of a primer binding region can disrupt optimal primer extension and thus PCR amplification. Of course, this failure to amplify depends on the PCR conditions, including the annealing temperature and amount of magnesium chloride used. In the situation described above, the vWA allele 19 was present in the sample but failed to be amplified by one of the primer sets. It was later reported that the null allele resulted from a rare A → T nucleotide change in the DNA template that occurred at the second base from the 3′-end of the AmpFlSTR vWA forward primer (Walsh 1998).

Potential null alleles resulting from allele drop-out can be predicted by statistical analysis of the STR typing data. The observed number of homozygotes can be compared to the expected number of homozygotes based on Hardy—Weinberg equilibrium (Chakraborty et al. 1992). An abnormally high level of homozygotes would indicate the possible presence of null alleles as it did with a group of samples from Guam for D8S1179 (D.N.A. Box 4.2). Thus, each set of population data should be carefully examined when new STR markers are being tested in a forensic DNA laboratory (see Chapter 10).

A number of primer concordance studies have been conducted in the past few years as use of various STR kits has become more prevalent. An examination of over 2,000 samples comparing the PowerPlex 16 kit to the Profiler Plus and COfiler kit results found 22 examples of allele drop-out due to a primer mismatch at 7 of the 13 core STR loci: CSF1PO, D8S1179, D16S539, D21S11, FGA, TH01, and vWA (Budowle et al. 2001, Budowle & Sprecher 2001). In a set of 200 unrelated samples

---

D.N.A. BOX 4.2

DETECTION OF A NULL ALLELE AT D8S1179 WITH SEVERE DEVIATIONS FROM HARDY—WEINBERG EQUILIBRIUM

An example of a significant difference between the observed and the expected number of homozygotes was seen at the D8S1179 locus when testing some Chamorros and Filipinos from Guam (Budowle et al. 2000). A total of 38.4% homozygotes were observed rather than the 22.8% expected in 97 Chamorros (p-value < 0.0001). Likewise, in 99 Filipinos the observed homozygosity was 25.8% rather than the expected 15.8% (p-value = 0.007). This excess homozygosity later led to discovery of a primer binding site polymorphism in the D8S1179 reverse primer for the original Profiler Plus kit (Leibelt et al. 2003). A second unlabeled (degenerate) D8S1179 reverse primer has been added to

the Identifiler and Profiler Plus ID kits as well as all subsequent kits released by Applied Biosystems. This degenerate primer contains a single nucleotide change of G → A 16 nucleotides from the 3′-end of the primer (and 56 bases from the STR repeat region) that matches the mutant A nucleotide and enables recovery of the null allele (Leibelt et al. 2003).

Sources: Budowle, B., et al. (2000). *Genetic variation at nine short tandem repeat loci in Chamorros and Filipinos from Guam.* Legal Medicine, 2, 26—30; Leibelt, C., et al. (2003). *Identification of a D8S1179 primer binding site mutation and the validation of a primer designed to recover null alleles.* Forensic Science International, 133, 220—227.

from the Kuwaiti population examined with MiniFiler, Identifiler, and PowerPlex 16, full concordance was observed in 198 out of 200 profiles (Alenizi et al. 2009). Allele drop-out was observed in D13S317 (loss of allele 10) with MiniFiler and D18S51 (loss of allele 18) with Identifiler.

NIST STR Kit Concordance Studies

Starting in 2009 with the adoption of additional STR loci in the European Standard Set (Schneider 2009), there has been a rapid expansion of new STR typing kits. Qiagen (Hilden, Germany) has also entered the marketplace in some parts of the world with Investigator STR kits such as the ESSplex and IDplex. In fact, of the 25 autosomal STR kits shown in Table 1.2, only eight existed before 2009. Kits including PowerPlex Fusion and GlobalFiler have been developed to meet an expanded set of U.S. core loci requested in April 2011 (Hares 2012a, Hares 2012b).

To help the worldwide forensic community understand potential concordance issues between STR kits, the Applied Genetics Group at the National Institute of Standards and Technology (NIST) has developed a pipeline for concordance studies (Hill et al. 2010). A primary driver for this work is to benefit measurement assurance between different commercial STR typing kits being used for casework and DNA databases around the world so that data may be shared confidently with minimal risk from null alleles. Agreements have been made with each of the STR kit manufacturers to enable concordance studies to be performed − typically, prior to kit release so that primer adjustments or additions may be made.

Accurate typing with full genotypes (i.e. no null alleles or at least characterized null alleles) is especially important in the development of NIST Standard Reference Materials (SRMs) that are used to calibrate DNA typing measurements. DNA samples used for forensic DNA SRMs are studied in STR kits commercially available at the time of preparation. Any issues arising from primer binding site mutations are characterized. For example, NIST SRM 2391b genomic DNA component 8 exhibits allele dropout at D16S539 with MiniFiler. The correct type is 9,11 with all other STR kits, but only the 9 is amplified with MiniFiler. The null allele 11 is due to a T→C mutation 34 bases downstream of the GATA repeat (Kline et al. 2011).

NIST concordance studies involve four S's (Hill et al. 2010). First, standard DNA extracts are run on every kit. Over 1,450 U.S. population samples and NIST SRM samples (2391b or 2391c) are routinely examined with STR kits (Hill et al. 2011). Second, software has been developed to compare data sets efficiently. Third, sequencing of samples exhibiting any differences is performed to understand the molecular basis for allele dropout (Kline et al. 2011). And, fourth, discordant results are shared first with kit suppliers to enable adjustments to primers before kit release and then with the community through presentations, publications, and the NIST STRBase website.

In one of the first NIST concordance studies, a total of 27 differences were observed between MiniFiler and Identifiler or PowerPlex 16 (Hill et al. 2007). A comparison of prototype PowerPlex ESX 17 and ESI 17 found 16 differences between these pre-release versions and other commercial kits or in-house assays (Hill et al. 2011). Most of these discordant results were corrected before final kit release by adding an additional D22S1045 forward primer in ESX 17 and redesigning the D1S1656 reverse primer in ESI 17 (Hill et al. 2011).

Figure 4.8 shows an example of genotyping results from several STR kits with D18S51 primers while Table 4.3 lists reported D18S51 discordant results from STRBase and the literature.

The D18S51 D172G→A mutation was observed frequently enough in samples from a Middle Eastern population that it gave rise to the only double null allele reported to date in the literature

FIGURE 4.8 (a) D18S51 typing results from three different STR kits. (b) Illustration of the two D18S51 alleles present in these samples with the relative positions of the reverse PCR primers for the various STR kits (with colors corresponding to the results in the top portion of the figure). The allele 13 possesses a G→A mutation at nucleotide position 172 downstream from the D18S51 repeat region. The NGM SElect kit reverse D18S51 primer spans this mutation and is disrupted from appropriately annealing thus causing an amplification failure that gives rise to the null allele. Data courtesy of Becky Hill, NIST (adapted from Hill et al. (2011)).

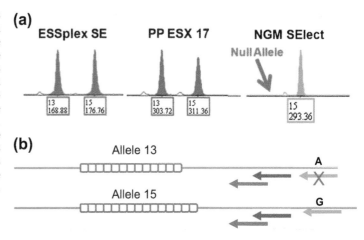

(Clayton et al. 2004). This double null situation occurred because both parents gave their child an allele with this mutation that causes D18S51 PCR amplification failure when using Identifiler, SGM Plus, or NGM SElect (see Figure 4.8) primers. This observation points out that while null alleles are typically rare, they can be concentrated in families. Often these primer binding site mutations are most efficiently uncovered during parentage testing (Dauber et al. 2011) where it is expected to have samples with alleles in common.

As of early 2014, more than one million allele comparisons have been performed with >125 kit-to-kit pairwise comparisons. Overall concordance between tested kits at NIST has been >99.9%. Similarly, a concordance study involving 26 European laboratories with four different STR kits found only 13 total discrepancies across 63,803 comparisons or a 99.98% concordance rate (Welch et al. 2012). Discordant results between STR kits observed in NIST studies, in the literature, or via submission are posted on the STRBase Null Allele page (STRBase 2014).

Solutions to Null Alleles

If a null allele is detected at an STR locus, there are several possible solutions. First, the problem PCR primer could be redesigned and moved away from the problematic site. This approach was taken early in the development of the D7S820 primers for the Promega PowerPlex 1.1 kit (Schumm et al. 1996), and more recently with a D16S539 flanking region mutation (Nelson et al. 2002). However, this solution could result in the new primer interfering with another one in the multiplex set of primers, or necessitate new PCR reaction optimization experiments. Clearly this solution is undesirable once a set of multiplex PCR primers has been implemented because it can be time-consuming and labor intensive to make adjustments.

A second solution is to simply drop the STR locus from the multiplex mix rather than attempting to redesign the PCR primers to avoid the site. This approach is only desirable early in the development cycle of a multiplex STR assay. The Forensic Science Service dropped the STR locus D19S253 from consideration in their prototype second-generation multiplex when a null allele was discovered (Urquhart et al. 1994).

TABLE 4.3 Summary of D18S51 Discordant Results Observed with Various STR Kits as Reported in the Literature due to Various Concordance Studies with Different PCR Primer Sets

STR Kits Compared	Null Allele (with kit)	Reason	Frequency	Reference
MiniFiler vs ID vs PP16	13 (Identifiler)	D172G → A	1 in 1308 0.077%	Hill et al. 2007
SGM vs SGM Plus	17, 18, 19, and 20 (SGM Plus)	D172G → A	9 in 4245 0.21%	Clayton et al. 2004, Kline et al. 2011
PP16 vs SGM Plus/ ProPlus	16 (PP16)	U71G → A	1 in 2055 0.049%	Delamoye et al. 2004
PP16 vs SGM Plus/ ProPlus	16 and 18 (SGM Plus)	D172G → A	2 in 2055 0.097%	Delamoye et al. 2004
PP16 vs SGM Plus	19 (SGM Plus)	D172G → A	2 in 1377 0.14%	Vanderheyden et al. 2007
PP16 vs SGM Plus	14 (PP16)	U71G → A	1 in 1377 0.073%	Vanderheyden et al. 2007
PP16 vs ID	14 (PP16)	U71G → A	1 in 18,314 0.0055%	STRBase submission (Apr 2014)
PP16 vs ID	18 and 20 (PP16)	U71G → A	2 in 18,314 0.011%	STRBase submission (Apr 2014)
PP16 vs ID	18 (PP16)	U71G → A	1 in 18,314 0.0055%	STRBase submission (Apr 2014)
	Totals	U71G → A	6 in 27,299 0.022%	
		D172G → A	14 in 27,299 0.051%	
		Both mutations	20 in 27,299 0.073%	

These discrepancies arise due to polymorphic nucleotides or insertions/deletions that occur in the tested DNA templates near the 3'-end of a primer binding site that disrupt proper primer annealing and result in allele drop-out upon PCR amplification. STR kits reported here include: PowerPlex 16 (PP16), Identifiler (ID), Profiler Plus (ProPlus), and SGM Plus. The primer binding site mutation "D172G → A" is 172 nucleotide downstream of the AAAG repeat region (see Figure 4.8) and 10 bases from the 3'-end of the ABI reverse primer. The U71G → A mutation is 71 nucleotides upstream of the AAAG repeat and 5 bases from the 3'-end of the PowerPlex 16 forward primer.

③ A third, and more favorable, solution is to add a "degenerate" primer that contains the known sequence polymorphism. This extra primer will then amplify alleles containing the problematic primer binding site sequence variant. This approach was taken with the AmpFlSTR kits for the D16S539 mutation mentioned previously (Holt et al. 2002). However, if the sequence variation at the primer binding site is extremely rare, it may not be worth the effort to add an additional primer to the multiplex primer mix.

④ A fourth possible solution to correct for allele drop-out that will work for some problematic primer binding sites is to re-amplify the sample with a lower annealing temperature and thereby reduce the stringency of the primer annealing. If the primer is only slightly destabilized, as detected by a peak height imbalance with a heterozygous sample (Figure 4.6, middle panel), then the peak height imbalance may be able to be corrected by lowering the annealing temperature during PCR.

It is important to recognize that *no primer set is completely immune to the phenomenon of null alleles*. However, when identical primer sets are used to amplify evidence samples and suspect reference samples, full concordance is expected from biological materials originating from a common source. If the DNA templates and PCR conditions are identical between two samples from the same individual, then identical DNA profiles should result regardless of how well or poorly the PCR primers amplify the DNA template.

The potential of null alleles is not a problem within a laboratory that uses the same primer set to amplify a particular STR marker. However, with the emergence of national and international DNA databases, which store only the genotype information for a sample, allele dropout could potentially result in a false negative or incorrect exclusion of two samples that come from a common source. To overcome this potential problem, the matching criteria in database searches can be made less stringent when searching a crime stain sample against the DNA database of convicted offender profiles. That is, the database search might be programmed to return profiles that are only a partial rather than a full match. This moderate stringency search is commonly used in searching the U.S. national DNA database to avoid missing null alleles from samples tested with different PCR primer pairs (see Butler 2012).

When primers are selected for amplification of STR loci, candidate primers are evaluated carefully to avoid primer binding site mutations (Schumm et al. 1996, Wallin et al. 2002), such as those illustrated in Figure 4.6. Sequence analysis of multiple alleles is performed, family inheritance studies are conducted, within-locus peak signal ratios for heterozygous samples are examined, apparent homozygous samples are re-amplified with lower annealing temperatures, and statistical analysis of observed versus expected homozygosity is performed on population databases (Walsh 1998). It is truly a challenge to design multiplex STR primer sets in which primer binding sites are located in sequence regions that are as highly conserved as possible and yet do not interfere with primers amplifying other loci.

Use of Degenerate Primers in Commercial Kits

In some cases, STR kit manufacturers have added an additional PCR primer to the assay that can hybridize properly to the alternative allele when it exists in a sample. This has been the preferred solution for Applied Biosystems (e.g. Wallin et al. 2002), while Promega has moved their primers to overcome allele drop-out problems (e.g. Nelson et al. 2002). According to their publications, Applied Biosystems has added an additional primer to correct for single-point mutations in AmpFlSTR primer binding sites for D16S539 (Wallin et al. 2002), vWA (Lazaruk et al. 2001), and D8S1179 (Leibelt et al. 2003).

Speculating on the potential impact of null alleles with DNA comparisons, it has been postulated that in a simulated DNA database containing 100 million unrelated samples, over 17,000 profiles would have discordant results at two out of the 13 CODIS STR loci if all loci possessed a 0.1% null allele rate and different primer sets were utilized (Davis et al. 2012). It is worth noting though that most concordance studies have found null allele rates to be less than 0.1% especially with kit modifications made by manufacturers after discovery of primer binding site mutations. For example, in their NGM SElect kit, Applied Biosystems added SNP-specific primers to correct rare false homozygotes observed in amelogenin (Albinsson et al. 2011), D2S441, and D22S1045 with the original NGM kit (Green et al. 2013).

While STR kit discordance is fairly rare overall, specific populations can sometimes exhibit higher frequencies of primer binding site mutations. For example, a double null, where both alleles were missing, was "observed" at D18S51 when performing relationship testing on some Kuwaiti population samples due to a high frequency of a mutation that impacts the Applied Biosystems kits' D18S51 reverse primer (Clayton et al. 2004). DNA sequence analysis uncovered a G-to-A mutation 172 nucleotides downstream of the STR repeat region, which is abbreviated as D172G → A, as the cause for this D18S51 null allele that appears to persist primarily in Middle Eastern populations (Kline et al. 2011, Vanderheyden et al. 2007). Likewise, the D8S1179 D56G → A mutation that gave rise to the extra D8S1179 reverse primer added in the Identifiler kit is primarily seen in Asians (Han et al. 2001) or Pacific Island groups (e.g. D.N.A. Box 4.2).

Throughout the years, Promega Corporation has been willing to move PCR primer sequences to avoid primer binding site mutations or to alter amplicon sizes as needed for new multiplex assays. Their primer changes have been accompanied by extensive concordance studies (e.g. Hill et al. 2011, McLaren et al. 2012). Applied Biosystems has chosen to maintain primer sequences across their kits and instead use mobility modifiers to adjust amplicon sizes as needed for different kit configurations (see Butler 2012).

While the Applied Biosystems' approach enables full comparison to legacy information with earlier kits, null alleles may go undetected if only STR kits from Applied Biosystems are used within a laboratory. With a desire for global expansion in data sharing capabilities, potential primer binding site mutations alleles need to be addressed. Therefore, Applied Biosystems has announced inclusion of several new SNP-specific degenerate primers (Mulero 2012, Life Technologies 2013) to reduce false homozygosity in their GlobalFiler kit (see Table 1.2 and Figure 1.6), which is a 24-plex assay intended to address the European Standard Set and expanded U.S. core loci. Table 4.4 includes a summary of the extra primers present in the GlobalFiler kit.

Discordance due to Insertions or Deletions Close to the STR Repeat Region

In a few rare instances, an insertion or deletion (InDel) close to the STR repeat region can result in discordant genotypes with different primer sets for the same STR locus (Butler et al. 2003, Rolf et al. 2011). Rather than false homozygotes where one of the alleles present in the sample fails to be amplified, these InDel situations are much more challenging to cope with since a size shift of a partial or even a full repeat can occur due to an InDel outside of one of the primers, but inside of another primer and therefore part of the amplicon. Fortunately, these situations are very rare and have only been reported thus far in D13S317 (Butler et al. 2003, Hill et al. 2007), SE33 (Hill et al. 2011, Rolf et al. 2011), and FGA (Rolf et al. 2011).

This phenomenon was reported with early miniSTR assay development (Butler et al. 2003, Drábek et al. 2004). The D13S317 locus has a four-base deletion of TGTC that is 24 nucleotides downstream of the TATC STR repeat (Boutrand et al. 2001). Knowing about this potential issue, Applied Biosystems designed the D13S317 reverse primer for the MiniFiler kit to lay across this deletion and thus would fail to amplify samples possessing this four-base deletion rather than exhibiting a shift of a single repeat unit that might be missed in a Q-K comparison with MiniFiler and Identifiler. Figure 4.9 shows D13S317 results from an African American sample with Identifiler, a NIST-developed miniSTR assay, and MiniFiler (Hill et al. 2007). While this D13S317 allele contains 11 TATC repeats with a TGTC deletion in flanking region, it measures as a "10" with Identifiler, an "11" with the miniSTR assay, and is not detected with MiniFiler.

TABLE 4.4   Information Regarding Additional 14 Primers Thought to Be Present in the GlobalFiler
             STR Kit to Account for Specific Primer Binding Site Mutations

Additional PCR Primer	SNP* (primary population if known)	Distance from 3'-end of primer	Reference
vWA-R	D(-2)C→T	4	Lazaruk et al. (2001)
D16S539-R	D38T→A	3	Wallin et al. (2002)
D8S1179-R	D56G→A (Asian)	16	Han et al. (2001), Leibelt et al. (2003)
Amelogenin-R	D41C→T	1	Mulero et al. (2011)
D22S1045-F	U15G→T	10	Green et al. (2013)
D2S441-F	U1insA (Asian)	1	Green et al. (2013)
D3S1358-R	D11G→C	5	Hill et al. (2011)
vWA-F	U52A→T	2	Walsh (1998), Alves et al. (2003)
D18S51-R	D172G→A (Middle East)	10	Delamoye et al. (2004)
D19S433-R	D32G→A (Asian)	20	Dauber et al. (2004), Kline et al. (2011)
TH01-R	D81C→T	6	Vanderheyden et al. (2007)
FGA-R	D71G→T	13	Ricci et al. (2007)
D5S818-R	D55G→T	10	Kline et al. (2011)
SE33-R	D15G→A (European)	8	Heinrich et al. (2004)

SNP positions are listed relative to the STR repeat region either downstream (D) or upstream (U) for the specified number of nucleotides (Life Technologies 2013).

The existence of flanking region size variation is a reminder of the fact that STR typing with capillary electrophoresis involves measuring an overall amplicon length. This amplicon encompasses the variable repeat region as well as flanking sequence information that also can in some instances vary in terms of its length. Different kit manufacturers use non-overlapping PCR primers to amplify the same STR loci in order to adjust overall PCR product length for a desired kit configuration of loci. Thus, a small degree of uncertainty exists in the actual classification of STR alleles into repeat lengths due to the possibility of insertions or deletions near to the repeat region being measured.

Likewise, due to possible primer binding site mutations causing primers not to anneal and extend during PCR, there is a small uncertainty related to genotype observations where null alleles and false homozygotes can occasionally occur. Perhaps future DNA sequencing techniques will enable a more complete characterization of STR repeats and their flanking regions.

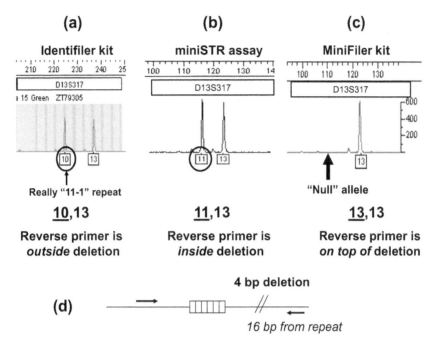

FIGURE 4.9 Comparison of D13S317 STR typing results on the same DNA sample from (a) Identifiler kit, (b) a NIST-developed miniSTR assay, and (c) MiniFiler kit. Allele calls are impacted because PCR primers are in different locations relative to a 4 base pair (bp) deletion that is located 16 bp downstream of the D13S317 repeat (d). Adapted from Hill et al. (2007).

Reading List and Internet Resources

Peak Height Ratios

Albinsson, L., et al. (2011). Verification of alleles by using peak height thresholds and quality control of STR profiling kits. *Forensic Science International Genetics Supplement Series, 3,* e251–e252.

Bright, J. A., et al. (2010). Examination of the variability in mixed DNA profile parameters for the Identifiler multiplex. *Forensic Science International Genetics, 4,* 111–114.

Buse, E. L., et al. (2003). Performance evaluation of two multiplexes used in fluorescent short tandem repeat DNA analysis. *Journal Forensic Sciences, 48,* 348–357.

Butler, J. M. (2012). *Advanced Topics in Forensic DNA Typing: Methodology.* San Diego: Elsevier Academic Press.

Debernardi, A., et al. (2011). One year variability of peak heights, heterozygous balance and inter-locus balance for the DNA positive control of AmpFlSTR Identifiler STR kit. *Forensic Science International Genetics, 5,* 43–49.

Gilder, J. R., et al. (2011). Magnitude-dependent variation in peak height balance at heterozygous STR loci. *International Journal Legal Medicine, 125,* 87–94.

Gill, P., et al. (1997). Development of guidelines to designate alleles using an STR multiplex system. *Forensic Science International, 89,* 185–197.

Hill, C. R., et al. (2011). Concordance and population studies along with stutter and peak height ratio analysis for the PowerPlex® ESX 17 and ESI 17 Systems. *Forensic Science International Genetics, 5*(4), 269–275.

Leclair, B., et al. (2004). Systematic analysis of stutter percentages and allele peak height and peak area ratios at heterozygous STR loci for forensic casework and database samples. *Journal Forensic Sciences, 49,* 968–980.

Kelly, H., et al. (2012). Modelling heterozygote balance in forensic DNA profiles. *Forensic Science International Genetics, 6,* 729–734.

Manabe, S., et al. (2013). Mixture interpretation: experimental and simulated reevaluation of qualitative analysis. *Legal Medicine, 15,* 66—71.

Moretti, T. R., et al. (2001). Validation of short tandem repeats (STRs) for forensic usage: performance testing of fluorescent multiplex STR systems and analysis of authentic and simulated forensic samples. *Journal Forensic Sciences, 46,* 647—660.

Moretti, T. R., et al. (2001). Validation of STR typing by capillary electrophoresis. *Journal Forensic Sciences, 46,* 661—676.

STR_AlleleFreq (2014): http://www.cstl.nist.gov/strbase/software.htm. Accessed March 23, 2014.

Wallin, J. M., et al. (1998). TWGDAM validation of the AmpFlSTR Blue PCR amplification kit for forensic casework analysis. *Journal Forensic Sciences, 43,* 854—870.

Stochastic Thresholds and Allele Dropout

Buckleton, J. (2009). Validation issues around DNA typing of low level DNA. *Forensic Science International Genetics, 3,* 255—260.

Bright, J. A., et al. (2012). A comparison of stochastic variation in mixed and unmixed casework and synthetic samples. *Forensic Science International Genetics, 6,* 180—184.

Gill, P., et al. (2009). The low-template-DNA (stochastic) threshold — its determination relative to risk analysis for national DNA databases. *Forensic Science International Genetics, 3,* 104—111.

Kirkham, A., et al. (2013). High-throughput analysis using AmpFlSTR® Identifiler® with the Applied Biosystems 3500xl Genetic Analyser. *Forensic Science International Genetics, 7,* 92—97.

Puch-Solis, R., et al. (2011). Practical determination of the low template DNA threshold. *Forensic Science International Genetics, 5,* 422—427.

Tvedebrink, T., et al. (2009). Estimating the probability of allelic drop-out of STR alleles in forensic genetics. *Forensic Science International Genetics, 3,* 222—226.

Tvedebrink, T., et al. (2012). Allelic drop-out probabilities estimated by logistic regression — further considerations and practical implementation. *Forensic Science International Genetics, 6,* 263—267.

Westen, A. A., et al. (2012). Assessment of the stochastic threshold, back- and forward stutter filters and low template techniques for NGM. *Forensic Science International Genetics, 6,* 708—715.

Weusten, J., & Herbergs, J. (2012). A stochastic model of the processes in PCR based amplification of STR DNA in forensic applications. *Forensic Science International Genetics, 6,* 17—25.

Concordance Studies and Null Alleles

Albinsson, L., et al. (2011). Swedish population data and concordance for the kits PowerPlex(R) ESX 16 System, PowerPlex(R) ESI 16 System, AmpFlSTR(R) NGM, AmpFlSTR(R) SGM Plus and Investigator ESSplex. *Forensic Science International Genetics, 5,* e89—e92.

Alenizi, M. A., et al. (2009). Concordance between the AmpFlSTR MiniFiler and AmpFlSTR Identifiler PCR Amplification kits in the Kuwaiti population. *Journal Forensic Sciences, 54,* 350—352.

Alves, C., et al. (2003). Multiplex STR genotyping: comparison study, population data and new sequence information. *Progress Forensic Genetics 9 ICS, 1239,* 131—135.

Boutrand, L., et al. (2001). Variations in primer sequences are the origin of allele dropout at loci D13S317 and CD4. *International Journal Legal Medicine, 114,* 295—297.

Budowle, B. (2000). STR primer concordance data — validation studies. *Proceedings 11ᵗʰ International Symposium Human Identification.* Available at http://www.promega.com/products/pm/genetic-identity/ishi-conference-proceedings/11th-ihsi-oral-presentations/. Accessed March 23, 2014.

Budowle, B., et al. (2000). Genetic variation at nine short tandem repeat loci in Chamorros and Filipinos from Guam. *Legal Medicine, 2,* 26—30.

Budowle, B., & Sprecher, C. J. (2001). Concordance study on population database samples using the PowerPlex 16 kit and AmpFlSTR Profiler Plus kit and AmpFlSTR COfiler kit. *Journal Forensic Sciences, 46,* 637—641.

Budowle, B., et al. (2001). STR primer concordance study. *Forensic Science International, 124,* 47—54.

Butler, J. M., et al. (2003). The development of reduced size STR amplicons as tools for analysis of degraded DNA. *Journal of Forensic Sciences, 48(5),* 1054—1064.

Butler, J. M. (2006). Genetics and genomics of core STR loci used in human identity testing. *Journal Forensic Sciences, 51,* 253—265.

Chakraborty, R., et al. (1992). Apparent heterozygote deficiencies observed in DNA typing data and their implications in forensic applications. *Annals of Human Genetics, 56,* 45—57.

Clayton, T. M., et al. (2004). Primer binding site mutations affecting the typing of STR loci contained within the AMPFlSTR SGM Plus kit. *Forensic Science International, 139*, 255—259.

Cortellini, V., et al. (2011). False homozygosity at D12S391 locus: a case report. *Forensic Science International Genetics Supplement Series, 3*, e253—e254.

Dakin, E. E., & Avise, J. C. (2004). Microsatellite null alleles in parentage analysis. *Heredity, 93*, 504—509.

Dauber, E. M., et al. (2004). New sequence data of allelic variants at the STR loci ACTBP2 (SE33), D21S11, FGA, vWA, CSF1PO, D2S1338, D16S539, D18S51 and D19S433 in Caucasoids. *Progress Forensic Genetics 10 ICS, 1261*, 191—193.

Dauber, E. M., et al. (2008). Two examples of null alleles at the D19S433 locus due to the same 4 bp deletion in the presumptive primer binding site of the AmpFlSTR Identifiler kit. *Forensic Science International Genetics Supplement Series, 1*, 107—108.

Dauber, E. M., et al. (2011). A primer binding site mutation at the D2S1338 locus resulting in a loss of amplification. *Forensic Science International Genetics Supplement Series, 3*, e87—e88.

Davis, C., et al. (2012). Variants observed for STR locus SE33: a concordance study. *Forensic Science International Genetics, 6*(4), 494—497.

Davis, C., et al. (2013). Prototype PowerPlex® Y23 System: A concordance study. *Forensic Science International Genetics, 7*, 204—208.

Delamoye, M., et al. (2004). False homozygosities at various loci revealed by discrepancies between commercial kits: implications for genetic databases. *Forensic Science International, 143*, 47—52.

Dion, D., et al. (2011). Concordance testing with the new STR kits and the influence on the Swiss National DNA database. *Forensic Science International Genetics Supplement Series, 3*, e85—e86.

Drábek, J., et al. (2004). Concordance study between miniplex STR assays and a commercial STR typing kit. *Journal Forensic Sciences, 49*, 859—860.

Forrest, S. W., et al. (2004). Two rare novel polymorphisms in the D8S1179 and D13S317 markers and a method to mitigate their impact on human identification. *Croatian Medical Journal, 45*, 457—460.

Garcia, O., et al. (2012). Population genetic data and concordance study for the kits Identifiler, NGM, PowerPlex ESX 17 System and Investigator ESSplex in Spain. *Forensic Science International Genetics, 6*, e78—e79.

Green, R. L., et al. (2013). Developmental validation of the AmpFlSTR® NGM SElect™ PCR Amplification Kit: A next-generation STR multiplex with the SE33 locus. *Forensic Science International: Genetics, 7*, 41—51.

Han, G. R., et al. (2001). Non-amplification of an allele of the D8S1179 locus due to a point mutation. *International Journal of Legal Medicine, 115*, 45—47.

Hares, D. R. (2012a). Expanding the CODIS core loci in the United States. *Forensic Science International: Genetics, 6*(1), e52—e54.

Hares, D. R. (2012b). Addendum to expanding the CODIS core loci in the United States. *Forensic Science International: Genetics, 6*(5), e135.

Hatzer-Grubwieser, P., et al. (2012). Allele frequencies and concordance study of 16 STR loci — including the new European Standard Set (ESS) loci — in an Austrian population sample. *Forensic Science International Genetics, 6*, e50—e51.

Heinrich, M., et al. (2004). Allelic drop-out in the STR system ACTBP2 (SE33) as a result of mutations in the primer binding region. *International Journal Legal Medicine, 118*, 361—363.

Hendrickson, B. C., et al. (2004). Accurate STR allele designations at the FGA and vWA loci despite primer site polymorphisms. *Journal Forensic Sciences, 49*, 250—254.

Hill, C. R., et al. (2007). Concordance study between the AmpFlSTR MiniFiler PCR Amplification Kit and conventional STR typing kits. *Journal Forensic Sciences, 52*, 870—873.

Hill, C. R., et al. (2010). Strategies for concordance testing. *Profiles DNA Promega, 13*(1). Available at http://www.promega.com/profiles/. Accessed March 23, 2014.

Hill, C. R., et al. (2011). Concordance and population studies along with stutter and peak height ratio analysis for the PowerPlex® ESX 17 and ESI 17 Systems. *Forensic Science International: Genetics, 5*, 269—275.

Holt, C. L., et al. (2002). TWGDAM validation of AmpFlSTR PCR amplification kits for forensic DNA casework. *Journal of Forensic Sciences, 47*, 66—96.

Kline, M. C., et al. (1998). Non-amplification of a vWA allele. *Journal Forensic Sciences, 43*(1), 250.

Kline, M. C., et al. (2011). STR sequence analysis for characterizing normal, variant, and null alleles. *Forensic Science International Genetics, 5*, 329—332.

Leibelt, C., et al. (2003). Identification of a D8S1179 primer binding site mutation and the validation of a primer designed to recover null alleles. *Forensic Science International, 133*, 220—227.

Lazaruk, K., et al. (2001). Sequence variation in humans and other primates at six short tandem repeat loci used in forensic identity testing. *Forensic Science International, 119*, 1—10.

I. DATA INTERPRETATION

Life Technologies. (2013). *GlobalFiler PCR amplification kit user guide*. Available at http://tools.lifetechnologies.com/content/sfs/manuals/4477604.pdf. Accessed March 23, 2014.

Maciejewska, A., & Pawlowski, R. (2009). A rare mutation in the primer binding region of the Amelogenin X homologue gene. *Forensic Science International Genetics, 3*, 265—267.

McLaren, R. S., et al. (2012). *Improved primer pair for the SE33 locus in the PowerPlex ESI 17 Pro System. Profiles in DNA*. Available at http://www.promega.com/resources/articles/profiles-in-dna/2012/improved-primer-pair-for-the-se33-locus-in-the-powerplex-esi-17-pro-system/.

Mulero, J., et al. (2011). Amelogenin SNP on chromosome X. *US Patent Application*, 2011/0237443 A1.

Mulero, J. (2012). Development of a "global" STR multiplex for human identification analysis. *Presentation given at the European Academy of Forensic Sciences (The Hague, Netherlands)*. Available at http://tools.lifetechnologies.com/downloads/EAFS2012.pdf. Accessed March 23, 2014.

Nelson, M. S., et al. (2002). Detection of a primer-binding site polymorphism for the STR locus D16S539 using the Powerplex 1.1 system and validation of a degenerate primer to correct for the polymorphism. *Journal Forensic Sciences, 47*, 345—349.

Raziel, A., et al. (2012). Discordance at D3S1358 locus involving SGM Plus and the European new generation multiplex kits. *Forensic Science International Genetics, 6*, 108—112.

Rolf, B., et al. (2011). Insertion/deletion polymorphisms close to the repeat region of STR loci can cause discordant genotypes with different STR kits. *Forensic Science International Genetics, 5*, 339—341.

Ricci, U., et al. (2007). A single mutation in the FGA locus responsible for false homozygosities and discrepancies between commercial kits in an unusual paternity test case. *Journal Forensic Sciences, 52*, 393—396.

Schneider, P. M. (2009). Expansion of the European Standard Set of DNA database loci—the current situation. *Profiles in DNA, 12*(1), 6—7.

Schumm, J. W., et al. (1996). *Automated fluorescent detection of STR multiplexes — development of the GenePrint™ PowerPlex™ and FFFL multiplexes for forensic and paternity applications*. Madison, Wisconsin: Proceedings of the International Symposium on Human Identification. Promega Corporation, pp. 70—88.

STRBase Null Allele page at http://www.cstl.nist.gov/strbase/NullAlleles.htm

Turrina, S., et al. (2011). Concordance study and allele frequencies for 5 new European standard set (ESS) loci in the North-East Italian population. *Forensic Science International: Genetics Supplement Series, 3*, e329—e330.

Tsuji, A., et al. (2010). A silent allele in the locus D19S433 contained within the AmpFlSTR Identifiler PCR Amplification Kit. *Legal Medicine, 12*, 94—96.

Urquhart, A., et al. (1994). Variation in short tandem repeat sequences — a survey of twelve microsatellite loci for use as forensic identification markers. *International Journal of Legal Medicine, 107*, 13—20.

Vallone, P. M., et al. (2011). Concordance study of direct PCR kits: PowerPlex 18D and Identifiler Direct. *Forensic Science International Genetics Supplement Series, 3*, e353—e354.

Vanderheyden, N., et al. (2007). Identification and sequence analysis of discordant phenotypes between AmpFlSTR SGM Plus and PowerPlex 16. *International Journal Legal Medicine, 121*(4), 297—301.

Wallin, J. M., et al. (2002). Constructing universal multiplex PCR systems for comparative genotyping. *Journal Forensic Sciences, 47*, 52—65.

Walsh, S. (1998). Commentary on Kline MC, Jenkins B, Rogers S. Non-amplification of a vWA allele. J Forensic Sci 1998 Jan; 43(1):250. *Journal Forensic Sciences, 43*, 1103—1104.

Welch, L. A., et al. (2012). European Network of Forensic Science Institutes (ENFSI): Evaluation of new commercial STR multiplexes that include the European Standard Set (ESS) of markers. *Forensic Science International Genetics, 6*, 819—826.

Yurrebaso, I., et al. (2011). Allele frequencies and concordance study between the Identifiler and the PowerPlex ESX17 systems in the Basque Country population. *Forensic Science International Genetics, 5*, e79—e80.

Zhai, X.-D., et al. (2010). False homozygosities at CSF1PO loci revealed by discrepancies between two kits in Chinese population. *International Journal Legal Medicine, 124*(5), 457—458.

5

STR Profiles
Multiplex PCR, Tri-Alleles, Amelogenin, and Partial Profiles

"Knowledge becomes serviceable only when it is used."

John Widtsoe

INTRODUCTION

Up to this point in the book we have been focusing on information derived from a single locus. Multiplex polymerase chain reaction (PCR) enables examination of many loci simultaneously, and this multi-locus genotyping information can increase interpretation capabilities beyond what is available from a single locus. Short tandem repeat (STR) profiles can be illustrated with simple triangles, line drawings, or more sophisticated tools for illustrating electropherograms (D.N.A. Box 5.1).

D.N.A. BOX 5.1

TOOLS TO CREATE EXAMPLE ELECTROPHEROGRAM DATA

To create example electropherograms for teaching purposes, triangles have been used to illustrate allele, genotype, or profile peaks. Simple line drawings can also be made using PowerPoint or other graphical tools as have been done in this book and previous editions of *Forensic DNA Typing*. However, new tools have been developed to create more realistic electropherogram data. Steven Myers (California Department of Justice, Richmond, CA) and Jo Bright (ESR, Auckland, New Zealand) have prepared some Excel macros that enable DNA electropherograms to be created with specific alleles and peak heights (e.g. Figure 1.5).

These programs are freely available on the NIST STRBase website: EPG Maker program from Steven Myers: http://www.cstl.nist.gov/strbase/tools/EPG-Maker(SPMv.3,Dec2-2011).xlt (13 Mb Excel file)

EPG Maker program from Jo Bright: http://www.cstl.nist.gov/strbase/tools/Bright-scaler.xlsx (113 kb Excel worksheet)

This chapter addresses single-source samples. An understanding of expected behavior of single-source DNA samples is important prior to attempting DNA mixtures containing multiple contributors, which are covered in Chapter 6.

Much can be learned during data interpretation by looking at the full profile. Did signal bleed-through lead to pull-up between dye channels? Viewing data as an overlap of dye colors can help assess this situation. Is there loss of signal with longer-sized PCR products due to DNA degradation or PCR inhibition? A comparison of peak heights between the shortest- and longest-size amplicons within a color channel will provide helpful clues. A "ski slope" with the smallest loci on the left side of the electropherogram producing significantly higher peak heights compared to the larger loci on the right side of the electropherogram suggests that PCR amplification has been compromised due to lack of target molecules from DNA degradation or lack of polymerase power due to PCR inhibition.

MULTIPLEX PCR CHALLENGES

There are a number of advantages of multiplex PCR, where more than one location is targeted and copied during the polymerase chain reaction. Multiplex PCR enables multiple regions of DNA to be examined from a small amount of original starting material.

For amplicons to be obtained from the targeted regions of DNA, PCR primer pairs need to be compatible with similar annealing temperatures. In addition, excessive regions of complementarity among the primers in the multiplex PCR reaction need to be avoided to prevent the formation of primer dimers that will reduce or prevent amplification of the desired target region. Sometimes mobility modifiers are added to specific primers and used to adjust overall PCR product sizes in order to maintain PCR primer positions with loci under different configurations in various STR kits (see Chapter 4 in Butler 2012).

Having primers that possess similar annealing temperatures and little-to-no complementarity among primers in the PCR reaction mix is only a starting point in generating effective STR profiles. In order to produce a *balanced* STR profile (such as illustrated in Figure 1.5), primer concentrations need to be optimized. A balanced profile enables comparison across loci, which can be particularly helpful in efforts to deconvolute a DNA mixture containing two or more contributors.

STR kit manufacturers spend a great deal of effort during kit development working on inter-locus balance within and across dye channels. This balance, which is demonstrated through developmental validation, is primarily performed with pristine samples using a range of DNA amounts. PCR amplification of evidentiary material, which is not pristine and may be limited in quantity, can yield partial profiles. PCR inhibitors in evidentiary samples may also result in uneven amplification across the tested STR loci.

STR PROFILE EVALUATION

STR data interpretation typically begins by looking at a DNA profile in its entirety. Off-scale data and the resultant pull-up peaks can suggest that too much DNA template was present in the multiplex PCR reaction. The loss of signal from longer-sized STR loci is an indicator of PCR inhibitors or degraded DNA. The presence of more than two alleles at a locus can suggest a potential mixture — although it is important to not focus on a single locus due to the possibility of tri-allelic patterns.

The ratio of X and Y alleles from the amelogenin sex-typing primer pair can also aid in DNA mixture interpretation. Inter-locus balance within a dye channel can help inform an analyst on potential PCR inhibition or DNA degradation. Inter-locus balance between dye channels can inform an STR kit developer on dye sensitivity and PCR primer balance.

Table 5.1 lists the fluorescent dyes employed in a number of STR kits and dye sets used with capillary electrophoresis (CE) to detect the STR kit amplicons. Newer STR kits typically involve five or six dyes with one dye channel reserved for an internal size standard (see Chapter 3).

There is a fairly narrow input range of DNA template quantities that produce optimal profiles. This is one of the reasons that human DNA quantitation is required on forensic samples by the FBI Quality Assurance Standards (FBI QAS 2011).

Because multiple dye colors are used to create DNA profiles, fluorescent can bleed through into adjacent color channels if data peaks are off-scale or the spectral calibration is not properly calibrated. These pull-up peaks from off-scale data can fall into allele size bins for STR loci in another color and need to be edited out of a properly interpreted profile. Alternatively, the DNA sample could be re-amplified with less DNA, or the original PCR products could be re-injected with a lower electrokinetic injection into the CE instrument to achieve on-scale data. Thus, pull-up peaks complicate STR profile interpretation.

Figure 5.1 illustrates some pull-up peaks that bleed through into adjacent dye channels from the off-scale TPOX 8,8 homozygote. Expert-systems software or a human performing manual data review must decide that the pull-up peaks are not real STR alleles based on their shape and position in the electropherogram. Other complications in STR data interpretation that can arise include the presence of tri-allelic patterns, amelogenin deletions, and STR alleles extending beyond their expected size ranges (see Chapter 3).

The European Network of Forensic Science Institutes (ENFSI) published principles related to testing STR multiplexes (Gill et al. 2000). Most developmental validation studies follow these principles, many of which are spelled out in the SWGDAM validation guidelines (SWGDAM 2012). An important part of validation is assessing stutter product formation, heterozygote balance, and inter-locus balance with various ranges of DNA amounts to define limits of reliability with low-template DNA samples. Stochastic effects with low amounts of DNA can cause STR profile inter-locus balance to deteriorate.

TABLE 5.1   STR Kits and Dye Sets Used

Example STR Kit	Dye Labels	Dye Set
Profiler Plus, SGM Plus, COfiler, Profiler	5-FAM, JOE, NED, ROX	F
Identifiler, MiniFiler, NGM, NGM SElect	6-FAM, VIC, NED, PET, LIZ	G5
GlobalFiler	6-FAM, VIC, NED, TAZ, SID, LIZ	J6 (3500)
PowerPlex 16, 16HS	FL, JOE, TMR, CXR	F
PowerPlex ESI 16/17, ESX 16/17, 18D, 21, Fusion	FL, JOE, TMR-ET, CXR-ET, CC5	G5
Qiagen Investigator Kits	B, G, Y, R, O	G5
Research assays	6-FAM, TET, HEX, ROX	C

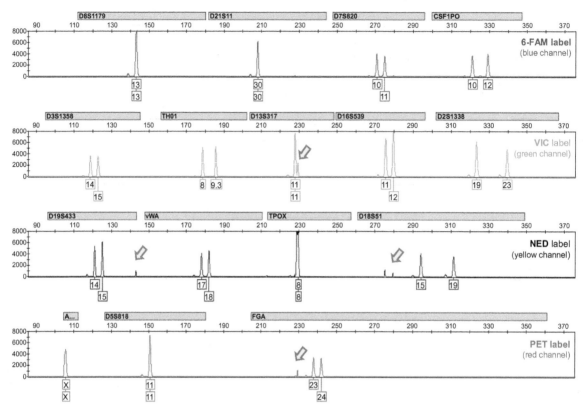

FIGURE 5.1   Identifiler kit STR profile from NIST SRM 2391b component 9 (9947A). Off-scale data leads to pull-up across dye channels (indicated by arrows). PCR conditions include 1-ng DNA template run at half-reaction and 28 cycles. Figure courtesy of Becky Hill, NIST.

TRI-ALLELIC PATTERNS

Occasionally three alleles can be observed at a locus in a single-source DNA profile (Figure 5.2). These tri-alleles or tri-allelic patterns are copy number variants (CNVs). They result from extra chromosome fragments being present in a sample that produce an additional PCR product when subjected to PCR primers for that locus. In some cases, an entire extra chromosome may be present, such as in trisomy 21 or Down syndrome. In fact, the detection of three alleles at D21S11 and other STR markers on chromosome 21 has been used as a diagnostic screen for Down syndrome detection (Pertl et al. 1994, Samura et al. 2001, Yoon et al. 2002).

Expanding efforts of human genome sequencing have discovered that CNVs are more common than originally thought (Freeman et al. 2006, Sjödin & Jakobsson 2012). Tri-allelic patterns are typically rare at a specific locus, but are likely to occur within a 15-locus STR profile about once every 1,000 samples (D.N.A. Box 5.2). An examination of 5,964 DNA profiles from Belgium found three cases of tri-allelic patterns, one with D8S1179 and two with D18S51 (Mertens et al. 2009).

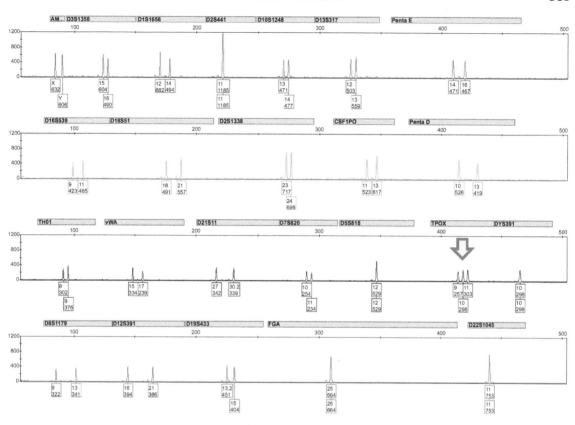

FIGURE 5.2 STR profile from a single-source DNA sample amplified with the PowerPlex Fusion kit that exhibits a tri-allelic pattern at TPOX (see arrow). Figure courtesy of Becky Hill, NIST.

Chromosomal duplication and triplication have also been observed in Y-chromosome STRs (Butler et al. 2005) and X-chromosome STRs (Lim et al. 2009).

Type 1 and Type 2 Tri-Alleles

Tim Clayton and colleagues at the UK Forensic Science Service developed a classification scheme for tri-allelic patterns (Clayton et al. 2004). Type 1, which is more common, involves triallelic patterns where the sum of peak heights from two of the alleles is similar to the peak height of the third allele. Type 2 triallelic patterns involve a fairly balanced set of three alleles (Figure 5.3). In 15 tri-allelic patterns reported by a study of 32,800 PowerPlex 16 profiles, 12 were Type 1 and 3 Type 2 with these tri-alleles seen in 10 of the 15 STRs examined (Huel et al. 2007).

More than 240 different tri-allelic patterns have been reported at all 13 CODIS STR loci with most of them being seen at TPOX, D18S51, D21S11, VWA, and FGA. A frequently updated listing of tri-allelic patterns may be found on the NIST STRBase web site (STRBase 2014). While only 7 different D18S51 tri-allelic patterns had been reported to STRBase through April 2005 (Butler 2006), as of

D.N.A. BOX 5.2

ESTIMATION OF AVERAGE FREQUENCY FOR TRI-ALLELIC PATTERNS IN STR PROFILES

Several years ago, DNA analyst Malena Jimenez from the Missouri State Highway Patrol supplied the NIST STRBase website with information on tri-alleles observed during analysis of 69,600 convicted offender samples. Below is a summary of the number of reported tri-alleles for each locus examined with their PowerPlex 16 single-source profiles.

Noting a total of 68 tri-alleles observed across these 69,600 samples, a tri-allelic pattern is expected to occur about once every one thousand samples on average. However, as can be seen with this data, the distribution of tri-allelic patterns is not even across loci.

Source: Steven Myers, California Department of Justice presentation provided to the author based on data collected from the NIST STRBase website at http://www.cstl.nist.gov/strbase/tri_tab.htm.

STR Locus	# Tri-Alleles	STR Locus	# Tri-Alleles	STR Locus	# Tri-Alleles
CSF1PO	1	D3S1358	2	D16S539	3
FGA	11	D5S818	1	D18S51	3
TH01	0	D7S820	0	D21S11	9
TPOX	9	D8S1179	2	Penta D	3
vWA	10	D13S317	4	Penta E	10

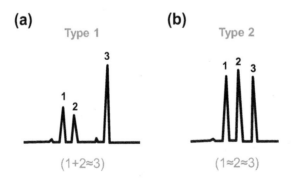

(a) Type 1   **(b)** Type 2

$(1+2\approx3)$ $(1\approx2\approx3)$

FIGURE 5.3 Illustration of tri-allelic patterns that are sometimes observed at a single locus in a multiplex STR profile. They may be classified into one of two different groups based on relative peak heights: (a) "Type 1" where the sum of two peak heights is almost equal to the third $(1 + 2 \approx 3)$ or (b) "Type 2" where fairly balanced peak heights are observed $(1 \approx 2 \approx 3)$.

TABLE 5.2   A Summary of 35 D18S51 Tri-Allelic Patterns Reported on STRBase (as of Jan 2014) Observed in Five Different Countries and Nine U.S. States

D18S51 Tri-Alleles	Reported Frequency (at time observed)	D18S51 Tri-Alleles	Reported Frequency (at time observed)
8, 11, 15	—	**14, 15, 16**	1 in 11,000
11, 13, 17	—	14, 15, 17	1 in 14,245
12, 13, 14	1 in 503	14, 15, 22	—
12, 13, 15 (2×)	1 in 15,000; other not reported	**14, 16, 17**	—
12, 13, 18	1 in 69,600	14, 16, 18	—
12, 14, 15	1 in 10,613	**14, 16, 22**	—
12, 14, 18	1 in 69,600	14, 18, 19	—
12, 15, 19	1 in 15,000	14, 19, 20	—
12, 16, 17	1 in 39,000	15, 16, 20	1 in 1120
12, 17, 18	—	**15, 17, 18**	—
12, 18, 19	—	15, 19, 20	—
13, 14, 15	—	**16, 17, 18** (3×)	2 in 16,046; 1 in 11,000
13, 14, 16	—	**16, 17, 19**	1 in 28,252
13, 14, 17	—	16, 17, 20	1 in 12,115
13, 14, 21	1 in 11,000	16, 19, 20	—
13, 15, 16 (2×)	1 in 11,500; 1 in 69,600	17, 18, 19 (3×)	—
13,15,19	—	**19, 20, 21**	—
		19, 22.2, 23.2	—

The tri-alleles listed in bold font were recognized as Type 1 (imbalanced) tri-allelic patterns. Most did not have reported frequencies (−).

January 2014 the number of different D18S51 tri-alleles had grown to 35 (Table 5.2). Thus, collection of more STR profiles is resulting in more observations of tri-allelic patterns.

Inheritance Studies

In order to better understand the origin of tri-allelic patterns, several studies have examined inheritance patterns (Rolf et al. 2002, Zamir et al. 2002, Lukka et al. 2006, Lane 2008, Vidal & Cassar 2008). These studies suggest that tri-alleles arise from inheritance of two chromosomes or chromosomal regions (e.g. a CNV duplication) from one parent.

A tri-allelic pattern at D3S1358 was observed in a tested child (17/**18/19**) during routine parentage testing (Vidal & Cassar 2008). Follow-up analysis found that the alleged paternal grandmother was also tri-allelic (15/**18/19**) while the mother exhibited a normal diploid genotype (15/**17**). Thus, the child likely inherited the 18/19 from her father and the 17 from her mother. Unfortunately, the father was unavailable for testing. DNA samples from the mother, child, and alleged paternal grandmother were further examined at 11 additional loci surrounding D3S1358 on chromosome 3. Only D3S1358 showed a duplication suggesting that the CNV duplication in this case was confined to a small portion of chromosome 3 (Vidal & Cassar 2008).

In another study (Rolf et al. 2002), in which the mother exhibited three alleles (18/19/33.2) at the SE33 (ACTBP2) locus, these three alleles segretated separately to her five children who appear to receive only one maternal allele each. With a father possessing a 29.2/31.2 SE33 genotype, the children had normal genotypes of 29.2/33.2, 29.2/33.2, 31.2/33.2, 19/31.2, and 18/31.2, where underlining is used to illustrate the maternal allele received. The authors of this study concluded that their data can best be explained by assuming somatic mosaicism, which is present in the tissues investigated as well as the maternal germ cells (Rolf et al. 2002). The 18 and 19 alleles are likely the mosaics and they may have arisen from an early mutation event during embryogenesis. This study concludes that because the frequency of somatic mosaicism is related to the mutation rate, loci with higher mutation rates will exhibit tri-allelic patterns more often.

The inheritance of a TPOX tri-allelic pattern was observed in a paternity trio where the child was 8/10/11, the mother was 8/8/10, and the father was 11/11 (Lukka et al. 2006). Analysis of neighboring STR loci to TPOX on the short arm of chromosome 2 support the assumption that the mother in this case supplied two alleles to the child while the father supplied one. Noting the TPOX tri-alleles are usually type 2 (Figure 5.3), the authors of this study suggest a relative high frequency of chromosomal rearrangements in the TPOX region near the telomere of chromosome 2 (Lukka et al. 2006). However, there may be another reason for the type 2 tri-allelic patterns frequently observed at TPOX (Lane 2008).

TPOX Tri-Alleles and "Allele 10"

A 2008 study reported that approximately 2.4% of indigenous South Africans have three rather than two TPOX alleles (Lane 2008). Data collected during routine paternity testing revealed that the extra allele is almost always allele 10 and that it appears to segregate independently of the other alleles at the main TPOX locus. Approximately twice as many females as males have TPOX tri-allelic genotypes, which suggests that the extra "allele 10" is on the X chromosome.

An analysis of STRBase submissions patterns provides support for the observation that allele 10 is extremely common in TPOX tri-allelic patterns. In 113 STRBase submissions involving 18 different TPOX tri-allelic patterns (reported as of January 2014), only 9 times (8%) is allele 10 not present. There are five 8/9/11, three 8/11/12, and one 9/11/12 tri-alleles. Likewise, 30 reports of the 113 submissions are 8/10/11. This 23% of reported TPOX tri-alleles correlates fairly well with the observed 8,11 genotype frequency of 27% found in the NIST 1036 dataset (Butler et al. 2012, Hill et al. 2013).

A set of 20 tri-allelic TPOX samples from the Dominican Republic containing either a tri-allele in a mother or her child found in all but two instances the presence of the "10" allele (Díaz et al. 2009). One of these instances was an 8/9/11 mother with no parental TPOX data available. In the other instance, the child (a son) was a TPOX 6/8/11 with an 8,8 mother. Thus, the father, who was not tested, likely transmitted a 6/11 to his son. Since a man will not pass on an X chromosome to his son, the absence of a TPOX "10" in the child agrees with the hypothesis that the duplicated "allele 10" is on the X chromosome (Lane 2008).

Frequency Estimates

It is challenging to determine an accurate frequency estimate for a specific tri-allele. While some STRBase submissions contain frequency information, it only pertains to a specific data set at the time submitted. For example, a CSF1PO 10,12,13 tri-allele was reported as 1 in 11,000 samples examined by the International Commission on Missing Persons and 1 in 31,330 samples tested by a laboratory in Korea. However, these values only reflect how many samples were tested by their lab at the time the information was submitted to STRBase. Thus, we only have limited information at best with which to estimate a frequency. If there are 12 million U.S. profiles with D18S51 results and likely more than 30 million profiles world-wide with D18S51, then perhaps these values could be used as the denominator in an estimate. However, not all observed tri-allelic patterns are submitted to STRBase, and therefore the numerator of such a frequency estimation would not be accurate due to incomplete information.

In some ways, tri-alleles are like heteroplasmy in mtDNA (Melton 2004) or duplication/deletions in Y-STR results (Butler et al. 2005). As can be seen in Table 5.2, the frequency of occurrence of each D18S51 tri-allele, when it was reported, ranges from 1 in 503 to 1 in 69,600.

Unfortunately, there is not a commonly accepted method to incorporate frequencies of tri-allelic patterns into the statistical calculation for STR profile rarity. My current recommendation would be to leave the tri-allele out of the statistical comparison because of the uncertainty with a proper numerator or denominator to use in the specific tri-allelic frequency estimate. However, the report should mention whether or not the question (Q) and known (K) samples qualitatively match at the locus containing the tri-allelic pattern. If they match, then you are strengthening the match statistic — we just do not know by how much.

Some authors have suggested not including tri-allelic information in case reports due to the possibility of clinically relevant data being inadvertently revealed if a chromosomal duplication, such as trisomy 21, is present (Lukka et al. 2006).

Tri-Allelic Anomalies

False tri-alleles may occur if an extreme off-ladder allele from an adjacent locus in the STR multiplex falls into the range of a neighboring locus — and sometimes even into a legitimate allele bin (see examples in Chapter 3). Thus, using different STR kits, with locus in different size and dye color confirmations, can be helpful in confirming tri-allelic patterns (e.g. Figure 3.8).

Abnormal DNA profiles may arise from various biological processes, including copy number variants either as duplications or deletions, somatic mutations (which could vary between different tissues tested), full chromosomal duplication (such as trisomy 21), and mosaicism.

Some true Type 1 tri-allelic patterns may be masked by what appears to be high stutter at a specific allele. Rather than being a DNA mixture of two individuals where the minor component is only being "observed" at a single locus, a sample possessing high stutter at a single allele may in fact be exhibiting mosaicism (a mixture of two cell types) within a single individual (Zimmer 2013). Scientists from the Washington State Patrol Crime Laboratory reported this phenomenon with an anomalous result at D3S1358 encountered in a sexual assault-homicide case (Shutler & Roy 2012) (D.N.A. Box 5.3).

D.N.A. BOX 5.3

ELEVATED STUTTER AT A SINGLE STR LOCUS: A DNA MIXTURE OR TRI-ALLELIC MOSAICISM?

Occasionally in what appears to be an otherwise single-source sample, the signal in the stutter position at a single STR locus will appear higher than expected. In the figure shown here, the second stutter peak is expected to be in the range of 12% to 15% rather than the 28% shown. The percentages shown are based on relative peak heights compared to the tallest allele peaks with relative fluorescence units of 414, 3863, 926, and 3,258 (for the peaks from left to right, respectively).

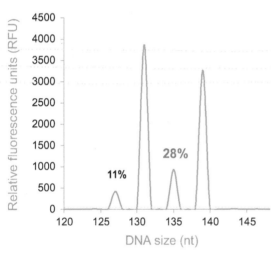

Assuming that other STR loci in the full profile do not show any other signs of a second contributor (i.e. all loci exhibit only one or two alleles and their accompanying stutter products) and that bleedthrough from another dye channel is not likely, then the reporting analyst is left with a difficult decision. Is this elevated stutter the only surviving evidence of a "mystery man" minor component where other alleles have dropped out or are being masked by the major component alleles and their stutter products? Or is there some other potential explanation for the

elevated stutter? For example, is this result from a low-template DNA sample amplified with an increased number of PCR cycles where elevated stutter is a definite possibility due to stochastic effects?

In a letter to the editor of *Forensic Science International: Genetics*, two scientists from the Washington State Patrol (WSP) Crime Laboratory reported some genetic anomalies that they believe are consistent with gonadal mosaicism (Shutler & Roy 2012). Mosaicism is the presence of genetically different tissues within a single individual. These different cells could potentially have different genotypes due to post-zygotic mutation either in somatic (non-germline) or gonadal (germline) cells. The figure shown here is a representation of D3S1358 results of a semen stain recovered from the suspect's pants in the WSP case study (their Supplemental Figure 4). The D3S1358 allele positions are 16, 17, 18, and 19. An oral reference sample from the suspect matched at all other loci with the exception of 11% stutter being seen in the 18 position, which is 28% in the semen stain result shown. The WSP authors conclude that the semen-derived profile could be explained as being consistent with a Type 1 tri-allelic pattern since the sum of the 18 and 19 allele peak heights (926 + 3258 = 4184 RFU) is approximately the same size as the allele 17 peak height (3863 RFU). This tri-allele (17/18/19) could have arisen "during mitosis leading to mosaicism and could be explained as being due to a sperm precursor cell somatic mutation" (Shutler & Roy 2012).

Source: Shutler, G., & Roy, T. (2012). Genetic anomalies consistent with gonadal mosaicism encountered in a sexual assault-homicide. Forensic Science International: Genetics, 6, *e159–e160. Electropherogram illustration of results from this study drawn with Jo Bright's EPG Marker available at http://www.cstl.nist.gov/strbase/tools/Bright-scaler.xlsx.*

GENDER IDENTIFICATION WITH AMELOGENIN

The ability to designate whether a sample originated from a male or a female source is useful in sexual assault cases, where distinguishing between the victim and the perpetrator's evidence is important. Likewise, missing persons and mass disaster investigations can benefit from gender identification of the remains. Over the years a number of gender identification assays have been demonstrated using PCR methods (Sullivan et al. 1993, Eng et al. 1994, Reynolds & Varlaro 1996). By far the most popular method for sex-typing today is the amelogenin system as it can be performed in conjunction with STR analysis.

Amelogenin is a gene that codes for proteins found in tooth enamel. The British Forensic Science Service was the first to describe the particular PCR primer sets that are used so prevalently in forensic DNA laboratories today (Sullivan et al. 1993). These primers flank a 6-bp deletion within intron 1 of the amelogenin gene on the X homolog (Figure 5.4). PCR amplification of this area with their primers results in 106-bp and 112-bp amplicons from the X and Y chromosomes, respectively.

An advantage in using a single primer set to amplify both chromosomes is that the X chromosome product itself plays a role as a positive control. This PCR-based assay is extremely sensitive. Mannucci and co-workers were able to detect as little as 20 pg ($\approx$3 diploid copies) as well as sample mixtures where female DNA was in 100-fold excess of male DNA (Mannucci et al. 1994).

Other regions of the amelogenin gene have size differences between the X and Y homologs and may be exploited for sex-typing purposes. A careful study found that 19 regions of absolute homology, ranging in size from 22 bp to 80 bp, exist between the human amelogenin X and Y genes that can be used to design a variety of primer sets (Haas-Rochholz & Weiler 1997). Thus, by spanning various deletions of the X and/or Y chromosome, it is possible to generate PCR products from the X and Y

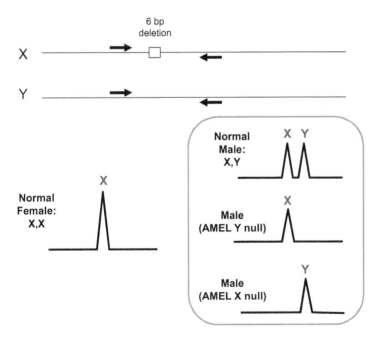

FIGURE 5.4 Schematic of the amelogenin sex-typing assay. The X and Y chromosomes contain a high degree of sequence homology at the amelogenin (AMEL) locus and primers, as depicted by the arrows, can target a 6 bp deletion that is present only on the X chromosome (Sullivan et al. 1993). In most circumstances, the presence of a single X peak indicates that the sample comes from a female, while two peaks identifies the sample's source as male. Both AMEL Y and AMEL X null alleles have been reported.

homologs that differ in size and contain size ranges that can be integrated into future multiplex STR amplifications. For example, an 80-bp amplicon from the X-chromosome and an 83-bp amplicon from Y-chromosome were used in the NIST 26plex assay (Hill et al. 2009).

While amelogenin is an effective method for sex-typing biological samples in most cases, the results are not foolproof either due to primer binding sites that lead to null alleles or chromosomal deletions. Amelogenin Y allele drop-outs have been observed due to loss of portions of the Y chromosome in some population groups. Amelogenin X allele drop-outs have been seen primarily due to primer binding site mutations.

Amelogenin Y Allele Drop-Out

Portions of the Y-chromosome can be deleted in normal males. It has been noted that a rare deletion of the amelogenin gene on the Y-chromosome can cause the Y-chromosome amplicon to be absent (Santos et al. 1998). In such a case, a male sample would falsely appear as a female with only the amelogenin X allele being amplified. This deletion of the Y chromosome amelogenin region appears to be more common in Indian populations (Thangaraj et al. 2002) than those of European or African origins. A study of almost 30,000 males in the Austrian National DNA database revealed that only six individuals lacked the amelogenin Y-amplicon (Steinlechner et al. 2002). These individuals were verified to be male with Y-STRs and amplification of the SRY region.

More recent studies have attempted to map the Y deletions in detail and to track the specific biogeographic ancestry of these interesting variants (Cadenas et al. 2007, Jobling et al. 2007). Through examining adjacent STR markers and sequence-specific tag sites, the extent of the Y chromosome deletion can be mapped (Takayama et al. 2009). When amplifying Y-STR loci, the locus DYS458 in Yfiler or PowerPlex Y23 is the most likely one to be lost with amelogenin Y deletions due to its close proximity to the AMEL Y.

A 2008 survey of paternity testing laboratories using the Applied Biosystems primers (i.e. Identifiler or Profiler Plus kits) noted an overall rate of 0.033% males (from 144,391 samples) that lacked the amelogenin Y allele (AABB, 2008). However, 1.8% East Asian males (6 of 505) exhibited a missing amelogenin Y allele demonstrating the population specificity with this particular Y-chromosome deletion.

Amelogenin X Allele Drop-Out

Amelogenin X allele drop-out has also been observed in males. In this case only the amelogenin Y-amplicon is present (Shewale et al. 2000, Alves et al. 2006, Maciejewska & Pawłowski 2009). In one study, this phenomenon was observed only three times out of almost 7,000 males examined (Shewale et al. 2000). The authors of this study felt that the AMEL X null was most likely a result of a rare polymorphism in the primer binding sites for the amelogenin primers used in commercial STR kits. A different set of amelogenin primers targeting the same 6-bp deletion on the X chromosome amplified both the X and Y alleles of amelogenin (Shewale et al. 2000). However, in some populations, this loss of the AMEL X allele is more common. In a study of 503 individuals from São Tomé Island (West Africa), 10 male individuals displayed only the Y allele from amelogenin amplification due to a primer binding site mutation in the AMEL X allele (Alves et al. 2006). A different mutation caused one male out of 5534 Polish males tested to display only the AMEL Y allele (Maciejewska & Pawłowski 2009).

A report of males examined in paternity testing labs using Applied Biosystems STR typing kits found that there were a higher number of African American males compared to other U.S. population groups showing only the AMEL Y allele (i.e. the AMEL X allele dropped out). Still, this AMEL X null is fairly rare, seen only 48 times in 144,391 males tested, or 0.03% of the time (AABB 2008).

In a 2011 U.S. Patent application, Life Technologies scientists reported a $C \rightarrow T$ SNP in the AMEL X sequence that impacts their reverse amelogenin primer (Mulero et al. 2011). Since it is located at the $3'$-end of their reverse primer, they report using a universal base to overcome possible sequence variants at this position.

Additional Male Confirmation Markers to Confirm Gender

Given the possibility of amelogenin Y being deleted and thus providing a false negative for male samples, additional Y-chromosome markers have sometimes been included in assays to confirm gender assignments. A group from the Israel Police DNA Laboratory proposed the addition of a Y-STR to help confirm male samples possessing an AMEL Y null allele (Oz et al. 2008).

In the announcement of the proposal for the U.S. core expansion (Hares 2012), DYS391 was included as a core locus for this purpose — to aid in male confirmation when deletions spanning AMEL Y occur. The megaplexes built to meet the proposed expanded U.S. core, AmpFlSTR GlobalFiler and PowerPlex Fusion, both contain DYS391 (see Chapter 1). Amplification of a portion of SRY, the sex-determining region of the Y-chromsome that is located at 2.65 Mb, has been used as well for a male confirmation marker (Kastelic et al. 2009, Giuliodori et al. 2011).

The GlobalFiler STR kit from Life Technologies (South San Francisco, CA) includes a Y insertion-deletion (InDel) that can be either "1" (deletion) or "2" (insertion). In a U.S. patent application laying out the GlobalFiler design, this Y-InDel is cited as rs2032678 (Hennessy & Wang 2012). Small ampli-con sizes of 81 bp or 86 bp enable successful results with degraded DNA samples.

Provided the GlobalFiler Y-InDel is rs2032678, it is a genetic marker originally known as M175 because it was the 175th marker discovered by Peter Underhill of Stanford University using dena-turing high-performance liquid chromatography (Underhill et al. 2007). M175 exhibits deletion of a five-base sequence "TTCTC" with Y-SNP haplogroup O individuals who typically are East or Southeast Asians (van Oven et al. 2012). Most samples will be "2," which is the ancestral "insertion" form, unless they are Asian in origin. M175 is located at 15.5 Mb on the reference Y-chromosome sequence, which is on the long arm of the Y-chromosome over 7 Mb from amelogenin that is at 6.74 Mb (Figure 5.5). Thus, a deletion around the amelogenin Y region is not expected to impact the rs2032678 Y-InDel or DYS391.

PARTIAL DNA PROFILES

A partial DNA profile is by definition one that is missing information that was sought as part of the initial genetic testing performed on a biological sample. For example, if a particular DNA test is performed that should amplify 16 loci, yet only 13 loci produced results, then the result is a partial profile that is missing information at three loci.

Allele drop-out is when only a single allele is missing at a tested locus, while locus drop-out involves missing both alleles in a single-source sample. Allele drop-out is most commonly due to stochastic effects when amplifying a DNA sample of low quantity or low quality (e.g. possesses

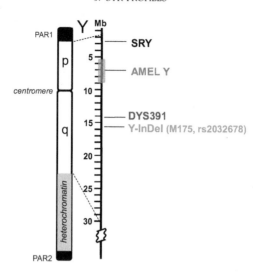

FIGURE 5.5　Relative positions of amelogenin (AMEL Y) and male confirmation markers found on the Y-chromosome. Red shading covers area that may be lost with AMEL Y null alleles due to deletion of that portion of the short arm of the Y-chromosome.

DNA size (bp) *relative to an internal size standard (not shown)*

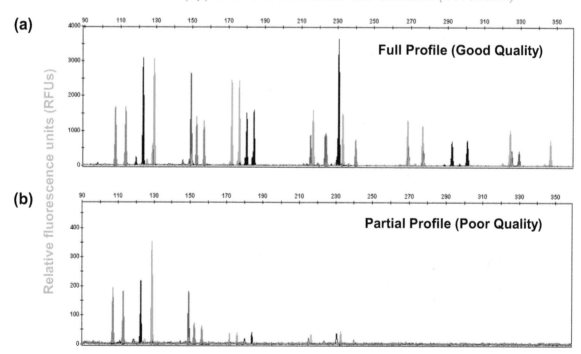

FIGURE 5.6　A comparison of DNA profiles originating from the same biological source but of different qualities. (a) Intact, good-quality DNA yields a full profile. (b) Degraded, poor-quality DNA yields a partial profile with only the shorter-size PCR products producing detectable signal. With the degraded DNA sample shown in (b), information is lost at the longer-sized STR loci. Also note the lower relative fluorescence units with the poor-quality partial profile in (b). Figure courtesy of Margaret Kline, NIST.

I. DATA INTERPRETATION

PCR inhibitors). Figure 5.6 illustrates a full profile versus a partial profile obtained from the same biological source. Chapter 7 will contain more on the interpretation challenges that arise with partial profiles. Chapter 13 covers statistical approaches attempting to account for allele drop-out in partial profiles, especially those arising with complex DNA mixtures.

Reading List and Internet Resources

Multiplex PCR Challenges

Butler, J. M. (2012). *Advanced Topics in Forensic DNA Typing: Methodology*. San Diego: Elsevier Academic Press, 167−211.

Edwards, M. C., & Gibbs, R. A. (1994). Multiplex PCR: advantages, development, and applications. *PCR Methods and Applications, 3*, S65−S75.

Gill, P., et al. (2005). A graphical simulation model of the entire DNA process associated with the analysis of short tandem repeat loci. *Nucleic Acids Research, 33*, 632−643.

Kimpton, C., et al. (1993). Automated DNA profiling employing 'multiplex' amplification of short tandem repeat loci. *PCR Methods and Applications, 3*, 13−22.

Kimpton, C. P., et al. (1996). Validation of highly discriminating multiplex short tandem repeat amplification systems for individual identification. *Electrophoresis, 17*, 1283−1293.

Wallin, J. M., et al. (2002). Constructing universal multiplex PCR systems for comparative genotyping. *Journal of Forensic Sciences, 47*, 52−65.

Walsh, P. S., et al. (1992). Preferential PCR amplification of alleles: mechanisms and solutions. *PCR Methods and Applications, 1*, 241−250.

STR Profile Evaluation

Bright, J. A., et al. (2010). Examination of the variability in mixed DNA profile parameters for the Identifiler multiplex. *Forensic Science International: Genetics, 4*, 111−114.

Bright, J. A., et al. (2011). Determination of the variables affecting mixed MiniFiler DNA profiles. *Forensic Science International: Genetics, 5*, 381−385.

Debernardi, A., et al. (2011). One year variability of peak heights, heterozygous balance and inter-locus balance for the DNA positive control of AmpFlSTR(c) Identifiler(c) STR kit. *Forensic Science International: Genetics, 5*, 43−49.

FBI QAS. (2011). http://www.fbi.gov/about-us/lab/biometric-analysis/codis/qas-standards-for-forensic-dna-testing-laboratories-effective-9-1-2011. Accessed March 23, 2014.

Gill, P., et al. (1997). Development of guidelines to designate alleles using an STR multiplex system. *Forensic Science International, 89*, 185−197.

Gill, P., et al. (2000). Report of the European Network of Forensic Science Institutes (ENFSI): formulation and testing of principles to evaluate STR multiplexes. *Forensic Science International, 108*, 1−29.

Hill, C. R., et al. (2011). Concordance and population studies along with stutter and peak height ratio analysis for the PowerPlex® ESX 17 and ESI 17 Systems. *Forensic Science International: Genetics, 5*(4), 269−275.

Kirkham, A., et al. (2013). High-throughput analysis using AmpFlSTR® Identifiler® with the Applied Biosystems 3500xl Genetic Analyser. *Forensic Science International: Genetics, 7*, 92−97.

Muller, K., et al. (2010). Casework testing of the multiplex kits AmpFlSTR SEfiler Plus PCR amplification kit (AB), PowerPlex S5 System (Promega) and AmpFlSTR MiniFiler PCR amplification kit (AB). *Forensic Science International: Genetics, 4*, 200−205.

Myers, B. A., et al. (2012). Evaluation and comparative analysis of direct amplification of STRs using PowerPlex® 18D and Identifiler® Direct systems. *Forensic Science International: Genetics, 6*, 640−645.

Petricevic, S., et al. (2010). Validation and development of interpretation guidelines for low copy number (LCN) DNA profiling in New Zealand using the AmpFlSTR SGM Plus multiplex. *Forensic Science International: Genetics, 4*, 305−310.

Poetsch, M., et al. (2011). Powerplex® ES versus Powerplex® S5 − casework testing of the new screening kit. *Forensic Science International: Genetics, 5*, 57−63.

Tvedebrink, T., et al. (2012). Performance of two 17 locus forensic identification STR kits − Applied Biosystems's AmpFlSTR® NGMSElect and Promega's PowerPlex® ESI17 kits. *Forensic Science International: Genetics, 6*, 523−531.

STR KIT Developmental Validation Studies

Butler, J. M. (2012a). Quality assurance and validation. Chapter 7. In *Advanced Topics in Forensic DNA Typing: Methodology* (pp. 167–211). San Diego: Elsevier Academic Press.

Collins, P. J., et al. (2004). Developmental validation of a single-tube amplification of the 13 CODIS STR loci, D2S1338, D19S433, and amelogenin: the AmpFlSTR Identifiler PCR amplification kit. *Journal of Forensic Sciences, 49*(6), 1265–1277.

Davis, C., et al. (2013). Prototype PowerPlex® Y23 System: a concordance study. *Forensic Science International: Genetics, 7*(1), 204–208.

Ensenberger, M. G., et al. (2010). Developmental validation of the PowerPlex 16 HS System: an improved 16-locus fluorescent STR multiplex. *Forensic Science International: Genetics, 4*, 257–264.

Ensenberger, M. G., et al. (2014). Developmental validation of the PowerPlex® 21 System. *Forensic Science International: Genetics, 9*, 169–178.

Green, R. L., et al. (2013). Developmental validation of the AmpFlSTR® NGM SElect PCR Amplification Kit: A next-generation STR multiplex with the SE33 locus. *Forensic Science International: Genetics, 7*, 41–51.

Greenspoon, S. A., et al. (2004). Validation and implementation of the PowerPlex 16 BIO System STR multiplex for forensic casework. *Journal of Forensic Sciences, 49*, 71–80.

Holt, C. L., et al. (2002). TWGDAM validation of AmpFlSTR PCR amplification kits for forensic DNA casework. *Journal of Forensic Sciences, 47*, 66–96.

Krenke, B. E., et al. (2002). Validation of a 16-locus fluorescent multiplex system. *Journal of Forensic Sciences, 47*, 773–785.

Krenke, B. E., et al. (2005). Validation of male-specific, 12-locus fluorescent short tandem repeat (STR) multiplex. *Forensic Science International, 151*, 111–124.

McLaren, R. S., et al. (2013). Developmental validation of the PowerPlex® ESI 17 Pro System. *Forensic Science International: Genetics, 7*(3), e69–e73.

Mulero, J. J., et al. (2006). Development and validation of the AmpFlSTR® Yfiler PCR amplification kit: a male specific, single amplification 17 Y-STR multiplex system. *Journal of Forensic Sciences, 51*, 64–75.

Mulero, J. J., et al. (2008). Development and validation of the AmpFlSTR® MiniFiler PCR Amplification Kit: a miniSTR multiplex for the analysis of degraded and/or PCR inhibited DNA. *Journal of Forensic Sciences, 53*, 838–852.

Mulero, J. J., et al. (2008). Developmental validation of the AmpFlSTR® SEfiler Plus™ PCR amplification kit: an improved multiplex with enhanced performance for inhibited samples. *Forensic Science International: Genetics Supplement Series, 1*, 121–122.

Oostdik, K., et al. (2013). Developmental validation of the PowerPlex® 18D System, a rapid STR multiplex for analysis of reference samples. *Forensic Science International: Genetics, 7*, 129–135.

SWGDAM.. (2012). Scientific Working Group on DNA Analysis Methods: Validation guidelines for DNA analysis methods. Available at http://swgdam.org/SWGDAM_Validation_Guidelines_APPROVED_Dec_2012.pdf. Accessed March 23, 2014.

Thompson, J. M., et al. (2013). Developmental validation of the PowerPlex® Y23 System: a single multiplex Y-STR analysis system for casework and database samples. *Forensic Science International: Genetics, 7*(2), 240–250.

Tucker, V. C., et al. (2011). Developmental validation of the PowerPlex® ESI 16 and PowerPlex® ESI 17 Systems: STR multiplexes for the new European standard. *Forensic Science International: Genetics, 5*, 436–448.

Tucker, V. C., et al. (2012). Developmental validation of the PowerPlex® ESX 16 and PowerPlex® ESX 17 Systems. *Forensic Science International: Genetics, 6*, 124–131.

Wallin, J. M., et al. (1998). TWGDAM validation of the AmpFlSTR Blue PCR amplification kit for forensic casework analysis. *Journal of Forensic Sciences, 43*, 854–870.

Wang, D. Y., et al. (2012). Developmental validation of the AmpFlSTR® Identifiler® Plus PCR Amplification Kit: an established multiplex assay with improved performance. *Journal of Forensic Sciences, 57*, 453–465.

Tri-Allelic Patterns

Butler, J. M. (2006). Genetics and genomics of core STR loci used in human identity testing. *Journal of Forensic Sciences., 51*(2), 253–265.

Butler, J. M., et al. (2005). Chromosomal duplications along the Y-chromosome and their potential impact on Y-STR interpretation. *Journal of Forensic Sciences, 50*, 853–859.

Clayton, T. M., et al. (2004). A genetic basis for anomalous band patterns encountered during DNA STR profiling. *Journal of Forensic Sciences, 49*, 1207–1214.

Crouse, C. A., et al. (1999). Analysis and interpretation of short tandem repeat microvariants and three banded patterns using multiple allele detection systems. *Journal of Forensic Sciences, 44,* 87–94.

Díaz, V., et al. (2009). The presence of tri-allelic TPOX genotypes in Dominican population. *Forensic Science International: Genetics Supplement Series, 2,* 371–372.

Freeman, J. L., et al. (2006). Copy number variation: new insights in genome diversity. *Genome Research, 16,* 949–961.

Hill, C. R., et al. (2013). U.S. population data for 29 autosomal STR loci. *Forensic Science International: Genetics, 7,* e82–e83.

Huel, R. L., et al. (2007). Variant alleles, triallelic patterns, and point mutations observed in nuclear short tandem repeat typing of populations in Bosnia and Serbia. *Croatian Medical Journal, 48,* 494–502.

Lane, A. B. (2008). The nature of tri-allelic TPOX genotypes in African populations. *Forensic Science International: Genetics, 2,* 134–137.

Lim, E. J., et al. (2009). Genetic polymorphism and haplotype analysis of 4 tightly linked X-STR duos in Koreans. *Croatian Medical Journal, 50,* 305–312.

Lukka, M., et al. (2006). Triallelic patterns in STR loci used for paternity analysis: evidence for a duplication in chromosome 2 containing the TPOX STR locus. *Forensic Science International, 164,* 3–9.

Melton, T. (2004). Mitochondrial DNA heteroplasmy. *Forensic Science Reviews, 16,* 1–20.

Mertens, G., et al. (2009). Observation of tri-allelic patterns in autosomal STRs during routine casework. *Forensic Science International: Genetics Supplement Series, 2,* 38–40.

Pertl, B., et al. (1994). Rapid molecular method for prenatal detection of Down's syndrome. *Lancet, 343,* 1197–1198.

Rolf, B., et al. (2002). Somatic mutations at STR loci — a reason for three-allele pattern and mosaicism. *Forensic Science International, 126,* 200–202.

Samura, O., et al. (2001). Diagnosis of trisomy 21 in fetal nucleated erythrocytes from maternal blood by use of short tandem repeat sequences. *Clinical Chemistry, 47,* 1622–1626.

Shutler, G., & Roy, T. (2012). Genetic anomalies consistent with gonadal mosaicism encountered in a sexual assault-homicide. *Forensic Science International: Genetics, 6,* e159–e160.

Sjödin, P., & Jakobsson, M. (2012). Population genetic nature of copy number variation. *Genomic Structural Variants: Methods in Molecular Biology, 838,* 209–223.

Tri-Allelic Patterns on NIST STRBase website. (2014). http://www.cstl.nist.gov/strbase/tri_tab.htm. Accessed March 23, 2014.

Vidal, C., & Cassar, M. (2008). A case of tri-allelic pattern at locus D3S1358 on chromosome 3p21 inherited from paternal grandmother. *Forensic Science International: Genetics, 2,* 372–375.

Yoon, H. R., et al. (2002). Rapid prenatal detection of Down and Edwards Syndromes by fluorescent polymerase chain reaction with short tandem repeat markers. *Yonsei Medical Journal, 43,* 557–566.

Zamir, A., et al. (2002). Presentation of a three-banded pattern — analysis and interpretation. *Journal of Forensic Sciences, 47,* 824–826.

Zimmer, C. (2013). DNA double take. *New York Times* (Sept 16, 2013). Available at http://www.nytimes.com/2013/09/17/science/dna-double-take.html. Accessed March 23, 2014.

Gender Identification with Amelogenin

Budowle, B., et al. (1996). Multiplex amplification and typing procedure for the loci D1S80 and amelogenin. *Journal of Forensic Sciences, 41,* 660–663.

Eng, B., et al. (1994). Anomalous migration of PCR products using nondenaturing polyacrylamide gel electrophoresis: the amelogenin sex-typing system. *Journal of Forensic Sciences, 39,* 1356–1359.

Francès, F., et al. (2007). Amelogenin test: From forensics to quality control in clinical and biochemical genomics. *Clinica Chimica Acta, 386,* 53–56.

Haas-Rochholz, H., & Weiler, G. (1997). Additional primer sets for an amelogenin gene PCR-based DNA-sex test. *International Journal of Legal Medicine, 110,* 312–315.

Hill, C. R., et al. (2009). A 26plex autosomal STR assay to aid human identity testing. *Journal of Forensic Sciences, 54*(5), 1008–1015.

Mannucci, A., et al. (1994). Forensic application of a rapid and quantitative DNA sex test by amplification of the X-Y homologous gene amelogenin. *International Journal of Legal Medicine, 106,* 190–193.

Reynolds, R., & Varlaro, J. (1996). Gender determination of forensic samples using PCR amplification of ZFX/ZFY gene sequences. *Journal of Forensic Sciences, 41,* 279–286.

Sullivan, K. M., et al. (1993). A rapid and quantitative DNA sex test: fluorescence-based PCR analysis of X-Y homologous gene amelogenin. *BioTechniques, 15,* 637–641.

I. DATA INTERPRETATION

Tschentscher, F., et al. (2008). Amelogenin sex determination by pyrosequencing of short PCR products. *International Journal of Legal Medicine, 122*, 333–335.

Amelogenin Anomalies and Null Alleles

AABB. (2008). *Annual Report Summary for Testing in 2008*. Available at http://www.aabb.org/sa/facilities/Documents/rtannrpt08.pdf. Accessed March 23, 2014.

Alves, C., et al. (2006). The amelogenin locus displays a high frequency of X homologue failures in Sao Tome Island (West Africa). In *Progress in Forensic Genetics 11, ICS 1288* (pp. 271–273).

Cadenas, A. M., et al. (2007). Male amelogenin dropouts: phylogenetic context, origins and implications. *Forensic Science International, 166*, 155–163.

Chang, Y. M., et al. (2007). A distinct Y-STR haplotype for Amelogenin negative males characterized by a large Y(p)11.2 (DYS458-MSY1-AMEL-Y) deletion. *Forensic Science International, 166*, 115–120.

Chen, W., et al. (2014). Detection of the deletion on Yp11.2 in a Chinese population. *Forensic Science International: Genetics, 8*, 73–79.

Davis, C., et al. (2012). A case of amelogenin Y-null: a simple primer binding site mutation or unusual genetic anomaly? *Legal Medicine, 14*, 320–323.

Jobling, M. A., et al. (2007). Structural variation on the short arm of the human Y chromosome: recurrent multigene deletions encompassing Amelogenin Y. *Human Molecular Genetics, 16*(3), 307–316.

Kumagai, R., et al. (2008). DNA analysis of family members with deletion in Yp11.2 region containing amelogenin locus. *Legal Medicine, 10*, 39–42.

Lattanzi, W., et al. (2005). A large interstitial deletion encompassing the *amelogenin* gene on the short arm of the Y chromosome. *Human Genetics, 116*, 395–401.

Maciejewska, A., & Pawlowski, R. (2009). A rare mutation in the primer binding region of the Amelogenin X homologue gene. *Forensic Science International: Genetics, 3*, 265–267.

Mitchell, R. J., et al. (2006). Amelogenin Y negative males: multiple origins. *Progress in Forensic Genetics 11, ICS, 1288*, 274–276.

Mulero, J., et al. (2011). Amelogenin SNP on chromosome X. U.S. Patent Application, US 2011/0237443 A1.

Murphy, K. M., et al. (2007). Constitutional duplication of a region of chromosome Yp encoding AMELY, PRKY, and TBL1Y: implications for sex chromosome analysis and bone marrow engraftment analysis. *Journal of Molecular Diagnostics, 9*, 408–413.

Ou, X., et al. (2012). Null alleles of the X and Y chromosomal amelogenin gene in a Chinese population. *International Journal of Legal Medicine, 126*, 513–518.

Raina, A., et al. (2010). Misinterpretation of results in medico-legal cases due to microdeletion in the Y-chromosome. *Molecular and Cellular Probes, 24*, 418–420.

Santos, F. R., et al. (1998). Reliability of DNA-based sex tests. *Nature Genetics, 18*(2), 103–103.

Shadrach, B., et al. (2004). A rare mutation in the primer binding region of the Amelogenin gene can interfere with gender identification. *Journal of Molecular Diagnostics, 6*(4), 401–405.

Shewale, J. G., et al. (2000). Anomalous amplification of the amelogenin locus typed by AmpFlSTR Profiler Plus amplification kit. *Forensic Science Communications, 2*(4). Available at http://www.fbi.gov/about-us/lab/forensic-science-communications/fsc/oct2000/index.htm/shewale.htm. Accessed March 23, 2014.

Steinlechner, M., et al. (2002). Rare failures in the amelogenin sex test. *International Journal of Legal Medicine, 116*(2), 117–120.

Takayama, T., et al. (2009). Determination of deletion regions from Yp11.2 of an amelogenin negative male. *Legal Medicine, 11*, S578–S580.

Thangaraj, K., et al. (2002). Is the amelogenin gene reliable for gender identification in forensic casework and prenatal diagnosis? *International Journal of Legal Medicine, 116*(2), 121–123.

Turrina, S., et al. (2009). Evaluation of deleted region from Yp11.2 of two amelogenin negative related males. *Forensic Science International: Genetics Supplement Series, 2*, 240–241.

Zehethofer, K., & Rolf, B. (2011). A molecular analysis of three amelogenin negative males in two routine paternity tests. *Forensic Science International: Genetics, 5*, 550–551.

Male Confirmation Markers

Giuliodori, A., et al. (2011). Rapid analysis for confirmation of amelogenin negative males characterized by a Yp11.2 deletion. *Forensic Science International: Genetics Supplement Series, 3,* e285–e286.

Hares, D. R. (2012). Expanding the CODIS core loci in the United States. *Forensic Science International: Genetics, 6,* e52–e54.

Hennessy, L., & Wang, D. (2012). Methods and kits for multiplex amplification of short tandem repeat loci. US Patent Application, US 2012/0122093 A1.

Kastelic, V., et al. (2009). Validation of SRY marker for forensic casework analysis. *Journal of Forensic Sciences, 54,* 551–555.

Oz, C., et al. (2008). A Y-chromosome STR marker should be added to commercial multiplex STR kits. *Journal of Forensic Sciences, 53,* 858–861.

Tozzo, P., et al. (2013). Deletion of amelogenin Y-locus in forensics: literature revision and description of a novel method for sex confirmation. *Journal of Forensic and Legal Medicine, 20,* 387–391.

Underhill, P. A., et al. (1997). Detection of numerous Y chromosome biallelic polymorphisms by denaturing high-performance liquid chromatography. *Genome Research, 7,* 996–1005.

van Oven, M., et al. (2012). A multiplex SNP assay for the dissection of human Y-chromosome haplogroup O representing the major paternal lineage in East and Southeast Asia. *Journal of Human Genetics, 57,* 65–69.

CHAPTER

6

DNA Mixtures

"Don't do mixture interpretation unless you have to."
Peter Gill (Mixture Workshop Conducted in Annapolis, Maryland in July 1998)

GENERAL INFORMATION

DNA mixtures arise when two or more individuals contribute to the sample being tested. Mixtures can be challenging to detect and interpret without extensive experience and careful training. DNA detection technologies have become more sensitive through polymerase chain reaction (PCR) amplification coupled with fluorescent measurements using capillary electrophoresis (CE). This detection sensitivity has improved the ability to see minor components in the DNA profile of mixed samples over that which was available with early DNA methods.

Likewise, the theoretical framework for statistical calculations involved in mixture interpretation has expanded in recent years (e.g. Clayton & Buckleton 2005, Gill et al. 2012). This chapter will focus on mixture detection and evaluation while Chapter 12 will cover statistical approaches to interpreting mixture comparisons to reference profiles. Chapter 13 discusses efforts to cope with allele drop-out that occurs in low-level and complex DNA mixtures.

Determining the Presence of a Mixture

Figure 6.1 provides an example of a DNA mixture from two contributors. This profile is part of the training data set available from (Boston University 2014). It represents the PCR amplification of 1 ng DNA from a two-person mixture (with a 4:1 mixture ratio) using the Identifiler STR kit. In Appendix 4, Dr. Michael Coble, from the National Institute of Standards and Technology (NIST) Applied Genetics Group, explores aspects of this mixture example and approaches for statistical analysis.

Several characteristics of this profile suggest that a DNA mixture is present. First, there are more than two alleles present at multiple loci (e.g. D8S1179 and D21S11). In fact, D2S1338 has four detected alleles. Second, several loci with only two detected alleles (e.g. D5S818 and D7S820) exhibit fairly extreme peak imbalance (peak height ratios of 13% and 17%, respectively), which exceeds typical peak height ratios expected for single-source samples. Third, the amelogenin X and Y alleles are imbalanced, which suggests a male-female mixture with the male as the minor contributor.

Advanced Topics in Forensic DNA Typing: Interpretation
http://dx.doi.org/10.1016/B978-0-12-405213-0.00006-3
2015 Published by Elsevier Inc.

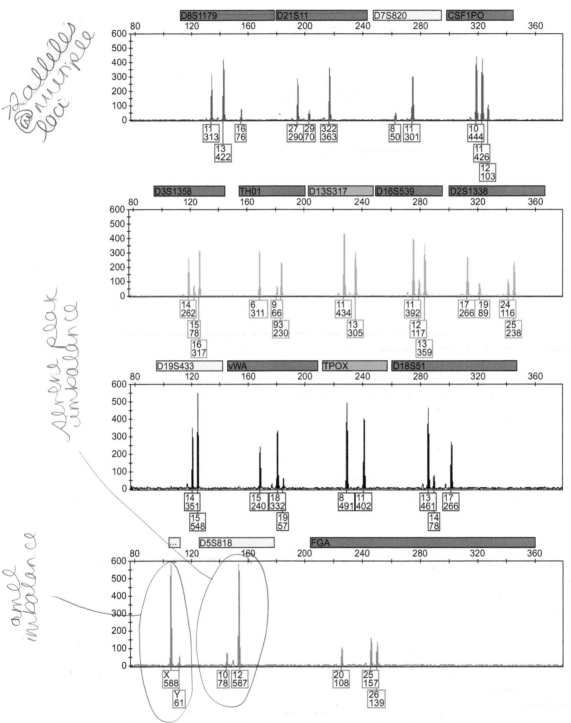

FIGURE 6.1 Example two-person DNA mixture with Identifiler. Output from GeneMapperID-X color codes STR loci names with green (appearance of single-source), yellow (imbalance with two or less peaks), and red (mixture evident). This example is worked in greater detail in Appendix 4. Data courtesy of Robin Cotton and Catherine Grgicak, Boston University.

I. DATA INTERPRETATION

Evaluation of the entire profile, rather than trying to focus on a single locus in isolation, is important for determining the presence of a mixture. In Figure 6.1 three loci have only two alleles, which are fairly well-balanced and if considered in isolation these loci could appropriately fit expected heterozygote peak height ratios (PHRs) for single-source samples. TPOX has a PHR of 81.9%, D13S317 has a PHR of 70.3%, and D19S433 has a PHR of 64.1%. However, this STR profile is clearly a mixture due to the aforementioned imbalances in other two-allele loci and the fact that nine loci exhibit three alleles and D2S1338 has four alleles.

The probability that a mixture will be detected improves with the use of more STR loci and genetic markers that have a high incidence of heterozygotes. Using highly polymorphic STR markers with more possible alleles translates to a greater chance of seeing differences between the two components of a mixture. For example, D18S51 has 73 possible alleles while TPOX only has 19 known alleles (Butler 2012), making D18S51 a more useful marker for detecting mixtures. D2S1338 is one of the most polymorphic loci in the Identifiler STR kit, and thus observing four alleles at this locus in the Figure 6.1 example is not unexpected. However, because D18S51 and D2S1338 are some of the larger-size loci, they may experience allele drop-out on a low-quality or low-quantity evidence sample.

The detectability of multiple DNA sources in a sample relates to the ratio of DNA present from each source, the specific combinations of genotypes, and the total amount of DNA amplified. In other words, some mixtures will not be as easily detectable as other mixtures.

Chromosomal abnormalities do exist and can give rise to extra allele peaks at a particular STR locus as discussed in Chapter 5 with tri-allelic patterns. Chromosomal translocations, somatic mutations, and trisomies may occur in the cells of the donor of a forensic stain. However, the STR profile from the individual with the chromosomal abnormality would most likely show only a single extra peak and the same pattern would be present in both the forensic stain and the reference sample from the matching suspect (Clayton et al. 1998). The rare cases where a chromosomal abnormality is observed can even help strengthen the final conclusions.

An excellent example of a chromosomal abnormality is found in the standard cell line K562. Three peaks are obtained at the D21S11 locus and at least five other STR loci have heterozygous peak patterns that are not balanced. At first glance, this sample might be suspected to have arisen from more than one source rather than a sample with an abnormal number of chromosomes. More than 240 different tri-allelic patterns have been reported spanning the 13 core STR loci used in the United States (NIST STRBase Tri-Allelic Patterns 2014).

Potential Sources of Mixtures

Several potential scenarios can result in a mixture DNA profile where cells from more than one individual are sampled. A vaginal swab following a sexual assault can contain cells from the victim as well as the perpetrator. There may also be residual cells from a prior consensual sexual partner as sperm can survive several days in the vaginal cavity. Likewise, blood or saliva from a perpetrator collected from the surface of a victim's skin is likely to contain cellular material from both the perpetrator and the victim. As will be discussed further, the collection of victim and consensual sexual partner reference samples can help decipher the expected components of a mixture result. With this additional information, it may thus be easier to derive the perpetrator portion of the mixture that can be evidence that a crime was committed.

It is also possible for a single-source sample to be contaminated at the crime scene by police or evidence collection staff or in the laboratory by staff handling the sample. For this reason, reference samples are commonly taken of crime scene investigators, DNA examiners, and people with access to the laboratory. DNA profiles developed from these reference samples then become part of an "elimination database" that can be examined following the observation of a mixture in order to eliminate contamination as a possible reason for the mixture result. Ideally, anyone with legitimate potential exposure to the biological evidence should have a reference sample on file for elimination purposes.

Finally, it has been observed that PCR reagents, tubes, pipet tips, or other plastic disposables used in the DNA testing process may contain contaminating DNA, usually at low levels (Gill & Kirkham 2004, Gefrides et al. 2010). Mixtures may then result when a single-source DNA sample is added to a tube containing a few contaminating cells from the manufacturer. For this reason, best practices encourage manufacturers of disposable plasticware to provide reference samples of employees to compare to any profiles found in negative controls, reagent blanks, or potential contamination mixtures (Gill et al. 2010). When evidentiary material is extremely limited, then a mixture from a few contaminating manufacturer cells becomes more significant.

Types of Mixtures Encountered Most Frequently

As an example of the number of mixture samples encountered in typical casework, a forensic laboratory in Spain reported on casework encountered over the four-year time period of 1997 to 2000 (Torres et al. 2003). Of 1,547 criminal cases involving a total of 2,424 samples, only 163 (6.7% of total samples) showed a mixed profile during this time period. Almost all of the observed mixtures (95%) were two-person mixtures. Only 8 of 163 samples (0.3% of the total 2,424 examined) had DNA profiles that suggested more than two individuals contributed to the biological sample (Torres et al. 2003).

A collection of casework sample data in 2007 and 2008 from 14 laboratories in North America found the majority of mixtures at that time were two-person mixtures (D.N.A. Box 6.1). From a total of 4,541 samples, about 55% were single-source (N = 2,489), 34% were two-person mixtures (N = 1,526), and just over 11% were DNA mixtures with more than two contributors (N = 526).

The types of samples being collected can make a difference in the types of DNA mixtures being observed in the laboratory. An examination of 8,470 casework profiles (either body fluids or trace evidence) from Lyon, France found that 71% were comprised of one contributor, 6% were two-person stains, and 23% were classified as unresolvable mixtures presumably containing more than two contributors (Haned et al. 2011a,b). The trace samples (N = 3,310) had 51% of DNA profiles with more than two contributors compared to the body fluids (N = 5,169) that only had 6% in this category (Haned et al. 2011a,b).

The number of complex mixtures containing more than two contributors has increased in recent years, probably in large measure due to the success of touch DNA evidence in aiding work with burglary cases (Roman et al. 2008). Higher volumes of sample submissions involving poor-quality and low-quantity DNA samples can create backlogs and lead to lower success rates (see Chapter 7 for further discussion).

Alternative Solutions to Avoid Mixture Results

Mixed sample stains are present in many forensic investigations and STR typing procedures have been demonstrated to be an effective means of differentiating components of a mixed sample. However, a case may contain multiple stains and not all of these will be mixtures. In fact, the proportions of a mixture can vary across the forensic stain itself. Thus, if additional samples can be tested that are

D.N.A. BOX 6.1

DATA COLLECTION ON MIXTURE TYPES IN 2007 AND 2008

In order to understand the types of samples and complexity of DNA mixtures that forensic DNA laboratories were processing when the Scientific Working Group on DNA Analysis Methods (SWGDAM) began work on revising the autosomal STR interpretation guidelines, case summary data were collected. From July 2007 to February 2008, Ann Marie Gross of the Minnesota Bureau of Criminal Apprehension, on behalf of the SWGDAM Mixture Interpretation Committee, coordinated the collection of case summary data. Participating forensic DNA laboratories were requested to fill out a spreadsheet with type of sample, type of substrate, quantity of DNA amplified, a minimum number of contributors (1, 2, 3, 4, or >4), if a predominant type or major profile was determined, if statistics were reported, and any comments as needed.

A total of 14 laboratories submitted information on 4780 samples: Centre for Forensic Sciences-Toronto (N = 276), Connecticut State Police (N = 610), Washington State Police (N = 419), Illinois State Police (N = 76), Montana State Crime Laboratory (N = 408), New Jersey State Police (N = 101), Georgia Bureau of Investigation (N = 19), Royal Canadian Mounted Police (N = 1555), U.S. Army Criminal Investigation Laboratory (N = 119), Michigan State Police (N = 225), California Department of Justice (N = 285), Kern County California Crime Lab (N = 31), Anne Arundel County Maryland Police Crime Laboratory (N = 322), and the Minnesota Bureau of Criminal Apprehension (N = 334). Some of the provided sample information was not complete which is why the total number of samples in the

table (N = 4551) differs from the 4780 sample information provided by the participating laboratories. The information in the table is divided by crime classifications: sexual assault, major crime (homicide), and high volume (burglary). Over half of the samples examined were single-source and ≈75% of all reported mixtures involved two contributors. The results of this case sample survey are why the SWGDAM 2010 interpretation guidelines were developed to focus on single-source samples and two-person mixtures.

	Minimum # of contributors					
Crime Class	**1**	**2**	**3**	**4**	**>4**	**N**
Sexual Assault	884	787	145	11	0	1,827
Major Crime	1,261	519	182	32	0	1,994
High Volume	344	220	140	11	5	720
Total	2,489	1,526	467	54	5	4,541
	54.8%	33.6%	10.3%	1.2%	0.1%	

Source: Ann Marie Gross presentation at AAFS Feb 2008 mixture workshop available at http://www.cstl.nist.gov/strbase/training/ AAFS2008_1_CaseworkSurvey.pdf; NIST 2008 poster available at http://www.cstl.nist.gov/strbase/pub_pres/Promega2008poster. pdf; Torres, Y., et al. (2003). DNA mixtures in forensic casework: a 4-year retrospective study. Forensic Science International, 134, 180–186; Clayton, T.M., et al. (1998). Analysis and interpretation of mixed forensic stains using DNA STR profiling. Forensic Science International, 91, 55–70.

easier to interpret, they should be sought after versus complicated mixtures (Gill et al. 1998b). Dr. Peter Gill, who at the time was head of research at the UK Forensic Science Service, provided some of the best advice on DNA mixtures in a workshop he gave in July 1998: "Don't do mixture interpretation unless you have to!"

Differential extraction can help in sexual assault cases to separate perpetrator sperm cells from victim vaginal epithelial cells (see Chapter 2 in Butler 2012). Laser microdissection combined with fluorescent *in-situ* hybridization (see Chapter 1 in Butler 2012) can also aid separation of male and female cells in some instances. Likewise, PCR amplification of Y-chromosome STRs (see Chapter 13 in Butler 2012) can enable differential amplification of male DNA components over female DNA, which may be in excess in biological samples recovered in sexual assault cases.

However, touch DNA samples do not have the same advantages of a physical or biological property that can be used to separate individual components prior to or during PCR amplification.

DNA Advisory Board Comments on DNA Mixtures

The DNA Advisory Board (DAB) was established by the United States Congress to provide guidance to the FBI Laboratory. The DAB issued the initial Quality Assurance Standards for U.S. forensic DNA laboratories. At the end of its five-year term in February 2000, the DAB provided recommendations on statistical and population genetic issues (DAB, 2000). Exerpts from these recommendations related to DNA mixtures are included here. Appendix 3 contains the entire text of the February 2000 document.

Mixtures, which for our purposes are DNA samples derived from two or more contributors, are sometimes encountered in forensic biological evidence. The presence of a mixture is evidenced typically by the presence of three or more peaks, bands, dots, and/or notable differences in intensities of the alleles for at least one locus in the profile. In some situations, elucidation of a contributor profile is straightforward. An example would be the analysis of DNA from an intimate swab revealing a mixture consistent with the composition of the perpetrator and the victim. When intensity differences are sufficient to identify the major contributor in the mixed profile, it can be treated statistically as a single-source sample. At times, when alleles are not masked, a minor contributor to the mixed profile may be elucidated. Almost always in a mixture interpretation, certain possible genotypes can be excluded. It may be difficult to be confident regarding the number of contributors in some complex mixtures of more than two individuals; however, the number of contributors often can be inferred by reviewing the data at all loci in a profile.

Interpretation of genotypes is complicated when the contributions of the donors are approximately equal (i.e. when a major contributor cannot be determined unequivocally) or when alleles overlap. Also, stochastic fluctuation during polymerase chain reaction (PCR) arising from a low quantity of DNA template can make typing of a minor contributor complicated. When the contributors of a DNA mixture profile cannot be distinguished, two calculations [probability of exclusion or likelihood ratio] convey the probative value of the evidence (DAB 2000).

It is useful to keep in mind that at the turn of the century when the DAB issued its recommendations simple two-person mixtures, mostly from sexual assault evidence, were the norm (e.g. Torres et al. 2003). In fact, all of the early theory and processes for DNA mixture interpretation were developed for two-person mixtures rather than more complex ones such as discussed in the next chapter. Therefore, this chapter will focus on principles involved with two-person mixture analysis.

TOOLS FOR MIXTURE INTERPRETATION

STR data obtained in CE electropherograms are a reflection of both the true sample components (i.e. what exists in the original biological sample) and the sample processing involved (Figure 6.2). PCR enables copying the original DNA sample material to a detectable level. However, the PCR amplification process can sometimes distort the allelic components. With low levels of DNA, alleles may fail to be copied due to stochastic variation in primer binding during the early PCR cycles. A primary purpose of validation studies where heterozygote balance (Chapter 4) and stutter ratios (Chapter 3) are characterized is to help establish the limits in accurately conveying true sample component *genotype information* through the sample processing steps for single-source samples. From the available CE electropherogram data, which depicts *decoupled allele information*, the goal of interpretation is to infer possible genotypes and determine the sample components. This task becomes more challenging as the number of contributors to a sample profile increases.

Potential allele overlap can lead to stacking of signal from multiple components. While there are many possible alleles with each STR locus, some alleles are more common than others — and thus more likely to be shared. In Figure 6.2 the true sample component genotypes at D18S51 are 13,17 and 13,14. Thus, the allele 13 is shared between two contributors. The electropherogram data exhibits allele 13 with a signal of 461 relative fluorescence units (RFU). The mixture ratio also impacts the relative allele signal that is produced from the combination of genotypes present in the original sample. Finally, because the total amount of DNA amplified is typically fixed at something like 1 ng (since an analyst will not know *a priori* how many

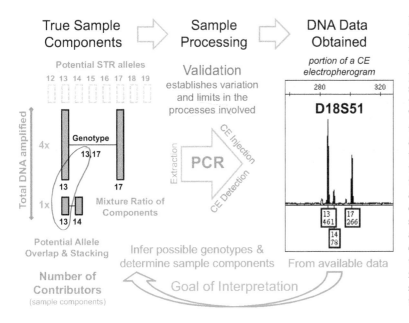

FIGURE 6.2 DNA data obtained in the form of STR peak heights in electropherograms are a reflection of the true sample components and the sample processing involved. Validation studies help establish the expected variation and limits in the processes. These processes include DNA extraction (that impacts the amount of DNA available for testing), PCR amplification (with potential stochastic effects that can unevenly sample elements of the true components) and CE injection and detection (that impact the amount of signal obtained). Aspects of the true sample components that influence the available biological material to be evaluated include the number of contributors, mixture ratio of the components, potential allele overlap and stacking, and the total amount of DNA template amplified.

contributors are present in a sample), the number of contributors (i.e. individual sample components) impact the DNA amount of each contributor.

Determining If a DNA Profile Contains a Mixture

Several clues exist to help determine that a mixture is present. Answers to the following questions can help ascertain the genotypes that make up the composite DNA profile of the mixture:

- Do any of the loci show more than two peaks in the expected allele size range?
- Is there a severe peak height imbalance between heterozygous alleles at a locus?
- Does the stutter product appear abnormally high (e.g. <15% to 20%)?

If the answer to any one of these three questions is yes, then the DNA profile may very well have resulted from a mixed sample. Mixture interpretation has been examined extensively by the Forensic Science Service (Clayton et al. 1998, Gill et al. 1998a, 1998b) and many of their strategies have been incorporated into this chapter's material.

Quantitative Capabilities with Peak Heights

The ability to obtain quantitative information from peaks in an electropherogram using an ABI Genetic Analyzer (see Chapter 2) permits relative peak heights or areas of STR alleles to be measured. This peak information can then be used to decipher the possible genotypes of the contributors to the mixed sample. Due to peak shape variation with slab gel analysis, use of peak areas was originally advocated as being superior to use of peak heights when comparing allele peak information (Gill et al. 1998a). However, STR allele peaks are much more symmetrical on capillary electrophoresis systems and thus peak heights are now more routinely used in most laboratories for mixture interpretation.

Figure 6.3 illustrates how typical single-source samples differ from mixed samples in their STR profiles. STR allele peak patterns for heterozygous samples will generally have stutter products that are less than 15% of the associated allele peak height. In addition, the peak height ratio, as measured by dividing the height of the lower quantity peak in relative fluorescence units by the height of the higher quantity allele peak, should be greater than approximately 60% in a single-source sample (Gill et al. 1997, Gill et al. 2006). Thus, if peaks fall in the region between 15% and 60% of the highest peak at a particular STR locus, a mixed sample that has resulted from two or more contributors is probable. The observation of three or more alleles at multiple loci is also a strong indicator of the presence of a mixture.

Mixture Ratios (Proportion)

A mixture ratio is the relative ratio of the DNA contributions of multiple individuals to a mixed DNA typing result, as determined by the use of quantitative peak height information (SWGDAM 2010). It may also be expressed as a percentage of one contributor in the overall sample mixture.

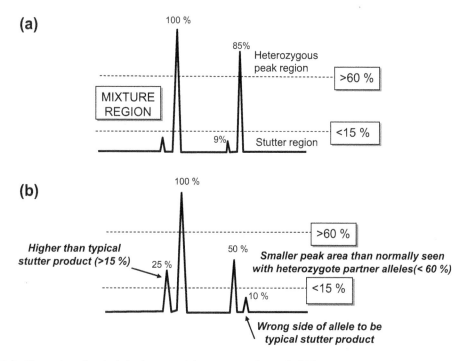

FIGURE 6.3 Illustration of typical single-source (a) versus mixed sample (b) heterozygote peak patterns. The relative peak heights due to the measured fluorescent signal are useful indicators to decipher the presence of a sample mixture. If the highest peak at a locus is set at 100%, then heterozygous alleles in single-source samples should have peak heights that are greater than about 60% of the highest alleles. Stutter products are typically less than 15% of their corresponding allele peak and shorter by four base pairs for tetranucleotide repeats.

As illustrated in Figure 6.2, there is an actual mixture ratio that exists in the true sample components which can only be estimated from relative peak height information in the observed electropherogram data. The deduced mixture proportion(s) can be expressed as a mixture ratio of the sum of peak heights for major alleles over minor alleles or mixture proportion (M_x), which has been referred to as the mass ratio (Wang et al. 2006) (D.N.A. Box 6.2).

Major and Minor Components

The quantity of each component in a mixture makes a difference in the ability to detect all contributors to the mixed sample. For example, if the two DNA sources are in similar quantities they will be much easier to detect than if one is present at only a fraction of the other.

Figure 6.2 illustrates the D18S51 genotype components of the mixture example in Figure 6.1. The 13,17 genotype is approximately four times the amount of the 13,14 genotype. The genotype in higher quantity is commonly called the "major" component and the genotype in the small quantity is called the "minor" component. The minor component of a mixture is usually not detectable for mixture ratios below the 5% level or 1:20. When the minor component is at a low level it is subject to stochastic effects that will be discussed in greater detail in the next chapter.

D.N.A. BOX 6.2

MIXTURE PROPORTION AND MIXTURE RATIO

With two-person mixtures, it is easiest to calculate a mixture proportion (M_x) or mixture ratio (M_R) by examining peak heights in STR loci with four alleles. The only locus in Figure 6.1 that has four alleles is D2S1338 (see figure insert). It may also be possible to calculate the M_x by using a three-allele locus where a high homozygote is present with two smaller alleles that can be assumed to be a heterozygous minor contributor genotype.

$$M_R = \frac{\varphi_{17} + \varphi_{25}}{\varphi_{19} + \varphi_{24}} = \frac{266 + 238}{89 + 116} = 2.46$$

$$M_x = \frac{\varphi_{17} + \varphi_{25}}{\varphi_{17} + \varphi_{25} + \varphi_{19} + \varphi_{24}}$$

$$= \frac{266 + 238}{266 + 238 + 89 + 116} = 0.711 = 71\%$$

In the equations, lower-case Greek letter phi (φ) represents peak height. The peak heights for alleles in the major component were put in the numerator. The calculation can also be done for the minor contributor, but it is typically easier to think in terms of the amount of the major contributor. This example is also discussed in Appendix 4 (see Table A4.1).

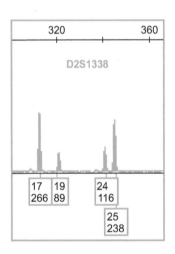

Impact of Allele Sharing

Usually a mixture is first identified by the presence of three or more prominent peaks at one or more loci. At a single locus, a sample containing DNA from two sources can exhibit one, two, three, or four peaks due to the possible genotype combinations listed below and illustrated in Figure 6.4. Table 6.1 displays the various genotype combinations using P, Q, R, and S as possible alleles.

When two contributors to a mixed stain share one or more alleles, the alleles are "masked" (i.e. covered up) and the contributing genotypes may not be easily decipherable. For example, if two

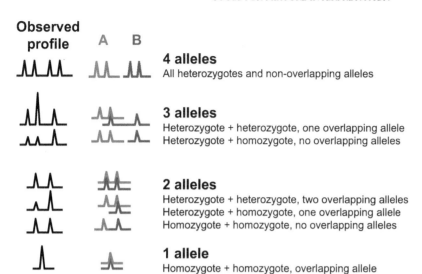

Observed profile A B

4 alleles
All heterozygotes and non-overlapping alleles

3 alleles
Heterozygote + heterozygote, one overlapping allele
Heterozygote + homozygote, no overlapping alleles

2 alleles
Heterozygote + heterozygote, two overlapping alleles
Heterozygote + homozygote, one overlapping allele
Homozygote + homozygote, no overlapping alleles

1 allele
Homozygote + homozygote, overlapping allele

FIGURE 6.4 With mixtures containing DNA from two contributors, each individual STR locus can exhibit 1, 2, 3, or 4 different alleles. There are a total of 14 different combinations of homozygotes and heterozygotes not considering the reciprocal possibilities (see Table 6.1). Hypothetical results from individual A are in red with individual B results in blue. In this example, the observed profile reflects relative peak height changes that would occur with allele stacking due to shared alleles and a 1:1 mixture ratio.

TABLE 6.1 Possible Genotype Combinations with Two-Person Mixtures Organized by the Number of Observed Alleles at a Locus

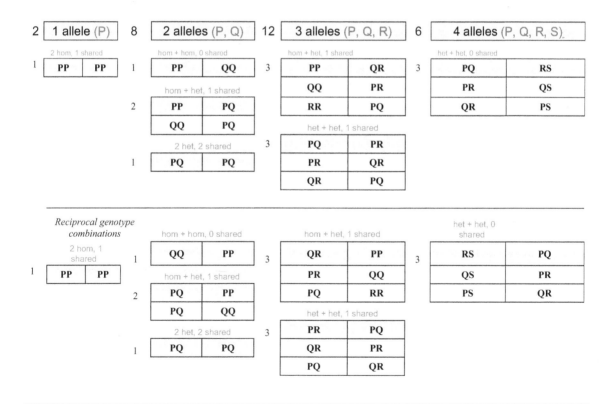

As illustrated in Figure 6.4, there are a total of 14 different genotype pairs of combinations of homozgyotes (hom) and heterozygotes (het). Below the line are the reciprocal genotype combinations when contributor order is important. Adapted from Overson (2009).

individuals at the FGA locus have genotypes 23,24 and 24,24, then a mixture ratio of 1:1 will produce a ratio of 1:3 for the 23:24 peak areas. In this particular case, the mixture could be interpreted as a homozygous allele with a large stutter product without further information. However, by examining the STR profiles at other loci that have unshared alleles, i.e. three or four peaks per locus, an analyst may be able to dissect or "deconvolute" this sample properly into its components.

In an effort to see whether it was possible for masking to occur at every locus in a multiplex, the Forensic Science Service conducted a simulated-mixture study with 120,000 individual STR profiles in their Caucasian database (Gill et al. 1997). This study found that the vast majority of these artificial mixtures showed 15 to 22 peaks across a 6-plex STR assay. The maximum number in a mixture of two heterozygous individuals with no overlapping alleles at six STRs would be 24 peaks. Thus, in this example with unrelated individuals, simple mixtures can be identified by the presence of three or more alleles at several loci. Out of more than 212,000 pairwise comparisons, there were only four examples where one or two alleles were observed at each locus in the 6-plex, and these could be designated mixtures because of peak imbalances (Gill et al. 1997).

The ability to confidently estimate the number of contributors goes down as the mixture becomes more complex (see Chapter 7).

German Classification Scheme for Mixtures

The German Stain Commission, which is composed of leaders from Institutes of Legal Medicine in Germany, proposed use of a simple classification system for mixture types (Schneider et al. 2009). This system also discusses how to handle the various types of mixtures from a statistical analysis point-of-view. This German classification scheme focuses on two-person mixtures and is based on earlier work by Tim Clayton and John Buckleton (Clayton & Buckleton 2005).

The three German mixture categories are Type A (where there is no obvious major contributor and no evidence of stochastic effects), Type B (where there is a clearly distinguishable major and minor and no stochastic effects), and Type C (where mixtures have no major contributor(s) and there is evidence of stochastic effects) (D.N.A. Box 6.3). The SWGDAM 2010 guidelines calls Type A mixtures "indistinguishable," Type B mixtures "distinguishable," and Type C mixtures "uninterpretable."

ELEMENTS OF MIXTURE INTERPRETATION

Mixture interpretation involves *interpretation of alleles and possible genotypes* from contributors followed by an *assessment of the statistical weight of evidence* if an association between the evidence DNA profile and the suspect's DNA profile can be made. With some two-person mixtures involving a major and a minor profile, it may be possible to reliably decipher the genotypes of the individual contributors at each tested genetic marker through a mixture deconvolution process. Good practice is driven by well-written protocols and a correct understanding of principles involved.

D.N.A. BOX 6.3

MIXTURE CLASSIFICATION SCHEME FROM THE GERMAN STAIN COMMISSION

Several years ago the German Stain Commission, a group of scientists from Germany's Institutes of Legal Medicine, developed a three-part classification scheme for DNA mixtures. Simple examples of what a Type A (no major contributor), Type B (major and minor contributors distinguishable), or Type C (low level DNA with stochastic effects) mixture might look like at a single STR locus are shown below:

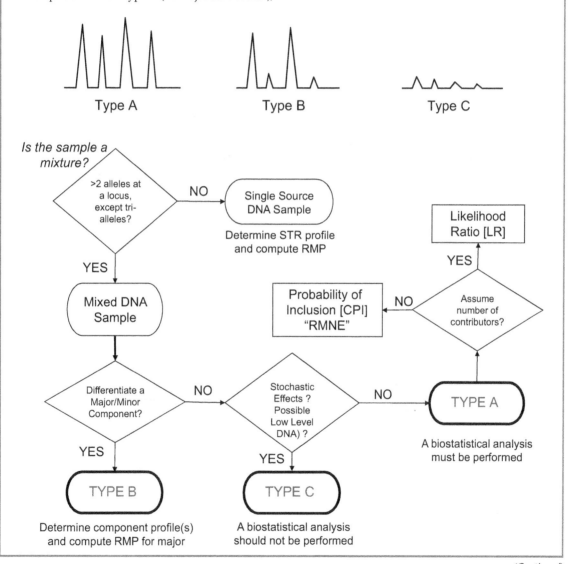

D.N.A. BOX 6.3—(cont'd)

Type A mixtures require a biostatistical analysis that can be performed with a likelihood ratio (LR) or combined probabiilty of inclusion (CPI), which is also known as random man not excluded (RMNE). Type B mixtures can be deconvoluted into the major and minor components, usually if they are present with consistent peak height ratios of approximately 4:1. The major component following deconvolution can be treated as a single-source profile with a random match probability (RMP) being calculated. For Type C mixtures, where all alleles may not be seen due to allele drop-out, a biostatistical interpretation is not appropriate, and a clear decision about whether to include or exclude a suspect may be difficult to reach.

Depending on laboratory interpretation thresholds, the DNA mixture in Figure 6.1 would probably be classified as a Type B or a Type C mixture. A mixture classification flowchart is shown on the previous page based on the three types of mixtures.

Source: Schneider, P.M., et al. (2009). The German Stain Commission: recommendations for the interpretation of mixed stains. International Journal of Legal Medicine, 123, 1–5. [Originally published in German in Rechtsmedizin (2006) 16:401–404].

Mixture Solving Strategies

This next section will review the principles described by Gill et al. (1998b) and Clayton et al. (1998) for interpreting mixed forensic stains using STR typing results. Seven primary steps for interpreting mixtures are outlined in Figure 6.5. The interpretation steps are discussed in the context of Figure 6.1, which is covered in more detail in the worked example shown in Appendix 4.

An understanding of how non-mixtures behave is essential to being able to proceed with mixture interpretation. Mixed DNA profiles need to be interpreted against a background of biological and technological artifacts. Chapter 3 and Chapter 4 discussed some of the prominent biological artifacts that exist for STR markers. These include stutter products and null alleles. In addition, chromosomal abnormalities, such as tri-allelic (three-banded) patterns resulting from trisomy (the presence of three chromosomes instead of the normal two) or duplication of specific chromosomal regions can occur. In addition, non-specific amplification products can occasionally occur and must be considered prior to making an attempt to decipher a mixed profile.

Stutter products represent the greatest challenge in confidently interpreting a mixture and designating the appropriate alleles. It is not always possible to exclude stutters since they are allelic products and differ from their associated allele by a single repeat unit. The general guideline for stutter identification of one repeat unit less than the corresponding allele and less than 15% of that allele's peak area is typically a useful one and can be used to mark suspected stutter products. The introduction of pentanucleotide repeat markers with stutter products of less than 1% or 2% has greatly simplified mixture interpretation for these loci (Bacher et al. 1999; Krenke et al. 2002).

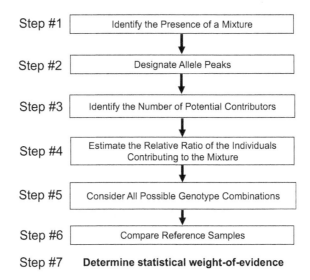

Step #1	Identify the Presence of a Mixture
Step #2	Designate Allele Peaks
Step #3	Identify the Number of Potential Contributors
Step #4	Estimate the Relative Ratio of the Individuals Contributing to the Mixture
Step #5	Consider All Possible Genotype Combinations
Step #6	Compare Reference Samples
Step #7	**Determine statistical weight-of-evidence**

FIGURE 6.5 Steps in mixture interpretation. Adapted from Clayton et al. (1998).

After a mixture has been identified as such and all of the alleles have been called, the next step (Figure 6.5, step #3) is to identify the number of potential contributors. For a two-person mixture, the maximum number of alleles at any given locus is four if both individuals are heterozygous and there is no allele overlap. Thus, if more than four alleles are observed at a locus then a complex mixture consisting of more than two individuals is possible. In the past, the overwhelming majority of mixtures encountered in forensic casework involved two-person mixtures (Clayton et al. 1998).

Mixtures can range from equal proportions of each component to one component being greatly in excess. The varying proportions of a mixture are usually referred to in a ratio format (e.g. 1:1 or 1:5). Mixtures of known quantities of DNA templates have shown that the mixture ratio is approximately preserved during PCR amplification (Gill et al. 1998a, Perlin & Szabady 2001). Thus, the peak areas and heights observed in an electropherogram can in most cases be related back to the amount of DNA template components included in the mixed sample.

An approximate mixture ratio can be best determined by considering the profile as a whole and looking at all of the information from each locus. The ratio of mixture components is most easily determined when there are no shared alleles at a locus. Thus, it is best to first examine loci with four alleles as a starting point for estimating the relative ratio of the two individuals contributing to the mixture. Determining the ratio when there are shared alleles is more complex because there may be more than one possible combination of alleles that could explain the observed peak patterns (Clayton et al. 1998).

The possible combinations of alleles for two-, three-, and four-allele peak patterns are illustrated in Figure 6.4. For four alleles at a locus, there are three possible pairwise comparisons that exist, if one does not worry about the reciprocal cases, i.e. which allele combinations belong to the minor

TABLE 6.2   Possible Amelogenin X and Y Allele Peak Height Ratios with Varying Quantities of DNA

| Mixture ratio | | Allele combination | | Ratio of X:Y peak heights |
Female (X,X)	Male (X,Y)	X	Y	X:Y
20	1	41	1	41:1
10	1	21	1	21:1
5	1	11	1	11:1
4	1	9	1	9:1
3	1	7	1	7:1
2	1	5	1	5:1
1	1	3	1	3:1
1	2	4	2	2:1
1	3	5	3	1.7:1
1	4	6	4	1.5:1
1	5	7	5	1.4:1
1	10	12	10	1.2:1
1	20	22	20	1.1:1

In Figure 6.1, the amelogenin X:Y peak height ratio (588 RFU: 61 RFU) is 9.6, which suggests that the relative ratio of female (major) to male (minor) is approximately 4:1.

contributor and which belong to the major contributor. For three alleles at a locus, there are six possible pairwise combinations, and for two alleles at a locus there are four possible pairwise combinations (Table 6.1).

Amelogenin, the sex-typing marker, is an effective marker for deciphering the contributions of genetically normal male and female individuals. The predicted X and Y allele peak ratios for a number of possible male and female mixture ratios are listed in Table 6.2. The amelogenin X and Y peak areas are especially useful in determining whether the major contributor to the mixture is male or female.

The next step in examining a mixture is to consider all possible genotype combinations at each locus (Figure 6.5, step #5). Peaks representing the allele calls at each locus are labeled with the designations P, Q, R, and so forth. The possible pairwise combinations from Table 6.1 are considered using the peak heights for each called allele. Each particular combination of alleles at the different loci is considered in light of the information determined previously regarding the mixture ratio for the sample under investigation (step #4). By stepping through each STR locus in this manner, the genotypes of the major and minor contributors to the mixture can be deciphered. In the example shown in Appendix 4 some of these calculations are demonstrated. Table 6.3 illustrates the possible major and minor genotypes for the D18S51 locus in Figure 6.1.

Many times specific combinations of genotypes can be eliminated or restricted due to the possible allele pair not meeting the expected levels of heterozygote balance or the needed mixture ratio for an

TABLE 6.3   Possible Genotype Combinations with D18S51
Data from Figure 6.1 Assuming Two Contributors

If the major genotype is	then the minor genotype is...
13,13	14,17
13,14	17,17 *or* 13,17 *or* 14,17
13,17	14,14 *or* **13,14** *or* 14,17
14,14	13,17
14,17	13,13 *or* 13,14 *or* 13,17
17,17	13,14

There are 12 possible genotype combinations with three alleles (see Table 6.1). Use of peak height information can help eliminate many of these possibilities. Making assumptions regarding mixture ratios can eliminate some other possibilities. In this situation with a 4:1 mixture, the correct genotypes are 13,17 for the major contributor and 13,14 for the minor contributor (shown in bold font).

overall STR profile. A restricted approach utilizes peak height information to help deconvolve a mixture (D.N.A. Box 6.4).

The sixth step in the interpretation of a mixture is to compare the resultant genotype profiles for the possible components of the mixture with the genotypes of reference samples (Figure 6.5, step #6). This is also known as the question-to-known (Q-to-K) profile comparison. In a sexual assault case, this reference sample could be the suspect and/or the victim. If the DNA profile from the suspect's reference sample matches the major or minor component of the mixture, then that person cannot be eliminated as a possible contributor to the mixed stain (Clayton et al. 1998).

Finally, with Q-to-K comparisons where the known profile cannot be excluded, a statistical weight-of-evidence is generated to provide context to the association being made. Chapter 12 will discuss several statistical approaches that can be taken.

RESOURCES AND GUIDANCE ON MIXTURE INTERPRETATION

ISFG 2006 and SWGDAM 2010 Recommendations

In July 2006, the DNA Commission of the International Society of Forensic Genetics (ISFG) published nine recommendations covering mixture interpretation principles (Gill et al. 2006). The DNA Commission endorsed the mixture interpretation steps covered in this chapter that were published in 1998 by the Forensic Science Service (Clayton et al. 1998). Since a number of prominent

---

D.N.A. BOX 6.4

UNRESTRICTED VERSUS RESTRICTED GENOTYPE COMBINATIONS

An *unrestricted* approach considers all combinations of genotypes possible because relative peak height differences are not utilized. It is as though all of the allele peaks are the same height in the electropherogram. With data near the limit of detection or where stochastic effects may cause allele drop-out, the ability to confidently eliminate some genotype possibilities may be reduced.

Quantitative data from allele peak heights can be used in some cases to eliminate possible genotype combinations (see figure). A *restricted* approach eliminates some of the possible genotype combinations based on relative peak heights. Alleles are paired into potential genotypes only where specific combinations are deemed possible using relative peak height information and validated heterozygote balance and stutter ratio ranges. The ability to restrict genotype combinations of possible contributors is based on assumptions made regarding the number of contributors, consideration of quantitative peak height information, and inference of contributor mixture ratios (SWGDAM 2010).

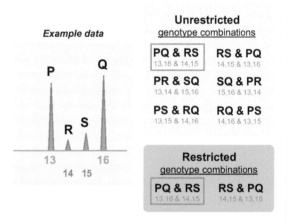

Figure caption: Example data exhibits what appears to be a PQ (13,16) major and a RS (14,15) minor. An unrestricted approach generates six possible genotype combinations, many of which are unreasonable in terms of heterozygote balance (e.g. PR and SQ). The restricted approach eliminates combinations that do have have reasonable heterozygote balance. Mixture ratio information, based on data from multiple loci, could also be used to help eliminate and restrict possible genotype combinations.

---

statisticians were part of this paper, these recommendations favor use of likelihood ratios (Evett et al. 1991, Weir et al. 1997).

Published support for the principles underlying the ISFG recommendations has come from the European DNA Profiling Group (EDNAP) and the European Network of Forensic Science Institutes (ENFSI) DNA working group (Morling et al. 2007), the UK DNA working group (Gill et al. 2008), an FBI-led mixture committee (Budowle et al. 2009), Australian and New Zealand forensic leadership (Stringer et al. 2009), and the German Stain Commission (Schneider et al. 2009). Further guidance on the use of probabilistic genotyping for statistical analysis of DNA mixtures having the potential of allele drop-out and drop-in was published by the ISFG DNA Commission in December 2012 (Gill et al. 2012). This material will be discussed in Chapter 13.

In January 2010 SWGDAM approved interpretation guidelines covering autosomal STR markers with guidance on mixture interpretation (SWGDAM 2010). Among other topics, these guidelines emphasized the importance of using a stochastic threshold in conjunction with a combined probability of inclusion statistical approach. Table 6.4 compares the ISFG 2006 recommendations for mixtures with sections of the SWGDAM 2010 guidelines that cover the same areas.

Software for Deciphering Mixture Components

Computer programs can be used to aid the process of deciphering mixture components and determining mixture ratios. Many laboratories have created their own spreadsheet programs to perform calculations needed in mixture interpretation.

A linear mixture analysis approach can derive estimated mixture ratios from quantitative STR peak information that are similar to known input mixture proportions (Perlin & Szabady 2001). This approach combined with probabilistic genotyping is the basis of the TrueAllele program from Cybergenetics (Perlin et al. 2011). Researchers at the University of Tennessee developed a least-squares deconvolution approach to decipher mixture components in an automated fashion (Wang et al. 2006). The UK Forensic Science Service developed a program named PENDULUM that evaluated potential genotype combinations with mixture ratios and heterozygote peak height balance to restrict possible genotypes (Bill et al. 2005). GeneMapper*ID-X* has a mixture analysis tool (Oldroyd & Shade 2008) that has been evaluated by researchers in Norway (Hansson & Gill 2011). A researcher at the U.S. Army Criminal Investigation Laboratory (USACIL) created a spreadsheet program called DNA_DataAnalysis (Overson 2009) that has been commercialized by NicheVision Forensics into Armed Xpert™ (2014). Other software tools for mixture deconvolution and statistical analysis are also listed on the STRBase website (NIST STRBase Mixture Information 2014).

Interlaboratory Studies

Five exploratory interlaboratory studies assessing DNA mixtures have been conducted by NIST over the time period of 1997 to 2013 (D.N.A. Box 6.5). Interlaboratory studies provide an interesting window into the practices and protocols under use at the time of a study. In addition, results from these studies expand the view of the community beyond each laboratory's focus on their own protocol and analyst performance.

STRBase Website and Training Materials

Since the NIST MIX05 interlaboratory study identified a large variability in DNA mixture interpretation results, a great deal of effort has gone into training and informing the community (NIST MIX05 2005). Over 50 workshops and presentations have been given by the author and NIST colleagues (Table 6.5). Our understanding of mixture interpretation has grown over the years and evolved with experiences in teaching the principles involved.

A few years ago a mixture section was established as part of the NIST STRBase website (NIST STRBase Mixture Information 2014). This website contains workshop materials and presentations given to help with mixture training, a listing of available software programs, and literature references.

TABLE 6.4   The DNA Commission of the International Society for Forensic Genetics (ISFG) 2006 Recommendations on DNA Mixture Interpretation (Gill et al. 2006) Are Compared with Corresponding Portions of the SWGDAM 2010 Guidelines (SWGDAM 2010)

ISFG (2006) recommendations	SWGDAM (2010) guidelines
Recommendation 1: The likelihood ratio is the preferred approach to mixture interpretation. The RMNE (probability of exclusion) approach is restricted to DNA profiles where the profiles are unambiguous. If the DNA crime stain profile is low level and some minor alleles are the same size as stutters of major alleles, and/or if drop-out is possible, then the RMNE method may not be conservative.	**4. Statistical Analysis of DNA Typing Results** In forensic DNA testing, calculations are performed on evidentiary DNA profiles that are established as relevant in the context of the case to aid in the assessment of the significance of an inclusion. These calculations are based on the random match probability (RMP), the likelihood ratio (LR), or the combined probability of exclusion/inclusion (CPE/CPI). **4.1.** The laboratory must perform statistical analysis in support of any inclusion that is determined to be relevant in the context of a case, irrespective of the number of alleles detected and the quantitative value of the statistical analysis.
Recommendation 2: Even if the legal system does not implicitly appear to support the use of the likelihood ratio, it is recommended that the scientist is trained in the methodology and routinely uses it in case notes, advising the court in the preferred method before reporting the evidence in line with the court requirements. The scientific community has a responsibility to support improvement of standards of scientific reasoning in the courtroom.	No equivalent guideline.
Recommendation 3: The methods to calculate likelihood ratios of mixtures (not considering peak area) described by Evett et al. (*J. Forensic Sci. Soc.* 1991;31:41–47) and Weir et al. (*J. Forensic Sci.* 1997;42:213–222) are recommended.	The Evett et al. (1991) and Weir et al. (1997) references are included in section 7 (Additional Suggested Readings). **5.4.2.3** Additional formulae for restricted and unrestricted LRs can be found in Fung and Hu (2008).
Recommendation 4: If peak height or area information is used to eliminate various genotypes from the unrestricted combinatorial method, this can be carried out by following a sequence of guidelines based on Clayton et al. (*Forensic Sci. Int.* 1998; 91:55-70).	The Clayton et al. 1998 reference is included in section 7 (Additional Suggested Readings).

Recommendation 5: The probability of the evidence under H_p is the province of the prosecution and the probability of the evidence under H_d is the province of the defense. The prosecution and defense both seek to maximize their respective probabilities of the evidence profile. To do this both H_p and H_d require propositions. There is no reason why multiple pairs of propositions may not be evaluated.	**5.4.2.** The calculation of the LR in a mixture is dependent upon the evidence profile, the comparison reference profile(s), and the individual hypotheses.
Recommendation 6: If the crime profile is a major/minor mixture, where minor alleles are the same size (height or area) as stutters of major alleles, then stutters and minor alleles are indistinguishable. Under these circumstances alleles in stutter positions that do not support H_p should be included in the assessment.	**3.5.8.3.** If a peak is at or below [a laboratory's established stutter percentage expectation], it is generally designated as a stutter peak. However, it should also be considered as a possible allelic peak, particularly if the peak height of the potential stutter peak(s) is consistent with (or greater than) the heights observed for any allelic peaks that are conclusively attributed (i.e. peaks in non-stutter positions) to the minor contributor(s).
Recommendation 7: If drop-out of an allele is required to explain the evidence under H_p: ($S = ab$; $E = a$), then the allele should be small enough (height/area) to justify this. Conversely, if a full crime stain profile is obtained where alleles are well above the background level, and the probability of drop-out approaches $Pr(D) \approx 0$, then H_p is not supported.	No equivalent guideline.
Recommendation 8: If the alleles of certain loci in the DNA profile are at a level that is dominated by background noise, then a biostatistical interpretation for these alleles should not be attempted.	No equivalent guideline.
Recommendation 9: In relation to low copy number, stochastic effects limit the usefulness of heterozygous balance and mixture proportion estimates. In addition, allelic drop-out and allelic drop-in (contamination) should be taken into consideration of any assessment.	[from Preamble] …this document is not intended to address the interpretation of analytical results from enhanced low template DNA techniques.

I. DATA INTERPRETATION

D.N.A. BOX 6.5

NIST INTERLABORATORY STUDIES INVOLVING DNA MIXTURES

Over the past two decades, the National Institute of Standards and Technology (NIST) has conducted 13 exploratory interlaboratory studies addressing DNA typing issues. Five of these studies (see table below) have dealt with DNA mixtures. Interlaboratory studies involve multiple labs examining the same samples or data to look for consistencies or differences in results, trends in laboratory practice, and potential opportunities for further training and reference material development. Mixed stain study 1 (MSS1) was conducted from April 1997 through November 1997 and focused on assessing how well participating laboratories could determine donor types given a complete set of reference sources. Data from MSS2 was collected from January 1999 to May 1999 with a focus on evaluating donor types given an incomplete set of references. The impact of DNA quantitation was also explored. MSS3, which ran from December 2000 to October 2001, examined the effect of DNA quantitation on STR typing performance.

These interlaboratory studies provide a brief snapshot in laboratory technology, methods, and practices used at the time of the study. For example, while only 20% of MSS1 participants used the ABI 310 single-capillary instrument, this number jumped to 47% of MSS2 and 72% of MSS3 participants as more laboratories moved to STR typing with capillary electrophoresis. Since there are inherent laboratory differences in DNA quantitation, PCR amplification, and instrument detection sensitivity, the MIX05 and MIX13 studies have only involved data interpretation based on supplied .fsa files from DNA mixtures

created at NIST with commonly used STR kits. Data files were then posted on the STRBase website for laboratories to download and test. This data-only approach significantly reduces the costs and logistics of preparing, packaging, and mailing DNA samples to participating laboratories. DNA samples were prepared with Profiler Plus, COfiler, SGM Plus, Identifiler, and Power-Plex 16 data for MIX05 and only Identifiler and PowerPlex 16 data for MIX13. These data sets reflect the STR kits in general use at the time the studies were conducted. A primary goal of MIX05 was to evaluate the "lay of the land" in order to determine future needs for training and tools for better mixture interpretation. Due to the wide range of variation seen within and among MIX05 participating laboratories, extensive mixture training has been conducted since 2005 (see Table 6.5). An important purpose of the MIX13 results was to examine whether consistency in mixture interpretation has improved across North America since the publication of the 2010 SWGDAM guidelines on autosomal STR interpretation. The MIX13 results were presented at the Technical Leader Summit held in Norman, Oklahoma in November 2013. A publication describing these results is planned.

Year (study)	# Labs	What was supplied
1997 (MSS1)	22	Mixed buffy coat cells on paper; six single-source, four two-person, one three-person (stains on paper).

Year (study)	# Labs	What was supplied
1999 (MSS2)	45	Bloodstains & semen on cotton cloth; Part A: four single-source, one two-person, one three-person (stains on paper); Part B: one two-person mixture at five different concentrations.
2001 (MSS3)	74	Extracted DNA samples supplied; one single-source, five two-person, one three-person (all extracts).
2005 (MIX05)	69	Electronic data supplied (covering five STR kits) mimicking sexual assault evidence; four two-person mixtures (all unrelated, male/female, various major/minor ratios).

Year (study)	# Labs	What was supplied
2013 (MIX13)	108	Electronic data (covering two STR kits) and case scenarios supplied mimicking sexual assault and touch evidence; five cases (two-, three-, >three-person; relatives, low-template, inclusion/exclusion).

Sources: *http://www.cstl.nist.gov/strbase/interlab.htm; Duewer, D.L., et al. (2001). NIST Mixed Stain Studies #1 and #2: interlaboratory comparison of DNA quantification practice and short tandem repeat multiplex performance with multiple-source samples.* Journal of Forensic Sciences, 46, 1199–1210; *Kline, M.C., et al. (2003). NIST mixed stain study 3: DNA quantitation accuracy and its influence on short tandem repeat multiplex signal intensity.* Analytical Chemistry, 75, 2463–2469; *Duewer, D.L., et al. (2004). NIST Mixed Stain Study #3: signal intensity balance in commercial short tandem repeat multiplexes,* Analytical Chemistry, 76, 6928–6934; *http://www.cstl.nist. gov/strbase/interlab/MIX05.htm; http://www.cstl.nist.gov/ strbase/interlab/MIX13.htm.*

TABLE 6.5   Summary of 51 DNA Mixture Workshops and Presentations Given by the Author or NIST Colleagues to More Than 7,000 Attendees Since 2005

Date	Meeting	Location	#Attendees (approximate)
27–28 September 2005	ISHI 2005 poster presentation	Grapevine, TX	poster
30 September 2005	ISHI 2005 HITA workshop	Grapevine, TX	70
20 February 2006	AAFS 2006	Seattle, WA	200
6 June 2006	NYC OCME training	New York City, NY	120
7 August 2006	MN BCA training	St. Paul, Mn	35
23 October 2006	CODIS Conference talk	Arlington, VA	400
5–6 December 2006	NJSP training	Hamilton, NJ	100
3–4 April 2007	Houston PD training	Houston, TX	50
11 September 2007	SAFS workshop	Atlanta, GA	50

(Continued)

I. DATA INTERPRETATION

TABLE 6.5 Summary of 51 DNA Mixture Workshops and Presentations Given by the Author or NIST Colleagues to More Than 7,000 Attendees Since 2005 (*cont'd*)

Date	Meeting	Location	#Attendees (approximate)
2–3 November 2007	NEAFS workshop	Bolton Landing, NY	40
19 February 2008	AAFS 2008	Washington, DC	200
10 April 2008	CE Users' Group	Ammendale, MD	40
25 April 2008	Virginia criminal defense seminar	Richmond, VA	650
12–13 May 2008	Florida statewide training	Indian Rocks Beach, FL	80
11 November 2008	CODIS Conference workshop	Crystal City, VA	350
23 January 2009	AFDIL training	Rockville, MD	20
27–28 January 2009	Harris County Texas training	Houston, TX	80
25 March 2009	NYC OCME training	New York City, NY	150
7 April 2009	Towson University class	Towson, MD	25
12 May 2009	Wisconsin DNA training	Milwaukee, WI	75
13–14 May 2009	Utah DNA training	Salt Lake City, UT	40
20 May 2009	NDAA lawyer training	Columbia, SC	50
20–24 July 2009	FIU DNA workshop	Miami, FL	15
22 September 2009	NWAFS workshop	Ft. Collins, CO	30
15 October 2009	ISHI TL session	Las Vegas, NV	50
29 October 2009	George Washington University	Washington, DC	40
11 October 2010	ISHI 2010 Mixture workshop	San Antonio, TX	200
22 February 2011	AAFS 2011 Mixture workshop	Chicago, IL	220
15–17 March 2011	NFSTC mixture workshop	Largo, FL	120
28 March 2011	Indiana State Police training	Indianapolis, IN	65
12 April 2011	Maryland DNA training	Pikesville, MD	60
26–27 April 2011	Florida DNA training	Palm Beach, FL	50
9–10 May 2011	Texas DNA training	Houston, TX	50
16–17 May 2011	Michigan DNA training	Lansing, MI	50
6–7 June 2011	Arizona DNA training	Mesa, AZ	50
1–3 August 2011	Hawaii DNA training	Honolulu, HI	10
3 October 2011	ISHI 2011 mixture workshop	Washington, DC	160
25 October 2011	CAC fall meeting	Sacramento, CA	100
18 April 2012	New York/New Jersey	New York City, NY	150
8 May 2012	Canada/RCMP training	Vancouver, BC	40

I. DATA INTERPRETATION

TABLE 6.5 Summary of 51 DNA Mixture Workshops and Presentations Given by the Author or NIST Colleagues to More Than 7,000 Attendees Since 2005 (*cont'd*)

Date	Meeting	Location	#Attendees (approximate)
6–7 June 2012	Taiwan DNA training	Taipei, Taiwan	60
20 June 2012	NIJ Conference mini-workshop	Crystal City, VA	150
13 September 2012	Washington State Patrol training	Seattle, WA	50
25 September 2012	MAFS workshop	Milwaukee, WI	50
15 October 2012	ISHI 2012 mixture workshop	Nashville, TN	120
12 April 2013	**NIST webcast**	Gaithersburg, MD	1100
18 April 2013	NACDL post-Conviction conference	Charlotte, NC	120
7 June 2013	ABA Fordham Law School talk	New York City, NY	150
2–3 Sept 2013	ISFG 2013 workshops	Melbourne, Australia	100
20–21 Nov 2013	**Technical Leaders' Summit**	Norman, OK	550
21 February 2014	AAFS 2014 talk	Seattle, WA	400

Feedback was collected from some meeting participants through audience response systems or written surveys. Slides and handouts are available on the NIST STRBase website (see http://www.cstl.nist.gov/strbase/NISTpub.htm or http://www.cstl.nist.gov/strbase/mixture.htm).

A number of the workshops were conducted in collaboration with Dr. Michael Coble from the NIST Applied Genetics Group, Boston University researchers Dr. Robin Cotton and Dr. Catherine Grgicak, and independent consultant Dr. Charlotte Word. Boston University received a training grant from the National Institute of Justice that funded the workshops performed in 2010, 2011, and 2012. In addition, Boston University (BU) has created a training website (Boston University DNA Mixture Training 2014) with about a dozen lessons that take a student through the various steps of mixture interpretation. The BU website also contains more than 2,700 .fsa files with single-source, two-person, three-person, and four-person mixtures at different mixture ratios and DNA amounts that can be downloaded and used in training programs.

COMPLICATING FACTORS IN MIXTURE DECONVOLUTION

Two of the primary complicating factors in deciphering mixture components are the potential for allele sharing that results in peak signal stacking (Figure 6.6) and handling potential alleles in the stutter position (Figure 6.7). The potential of N+4 forward stutter (see Chapter 3) can also complicate mixture interpretation.

These complicating factors increase interpretation uncertainty in some STR profiles. Some forensic DNA laboratories may decide not to go through the trouble of fully deciphering the genotype possibilities and assigning them to the major and minor contributors even for simple two-person

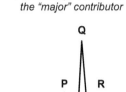

FIGURE 6.6   Illustration of the impact of allele sharing. This type of result where allele Q appears to be from a "major" contributor is possible with a three-person mixture containing fairly equal amounts of each genotype (PQ + QQ + QR).

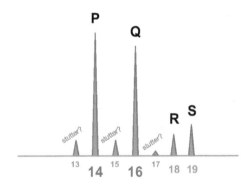

FIGURE 6.7   Hypothetical example of STR mixture data at the D18S51 locus illustrating that when minor components are similar in peak height to stutter products of the major alleles these stutter products need to be considered as possible alleles from another minor contributor.

mixtures. An easier approach is to simply include or exclude a suspect's DNA profile from the crime scene mixture profile. If all of the alleles from a suspect's DNA profile are represented in the crime scene mixture, then the suspect cannot be excluded as contributing to the crime scene stain. Likewise, the alleles in a victim's DNA profile could be subtracted from the mixture profile to simplify the alleles that need to be present in the perpetrator's DNA profile. Approaches to attaching a statistical value to mixture results are presented in Chapter 12.

Reading List and Internet Resources

General Information

Bacher, J. W., et al. (1999). Pentanucleotide repeats: highly polymorphic genetic markers displaying minimal stutter artifact. *Proceedings of the 9th International Symposium on Human Identification*, 24–37.
Butler, J. M. (2012). *Appendix 1 in* Advanced Topics in Forensic DNA Typing: Methodology. San Diego: Elsevier Academic Press. pp. 549–602.

Clayton, T., & Buckleton, J. (2005). *Mixtures. Chapter 7 in* Forensic DNA Evidence Interpretation. In J. Buckleton, C. M. Triggs, & S. J. Walsh (Eds.) (pp. 217–274). CRC Press.

DNA Advisory Board (DAB 2000). Statistical and population genetics issues affecting the evaluation of the frequency of occurrence of DNA profiles calculated from pertinent population database(s). Forensic Science Communications, 2(3). Available at http://www.fbi.gov/about-us/lab/forensic-science-communications/fsc/july2000/dnastat.htm/. Accessed March 24, 2014.

Gefrides, L. A., et al. (2010). UV irradiation and autoclave treatment for elimination of contaminating DNA from laboratory consumables. *Forensic Science International: Genetics, 4,* 89–94.

Gill, P., & Kirkham, A. (2004). Development of a simulation model to assess the impact of contamination in casework using STRs. *Journal of Forensic Sciences, 49*(3), 485–491.

Gill, P., et al. (2010). Manufacturer contamination of disposable plastic-ware and other reagents — an agreed position statement by ENFSI, SWGDAM and BSAG. *Forensic Science International: Genetics, 4,* 269–270.

Gonzalez-Andrade, F., et al. (2006). DNA mixtures in forensic casework resolved with autosomic STRs. *Progress in Forensic Genetics 11, ICS, 1288,* 580–582.

Kamodyova, N., et al. (2013). Prevalance and persistence of male DNA identified in mixed saliva samples after intense kissing. *Forensic Science International: Genetics, 7,* 124–128.

Nurit, B., et al. (2011). Evaluating the prevalence of DNA mixtures found in fingernail samples from victims and suspects in homicide cases. *Forensic Science International: Genetics, 5,* 532–537.

Roman, J. K., et al. (2008). *The DNA field experiment: cost-effectiveness analysis of the use of DNA in the investigation of high-volume crimes.* Available at https://www.ncjrs.gov/pdffiles1/nij/grants/222318.pdf. Accessed March 24, 2014.

Tomsey, C. S., et al. (2001). Case work guidelines and interpretation of short tandem repeat complex mixture analysis. *Croatian Medical Journal, 42,* 276–280.

Torres, Y., et al. (2003). DNA mixtures in forensic casework: a 4-year retrospective study. *Forensic Science International, 134,* 180–186.

Torres, Y., & Sanz, P. (2006). Variability in the detection of mixed profiles in four commercial autosomic STR multiplexes. *Progress in Forensic Genetics 11, ICS, 1288,* 501–503.

Word, C. J. (2011). Mixture interpretation: why is it sometimes so hard? *Profiles in DNA, 14*(1). Available at http://www.promega.com/resources/profiles-in-dna/2011/mixture-interpretation-why-is-it-sometimes-so-hard/. Accessed March 24, 2014.

Tools for Mixture Interpretation

Recommendations

Budowle, B., et al. (2009). Mixture interpretation: defining the relevant features for guidelines for the assessment of mixed DNA profiles in forensic casework. *Journal of Forensic Sciences, 54,* 810–821.

Gill, P., et al. (2006). DNA commission of the International Society of Forensic Genetics: Recommendations on the interpretation of mixtures. *Forensic Science International, 160,* 90–101.

Gill, P., et al. (2008). National recommendations of the technical UK DNA working group on mixture interpretation for the NDNAD and for court going purposes. *Forensic Science International: Genetics, 2,* 76–82.

Morling, N., et al. (2007). Interpretation of DNA mixtures — European consensus on principles. *Forensic Science International: Genetics, 1,* 291–292.

Schneider, P. M., et al. (2006). Editorial on the recommendations of the DNA commission of the ISFG on the interpretation of mixtures. *Forensic Science International, 160,* 89-89.

Schneider, P. M., et al. (2009). The German Stain Commission: recommendations for the interpretation of mixed stains. *International Journal of Legal Medicine, 123,* 1–5 (originally published in German in 2006 — Rechtsmedizin 16: 401-404).

Stringer, P., et al. (2009). Interpretation of DNA mixtures — Australian and New Zealand consensus on principles. *Forensic Science International: Genetics, 3,* 144–145.

SWGDAM. (2010). *SWGDAM interpretation guidelines for autosomal STR typing by forensic DNA testing laboratories.* Available at http://www.swgdam.org. Accessed March 24, 2014.

Wickenheiser, R. A. (2006). General guidelines for categorization and interpretation of mixed STR DNA profiles. *Canadian Society of Forensic Science Journal, 39,* 179–216.

Elements of Mixture Interpretation

Clayton, T. M., et al. (1998). Analysis and interpretation of mixed forensic stains using DNA STR profiling. *Forensic Science International, 91*, 55–70.

Mixture Detection and Component Profile Deconvolution

Bright, J. A., et al. (2010). Examination of the variability in mixed DNA profile parameters for the Identifiler multiplex. *Forensic Science International: Genetics, 4*, 111–114.

Cowell, R. G., et al. (2007). Identification and separation of DNA mixtures using peak area information. *Forensic Science International, 166*, 28–34.

Evett, I. W., et al. (1991). A guide to interpreting single locus profiles of DNA mixtures in forensic cases. *Journal of Forensic Science Society, 31*, 41–47.

Evett, I. W., et al. (1998a). Taking account of peak areas when interpreting mixed DNA profiles. *Journal of Forensic Sciences, 43*, 62–69.

Evett, I. W., et al. (1998b). Using a tree diagram to interpret a mixed DNA profile. *Journal of Forensic Sciences, 43*, 472–476.

Fung, W. K., & Hu, Y.-Q. (2008). *Statistical DNA Forensics: Theory, Method and Computation.* John Wiley & Sons, Ltd.

Gill, P., et al. (1997). Development of guidelines to designate alleles using an STR multiplex system. *Forensic Science International, 89*, 185–197.

Gill, P., et al. (1998a). Interpreting simple STR mixtures using allelic peak areas. *Forensic Science International, 91*, 41–53.

Gill, P., et al. (1998b). Interpretation of simple mixtures when artifacts such as stutters are present — with special reference to multiplex STRs used by the Forensic Science Service. *Forensic Science International, 95*, 213–224.

Leclair, B., et al. (2004). Systematic analysis of stutter percentages and allele peak height and peak area ratios at heterozygous STR loci for forensic casework and database samples. *Journal of Forensic Sciences, 49*, 968–980.

Manabe, S., et al. (2013). Mixture interpretation: experimental and simulated reevaluation of qualitative analysis. *Legal Medicine, 15*, 66–71.

Shrestha, S., et al. (2006). Unknown biological mixtures evaluation using STR analytical quantification. *Electrophoresis, 27*, 409–415.

Weir, B. S., et al. (1997). Interpreting DNA mixtures. *Journal of Forensic Science, 42*, 213–222.

Estimating the Number of Contributors

Biedermann, A., et al. (2012). Inference about the number of contributors to a DNA mixture: comparative analyses of a Bayesian network approach and the maximum allele count method. *Forensic Science International: Genetics, 6*, 689–696.

Buckleton, J. S., et al. (2007). Towards understanding the effect of uncertainty in the number of contributors to DNA stains. *Forensic Science International: Genetics, 1*, 20–28.

Egeland, T., et al. (2003). Estimating the number of contributors to a DNA profile. *International Journal of Legal Medicine, 117*, 271–275.

Haned, H., et al. (2011). The predictive value of the maximum likelihood estimator of the number of contributors to a DNA mixture. *Forensic Science International: Genetics, 5*, 281–284.

Haned, H., et al. (2011b). Estimating the number of contributors to forensic DNA mixtures: does maximum likelihood perform better than maximum allele count? *Journal of Forensic Sciences, 56*, 23–28.

Lauritzen, S. L., & Mortera, J. (2002). Bounding the number of contributors to mixed DNA stains. *Forensic Science International, 130*, 125–126.

Paoletti, D. R., et al. (2005). Empirical analysis of the STR profiles resulting from conceptual mixtures. *Journal of Forensic Sciences, 50*, 1361–1366.

Paoletti, D. R., et al. (2012). Inferring the number of contributors to mixed DNA profiles. *IEEE/ACM Transactions on Computational Biology and Bioinformatics, 9*, 113–122.

Perez, J., et al. (2011). Estimating the number of contributors to two-, three-, and four-person mixtures containing DNA in high template and low template amounts. *Croatian Medical Journal, 52*(3), 314–326.

Presciuttini, S., et al. (2003). Allele sharing in first-degree and unrelated pairs of individuals in the Ge.F.I. AmpFlSTR Profiler Plus database. *Forensic Science International, 131*, 85–89.

Mixture Ratios & Deconvolution

Armed Xpert™; (2014): http://www.armedxpert.com/. Accessed March 24, 2014

Clayton, T. M., et al. (1998). Analysis and interpretation of mixed forensic stains using DNA STR profiling. *Forensic Science International, 91,* 55–70.

Cowell, R. G., et al. (2007). Identification and separation of DNA mixtures using peak area information. *Forensic Science International, 166,* 28–34.

Evett, I. W., et al. (1998). Taking account of peak areas when interpreting mixed DNA profiles. *Journal of Forensic Sciences, 43,* 62–69.

Gill, P., et al. (1998). Interpreting simple STR mixtures using allelic peak areas. *Forensic Science International, 91,* 41–53.

Kline, M. C., et al. (2011). The new Standard Reference Material® 2391c: PCR-based DNA profiling standard. *Forensic Science International: Genetics Supplement Series, 3,* e355–e356.

NIST STRBase Tri-Allelic Patterns. (2014). http://www.cstl.nist.gov/strbase/tri_tab.htm. Accessed March 24, 2014.

Overson, T. L. (2009). *System and method for the deconvolution of mixed DNA profiles using a proportionately shared allele approach.* US Patent Application 2009/0270264 A1.

Perlin, M. W., & Szabady, B. (2001). Linear mixture analysis: a mathematical approach to resolving mixed DNA samples. *Journal of Forensic Sciences, 46,* 1372–1378.

Tvedebrink, T., et al. (2012). Identifying contributors of DNA mixtures by means of quantitative information of STR typing. *Journal of Computational Biology, 19*(7), 887–902.

Wang, T., et al. (2006). Least-squares deconvolution: a framework for interpreting short tandem repeat mixtures. *Journal of Forensic Sciences, 51,* 1284–1297.

Resources to Aid Mixture Interpretation

STR Data Analysis and Interpretation (on-line training): http://www.nij.gov/training/courses/analyst-str-data.htm. Accessed March 24, 2014.

Boston University DNA Mixture Training (2014): http://www.bu.edu/dnamixtures/. Accessed March 24, 2014.

NIST DNA Analyst Training on Mixture Interpretation: http://www.nist.gov/oles/forensics/dna-analyst-training-on-mixture-interpretation.cfm. Accessed March 24, 2014.

NIST 2013 webcast: http://www.nist.gov/oles/forensics/dna-analyst-training-on-mixture-interpretation-webcast.cfm. Accessed March 24, 2014.

NIST STRBase Mixture Information. (2014). http://www.cstl.nist.gov/strbase/mixture.htm. Accessed March 24, 2014.

Guidance for DNA Interpretation

Butler, J. M. (2013). *Forensic DNA advisory groups: DAB, SWGDAM, ENFSI, and BSAG* (2nd ed.). New York: Elsevier Academic Press. Encyclopedia of Forensic Sciences.

DNA Commission of the ISFG: http://www.isfg.org/Publications/DNA+Commission. Accessed March 24, 2014.

European Network of Forensic Science Institutes (ENFSI) DNA Working Group: http://www.enfsi.eu/about-enfsi/structure/working-groups/dna?uid=98. Accessed March 24, 2014.

Gill, P., et al. (2006). DNA Commission of the International Society of Forensic Genetics: Recommendations on the interpretation of mixtures. *Forensic Science International, 160,* 90–101.

Gill, P., et al. (2008). National recommendations of the technical UK DNA working group on mixture interpretation for the NDNAD and for court going purposes. *Forensic Science International: Genetics, 2,* 76–82.

Gill, P., Guiness, J., & Iveson, S. (2012). *The interpretation of DNA evidence (including low-template DNA).* Available at http://www.homeoffice.gov.uk/publications/agencies-public-bodies/fsr/interpretation-of-dna-evidence. Accessed March 24, 2014.

Gill, P., et al. (2012). DNA Commission of the International Society of Forensic Genetics: recommendations on the evaluation of STR typing results that may include drop-out and/or drop-in using probabilistic methods. *Forensic Science International: Genetics, 6,* 679–688.

Hobson, D., et al. (1999). *STR analysis by capillary electrophoresis: development of interpretation guidelines for the Profiler Plus and COfiler systems for use in forensic science.* Proceedings of the 10th International Symposium on Human Identification. Available at http://www.promega.com/products/pm/genetic-identity/ishi-conference-proceedings/10th-ishi-oral-presentations/. Accessed March 24, 2014.

Puch-Solis, R., et al. (2012). *Assessing the probative value of DNA evidence: Guidance for judges, lawyers, forensic scientists and expert witnesses*. Available at http://www.maths.ed.ac.uk/~cgga/Guide-2-WEB.pdf. Accessed March 24, 2014.

QAS. (2011). *Quality Assurance Standards for Forensic DNA Testing Laboratories effective 9-1-2011*. See http://www.fbi.gov/about-us/lab/codis/qas-standards-for-forensic-dna-testing-laboratories-effective-9-1-2011. Accessed March 24, 2014.

Schneider, P. M., et al. (2009). The German Stain Commission: recommendations for the interpretation of mixed stains. *International Journal of Legal Medicine, 123*, 1–5 (originally published in German in 2006 – Rechtsmedizin 16:401–404).

Scientific Working Group on DNA Analysis Methods (SWGDAM): http://www.swgdam.org. Accessed March 24, 2014.

SWGDAM. (2010). *SWGDAM Interpretation Guidelines for Autosomal STR Typing by Forensic DNA Testing Laboratories*. Available at http://www.swgdam.org/Interpretation_Guidelines_January_2010.pdf. Accessed March 24, 2014.

SWGDAM. (2012). *Validation Guidelines for DNA Analysis Methods*. Available at http://swgdam.org/SWGDAM_Validation_Guidelines_APPROVED_Dec_2012.pdf. Accessed March 24, 2014.

Software

Bill, M., et al. (2005). PENDULUM-a guideline-based approach to the interpretation of STR mixtures. *Forensic Science International, 148*, 181–189.

Hansson, O., & Gill, P. (2011). Evaluation of GeneMapperID-X mixture analysis tool. *Forensic Science International: Genetics Supplement Series, 3*, e11–e12.

Mortera, J., et al. (2003). Probabilistic expert system for DNA mixture profiling. *Theoretical and Population Biology, 63*, 191–205.

Oldroyd, N., & Shade, L. L. (2008). Expert assistant software enables forensic DNA analysts to confidently process more samples. *Forensic Magazine Dec 2008/Jan, 2009*, 25–28. Available at http://www.forensicmag.com/articles.asp?pid=240. Accessed March 24, 2014.

Perlin, M. W., & Szabady, B. (2001). Linear mixture analysis: a mathematical approach to resolving mixed DNA samples. *Journal of Forensic Sciences, 46*, 1372–1378.

Perlin, M. W. (2006). Scientific validation of mixture interpretation methods. *Proceedings of Promega's Seventeenth International Symposium on Human Identification*. Available at http://www.promega.com/products/pm/genetic-identity/ishi-conference-proceedings/17th-ishi-oral-presentations/. Accessed March 24, 2014.

Perlin, M. W., et al. (2011). Validating TrueAllele DNA mixture interpretation. *Journal of Forensic Sciences, 56*(6), 1430–1447.

Tvedebrink, T. (2011). Mixsep: an R-package for DNA mixture separation. *Forensic Science International: Genetics Supplement Series, 3*, e486–e488.

Tvedebrink, T., et al. (2012). Identifying contributors of DNA mixtures by means of quantitative information of STR typing. *Journal of Computational Biology, 19*, 887–902.

NIST Interlaboratory Studies on Mixture Interpretation

Duewer, D. L., et al. (2001). NIST mixed stain studies #1 and #2: interlaboratory comparison of DNA quantification practice and short tandem repeat multiplex performance with multiple-source samples. *Journal of Forensic Sciences, 46*, 1199–1210.

Duewer, D. L., et al. (2004). NIST mixed stain study 3: signal intensity balance in commercial short tandem repeat multiplexes. *Analytical Chemistry, 76*, 6928–6934.

Kline, M. C., et al. (2003). NIST mixed stain study 3: DNA quantitation accuracy and its influence on short tandem repeat multiplex signal intensity. *Analytical Chemistry, 75*, 2463–2469.

Krenke, B. E., et al. (2002). Validation of a 16-locus fluorescent multiplex system. *Journal of Forensic Sciences, 47*, 773–785.

NIST Interlaboratory Mixture Interpretation Study (MIX05, 2005): http://www.cstl.nist.gov/strbase/interlab/MIX05.htm. Accessed March 24, 2014.

NIST MIX13 study: http://www.cstl.nist.gov/strbase/interlab/MIX13.htm. Accessed March 24, 2014.

Low-Level DNA and Complex Mixtures

"The limits of each DNA typing procedure should be understood, especially when the DNA sample is small, is a mixture of DNA from multiple sources, or is contaminated with interfering substances."

NRC I, 1992, p. 8

"For the complex DNA profile, there is no predominant or overarching standard interpretation method."
Peter Gill (Gill et al. 2012, report to the UK Forensic Science Regulator, p. 18)

INTERPRETATION CHALLENGES WITH LOW TEMPLATE DNA

Short tandem repeat (STR) typing works best when using optimal amounts of DNA. The multiplex polymerase chain reaction (PCR) for most STR kits typically is designed by manufacturers to work best with DNA input amounts in the range of 0.5 ng to 1.5 ng. Larger multiplexes (e.g. 16plex) appear to have a tighter optimal DNA quantity range than smaller multiplexes (e.g. 3plex). While DNA quantitation can help make decisions on how best to proceed with processing a specific sample, in the end the resulting capillary electrophoresis (CE) electropherogram after PCR and CE provides the most useful metric of the amount of DNA per allele, per locus, and per contributor if a mixture is present (Gill et al. 2012). In addition, examining the STR profile as a whole will provide an indication of potential DNA degradation effects.

Complex mixtures, which are defined here as biological samples containing DNA with three or more contributors, exhibit several significant challenges. First, *allele sharing will occur* at many of the loci tested, making it challenging to unambiguously discern the full genotypes of the mixture contributors. Second, complex mixtures are *likely to contain low-template DNA* (LTDNA) for one or more of the contributors since PCR reactions are usually run with 1 ng or less of total DNA. Each additional contributor to a mixture means a dilution of one or more of the contributors into the stochastic danger zone where allele drop-out is more likely. Concepts developed for two-person mixtures like stochastic thresholds will not always be applicable with mixtures containing three or more contributors, largely because of the possibility of allele sharing.

With more contributors, there will be more allele sharing and thus more stacking of allelic contribution at each observed allele. In the hypothetical example shown in Figure 7.1, four contributor genotypes (10,11 & 10,12 & 10,10 & 11,12) combine to produce only three observed alleles. Allele 10 is the highest peak in the example data illustrated in Figure 7.1(a).

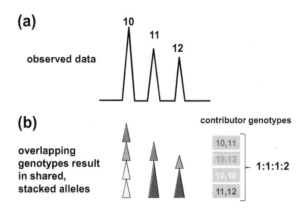

FIGURE 7.1   Illustration of (a) hypothetical observed data from a complex mixture for a single STR locus exhibiting alleles 10, 11, and 12 and (b) allele stacking from a set of contributor genotypes present in a 1:1:1:2 ratio.

Depending on the relative peak heights of allele 10 compared to alleles 11 and 12, a poorly designed mixture interpretation protocol might inappropriately consider the 10 allele as the major contributor in the mixture without considering the impact of allele stacking from multiple contributor genotypes.

Of course, in actual casework, the full identity of all contributor genotypes and mixture ratios is not known and must be inferred based on assessing the evidentiary DNA profile as a whole. As a general principle, the greater the number of contributors to a mixture, the lower the probability that the complete DNA profiles creating the mixture can be deciphered.

When lower amounts of DNA are PCR-amplified, there is a higher degree of stochastic variation. Thus, the relative ratios of the heterozygous alleles illustrated by different pairs of colored triangles in Figure 7.1(b) may become more skewed. When more stochastic variation occurs in heterozygote peak height ratios and stutter ratios, it becomes increasingly difficult to pair alleles into genotypes from individual contributors.

In an evaluation of low copy number (LCN) DNA profiling results in New Zealand, scientists from the Institute of Environmental Science and Research (ESR) evaluated 20 DNA samples that were fully heterozygous at the 10 STR loci in the SGM Plus kit (Petricevic et al. 2010). Lower heterozygote balance (Hb) and higher stutter ratios were observed with 12.5 pg or 25 pg examined at 34 PCR cycles versus 1 ng examined at 28 PCR cycles (Figure 7.2).

Figure 7.3 illustrates how the overlap of high stutter and low heterozygote balance with stochastic variation makes the use of peak height information for restricting genotype combinations more difficult from low-level DNA results. DNA results from high-signal two-person mixtures containing discernable major/minor profiles can exploit the gap between the stutter ratio and heterozygote balance (Figure 7.3(a)) and enable mixture devolution through restricting possible genotype combinations.

However, when one or more of the contributors fall into the stochastic range (e.g. <100 pg amplified for that particular contributor's DNA), higher levels of stochastic variation can lead to more variability in peak height ratios of heterozygotes and more significant stutter products (Figure 7.3(b)). This variation leads to a lower confidence in appropriately associating allele pairs into individual contributor genotypes. Quoting the 2010 ESR

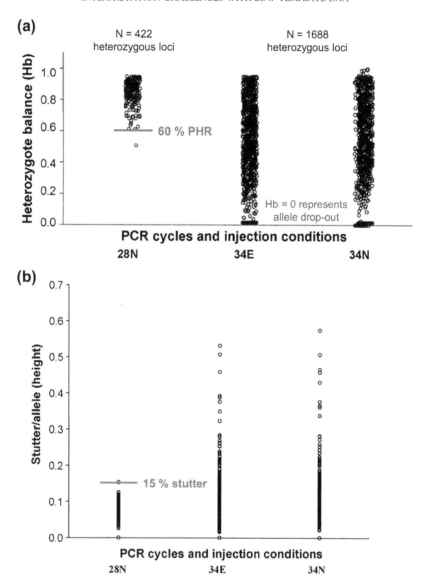

FIGURE 7.2   (a) Heterozygote balance across 10 STR loci in 20 fully heterozygous samples tested with SGM Plus at the ESR Laboratory in New Zealand compared among three sets of conditions: 28N = 1 ng target DNA tested with 28 PCR cycles and normal CE injection (10s @ 3kV); 34E = 12.5 pg and 25 pg target DNA tested in duplicate with 34 PCR cycles and enhanced CE injection (15 s @ 5 kV); 34N = 12.5 pg and 25 pg target DNA tested in duplicate with 34 PCR cycles and normal CE injection. (b) Stutter ratio data under the same conditions. Adapted from Petricevic et al. (2010).

study: "Because of the greater stochastic effects, the interpretation of mixed LCN profiles should utilize models that place much less emphasis on peak heights/area differences. ... However in some instances it is still possible to infer a strong major component of mixtures" (Petricevic et al. 2010).

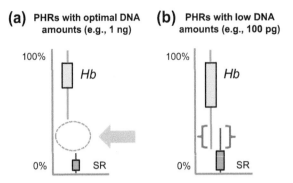

FIGURE 7.3   Impact of template DNA amount on variation in peak height ratios (PHRs). The observed spread in stutter ratio (SR) and heterozygous balance (*Hb*) are illustrated using box and whisker plots with (a) optimal versus (b) lower levels of DNA template being amplified. The gap between the SR and *Hb* (noted with the large gray arrow) is what enables mixture deconvolution through assuming restricted genotype combinations. The larger box and longer whiskers in the low-level DNA plot (b) reflect a larger variance causing the potential ranges of Hb and SR to overlap (noted by red brackets) and therefore greater uncertainty exists in reliably associating alleles into genotypes due to inherent stochastic effects during PCR.

Potential DNA Amounts in Mixtures

Table 7.1 compares the quantity of DNA and theoretical cell counts with single-source, two-person, three-person, and four-person mixtures with selected DNA mixture ratios. Studies with single-source samples have shown that stochastic effects such as elevated stutter and allele drop-out occur at around 15 to 20 cells or 100 pg to 125 pg (Butler & Hill 2010). Thus, the minor component in a 0.5-ng two-person mixture at a 4:1 ratio may experience adverse stochastic effects. Likewise, all four contributors in a 0.5-ng four-person mixture at a 1:1:1:1 ratio could potentially experience allele drop-out. Some amount of allele drop-out is highly likely when amplifying 0.25 ng total DNA containing a three-person or a four-person mixture with *any* mixture ratio.

Enhanced detection methods, such as the 34 PCR cycles used in the ESR study (Petricevic et al. 2010), may enable more alleles to be detected, but lead to greater variability in heterozygote balance and increased stutter product formation as shown in Figure 7.2.

Limitations of SWGDAM 2010 Guidelines

In January 2010, the FBI Laboratory's Scientific Working Group on DNA Analysis Methods (SWGDAM) approved interpretation guidelines for autosomal STR analysis (SWGDAM 2010). The SWGDAM 2010 guidelines, which discuss among other topics the use of a stochastic threshold, were primarily designed to cover single-source samples and two-person mixtures. The Frequently Asked Questions (FAQs) section of the SWGDAM website (SWGDAM FAQs 2014) states:

Question: *Are the 2010 SWGDAM Interpretation Guidelines applicable to all DNA mixtures?*

SWGDAM Response: *These guidelines were written with single-source samples and two-person mixtures in mind, and are not intended to replace a laboratory's previously validated mixture interpretation guidelines and/or*

TABLE 7.1   Comparison of the Quantity of DNA and Theoretical Cell Counts with Various Numbers of Contributors and DNA Mixture Ratios

Amount of DNA in PCR	Single-source	Two-person mixture	Three-person mixtures		Four-person mixtures	
		4:1	1:1:1	5:2:1	1:1:1:1	5:2:2:1
1 ng	1	0.8 + 0.2	0.33 × 3	0.6 + 0.25 + 0.13	0.25 × 4	0.5 + 0.2 + 0.2 + 0.1
	150	120 + 30	50 × 3	94 + 38 + 19	38 × 4	75 + 30 + 30 + 15
0.5 ng	0.5	0.4 + 0.1	0.16 × 3	0.31 + 0.12 + 0.06	0.125 × 4	0.25 + 0.1 + 0.1 + 0.05
	75	60 + 15	24 × 3	47 + 18 + 9	19 × 4	38 + 15 + 15 + 7
0.25 ng	0.25	0.2 + 0.05	0.08 × 3	0.15 + 0.06 + 0.03	0.062 × 4	0.12+0.05+0.05+0.02
	38	30 + 7	12 × 3	23 + 9 + 4	9 × 4	18 + 7 + 7 + 3
0.1 ng	0.1	0.075 + 0.025	0.03 × 3	0.062+0.02+0.01	0.025 × 4	0.05+0.02+0.02+0.01
	15	11 + 4	5 × 3	10 + 3 + 1	4 × 4	7 + 3 + 3 + 1
0.05 ng	0.05	0.04 + 0.01	0.016 × 3	0.03+0.012+0.006	0.0125 × 4	0.025+0.01+0.01+0.005
	7	6 + 1	2 × 3	5 + <2 + <1	2 × 4	4 + 1 + 1 + <1

Under each amount of DNA, the top row shows the approximate amount of DNA per person in nanograms (ng) and the bottom row provides the approximate number of cells assuming 6 picograms (pg) per diploid cell. Information courtesy of Dr. Charlotte Word.

policy. The basic concepts outlined in the 2010 SWGDAM Mixture Interpretation Guidelines hold true as they relate to DNA mixtures of three or more contributors, low-level DNA samples, and mixtures containing biologically related individuals. However, there are nuances and limitations to the interpretation of these more complex mixtures, which are not fully explored in the 2010 guidelines. The Autosomal STR Interpretation Committee is tasked with reviewing and revising these SWGDAM guidelines. Laboratories are encouraged to perform additional validation studies of complex mixtures to further their understanding of the issues related to these challenging samples.

Understanding the original designed scope of the 2010 SWGDAM guidelines is important as well to discussions on possible statistical approaches for coping with more complex mixtures that will be covered in Chapter 13.

Limitations of a Stochastic Threshold

Chapter 4 briefly discussed methods for establishing a stochastic threshold, which is used to assess the possibility of allele drop-out. When allelic peaks are seen below a stochastic threshold with a two-person mixture, then the possibility exists that a sister allele may not be detected because it was not amplified to a detectable level. Thus, a stochastic threshold is intended as a warning indicator of possible allele drop-out.

However, the potential of allele stacking, especially with more than two contributors (see Figure 7.1), can limit the usefulness of a stochastic threshold. Just because allelic peaks at a locus are above an established stochastic threshold does not mean that no allele drop-out has occurred in a complex mixture. Of course, if peaks are observed below a stochastic threshold in a complex mixture, then allele drop-out of a sister allele is possible as with simple two-person mixtures and the detected allele could be a false homozygote.

Validation Needs to Match Sample Types

If a laboratory desires to develop appropriate protocols that will enable reliable interpretation of DNA from low-level DNA or mixtures involving three or more contributors, then validation studies need to be performed with known samples that mimic the amounts of DNA and complexity of profiles where stochastic effects and allele dropout are expected. In short, three- or four-person mixtures of known genotypes should be mixed at specific ratios and amplified multiple times. Then these complex mixture profiles should be subjected to interpretation approaches to see if a true contributor is appropriately associated with the mixture and if non-contributors are appropriately excluded.

In my opinion, a laboratory cannot run a single two-person mixture series (e.g. 9:1, 5:1, 3:1, 1:1, 1:3, 1:5, and 1:9) and feel confident that minimum requirements for "mixture validation" have been met. This type of a limited validation may simply be able to help determine that a minor contributor can be detected down to a certain level. Determining that a mixture exists is not the same as fully interpreting a mixture. Developing robust interpretation protocols will require considering more samples — especially ones that go beyond a cursory combination of control samples 9947A and 9948 (D.N.A. Box 7.1).

D.N.A. BOX 7.1

LIMITATIONS OF CREATING MIXTURES WITH STANDARD CONTROL SAMPLES 9947A AND 9948

Cell lines 9947A and 9948 have been used since the mid-1990s as control samples for forensic DNA testing (Fregeau et al. 1995). Genomic DNA from these cell lines were included in NIST Standard Reference Material (SRM) 2391, 2391a, and 2391b as well as positive controls in STR typing kits for a number of years. Many forensic laboratories have, for the sake of convenience and availability, used the STR kit positive control 9947A in their heterozygous balance studies and mixed 9947A and 9948 together for simple mixture validation studies. Unfortunately, due to the large number of homozygotes (with five of the original 13 CODIS core loci), allele drop-out cannot be effectively measured across all loci with these

samples. For example, because TPOX, D5S818, D8S1179, D13S317, and D21S11 are homozygous in 9947A, it is not possible to examine heterozygote balance or to look for missing sister alleles at these loci when replicate low-level, serial dilutions are studied. Validation studies involving fully heterozygous samples are more effective at studying allele drop-out across all loci. Likewise, there is a great deal of allele sharing between 9947A and 9948 making them less than ideal candidates for studying detection of minor components in 2-person mixtures. The table below shows the observed alleles at 9947A and 9948 as well as the number of alleles seen when these two DNA samples are mixed together.

Locus	9947A	9948	Mixture of 9947A & 9948	#alleles
Amelogenin	**X,X**	X,Y	male & female	–
CSF1PO	10,12	10,11,12	10,11,12	3
FGA	23,24	24,26	23,24,26	3
TH01	8,9.3	6,9.3	6,8,9.3	3
TPOX	**8,8**	8,9	8,9	2
vWA	17,18	**17,17**	17,18	2
D3S1358	14,15	15,17	14,15,17	3
D5S818	**11,11**	11,13	11,13	2
D7S820	10,11	**11,11**	10,11	2
D8S1179	13,13	12,13	12,13	2
D13S317	**11,11**	**11,11**	11	1
D16S539	11,12	**11,11**	11,12	2
D18S51	15,19	15,18	15,18,19	3
D21S11	**30,30**	29,30	29,30	2
Penta D	**12,12**	8,12	8,12	2
Penta E	12,13	**11,11**	11,12,13	3
D2S1338	19,23	23,23	19,23	2
D19S433	14,15	13,14	13,14,15	3
D1S1656	**18.3,18.3**	14,17	14,17,18.3	3
D2S441	10,14	11,12	10,11,12,14	4
D10S1248	13,15	12,15	12,13,15	3
D12S391	18,20	18,24	18,20,24	3
D22S1045	11,14	16,18	11,14,16,18	4
SE33	19,29.2	23.2,26.2	19,23.2,26.2,29.2	4
D6S1043	12,18	**12,12**	12,18	2

Life Technologies (formerly as Applied Biosystems) has supplied a control DNA sample "007" with many of its kits since the launch of the AmpFlSTR SGM Plus kit in 1999 largely because the 007 sample was fully heterozygous at all 11 tested SGM Plus kit. In 2012, Promega began using as its positive STR kit control a sample labeled "2800M Control DNA," which is heterozygous at 21 of the 24 STR loci shown here (the three homozygotes are CSF1PO, TPOX, and D22S1045).

It is well known that low amounts of DNA template (e.g. 50 pg) do not behave as consistently as optimal DNA target quantities (e.g. 1 ng) and that additional measures which account for potential allele drop-out are necessary (see Butler 2012, Gill et al. 2012). A meaningful and reliable protocol to benefit work conducted with complex mixtures requires developing an understanding of allele drop-out and the impact of potential allele sharing.

Assessing allele drop-out can begin with replicate amplifications of low-level DNA from a dilution series of single-source samples possessing fully heterozygous genotypes. For example, five or ten replicates from single-source DNA samples containing 100 pg, 50 pg, 30 pg, and 10 pg will enable gathering data in a range where allele drop-out is expected (NIST Low Template DNA Testing 2014). Protocols should be regularly queried with controls (i.e. samples with known genotypes). Results obtained with these controls and a specific method should be carefully examined to see whether the expected alleles and genotypes are obtained.

Laboratories cannot adequately understand performance characteristics of low-template, complex DNA mixtures from having run a few high-template, simple DNA mixtures such as a few mixtures of 9947A and 9948. Attempts at *validation extrapolation*, where a simple two-person mixture study is expected to provide guidance for proper interpretation of less optimal mixtures, will not enable creation of robust protocols that provide consistent, reliable results. Every DNA interpretation protocol should be based on validation data, the scientific literature, and experience (SWGDAM 2010). Empirical data are always needed to establish limitations for a technique.

Some Complex Mixture Studies

Several published studies have examined complex DNA mixtures with controlled validation experiments. For laboratories pursuing their own STR validation studies involving more than two contributors, reviewing these and other articles would be a good starting point.

The Netherlands Forensic Institute (NFI) assessed four mock cases involving LTDNA containing two, three, or four contributors in which some of the contributors were brothers (Benschop et al. 2012). Four DNA mixtures were amplified in quadruplicate and reviewed by eight different NFI reporting officers with known samples being examined after profile interpretation. Likelihood ratio calculations were performed with a probabilistic genotyping tool LRmix (Gill & Haned 2013). The results from the eight reporting officers were then classified into one of four categories used at NFI: (a) exclusion, (b) match with statistical evaluation, (c) match without statistical evaluation, and (d) cannot be included or excluded (i.e. inconclusive). Because reporting officers provided conclusions similar to those expected for known samples, this study "gives the impression that the evaluation of LTDNA profiles is feasible" (Benschop et al. 2012). The use of pooled samples has also been found to aid complex LTDNA mixture interpretation (Benschop et al. 2013, Budimliga & Caragine 2012).

A German team from Institutes of Legal Medicine in Ulm and Hannover studied two types of degraded samples with DNA amounts as little as 50 pg and 100 pg per contributor (Pfeifer et al. 2012). They selected six contributors and combined these DNA samples into ten mixtures with up to four contributors for study. Different STR kits were evaluated as were the composite and consensus models (see below) for combining information from replicate PCR amplifications (Pfeifer et al. 2012).

Genotype Possibilities with Three or More Contributors

With each additional contributor to a mixture, the number of possible genotype combinations increases. A single-source sample (one contributor) has two possible genotype combinations: either a homozygote (PP) or a heterozygote (PQ). Two-person mixtures (two contributors) have 14 different genotype combinations. DNA mixtures consisting of three contributors have 150 possible combinations of genotypes at each locus and mixtures with four contributors have more than 600 possible genotype combinations at each locus (D.N.A. Box 7.2).

D.N.A. BOX 7.2

NUMBER OF POSSIBLE GENOTYPE COMBINATIONS

Evaluation of numbers of possible genotype combinations with specific numbers of alleles (vertical) and number of contributors (horizontal).

Bruce Heidebrecht (Maryland State Police Forensic Laboratory) helped check some of this information.

	1 contributor (either hom or het)	# (2)	2 contributors (7 classes)	# (14)	3 contributors (23 classes)	# (150)	4 contributors (41 classes)	# (>600)
1 allele (1 hom, 0 het)	homozygote (hom)	1	(a) 2 hom, 1 shared	1	(a) 3 hom, 1 shared	1	(a) 4 hom, 1 shared	1
2 alleles (2 hom, 1 het)	heterozygote (het)	1	(a) hom + hom, 0 shared (b) hom + het, 1 shared (c) hom + het, 2 shared	1 2 1	(a) 2 hom + hom, 0 shared (b) 2 hom + het, 1 shared (c) hom + hom + het, 2 shared (d) hom + 2 het, 2 shared (e) 3 het, 2 shared	2 2 1 2 1	(a) 3 hom + hom, 1 shared (b) 2 hom + 2 hom, 2 shared (c) 3 hom + het, 1 shared (d) 2 hom + hom + het, 2 shared (e) 2 hom + 2 het, 2 shared (f) hom + hom + 2 het, 2 shared (g) hom + 3 het, 2 shared (h) 4 het, 2 shared	2 1 2 2 1 1 2 1
3 alleles (3 hom, 3 het)	*possible tri-allele?*	--	(a) hom + het, 1 shared (b) het + het, 1 shared	3 3	(a) hom + hom + hom, 0 shared (b) hom + hom + het, 0 shared (c) hom + hom + het, 1 shared (d) hom + 2 het, 2 shared (2:2:2) (e) hom + het + het, 2 shared (4:1:1) (f) hom + het + het, 2 shared (3:2:1) (g) het + het + het, 2 shared (3:2:1) (h) het + het + het, 3 shared (2:2:2)	1 3 6 3 3 6 6 1	(a) 2 hom + hom + hom, 1 shared (b) 3 hom + het, 1 shared (c) hom + hom + hom + het, 2 shared (d) hom + hom + het + het, 2 shared (e) hom + 2 het + het, 2 shared (f) hom + het + het + het, 3 shared (g) 3 het + het, 2 shared (h) 2 het + 2 het, 3 shared (i) 2 het + het + het, 3 shared	3 3 3 5 9 3 6 2 3
4 alleles (4 hom, 6 het)	--	--	(a) het + het, 0 shared	3	(a) hom + hom + het, 0 shared (b) hom + het + het, 1 shared (3:1:1:1) (c) hom + het + het, 1 shared (2:2:1:1) (d) 2 het, 2 shared (2:2:1:1) (e) het + het + het, 1 shared (3:1:1:1) (f) het + het + het, 2 shared (2:2:1:1)	6 12 12 6 4 12	(a) hom + hom + hom + het, 0 shared (b) 2 hom + hom + het, 1 shared (4:2:1:1) (c) hom + hom + hom + het, 1 shared (3:2:2:1) (d) hom + hom + 2 het, 2 shared (2:2:2:2) (e) hom + hom + het + het, 2 shared (3:2:2:1) (f) het + het + het + het, 4 shared (2:2:2:2) (g) het + het + het + het, 3 shared (3:2:2:1) (h) 2 hom + het + het, 2 shared (4:2:1:1) (i) hom + het + het + het, 3 shared (3:2:2:1) (j) 2 het + het + het, 3 shared (3:2:2:1) (k) 2 het + het + het, 3 shared (4:2:1:1) (l) 2 het + het + het, 2 shared (3:3:1:1)	1 12 12 6 24 2 8 12 24 24 12 24
5 alleles (5 hom, 10 het)	--		--		(a) hom + het + het, 0 shared (b) het + het + het, 1 shared	15 30	(a) hom + hom + hom + het, 0 shared (b) hom + hom + het + het, 1 shared (c) hom + het + het + het, 2 shared (d) het + het + het + het, 3 shared (2:2:2:1:1) (e) 2 het + het + het, 2 shared (3:2:1:1:1)	10 30 30 >4 >11
6 alleles (6 hom, 15 het)	--		--		(a) het + het + het, 0 shared	15	(a) hom + hom + het + het, 0 shared (b) hom + het + het + het, 1 shared (c) het + het + het + het, 2 shared	30 48 >13
7 alleles (7 hom, 21 het)	--		--		--		(a) hom + het + het + het, 0 shared (b) het + het + het + het, 1 shared	70 >35
8 alleles (8 hom, 28 het)	--		--		--		(a) het + het + het + het, 0 shared	105

The different groupings of genotype combinations for a three-person mixture are shown in Figure 7.4. If we designate detected alleles as capital letters in sequential fashion starting with P, then we could have alleles P, Q, R, S, T, or U. Working all of these potential genotype combinations out by hand becomes increasingly difficult without a computer program.

With a three-person mixture, genetic loci exhibiting only a single allele would be comprised of PP homozygotes from all three contributors (Figure 7.4). Loci with two alleles could be composed of one

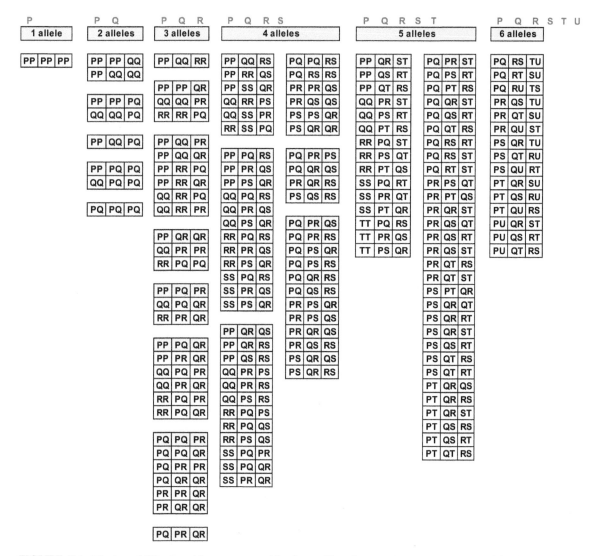

FIGURE 7.4　Display of 150 potential genotype combinations with a three-person mixture organized by the number of detected alleles. There are 23 different classes or groupings of genotype combinations with the first one in each group being highlighted in yellow. Adapted from Overson (2009) *(allele nomenclature changed from ABCDEF to PQRSTU).*

I. DATA INTERPRETATION

of eight possible combinations from five different "families" or classes of genotype combinations, which include: (1) two homozygous genotypes (PP + PP + QQ or PP + QQ + QQ), (2) a homozygous + a heterozygous combination sharing one allele (PP + PP + PQ or QQ + QQ + PQ), (3) two individual homozygotes coupled with a heterozygote sharing one allele (PP + QQ + PQ), (4) a homozygote with two heterozygotes sharing one allele (PP + PQ + PQ or QQ + PQ + PQ), or (5) three homozygotes sharing both alleles (PQ + PQ + PQ).

Three allele loci have eight families of genotype combinations, four allele loci have six families, five allele loci have two families, and six allele loci possess a single family of genotype combinations. There are 15 different combinations of heterozygotes with non-overlapping alleles (e.g. PQ + RS + TU or PQ + RT + SU, and so forth). The probability of observing a particular number of alleles at each locus in a mixture is related to the allele frequencies for each locus. More polymorphic loci such as D18S51 or D2S1338 will exhibit a greater number of alleles than a less polymorphic locus such as TPOX.

Difficulties with Estimating the Number of Contributors

The most common approach to estimating the number of contributors in a mixture is through using a maximum allele count. If contributor genotypes are heterozygous at a locus and there is no overlap in the alleles observed, then there would be twice as many alleles at an examined locus as there are contributors to the mixture. Thus, seeing four alleles at one or more loci would be an indication that two people contributed to the mixture whereas observing six alleles at one or more loci would suggest that three individuals contributed to the mixed DNA sample.

Unfortunately it is not this easy. Some alleles are fairly common and thus homozygotes occur as well as overlapping heterozygous alleles. This allele sharing makes accurately deducing the number of contributors challenging — and the challenge only grows with each additional contributor to a DNA mixture. Use of a maximum likelihood estimator that incorporates allele frequency information with the maximum allele count can help somewhat with improving the accuracy of estimating the number of contributors (Haned et al. 2011a,b). A Bayesian network approach has also been used (Biedermann et al. 2012). The most recent approach is a computational tool named NOC*It* that calculates the probability distribution for the number of contributors to a DNA sample (Swaminathan et al. 2013).

The examination of mixtures with more STR loci does help with estimating the number of contributors, particularly when using loci that have a high heterozygosity rate such as D18S51, D12S391, or SE33. Table 7.2 provides a summary of the benefit from adding nine additional STR loci to the 13 core STR loci used with the U.S. Combined DNA Index System (CODIS).

While it is fairly unlikely to mistake a four-person mixture as a single-source sample (with 13 STRs, the probability in Table 7.2 is 7×10^{-25}), as the number of contributors increases so does the potential for overlap with alleles between the contributors. For example, a five-person mixture has a 41% chance of being mistaken as a three-person mixture due to having at most six alleles at any of the 13 STRs examined. By using the 22 STR loci available in the GlobalFiler STR kit, this possibility of mistaking a five-person mixture for a three-person mixture drops to a probability of occurring a mere 0.48% of the time. Note, however, that a six-contributor DNA profile (based on the maximum allele count approach) would appear like a five-person mixture 99.9% of the time using 13 STRs and only drop to 86% with 22 STRs.

TABLE 7.2   Allele Sharing Impacts Number of Contributors Determination

		1	2	3	4	5
		2 alleles	*4 alleles*	*6 alleles*	*8 alleles*	*10 alleles*
6	CODIS 13	1.75×10^{-40}	6.34×10^{-9}	0.161	0.946	0.999
	22 STRs	$0\ (<10^{-99})$	9.59×10^{-21}	5.32×10^{-5}	0.188	0.860
5	CODIS 13	9.78×10^{-33}	2.10×10^{-6}	0.414	0.990	
	CODIS22	6.36×10^{-61}	7.01×10^{-15}	0.00484	0.610	
4	CODIS 13	7.02×10^{-25}	0.00052	0.786		
	22 STRs	3.50×10^{-46}	3.49×10^{-9}	0.165		
3	CODIS 13	8.42×10^{-17}	0.05949			
	22 STRs	5.77×10^{-31}	0.00043			
2	CODIS 13	1.70×10^{-8}				
	22 STRs	2.05×10^{-15}				

There is a limited ability to reliably decipher the number of contributors to a mixture based on a maximum allele count observed at any STR loci tested. As more loci are evaluated, the chance of incorrectly deciphering the number of contributors is reduced. The 13 Combined DNA Index System (CODIS) STR loci are compared to the 22 STRs discussed in the possible U.S. core expansion set (Hares 2012). The values in this table were determined using U.S. Caucasian allele frequencies (Hill et al. 2013, see Appendix 1) and reflect the probability of incorrectly assigning a specific number of contributors based on the maximum number of observed alleles at one or more loci (listed across the top) compared to the true number of contributors (listed down the left side). For example, four contributors would look like three contributors (with a maximum of 6 alleles at one or more STR locus) about 79% of the time when examining results from the 13 CODIS STRs. However, adding 9 STR loci reduces the probability of four contributors appearing as three contributors from 79% to 16%. This maximum allele count method does not consider any relative peak height imbalances in DNA mixtures. Data kindly provided by Mike Coble based on work by James Curran, Jo Bright, Mike Coble, and John Buckleton.

As illustrated in Table 7.2, mixture *detectability* will improve with use of more STR loci. However, mixture *interpretation* will take longer with the larger PCR multiplexes since there is more data to review. Also the chance of some or most of the contributors being in the LTDNA stochastic realm increases as the number of mixture contributors increases.

LOW-QUANTITY AND LOW-QUALITY DNA

Low-quantity and low-quality DNA templates are subject to stochastic processes during PCR amplification, which can skew the normal stutter product amounts and heterozygote balance (Butler & Hill 2010, Butler 2012). Generally an analyst will know that the DNA profile they are evaluating has components that are in the stochastic range based on allele peak heights. However, there is no clear distinction between LTDNA and conventional DNA profiles. Peter Gill and colleagues have written: "Because [stochastic] effects increase progressively as the amount of DNA decreases, there is no *natural* delineator that can be used to differentiate between *conventional* and *low-level* DNA profiles" (Gill et al. 2012).

Degraded DNA may exhibit both low-level DNA characteristics with the longer STR loci in a multiplex and conventional performance at the low relative molecular mass end of the electropherogram (Gill et al. 2012). Although there may be sufficient total DNA molecules available to render a DNA quantitation value in the conventional target range (e.g. 500 pg), a degraded DNA sample may have a limited number of intact molecules for the larger molecular mass STR markers. Thus, the larger STR marker targets may only be present at a sub-optimal level (e.g. 20 pg).

Replicate Testing to Form a Consensus or a Composite Profile

Results from replicate PCR amplifications can be combined to form either consensus or composite profiles (Figure 7.5). The requirement for repeated observations of an allele with the consensus method has made it a typical method of choice (Gill et al. 2000).

Replicate testing helps eliminate problems with random allele drop-in events but consumes more DNA sample (Cowen et al. 2011). One study found that consensus profiling did eliminate any drop-in spurious alleles from the final profile, but the act of subdividing an already low-quantity sample into multiple aliquots increased the total amount of allele and locus drop-out (Grisedale & van Daal 2012). There is a balance that must be struck between running as much DNA as possible in a single PCR versus splitting the sample to have replicate results, albeit from smaller amounts of DNA that could exhibit more variation and individual amplification ambiguity.

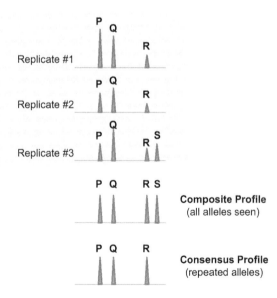

FIGURE 7.5 Replicate amplifications are often performed with low-template DNA (LTDNA) samples to aid overall result reproducibility. Detected alleles are labeled P, Q, R, and S. A composite profile contains all detected alleles (P, Q, R, and S) whereas a consensus profile only includes alleles that occur in more than one replicate amplification (P, Q, and R).

Combining the composite and consensus approaches, a team from Belgium created what they call a "Bracket" method (Bekaert et al. 2012). Clearly identifiable dominant profiles are separated from minor alleles that are enclosed in either soft () or hard [] brackets depending on their reproducibility in the replicate amplifications tested. This group typically refrains from attempting to determine minor DNA profiles due to the possibility of multiple minor contributors or extensive allele drop-out.

Challenges with Allele Drop-Out

At a particular locus, an evidentiary sample may possess one or more alleles that fail to be amplified during the PCR process due to stochastic effects. Thus, a reference sample from the suspect might contain a heterozygous genotype of PQ while the evidentiary sample only displays a P. This nonconcordance may be the result of the Q allele being lost due to allele drop-out (the prosecution's hypothesis) or the real perpetrator is homozygous PP and the evidence does not have a Q allele because the PQ suspect did not commit the crime (the defense's hypothesis).

There are several other possible explanations as well that include: (a) the real perpetrator is a heterozygote PF where F represents another allele besides Q that has dropped out; in this situation, P is considered a true allele and not due to drop-in; (b) the real perpetrator is a homozygote FF (not Q), but the F allele has dropped out, and the P allele is due to allele drop-in; or (c) the real perpetrator is a heterozygote FF' but these alleles have dropped out and the P allele is due to allele drop-in (Gill et al. 2012).

To address these possible explanations, the probability of drop-out, or Pr(D), and the probability of drop-in due to contamination, or Pr(C), have to be determined. It should also be demonstrated that Pr(D) and Pr(C) are consistent over time if constant values are going to be used in probabilistic approaches. One of the principles advocated by Peter Gill in his 2012 report to the UK Regulator is that "interpretation methodology should incorporate a probabilistic consideration of drop-out and additional alleles, such as drop-in, stutters, gross contamination and additional contributors" (Gill et al. 2012).

Assessing the Probability of Drop-Out

The Pr(D) is an estimate of how often alleles are expected to fail to amplify under certain PCR amplification conditions typically involving low-template DNA amounts. The Forensic Science Service introduced the concepts of allele drop-out and allele drop-in in their 2000 landmark LCN paper (Gill et al. 2000). However, almost a decade went by before statistical methods and interpretation approaches began to put these concepts into practice (Gill et al. 2009, Gill & Buckleton 2010). An important point in determining and using the Pr(D) concept is that alleles with lower peak heights have a greater chance of a sister allele in the allele pair failing to amplify due to stochastic effects if a heterozygous genotype is truly present.

Torben Tvedebrink and colleagues from the University of Copenhagen demonstrated a useful method for assigning the probability of drop-out on a per locus basis using logistical regression and the heights of the surviving sister allele in a heterozygote (Tvedebrink et al. 2009). Table 7.3 lists the allele drop-out probabilities with various STR loci at specific peak height levels.

TABLE 7.3 Average Peak Heights (in Relative Fluorescence Units) for Various Allele Drop-Out Probabilities [Pr(D)] across 10 STR Loci Present in the SGM Plus Kit

Pr(D)	D3S1358	vWA	D16S539	D2S1338	D8S1179	D21S11	D18S51	D19S433	TH01	FGA	Overall
0.0001	556	577	622	562	558	461	531	722	723	692	648
0.0005	384	399	430	388	385	318	367	499	499	478	439
0.001	327	340	366	331	328	271	313	425	426	407	371
0.005	226	235	253	228	226	187	216	293	294	281	251
0.01	192	200	215	194	193	159	184	250	250	239	212
0.05	132	137	147	133	132	109	126	171	171	164	142
0.1	111	115	124	112	111	92	106	144	144	138	119
0.2	92	95	103	93	92	76	88	119	120	114	98
0.3	81	84	91	82	81	67	78	105	106	101	86
0.4	73	76	82	74	74	61	70	95	95	91	77
0.5	67	69	75	68	67	55	64	87	87	83	70
0.6	61	63	68	62	61	50	58	79	79	76	63
0.7	55	57	62	56	55	46	53	71	71	68	57
0.8	49	50	54	49	49	40	46	63	63	60	50
0.9	40	42	45	41	40	33	39	52	52	50	41
0.95	34	35	38	34	34	28	32	44	44	42	34
0.99	23	24	26	23	23	19	22	30	30	29	23

Based on the data used to produce this model of allelic behavior, if a D18S51 peak was detected at 126 RFU, there is about a 5% chance of the sister allele in a heterozygote dropping-out (i.e. being below a 50 RFU detection threshold). Data reproduced with permission from Tvedebrink et al. (2009).

Monitoring Allele Drop-In Rates

Increased sensitivity with newer STR kits means that contamination risks are real. Sometimes consumables such as pipet tips and PCR tubes are not fully DNA-free (Gill et al. 2010). Allele drop-in relates to one or two extra alleles that cannot be attributed to the known reference sample whereas gross contamination refers to the transfer or a partial or even a full DNA profile from another source (Gill et al. 2012).

The probability of drop-in, Pr(C), is commonly estimated through detection of extra alleles in negative controls where it is expected that no DNA is present. A laboratory should maintain some kind of record of any spurious alleles noted while examining negative control data in order to record drop-in and gross contamination events (Gill & Kirkham 2004, Gill et al. 2012). This record not only serves as a monitor over time but can also be used to provide data for probabilistic models.

PROBABILISTIC GENOTYPING

Given that allele drop-out and allele drop-in are real issues faced with low-template DNA and complex mixtures, movement is underway towards *probabilistic genotyping* that involves calculating the probability of potential genotype combinations at each STR locus in an effort to best explain DNA mixture results (Kelly et al. 2014). Probabilistic genotyping is often divided into two general approaches: (1) semi-continuous model and (2) fully continuous model. Both of these approaches can incorporate Pr(D) and Pr(C).

Under the *semi-continuous* approach, the presence or absence of alleles is used to make decisions about potential genotype combinations. Peak height information is not considered. The *fully continuous* model utilizes allele and peak height information along with parameters such as heterozygote balance, mixture ratios, and stutter ratios to ascertain what contributor genotypes may be present. Statistical aspects of probabilistic genotyping and software programs that utilize the semi-continuous or fully continuous models are discussed in Chapter 13.

HIGH-DENSITY SNP ARRAYS?

In August 2008, a group of scientists led by David Craig at the Translational Genomics Research Institute in Phoenix, Arizona, published an article entitled "Resolving individuals contributing trace amounts of DNA to highly complex mixtures using high-density SNP genotyping microarrays" (Homer et al. 2008). These researchers claimed that by examining 500,000 single nucleotide polymorphisms (SNPs) using high-density SNP genotyping microarrays they could identify the presence of genomic DNA of specific individuals within highly complex mixtures, including mixtures where an individual contributes less than 0.1% (1 part in a thousand) of the total genomic DNA. Their high-density SNP array method utilizes differences of individual alleles from a reference set of population allele frequencies to infer whether or not a specific individual is present in the mixture.

The authors of this paper (Homer et al. 2008) boldly claimed the utilities of their approach for identifying individual trace contributors within a forensic mixture — although the test required hundreds of nanograms of pristine DNA. Given the potential for allele drop-out at numerous loci when testing forensically relevant amounts of DNA for a few nanograms or less, the initial theoretical claims of Homer et al. (2008) have yet to be substantiated. A number of follow-up studies discussed the approach taken and its potential limitations (Visscher & Hill 2009, Braun et al. 2009, Jacobs et al. 2009, Sampson & Zhao 2009, Clayton 2010).

In a follow-up study focused on addressing potential forensic applications, Thore Egeland and several Norwegian colleagues found that it was not possible to reliably infer the presence of minor contributors to mixtures following the approach described by David Craig's team in 2008 (Egeland et al. 2012). Egeland and his colleagues prepared 25 mixtures consisting of two, three, four, or five contributors with mixture proportions ranging from 0.01 to 0.99 and examined them in a blinded experiment with 360 SNPs (rather than the 500,000 SNPs studied by Homer et al. 2008).

The Norwegian study found that major contributors and all samples with mixture proportions exceeding 0.33 could be correctly identified (Egeland et al. 2012). Of 39 people not in a tested mixture, the SNP method always correctly excluded them. However, in 11% of the cases examined, low-level mixture contributors were incorrectly assigned as non-contributors. In addition, an inconclusive result was obtained in 24% of the cases studied. The Norwegians conclude that "contrary to Homer et al. 2008, it is not possibl[e] to accurately infer the presence of contributors to unbalanced mixtures following the suggested approach" (Egeland et al. 2012).

Dr. Kevin McElfresh, a forensic research scientist formerly of LifeCodes and Bode Technology Group, first spoke on the topic of high-density SNP typing for forensic mixtures at the October 2009 International Symposium on Human Identification (ISHI) meeting (McElfresh et al. 2009). He presented further SNP typing work with a poster presentation at the 2011 ISHI meeting (McElfresh et al. 2011) and in 2013 started a new company to pursue SNP typing, The Center for Advanced Forensic DNA Analysis™ (CAFDA 2014).

Two Israeli scientists have proposed using a panel of 1,000 to 3,000 SNPs with each SNP having a relatively low minor allele frequency in the target population (Voskoboinik & Darvasi 2011). They predict that this approach can differentiate even brothers in a mixture composed of up to 10 contributors. While, as noted in this section, there have been several theoretical studies claiming benefits of high-density SNP typing, substantiating data has been slow to be released. Only time will tell what kind of role high-density SNP typing will play in handling complex forensic DNA mixtures of the future.

MORE POOR-QUALITY SAMPLES BEING SUBMITTED

Due to the success of DNA testing and its value to the criminal justice system, many laboratories are seeing an increasing number of poor quality/quantity samples being submitted. For example, at the International Society of Forensic Genetics (ISFG) 2009 meeting, Sabine Michel from the Regional Center of Identification in Gosselies, Belgium reported that the number of samples with <100 pg of DNA had increased from 19% in 2004 to 45% in 2008 (Michel 2009). Laboratories in the United States are processing more "touch evidence" samples since the 2008 National Institute of Justice funded study on the value of using DNA to help solve burglary cases (Roman et al. 2008). This mentality of swab first and ask questions (i.e. try to interpret results) later has led to what Ted Hunt, a prosecutor from Kansas City, Missouri, terms "swab-a-thons" by the police looking for any useful DNA results (Hunt 2014).

Many laboratories have not adopted stringent case acceptance policies and are being drowned in a tsunami of sample submissions. At the same time, the ability to recover information from low-level DNA samples has increased as the sensitivity of DNA testing methods has improved. Sensitivity is in many ways a two-edge sword — although more information can be recovered, interpretation becomes more challenging and time-consuming. Contamination and potential secondary or tertiary transfer becomes a more significant issue when working to recover low-level DNA (see Chapter 16). Depending on the case context, recovering DNA information from the equivalent of a few cells may not be considered probative.

From 2008 to 2010, the Swedish National Laboratory for Forensic Science collected 2,033 samples containing low template DNA in 417 cases (Dufva & Nilsson 2011). The results were grouped into four categories: (1) a useful DNA profile relevant to the case, (2) a useful DNA profile but not relevant to the case, (3) complex, and (4) weak. A "successful" case was defined as having at least one sample with results in category 1. This Swedish study found an overall success rate of 38%. Results recovered from knives provided a useful DNA profile relevant to the case about 19% of the time (Dufva & Nilsson 2011).

At the American Academy of Forensic Sciences (AAFS) meeting in February 2014, two presentations discussed poor success rates seen in their laboratories with swabs from gun cases and other touch evidence (Bitner et al. 2014, Samples et al. 2014). Only about 10% of profiles obtained from over 9,500 touch evidence swabs received from 2007 to 2011 produced usable DNA results in New York City (Samples et al. 2014). Improving the swab collection training for the evidence collection teams and altering laboratory DNA extraction procedures have helped improve recovery in recent years, but overall their laboratory continues to see more inconclusive results than not for many types of touch evidence cases (Samples et al. 2014). A review of touch DNA items processed by the Allegheny County Office of the Medical Examiner Forensic Laboratory from 2008 to 2013 grouped sample types into firearms, magazines, baseball caps, masks, car door handles, doorknobs, shirts, and gloves (Bitner et al. 2014).

No formal analysis of the collection of DNA evidence has been performed and reported in recent years. However, based on feedback the author has received from discussions with forensic laboratories around the world, the number of complex mixtures (those containing three or more contributors) appears to have risen significantly. It is important to keep in mind that increased complexity in sample results can lead to decreased confidence in the interpretation of the evidence. Uninterpretable results lead to reporting inconclusive findings. Laboratories may want to consider increasing the stringency of their case/sample acceptance policy in order to avoid a "garbage in, garbage out" situation.

A COMPLEXITY THRESHOLD?

Some DNA mixtures will be too complex to solve. Laboratories may benefit from developing criteria for when to stop working on a sample or on a case based on a preliminary analysis of samples received. This might be termed a "complexity threshold" (Rudin & Inman 2012). One idea for creating a complexity threshold is the use of receiver operator characteristics (ROC) curves that correlate the number of false positives and false negatives under certain conditions (Gordon 2012, Grgicak 2012). For example, simulations can be run and visualized via ROC curves to determine how many non-concordant results (i.e. missing alleles in the evidence sample) are permitted before there is a chosen probability of falsely including an innocent person (Gordon 2012).

In one of their complex mixture studies, NFI proposed to develop criteria for assessing the peak heights, position of allele calls (such as in potential stutter positions), the consistency of allele calls among replicates, and a maximum number of allele drop-outs that could be considered for non-concordance (Benschop et al. 2012). Presumably studying the variability of these parameters in validation studies with known mixture contributors could lead to an effective complexity threshold.

In April 2012, an international conference was held in Rome, Italy, entitled "The hidden side of DNA profiles: artifacts, errors and uncertain evidence" (Pascali & Prinz 2012). Peter Schneider, a forensic DNA researcher from Cologne, Germany, shared his thoughts on what to do when evidence becomes too complex to reliably interpret: "If you cannot explain your evidence to someone that is not from the field (like a judge) — and you need a lot of technical excuses to report something — then the result is not good. You should leave it on your desk and not take it to court. This is a very common sense approach to this problem" (Rome 2012).

Low-level DNA and complex mixtures are challenging to interpret. Not every DNA result can or should be interpreted. When there is a high degree of interpretation uncertainty from an evidentiary sample, it makes little sense to try and draw conclusions (either inclusion *or* exclusion of reference samples) — and expect those conclusions to be reliable.

With stochastic effects ever-present in low-level DNA PCR amplifications, allele drop-out and potential allele sharing from multiple contributors lead to greater uncertainty in the specific genotype combinations that can be reliably assumed. Furthermore, stochastic thresholds often lose their value and meaning when allele sharing is possible with three or more contributors to a DNA mixture. Probabilistic genotyping approaches (see Chapter 13) using computer simulations that estimate relative contributions of potential contributors are being developed to try and explain observed data.

Another approach may be to develop a complexity threshold in order to halt efforts on poor quality data. Sensitive DNA detection technology has the potential to outpace reliable interpretation. The forensic DNA community needs to be vigilant in efforts to appropriately interpret challenging evidence without pushing too far.

Reading List and Internet Resources

Interpretation Challenges

Anjos, M. J., et al. (2006). Low copy number: interpretation of evidence results. *Progress in Forensic Genetics 10, ICS, 1288*, 616—618.

Anslinger, K., & Bayer, B. (2011). The effect of increased cycle numbers using the Quantifiler Duo DNA Quantitation Kit (AB) on the detection of minute amounts of male DNA in mixtures and its application in routine case work. *Forensic Science International: Genetics Supplement Series, 3*, e277—e278.

Balding, D. J., & Buckleton, J. (2009). Interpreting low template DNA profiles. *Forensic Science International: Genetics, 4*, 1—10.

Budowle, B., et al. (2009). Validity of low copy number typing and applications to forensic science. *Croatian Medical Journal, 50*, 207—216.

Butler, J. M., & Hill, C. R. (2010). Scientific issues with analysis of low amounts of DNA. *Profiles in DNA, 13*(1). Available at http://www.promega.com/profiles/1301/1301_02.html. Accessed March 24, 2014.

Butler, J. M. (2012). Chapter 11 — Low-Level DNA testing: issues, concerns, and solutions. In *Advanced Topics in Forensic DNA Typing: Methodology* (pp. 311—346). San Diego: Elsevier.

Caragine, T., et al. (2009). Validation of testing and interpretation protocols for low template DNA samples using AmpFlSTR Identifiler. *Croatian Medical Journal, 50*(3), 250—267.

Carracedo, A., et al. (2012). Focus issue — Analysis and biostatistical interpretation of complex and low template DNA samples. *Forensic Science International: Genetics, 6*(6), 677—678.

Cowen, S., et al. (2011). An investigation of the robustness of the consensus method of interpreting low-template DNA profiles. *Forensic Science International: Genetics, 5*, 400—406.

Decorte, R., et al. (2011). An automated approach for generating consensus profiles from low template STR typing results. *Forensic Science International: Genetics Supplement Series, 3*, e435—e436.

Forster, L., et al. (2008). Direct comparison of post-28-cycle PCR purification and modified capillary electrophoresis methods with the 34-cycle 'low copy number' (LCN) method for analysis of trace forensic DNA samples. *Forensic Science International: Genetics, 2*, 318—328.

Fregeau, C. J., et al. (1995). Characterization of human lymphoid cell lines GM9947 and GM9948 as intra- and interlaboratory reference standards for DNA typing. *Genomics, 28*, 184—197.

Gill, P., et al. (2000). An investigation of the rigor of interpretation rules for STRs derived from less than 100 pg of DNA. *Forensic Science International, 112*, 17—40.

Gill, P., et al. (2006). DNA commission of the International Society of Forensic Genetics: Recommendations on the interpretation of mixtures. *Forensic Science International, 160*, 90—101.

Gill, P., et al. (2007). LoComatioN: a software tool for the analysis of low copy number DNA profiles. *Forensic Science International, 166*, 128—138.

Gill, P., et al. (2008). Interpretation of complex DNA profiles using empirical models and a method to measure their robustness. *Forensic Science International: Genetics, 2*, 91—103.

Gill, P., & Buckleton, J. (2010). A universal strategy to interpret DNA profiles that does not require a definition of *low-copy-number*. *Forensic Science International: Genetics, 4,* 221–227.

Gill, P., et al. (2012). The interpretation of DNA evidence (including low-template DNA). Available at http://www.homeoffice.gov.uk/publications/agencies-public-bodies/fsr/interpretation-of-dna-evidence. Accessed March 24, 2014.

Gross, T., et al. (2009). A review of low template STR analysis in casework using the DNA SenCE post-PCR purification technique. *Forensic Science International: Genetics Supplement Series, 2,* 5–7.

Kloosterman, A. D., & Kersbergen, P. (2003a). Efficacy and limits of genotyping low copy number (LCN) DNA samples by multiplex PCR of STR loci. *Journal de la Société de Biologie, 197,* 351–359.

Kloosterman, A. D., & Kersbergen, P. (2003b). Efficacy and limits of genotyping low copy number DNA samples by multiplex PCR of STR loci. *Progress in Forensic Genetics 9, ICS1239,* 795–798.

Michel, S., et al. (2009). Interpretation of low-copy-number DNA profile after post-PCR purification. *Forensic Science International: Genetics Supplement Series, 2,* 542–543.

NIST Low Template DNA Testing: Available at http://www.cstl.nist.gov/strbase/LTDNA.htm. Accessed March 24, 2014.

Noël, J., et al. (2009). Searching a DNA databank with complex mixtures from two individuals. *Forensic Science International: Genetics Supplement Series, 2,* 464–465.

Overson, T. L. (2009). System and method for the deconvolution of mixed DNA profiles using a proportionately shared allele approach. *US Patent Application 2009/0270264 A1.*

Pedersen, L. M. I., et al. (2011). Purification and concentration of PCR products leads to increased signal intensities with fewer allelic drop-outs and artifacts. *Forensic Science International: Genetics Supplement Series, 3,* e347–e348.

Petricevic, S., et al. (2010). Validation and development of interpretation guidelines for low copy number (LCN) DNA profiling in New Zealand using the AmpFlSTR SGM Plus multiplex. *Forensic Science International: Genetics, 4,* 305–310.

Roeder, A. D., et al. (2009). Maximizing DNA profiling success from sub-optimal quantities of DNA: a staged approach. *Forensic Science International: Genetics, 3,* 128–137.

Romanini, C., et al. (2011). A comparison of AmpFlSTR Identifiler kit versus AmpFlSTR Identifiler Plus kit in challenging bone samples by using normal and increased PCR cycle number. *Forensic Science International: Genetics Supplement Series, 3,* e514–e515.

Smith, P. J., & Ballantyne, J. (2007). Simplified low-copy-number DNA analysis by post-PCR purification. *Journal of Forensic Sciences, 52,* 820–829.

SWGDAM. (2010). *SWGDAM interpretation guidelines for autosomal STR typing by forensic DNA testing laboratories.* Available at http://www.swgdam.org. Accessed March 24, 2014.

SWGDAM FAQs. (2014). Available at http://swgdam.org/faq.html. Accessed March 24, 2014.

Westen, A. A., et al. (2009). Higher capillary electrophoresis injection settings as an efficient approach to increase the sensitivity of STR typing. *Journal of Forensic Sciences, 54,* 591–598.

Westen, A. A., et al. (2012). Assessment of the stochastic threshold, back- and forward stutter filters and low template techniques for NGM. *Forensic Science International: Genetics, 6,* 708–715.

Weusten, J., & Herbergs, J. (2012). A stochastic model of the processes in PCR based amplification of STR DNA in forensic applications. *Forensic Science International: Genetics, 6,* 17–25.

Whitaker, J. P., et al. (2001). A comparison of the characteristics of profiles produced with the AMPFlSTR SGM Plus multiplex system for both standard and low copy number (LCN) STR DNA analysis. *Forensic Science International, 123,* 215–223.

Word, C. J. (2011). Mixture interpretation: why is it sometimes so hard? *Profiles in DNA.* Available at http://www.promega.com/resources/profiles-in-dna/2011/mixture-interpretation-why-is-it-sometimes-so-hard/. Accessed March 24, 2014.

Low–Level Complex DNA Mixtures

Bekaert, B., et al. (2012). Automating a combined composite – consensus method to generate DNA profiles from low and high template mixture samples. *Forensic Science International: Genetics, 6(5),* 588–593.

Benschop, C. C., et al. (2011). Low template STR typing: effect of replicate number and consensus method on genotyping reliability and DNA database search results. *Forensic Science International: Genetics, 5,* 316–328.

Benschop, C. C. G., et al. (2012). Assessment of mock cases involving complex low template DNA mixtures: a descriptive study. *Forensic Science International: Genetics, 6(6),* 697–707.

Benschop, C. C. G., et al. (2013). Consensus and pool profiles to assist in the analysis and interpretation of complex low template DNA mixtures. *International Journal of Legal Medicine, 127,* 11–23.

Bright, J. A., et al. (2012). Composite profiles in DNA analysis. *Forensic Science International: Genetics, 6,* 317–321.

Buckleton, J. (2009). Validation issues around DNA typing of low level DNA. *Forensic Science International: Genetics, 3,* 255–260.

Budimlija, Z. M., & Caragine, T. A. (2012). Interpretation guidelines for multilocus STR forensic profiles from low template DNA samples. *Methods in Molecular Biology, 830,* 199–211 [Alonso, A. (ed.), *DNA Electrophoresis Protocols for Forensic Genetics*].

Haned, H., et al. (2012). Exploratory data analysis for the interpretation of low template DNA mixtures. *Forensic Science International: Genetics, 6,* 762–774.

Kelly, H., et al. (2012). The interpretation of low level DNA mixtures. *Forensic Science International: Genetics, 6,* 191–197.

Mitchell, A. A., et al. (2011). Likelihood ratio statistics for DNA mixtures allowing for drop-out and drop-in. *Forensic Science International: Genetics Supplement Series, 3,* e240–e241.

Mitchell, A. A., et al. (2012). Validation of a DNA mixture statistics tool incorporating allelic drop-out and drop-in. *Forensic Science International: Genetics, 6,* 749–761.

Pfeifer, C., et al. (2012). Comparison of different interpretation strategies for low template DNA mixtures. *Forensic Science International: Genetics, 6(6),* 716–722.

Prieto, L., et al. (2014). Euroforgen-NoE collaborative exercise on LRmix to demonstrate standardization of the interpretation of complex DNA profiles. *Forensic Science International: Genetics, 9,* 47–54.

Weiler, N. E. C., et al. (2012). Extended PCR conditions to reduce drop-out frequencies in low template STR typing including unequal mixtures. *Forensic Science International: Genetics, 6,* 102–107.

Wetton, J. H., et al. (2011). Analysis and interpretation of mixed profiles generated by 34 cycle SGM Plus amplification. *Forensic Science International: Genetics, 5(5),* 376–380.

Determining Number of Contributors

Biedermann, A., et al. (2012). Inference about the number of contributors to a DNA mixture: comparative analyses of a Bayesian network approach and the maximum allele count method. *Forensic Science International: Genetics, 6,* 689–696.

Buckleton, J. S., et al. (2007). Towards understanding the effect of uncertainty in the number of contributors to DNA stains. *Forensic Science International: Genetics, 1,* 20–28.

Egeland, T., et al. (2003). Estimating the number of contributors to a DNA profile. *International Journal of Legal Medicine, 117,* 271–275.

Haned, H., et al. (2011a). The predictive value of the maximum likelihood estimator of the number of contributors to a DNA mixture. *Forensic Science International: Genetics, 5(5),* 281–284.

Haned, H., et al. (2011b). Estimating the number of contributors to forensic DNA mixtures: does maximum likelihood perform better than maximum allele count? *Journal of Forensic Sciences, 56(1),* 23–28.

Hares, D. R. (2012). Expanding the CODIS core loci in the United States. *Forensic Science International: Genetics, 6(1),* e52–e54.

Hill, C. R., et al. (2013). U.S. population data for 29 autosomal STR loci. *Forensic Science International: Genetics, 7,* e82–e83.

Lauritzen, S. L., & Mortera, J. (2002). Bounding the number of contributors to mixed DNA stains. *Forensic Science International, 130,* 125–126.

Paoletti, D. R., et al. (2005). Empirical analysis of the STR profiles resulting from conceptual mixtures. *Journal of Forensic Sciences, 50,* 1361–1366.

Paoletti, D. R., et al. (2012). Inferring the number of contributors to mixed DNA profiles. *IEEE/ACM Transactions on Computational Biology and Bioinformatics, 9(1),* 113–122.

Perez, J., et al. (2011). Estimating the number of contributors to two-, three-, and four-person mixtures containing DNA in high template and low template amounts. *Croatian Medical Journal, 52(3),* 314–326.

Presciuttini, S., et al. (2003). Allele sharing in first-degree and unrelated pairs of individuals in the Ge. F.I. AmpFlSTR Profiler Plus database. *Forensic Science International, 131,* 85–89.

Swaminathan, H., et al. (2013). NOCIt – a computational tool to infer the number of contributors to a forensic DNA sample. Available at. In *Proceedings of the 24th International Symposium on Human Identification.* http://www.promega.com/ products/pm/genetic-identity/ishi-conference-proceedings/24th-ishi-oral-presentations/. Accessed March 24, 2014.

Tvedebrink, T., et al. (2012). Identifying contributors of DNA mixtures by means of quantitative information of STR typing. *Journal of Computational Biology, 19(7),* 887–902.

Tvedebrink, T. (2012). On the exact distribution of the numbers of alleles in DNA mixtures. *International Journal of Legal Medicine, 128(3),* 427–437.

Low-Quantity and Low-Quality DNA

Benschop, C. C. G., et al. (2010). Low template STR typing: effect of replicate number and consensus method on genotyping reliability and DNA database search results. *Forensic Science International: Genetics, 5*(4), 316–328.

Buckleton, J., et al. (2014). Utilising allelic dropout probabilities estimated by logistic regression in casework. *Forensic Science International: Genetics, 9*, 9–11.

Butler, J. M. (2012). Low-level DNA testing: issues, concerns, and solutions. Chapter 11. In *Advanced Topics in Forensic DNA Typing: Methodology* (pp. 311–346). San Diego: Elsevier Academic Press.

Gill, P., et al. (2000). An investigation of the rigor of interpretation rules for STRs derived from less than 100 pg of DNA. *Forensic Science International, 112*, 17–40.

Gill, P., & Kirkham, A. (2004). Development of a simulation model to assess the impact of contamination in casework using STRs. *Journal of Forensic Sciences, 49*, 485–491.

Gill, P., et al. (2009). The low-template-DNA (stochastic) threshold—its determination relative to risk analysis for national DNA databases. *Forensic Science International: Genetics, 3*, 104–111.

Gill, P., et al. (2010). Manufacturer contamination of disposable plastic-ware and other reagents – an agreed position statement by ENFSI, SWGDAM and BSAG. *Forensic Science International: Genetics, 4*, 269–270.

Grisedale, K. S., & van Daal, A. (2012). Comparison of STR profiling from low template DNA extracts with and without the consensus profiling method. *Investigative Genetics, 3*, 14.

Hedman, J., et al. (2011). Evaluation of three new forensic DNA profiling kits on PCR-inhibitory crime scene samples. *Forensic Science International: Genetics Supplement Series, 3*, e457–e458.

Tvedebrink, T., et al. (2009). Estimating the probability of allelic drop-out of STR alleles in forensic genetics. *Forensic Science International: Genetics, 3*, 222–226.

Tvedebrink, T., et al. (2011). Statistical model for degraded DNA samples and adjusted probabilities for allelic drop-out. *Forensic Science International: Genetics Supplement Series, 3*, e489–e491.

Tvedebrink, T., et al. (2012). Statistical model for degraded DNA samples and adjusted probabilities for allelic drop-out. *Forensic Science International: Genetics, 6*, 97–101.

Tvedebrink, T., et al. (2012). Allelic drop-out probabilities estimated by logistic regression – further considerations and practical implementation. *Forensic Science International: Genetics, 6*, 263–267.

Probabilistic Genotyping Approach

Ballantyne, J., Hanson, E. K., & Perlin, M. W. (2012). DNA mixture genotyping by probabilistic computer interpretation of binomially-sampled laser captured cell populations: combining quantitative data for greater identification information. *Science & Justice, 53*(2), 103–114.

Cowell, R. G., et al. (2008). Probabilistic modelling for DNA mixture analysis. *Forensic Science International: Genetics Supplement Series, 1*, 640–642.

Cowell, R. G., et al. (2011). Probabilistic expert systems for handling artifacts in complex DNA mixtures. *Forensic Science International: Genetics, 5*(3), 202–209.

Curran, J. M. (2008). A MCMC method for resolving two-person mixtures. *Science & Justice, 48*, 168–177.

Gill, P., & Buckleton, J. (2010). Commentary on: Budowle B, Onorato AJ, Callaghan TF, Della Manna A, Gross AM, Guerrieri RA, Luttman JC, McClure DL. Mixture interpretation: defining the relevant features for guidelines for the assessment of mixed DNA profiles in forensic casework. *J Forensic Sci 2009, 54*(4), 810–821. Journal of Forensic Sciences, 55(1), 265–268.

Gill, P., et al. (2012). DNA Commission of the International Society of Forensic Genetics: Recommendations on the evaluation of STR typing results that may include drop-out and/or drop-in using probabilistic methods. *Forensic Science International: Genetics, 6*(6), 679–688.

Gill, P., & Haned, H. (2013). A new methodological framework to interpret complex DNA profiles using likelihood ratios. *Forensic Science International: Genetics, 7*, 251–263.

Kelly, H., et al. (2014). A comparison of statistical models for the analysis of complex forensic DNA profiles. *Science & Justice, 54*, 66–70.

Perlin, M. W., et al. (2011). Validating TrueAllele DNA mixture interpretation. *Journal of Forensic Sciences, 56*(6), 1430–1447.

Perlin, M. W. (2012). Easy reporting of hard DNA: computer comfort in the courtroom. *Forensic Magazine, 9*(4), 32–37. Available at http://www.cybgen.com/information/publication/page.shtml. Accessed March 24, 2014.

High-Density SNP Arrays?

Braun, R., et al. (2009). Needles in the haystack: identifying individuals present in pooled genomic data. *PLoS Genetics, 5*(10), 1–8.

The Center for Advanced Forensic DNA Analysis™. Available at http://advancedforensicdna.com/. Accessed March 24, 2014.

Clayton, D. (2010). On inferring presence of an individual in a mixture: a Bayesian approach. *Biostatistics, 11*(4), 661–673.

Egeland, T., et al. (2012). Complex mixtures: a critical examination of a paper by Homer, et al. *Forensic Science International: Genetics, 6*, 64–69.

Homer, N., et al. (2008). Resolving individuals contributing trace amounts of DNA to highly complex mixtures using high-density SNP genotyping microarrays. *PLoS Genetics, 4*(8), 1–9.

Jacobs, K. B., et al. (2009). A new statistic and its power to infer membership in a genome-wide association study using genotype frequencies. *Nature Genetics, 41*(11), 1253–1257.

McElfresh, K. C., et al. (2009). Utilizing 300,000 or more single nucleotide polymorphisms for the identification of individuals within a forensic mixture. In *Proceedings of the 20th International Symposium on Human Identification*. Available at http://www.promega.com/ ~ /media/files/resources/conference%20proceedings/ishi%2020/oral%20presentations/mcelfresh.pdf?la=en. Accessed March 24, 2014.

McElfresh, K. C., et al. (2011). Utilizing ultra-high-density SNP arrays to analyze forensic mixtures: an operational assessment. In *Proceedings of the 22th International Symposium on Human Identification*. Available at http://www.promega.com/ ~ /media/files/resources/conference%20proceedings/ishi%2021/poster%20abstracts/poster_24.pdf?la=en. Accessed March 24, 2014.

Sampson, J., & Zhao, H. (2009). Identifying individuals in a complex mixture of DNA with unknown ancestry. *Statistical Applications in Genetics and Molecular Biology, 8*(1), 37.

Visscher, P. M., & Hill, W. G. (2009). The limits of individual identification from sample allele frequencies: theory and statistical analysis. *PLoS Genetics, 5*(10), 1–6.

Voskoboinik, L., & Darvasi, A. (2011). Forensic identification of an individual in complex DNA mixtures. *Forensic Science International: Genetics, 5*, 428–435.

Poor-Quality Samples Being Submitted

Bitner, S. E., et al. (2014). A touch-ing retrospective: a review of five years of touch DNA samples. *Proceedings of the American Academy of Forensic Sciences 66th Annual Scientific Meeting, 20*, 98–99.

Dieltjes, P., et al. (2011). A sensitive method to extract DNA from biological traces present on ammunition for the purpose of genetic profiling. *International Journal of Legal Medicine, 125*, 597–602.

Dufva, C., & Nilsson, A. (2011). Success rate of LT DNA analyses in casework. *Forensic Science International: Genetics Supplement Series, 3*, e271–e272.

Hunt, T. R. (2014). It's rapid, but is it relevant? Balancing speed and evidentiary significance in the coming age of real-time DNA analysis. *Proceedings of the American Academy of Forensic Sciences 66th Annual Scientific Meeting, 20*, 265–266.

Irwin, J. A., et al. (2007). Application of low copy number STR typing to the identification of aged, degraded skeletal remains. *Journal of Forensic Sciences, 52*, 1322–1327.

Pizzamiglio, M., et al. (2004). Forensic identification of a murderer by LCN DNA collected from the inside of the victim's car. *Progress in Forensic Genetics, 10*(ICS 1261), 437–439.

Prinz, M., et al. (2006). Maximization of STR DNA typing success for touched objects. *Progress in Forensic Genetics, 11*(ICS 1288), 651–653.

Raymond, J. J., et al. (2008). Trace DNA analysis: do you know what your neighbour is doing? a multi-jurisdictional survey. *Forensic Science International: Genetics, 2*, 19–28.

Raymond, J. J., et al. (2009). Trace DNA success rates relating to volume crime offences. *Forensic Science International: Genetics Supplement Series, 2*, 136–137.

Raymond, J. J., et al. (2009). Trace evidence characteristics of DNA: a preliminary investigation of the persistence of DNA at crime scenes. *Forensic Science International: Genetics, 4*, 26–33.

Roman, J. K., et al. (2008). *The DNA field experiment: cost-effectiveness analysis of the use of DNA in the investigation of high-volume crimes*. Washington, DC: Urban Institute Justice Policy Center. Available at https://www.ncjrs.gov/pdffiles1/nij/grants/222318.pdf. Accessed March 24, 2014.

Samples, M., Vasquez, T. L., & Umback, N. J. (2014). What's in a name? That which we call 'touch DNA' perhaps should be split in twain. *Proceedings of the American Academy of Forensic Sciences 66th Annual Scientific Meeting, 20*, 96.

Complexity Threshold

Geddes, L. (2010). Fallible DNA evidence can mean prison or freedom. *New Scientist*, (issue 2773). Available at http://www.newscientist.com/article/mg20727733.500-fallible-dna-evidence-can-mean-prison-or-freedom.html. Accessed March 24, 2014.

Gordon, J. S. (2012). Characterization of error tradeoffs in human identity comparisons: determining a complexity threshold for DNA mixture interpretation. *Unpublished master's thesis for Boston University School of Medicine Forensic Science Program.*

Grgicak, C. M. (2012). Complexity thresholds and exclusion criteria. In *Presentation at ISHI 2012 Mixture Interpretation Workshop.* Available at http://www.cstl.nist.gov/strbase/training/ISHI2012-MixtureWorkshop-ComplexityThreshold.pdf. Accessed March 24, 2014.

Pascali, V., & Prinz, M. (2012). Highlights of the conference "The hidden side of DNA profiles: Artifacts, errors and uncertain evidence." *Forensic Science International: Genetics, 6*, 775–777.

Rome meeting (2012). Video of conference entitled "The hidden side of DNA profiles: artifacts, errors and uncertain evidence" kindly provided by Vince Pascali to Author following the April 27–28, 2012 meeting.

Rudin, N., & Inman, K. (2012). The discomfort of thought — a discussion with John Butler. *The CACNews. 1st Quarter, 2012*, 8–11.

8

Troubleshooting Data Collection

It's not that I'm so smart; it's just that I stay with problems longer.

Albert Einstein

Men give me some credit for genius, but all of the genius I have lies in this. When I have a subject in mind,
I study it profoundly, day and night it is before me. I explore it in all its bearings. My mind becomes pervaded with
it. The result is what some people call the fruits of genius, whereas it is in reality the fruits of study and labor.

Alexander Hamilton

INTRODUCTION

DNA labs often encounter challenges when working with the many variables involved during the polymerase chain reaction (PCR) amplification of short tandem repeat (STR) markers and capillary electrophoresis (CE) separation and detection of fluorescently-labeled DNA molecules. My graduate research, conducted at the FBI Laboratory with Bruce McCord from 1993 to 1995, involved pioneering CE analysis of PCR products including the first demonstration of STR typing with CE (Butler 1995, Butler et al. 1994, Butler et al. 1995). Instruments have improved immensely over the past two decades but the general principles of DNA separation and detection remain the same. Our group at NIST has worked with numerous CE systems including the Applied Biosystems (ABI) 310, 3100, 3130xl, 3500, and 3500xl Genetic Analyzers.[1] This chapter shares lessons learned in our laboratory as well as some reported by other scientists in the literature or through correspondence with the author.

Troubleshooting is all about understanding your analytical system and how DNA typing data are generated during the PCR process and subsequent separation and detection of STR alleles via CE with fluorescence detection. Thus, this chapter begins with a brief review of the principles and processes of CE.

---

[1] Certain commercial equipment, instruments, and materials are identified in order to specify experimental procedures as completely as possible. In no case does such identification imply a recommendation or endorsement by the National Institute of Standards and Technology nor does it imply that any of the materials, instruments, or equipment identified are necessarily the best available for the purpose.

PRINCIPLES AND PROCESSES INVOLVED WITH
CAPILLARY ELECTROPHORESIS

Chapter 6 in *Advanced Topics in Forensic DNA Typing: Methodology* (Butler 2012) covers fundamental principles of CE injection, separation, and detection. Pertinent information is also available in a 2004 *Electrophoresis* review article (Butler et al. 2004). Readers are encouraged to examine information found in Chapter 2 of this book on fluorescence detection in ABI Genetic Analyzer instruments. Because ABI 3130 and 3500 series Genetic Analyzers are currently the most widely-used instruments, Figure 8.1 includes labeled photos of the primary parts of these instruments.

Initial Calibrations

Before color-separated data can be collected on multicapillary ABI Genetic Analyzers, spatial and spectral calibrations must be performed. These steps prepare the instrument for examining DNA data in specific capillary array and STR kit configurations. If these initial calibrations are not performed properly, similar to poor alignment of tires on a car giving rise to a wobbly ride, the data analysis "ride" will be rougher than need be — and may not even be possible.

Spatial Calibration

A spatial calibration maps the location of fluorescence from each capillary onto the charged-coupled device (CCD) detector and should be carried out whenever installing a new capillary array or replacing an array that has been previously used. Also if the detection cell door has been opened or the instrument has been moved, running a new spatial calibration is important as misalignment of the emitted fluorescent light will result in loss of signal reaching the CCD detector.

A proper spatial calibration will have evenly spaced peaks with similar heights and good morphology (meaning fairly narrow peaks in a Gausian shape). Typically peak spacing will be about 15 pixels between the tops of each detected peak. The data collection software places a small orange cross on top of peaks that are recognized as potential capillary positions. The number of peaks should equal the number of capillaries in the array (e.g. 16 peaks for an ABI 3130xl or 8 peaks for an ABI 3500). For more information and for examples of good and bad spatial calibration results, see the user manual for the specific ABI Genetic Analyzer of interest.

If a spatial calibration fails, the capillary array may be improperly positioned, the detector cell may need to be cleaned, or individual capillaries in the array may not be completely filled with the separation buffer and polymer. With each of these possibilities, laser light is not passing properly through the detection region. Any particles or air bubbles that block or deflect light can adversely impact the signal detected by the CCD camera. The array detector cell can usually be cleaned with methanol and blotted dry with a Kimwipe. Polymer leaks, which result in incomplete filling of the capillary array, can be due to failure to tighten fittings fully when inserting the array or connecting lines to the polymer block. More rarely, a cracked detection cell can result in a polymer leak.

Spectral Calibration

A matrix correction (as it was originally called with the ABI 310) or a spectral calibration (for multi-capillary systems) involves determining the contribution of different colored light emitted from fluorescent dyes that falls within a defined set of wavelengths collected on the CCD detector. Following

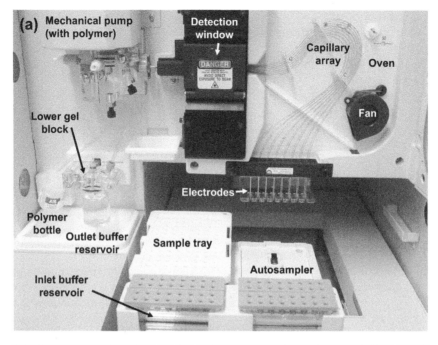

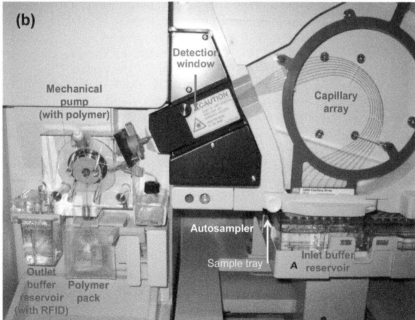

FIGURE 8.1 (a) Photograph of ABI 3130xl Genetic Analyzer with a 16-capillary array. (b) Photograph of ABI 3500 Genetic Analyzer with an 8-capillary array.

I. DATA INTERPRETATION

the analysis of spectral calibration standards, which should exhibit a single peak for each dye being calibrated in multicapillary CE instruments, a proprietary mathematical matrix is applied within the data collection software. As noted in Chapter 1, this matrix separates fluorescence signal from any DNA molecules labeled with a specific fluorescent dye into a defined color that is then displayed by the data analysis software.

STR kit manufacturers supply spectral calibration standards with which to calibrate a laboratory's Genetic Analyzer for use with a specific set of fluorescent dyes present in an STR kit. These spectral calibration standards are DNA samples containing individual fluorescent dyes that match the dye-labeled PCR primers present in an STR kit.

Failure to establish an appropriate spectral calibration that matches the fluorescent dyes present in a specific STR kit will result in signal bleedthrough between different dye channels, commonly referred to as "pull-up." Pull-up can also result from a saturated CCD detector signal when an over-abundance of dye-labeled DNA molecules are present. Signal from an overloaded sample effectively spills over into adjacent dye colors. For example, an off-scale homozygous TH01 allele labeled with a green-colored dye may cause a false peak to appear in the blue dye channel and perhaps in the yellow dye channel as well at the same time point in the electropherogram.

With high levels of multiplexing in commercially available STR kits, there may be loci in adjacent colors with alleles that are similar in size to potential pull-up peaks. If a pull-up peak falls into an allele sizing bin for an STR marker in an adjacent dye color, the pull-up peak will be labeled by the genotyping software as though it were a true allele for this different locus. An observant analyst will then need to remove this pull-up "allele" to avoid creating an incorrect DNA profile that does not represent the original biological sample. Thus, pull-up peaks in adjacent dye colors can result from either an overloaded signal or because of poor alignment of the spectral calibration to the fluorescence being emitted by the dye-labeled PCR products in the sample.

A spectral calibration file specifies criteria that are used to determine if a spectral calibration passes. A Q-value (quality value) sets the tolerance for pull-up or pull-down peaks. (Pull-down peaks result from an overcompensation of signal subtraction and the electrophoretic trace artificially dipping.) Typically, a Q-value is set at 0.95 (although it may be adjusted slightly) where a value of 1.0 signifies a theoretically perfect spectral separation with no detectable pull-up/pull-down peaks. Essentially a Q-value of 0.95 means that up to 5% bleedthrough can be tolerated in a "passing spectral." If a spectral calibration fails for a few of the capillaries in some of the multicapillary CE instruments, then successful calibrations can be "borrowed" to aid adjacent capillaries. Spectral performance across the capillary array will be better if all of the capillaries pass. Capillaries with borrowed spectral calibrations are more likely to exhibit pull-up peaks over time as the spectral conditions in the specific capillary are not an optimal match. For the four-capillary 3130, all four capillaries must pass.

Condition bounds, defined by C-values, reflect the amount of overlap between fluorescent dye emission spectra for a specific set of dyes. A C-value of 1.0 would be equivalent to no overlaps between dyes. Higher C-values reflect a higher overlap in a dye set. Default C-value bounds are 6–12 for Dye Set F and 7–12 for Dye Set G5. All fluorescence dyes commonly used in STR kits exhibit some degree of spectral overlap in emission spectra.

Over time, a spectral calibration will drift, and pull-up peaks will begin to appear in electropherograms even when the peak signals are not off-scale (Shewale et al. 2012). For this reason, spectral calibrations need to be repeated on a periodic basis to ensure that data are being collected as cleanly as possible. In addition, new spectral calibrations are needed whenever anything significant has been changed on the instrument that would impact the optics or fluorescence of the dye sets in use (e.g. replacement of a CCD camera or optics adjustments by a service engineer). Of course, data can still be interpreted with some degree of pull-up. However, mixture interpretation, which is hard enough by itself, can be made even more difficult when true alleles must be distinguished from pull-up peaks.

Variable Binning

Another thing to be aware of is that since the introduction of data collection software v1.1 for the ABI 3100 in 2002 and subsequent instruments (ABI 3130 and 3500 series), ABI has used "variable binning" (Applied Biosystems 2003) where more pixels on the CCD detector are combined to inflate the amount of light collected for the weaker red-dye color channels (D.N.A. Box 8.1).

D.N.A. BOX 8.1

VARIABLE BINNING AND ITS IMPACT

Since not all of the fluorescent dyes used to label PCR products in STR kits are equally sensitive when excited with a single laser wavelength, electronic signal enhancement has been used with newer versions of software to strengthen the weaker signals. The expansion of data collection with a wider window for fluorescence emission wavelengths enhances sensitivity making red-dye channel peaks appear larger (see figure) but may also lead to more noise in these channels. As discussed in Chapter 2, the four-fold expansion of the relative fluorescence unit (RFU) scale in ABI 3500 and 3500xl Genetic Analyzers (relative to earlier ABI 3100 and 3130 series instruments) can lead to significantly different noise levels in each dye channel. In spite of this observation, most labs choose to use a common analytical threshold (e.g. 100 RFU) to simplify data interpretation. While dye-specific analytical thresholds may be used (e.g. 55 RFU for the blue channel and 120 RFU for the red channel), interpretation protocols become more complicated.

In the figure (see right), a portion of the same Identifiler DNA profile was analyzed using different ABI 3100 and 3130xl data collection versions. The relative peak height differences (y-axis) are due to "variable binning" with newer ABI data collection versions that increase the amount of emitted light collected from the red dye region to improve the balance between the color channels in a DNA profile. The difference in STR allele relative mobilities as exhibited by the relative peak positions (x-axis) in this particular example are due to using different polymers for separation (POP-6 with the ABI 3100 and POP-7 with the ABI 3130xl).

(a)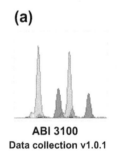

(b)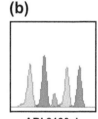

| **ABI 3100** | **ABI 3130xl** |
| Data collection v1.0.1 | Data collection v3.0 |

The same PCR products examined with different data collection versions. In (a) there is an equal number of pixels of light collected from the CCD camera for the blue-labeled and red-labeled peaks. In (b) the signal increase in the red dye-labeled PCR products is accomplished with "variable binning" where more pixels of light are collected from the CCD camera in the red channel to help balance the less sensitive red dye with blue dye-labeled amplicons.

Analytical Requirements

Once the initial spatial and spectral calibrations have been performed, the instrument is able to collect data for the purposes of generating DNA profiles. In order to perform effective STR typing, three analytical requirements must be met: (1) *spectral resolution* of fluorescent dyes in order to distinguish different dye labels on PCR products, (2) *analytical size resolution* in order to distinguish STR alleles from one another that may differ by as little as a single nucleotide, and (3) *tight run-to-run precision* so that sequentially run samples may be compared and analyzed relative to allelic ladders.

Spectral Resolution

Distinguishing signal from different fluorescent dyes is crucial with modern STR kits that involve many loci with overlapping size ranges. Software manipulations of color-separated data are performed once emitted light at dye-specific wavelengths is collected onto CCD detectors. Because fluorescence emission spectra overlap from each of the fluorescent dyes used to label STR alleles, a spectral calibration must be used to create a mathematical relationship between the levels of adjacent colors found in each color. For example, the blue color virtual bin contains some contribution from green, yellow, and red dyes. This spectral correction is used by the data collection software to correct for the spectral overlap of the dyes.

There are different dye sets used for various STR kits (see Table 5.1). Once spectral calibration has been performed for a specific dye set, it is important to use this dye set with an appropriate STR kit. For example, accidently running Identifiler PCR products, which should be matched to a five-dye G5 spectral calibration, with a four-dye F spectral calibration (that is used for Profiler Plus or SGM Plus kits) will result in pull-up and failure to collect meaningful data since a four-dye filter is being placed on a five-dye system.

On the single-capillary ABI 310 instrument, spectral calibration (referred to as a matrix) can be applied at the time of data analysis (as opposed to *during* data collection) enabling spectral contribution values to be manually tweaked or new matrices to be applied *after* running samples. However, on all multicapillary instruments since the 3100 was introduced, color correction from the spectral calibration is applied *as the data are collected* on the CCD detector. Thus, as noted previously, successful spectral calibrations are required to be assigned to every capillary before samples can be processed.

Analytical Size Resolution

While most of the STR markers used in forensic human identification are tetranucleotides, and therefore would be expected to have closely spaced heterozygous alleles differing in size by four nucleotides, the existence of variant alleles with as little as a single nucleotide variation in size increases the stringency of resolution requirements. In a population study involving 700 DNA samples and over 10,000 allele measurements across 15 autosomal STR loci (Butler et al. 2003), there were 160 observations of heterozygous alleles that differed by one, two, or three nucleotides, such as TH01 9.3 and 10 which differ by a single nucleotide. Thus, an instrument system capable of only resolving alleles that differed by four nucleotides could miss calling closely spaced heterozygous samples about 1.5% of the time.

A qualitative assessment of resolution in an electropherogram can usually be made through a visual inspection of peak shape, breadth, and separation. Peaks that are poorly shaped, overly broad, merged, or lack appropriate baseline separation indicate deteriorated system performance. For

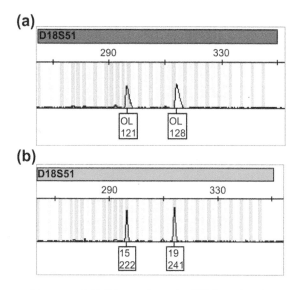

FIGURE 8.2 Results from a positive control 9947A sample at the STR locus D18S51 using (a) poor quality formamide versus (b) fresh high quality formamide. Peak labels indicate allele call and height in relative fluorescence units. Note that in (a) the STR alleles are not typed correctly (called off-ladder "OL" alleles) and have a smaller peak height. The peak tailing and wider peaks with lower peak heights are indicative of an injection from a salty sample. Figure courtesy of Amy Decker.

example, Figure 8.2 compares a good- and poor-resolution DNA separation at a single locus of the same STR sample. Visual inspections of electropherogram peak shapes can offer an excellent qualitative gauge of the system's resolution.

Resolution measurements can be conducted if a non-subjective approach is desired to evaluate casework electropherograms. For casework analysis this may take the form of evaluating the resolution of the allelic ladders typically bracketing casework samples or by evaluating the samples themselves. The allelic ladder typically contains multiple peaks that span the breadth of the electrophoretic run and are consistently applied from run to run. These factors make the allelic ladder an excellent sample to assess the performance of the system. Assessing individual-sample resolution may be approached by evaluation of the sample peak shapes or through the assessment of peaks present in the internal size standard (ISS).

Run-to-Run Precision

Minor temperature and electrophoresis changes occur between each run impacting electrophoretic mobility of DNA molecules traveling through the capillary. Even capillaries run in parallel at the same time in a capillary array have slightly different electrophoresis environments. Thus, all analyses need to be calibrated to achieve capability for full comparison of results.

Size calibration is achieved using ISSs that are mixed with the DNA samples and co-electrophoresed to put data on a common sizing scale. This calibration through minor measurement adjustments enables data to be compared over time and across samples. Size bins for each common allele can be established using allelic ladder alleles. Peaks present in samples can then be aligned to these size bins in order to make allele assignments for each locus.

When run-to-run precision has a standard deviation (SD) of less than 0.15 nucleotides, then it is possible to effectively distinguish sequence variants that differ by as little as a single nucleotide (D.N.A. Box 8.2). Common validation experiments involve injecting an allelic ladder multiple times to assess the size precision across the entire range of alleles.

D.N.A. BOX 8.2

SIZING PRECISION

An important set of experiments to perform when setting up a CE instrument involves sizing precision. The easiest way to conduct the experiments is to reinject an allelic ladder multiple times. The sizing results for each allele (relative to the ISS) are then evaluated across the multiple injections. An average and SD for each allele are established from the data (see figure on right). Ideally, the SD should be <0.15 bp so that 3 SD will be <0.5 bp. With a 3 SD of <0.5 bp, then over 99% of the time (assuming a normal, random variation in the sizing results) alleles differing by a single base pair can be distinguished from one another.

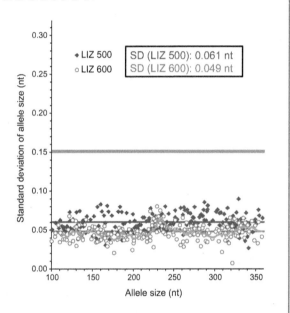

Average sizes of alleles in nucleotides (nt) from 16 injections of Identifiler STR kit allelic ladders on an ABI 3500 using two different size standards. The overall SD is slightly lower with the LIZ 600 (0.049 nt) compared to the LIZ 500 (0.061 nt). Figure courtesy of Erica Butts, NIST.

It helps to remember what is being measured when performing STR typing. Each peak that is produced in an electropherogram reflects the overall electrophoretic mobility of a single-stranded DNA (ssDNA) molecule that has a fluorescent tag (and perhaps mobility modifiers) on one end. The peak's mobility, as measured by data collection scan number, is converted to apparent nucleotide size with an ISS and size fitting algorithm. A peak's apparent size is then converted to an equivalent number of STR repeat units by comparison to an allelic ladder that contains the well-characterized commonly occurring alleles for each STR locus.

TABLE 8.1   Potential Issues and Solutions with Multicolor Capillary Electrophoresis

Issue	Cause/Result with Failure	Potential Solutions
Spectral resolution (color separation)	High RFU peaks	Inject less DNA into the CE capillary to avoid overloading the detector
	Bleedthrough or pull-up off of high RFU peaks that create artificial peaks in adjacent dye channels(s)	
Analytical size resolution	Inner capillary wall coating failure	Reinject sample (if a bubble causes poor polymer filling for a single run)
	Inability to resolve closely spaced STR alleles and in some cases incorrect allele calls could be made	Replace pump (if polymer is not being routinely delivered to fully fill the capillaries)
Run-to-run precision	Room temperature changes	Monitor room temperature and make adjustments to have more consistency
	Sample alleles run differently compared to allelic ladder alleles (and internal size standard cannot compensate) and false "off-ladder" alleles are typed	Reinject samples with an allelic ladder run in an adjacent capillary or a subsequent run

Assessing Analytical Performance

Table 8.1 lists some of the common problems and potential solutions related to spectral resolution, analytical size resolution, and run-to-run precision.

Analytical performance is dynamic in a CE environment. Resolution changes as capillaries begin to fail and eventually need to be replaced — usually after hundreds of injections. Room temperature variation may adversely impact size precision and run-to-run comparisons necessary to correlate allelic ladder allele sizes with sample allele sizes. Pull-up peaks from dye-channel bleedthrough may begin to appear over time as instrument settings drift from adequate spectral calibration.

Continually assessing adequacy of analytical performance is an important quality assurance measure. A simple way to do this assessment is to evaluate multiple allelic ladders over time. Because allelic ladders possess numerous DNA fragments, they provide an effective means of assessing spectral and spatial resolution. For example, the ability to resolve alleles 9.3 and 10 in the TH01 allelic ladder demonstrates single-base resolution in the size range of these PCR products.

Verification of appropriate run-to-run precision can be observed through purposeful repeated injections of allelic ladder samples as is commonly performed during validation precision studies. Alternatively, from a batch of samples containing multiple allelic ladders, an analyst can designate only one of the allelic ladder samples as "ladder" in the genotyping software and treat the remainder of the allelic ladders as "samples." For example, with a 16-capillary instrument, if an allelic ladder is included with each set of 15 samples, then six allelic ladders will be run during the processing of a full 96-well tray. Typically all six ladders are used to provide an averaged size-to-allele calibration across the plate. However, five of the ladders could be set as "samples" during the analysis of the plate with a single "ladder" providing size-to-allele calibration. If all of the alleles in the allelic ladder "samples" are appropriately assigned by the software, then an analyst can have confidence that run-to-run precision across the STR kit size range is sufficient for reliable allele calling across the entire 96-well plate of samples.

TABLE 8.2 Overview of Steps in STR Typing Process

Process What?	Protocol How?	Purpose Why?	Potential Problems What Can Go Wrong?
Biological sample collected	Swab obtained from evidentiary item or reference sample	Enables sample to be brought back to the lab for processing; represents individual(s) from whom sample came	Sample may not be collected fully; improper storage can result in the DNA degrading after collection; DNA contamination may occur by collector or manufacturer of swab
DNA template isolated (extracted) and quantified	DNA is chemically extracted from its cellular environment; amount of amplifiable DNA is assessed with a quantitative PCR assay	Isolates and hopefully purifies the DNA template(s) for further use; quantitation step determines amount of *human* DNA present so an optimal level can be added to the multiplex PCR reaction in order to achieve the best possible DNA profile	Sample may have a low amount of DNA and/or possess DNA from multiple contributors; poor recovery of the initial sample with low DNA extraction efficiency; PCR inhibitors may not be removed during extraction
Multiplex PCR amplification of STR markers performed	DNA template (in optimal amount) is mixed with DNA polymerase, a buffer, dNTPs, and a pair of primers specific for each locus with one primer containing a fluorescent dye; STR kits can contain a mixture of >30 primers	Copies DNA template regions to a detectable level and puts dye label on amplicons generated from specific locations (e.g. STR loci) within the DNA template	A sequence difference in a primer binding region can result in failure to amplify the desired target (null allele); DNA template may be damaged or fragmented or PCR inhibitors may be present and lead to loss or reduction of amplification product at some or all of the STR loci
Samples prepared for capillary electrophoresis (CE) analysis	An aliquot of multiplex PCR products is added to formamide along with a size standard containing a series of DNA molecules all labeled with a fluorescent dye different from the dyes used to create the PCR products; samples are covered with a septa to prevent evaporation while inside the CE instrument	Denatures amplicons into ssDNA; internal size standard added to facilitate comparison between samples and allelic ladders	Sample mix-up (switch) could happen with manual sample transfers if control processes not in place; sample switches are less likely with liquid transfer being performed using automation; poor quality formamide can result in poor CE injections and low peak signal; unclean septa can introduce a small amount of sample carryover from a previous injection
CE injection	The PCR sample diluted in formamide is placed into a CE instrument and raised onto the end of a capillary by an autosampler during the course of a "run," and a voltage is applied for a specific period of time (e.g. 3000 V for 10 s) pulling charged molecules into the capillary	Loads negatively charged molecules (including DNA) into the capillary	Presence of other ions such as chloride present from the PCR reaction buffer (or poor quality formamide breakdown products) can reduce the amount of DNA loaded onto the capillary; uneven autosampler tray can result in some sample positions not being injected properly due to the capillary and electrode not reaching the sample

CE separation	Negatively-charged ssDNA molecules interact with polymer strands in solution as they are being pulled by an electric field towards the positive electrode; longer DNA moves slower in a linear fashion below about 500 nucleotides	Separates charged molecules by size through interaction with polymer strands (e.g. POP-4) inside capillary	Dye artifacts (blobs) from primer impurities can comigrate with the DNA molecules; failure to completely fill capillaries with polymer or formation of electroosmotic flow due to capillary inner wall coating issues can lead to loss of resolution and thus failure to resolve similarly sized STR alleles
CE detection	Laser-excitation generates fluorescence of dye-labeled molecules as they pass the detector; emitted light passes through filters and mirrors onto a diffraction grating to separate the light into component colors that are captured on a CCD camera	Detects fluorescent signals that are converted into peaks in CE electropherogram where peak signal height can be correlated to PCR product amount and peak position (time since injection) can be correlated to relative size when compared to an internal size standard	Overloading of signal (including off-scale data) can lead to bleedthrough between dye channels and pull-up of false signals in adjacent dye colors; laser failure or detection optics that are not properly aligned or dirty (e.g. fingerprints on capillary window) can result in loss of fluorescence signal
Data collection software utilized	Creates .fsa (310/31xx) or .hid (3500) file after converting CCD detector intensities at specific wavelengths across thousands of scans; virtual filters assign ranges of wavelengths to specific colors; variable binning is now used to increase signal coming from weaker dye intensities	Applies spatial and spectral calibration (previously collected on the CE instrument) to create sample electropherograms	Application of an improper spectral calibration could result in excessive pull-up; noise levels in different dye channels can be different due in part to variable binning
Genotyping software applied	Peak data are converted to size information with internal size standard (using local Southern sizing algorithm) and into allele calls with allelic ladders (and stutter filters)	Enables correlation of PCR product size, fluorescence value and amount to STR loci allele calls and STR profile genotypes (and potentially contributor amounts if a 2-person mixture is present)	Analyst reviewing data could accidently remove the label on a true allele during initial data review (hopefully would be caught and corrected during technical review); inconsistent treatment of DNA mixtures

I. DATA INTERPRETATION

Overview of Process

Table 8.2 summarizes the principles, protocols, purposes, and potential problems for each step in the process of DNA typing using STR markers and CE.

Prior to electrophoresis, an aliquot of each DNA sample is typically diluted in formamide and mixed with an ISS. Following this sample preparation step, DNA molecules are injected onto the capillary and separated based on size through interaction with a sieving polymer matrix until the dye-labeled molecules pass a detector region where the fluorophore tags are excited by a laser and emitted light is detected and separated into different color channels for processing by genotyping software.

Sample Preparation

Sample preparation can impact electrokinetic injection. The PCR products created from amplifying a genomic DNA sample with STR typing kits are typically diluted to levels of approximately 1 in 10 with deionized formamide (e.g. 1 μL PCR product into 9 μL of formamide) both to help denature the double-stranded DNA (dsDNA) molecules and to help reduce the salt levels and aid the electrokinetic injection process (see next section).

Since formamide is a strong denaturant, it is commonly used in the preparation of ssDNA samples for CE. Merely placing a sample in formamide is usually sufficient to separate the two hybridized strands of DNA. However, heating a sample to 95°C for several minutes followed by rapid cooling to around 4°C (commonly referred to as "snap-cooling") is often performed to ensure that the two complementary DNA strands are separated or denatured. In our experience at NIST, STR samples do not need to be heated and snap-cooled after dilution in formamide in order to obtain reliable results.

Use of high-quality formamide with low conductivity is important. As formamide degrades it produces ionic decomposition products, including formic acid, which are negatively charged at a neutral pH and will be preferentially injected into the capillary. The formamide by-products can cause problems in both sensitivity and resolution (Buel et al. 1998). The quality of formamide can be easily measured using a portable conductivity meter and should be approximately 100 μS/cm (the SI unit of conductivity is Siemens per meter) or lower to obtain the best results.

The Hi-Di formamide (Life Technologies, South San Francis co, CA) used by most forensic DNA laboratories has a conductivity of <25 μS/cm. Many laboratories purchase ultrapure formamide and freeze aliquots immediately to ensure sample quality. The differences in peak shapes observed in Figure 8.2(a) and (b) are due to formamide quality.

Injection

The most common method used to introduce DNA samples into a capillary is a process known as *electrokinetic injection*, whereby a voltage is applied to a liquid sample immersed in one end of a capillary for a defined time. As DNA molecules are negatively charged in a neutral pH environment, a positive voltage draws the DNA molecules into the capillary. Electrokinetic injections produce narrow injection zones that permit high-resolution DNA separations to occur in a relatively short separation distance.

In order to get DNA molecules onto the CE capillary, an electric voltage is applied while the end of the capillary is immersed into the liquid DNA sample. A platinum electrode (cathode), which is adjacent to the single capillary in the ABI 310 instrument or surrounds each capillary in multicapillary systems, delivers voltage to the sample being tested. The flow of current, which is generated by the voltage applied and resistance experienced, pulls the negatively charged DNA molecules into the end of the capillary. CE injections of DNA are highly sensitive to the sample matrix. In particular, the ionic strength of small negative ions, such as chloride from the PCR solution, provide competition for larger, slower DNA molecules in entering the end of the capillary.

The quantity of DNA injected into a CE column ([DNA$_{injected}$]) is a function of the voltage or electric field applied (E), the injection time (t), the concentration of DNA in the sample ([DNA$_{sample}$]), the area of the capillary opening (πr^2), and the ionic strength of the sample (λ_{sample}) versus the buffer (λ_{buffer}). The electrophoretic mobility (μ_{ep}), or how quickly a charged molecule moves when experiencing an electric field, also impacts the quantity of the DNA loaded into a capillary as does the electroosmotic flow (μ_{eof}), which will be explained further in the next section. The equation for amount of DNA injected—and hence detected—in a CE system is (Butler et al. 2004, Rose & Jorgenson 1988):

$$\left[DNA_{injected} \right] = \frac{Et\left(\pi r^2\right)\left(\mu_{ep} + \mu_{eof}\right)\left[DNA_{sample} \right]\left(\lambda_{buffer}\right)}{\lambda_{sample}}.$$

This equation reveals how high ionic strength in a sample can impact the amount of DNA injected. Chloride (Cl^-) ions and other buffer ions present in PCR samples contribute to the sample conductivity and compete with DNA for injection onto the capillary. This inverse relationship between sample conductivity (caused by its salt content) and amount of DNA injected into the capillary is the reason that post-PCR purification can increase the CE signal. An increase in amount of DNA injected and detected has been reported using post-PCR purification products such as MinElute (Qiagen, Germantown, MD) or Montage (Millipore, Billerica, MA).

Separation

There are several components that impact DNA separations within CE systems: the polymer, the capillary, the electrophoresis buffer, and the voltage applied or electric field strength (Buel et al. 2003, Butler 1995). DNA moves with the electrophoretic flow from the negative electrode (cathode) towards the positive electrode (anode). Strands of entangled polymer form transient pores that serve as obstacles to inhibit progress of DNA molecules based on their size. Smaller DNA molecules are able to move more easily through the obstructions.

The commercially available poly-dimethyl-acrylamide POP-4, POP-6, and POP-7 polymers are successfully used in DNA genotyping by CE because they provide a sieving matrix for the separation of ssDNA and, at the same time, suppress electroosmotic flow that occurs due to negative charges that occur on the inner wall of the capillary (Rosenblum et al. 1997). POP-4 consists of 4% linear dimethylacrylamide, 8 mol/L urea, and 5% 2-pyrrolidinone (Rosenblum et al. 1997, Wenz et al. 1998). A common cause of poor resolution is failure to fully fill the capillary with polymer solution due to a leak in the syringe, pump, or capillary connection to the instrument.

Manufacturers of capillaries often suggest replacing a capillary at around 100 or 150 injections to avoid problems with resolution failure. With good sample preparation, many forensic laboratories see capillary lifetimes extend far past the 100 or 150 injections recommended by the manufacturer. Through effective monitoring of sample resolution, capillaries can be replaced when resolution declines (Buel et al. 2003).

To accomplish optimal resolution of samples during STR analysis, the amplified DNA fragments need to remain denatured. To accomplish this DNA denaturation, the CE run temperature is set higher than room temperature, and buffer additives such as formamide, urea, and 2-pyrrolidinone are added to keep the DNA from reannealing. Even under strong denaturing conditions, DNA

I. DATA INTERPRETATION

molecules can assume various conformations due to intramolecular attractions. Therefore, capillary run temperatures of 60°C are commonly employed to help reduce secondary structure in DNA (Rosenblum et al. 1997). Even with these measures, CE instruments need a stable ambient temperature, as temperature variations can have profound effects on allele migration (D.N.A. Box 8.3).

D.N.A. BOX 8.3

UNDERSTANDING CE INSTRUMENT SENSITIVITY TO ROOM TEMPERATURE CHANGES

Swings in room temperature of more than $\approx 2°C$ have been shown to adversely impact sizing precision when DNA separations are occurring in an ABI 310 or other Genetic Analyzer. This imprecision can lead to improperly calling "off-ladder" alleles when comparisons are made to sequentially-run allelic ladders. The reasons why temperature variation leads to imprecise measurements and inaccurate allele calls are enumerated below.

Voltage is determined by current times resistance ($V = I \times R$), which is also known as Ohm's law after Georg Ohm, who discovered this relationship in 1827. Rearranging this equation, current is equal to voltage divided by resistance. Voltage is the energy put into the system by the power supply. In the case of an ABI 310 or 3100 Genetic Analyzer, the voltage delivered for the separation step is typically 15,000 V or 15 kV. For the injection step, a lower voltage and hence lower current is often used to coax the DNA molecules into the end of the capillary. While thousands of volts may seem like a lot of energy, it is the current, or the flow of electrons or charged particles, that matters with electricity and electrophoresis. The speed at which the DNA molecules move is directly related to the current flow — not the voltage delivered. Resistance is high inside of a narrow glass capillary filled with a viscous polymer solution so current flow is typically in the (10−100) microampere region.

Excessive room temperature changes (swings of more than several degrees Celsius) can lead to temperature variation inside the CE instrument and inside the capillary itself. Temperature changes that occur inside the capillary change the viscosity of the polymer which in turn alters the resistance experienced by the DNA molecules and other ions flowing during electrophoresis. As the polymer concentration inside the capillary effectively changes due to this temperature change, the mobility, or speed of movement, of DNA molecules shifts. If the temperature goes up, the polymer network of transient pores inside the capillary becomes more flexible (essentially less concentrated) and the DNA molecules move more quickly. Thus, while the voltage may be constant between runs, the resistance can change — leading to shifting in the current experienced by the DNA molecules undergoing electrophoresis.

Different length DNA sequences have different electrophoretic mobilities because they tumble or gyrate through a gel at different rates. Longer DNA molecules have a larger radius of gyration, which means that they will interact more frequently with polymer strands that effectively slow the DNA molecules and their movement through the capillary. Sequence differences in DNA molecules impact their 3-dimensional structure (their radius of gyration). Thus, in some cases, it is possible to separate two DNA molecules with the same length but different internal sequence (or to see a shift in the apparent size between them). This is the reason that allelic ladders are necessary in order to accurately genotype STR alleles separated and sized by electrophoresis. *The allelic ladder alleles have the same DNA sequence as the STR allele being measured and thus possess the same radius of gyration when exposed to the same electrophoresis conditions.*

How does this information relate to loss of precision in CE systems when room temperature varies? DNA sizes measured in CE are determined relative to an ISS, which contains a series of DNA fragments. These fragments have a different internal sequence compared to STR alleles. When the electrophoresis conditions change between two runs of the CE instrument (e.g. due to a room temperature shift that ultimately alters the polymer concentration in the capillary), the differential movement of the size standard peaks compared to the STR alleles may be sufficient between sequential runs to alter the apparent size of the STR alleles. If this happens, then the allelic ladder allele corresponding to the sample allele being measured may appear slightly different in size. If it falls outside of the ±0.5 bp genotyping bin, then the sample allele is incorrectly labeled as "off-ladder." Thus, precise temperature control either within the instrument itself or the room where the instrument is housed, or both, is critical to obtaining quality STR typing results.

Detection

The amount of detected signal in an electropherogram is influenced by the excitation laser power, the fluorescent dyes used, the optical path of emitted light, the detector, and the software algorithms used to filter and adjust observed signal. Intensity of the light emitted by a fluorophore is directly dependent on the amount of light that the dye has absorbed. Thus, the excitation source is very important in the behavior of a fluorophore. Other important instrument parameters include optical filters used for signal discrimination and the sensitivity and spectral response of the detector.

Dye-labeled PCR primers label only a single strand of a PCR product. This simplifies data interpretation because the complementary DNA strand is not visible to the detector. However, as will be discussed later in the chapter, labeled single-strand DNA molecules can re-hybridize to their complementary strands and produce labeled dsDNA molecules that migrate through the capillary at a faster rate.

A key capability of the technology used to produce STR profiles is that dye-labeled primers enable multiple PCR products to be labeled simultaneously during the PCR amplification process in an independent fashion. Therefore, multiple sites in an individual's genome can be probed in parallel enabling higher-throughput genotyping with amplicons of overlapping size being distinguished from one another by their dye labels.

INSTRUMENT MAINTENANCE & COMMON PROBLEMS

Obtaining high-quality data from Genetic Analyzers requires appropriate maintenance of the CE and being aware of common problems that can result during the course of instrument use.

Instrument Maintenance

Environment and Power

A key aspect of obtaining the best possible results from ABI Genetic Analyzers, or any CE instrument for that matter, is to maintain a clean environment. Dust or any particulate matter in the detection region can block light travel through the filters and optical path and thus adversely impact the amount of detected signal. Maintaining consistent power is also important, particularly since DNA separations are typically occurring at 15,000 V. An electrical surge protector and uninterrupted power supply battery backup can help avoid voltage spikes.

Seals, Syringes, and Pumps

For robust, reliable DNA separations, capillaries must fully fill with the buffer and polymer solution. Capillaries are long thin tubes and thus require a lot of pressure to properly fill. Resistance is encountered when trying to push a viscous polymer solution into a 50 μm internal diameter tube. Leaks in fittings to the pump block or loose syringe barrels prevent desired filling of the capillary. Pumps on the ABI 3130 and 3500 series instruments can sometimes fail and need to be replaced. Poor resolution on a new capillary array is a common indication that there is a leak in the system or a pump is not working properly.

Air Bubbles

Air bubbles in a narrow capillary or the tubing connecting the polymer, buffer, and capillaries present a significant problem because electric current cannot flow properly through the air pocket. Buffer and polymer solutions should be devoid of bubbles. The manufacturer recommends allowing polymer solution to sit at room temperature for at least an hour with the cap loosened before installing on the instrument to avoid bubble formation (Applied Biosystems 2011). When capillaries, polymer, and buffer are initially placed on the CE instrument, solutions are pushed through the tubing and pump block to try to remove all bubbles before closing the system. In addition, pre-electrophoresis is performed prior to each sample injection in order to try to remove any bubbles that have entered the closed system. Sample plates are commonly centrifuged prior to loading them onto the CE autosampler in order to remove air bubbles that would adversely impact electrokinetic injection.

Capillary Tips

Both ends of capillaries need to be stored in water or buffer once the tips of the capillaries are exposed to buffer or polymer solutions. Buffer and polymer solutions used for DNA separations contain high concentrations of urea. If these solutions are allowed to evaporate, urea crystals can form in the narrow opening of a capillary and block the flow of current. Because openings of CE capillaries are so small, it can be extremely difficult to redissolve the crystalline urea and unblock the capillary opening.

Regular Reagent Replacement

When routinely processing samples, buffer solutions should be replaced regularly (e.g. every few days) due to buffer depletion from electrolysis of solutions coming in direct contact with the electrodes. While the manufacturer may encourage weekly replenishment of polymer solutions, our experience at NIST has confirmed that keeping the system closed for multiple weeks is preferable to avoid the introduction of air bubbles and formation of urea crystals as solutions evaporate when the pump block is opened and cleaned. In addition, precious polymer solution is lost pushing out air bubbles when the pump block and lines are filled before closing the system.

Polymer and buffer solutions have manufacturer-warrantied shelf lives. While it is recognized that accredited labs must follow manufacturer expiration dates as a requirement of their quality systems, it is worth noting that DNA profile quality is not necessarily diminished if "expired" reagents are used. As long as the urea in the buffer or polymer solution has not come out of solution (typically due to evaporation from improperly sealed containers), then quality DNA separations may be obtained even years after the official expiration date provided by the manufacturer. In previous discussions with manufacturers, we have learned that some expiration dates may have been set for business rather than scientific reasons.

Common Artifacts and Problems

CE instruments are not discriminating towards (i.e. specific to detecting) STR alleles. Electrokinetic injection will inject any ion of the appropriate charge. The rate of entry into the capillary will be largely dependent on the ion's mobility. Thus, smaller ions typically will travel faster than larger DNA molecules and be preferentially loaded into the capillary. In addition, anything that causes the CCD camera to produce a signal in the specified wavelength range will be considered signal with the assigned dye color and appear in the final electropherogram as a peak that represents the level of fluorescent signal detected.

If a peak signal occurs above the detection or analytical threshold (see Chapter 2) and falls in an STR allele bin (a kit-specific color and size range), it will be designated as an allele by genotyping software. An important exception involves stutter products that can be filtered out with threshold settings in the genotyping software. Following the initial allele determinations by the software, a DNA analyst, or an expert system software program, as part of the interpretation process, assesses whether or not a labeled peak is in fact a true STR allele. If it is deemed to be an artifact, then the allele label is removed — typically with notation as to the reason for removal.

Several of the common artifacts seen in CE electropherograms are discussed below.

Dye Artifacts

Dye artifacts (commonly referred to as "dye blobs") are fluorescent dye molecules that coexist with dye-labeled primers and are injected and separated during DNA separation using CE. These dye artifacts arise from incomplete coupling of the fluorescent dye during primer synthesis and have slipped past a manufacturer's primer purification process. These dye blobs, which are usually broad low-level peaks at specific locations and dye colors in an electropherogram, are thus minor contaminants that primarily interfere with low-level DNA detection.

Each STR kit lot can possess a different level of dye artifacts. Dye artifacts can be most easily seen in PCR negative controls and will migrate through the CE capillary at characteristically consistent sizes. For example, there is a prominent fluorescein dye blob that migrates, depending on electrophoresis conditions, at an apparent size of approximately 120 nt.

Dye artifacts can be removed with post-PCR purification (Butler et al. 2003) using Dye-Terminator Removal filtration columns from Edge Biosystems (Gaithersburg, MD). This solution is not ideal as it adds additional steps and expense. STR kit manufacturers have improved their primer synthesis and purification processes in recent years, and therefore dye artifacts are not as much of a problem today as they once were.

Spikes

Spikes are manifest as sharp peaks that may occur in a single color or be exhibited across multiple colors. Most spikes in electropherograms are not reproducible since they are not an inherent part of the sample being separated and detected. Thus, if a sample is reinjected, the initial spike will not be observed.

Possible causes of spikes include dust or lint from non-lint free tissues, dried polymer deposits, dried buffer deposits, old or poor quality formamide, air bubbles, power surges, poor/exhausted capillary/array, improper use of canned air, or use of powdered gloves (Applied Biosystems 2011). The frequency of occurrence of spikes, which were fairly common in the early days of STR typing with the ABI 310 Genetic Analyzer, has been significantly reduced. This reduction in spikes is likely due to better quality control in the polymer and buffers used and perhaps improved electrical stability with newer instruments.

Pull-up (Bleedthrough)

As was discussed earlier in this chapter, peak signal that carries over to adjacent color channels is referred to as pull-up or bleedthrough (Figure 8.3). Pull-up results from failure of the spectral calibration to compensate for the observed signal on the CCD detector. Typically this bleedthrough is a result of exceeding the linear range of detection for the instrument and can be reduced by reinjecting samples using a lower CE injection time or voltage (or a combination, such as 5 s @ 2 kV instead of 10 s @ 3 kV).

Pull-up can especially be a problem when STR loci in different colors have allele size bins that fall directly in line. For example in the SGM Plus kit, many of the vWA allele bins (in the blue dye

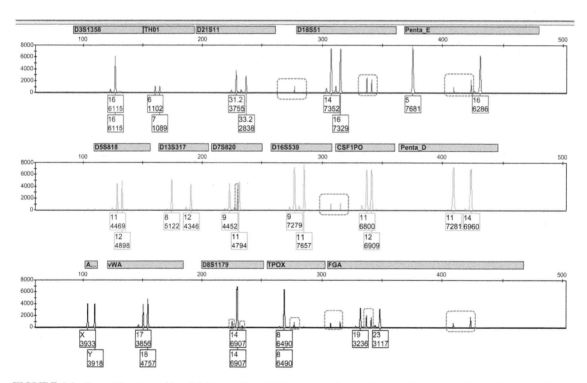

FIGURE 8.3 PowerPlex 16 profile exhibiting pull-up (circled peaks) due to off-scale data at several loci. Figure courtesy of Becky Hill, NIST.

channel) and TH01 allele bins (in the yellow dye channel) have the same sizes. With an overloaded sample and poor spectral color separation, one group reported missing a TH01 allele that was hidden under a vWA peak (Bardill et al. 2006).

Poor Resolution (Wide Peaks)

Wide peaks result in poor resolution. A common measure of peak resolution is the TH01 9.3 and 10 alleles (Figure 8.4). High-resolution results in CE are dependent on using a focused injection to keep the initial plug of DNA molecules together, a well-coated inner capillary wall that prevents DNA from sticking to it, and a uniform polymer solution designed to resolve closely sized DNA molecules. In addition, DNA separations work best when the DNA molecules are in a single-stranded state as it is more flexible than dsDNA. Flexible molecules are more likely to interact with the polymer strands in the capillary and be distinguished from other molecules of similar size. Dilution of samples in formamide, use of denaturants such as urea in run buffers, and performing electrophoresis at elevated temperatures (e.g. 60°C) all help make and keep the DNA in a single-stranded form.

A DNA separation is like a marathon race. DNA molecules are lined up at the opening of a capillary during the injection process just like runners line up at a starting line for a race. Once the electrophoresis voltage is applied, the DNA molecules run the capillary course based on their interactions with polymer strands. Smaller, lighter DNA molecules move through the polymer strand obstacles more easily than larger, heavier molecules and thus make it to the detector (finish line) first. The race time for each molecule is recorded as it crosses the finish line. Note that if runners are spread out in a straight line across the starting line at the start of a race, they will be separated by their running speed *during* the course of the race. If, instead, the initial runners start at slightly different times, then those who start later will be at a disadvantage as they lose time while they are in the starting area. Two runners with the same ability (i.e. DNA size) that do not start at the same time will cross the finish line at slightly different times. This would be equivalent to a wide peak rather than a narrow one.

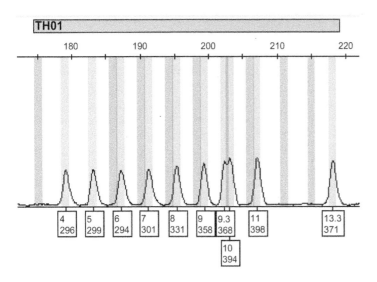

FIGURE 8.4 Poor resolution of TH01 alleles 9.3 and 10 in NGM SElect STR kit allelic ladder. The broad peak bases suggest that the capillary array needs to be replaced. Data courtesy of Becky Hill, NIST.

Having a focused plug of DNA molecules at the starting line results in sharper peaks. Poor quality formamide leads to spreading out of the DNA molecules at the starting line, which in turn creates broader peaks (see Figure 8.2(a)). After many injections, the inner wall of a capillary fails to be coated properly and the capillary needs to be replaced to overcome the resulting poor resolution (see Figure 8.4).

The most common cause of peak broadening is incomplete filling of the capillary array. This may occur because of a pump failure (or syringe barrel leakage on earlier instruments). Poor polymer delivery to the capillary can also be caused by failure to fully close the check valve or buffer pin valve that "seals" the system before polymer is pushed into the capillary prior to each run. If the check valve is not closed completely, then polymer will leak into the outlet buffer vial and not fully fill the capillary.

Sample Carryover

In a July 2010 *Forensic News* article (Applied Biosystems 2010) and a June 2012 technical note (Applied Biosystems 2012), ABI scientists discuss sample carryover, which is the physical transfer of DNA from one injection to the next. They note that after sample injection, capillaries are moved from the sample plate to a water reservoir to rinse off any excess sample. The capillaries pass through septa covering the water wash container. If some sample residue remains on the septa, it could be picked up during the next injection cycle, resulting in contaminating signal in the next electropherogram. Of course the degree of impact from sample carryover is dependent on several factors, including: (1) the concentration of the DNA in the original source well, (2) whether the septa retained liquid residue, and (3) the integrity of the capillary tip, which if cracked could theoretically harbor and transfer minute amounts of liquid during the wash step. While significant sample carryover is unlikely to occur, it has been observed at low levels.

Crosstalk between Capillaries

Adjacent capillaries in an array can experience crosstalk where high signal in one capillary can effectively bleedthrough into a capillary next to it. These observations are most commonly seen with CE instruments containing 48 or 96 capillaries, such as the ABI 3700 or 3730, and when a high-signal sample is next to one containing little or no DNA.

Loss of Data or Poor Signal

Failure to get the DNA sample onto the capillary during electrokinetic injection can result in a loss of data or poor signal, as can problems with detection. Reasons for injection failure include an air bubble in the sample tube, no current between electrode and capillary due to an air bubble in the electrophoresis system, sample volume in the tubes is too low, the sample and/or size standard were not added, suboptimal autosampler calibration, and a clogged capillary within the array (Applied Biosystems 2011). Detection problems may result from a dead laser (in which case there would be no excitation of the fluorescent dyes) or poor spatial calibration (leading to looking at the wrong place on the CCD detector for signal) (Applied Biosystems 2011).

Occasionally some other process in the laboratory may adversely impact PCR amplification. In a rather curious discovery, a group in New Zealand (Bright et al. 2011) found that a level of 0.004% of the cleaning agent TriGene ADVANCE (MediChem International, Kent, UK) caused PCR inhibition and loss of three specific STR loci D7S820, D18S51, and FGA from Identifiler PCR amplifications.

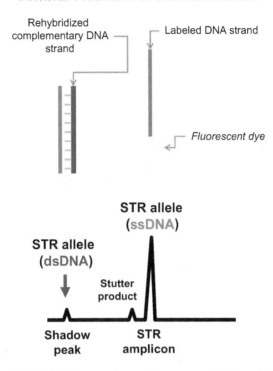

FIGURE 8.5 Double-stranded DNA (dsDNA) molecules, which are more rigid than their corresponding single-stranded DNA (ssDNA) counterparts, migrate more quickly through the polymer network inside of a capillary. When CE conditions permit rehybridization of the complementary strand, then a shadow peak occurs in front of its corresponding labeled STR allele (or internal size standard DNA fragment).

Shadow Peaks

Occasionally extra peaks can appear in DNA profiles that are on the order of 10 or more nucleotides in front of PCR products being measured. These so-called shadow peaks, which are relatively small in height, can result from dsDNA. These dsDNA molecules are due to incomplete denaturation or rehybridization of the two complementary DNA strands (Figure 8.5).

Shadow peaks usually appear in the ISS as well as the STR profile. dsDNA runs faster through the polymer network inside the capillary than ssDNA because dsDNA is not as flexible and therefore does not interact as strongly with the polymer. Post-injection hybridization with a sacrificial hybridization sequence has been used to eliminate dsDNA artifacts that occur at the vWA locus in Power-Plex 16 kits (McLaren et al. 2008).

Split Peaks in STR Profile

Split peaks in STR profile may be due to incomplete adenylation. This situation is often an indication of poor quality deoxyribonucleotide triphosphates (dNTPs) or not enough magnesium chloride in the STR kit. If the building blocks for the PCR reaction are not functioning properly, the PCR products will not be fully extended. The presence of −A peaks (see Chapter 3) is an indication that the PCR reaction is not working optimally. Depending on the STR kit, specific loci are more prone to exhibit a lack of full adenylation. Applied Biosystems has observed some situations where split peaks occurred in the smaller PCR products when the room temperature where the CE instrument is housed is below 20°C (Applied Biosystems 2011).

Poor Run-to-Run Precision

As noted in D.N.A. Box 8.3, room temperature variation impacts run-to-run precision. Certain loci may be more likely to exhibit migration shifts with room temperature changes (Hartzell et al. 2003). For example, studies in which run temperature was varied from 45 to 70°C found that D18S51 alleles change apparent size (relative to the ISS) much faster than D21S11 alleles (Butler & McCord 2008).

Sample Contaminants

Materials that fluoresce in the visible region of the spectrum ($\approx 500-600$ nm) may interfere with DNA typing when using fluorescent scanners or a fluorescence detection CE system, by appearing as identifiable peaks in the electropherogram. In some early studies conducted by the UK's Forensic Science Service (Urquhart et al. 1994), a number of fluorescent compounds were examined to determine their apparent mobility when electrophoresed in a polyacrylamide gel. All of the compounds studied, which included antibiotics, vitamins, polycyclic aromatics, fluorescent brighteners, and various textile dyes, could be removed with an organic extraction (i.e. phenol/chloroform, as is commonly used to extract DNA from cells). Fortunately, these interfering peaks were usually wide and possessed a broader fluorescent spectrum, which made it fairly easy to distinguish them from the fluorescent dye-labeled PCR products. More recently, Bruce McCord's group observed problems with divalent metal ions (e.g. nickel or iron) impacting DNA separation quality depending on the sample pH (Hartzell & McCord 2005). Poor quality water could be a source of contaminants that interfere with obtaining high-quality results.

RECOMMENDED STEPS FOR TROUBLESHOOTING

Troubleshooting is more than simply following laboratory protocols. It involves paying close attention to details in the data produced. In order to be effective at troubleshooting, an analyst must first know expected normal ranges for results. Instrument diagnostics are collected for each injection on a CE instrument. While the ABI 3500 Genetic Analyzer has locked down many parameters and provides less operational flexibility compared to the ABI 310 or 3130, there are still aspects of these CE instruments and data that can be monitored to aid troubleshooting efforts.

Monitor Instrument Run Conditions and Data Quality

A carefully controlled laboratory environment is essential to obtaining the best quality data. Room temperature and humidity need to remain fairly consistent and within appropriate levels so that CE instruments can function properly. Below are a few suggestions for aspects of CE data to monitor as part of troubleshooting when things go wrong and poor quality data is generated.

Monitor Run Current

Monitoring the run current is an excellent first step to knowing when something is wrong. Because the voltage (V) is fixed in a CE separation, changes in resistance (R) within the capillary will be reflected in the current (I) observed: Ohm's Law is $V = IR$, which rearranges to $I = V/R$. A significant drop in current flow can occur if air bubbles or urea crystals are increasing resistance. Examine run currents on good quality data to gain a baseline understanding of what the current levels should look like in your instrument. Current levels can vary based on the length of capillary as well as the buffer and polymer concentration used. When poor quality data are observed, compare the current levels in these runs with the current levels obtained during good quality data runs. Changing the cathode and anode (the inlet and outlet) run buffer solutions will often restore current levels that have been impacted by buffer depletion.

Observe Syringe Position and Movement

In ABI 310 and 3100 instruments, the polymer syringe position before and after each injection is noted in a log file. Monitoring the syringe movement through a batch of samples is an effective way to see if polymer is being delivered appropriately. Insufficient filling of a capillary with polymer solution can result in a "meltdown" where peak resolution grows worse as DNA profile peaks pass the detector so that the larger sized peaks are mere blobs (Figure 8.6(a)).

Too little movement of the polymer delivery syringe suggests that excessive resistance is a problem perhaps due to urea crystals blocking a channel in the pump block or capillary tip. Excessive movement of the syringe position between each run indicates that a leak is present in the system perhaps because the capillary is cracked or a pump block fitting needs to be tightened.

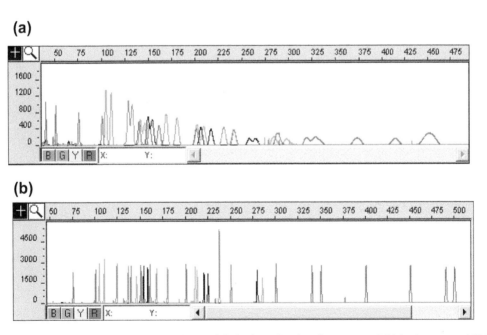

FIGURE 8.6 Comparison of (a) poor quality data and (b) high quality data from sequential injections on an ABI 310. The loss of resolution in panel (a), termed a "meltdown," comes from incomplete filling of the capillary with polymer due to a leaky syringe. Data courtesy of Margaret Kline, NIST.

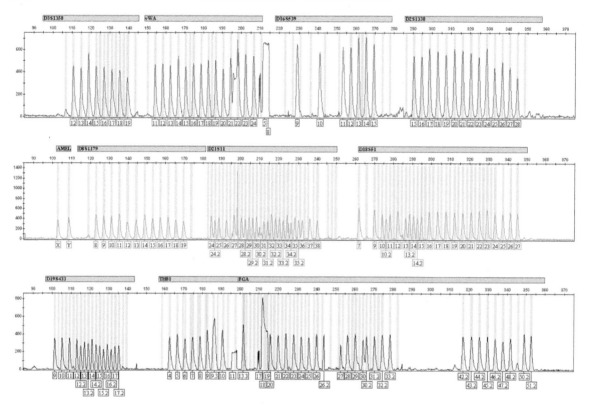

FIGURE 8.7   SGM Plus allelic ladder result just before a faulty CCD camera was replaced. Figure courtesy of Becky Hill, NIST.

Newer CE instruments contain pumps rather than syringes. Thus, the 3130 and 3500 Genetic Analyzers are not as accessible to monitoring polymer delivery. However, in our experience at NIST, we have found polymer pump failure to be a primary cause of poor quality data in our ABI 3130xl instruments and our pumps have been replaced multiple times in order to restore quality in data collection.

Examine Baseline Noise

Look at "Raw Data" traces within the data analysis software. If the starting fluorescence signals for the various colors are spread apart on the y-axis, then the detection window may need to be cleaned. Being aware of the typical levels of baseline noise in negative controls can also be helpful so that significant differences can be recognized as such if poor quality data is suddenly observed. If spikes or extra peaks begin appearing in data, then the CCD detector may need to be replaced (Figure 8.7).

Examine Peak Shapes and Resolution

Examining peak shapes and resolution of closely spaced alleles in allelic ladders is helpful to track when capillaries are failing and the array needs to be replaced. Many laboratories use the TH01 alleles

9.3 and 10 in STR kit allelic ladders as such a resolution indicator (see Figure 8.4). General peak shapes and positions for DNA fragments in the ISS can also be monitored.

Laboratories typically use the same positive control in various batches of samples being processed to confirm that correct allele calls are being made. Tracking peak heights and heterozygote balance in the positive control can also yield valuable data to help monitor instrument sensitivity and performance over time (Debernardi et al. 2011). A program called Multiplex_QA was developed several years ago to help with monitoring control samples and ISS peaks over time (Duewer & Butler 2006).

Use of Internal Size Standard Peak Characteristics

Many laboratories assess an internal standard peak, such as the 250 peak in the ABI GS500 internal standard which is particularly sensitive to temperature variation (Rosenblum et al. 1997), to demonstrate that their CE systems are stable and well-calibrated (Klein et al. 2003). CE analysis of DNA fragments at elevated pH conditions, where the DNA molecule is predominantly denatured, suggests that DNA secondary structure is responsible for the variations observed in DNA size determinations with fluctuating temperatures (Nock et al. 2001). By carefully controlling the run conditions, i.e. pH, buffer, denaturants, and temperature, variations within and between runs can be minimized and overall run precision improved. Run-to-run precision can also be enhanced using a global Southern sizing algorithm rather than the traditional local Southern sizing (Hartzell et al. 2003, Klein et al. 2003).

While examining success rates for detecting direct PCR amplification using PowerPlex 18D and Identifiler Direct, a group at the University of North Texas proposed use of fragment ratio analysis (FRA) to look for injection problems (Myers et al. 2012). Their FRA value is determined by dividing the peak height of the smallest ISS peak by the peak height of the largest ISS peak. An average FRA of 0.66 ($\pm$0.020) was observed across 400 samples examined with PowerPlex 18D and 0.60 ($\pm$0.015) with Identifiler Direct (Myers et al. 2012).

Replace Reagents with Fresh Materials

Consider the length of time that reagents have been on the instrument. The 3500 and 3500xl Genetic Analyzers have reagent usage information built into the data collection software. Sometimes simply replacing old reagents with fresh materials can improve data quality. Formamide is a critical reagent and using a fresh lot of formamide can restore data quality (see Figure 8.2).

SUMMARY

A multiplex PCR amplification of STR markers produces a number of DNA molecules that must be separated based on DNA size and fluorescent dye label to produce a coherent DNA profile. Troubleshooting involves understanding your analytical system and how DNA typing data are generated during the PCR process and subsequent separation and detection of STR alleles via CE with fluorescence detection. This chapter has reviewed principles and processes of CE and a few examples of common problems have been discussed. For additional material on CE instrumentation and the injection, separation, and detection processes, see Chapter 6 in *Advanced Topics in Forensic DNA Typing: Methodology* (Butler 2012).

Reading List and Internet Resources

Principles & Processes for Capillary Electrophoresis

Butler, J. M. (2010). *Fundamentals of forensic DNA typing*. San Diego: Elsevier Academic Press (see Chapter 9, Fundamentals of DNA separation and detection, pp. 175–203).

Butler, J. M., et al. (2004). Forensic DNA typing by capillary electrophoresis using the ABI Prism 310 and 3100 genetic analyzers for STR analysis. *Electrophoresis, 25*, 1397–1412.

Shewale, J. G., et al. (2012). Principles, practice, and evolution of capillary electrophoresis as a tool for forensic DNA analysis. *Forensic Science Review, 24*, 79–100.

Early CE Work with STR Typing

Butler, J. M. (1995). *Sizing and quantitation of polymerase chain reaction products by capillary electrophoresis for use in DNA typing (Ph.D. dissertation)*. Charlottesville: University of Virginia. Available at http://www.cstl.nist.gov/strbase/pub_pres/JohnButler-PhD-Dissertation-1995.pdf Accessed 25.03.14.

Butler, J. M., et al. (1994). Rapid analysis of the short tandem repeat HUMTH01 by capillary electrophoresis. *BioTechniques, 17*, 1062–1070.

Butler, J. M., et al. (1995). Application of dual internal standards for precise sizing of polymerase chain reaction products using capillary electrophoresis. *Electrophoresis, 16*, 974–980.

Spectral Calibration

Applied Biosystems. (2003). *ABI Prism® 3100/3100-Avant Genetic Analyzers using data collection software v2.0*. Available at http://tools.invitrogen.com/content/sfs/manuals/cms_041446.pdf Accessed 25.03.14.

Buel, E., et al. (1998). Capillary electrophoresis STR analysis: comparison to gel-based systems. *Journal of Forensic Sciences, 43(1)*, 164–170.

Singer, V. L., & Johnson, I. D. (1997). Fluorophore characteristics: making intelligent choices in application-specific dye selection. In *Proceedings of the eighth international symposium on human identification* (pp. 70–77). Madison, Wisconsin: Promega Corporation.

Whittle, M. R., et al. (2011). Use of matrix standards for new fluorophores in capillary sequencers. *Forensic Science International: Genetics Supplement Series, 3*, e73–e74.

Sample Preparation

Amresco formamide: http://www.amresco-inc.com/ Accessed 25.03.14.

Biega, L. A., & Duceman, B. W. (1999). Substitution of H$_2$O for formamide in the sample preparation protocol for STR analysis using the capillary electrophoresis system: the effects on precision, resolution, and capillary life. *Journal of Forensic Sciences, 44*, 1029–1031.

Hi-Di formamide: http://www.appliedbiosystems.com Accessed 25.03.14.

Janssen, L., et al. (2009). Increased sensitivity for amplified STR alleles on capillary sequencers with BigDye XTerminator. *Forensic Science International: Genetics Supplement Series, 2*, 123–124.

Injection

Butler, J. M. (1997). Effects of sample matrix and injection on DNA separations. In C. Heller (Ed.), *Analysis of nucleic acids by capillary electrophoresis* (pp. 125–134). Germany: Viewig.

Rose, D. J., & Jorgenson, J. W. (1988). Characterization and automation of sample introduction methods for capillary zone electrophoresis. *Analytical Chemistry, 60*, 642–648.

DNA Separation

Barron, A. E., & Blanch, H. W. (1995). DNA separations by slab gel and capillary electrophoresis. *Separation and Purification Methods, 24*, 1–118.

Boulos, S., et al. (2008). Development of an entangled polymer solution for improved resolution in DNA typing by CE. *Electrophoresis, 29*, 4695–4703.

Buel, E., et al. (2001). Evaluation of capillary electrophoresis performance through resolution measurements. *Journal of Forensic Sciences, 46*(2), 341–345.

Buel, E., et al. (2003). Using resolution calculations to assess changes in capillary electrophoresis run parameters. *Journal of Forensic Sciences, 48*, 77–79.

Hahn, M., et al. (2001). Influence of fluorophor dye labels on the migration behavior of polymerase chain reaction-amplified short tandem repeats during denaturing capillary electrophoresis. *Electrophoresis, 22*, 2691–2700.

Hartzell, B., et al. (2003). Response of short tandem repeat systems to temperature and sizing methods. *Forensic Science International, 133*, 228–234.

Hjertén, S. (1985). High-performance electrophoresis: elimination of electroendosmosis and solute adsorption. *Journal of Chromatography, 347*, 191–198.

Klein, S. B., et al. (2003). Addressing ambient temperature variant effects on sizing precision of AmpFlSTR Profiler Plus alleles detected on the ABI Prism 310 Genetic Analyzer. *Forensic Science Communications, 5*(1). Available at http://www.fbi.gov/about-us/lab/forensic-science-communications/ Accessed 25.03.14.

Lazaruk, K., et al. (1998). Genotyping of forensic short tandem repeat (STR) systems based on sizing precision in a capillary electrophoresis instrument. *Electrophoresis, 19*, 86–93.

Leclair, B., et al. (2004). Precision and accuracy in fluorescent short tandem repeat DNA typing: assessment of benefits imparted by the use of allelic ladders with the AmpF/STR Profiler Plus kit. *Electrophoresis, 25*, 790–796.

Madabhushi, R. (2001). DNA sequencing in noncovalently coated capillaries using low viscosity polymer solutions. *Methods in Molecular Biology, 163*, 309–315.

Madabhushi, R. S. (1998). Separation of 4-color DNA sequencing extension products in noncovalently coated capillaries using low viscosity polymer solutions. *Electrophoresis, 19*, 224–230.

Madabushi, R. S., et al. (1996). Polymers for separation of biomolecules by capillary electrophoresis. *U.S. Patent 5,552,028*.

Mansfield, E. S., et al. (1996). Sensitivity, reproducibility, and accuracy in short tandem repeat genotyping using capillary array electrophoresis. *Genome Research, 6*, 893–903.

Mayrand, P. E., et al. (1992). The use of fluorescence detection and internal lane standards to size PCR products automatically. *Applied & Theoretical Electrophoresis, 3*, 1–11.

Nock, T., et al. (2001). Temperature and pH studies of short tandem repeat systems using capillary electrophoresis at elevated pH. *Electrophoresis, 22*, 755–762.

Rosenblum, B. B., et al. (1997). Improved single-strand DNA sizing accuracy in capillary electrophoresis. *Nucleic Acids Research, 25*, 3925–3929.

Shewale, J. G., et al. (2003). Variation in migration of the DNA fragments labeled with fluorescent dyes on the 310 Genetic Analyzer and its implications in the genotyping. *Journal of the Association of Genetic Technologists, 29*, 60–63.

Smith, R. N. (1995). Accurate size comparison of short tandem repeat alleles amplified by PCR. *BioTechniques, 18*, 122–128.

Viovy, J.-L., & Duke, T. (1993). DNA electrophoresis in polymer solutions: Ogston sieving, reptation and constraint release. *Electrophoresis, 14*, 322–329.

Wenz, H. M., et al. (1998). High-precision genotyping by denaturing capillary electrophoresis. *Genome Research, 8*, 69–80.

Fluorescence Detection

Mansfield, E. S., & Kronick, M. N. (1993). Alternative labeling techniques for automated fluorescence based analysis of PCR products. *BioTechniques, 15*, 274–279.

Singer, V. L., & Johnson, I. D. (1997). Fluorophore characteristics: making intelligent choices in application-specific dye selection. In *Proceedings of the eighth international symposium on human identification* (pp. 70–77). Madison, Wisconsin: Promega Corporation.

Watts, D. (1998). Genotyping STR loci using an automated DNA sequencer. In P. J. Lincoln, & J. Thomson (Eds.), *Forensic DNA profiling protocols* (pp. 193–208). Totowa, NJ: Humana Press.

CE Instrument Maintenance & Common Problems

Applied Biosystems. (Oct 2007). Troubleshooting amplification and electrophoresis of the AmpFlSTR kits. *Forensic News.* http://www.lifetechnologies.com/content/dam/LifeTech/migration/us-media-library/product—services/services/pdf.par.46654.file.dat/forensic-news-oct-2007.pdf (available on pages 13–24).

I. DATA INTERPRETATION

Applied Biosystems. (2010). *FAS Corner: Maximizing the performance of capillary electrophoresis systems. The Maximizing Data Quality Series—Part 4.* Available at http://www.lifetechnologies.com/content/dam/LifeTech/migration/us-media-library/product—services/services/pdf.par.90589.file.dat/forensic-news-july-2010.pdf (available on pages 27—33).

Applied Biosystems. (2011). *Slides kindly provided to the author by Lisa Calandro on "Common 3130 Errors/Issues".*

Applied Biosystems. (2012). *Technical note: Considerations for evaluating carryover on Applied Biosystems capillary electrophoresis platforms in a HID laboratory.* Provided to the author by Jeff Sailus. Life Technologies.

Bardill, S. C., et al. (2006). Validation and evaluation of the ABI 3100 genetic analyser for use with STR analysis of buccal swabs—report of erroneous SGM Plus profiles caused by poor spectral calibration. *Progress in Forensic Genetics, 11, ICS 1288,* 507—509. Available at http://www.isfg.org/Publications/Congress+Proceedings Accessed March 25, 2014.

Butler, J. M. (2012). *Advanced Topics in Forensic DNA Typing: Methodology.* San Diego: Elsevier.

Butts, E. L. R., & Vallone, P. M. (February 2012). 3500 Genetic Analyzer: validation studies. *Forensic News.* Available at http://www.lifetechnologies.com/us/en/home/industrial/human-identification/3500-series-genetic-analyzer.html Accessed 06. 04. 2014.

Butts, E. L. R., et al. (2011). NIST validation studies on the 3500 Genetic Analyzer. *Forensic Science International: Genetics Supplement Series, 3,* e184—e185.

Forensic News: http://www.lifetechnologies.com/us/en/home/industrial/human-identification/forensic-news.html Accessed 06. 04. 2014.

McLaren, R. S., et al. (2008). Post-injection hybridization of complementary DNA strands on capillary electrophoresis platforms: a novel solution for dsDNA artifacts. *Forensic Science International: Genetics, 2,* 257—273.

Shewale, J. G., et al. (2000). Detection and correction of a migration anomaly on a 310 genetic analyzer. *Journal of Forensic Sciences, 45,* 1339—1342.

Common Artifacts and Problems

Butler, J. M., et al. (2003). The development of reduced size STR amplicons as tools for analysis of degraded DNA. *Journal of Forensic Sciences, 48*(5), 1054—1064.

Hartzell, B., & McCord, B. (2005). Effect of divalent metal ions on DNA studied by capillary electrophoresis. *Electrophoresis, 26,* 1046—1056.

Murphy, K. M., et al. (2005). Capillary electrophoresis artifact due to eosin: implications for the interpretation of molecular diagnostic assays. *Journal of Molecular Diagnostics, 7,* 143—148.

Sparkes, R., et al. (1996). The validation of a 7-locus multiplex STR test for use in forensic casework. (II), Artefacts, casework studies and success rates. *International Journal of Legal Medicine, 109,* 195—204.

Urquhart, A., et al. (1994). Multiplex STR systems with fluorescent detection as human identification markers. In *Proceedings from the fifth international symposium on human identification* (pp. 73—83). Madison, Wisconsin: Promega Corporation.

Troubleshooting

Bright, J. A., et al. (2011). The effect of cleaning agents on the ability to obtain DNA profiles using the Identifiler and PowerPlex Y multiplex kits. *Journal of Forensic Sciences, 56,* 181—185.

Butler, J. M., & McCord, B. R. (2008). *Workshop on troubleshooting common laboratory problems at the 19th international symposium on human identification.* Available at http://www.cstl.nist.gov/biotech/strbase/training.htm Accessed 25.03.14.

Butler, J. M., & McCord, B. R. (2011). *Workshop on troubleshooting common laboratory problems at the 22nd international symposium on human identification.* Available at http://www.cstl.nist.gov/biotech/strbase/training.htm Accessed 25.03.14.

Debernardi, A., et al. (2011). One year variability of peak heights, heterozygous balance and inter-locus balance for the DNA positive control of AmpFlSTR Identifiler STR kit. *Forensic Science International: Genetics, 5,* 43—49.

Duewer, D. L., & Butler, J. M. (2006). Multiplex_QA: an exploratory quality assessment tool for multiplexed electrophoretic assays. *Electrophoresis, 27,* 3735—3746. User manual and software available at http://www.cstl.nist.gov/strbase/software.htm Accessed 25.03.14.

McCord, B. (2003). Troubleshooting capillary electrophoresis systems. *Profiles in DNA, 6*(2), 10—12. Available at http://www.promega.com/resources/articles/profiles-in-dna/2003/troubleshooting-capillary-electrophoresis-systems/ Accessed 25.03.14.

Myers, B. A., et al. (2012). Evaluation and comparative analysis of direct amplification of STRs using PowerPlex 18D and Identifiler Direct systems. *Forensic Science International: Genetics, 6,* 640—645.

STATISTICAL INTERPRETATION

Statistical Interpretation Overview

"Statistical thinking will one day be as necessary for efficient citizenship as the ability to read and write."
Attributed to H.G. Wells by Darrell Huff in How to Lie with Statistics *(1954)*

ROLE OF STATISTICS IN FORENSIC DNA

The first section of this book has covered data interpretation. Assuming that appropriate data interpretation has taken place, such as filtering out stutter products and discerning heterozygotes versus homozygotes at each STR locus, we can turn our attention in the second half of the book to understanding the meaning of the data obtained.

As James Curran, from the Department of Statistics at the University of Auckland in New Zealand, notes in a recent editorial (Curran 2013): "As an expert presenting evidence to the court, I have an obligation to use the best scientific methods available to me, not the ones that are the easiest to explain." He then outlines some of the reasons why many forensic DNA scientists are not using the latest statistical methods.

Curran comments: "Many statisticians come across as simply too academic. That is, they are unable or unwilling to simplify explanation to facilitate better understanding." Speaking to statisticians, he states: "To be an effective and useful statistician requires one to engage with the specialists in that discipline, take time to understand the nature of the problem, and the issues that may affect the interpretation of the results" (Curran 2013).

Speaking to forensic practitioners, Curran opines: "There is a fundamental fear of statistics, both in the general public, and in the scientific community…forensic science trainees need to recognize that they must use statistics as part of the job." He comments on the need to educate the legal community that uses forensic evidence and adds, "for any solution to be effective there has to be the desire to change." Curran concludes: "Statistical interpretation is a vital part of a modern forensic scientist's toolbox. It is incumbent upon us, as a community, to make sure that we have the best tool set available and that everyone knows how to use it" (Curran 2013).

When Is Statistical Interpretation Needed?

As noted in the introduction to the FBI's DNA Advisory Board (DAB) statistics document (Appendix 3): "When a comparison of DNA profiles derived from evidence and reference samples *fails to exclude* an individual(s) as a contributor(s) of the evidence sample, statistical assessment and/or probabilistic reasoning are used to evaluate the significance of the association. *Proper statistical inference requires careful formulation of the question to be answered*, including, in this instance, the requirements of the legal system. Inference must take into account how and what data were collected, which, in turn, determine how the data are analyzed and interpreted" (DNA Advisory Board 2000; emphasis added).

Of the three possible traditional outcomes of a DNA test — "exclusion," "inconclusive/uninterpretable," or "inclusion" between samples examined — only the third requires statistics. The 2010 SWGDAM STR Interpretation Guidelines reinforce this principle: "*Statistical interpretation for reported inclusionary results provides weight to the inclusionary statement*. Statistical analysis is not required for exclusionary conclusions, comparisons between multiple questioned samples without a comparison to a known sample, nor application to inconclusive/uninterpretable results" (emphasis added).

Statistics attempt to provide meaning to the DNA match or association between a question (Q) or evidence sample and a known (K) or reference sample. This chapter will discuss some principles of statistics and probability and the framework for generating a match probability statistic. A DNA profile rarity estimate, commonly called a *random match probability*, is based on (1) the alleles/genotypes present in a DNA profile, (2) population frequency estimates of the alleles/genotypes, and (3) genetic formulas used to account for population substructure or degree of relatedness (Figure 9.1).

To estimate this match probability, allele frequencies are collected from various ethnic/racial sample sets. Information is gathered from different groups to provide a range of allele frequency values to be used in calculating possible profile frequency estimates. Based on their allele frequencies from validated databases, population genetic principles are applied to infer how reasonable it is that a random, unrelated individual could have contributed the DNA profile in question. This DNA profile rarity estimate is produced using allele frequencies gathered from one or more population groups, considering the specific alleles present in the DNA profile of interest, and applying appropriate genetic formulas.

Subsequent chapters will address how population data are collected and validated in gathering allele frequency information (Chapter 10) that may then be used to calculate the profile frequency (Chapter 11) or assess the rarity of genotype combinations in mixtures (Chapter 12). As will be shown in the following chapters, there are several different approaches that may be taken in stating rarity of a match with a Q-to-K comparison.

If a DNA profile from a suspect does not match evidence from a crime scene — and the testing has been performed properly based on robust quality assurance measures — then we can reliably

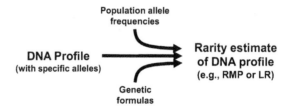

FIGURE 9.1   The rarity estimate for a specific DNA profile (in the form of a random match probability, RMP, or likelihood ratio, LR) is determined based on the alleles present in the profile, the population allele frequencies used, and genetic formulas that account for population substructure or degree of relatedness.

conclude that the individual in question did not contribute the biological sample recovered from the crime scene. However, allele drop-out due to stochastic amplification effects from low DNA template quantities in a mixture component may be another explanation for lack of full agreement in the Q-to-K comparison (Chapter 13). Methods are being developed to cope with missing alleles using a probability of drop-out, often abbreviated as Pr(D) (Gill et al. 2012).

If an evidentiary DNA profile matches a suspect, we need to determine the rarity of the association made. Are the evidence profile and the suspect profile from the same source or is there someone else out there who just happens to match the evidence in question? Since we do not have the luxury of access to DNA profiles of everyone living on planet Earth, we must use smaller population data sets to extrapolate the possibility of a random or coincidental match. In other words, models are used to try to describe the observations.

Because of the genetic inheritance properties involved, statistical calculations with close relatives (Chapter 14) or with lineage marker data (Chapter 15) use different models than autosomal DNA calculations that assume unrelated individuals.

It is important to distinguish between unrelated and related individuals in assumptions being made for the calculations that follow. Related individuals have DNA profiles that are more similar than unrelated individuals who are compared. In most equations that will be used in this and the next two chapters, we will be assuming that unrelated individuals are involved. In Chapter 14, applications are considered where assumptions are made that individuals are related, such as paternity testing and disaster victim identification using biological relatives.

Framing the Questions to be Answered

John Tukey, an American statistician who among other things coined the words "software" and "bit" (Brillinger 2002), is credited with saying: "Far better an approximate answer to the right question, which is often vague, than the exact answer to the wrong question, which can always be made precise." In other words, answering the right question should always be the goal of statistical analysis. The DNA Advisory Board statement on statistics for forensic DNA agrees: "Proper statistical inference requires careful formulation of the question to be answered … Inference must take into account how and what data were collected, which, in turn, determine how the data are analyzed and interpreted" (DNA Advisory Board 2000).

The scientific method involves developing questions to be answered by experimental evidence. These questions are termed *hypotheses*. Comparison of observations made with experimental evidence to the initial question then helps to form *theories* and inform conclusions that can be drawn. Chapter 16 discusses drawing conclusions and effectively writing reports to communicate those conclusions. However, it all begins with trying to ask the right question.

Multiple Approaches to Statistical Analysis

Just as there are multiple ways to move between point A and point B, there can be multiple statistical approaches to describe results. Although just as with the point A to point B analogy, some statistical approaches are more direct than others.

The DNA Advisory Board notes: "Rarely is there only one statistical approach to interpret and explain the evidence. The choice of approach is affected by the philosophy and experience of the user, the legal system, the practicality of the approach, the question(s) posed, available data, and/or assumptions. *For forensic applications, it is important that the statistical conclusions be conveyed meaningfully.* Simplistic or less rigorous approaches are often sought. Frequently, calculations such as the random match probability and probability of exclusion convey to the trier of fact the probative value of the evidence in a straightforward fashion. *Simplified approaches are appropriate, as long as the analysis is conservative or does not provide false inferences"* (DNA Advisory Board 2000; emphasis added).

A commonly accepted opinion in forensic science is that reported results should be "conservative" (i.e. generate a weaker statement) in order to be fair to defendants. In other words, a statistical calculation is often selected that provides a lower weight-of-evidence against the defendant. However, Ian Evett points out that by understating of the evidence we can open the door for the defense to show that there may be another method that is even more conservative – and when taken to the extreme someone could say that the evidence has no value (Evett 1996).

Significant Figures

Keep in mind that statistical results are estimates – not precise numbers. Thus, reports that proffer many significant figures in the final values (e.g. 1 in 155,373,205.82) are doing a disservice to the science and may leave an impression of greater accuracy than really exists. My personal preference is two or maybe three signficant figures (e.g. 1 in 1.6×10^8 or 1 in 155 million).

To help keep this level of imprecision in mind, allele frequencies in Appendix 1 have been provided to only three significant figures. When calculations are being performed (e.g. combining genotype frequencies across independent loci through product rule multiplication), it is fine to keep as many significant figures as possible, but the final result should be expressed in two or three significant figures at the most. Doing this will help convey that estimates have a level of uncertainty about them based on assumptions being made and foundational data including the STR allele frequencies.

Helpful Information Sources

A number of books have been written on forensic DNA evidence interpretation. Some helpful sources for further information on statistical interpretation of DNA profiles are briefly described below.

The Evaluation of Forensic DNA Evidence by the National Research Council (National Academy Press 1996) – better known as NRC II – is often viewed as the definitive source on DNA interpretation for many U.S. forensic DNA analysts and courts.
Introduction to Statistics for Forensic Scientists by David Lucy (Lucy 2005) provides a basic overview of statistical methods with 17 chapters and 10 appendices. Chapter 14 provides an introduction to population genetics including Hardy–Weinberg equilibrium and subpopulation issues. Chapter 15 describes parentage testing and database search problems. A few review questions are included at the end of many of the chapters with worked solutions in Appendix A. Overall this book provides a great starter to appreciating the vast banquet that is statistics and probability.
Interpreting DNA Evidence: Statistical Genetics for Forensic Scientists by Ian Evett and Bruce Weir (Evett & Weir 1998) was the first full text to address DNA evidence interpretation, and probably the best book on the topic for many years. Its nine chapters cover probability theory, transfer evidence, basic statistics, population genetics, statistical genetics, parentage testing,

mixtures, calculating match probabilities, and presenting evidence. It has been out of print for a number of years, and the authors are not planning an updated version. In some ways, John Buckleton's book, below, is an extension of this one (Buckleton 2005).

Weight-of-Evidence for Forensic DNA Profiles by David Balding (Balding 2005a) provides a nice overview of the issues and principles behind DNA interpretation. Nine chapters examine topics involving the application of Balding's weight-of-evidence formula, which hinges on a Bayesian approach requiring prior probabilities to be estimated. Solutions to several exercises from each chapter are provided at the end of the book.

Forensic DNA Evidence Interpretation edited by John Buckleton, Christopher Triggs, and Simon Walsh (Buckleton et al. 2005), with contributions from Peter Gill, Tim Clayton, James Curran, and SallyAnn Harbison, is probably the most thorough book on DNA evidence interpretation currently available. Twelve chapters provide coverage of population genetic models, mixtures, low copy number, parentage testing, and disaster victim identification among other subjects. However, as noted by David Balding in a review of this book: "Trainees will need to look elsewhere for a first introduction …[as] this book does not provide an accessible tutorial for beginners…. Some statistical or mathematical maturity is needed to absorb the more advanced developments" (Balding 2005b). John Buckleton plans to release a second edition soon.

Statistical DNA Forensics: Theory, Methods and Computation by Wing Kam Fung and Yue-Qing Hu (Fung & Hu 2008) covers basic statistical and population genetics topics and demonstrates examples with the EasyDNA software developed by the authors. Following the eight chapters that cover the topics of the book, there are solutions to problems presented throughout the book for readers to work as well as two appendices with standard normal distribution and chi-squared distribution tables.

Statistics and the Evaluation of Evidence for Forensics Scientists, Second Edition by Colin Aitken and Franco Taroni (Aitken & Taroni 2004) contains 14 chapters covering a wide range of topics over its almost 500 pages of text. Chapter 13 deals specifically with DNA profiling and reviews population genetics, likelihood ratios, related individuals, database searching, mixtures, and error rate (Aitken & Taroni 2004).

"Better Know a Statistician"

Science, in any field, develops and grows from the effort of numerous contributors. Understanding connections between people and the foundations they have laid can often provide a deeper understanding to current activities in any scientific endeavor. As many readers will be unfamiliar with statisticians who have had an impact on forensic DNA analysis, brief summaries of their backgrounds and contributions to the field are included below.

The following individuals, who are listed in alphabetical order by last name with their current position or their birth/death dates, have contributed to the forensic DNA community's understanding and use of statistics, some more recently than others. While the list is not comprehensive, it has been included to provide recognition to those efforts that have brought us to where we are today.

Colin Aitken (University of Edinburgh, Scotland, School of Mathematics): author of several texts including the 2004 "Statistics and the Evaluation of Evidence for Forensic Scientists" (Aitken & Taroni 2004).

Karen Ayres (University of Reading, UK, Department of Mathematics and Statistics): developed formulas for relatedness testing and forensic identification under tutelage of David Balding.

David Balding (University College London, Statistical Genetics): author of an important 1994 article introducing the Balding-Nichols equations (Balding & Nichols 1994) as well as a useful 2005 text "Weight-of-Evidence for Forensic DNA Profiles" (Balding 2005a); in July 2013 he published an article entitled "Evaluation of mixed-source, low-template DNA profiles in forensic science" that describes his likeLTD software to solve mixtures (Balding 2013).

Max Baur (University of Bonn, Germany): professor and chair of his university's medical department with expertise in relationship testing; has taught numerous forensic statistics courses over the years including courses at ISFG 2009 and 2011 meetings.

Thomas Bayes (1701–1761): an English mathematician and Presbyterian minister who is credited with Bayes' theorem, which connects prior probabilities to posterior probabilities through use of a likelihood ratio; two years after his death, his friend Richard Price presented Bayes' work as "An essay towards solving a problem in the doctrine of chances" and published it in the *Philosophical Transactions of the Royal Society of London*; since the 1950s, Bayesian statistics have experienced a rebirth due to advances in computer technology that enable random walk techniques, such as Markov chain Monte Carlo simulations.

Donald Berry (University of Texas M.D. Anderson Cancer Center, Department of Biostatistics): wrote articles in early 1990s on statistics used in forensic DNA profiling; author of 1995 textbook "Statistics: A Bayesian Perspective"; his work today is focused on designing clinical trials for medical research.

George Box (1919–2013): industrial statistician who wrote texts on experimental design; professor at University of Wisconsin-Madison; attributed with famous quote: "all models are wrong but some are useful"; son-in-law of Ronald Fisher.

Charles Brenner (consultant in forensic mathematics): creator of DNA-View software that is widely used for kinship analysis; aided disaster victim identification work including World Trade Center investigation and Hurricane Katrina; served on ISFG DNA Commission on mixture interpretation; in 2010 he published his kappa model for describing a new approach to evaluating rare haplotypes in Y-STR and mtDNA testing (Brenner 2010).

John Buckleton (Institute of Environmental Science and Research, Auckland, New Zealand): primary author of 2005 text "Forensic DNA Evidence Interpretation" and more than 100 research articles on interpretation issues in forensic science; is a leading proponent of likelihood ratio methods in DNA evidence evaluation and with colleagues is promoting STRmix as a tool for fully continuous DNA mixture interpretation.

Bruce Budowle (University of North Texas Health Science Center): although not formally trained as a statistician, in his role as the lead FBI DNA scientist during his 26-year tenure there, he strongly influenced U.S. laboratories to adopt specific DNA marker systems and to use combined probability of inclusion/exclusion statistics; has published more than 400 articles, many of them analyzing forensic population databases for various RFLP and PCR DNA marker systems.

George Carmody (1938–2011): taught evolutionary biology and population genetics for over 40 years at Carleton University in Ottawa, Ontario, Canada; consultant to FBI, RCMP, and other forensic labs; aided disaster victim identification work on Swissair Flight 111, World Trade Center investigation, and Hurricane Katrina.

Ranajit Chakraborty (University of North Texas Health Sciences Center): author of over 500 articles, many of them related to forensic DNA population genetics; co-wrote 1991 *Science* article with Ken Kidd countering concerns raised by early forensic DNA detractors (Chakraborty and Kidd 1991); has worked closely with Bruce Budowle over the past two decades; created DNAType program used extensively by Bruce Budowle, then of the FBI Laboratory, to analyze forensic population databases for RFLP and STR data.

Robert Cowell (Cass Business School, City University, London, UK): statistician who has worked on DNA mixture interpretation models using Bayesian networks with Philip Dawid (Cambridge) and Steffen Lauritzen (Oxford).

James Crow (1916–2012): professor of genetics at the University of Wisconsin-Madison; authored multiple textbooks on population genetics and chaired the NRC II committee that produced the 1996 report "The Evaluation of Forensic DNA Evidence" (see Appendix 2).

James Curran (University of Auckland, New Zealand, Department of Statistics): postdoc with Bruce Weir; regular collaborator with John Buckleton; has written a book on *R*-programming for forensic research; in 2013 he wrote an editorial in *Science and Justice* entitled "Is forensic science the last bastion of resistance against statistics?" (Curran 2013).

Alexander Philip Dawid (retired from Cambridge University): emeritus professor of statistics best known for his work with Bayesian networks; has published almost 200 articles and several textbooks.

Bernie Devlin (University of Pittsburgh, Department of Psychiatry): researcher primarily known for studies in the genetics of brain diseases; although he has had little interaction with the forensic community for the past two decades, he helped develop early statistical methods used in the analysis of VNTRs; his 1993 article entitled "Forensic inference from genetic markers" published in the journal *Statistical Methods in Medical Research* (Devlin 1993) was cited by the 2000 DNA Advisory Board (see Appendix 3) as the basis for the probability of exclusion (CPI/CPE) calculations used in many U.S. labs today; he is married to Kathryn Roeder who is a professor of statistics at Carnegie Mellon University.

Peter Donnelly (University of Oxford): professor of statistical science and Director of the Wellcome Trust Centre for Human Genetics; wrote important articles in the mid-1990s with David Balding on forensic inference from DNA profiles.

Thore Egeland (Norwegian University of Life Sciences, Norway): an applied statistician and mathematician who has published more than 200 articles and created the *familias* computer program used for relationship testing; part of the EuroForGen project (see D.N.A. Box 13.3).

Ian Evett (Principal Forensic Services, UK): chief statistician at the UK Forensic Science Service before its 2012 demise; authored numerous articles on statistics to aid forensic analysis of trace evidence and DNA; co-authored 1998 book "Interpreting DNA Evidence" with Bruce Weir; in the late 1990s with colleagues from the Forensic Science Service Roger Cook, Phil Jones, Graham Jackson, and Jim Lambert, he developed a "case assessment and interpretation" model that introduces a "hierarchy of propositions" (see Chapter 16); his thinking in Bayesian analysis has been influenced by Dennis Lindley (Evett 1991); he has collaborated extensively with John Buckleton and James Curran.

R.A. (Ronald Aylmer) Fisher (1890–1962): British statistician and geneticist who pioneered the application of statistical procedures to the design of scientific experiments that included randomization; developed the concept of analysis of variance (ANOVA) and the Fisher's exact test for statistical significance; introduced the concept of likelihood, where the likelihood of a parameter is proportional to the probability of the data.

II. STATISTICAL INTERPRETATION

Wing Kam Fung (University of Hong Kong, Department of Statistics and Actuarial Science): co-authored 2008 book "Statistical DNA Forensics: Theory, Methods and Computation" and the Easy DNA program.

Peter Gill (University of Oslo, Norway): early pioneer in forensic DNA typing and prolific researcher of the former UK Forensic Science Service; currently chair of ISFG DNA Commission that has provided important DNA mixture recommendations in 2006 and 2012; part of the EuroForGen project (see D.N.A. Box 13.3).

David Gjerten (UCLA, Department of Biostatistics): paternity testing expert who authored the 2007 ISFG recommendations on biostatistics in paternity testing.

J.B.S. (John Burdon Sanderson) Haldane (1892−1964): professor of genetics at the University College London who is considered one of the founders of population genetics along with Ronald Fisher and Sewall Wright.

Hinda Haned (Netherlands Forensic Institute): developer of LRmix and collaborator with Peter Gill; part of the EuroForGen project (see D.N.A. Box 13.3).

Godfrey Harold "G.H." Hardy (1877−1947): considered to be the leading English mathematician of his day who in a brief 1908 *Science* letter to the editor showed how a binomial distribution reflected Mendelian inheritance of alleles from generation to generation; he was later credited for his observation by inclusion of his name in the cornerstone principle of diploid genetics − Hardy-Weinberg equilibrium.

Daniel Hartl (Harvard University): a prominent evolutionary geneticist and professor of biology who has written widely used textbooks on population genetics; he studied under James Crow at the University of Wisconsin-Madison for his PhD; in 1991, he along with Richard Lewontin wrote an article in *Science* critical of forensic DNA statistical approaches being used at the time (Lewontin & Hartl 1991).

Ken Kidd (Yale University School of Medicine, Department of Genetics): researcher with over 500 publications; co-wrote 1991 *Science* article with Ranajit Chakraborty countering concerns raised by early forensic DNA detractors; creator of ALFRED (The ALlele FREquency Database); aided disaster victim identification work on the World Trade Center investigation and Hurricane Katrina.

Dan Krane (Wright State University): founder of Forensic Bioinformatics, which provides DNA data analysis for defense attorneys; was a postdoc under Daniel Hartl.

Michael Krawczak (Christian-Albrechts University, Kiel, Germany): professor of medical genetics and statistics who has authored several books and more than 230 peer-reviewed publications; served on ISFG DNA Commission on mixture interpretation.

Eric Lander (Broad Institute, MIT and Harvard University): well-known for his work with leading the Whitehead Institute and completing the Human Genome Project initial draft sequence in 2001; uncovered problems with forensic DNA analysis in the infamous *NY v Castro* case; NRC I architect of the controversial ceiling principle in 1992; co-published a 1994 article in *Nature* with Bruce Budowle declaring the DNA statistical wars over (Lander & Budowle 1994).

Richard Lewontin (retired from Harvard University): evolutionary biologist and geneticist who in 1972 demonstrated that most human genetic variation ($\approx 85\%$) is among individuals rather than between traditional racial groups; he received his PhD from Columbia University under the prominent evolutionary biologist Theodosius Dobzhansky; in 1991, he along with Daniel Hartl wrote an article in *Science* critical of forensic DNA statistical approaches being used at the time.

Dennis Lindley (retired from University College London): prominent British statistician and a leading advocate of Bayesian statistics; wrote 2006 text "Understanding Uncertainty" (Lindley 2006); his 1977 article in *Biometrika* entitled "A problem in forensic science"(Lindley 1977) led Ian Evett to begin his work with the likelihood ratio and Bayesian approaches to forensic evidence (Evett 1991).

David Lucy (Lancaster University, UK, Department of Mathematics and Statistics): wrote 2005 text "Introduction to Statistics for Forensic Scientists" (Lucy 2005).

Erik Essen-Möller (1901−1992) (Lund University, Sweden, Professor of Psychiatry): wrote a 1938 seminal article on the theoretical basis for determining statistical evidence of paternity (Essen-Möller 1938).

Laurence Mueller (University of California-Irvine): a professor of Ecology and Evolutionary Biology who testifies regularly for the defense on issues pertaining to population genetics and the statistics associated with forensic DNA profiling.

Masatoshi Nei (Pennsylvania State University, Biology): wrote 1987 classic text "Molecular Evolutionary Genetics"; served on the NRC II committee; mentored Ranajit Chakraborty.

Richard A. Nichols (University of London, Evolutionary Genetics): published 1994 article on match probabilities with David Balding (Balding & Nichols 1994); the Balding-Nichols equations are cited in NRC II 4.10 (see Appendix 2).

Anders Nordgaard (Swedish National Laboratory of Forensic Science): also teaches statistics at Linköping University; published 2012 article on "Scale of conclusions for the value of evidence" in *Law, Probability and Risk* (Nordgaard et al. 2012).

Egon Pearson (1895−1980): son of Karl Pearson; succeeded his father as professor of statistics at University College London and as editor of the journal *Biometrika*; with C.J. Clopper, established the Clopper-Pearson binomial proportion (exact) confidence interval in 1934 (Clopper & Pearson 1934).

Karl Pearson (1857−1936): English mathematician; founded the world's first university statistics department in 1911 at University College London; was a protégé of Francis Galton; in 1901 founded the journal *Biometrika* to help develop statistical theory; developed principle component analysis (PCA).

Mark Perlin (Cybergenetics): developer of TrueAllele software for computing probabilistic genotypes with DNA mixtures.

Kathryn Roeder (Carnegie Mellon University, Department of Statistics): in 1993−1995 she published critiques on the NRC I report and worked as an advisor to the FBI and National Research Council on NRC II; she is married to Bernie Devlin.

Franco Taroni (University of Lausanne, Switzerland, School of Criminal Justice): has co-authored three books on data analysis, statistics, and Bayesian networks and is an active researcher addressing topics of decision-making and forensic interpretation.

William Thompson (University of California, Irvine): professor and chair of the Department of Criminology, Law & Society who has written extensively about the use and misuse of DNA evidence.

Chris Triggs (University of Auckland, New Zealand, Department of Statistics): co-author of 2005 book "Forensic DNA Evidence Interpretation."

Wilhelm Weinberg (1862−1947): a German physician who discovered and described the principles of genetic equilibrium independent of G.H. Hardy; because his 1908 article was written

222   9. STATISTICAL INTERPRETATION OVERVIEW

in German in the *Annals of the Society of the National Natural History in Württemberg*, it would be 35 years before geneticist Curt Stern connected Weinberg's work with Hardy's, creating the now famous Hardy — Weinberg principle.

Bruce Weir (University of Washington, Biostatistics): testified for the prosecution in O.J. Simpson trial; co-authored 1998 book with Ian Evett "Interpreting DNA Evidence" (Evett & Weir 1998); has written numerous articles on population substructure and theta corrections; a close collaborator with John Buckleton and a postdoc advisor to James Curran.

Sewell Wright (1889—1988): American geneticist known for his influential work on evolutionary theory and also for his work on path analysis; with R.A. Fisher and J.B.S. Haldane, he was a founder of theoretical population genetics; he is the discoverer of the inbreeding coefficient and methods of computing it in pedigrees.

PROBABILITY

Probability is the number of times an event happens divided by the number of opportunities for it to happen (i.e. the number of trials). The concepts of probabilities can be difficult to grasp because we are often in the mindset of thinking simply that something either happened or it did not. Probability is usually viewed on a continuum between zero and one. At the lower extreme of zero, it is not possible for the event to occur (or to have occurred). In other words, there is a certainty of non-occurrence. At the upper end, where the probability is equal to one, the event being measured or calculated did in fact occur. Quite often in scientific determinations, the probability of an event occurring is understood to never be completely zero or completely one. Thus, decisions in science, as in life, often need to be made in the face of uncertainty.

If a weather bureau predicts a 60% chance of rain, experience has shown that under similar meteorological conditions it has rained six out of ten times. If one of two events is equally possible, such as heads or tails when flipping a coin, then the probability is considered 50% or 0.5 for either one of the events. Probabilities are mathematically described with symbols, such as P or Pr. The probability that an event can occur is given by the notation or formula: $P(H|E)$ or $Pr(H|E)$. This notation is shorthand for stating "the probability of event H occurring given evidence E is equal to ...." Every probability is conditional on knowing something or on something else occurring.

In the case of a rape or murder, there may be no witnesses available to assist in verification of who was the actual perpetrator of the crime. Therefore, DNA evidence developed as part of a criminal investigation of necessity has to be interpreted in the face of uncertainty. While a crime scene sample may match the DNA profile of a suspect, the result is typically cast in the language of probabilities rather than certainty. Probability statements are designed to attach numerical values to issues of uncertainty. As Ian Evett has noted: "There is no situation in which one can have a probability without making at least one assumption" (Evett 1996).

Laws of Probability

Nomenclature for probability commonly uses these symbols: Event A $= A$, not Event $A = \bar{A}$, probability of event A occurring $= Pr(A)$, Probability of event A not occurring $= Pr(\bar{A})$. The three laws of probability can be summarized as follows.

First, as stated earlier, probabilities can take place in the range zero to one. Events that are certain have a probability of one while those that are not possible have a probability of zero. Thus, if a proposition or possibility is false, it has a probability of zero. In mathematical terms, with Pr standing for probability: $0 \leq Pr(A) \leq 1$. Or verbally, the probability that event "A" will occur is greater than or equal to 0 and less than or equal to 1. *Note that there are no negative probabilities or probabilities greater than one.*

Either event A happens, $Pr(A)$, or it does not, $Pr(\overline{A})$. Within a single set of events, the probability of all possible events occurring must sum to one, or in formula form: $Pr(A) + Pr(\overline{A}) = 1$. Therefore, the probability of A not occurring (not A) is one minus the probability of A, or as a formula: $Pr(\overline{A}) = 1 - Pr(A)$, and the probability of A occurring is one minus the probability of A not occurring, or $Pr(A) = 1 - Pr(\overline{A})$.

Second, events can be mutually exclusive, meaning that if any one of a particular set of events has occurred, then none of the others has occurred. If two events are mutually exclusive and we wish to know the probability that one or other of them is true, then we can simply add their probabilities. This concept can be written out in the form:

$$Pr(G \ or \ H|E) = Pr(G|E) + Pr(H|E)$$

or verbally, the probability of events G or H occurring given evidence E is equal to the probability of event G occurring given evidence E plus the probability of event H occurring given evidence E. In this example, all possibilities are captured by events G or H. Thus, if event G occurred, then event H did not and vice versa. Another way to write this concept is that $Pr(G|E) + Pr(H|E) = 1$ and therefore upon rearranging the equation $Pr(H|E) = 1 - Pr(G|E)$. This then means that the probability that H is false is equal to one minus the probability that H is true.

The third law of probability centers on the fact that when two events are independent of one another, their probabilities can be multiplied by one another:

$$Pr((G \ and \ H)|E) = Pr(G|E) \times Pr(H|G, E)$$

or verbally, the probability of events G and H occurring given evidence E is equal to the probability of event G given evidence E multiplied by the probability of event H given event G and evidence E.

If the conditioning information (evidence E) is clearly specified and consistent for all possible events, then we can drop the "|E" or "given evidence E" portion of the equation to arrive at:

$$Pr(G \ and \ H) = Pr(G) \times Pr(H|G)$$

And if G and H are statistically independent or unassociated events then:

$$Pr(G \ and \ H) = Pr(G) \times Pr(H)$$

To summarize, probabilities fall in the range of 0 to 1. When considering the possibilities of two events occurring, if either one of two mutually exclusive events can occur, their individual probabilities are added (sum rule). Alternatively, if we wish to consider the probability of two independent events occurring simultaneously, then the individual probabilities can be multiplied (product rule).

II. STATISTICAL INTERPRETATION

It is often easier to think of situations in terms of odds rather than probability. Odds reflect the probability of an event occurring divided by the probability of the event not occurring. D.N.A. Box 9.1 reviews the mathematical relationship between probability and odds.

Bayesians vs. Frequentists

There are two widely used philosophical approaches to the nature of probability. These two approaches debate essentially idealistic versus realistic positions. "Bayesians" are a school of statisticians who try to use Bayes' theorem, which is a method originally developed by Thomas Bayes almost 250 years ago, to relate unconditional probabilities to conditional probabilities (Bayes, 1763). Frequentists, on the other hand, relate probability to the frequency of observing an event in a large number of experimental tests (D.N.A. Box 9.2).

David Lucy notes in his book *Introduction to Statistics for Forensic Scientists* (p. 191): "Statistical science has been undergoing a fundamental change since the early 1990s from frequentist implementations and interpretations, to more and more Bayesian approaches. This change has been enabled by

---

D.N.A. BOX 9.1

THE RELATIONSHIP BETWEEN PROBABILITY AND ODDS

Odds are the probability of an event (A) occurring divided by the probability of the event not occurring ($\bar{A}$), where the bar above the A mean "not." Either an event occurs or it does not. There are no other options. Stated as a formula: $\Pr(A) + \Pr(\bar{A}) = 1$, or with rearrangement $\Pr(\bar{A}) = 1 - \Pr(A)$. Thus,

$$odds = \frac{\Pr(A)}{\Pr(\bar{A})} = \frac{\Pr(A)}{1 - \Pr(A)}$$

The odds against event (A) occurring is the inverse

$$odds = \frac{\Pr(\bar{A})}{\Pr(A)} = \frac{1 - \Pr(A)}{\Pr(A)}$$

To put the $\Pr(A)$ in terms of the odds

$$\frac{\Pr(A)}{1 - \Pr(A)} = odds$$

...multiply both sides by $(1 - \Pr(A))$

$$\Pr(A) = odds(1 - \Pr(A))$$

...distribute *odds* on right side of equation

$$\Pr(A) = odds - \Pr(A)\,odds$$

...add $\Pr(A)\,odds$ to both sides

$$\Pr(A) + \Pr(A)\,odds = odds$$

...factor out $\Pr(A)$ on left side of equation

$$\Pr(A)[1 + odds] = odds$$

...divide both sides by $[1 + odds]$

$$\Pr(A) = \frac{odds}{1 + odds}$$

D.N.A. BOX 9.2

TWO PHILOSOPHIES OF STATISTICS: FREQUENTIST AND BAYESIAN

Frequentists define the probability of an event as the frequency with which the event occurs in the long-run of a sequence of identical trials where the event may or may not occur. Bayesians define the probability of an event as the degree of belief in the truth of the proposition that asserts that it will occur. Since statistical methods use data to produce inferences that include probabilistic qualifications, those two definitions assign different meanings to these inferences.

The frequentist interpretation applies only to situations that are, at least in principle, repetitive and repeatable in identical circumstances. However, most of the situations that, in forensic examinations, require that a conclusion be qualified probabilistically are one-off and unique in many ways. These situations therefore are essentially different from games of chance, like roulette, that lie at the origin of the frequentist interpretation of probability.

Frequentist statistics focuses on the probability of the evidence given a hypothesis, $Pr(E|H)$, and interprets the evidence in the context of all the conceivable evidence that is consistent with the hypothesis, none of which will have been observed except the evidence in hand. Bayesian statistics aims to produce the probability of a hypothesis given the evidence, $Pr(H|E)$. It does this using not only the sole ingredient that the frequentists use, $Pr(E|H)$, but also the probability $Pr(H)$ of the hypothesis H, in the context of all the hypotheses that might conceivably have produced the evidence in hand. The $Pr(H|E)$ is produced using a technical device known as Bayes' theorem, which is attributed to the Reverend Thomas Bayes who lived in the 18th century.

The difference between frequentist and Bayesian statistics lies deeper than just this "inversion' of probability [i.e. calculating $Pr(H|E)$ from $Pr(E|H)$ and prior probabilities]. For frequentists, statistical inferences are legitimate only in situations involving random sampling, while for Bayesians statistical inferences apply whenever one uses incomplete information and employs probability distributions to describe states of knowledge. Bayesian approaches typically involve simulations that can require extensive computing power. The availability of increasing computing power over the past several decades has led to a resurgence in Bayesian efforts.

Given two alternative explanations for the same evidence E, formulated as two mutually exclusive hypotheses H_1 and H_2, the frequentist bases conclusions on the likelihood ratio $Pr(E|H_1)/Pr(E|H_2)$. The Bayesian approach bases conclusions on the posterior odds instead (see Figure 9.2), which include consideration of the relative plausibility of H_1 and H_2 *a priori*, that is, before gathering the evidence or considering its weight. A difficult challenge with the Bayesian approach is coming up with an appropriate prior probability. In paternity testing where Bayesian analysis is regularly used (see Chapter 14), the prior probability is set to 0.5 (50%). In other words, it is equally likely that the alleged father is the biological father of the tested child versus not being the father of the tested child.

George Casella, from the Department of Statistics at the University of Florida, notes that Bayesians view the world probabilistically rather than as a set of fixed phenomena that are either known or unknown, while frequentists view the parameters of interest as fixed and unchanging under all realistic circumstances. Statistician David Lucy comments (Lucy 2005, p. 6): "The differences between Bayesians and frequentists are not mathematical... The differences are in this interpretation of the nature of probability. Frequentists tend to argue against subjective

(Continued)

D.N.A. BOX 9.2—(*cont'd*)

---

probabilities, and for long-run frequency-based interpretations of probability. Bayesians are in [favor] of subjective notions of probability, and think that all quantities which are uncertain can be expressed in probabilistic terms."

Lucy goes on to note the challenges for forensic scientists (Lucy 2005, p. 6): "... [The difference between Bayesians and frequentists] leads to a rather interesting position for forensic scientists. On the one hand they do experimental work in the laboratory where long runs of repeated results are possible; on the other hand they have to interpret data as evidence which relates to singular events. The latter aspect of the work of the forensic scientist is explicitly idealistic because events in a criminal or civil case happened once and only once, and require a subjective interpretation of probability to interpret probabilities as degrees of belief..."

The choice between frequentist and Bayesian statistics comes down to whether probabilities are intrinsic attributes of the world, or whether they quantify relations between knowing subjects and the world they study, thus conveying states of knowledge about the world. The Bayesian interpretation certainly makes probabilistic conclusions meaningful under much broader circumstances than the frequentist interpretation. Furthermore, the frequentist approach is rather

prone to the "prosecutor's fallacy" of equating $Pr(E|H)$ with $Pr(H|E)$. An example of a prosecutor's fallacy was shared in a presentation by Philip Dawid a few years ago: if the probability is 1 in 73 million that both of Sally Clark's babies would have died of natural causes, then the prosecutor's fallacy is that 1 in 73 million is the probability that she is innocent of double infanticide (Dawid 2005).

Forensic DNA analysts, especially in the United States, have usually used a frequentist approach with the calculation of random match probabilities (see Chapter 11) based on information from allele frequency population databases (Chapter 10). Recent efforts with complex DNA mixture interpretation involving probabilistic genotyping (see Chapter 13) employ a Bayesian approach.

Sources: *Antonio Possolo, Chief of Statistical Engineering Division at the National Institute of Standards and Technology; Dawid, A.P. (2005). Probability and statistics in the law. In Proceedings of the Tenth International Workshop on Artificial Intelligence and Statistics, January 6—8, 2005 available at http:// tinyurl.com/br8f1. Jeremy Fox on Oikos blog October 11, 2011 available at http://oikosjournal.wordpress.com/2011/10/11/ frequentist-vs-bayesian-statistics-resources-to-help-you-choose/; George Casella presentation available at http://www.stat.ufl.edu/ archived/casella/Talks/BayesRefresher.pdf;* Lucy, D. (2005). Introduction to Statistics for Forensic Scientists. *Hoboken, New Jersey: John Wiley & Sons.*

---

statisticians' increased ability to make complex calculations in highly multivariate spaces, and driven by data and propositions of greater complexity. It should not be thought that classical type hypothesis tests are in some sense wrong. They are not. They have exactly the same firm grounding in probability theory that later approaches have. *It all depends on where and how the classical tests are applied, and the interpretation one expects to be able to place upon their results"* (Lucy 2005; emphasis added).

Likelihood Ratios and Bayesian Statistics

A *likelihood ratio* (LR) involves a comparison of the probabilities of the evidence under two alternative propositions. In forensic DNA settings, these mutually exclusive hypotheses represent the position of the prosecution — namely that the DNA from the crime scene originated from the suspect — and the position of the defense — that the DNA just happens to coincidently match the defendant and is instead from an unknown person out in the population at large. In mathematical terms, the likelihood ratio is written as:

$$Likelihood\ Ratio = \frac{Hypothesis\ 1}{Hypothesis\ 2} = \frac{Hypothesis\ of\ prosecution\ \left(H_p\right)}{Hypothesis\ of\ defense\ (H_d)}$$

The likelihood ratio is used in Bayes' theorem to relate the probabilities of the propositions after the evidence to the probabilities prior to the evidence:

$$\frac{Pr(H_p)}{Pr(H_d)} \times \underbrace{\frac{Pr(E \mid H_p)}{Pr(E \mid H_d)}}_{\substack{\text{Likelihood} \\ \text{Ratio}}} = \frac{Pr(H_p \mid E)}{Pr(H_d \mid E)}$$

or the prior odds multiplied by the likelihood ratio equals the posterior odds.

Prior odds relates to the relative guilt or innocence of the suspect. Thus, in order to perform this calculation, one must make assumptions about the prior odds of guilt or innocence. As you might imagine, this approach has not caught on in the United States where the judicial system tries to maintain "innocent until proven guilty." However, there is nothing wrong with using the likelihood ratio by itself and having the judge and jury decide on the prior and post odds of guilt or innocence.

A strong DNA typing result should provide large likelihood ratios when the defendant and the perpetrator of a crime are the same person. Likewise, if they are different people, then the likelihood ratio should be less than 1 because the question (Q) evidence DNA profile and known (K) reference DNA profile do not match. Relative levels of likelihood ratios are discussed in Chapter 11.

Perhaps using the order of E and H in the English language alphabet can be helpful to avoid the transposed conditional when describing results with a likelihood ratio. Always describe the "E" (evidence) before the "H" (hypothesis) when reporting a likelihood ratio. For example, with an LR of 50, this could be verbally stated as the evidence is 50 times more likely if hypothesis 1 (e.g. suspect profile is in the evidence profile) is correct than if hypothesis 2 (e.g. an unrelated individual's profile is in the evidence profile) is correct.

Figure 9.2 illustrates the relationship between the frequentist approach involving a single hypothesis, the likelihood ratio approach that compares two mutually exclusive hypotheses, and the full Bayesian approach that combines the calculated likelihood ratio with a prior probability in order to infer a posterior probability.

Over the past two decades a great deal has been written on the value of using a likelihood ratio approach, including books by Ian Evett and Bruce Weir (Evett & Weir 1998) and John Buckleton and colleagues (Buckleton et al. 2005). Writing in 1996, Ian Evett noted: "A scientist cannot speculate

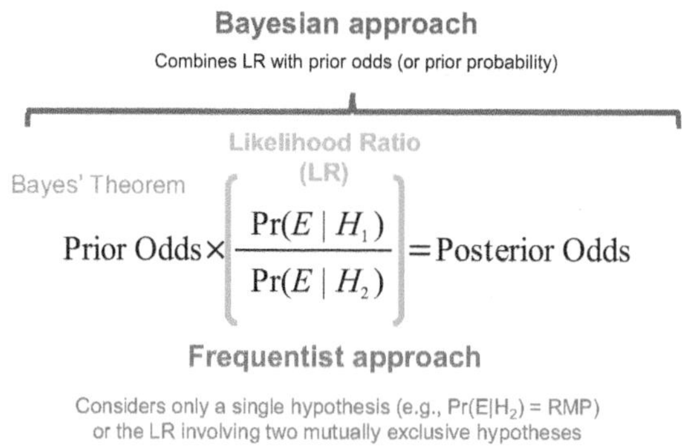

Bayesian approach

Combines LR with prior odds (or prior probability)

Bayes' Theorem

Likelihood Ratio
(LR)

$$\text{Prior Odds} \times \left[\frac{\Pr(E \mid H_1)}{\Pr(E \mid H_2)} \right] = \text{Posterior Odds}$$

Frequentist approach

Considers only a single hypothesis (e.g., $\Pr(E|H_2) = RMP$)
or the LR involving two mutually exclusive hypotheses

FIGURE 9.2   An illustration of the relationship between different statistical approaches to the evaluation of forensic DNA results. The frequentist approach considers either a single hypothesis (H) and probability of the evidence given the hypothesis, $\Pr(E|H)$, which is the random match probability (RMP) of a DNA profile in a single-source sample, or the likelihood ratio $\Pr(E|H_1)/\Pr(E|H_2)$ involving two mutually exclusive hypotheses. The Bayesian approach allows for the inclusion of prior beliefs about the truth of H_1 and H_2, and updates these with the evidence (via Bayes' formula), to produce posterior odds of the two hypotheses given the evidence.

about the truth of a proposition without considering at least one alternative proposition. Indeed, an interpretation is without meaning unless the scientist clearly states the alternatives he has considered" (Evett 1996).

STATISTICS

Statistics is a mathematical science involving the collection, analysis, and interpretation of numerical data. It provides a sense of how reliable a measurement is when the measurement is made multiple times. Statistics involves using samples to make inferences about populations. A *population* is considered in this context to be a set of objects of interest, which may be infinite or otherwise unmeasurable in their entirety. In effect, statistics involves modeling data to create a framework that can be used, it is hoped, to understand future sets of data collected.

An observable subset of a population can be referred to as a *sample* with a *statistic* being some observable property of the sample. In the context of DNA testing, the "population" would be the entire group of individuals who could be considered (e.g. billions of people around the world or those living within a particular country or region). The "sample" would be a set of individuals from the population at large (e.g. 100 males) who were selected at random and tested at particular genetic markers to try to establish a reliable representation of the entire population. The "statistic" examined might be the observed allele or genotype frequencies for the tested genetic markers.

There are two basic types of statistics: descriptive and inferential (see CIDM 1998). *Descriptive statistics* summarize a set of data from a complete population (e.g. the average height or weight of everyone in your family). When based upon a truly complete national census, statistical summaries of data collected during the census are purely descriptive of that nation's population.

Inferential statistics help predict or infer information regarding some aspect of a large population by sampling a subset of the population. Inferential statistics are used when it is essentially impossible to collect data on every member of a particular population. Political election polls and population allele frequency DNA databases (see Chapter 10) are examples where inferential statistics are used.

Uncertainty and Assumptions

Uncertainty exists in the real world. Statistics is the science of uncertainty — an effort to place meaning on the level of uncertainty. Ian Evett and Bruce Weir point out in their 1998 book (p. 217) that they "do not accept that DNA statistics are objective in the sense of being independent of human judgment. In spite of the often elegant mathematical arguments [they] have presented, [they] stress that *the final statistical values depend wholly on the initial assumptions*. The validity of these assumptions in any given case is a matter for expert opinion, so that [they] claim "objective science" can exist only within the framework of subjective judgment" (Evett & Weir 1998; emphasis added).

Hypothesis Testing for Statistical Significance

One of the most important things to understand about statistics is the concept of hypothesis testing. *Hypothesis testing* is the formal procedure for using statistical concepts and measures in performing decision-making. This concept forms the basis for likelihood ratios that were mentioned briefly in the previous section (see also Chapter 11).

Six steps are typically involved in making a statistical analysis of a hypothesis (Figure 9.3): (1) formulate two competing hypotheses; (2) select the appropriate statistical model (theorem) that identifies the test statistic; (3) specify the level of significance, which is a measure of risk; (4) collect a sample of data and compute an estimate of the test statistic; (5) define the region of rejection for the test statistic; and (6) select the appropriate hypothesis.

The first step is to formulate usually two hypotheses for testing. The first hypothesis is called the *null hypothesis*, and is denoted by H_0. The null hypothesis is formulated as an equality and indicates

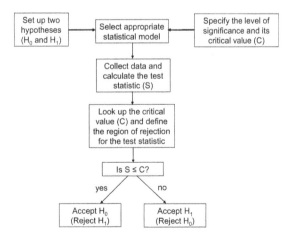

FIGURE 9.3 Flow chart illustrating the steps in hypothesis testing. The null hypothesis (H_0) is mutually exclusive of the alternative hypothesis (H_1). Adapted from Graham (2003).

that a difference does not exist. The second hypothesis is usually referred to as the *alternative hypothesis* and is denoted by H_1 or H_A. The null and alternative hypotheses are set up to represent mutually exclusive conditions so that when a statistical analysis of the sampled data suggests that the null hypothesis should be rejected, the alternative hypothesis must be accepted. Thus, the data collected (evidence gathered) should tip the scales towards either the null hypothesis or the alternative hypothesis.

In the context of a forensic DNA evidence examination, the null hypothesis put forward by the prosecution is that the defendant contributed the crime scene DNA profile while the alternative hypothesis championed by the defense is that someone else other than the defendant contributed the crime scene DNA profile in question. These two hypotheses are then expressed in the form of a likelihood ratio with H_1 or H_p (hypothesis of the prosecution) in the numerator and H_2 or H_d (hypothesis of the defense) in the denominator.

The available situations and potential decisions/outcomes of a hypothesis test are shown in Figure 9.4. There are two types of errors that can be made with hypothesis testing. A type I error involves rejecting the null hypothesis when in fact it is really true. This might be considered a "false positive." A type II error on the other hand involves failing to reject (i.e. accepting) the null hypothesis when in fact it is really false. A type II error is a "false negative."

The level of significance, which is a primary element of the decision-making process in hypothesis testing, represents the probability of making a type I error and is denoted by α (D.N.A. Box 9.3). The value chosen for α is typically based on convention, with values for α of 0.05 and 0.01 being selected frequently. The value of 0.05 is equivalent to a 95% "confidence limit," while α of 0.01 represents a 99% confidence limit. When we select the significance level (α) of a test, we are setting the

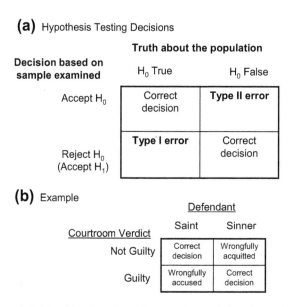

FIGURE 9.4   (a) Comparison of decisions based on hypothesis testing and the relationship of type I and type II errors. (b) Example demonstrating how type I and type II errors correlate to false positive and false negative results. Adapted from Graham (2003).

D.N.A. BOX 9.3

WHAT DOES IT MEAN TO BE "STATISTICALLY SIGNIFICANT"?

Connected to the process of hypothesis testing is the concept of a statistically significant result, which involves a probability value or "p-value." A p-value reflects the probability that a variable being measured would assume a value greater than or equal to the observed value strictly by chance. In mathematical terms this can be described as $\Pr(z \geq z_{observed})$. The threshold whereby a p-value is considered significant is set by an "alpha value" (α). With the commonly used 95% confidence limit, $\alpha = 0.05$ (since $100\% - 95\%$ is 5% or 0.05).

A variety of alpha values are used in different fields, but probably the most common is 0.05 for a 95% confidence interval around a measurement. Thus, if a p-value is <0.05, then the test statistic and comparison are considered "not significant." If the p-value is computed to be between 1% and 5%, then it is generally considered "significant," in which case the value can be denoted with an asterisk (e.g. 0.0435*). When the computed p-value is less than 1%, it is thought to be "highly significant" and can be marked with a double asterisk (e.g. 0.00273**).

Thus, in cases where the p-value, which is the probability of obtaining an observed result or a more extreme result, is less than the conventional 0.05, we conclude that there is a "significant relationship" between the two classification factors. However, it is important to keep in mind that the outcome of the significance testing is very much dependent on how the question is framed as part of the hypothesis testing.

Sources: Graham, A. (2003) Teach Yourself Statistics. Blacklick, Ohio: McGraw-Hill. http://mathworld.wolfram.com/ Significance.html; http://mathworld.wolfram.com/AlphaValue. html; http://mathworld.wolfram.com/P-Value.html; Taylor, C. (2014). What is the difference between alpha and p-values? Available at http://statistics.about.com/od/Inferential-Statistics/ a/What-Is-The-Difference-Between-Alpha-And-P-Values.htm

probability of a type I error ("wrongfully accused"). Small p-values lead to rejection of the null hypothesis (and acceptance of the alternative hypothesis) while large p-values favor the null hypothesis.

The null hypothesis is rejected when the computed p-value lies in the region of rejection, which is usually $p < 0.05$. Rejection of the null hypothesis implies acceptance of the alternative hypothesis. When multiple analyses are being performed simultaneously for significance testing, the Bonferroni correction may be applied (D.N.A. Box 9.4).

It is important to recognize that by chance 5% of tests will have p-values below $p = 0.05$. In other words, the true null hypothesis will be rejected about one out of twenty times tested. Thus, just because a test of significance is below a certain value, the null hypothesis should not necessarily be rejected.

Chi-Squared Test

Chi-squared test is a "goodness-to-fit" test. In other words, how close do observations of an event come to the expected results? The chi-square (χ^2) is determined by summing the squared value of

D.N.A. BOX 9.4

THE BONFERRONI CORRECTION

Carlo Emilio Bonferroni (1892–1960) was an Italian mathematician who developed theories for simultaneous statistical analysis. The Bonferroni correction is a multiple-comparison correction used when several independent statistical tests are being performed simultaneously. While a given alpha value (e.g. 0.05) may be appropriate for each individual comparison, it is probably not sufficient for the set of all comparisons. Thus, the alpha value needs to be lowered to account for the number of comparisons being performed.

The Bonferroni correction lowers the significance level for the entire set of n comparisons by dividing n into the alpha value for each comparison. The adjusted significance level becomes:

$$1 - (1 - \alpha)^{1/n} \approx \alpha/n$$

Thus, a set of 10 comparisons would lower the alpha value from 0.05 to 0.005 (0.05/10) so only p-values below 0.005 would be considered statistically significant rather than the conventional $p < 0.05$.

In the analysis of genetic data for Hardy–Weinberg equilibrium, application of the Bonferroni correction almost always removes the stigma of a locus being below the 5% threshold level. Applying the Bonferroni correction means that the more STR loci being examined, the less sensitive the statistical test since the alpha value threshold has been lowered.

Sources: *http://mathworld.wolfram.com/BonferroniCorrection. html; Perneger, T.V. (1998). What's wrong with Bonferroni adjustments. British Medical Journal, 316, 1236–1238; Weir, B.S. (1996). Genetic Data Analysis II, Multiple Tests, pp. 133–135.*

the difference between the observed results (obs) and expected results (exp) divided by the expected results.

$$\chi^2 = \sum_{i=1}^{k} \frac{(\text{obs}_i - \text{exp}_i)^2}{\text{exp}_i}$$

The resultant chi-square value is then compared against a table of numbers to see if there is a significant deviation from the "normal" values expected. High chi-square values indicate discrepancies between observed and expected results. Different "degrees of freedom" may be applied to data depending on the situation. Paul Lewis at the University of Connecticut has created a nice freeware program that can quickly relate user-input chi-square values and degrees of freedom to their p-value. This program is available at his website (Lewis 2014).

Confidence Intervals

Another important statistical concept is that of confidence intervals. Confidence intervals are useful for determining the reliability of a point estimate. Typically a 95% confidence interval is computed reflecting the probability that in 95% of samples drawn from the same population, the point estimate will be contained within the interval.

A 95% confidence interval effectively is the sample average plus or minus two standard deviations (see D.N.A. Box 2.4). A confidence interval around some point estimate x is a function of the probability (p) of observing x and the number of individuals or items sampled in a population (n). For a *binomial distribution*, which is the probability distribution of the number of successes in a sequence of independent yes or no experiments, the confidence interval is

$$p - z_{\alpha/2}\sqrt{\frac{p(1-p)}{n}} \leq x \leq p + z_{\alpha/2}\sqrt{\frac{p(1-p)}{n}}$$

For 95 % confidence intervals, $z_{0.025} = 1.96$.

$$p - 1.96\sqrt{\frac{p(1-p)}{n}} \leq x \leq p + 1.96\sqrt{\frac{p(1-p)}{n}}$$

Note that the upper bound of 95% confidence interval has been used for the Y-STR haplotype and mitochondrial DNA frequency estimates with the counting method (see Chapter 15).

Randomization Tests

To confirm the validity of data sets, resampling and randomization tests are often performed, usually with the aid of computer programs. These randomization tests permit an investigator to ask the question if the data were collected differently, could the overall results be significantly different. Permutation tests, such as the "exact test," shuffle the original set of genotypes obtained in a population database to examine how unusual the original sampling of genotypes is. This shuffling generates a new genotypic distribution that can be compared to the original one.

Resampling tests referred to as "bootstrapping" or "jack-knifing" can be performed on data sets as well. Bootstrapping is a computer simulation where the original n observations are resampled with replacement. Jack-knifing involves re-sampling by leaving one observation out of the original n observations to create n samples, each of size $n - 1$. Most papers in the literature describing population data sets utilize the exact test with 2,000 shuffles, although some have reported shuffling as many as 100,000 times.

Since we are only sampling a DNA profile one time in most cases, we perform statistical tests to estimate expected variability if the test were performed again. In the end, a number of statistical tests are performed on genetic data to estimate genotype frequencies since many genotypes are rare and may not be seen in population samples tested.

D.N.A. BOX 9.5

FUNDAMENTAL MATH REVIEW

As some readers may be a bit out of practice with their algebra and fundamental math skills, a few important mathematical concepts are reviewed here to help aid understanding of statistical and population genetic formula manipulations used in this book.

Fractions:

- With addition and subtraction, the same denominator is required

$$\left(\frac{1}{2} - \frac{3}{8} = \frac{4}{8} - \frac{3}{8} = \frac{4-3}{8} = \frac{1}{8}\right)$$

- With multiplication and division, different denominators are okay

$$\left(\frac{2}{3} \times \frac{1}{2} = \frac{2 \times 1}{3 \times 2} = \frac{2}{6} = \frac{1}{3}\right)$$

- When dividing two fractions, invert the denominator fraction and multiply it with the numerator fraction

$$\left(\frac{2/3}{1/4} = \frac{2}{3} \times \frac{4}{1} = \frac{2 \times 4}{3 \times 1} = \frac{8}{3} = 2\frac{2}{3}\right)$$

- Equivalent values in the numerator and denominator can be canceled to reduce the fraction

$$\left(\frac{3/8}{1/8} = \frac{3/\cancel{8}}{1/\cancel{8}} = \frac{3}{1} = 3\right)$$

Exponents:

- Provide a way to indicate when something is multiplied by itself (e.g. $p \times p = p^2$)
- Anything to the "0" exponent = 1
  ($10^0 = 1$; $100^0 = 1$; $a^0 = 1$)
- When exponents are fractions, take the root of the number
  ($16^{1/2} = \sqrt{16} = 4$)
- With addition and subtraction, do not combine the exponents
  ($a^2 + a^2 = 2a^2$; $a^2 + b^3 = a^2 + b^3$)
- With multiplication and division, exponents are combined
  ($p^2 \times p^2 = p^{2+2} = p^4$)
- With multiplication and division, values with the same exponent can be combined
  ($2^2 \times 3^2 = (2 \times 3)^2 = 6^2 = 36$)

Some basic algebra:

- The distributive property
  $2 \times (a + b) = 2a + 2b$

Sources: notes from a California Criminalistics Institute Kinship Analysis course, taught February 14–17, 2011 by Brian Harmon and Steven Myers (see http://oag.ca.gov/cci/description/kinship-analysis); see also http://www.rapidtables.com/math/index.htm.

Additional Topics and Tools

It is important to recognize that not all approaches are universally accepted, and discussion and debate still exist regarding the application of some statistics to forensic DNA typing results (e.g. Bayesian approaches). Models are used in statistics to help interpret data (see Chapter 2). Yet there are usually assumptions involved so these models are simplified versions of true genetic processes and are attempts to model the real world.

The examples provided in this text will be those approaches that are most widely used today, largely due to the acceptance of the National Research Council's report on *The Evaluation of Forensic*

D.N.A. BOX 9.6

IT'S ALL GREEK TO ME!

Reading a scientific paper or book on statistical aspects of forensic genetics can be an exercise in recognition of Greek letters and their meaning. For example, an inspection of Ian Evett and Bruce Weir's 1998 landmark book *Interpreting DNA Evidence* finds $\Sigma, \Pi, \pi, \alpha, \beta, \Gamma, \varepsilon, \chi, \lambda, \theta, \delta, \Delta, \gamma$ and a host of other variables used to convey concepts of allele inheritance in statistical genetics. Some of these variables have specific meaning and are routinely used in statistics, such as uppercase sigma. Others are just variables defined by the author(s) to convey some aspect of genetics. A careful reading of an article's text preceeding the first use of a symbol will often provide a clue and some context as to the intended purpose of the variable. Below, several commonly used Greek letters are summarized.

Symbol	Greek letter	Common use in statistics or genetics
Σ	Sigma (uppercase)	Summation of a series of values over a defined range
Π	Pi (uppercase)	Product of a series of values over a defined range
σ	Sigma (lowercase)	Standard deviation (square root of variance)
μ	mu (lowercase)	Average value (typically a population mean)

Symbol	Greek letter	Common use in statistics or genetics
α	alpha (lowercase)	Used in hypothesis testing to reflect the level of statistical significance being evaluated (e.g. 95% level of confidence has an α value of 0.05)
θ	theta (lowercase)	Inbreeding coefficient ($\approx F_{ST}$)
Δ, δ	Delta (uppercase), delta (lowercase)	Difference or change between two values
ϕ or φ	phi (lowercase)	A common descriptor of heterozygote balance often used by John Buckleton and James Curran

Thinking in terms of letters instead of numbers or words can be challenging and requires practice. Like learning a new language, grammar rules must be understood and an individual needs to be exposed to key elements and nomenclature before they can learn to effectively converse. The language of statistics involves Greek letters used in algebraic equations to present possibilities in a general sense as models are being developed and applied. A full listing of Greek alphabet letters and pronunciations is available at http://www.rapidtables.com/math/symbols/greek_alphabet.htm.

DNA Evidence, which was published in 1996 and is commonly referred to as "NRCII." Both the NRCII report (Appendix 2) and the DNA Advisory Board (DAB) recommendations on statistics (Appendix 3) recognize that rarely is there only one statistical approach to interpret and explain evidence. In fact, the DAB recommendations state: "The choice of approach is affected by the philosophy and experience of the user, the legal system, the practicality of the approach, the question(s) posed, available data, and/or assumptions" (DAB 2000). The DAB further states that simplistic and less rigorous approaches can be employed, as long as false inferences are not conveyed.

Statistical calculations involve basic arithmetic and algebraic manipulation. Some fundamental math information is provided as a review for readers as needed (D.N.A. Box 9.5). As is done in many scientific fields, statisticians often communicate with Greek letters in their publications. These Greek letters are used to express specific functions in some cases, or just variables selected by the authors as placeholders in describing mathematical relations among variables (D.N.A. Box 9.6). Greek symbols can sometimes make statistical articles inaccessible at first glance.

Many statisticians write computer programs in a programming language known as "R," which is free and runs on UNIX, Windows, and Mac platforms to provide computing and graphic capabilities. The R program can be downloaded from the R project website (R Project 2014), which is hosted by the Institute of Statistics and Mathematics at the Vienna University of Economics and Business. For those interested in new R programs and applications, the *R Journal* is an open-access, refereed journal of the R project for statistical computing (R Journal 2014). James Curran recently published a book entitled "Introduction to Data Analysis with R for Forensic Scientists" to help forensic scientists design experiments and use R for data analysis (Curran 2010).

Reading List and Internet Resources

Role of Statistics in Forensic DNA

Aitken, C., & Taroni, F. (2004). *Statistics and the Evaluation of Evidence for Forensic Scientists* (2nd ed.). Chichester, England: John Wiley & Sons.

Balding, D. J. (2005a). *Weight-of-Evidence for Forensic DNA Profiles*. Hoboken, New Jersey: John Wiley & Sons.

Balding, D. J. (2005b). Review of: Forensic DNA Evidence Interpretation. *Journal Forensic Sciences, 50*, 1.

Balding, D. J., & Buckleton, J. (2009). Interpreting low template DNA profiles. *Forensic Science International Genetics, 4*, 1–10.

Balding, D. J. (2013). Evaluation of mixed-source, low-template DNA profiles in forensic science. *Proceedings National Academy Sciences United States America, 110*(30), 12241–12246.

Balding, D. J., & Nichols, R. A. (1994). DNA profile match probability calculation: how to allow for population stratification, relatedness, database selection and single bands. *Forensic Science International, 64*, 125–140.

Brenner, C. H. (2010). Fundamental problem of forensic mathematics—the evidential value of a rare haplotype. *Forensic Science International Genetics, 4*, 281–291.

Buckleton, J., Triggs, C. M., & Walsh, S. J. (2005). *Forensic DNA Evidence Interpretation*. London: CRC Press.

Buckleton, J., & Roux, C. (2005). Review of: Statistics and the Evaluation of Evidence for Forensic Scientists, 2nd Ed. *Journal Forensic Sciences, 50*, 1265

Chakraborty, R., & Kidd, K. K. (1991). The utility of DNA typing in forensic work. *Science, 254*, 1735–1739.

Clopper, C. J., & Pearson, E. S. (1934). The use of confidence or fiducial limits illustrated in the case of the binomial. *Biometrika, 26*, 404–413.

Devlin, B. (1993). Forensic inference from genetic markers. *Statistical Methods Medical Research, 2*, 241–262.

DNA Advisory Board. (2000). Statistical and population genetic issues affecting the evaluation of the frequency of occurrence of DNA profiles calculated from pertinent population database(s). *Forensic Sci. Comm, 2*(3). Available at http://www.fbi.gov/about-us/lab/forensic-science-communications/fsc/july2000/index.htm/dnastat.htm. Accessed March 23, 2014.

Evett, I. W., & Weir, B. S. (1998). *Interpreting DNA Evidence: Statistical Genetics for Forensic Scientists*. Sunderland, MA: Sinauer Associates.

Forensic DNA statistics (Peter Gill). Available at https://sites.google.com/site/forensicdnastatistics/

Fung, W. K., & Hu, Y.-Q. (2008). *Statistical DNA Forensics: Theory, Methods and Computation*. Hoboken, NJ: Wiley.

Gill, P., & Buckleton, J. (2005). Book review: David J. Balding. Weight-of-Evidence for Forensic DNA Profiles, John Wiley and Sons Ltd. *Forensic Science International, 152*, 319.

Gill, P., et al. (2012). DNA Commission of the International Society of Forensic Genetics: recommendations on the evaluation of STR typing results that may include drop-out and/or drop-in using probabilistic methods. *Forensic Science International Genetics, 6*, 679–688.

Lander, E. S., & Budowle, B. (1994). DNA fingerprinting dispute laid to rest. *Nature, 371*, 735–738.

Lewontin, R. C., & Hartl, D. L. (1991). Population genetics in forensic DNA typing. *Science, 254*, 1745–1750.

Lindley, D. (1977). A problem in forensic science. *Biometrika, 64*, 207–213.

Morton, N. E. (1995). *Alternative approaches to population structure. Human Identification: The Use of DNA Markers*. In B. S. Weir (Ed.) (pp. 139–144). Boston: Kluwer Academic Publishers.

National Research Council Committee on DNA Forensic Science. (1996). *The Evaluation of Forensic DNA Evidence*. Washington, DC: National Academy Press.

Nordgaard, A., et al. (2012). Scale of conclusions for the value of evidence. *Law Probability Risk, 11*(1), 1–24.

SWGDAM. (2010). *SWGDAM Interpretation Guidelines for Autosomal STR Typing by Forensic DNA Testing Laboratories*. Available at http://www.fbi.gov/about-us/lab/codis/swgdam-interpretation-guidelines.

Weir, B. S. (2009). Review of: Statistical DNA Forensics: Theory, Methods, and Computation. *Journal Forensic Sciences, 54*, 1195.

Probability

Ayyub, B. M., & McCuen, R. H. (2003). *Probability, Statistics, and Reliability for Engineers and Scientists* (2nd ed.). Washington, DC: Chapman & Hall/CRC.

Barnard, G. A., & Bayes, T. (1958). Studies in the history of probability and statistics: IX. Thomas Bayes's essay towards solving a problem in the doctrine of chances. *Biometrika, 45*, 293–315.

Bayes, T. (1763). An essay towards solving a problem in the doctrine of chances. *Philosophical Transactions Royal Society, 53*, 370–418.

Lindley, D. V. (2006). *Understanding Uncertainty*. Hoboken, New Jersey: John Wiley & Sons.

Statistics

Aitken, C. G. G., & Taroni, F. (2004). *Statistics and the Evaluation of Evidence for Forensic Scientists* (2nd ed.). Hoboken, New Jersey: John Wiley & Sons.

Berger, J. O., & Berry, D. A. (1988). Statistical analysis and the illusion of objectivity. *American Scientist, 76*, 159–165.

Brillinger, D. R. (2002). John W. Tukey: his life and professional contributions. *Annals Statistics, 30*(6), 1535–1575.

CIDM — Center for Informed Decision Making. (1998). *Statistics*. Available at http://cygnus-group.com/CIDM/stats.html. Accessed March 23, 2014.

Curran, J. M. (2010). *Introduction to Data Analysis with R for Forensic Scientists*. Boca Raton, Florida: CRC Press.

Curran, J. M. (2013). Is forensic science the last bastion of resistance against statistics? *Science Justice, 53*, 251–252.

Essen-Möller, E. (1938). Die Beweiskraft der Ähnlichkeit im Vaterschaftsnachweis — theoretische Grundlagen. *Mitt Anthropol Ges (Wien), 68*, 9–53.

Evett, I. W. (1991). *Interpretation: a personal odyssey. Preface to The Use of Statistics in Forensic Science*. In C. G. G. Aitken, & D. A. Stoney (Eds.) (pp. 9–22). New York: Taylor & Francis.

Evett, I. W. (1996). Expert evidence and forensic misconceptions of the nature of exact science. *Science Justice, 36*, 118–122.

Graham, A. (2003). *Teach Yourself Statistics*. Blacklick, Ohio: McGraw-Hill.

Huff, D. (1954). *How to Lie with Statistics*. New York: W.W. Norton & Co.

Lewis, P. (2014). http://www.eeb.uconn.edu/people/plewis/software.php. Accessed March 23, 2014.

Lucy, D. (2005). *Introduction to Statistics for Forensic Scientists*. Hoboken, New Jersey: John Wiley & Sons.

Planz, J. (2003) Introduction to Forensic Statistics: Probability and Statistics. Workshop presented at the 14th International Symposium on Human Identification; see http://www.promega.com/products/pm/genetic-identity/ishi-conference-proceedings/14th-ishi-statistics-workshop/. Accessed March 23, 2014.

R Journal: http://journal.r-project.org/. Accessed March 23, 2014.

R Project: http://www.r-project.org/. Accessed March 23, 2014.

Rumsey, D. (2003). *Statistics for Dummies*. Indianapolis, Indiana: Wiley Publishing, Inc.

II. STATISTICAL INTERPRETATION

STR Population Data Analysis

"By a small sample, we may judge of the whole piece."

Miguel de Cervantes from Don Quixote

A DNA profile rarity estimate, commonly called a *random match probability*, is based on (1) the alleles/genotypes present in a DNA profile, (2) population frequency estimates of the alleles/genotypes, and (3) genetic formulas used to account for population substructure or degree of relatedness (see Figure 9.1). The first half of this book focused on the determination of alleles and genotypes present in a DNA profile. This chapter addresses the second two points — how population allele frequency estimates are determined and how genetic formulas are used to address population substructure or potential relatives. The next chapter covers how the rarity of a particular set of STR alleles can be estimated and expressed. Example equations are examined and discussed using the U.S. population allele frequencies found in Appendix 1.

INTRODUCTORY GENETIC PRINCIPLES

Genetics involves the study of patterns of inheritance of specific traits between parents and offspring. Rather than study inheritance patterns in single families, much of genetics today involves examining populations. *Populations* are groups of individuals and are often classified by grouping together those sharing a common ancestry. Population genetics assesses variation in the specific traits under consideration (e.g. STR alleles) among a group of individuals residing in a given area at a given time. Thus, *population genetics* is the study of inherited variation and its modulation in time and space. It is an attempt to quantify the variation observed within a population group or among different population groups in terms of allele and genotype frequencies.

Great genetic variation exists within species at the individual nucleotide level. In humans, a million nucleotides can differ between individuals. In addition, recent comparative genomic studies have revealed that entire sections of chromosomes can be deleted or duplicated (Freeman et al. 2006). The genetic difference between individuals within human population groups is usually much greater than the average difference between populations. An early evaluation of human genetic variation from 17 protein markers demonstrated that on average about 85% of variation occurs among individuals *within* population groups rather than *between* the groups (Lewontin 1972). Twenty-five years later a similar level of genetic apportionment was observed using 109 DNA markers (Barbujani et al. 1997).

Laws of Mendelian Genetics

Gregor Mendel (1822–1884) is credited with being the "father of modern genetics" for his mid-19th century studies tracking multiple characteristics of pea plants through several successive generations (Castle 1903, Sandler 2000). Mendel correctly determined that each individual has two forms of each trait (gene or DNA sequence) — one coming from each parent. The observations of heredity that Mendel first described are now commonly referred to as Mendel's Laws of Heredity or *Mendelian inheritance*. These two laws are the Law of Segregation and the Law of Independent Assortment.

These basic laws or principles of genetics first described by Mendel form the foundation for interpretation of DNA evidence. The *Law of Segregation* states that the two members of a gene pair segregate (separate) from each other during sex-cell formation (meiosis), so that one-half of the sex cells carry one member of the pair and the other one half of the sex cells carry the other member of the gene pair. In other words, chromosome pairs separate during meiosis so that the sex cells (gametes) become haploid and possess only a single copy of a chromosome.

Figure 10.1 illustrates the chromosomes present in the human genome and the maternal and paternal contributions to a child's full genome. A mother contributes a single member of each of the 22 autosomal chromosomes, an X chromosome, and her mitochondrial DNA (mtDNA). A father contributes a single member of each of the 22 autosomal chromosomes and either an X or a Y chromosome (and no mtDNA). Thus, the sex chromosome from the father's sperm (X or Y) when it combines with the mother's egg (containing an X) determines the sex of the zygote—either X,X for female or X,Y for male.

The *Law of Independent Assortment* states that different segregating gene pairs behave independently due to recombination when genetic material is shuffled between generations. The Law of Segregation and the Law of Independent Assortment are the basis for linkage equilibrium and Hardy–Weinberg equilibrium (HWE) that are tested for when examining DNA population databases.

Hardy–Weinberg Equilibrium and Linkage Equilibrium

For a genetic marker with two alleles A and a in a random-mating population, the expected genotype frequencies of AA, Aa, and aa are given by p^2, $2pq$, and q^2, where p and q are the allele frequencies of A and a, respectively, with $p + q = 1$ (Hartl & Jones 1998). Note that the use of p and q for allele frequencies should not be confused with the "p" and "q" labels used for chromosomal positions. While p and q are used in this book, a number of different symbols have been used for alleles and allele frequencies in the literature (D.N.A. Box 10.1).

Figure 10.2 illustrates these principles, which constitute HWE. This graphical representation of the cross between alleles A and a from both parents is referred to as a *Punnett square*. Godfrey Hardy (1877–1947) and Wilhelm Weinberg (1862–1937) both independently discovered the mathematics for independent assortment that is now associated with their names as the Hardy–Weinberg principle (Crow 1999). HWE proportions of genotype frequencies can be reached in a single generation of random mating. HWE is simply a way to relate allele frequencies to genotype frequencies.

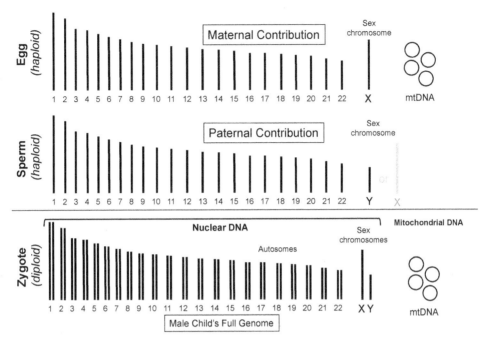

FIGURE 10.1 Human genome and inheritance. The haploid complement of chromosomes from a female's egg combines with the haploid chromosomal complement of a male's sperm to create a fully diploid zygote, which eventually develops into a child whose non-gamete cells each contain the same genome. Half of the 22 autosomes come from each parent while mtDNA is only inherited from the mother. The father's contribution of either an X or a Y chromosome determines the child's sex.

Checking for HWE is performed by taking the observed allele frequencies and calculating the expected genotype frequencies based on the allele frequencies. If the observed genotype frequencies are close to the expected genotype frequencies calculated from the observed allele frequencies, then the population is in HWE and allele combinations are assumed to be independent of one another.

One of the principal implications of HWE is that the allele and genotype frequencies remain constant from generation to generation (Hartl & Jones 1998). Another implication is that when an allele is rare, the population contains more heterozygotes for the allele than it contains homozygotes for the same allele.

Genes (or genetic markers like STR loci) that are in random association are said to be in a state of *linkage equilibrium*, while those genes or segments of the genome that are not in random association (i.e. are inherited together as a block) are said to be in *linkage disequilibrium*. Computer programs are used to check for linkage equilibrium in order to verify that a genetic marker is independent of other genetic markers being examined.

Relationship between Allele Frequency and Genotype Frequency

Allele frequency refers to the number of copies of an allele in a tested group of individuals divided by the total number of all alleles observed in this population. Since there are two copies of each allele

D.N.A. BOX 10.1

AN ALLELE NOMENCLATURE ROSSETTA STONE

One of the most confusing aspects of reading scientific publications describing theoretical population genetics involves the use of different symbols or letters to reflect quite-often straight-forward concepts. To create a generic allele in order to perform algebraic functions, authors will usually draw from letters of the English alphabet beginning with P, Q, R, … or A, B, C, …. Sometimes a capital A with subscripts is used to denote alleles while a lower case p with subscripts is used to reflect specific allele frequencies.

Although each author typically introduces his or her specific variables for alleles, genotypes, and allele frequencies, looking across articles by different authors (and even different publications from the same authors) can lead to confusion unless this variation in nomenclature is recognized. The table below illustrates some of the allele, genotype, and allele frequency nomenclatures used in the literature.

Having observed that subscripted i and j letters can sometimes be very challenging to differentiate in complex genetic equations, all of the examples used in this book follow a consistent nomenclature of P, Q, R, etc. for alleles and p, q, r, etc. (*italicized lower case letters*) for allele frequencies in order to avoid subscript characters.

Alleles	Genotype	Allele frequency	Reference
P, Q	PQ	p, q	This book
P, Q	PQ	p, q	SWGDAM (2010)
p, q	*pq*	p, q	Brenner (1997)
A_u, A_v	$A_u A_v$	p_u, p_v	Weir (2007)
A_i, A_j	$A_i A_j$	p_i, p_j	NRC II (1996)
A_i, A_j	$A_i A_j$	p_i, p_j	Fung & Hu (2008), Weir (2013)
A_1, A_2	$A_1 A_2$	p_1, p_2	Evett & Weir (1998)
A, B	AB	Pr_A, Pr_B	Lucy (2005)
a, b	ab	p_a, p_b	Buckleton et al. (2005)
A, B	AB	p_A, p_B	Balding (2005); Buckleton et al. (2011)
a, b	ab	f_a, f_b	Evett (1992)

Examples in this book are worked using allele frequencies from U.S. Caucasians (one of four U.S. population groups included in Appendix 1).

Sources: *See chapter reference list.*

per individual, when there are N individuals in a population there are 2N alleles. Genotypes, which are created by combining the (typically) two alleles present in an individual at a specific locus, are equal to the number of individuals. Thus, the genotype frequency refers to the number of individuals with a particular genotype divided by the total number of individuals examined. Figure 10.3 depicts the relationships between allele frequencies and genotype frequencies. The sum of the genotype frequencies always adds up to 100%. Thus, if the genotype Aa is seen in 50% of the individuals examined, then genotype AA and genotype aa would each be expected to occur in 25% of the population (see center of Figure 10.3).

Diploid individuals have two copies of each autosomal gene (or DNA marker): one of paternal origin (sperm) and one of maternal origin (egg). If the alleles obtained from the sperm and the egg

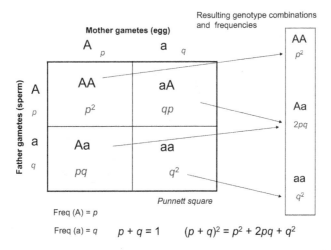

FIGURE 10.2 A cross-multiplication (Punnett) square showing Hardy–Weinberg frequencies resulting from combining two alleles A and a with frequencies p and q, respectively. Note that $p + q = 1$ and that the Hardy–Weinberg genotype proportions are simply a binomial expansion of $(p + q)^2$, or $p^2 + 2pq + q^2$.

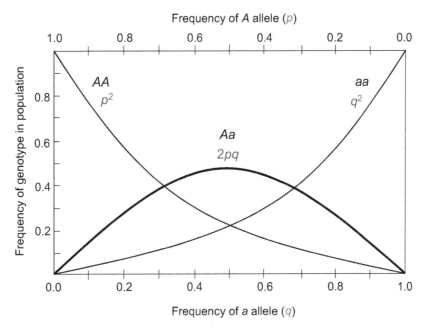

FIGURE 10.3 Graph depicting genotype frequencies for AA, Aa, and aa when Hardy–Weinberg equilibrium (HWE) conditions are met. The highest amount of heterozygotes Aa are observed when alleles frequencies for both A and a are 0.5. Adapted from Hartl & Clark (1997).

II. STATISTICAL INTERPRETATION

differ, then they are termed *heterozygous* for that locus whereas if the individual received two identical alleles from both parents they are described as being *homozygous*.

Variability within a locus has to be stable enough to accurately pass the allele to the next generation (i.e. possess a low mutation rate) yet not be too stable or else only a few alleles would exist over time and the locus would not be as informative (i.e. useful in human identity testing applications). The simplest description of variation is the frequency distribution of genotypes. A measure of this variation is the number of heterozygote individuals present in a population or the *heterozygosity* of the genetic marker.

Genetic Variability

The human population is genetically quite variable. This is evidenced by the observation that, with the exception of identical twins, we all appear different from each other. To gain a better appreciation for how the numbers of alleles present at a particular locus impact the variability, consider the ABO blood group. Three alleles are possible: A, B, and O. These three alleles can be combined to form three possible homozygous genotypes (AA, BB, and OO) and three heterozygous genotypes (AO, BO, and AB). Thus, with three alleles, there are six possible genotypes. However, because AA and AO are phenotypically equal as are BB and BO, there are only four phenotypically expressed blood types: A, B, AB, and O. The alleles (A and a) and genotypes (AA, Aa, and aa) represented in Figure 10.3 depict the frequency of occurrence of alleles with individuals as well as in the general population.

With larger numbers of alleles for a particular DNA marker, a great number of genotypes result. In general, if there are n alleles, there are $n(n + 1)/2$ genotypes possible of which there are n homozygous genotypes and $n(n - 1)/2$ heterozygous ones. Thus, a locus with 10 possible alleles could exhibit 10 homozygous possibilities plus $[10 \times (10\text{-}1)]/2$ heterozygous possibilities or $10 + 45 = 55$ total genotypes. A locus with 20 possible alleles could exhibit $20 + (20 \times 19)/2$ or 210 genotypes.

A combination of 10 loci with 10 alleles in each locus would have over 2.5×10^{17} possible genotypes ($55 \times 55 \times 55 \times ...$), whereas the use of four loci with 30 alleles in each locus would have 465 genotypes for each locus and 4.7×10^{10} possible genotypes ($465 \times 465 \times 465 \times 465$). The number of observed alleles per locus and the number of loci per DNA test both help produce a large number of genetically possible genotypes.

Short tandem repeat (STR) multiplexes now exist (e.g. GlobalFiler and PowerPlex Fusion) that can simultaneously amplify 22 autosomal STRs. If these 22 STRs have at least 10 common alleles (and thus 55 possible genotypes), then this would lead to somewhere on the order of 55^{22} or 1.9×10^{38} theoretical genotype combinations! However, with any particular locus and population group, the observed number is typically far lower than the number of theoretical possibilities.

For example, at the locus D18S51 in the NIST 1036 data set (see D.N.A. Box 1.4), we observed 22 alleles and 93 genotypes (Butler et al. 2012). Yet with 22 alleles, there are $n(n + 1)/2$ or 253 possible genotype combinations. In other words, 160 genotypes were not observed, or 63% of what could be possible based on the number of alleles seen. Some D18S51 alleles are simply more common than others. These common alleles are more likely to occur in combination with themselves to form homozygotes or with other commonly occurring alleles to create higher frequency heterozygotes.

Table 10.1 displays the number of observed alleles and genotypes across all 29 autosomal STRs measured in the NIST 1036 data set. SE33, with 52 alleles and 304 genotypes, exhibited the highest degree of variability while F13B, with 7 alleles and 20 genotypes, was least variable. Note that even when loci display the same number of alleles, there can be a different number of observed genotypes. For example, FGA, D6S1043, and D21S11 all showed 27 alleles yet D6S1043 (with 109) had 23 more genotypes than D21S11 (with 86). Thus, D6S1043 exhibits a greater degree of genetic variability in this data set than D21S11 even though these two loci possess the same number of alleles. The different number of observed genotypes compared to observed alleles illustrates that not all loci perform equally to aid human identity testing. Other measures of genetic variability will be discussed later in this chapter.

POPULATION DATA

Like the data models discussed in Chapter 2, forensic DNA statistical calculations also involve theoretical models to describe population information. An important model in population genetics is the Hardy—Weinberg principle that relates allele frequencies to genotype frequencies. Model validation may be performed by gathering data from various population groups and examining these data with various statistical tests to assess the correlation of the real-world data to the population model.

In order to assess how common or rare a particular allele and allele combination are, data are gathered from representative groups of individuals. It is possible to run a small subset of the population and reliably predict allele and genotype frequencies in the entire population — much like a telephone survey of several hundred individuals is used to predict the outcome of a political election. The key is collecting information from enough individuals to reliably estimate the frequency of the major alleles for a genetic locus.

Addressing the topic of population genetic issues in DNA forensics, Eric Lander of the Whitehead Institute for Biomedical Research stated in 1989 that the accurate determination of genotype frequencies depends on four underlying assumptions: (1) the correct population has been identified, (2) the sample is large enough that the observed frequencies accurately represent the true population frequencies, (3) the sample is truly random, and (4) the population is homogeneously mixed so that each locus is in HWE and the loci are together in linkage equilibrium (Lander 1989).

Generating a Population DNA Database

The primary goal of generating a population database is to find all "common" alleles and sample these alleles multiple times in order to reliably estimate the frequency of alleles present in the population under consideration. It is worth noting that some alleles, particularly variant alleles, have only been observed a few times and are therefore rather rare. Appendix 1 lists allele frequencies for African American, U.S. Caucasian, U.S. Asian, and U.S. Hispanic populations at the 13 core STR loci used in the United States as well as 16 additional loci used in various commercial STR kits (see Table 1.2). These allele frequencies are used throughout the book in example calculations to illustrate the principles being taught. However, for specific use in areas of the world outside of the United States, a laboratory may wish to replace the allele frequencies with those from their specific population(s) of interest.

TABLE 10.1   Comparison of Numbers of Alleles and Genotypes Observed at 29 Autosomal STRs in a Set of 1,036 Unrelated U.S. Samples (see D.N.A. Box 1.4) vs. the Theoretical Number of Genotypes Possible

Locus	Alleles Observed (n)	Genotypes Observed	Number of Theoretical Genotypes Possible (n×(n+1))/2	Heterozygosity
SE33	52	304	1378	0.935
FGA	27	96	378	0.874
D6S1043	27	109	378	0.849
D21S11	27	86	378	0.833
D12S391	24	113	300	0.881
Penta E	23	138	276	0.900
D18S51	22	93	253	0.869
Penta D	16	74	136	0.855
D19S433	16	78	136	0.812
F13A01	16	56	136	0.781
D1S1656	15	93	120	0.889
D2S441	15	43	120	0.783
D2S1338	13	68	91	0.879
Penta C	12	49	78	0.773
D10S1248	12	39	78	0.782
FESFPS	12	36	78	0.723
D8S1179	11	46	66	0.799
vWA	11	39	66	0.806
D7S820	11	32	66	0.794
D3S1358	11	30	66	0.752
D22S1045	11	44	66	0.761
D16S539	9	28	45	0.776
CSF1PO	9	31	45	0.756
D5S818	9	34	45	0.730
LPL	9	27	45	0.703
TPOX	9	28	45	0.690
D13S317	8	29	36	0.767
TH01	8	24	36	0.747
F13B	7	20	28	0.691

Loci are sorted by the number of alleles observed with the original 13 U.S. core loci in bold font. Heterozygosity reflects the fraction of heterozygotes observed in the data set.

II. STATISTICAL INTERPRETATION

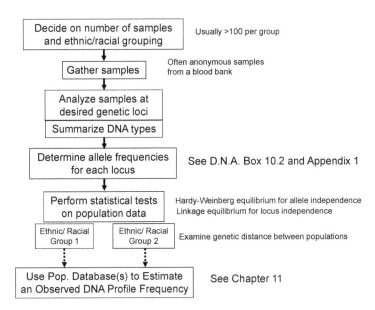

FIGURE 10.4 Steps in generating and validating a population database that can then be used to estimate the frequency of an observed DNA profile in the population.

The primary steps in generating and testing a population database are illustrated in Figure 10.4. A laboratory must first decide on the number of samples that will be tested and what particular ethnic/racial groups are relevant to estimating DNA profile frequencies that might be encountered by the lab. Population databases are often generated by gathering a set of biological samples in the form of liquid blood from a local hospital or blood bank. Usually the individuals selected are healthy and, it is hoped, unrelated to one another so that they reliably represent the population of interest. These "convenience" samples are deemed reliable since they are similar to other data sets from similar population groups (Fung 1996b). The individual samples are provided devoid of identifiers that could be used to link the DNA typing results back to the donor.

After biological samples have been gathered, DNA extraction is performed followed by PCR amplification and genotyping at the STR loci of interest, such as the 13 core loci used in the FBI's Combined DNA Index System (CODIS). These single-source samples are typically processed using commercial STR kits and standard interpretation guidelines to designate alleles.

Following the gathering of the genotype data, the information is converted into allele frequencies by counting the number of times each allele is observed. D.N.A. Box 10.2 shows an example of allele counting with the STR locus D18S51 used to determine the Caucasian data in Appendix 1.

Allele frequency information allows for more compact data storage and enables HWE testing to be performed (see below). Typically the sample genotypes and allele frequencies associated with a particular ethnic/racial group are segregated to enable both intra- and inter-group comparisons.

In forensic DNA testing, a population is a group of individuals with similar genetic characteristics. Within the U.S., population groups termed "Caucasian" and "Hispanic" are commonly used, although these group names do not have a genetic basis and can mean different things to different people (D.N.A. Box 10.3). Likewise, Africans may be classified differently from African Americans ("Black").

D.N.A. BOX 10.2

CONVERTING COLLECTED STR GENOTYPES INTO OBSERVED ALLELE FREQUENCIES

Following the gathering of the genotype data at each STR locus, the information is converted into allele frequencies by counting the number of times each allele is observed. The table below shows an example of allele and genotype counting for the locus D18S51 measured from 361 U.S. Caucasians. The observed alleles, ranging from 10 to 22 repeats, are listed across the top and down the left side. At the intersection of the rows and columns, the numbers of observed genotypes are listed. The number of homozygotes appear in the diagonal shaded boxes. Allele counts and frequencies are listed on the far left side of the table. Only the final allele frequencies are reported in Appendix 1.

Across the 361 individuals in this data set, allele 10 is observed 6 times out of 722 (2N, where N = 361) chromosomes measured for a frequency estimate of 0.00831 (0.831%). There were no 10,10 homozygotes observed in this data set. Six heterozygotes contained allele 10: 10,12 (seen three times), 10,13 (seen twice), and 10,14 (seen once).

Allele 15 was the most common allele in this data set, being seen in 123 out of 722 chromosomes for a frequency of 0.170 (17.0%). A total of 105 heterozygotes containing allele 15 were seen − from the vertical column: 11,15 (1×), 12,15 (15×), 13,15 (17×), 14,15 (12×); and 14.2,15 (1×) and from the horizonal row: 15,16 (14×), 15,17 (20×), 15,18 (19×), 15,19 (3×), 15,20 (2×), and

D18S51									Allele								
Count	Frequency	Allele	10	11	12	13	14	14.2	15	16	16.2	17	18	19	20	21	22
6	0.00831	10			3	2	1										
7	0.00970	11			1	1	1		1	1		1				1	
82	0.114	12			7	6	9		15	13		11	5	2		2	1
89	0.123	13				5	11		17	10		18	6	3	4	1	
97	0.134	14					10		12	12		17	4	5	3	1	1
1	0.00139	14.2							1								
123	0.170	15							9	14		20	19	3	2		1
106	0.147	16								12		9	13	7	1	1	1
1	0.00139	16.2											1				
100	0.139	17										7	4	4	1	1	
56	0.0776	18											1	2			
29	0.0402	19												1	1		
13	0.0180	20															1
7	0.00970	21															
5	0.00693	22															

15,22 (1×). There are nine 15,15 homozygotes, which get counted twice in the allele count since both chromosomes in these individuals contain allele 15 at D18S51. Thus, we have $1 + 15 + 17 + 12 + 1 + 14 + 20 + 19 + 3 + 2 + 1 + [2 \times 9] = 123$ alleles.

Note that the 14.2 and 16.2 variant alleles are rare, occurring only once each in a 14.2,15 genotype and in a 16.2,18 genotype. Using a minimum allele frequency approach of 5/2N, or 0.00693 when N = 361 individuals are tested, the allele frequency values for 14.2 and 16.2 would be adjusted from 0.00139 to 0.00693 in any statistical calculations made.

Source: NIST 1036 data available at http://www.cstl.nist.gov/ strbase/NISTpopdata/NIST-US1036-29aSTRs-23YSTRs.xls processed with Excel-macro available at http://www.cstl.nist.gov/ strbase/tools/STR_Genotype.xlsm

---

D.N.A. BOX 10.3

COMMONLY USED U.S. RACIAL CLASSIFICATIONS "CAUCASIAN" AND "HISPANIC"

In the United States the term "Caucasian" is commonly used to describe people with light-colored skin who have their primary ancestry from Western Europe. Strictly speaking, *Caucasian* refers to someone from the Southern Caucasus region, which is now the countries of Georgia, Armenia, and Azerbaijan. A German philosopher, Christoph Meiners, came up with the term Caucasian in his 1785 book *The Outline of History of Mankind*. Some publications describe this U.S. population group as individuals with Western European ancestry.

Hispanic is actually a language classification rather than a genetic one. The name originates from the Latin word for Spain and has been used to describe all Spanish-speaking people in Europe as well as the Western Hemisphere. The term Hispanic was adopted by the United States government in the early 1970s. It has been used in the U.S. Census for the past three decades. *Latino*, meaning someone from Latin America, has been adopted as well in recent years. *Hispanic* is a narrower term that mostly refers to persons of Spanish-speaking origin or ancestry, while *Latino* is more frequently used to refer more generally to anyone of Latin American origin or ancestry, including Brazilians (who speak Portuguese). *Hispanic* thus includes persons from Spain and Spanish-speaking Latin Americans, excluding Brazilians, while *Latino* excludes persons from Spain but includes both Spanish-speaking and Portuguese-speaking Latin Americans.

Due to some perceived allele frequency differences in early population data sets, the FBI designed their PopStats program to classify and report Southeast Hispanics (SEH) separate from Southwest Hispanics (SWH). SEH (e.g. from Florida) often have more African admixture while SWH (e.g. from Arizona) contain more Native American ancestry.

Recognizing that these terms "Caucasian" and "Hispanic" are not optimal, they have nevertheless been used in this book due to familiarity with them in the U.S. forensic DNA community.

Sources: http://en.wikipedia.org/wiki/Caucasian_race; http://en. wikipedia.org/wiki/Hispanic_and_Latino_Americans.

Allele Frequencies across Population Groups

Allele frequencies differ among population groups. Figure 10.5 provides a visual illustration of this difference with a bar graph of D18S51 allele frequencies for the U.S. population groups from the NIST 1036 data set contained in Appendix 1. Note particularly the differences in allele 13 and allele 14 between the Black and the Asian allele frequencies. Other allele frequencies, such as those for allele 15 and allele 21, are similar across all of these U.S. groups.

Hundreds of publications in the literature contain information on allele frequencies measured from common STR loci across various population groups from around the world (see reference listing available on the NIST STRBase website (STRBase 2014). Table 10.2 summarizes several sets of population data that have been published in the literature next to the D18S51 allele frequencies listed in Appendix 1 for U.S. population groups.

An examination of allele 14 in Table 10.2 is instructive. Values range from about 7% to almost 24%. Clearly genotype frequency calculations will differ depending on which population data are used. The potential difference that can exist between population groups is a primary reason that the National Research Council in its 1992 report recommended that "data on at least three major 'races' (e.g. Caucasians, Blacks, Hispanics, Asians, and Native Americans) should be analyzed" (NRC 1992, p. 15; see also Appendix 2). It is therefore common practice in forensic DNA laboratory reports to include statistical calculations from multiple population groups in order to provide a range for potential DNA profile frequency estimates.

Sample Sizes Used for Allele Frequency Estimation

Most published population data includes on the order of 100 to 200 STR types per locus per population examined. In a key paper in 1992 entitled "Sample size requirements for addressing the population genetic issues of forensic use of DNA typing," Ranajit Chakraborty concluded that 100 to 150 individuals per population could provide an adequate sampling for a genetic locus provided that allele frequencies below 1% were not used in forensic calculations. Others have arrived at similar conclusions, namely that 100 to 120 individuals per locus per population are sufficient for robust likelihood calculations (Evett & Gill 1991). Collecting information from more samples usually only improves the accuracy of frequency estimates for rare alleles. Comparisons of data collected with typical population sizes versus thousands of individuals show similar allele frequency results (D.N.A. Box 10.4).

One of the largest published population data studies involves over 100,000 samples from various regions around Brazil examined with the PowerPlex 16 kit (Aguiar et al. 2012). With D18S51, 136,739 genotypes were analyzed. A total of 41 D18S51 alleles were observed, including rare alleles 4, 5, 6, 7, 12.2, 12.3, 13.3, 14.3, 18.2, 20.2, 23.2, 27, and 28 that were not reported in the studies described in D.N.A. Box 10.4.

A Colombian study found that increasing their population database from 560 individuals to 4,652 individuals expanded the total number of detected alleles by 17% (Restrepo et al. 2011). However, most of the newly detected alleles (73%) were below the minimum allele frequency, and thus their specific frequencies would not be used in calculations (see below). Although the expanded population database contained 4,092 more samples, six loci (TPOX, D5S818, D7S820, Penta E, vWA, and D2S1338) did not contain any additional alleles.

Population comparison DNA databases are often generated by individual forensic laboratories to assess variation in common local populations. This is particularly important to locales that may have

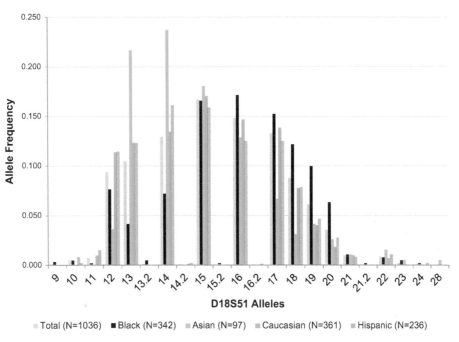

FIGURE 10.5 Comparison of D18S51 allele frequencies observed in four U.S. population groups (see Appendix 1).

an isolated population within its jurisdiction. For example, in Arizona it would be helpful to have a population database involving Native Americans such as Apaches and Navajos since they live in fairly close-knit communities within Arizona and would be expected to have different genotype frequencies compared to Caucasians or African Americans living in Arizona.

Minimum Allele Frequency

In order to make a reliable estimation of an allele frequency, it is important to collect more than one data point for that allele. There are several approaches to ensuring sufficient sampling of alleles. The most common of which in the U.S. is to utilize a minimum allele frequency, which was advocated by the 1996 National Research Council (NRC II).

NRC II states that an estimate of an allele frequency can be very inaccurate if the allele is so rare that it is represented only once or a few times in a database. Some rare alleles might not be represented at all. Thus, it is recommended that each allele should be observed at least five times to be included in reliable statistical calculations (NRC 1996, p. 148). The minimum allele frequency is therefore 5/(2N), where N is the number of individuals sampled from a population and 2N is the number of chromosomes counted because autosomes are in pairs due to inheritance of one allele from each parent.

When an observed allele frequency falls below the minimum allele frequency of 5/2N, such as the D18S51 allele 14.2 in D.N.A. Box 10.2, then the minimum allele frequency is used instead. Thus, with the D18S51 allele 14.2 example, a value of 0.00693 (5/[2 × 361]) would be used in allele frequency calculations rather than the 0.00139 actually reported in the study described in D.N.A. Box 10.2. Keep in mind that minimum allele frequency values change with the number of individuals sampled (Table 10.3).

TABLE 10.2   Comparison of D18S51 Allele Frequencies between Different Population Studies (see Appendix 1)

Allele	N=342 U.S. Black	N=650 Japan (Tokyo)	N=97 U.S. Asian	N=509 Argentina (Buenos Aires)	N=236 U.S. Hispanic	N=296 Sweden (Stockholm)	N=361 U.S. Caucasian
9	0.00292*	—	—	—	—	—	—
10	0.00439*	—	—	0.00982	0.00212*	0.007*	0.00831
11	0.00146*	0.008	—	0.01179	0.0148	0.005*	0.0097
12	0.076	0.052	0.0361	0.12377	0.114	0.118	0.114
13	0.0409	0.193	0.216	0.13261	0.123	0.155	0.123
13.2	0.00439*	0.003*	—	—	—	—	—
14	0.0716	**0.196**	**0.237**	**0.20629**	**0.161**	**0.194**	0.134
14.2	—	0.002*	—	0.00196*	0.00212*	—	0.00139*
15	0.165	0.166	0.180	0.12574	0.159	0.137	**0.170**
15.2	0.00146*	—	—	—	—	—	—
16	**0.171**	0.159	0.129	0.12967	0.125	0.113	0.147
16.2	—	—	—	—	—	—	0.00139*
17	0.152	0.082	0.067	0.10904	0.125	0.113	0.139
18	0.121	0.044	0.0309	0.07957	0.0784	0.083	0.0776
19	0.0994	0.026	0.0412	0.03438	0.0466	0.041	0.0402
20	0.0629	0.027	0.0258	0.02063	0.0275	0.012	0.018
21	0.0102	0.026	0.0103*	0.00786	0.00847*	0.014	0.0097
21.2	0.00146*	—	—	—	—	—	—
22	0.00731	0.006	0.0155*	0.00393*	0.0106	0.008*	0.00693
23	0.00439*	0.005	0.00515*	0.00196*	—	—	—
24	0.00146*	0.003*	—	0.00098	0.00212*	—	—
25	—	0.002*	—	—	—	—	—
28	—	—	0.00515*	—	—	—	—
Minimum allele frequency	0.00731	0.00385	0.0258	0.00491	0.0106	0.00845	0.00693

Data sets are grouped according to ethnic/racial classification which categories are often defined by self-declaration when samples are collected. Alleles with an asterisk are below the recommended minimum allele frequency of 5/2N (NRC 1996). Bold font highlights the most frequent allele in each group. Results are listed according to number of significant figures reported in the original publication.

II. STATISTICAL INTERPRETATION

D.N.A. BOX 10.4

COMPARISON OF STR ALLELE FREQUENCIES FROM A "NORMAL" VERSUS A LARGER POPULATION STUDY

Most population data sets used in estimating STR allele frequencies come from roughly a hundred to a few hundred individuals. To demonstrate that collection of data from a few hundred individuals can provide reliable STR allele frequency estimates, comparisons of individual allele frequencies can be made to much larger data sets. In the table below, a comparison of a typical population study with a few hundred individuals (Hill et al. 2013) is made to a much larger study involving thousands of samples (Einum & Scarpetta 2004). In both African American and Caucasian data sets, many of the allele frequencies are very similar. For example,

D18S51 allele 15 in African Americans was seen in 16.6% of the individuals tested in the 7,463-sample study and 16.5% with the 342-sample study. Most allele frequencies are not that close. Note that with the larger sample set, more rare alleles are observed (e.g. alleles 8, 10.2, 25, and 26). Also, in the larger data set, there can be fewer allele frequencies below the minimum allele frequency (MAF), which are designated with an asterisk. With the African American set, the 7,463-group has three below MAF while the 342-group has eight below MAF. In the Caucasian comparison, 7,628 has two below MAF and 361 has two below MAF.

D18S51	African American (Black)		North American Caucasian	
Alleles	N = 7,463	N = 342	N = 7,628	N = 361
8	0.0001*	—	—	—
9	0.0013	0.00292*	0.0008	—
10	0.0019	0.00439*	0.0091	0.00831
10.2	0.0016	—	—	—
11	0.0050	0.00146*	0.0112	0.00970
12	0.0625	0.0760	0.1450	0.114
13	0.0476	0.0409	0.1260	0.123
13.2	0.0050	0.00439*	0.0001*	—
14	0.0658	0.0716	0.1640	0.134
14.2	0.0037	—	—	0.00139*
15	0.1660	0.165	0.1440	0.170
15.2	0.0001*	0.00146*	—	—
16	0.1810	0.171	0.1280	0.147

(Continued)

D.N.A. BOX 10.4—(*cont'd*)

D18S51	African American (Black)		North American Caucasian	
16.2	—	—	—	0.00139*
17	0.1640	0.152	0.1160	0.139
18	0.1160	0.121	0.0773	0.0776
19	0.0913	0.0994	0.0440	0.0402
19.2	0.0004	—	—	—
20	0.0537	0.0629	0.0173	0.0180
21	0.0222	0.0102	0.0098	0.00970
21.2	—	0.00146*	—	—
22	0.0086	0.00731	0.0046	0.00693
23	0.0021	0.00439*	0.0014	—
24	0.0003	0.00146*	0.0005	—
25	0.0002*	—	—	—
26	—	—	0.0001*	—
Minimum allele frequency (5/2N)	0.000335	0.00731	0.000328	0.00693

Sources: Hill, C.R., et al. (2013). U.S. population data for 29 autosomal STR loci. Forensic Science International: Genetics, 7, e82—e83; Einum, D.D., & Scarpetta, M.A. (2004). Genetic analysis of large data sets of North American Black, Caucasian, and Hispanic populations at 13 CODIS STR loci. Journal of Forensic Sciences, 49, 1381—1385.

TABLE 10.3   Illustration of How Minimum Allele Frequency Values Change with Increasing the Number of Individuals Sampled

Number of Individuals (N)	Chromosomes Sampled (2N)	Minimum Allele Frequency (5/2N)
100	200	0.025
200	400	0.0125
500	1,000	0.005
1,000	2,000	0.0025
10,000	20,000	0.00025
100,000	200,000	0.000025

II. STATISTICAL INTERPRETATION

An examination of the D18S51 U.S. population data in Appendix 1 finds that 13 out of 22 observed alleles are below the minimum allele frequency in at least one population group. Most of these are variant alleles, such as alleles 13.2 or 14.2, or alleles on the upper or lower end of the observed allele range, such as alleles 9 and 10 or alleles 23, 24, and 28.

STR loci that are more polymorphic often exhibit more rare alleles that need to be adjusted using the minimum allele frequency approach. For example, the most polymorphic STR locus in Appendix 1 is SE33, which has 52 observed alleles. From these 52 alleles, 38 alleles (73%) have five or less observations in at least one population group. Thus, the minimum allele frequency may be commonly used with some loci. On the other extreme is D13S317, which has eight observed alleles and only one (allele 15) with less than five observations in the two population groups were this rare allele is observed.

The minimum allele frequency serves as a statistical "floor" in calculations for genotype and profile frequency. The more alleles sampled, the greater the chance of observing a rare allele, all things being equal. What may be a "rare" allele with lower sampling may become more common and cross the minimum allele frequency threshold given further data collection.

Sources of Samples for Population Databases

Individuals whose DNA profiles will be used to construct a population database for allele frequency estimation purposes should be selected without prior knowledge of genotypes at the loci under examination to ensure randomness of the samples. A frequent practice is to collect samples from blood donors or hospital volunteers (Fung 1996b). For example, the samples used to generate the STR typing data used in Appendix 1 were purchased from two different blood banks and represent anonymous blood donors with self-identified ethnicities.

Well-characterized population samples with anthropological descriptions would be desirable in many cases to carefully define population groups, but are not necessary to obtain valid information in forensic DNA population databases. Self-declaration of ethnicity can be a suitable method of categorizing samples on the basis of ethnicity. In some cases, ancestry-informative markers can be used to verify sample categories (Lao et al. 2010). The correlation of autosomal, Y-chromosome, and mtDNA information strengthens the confidence in the classification of samples into various population groups.

Broad racial/ethnic categories are usually adequate for most forensic population databases, unless an isolated population is of interest, such as a Native American tribal group or an Amish community. It is also desirable to use unrelated individuals in creating a population database in order to improve the precision of allele frequency estimates by increasing the number of independent alleles sampled.

Most institutions now require institutional review board (IRB) approval when performing tests on human subjects or examining genetic material from human subjects. These IRB approvals typically request that informed consent be provided by those who contribute the DNA samples and often require that DNA samples be made completely anonymous to the testing laboratory so that genetic information cannot be reconnected with the tested individual. Government funding agencies may not provide funding for research unless a DNA laboratory has an IRB in place.

Statistical Tests on Population Data

Once STR genotypes have been generated from population samples, the data are typically evaluated with statistical tests to ensure that the allele frequencies are reasonable based on genetic

TABLE 10.4   Computer Programs Available for Performing Statistical Tests on Genetic Data

ARLEQUIN (version 3.5); available for download: http://popgen.unibe.ch/software/arlequin35/; ≈7 Mb
Developed by Laurent Excoffier and colleagues at the University of Bern, Switzerland. This software suite is widely used in population genetics because of its flexibility in handling large samples of DNA sequences, STR, or SNP information.

DNATYPE (Windows 95/NT version); *Contact program authors for availability*
A collection of computer programs developed in the 1990s by Ranajit Chakraborty, David Stivers, and Yixi Zhong (then at University of Texas Health Science Center in Houston). The programs run in DOS windows that pop up when they are executed through a Windows interface added more recently by Snehit Cherian and Robert Gaensslen (University of Chicago-Illinois). This suite of programs has been used extensively by Bruce Budowle (while he was at the FBI Laboratory) and others to analyze forensic population databases for both RFLP and STR data.

DNA-VIEW; see http://www.dna-view.com/; costs approximately $7500
Program written by Charles Brenner to enable a wide variety of DNA tests including kinship analysis and parentage testing.

GDA (Genetic Data Analysis) version 1.0; ≈750 kb as zipped file
Free program distributed by the authors Paul Lewis and Dmitri Zaykin via download: http://phylogeny.uconn.edu/software/. Can perform a variety of genetic tests described in Weir's *Genetic Data Analysis II* (1996).

GENEPOP (version 4.2); (see Raymond & Rousset 1995, Rousset 2008)
A web-based browser version is accessible: http://wbiomed.curtin.edu.au/genepop/index.html. This program can do a variety of statistical tests necessary for validating STR population frequency database including Hardy-Weinberg exact tests and a linkage disequilibrium test.

MENDEL (version 13); (see Lange et al. 2013)
Available at http://www.genetics.ucla.edu/software/mendel. This program is capable of identifying deviations from Hardy−Weinberg and linkage equilibrium and testing for paternity or other pedigree relationships.

PopStats (version 5.3; updated with newer versions of CODIS); standalone version is not publicly available.
Used as part of the FBI's Combined DNA Index System (CODIS) software to perform population statistical analyses and DNA profile frequency estimates.

PowerMarker (version 3.07); available for download: http://statgen.ncsu.edu/powermarker/
Developed by Jack Liu at North Carolina State University, and is capable of performing a wide range of summary and population statistics.

PowerStats (version 1.2) from Promega Corporation (see Tereba 1999); ≈3 Mb
No longer available from Promega website, but is still used by authors who had previously downloaded it. Uses a Microsoft Excel workbook template to obtain statistics on allele distributions within populations examined. Summary statistics include frequency of each allele, polymorphism information content, probability of a match, power of discrimination, power of exclusion, and the paternity index.

TFPGA (Tools for Population Genetic Analyses) version 1.3; ≈350 kb as zipped file
Available for free download from statistician Mark Miller at: http://www.marksgeneticsoftware.net/. Performs a variety of tests including Hardy−Weinberg and F-statistic calculations. Interpopulation comparisons can be performed using another program to perform analysis of R×C contingency tables.

A list of over 600 genetic analysis software programs is regularly updated and is available at http://lab.rockefeller.edu/ott/geneticsoftware.

inheritance principles. Computer programs are used to conduct statistical tests for HWE and linkage equilibrium in order to assess independence of alleles and loci. A list of commonly used computer programs for HWE and other statistical calculations is shown in Table 10.4.

II. STATISTICAL INTERPRETATION

GENETIC MODELS AND FORMULAS

Population genetics theory involves models and assumptions, some of which are better than others. As Ian Evett and Bruce Weir note: "Models that are simple enough for tractable mathematical analysis are not true in the real world. With every model there is a compromise between simplicity and reality" (Evett & Weir 1998, p. 79).

DNA profiles are composed of genotypes at individual loci, and these genotypes are made up of maternal and paternal alleles (Figure 10.6). Tests for HWE are used to assess independence of alleles and genotypes while linkage equilibrium is examined to determine if the loci are genetically independent.

Factors Involved

Two primary forces are at play in population genetics: genetic drift and mutation. *Genetic drift* results as allele frequencies change over multiple generations. While some alleles drift to become more common, other alleles will be lost in the population due to biological parents not passing on a specific allele to their offspring. Over multiple generations with high levels of inbreeding, genetic loci can be driven to *fixation*, in other words the multiple alleles present at a locus converge to a single, unchanging allele.

Mutation is an alteration or change of an allele at a genetic locus resulting in a genetic inconsistency between a biological parent and offspring. Mutation counteracts genetic drift by introducing new alleles into the population. *Selection* and *migration* can also play a role in changing allele proportions in a population.

When comparing individual alleles between a question sample (Q) and a known reference sample (K), it is not always possible to tell if the two alleles are *identical by state* (IBS) or are *identical by descent* (IBD). Due to the possibility of a mutation, a measured allele 14 at an STR locus may be present because the source of the sample directly inherited the allele 14 from one of their parents (IBD), or it could have mutated (e.g. parent has a 13 but this allele mutates to a 14 that is then inherited by the offspring) into an allele 14 (IBS). *Homoplasy* is the term given to allelic states that are identical without the alleles being identical by descent (Hamilton 2009, p. 169).

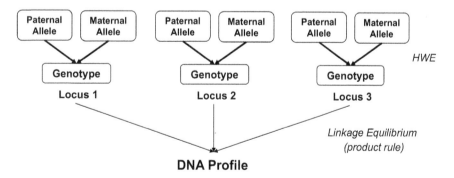

FIGURE 10.6 A DNA profile is made up of genotypes from individual genetic loci. The genotype at each locus results from inheritance of paternal and maternal alleles. Hardy–Weinberg equilibrium (HWE) tests evaluate the independence of alleles within a genetic locus while linkage equilibrium tests ascertain the independence of alleles between loci. Independent loci and alleles enable use of the product rule.

TABLE 10.5   Assumptions with Hardy–Weinberg equilibrium.

The Assumption	The Reason
Large population	Many possible allele combinations
No natural selection	No restriction on mating so all alleles have equal chance of becoming part of next generation
No mutation	No new alleles being introduced
No immigration/emigration	No new alleles being introduced or leaving
Random mating	Any allele combination is possible

Most of the examples that are worked in this book utilize the simple HWE model for the genetic formulas applied (i.e. $2pq$ for heterozygotes and p^2 for homozygotes). However, real-world populations often need adjustments to correct for what is known as *population substructure.*

To teach concepts of population genetics, including genetic drift and population substructure, Duncan Taylor from Forensic Science South Australia (Adelaide) uses an imaginary "Hardy Weinberg Island" (Taylor 2013). Smaller, more isolated population groups will experience the effects of genetic drift more significantly. Thus, subpopulation correction factors need to be larger to model these effects as will be described below.

HWE Model

STR alleles are inherited by an individual from their mother and father in a Mendelian fashion and frequencies of occurrence follow a predictable pattern of probability. If two alleles P and Q occur with frequencies p and q in the population, then the genotype PP (a homozygote) should occur p^2 and the genotype PQ (heterozygote) should occur with frequency $2pq$ (pq or qp) (see Figure 10.2). Allele frequencies are used to generate expected genotype frequencies that are then compared to the observed genotype frequencies. If observed and expected values are similar then it is assumed that alleles within the genetic locus are stable across generations, or in other words, "in equilibrium."

HWE predicts the stability of allele and genotype frequencies from one generation to the next. The primary purpose in testing for HWE is to determine if alleles within a locus are independent of each other. Frequencies should not change over the course of many generations if the locus is genetically stable. However, natural populations usually violate HWE to some degree and thereby cause allele frequencies to change over time.

HWE assumes a random mating population of infinite size with no migration or mutation to introduce new alleles, which of course does not exist in real human populations. The ideal population is one that follows Hardy–Weinberg assumptions (Table 10.5). A locus is in HWE when allele and genotype frequencies in a population remain constant from generation-to-generation.

If minor departures are seen from HWE, there is generally no major cause for concern with using a particular population data set. Some authors will do little more than note that there is a statistically significant departure from HWE for a particular locus in their population data set. It is important to keep in mind that there are three principal reasons for observations of major differences (departures) from HWE: (1) parents might be related, leading to inbreeding and a higher than expected number of homozygotes; (2) population substructure; and (3) selection because people with different genotypes might survive and reproduce at different rates.

Another purpose of performing an HWE test is to look for any indications of excess homozygosity. The primary explanation for excess homozygosity is allelic drop-out or "null alleles" from a primer binding site mutation where only one allele is observed from a truly heterozygous individual. An example of this observation of excess homozygosity leading to discovery of a primer binding set mutation is reported in D.N.A. Box 4.2.

Independence of Loci — Linkage and Linkage Disequilibrium

The closer two sections of DNA are to one another on a chromosome, the more likely it is that they will be inherited together. If recombination occurs between the two sections of DNA under investigation, then the shuffling of genetic material during meiosis means that the two sections are not inherited together.

With the assumption of independence, it then becomes possible to equate the overall profile match probability with the product of the locus-specific match probabilities. This combination of locus-specific match probabilities is referred to as the *product rule*. In other words, the match probability for the STR locus D18S51 can be combined with additional STR loci such as TH01 and D21S11 to decrease the odds of a random match to an unrelated individual.

Loci co-located on the same arm of a chromosome are called *syntenic loci*. Alleles from closely spaced markers are not inherited independently. In other words, recombination does not shuffle the individual allele combinations along the chromosome with each generation. When this occurs, genotype results are not independent and their frequencies cannot be multiplied together. Typically genetic markers used in forensic genetics are selected that are far enough apart to be independent of one another. Exceptions include lineage markers such as Y-chromosome STRs, X-chromosome STRs, and mitochondrial DNA sequence information (see Chapter 15).

As noted by Tillmar et al. (2008), *linkage* is the co-segregation of closely located loci in a pedigree while *linkage disequilibrium* (LD) measures the allele co-segregation at a population level. Linkage refers to physical dependency between loci, and LD relates to allelic dependency between alleles at different loci (Ott 1999). Linkage can be measured between two or more genetic markers through obtaining recombination frequencies using family samples. LD is estimated from allele frequencies and haplotype frequencies measured in unrelated population samples. Computer programs, such as Mendel or Genetic Data Analysis (GDA) (see Table 10.4), are typically used to assess linkage and LD with either family or population sample sets, respectively.

Table 10.6 lists sets of *syntenic STR loci* that occur on the same arm of a chromosome. The recombination activity between two genetic markers is more important than the physical distance in terms of ensuring independent genotype assortments in multiplex DNA profiles (Phillips et al. 2012). For widely used STR kits, the two closest loci are vWA and D12S391.

Closely Spaced STR Loci: D12S391 and vWA

Two of the loci selected in 2009 by the European DNA community (see Butler 2012, Chapter 5) are vWA and D12S391, which are located only 6.36 Mb apart on the short arm of human chromosome 12. Studies involving father—son pairs suggest that LD between vWA and D12S391 may be an issue with related individuals and therefore the results from these loci should not be multiplied together as they may not be statistically independent (O'Connor & Tillmar 2012). However, studies involving

TABLE 10.6　Syntenic Autosomal STR Loci Ranked by Their Physical Distance

Chromosome Position	Syntenic STR Pair	Physical Distance (Mb)	Genetic Distance (cM)	Recombination Fraction	STR Kits Where Both Loci Appear (see Table 1.2)
6q	SE33 − D6S1043	3.463	4.414	0.0440	*None currently*
15q	FESFPS − Penta E	5.949	18.96	0.1810	PowerPlex CS7
12p	vWA − D12S391	6.357	11.94	0.1172	NGM, NGM SElect, PowerPlex ESI 16/17, ESX 16/17, PowerPlex 21, GlobalFiler, PowerPlex Fusion, ESSplex, ESSplex SE, Nonaplex ESS, SinoFiler
21q	D21S11 − Penta D	24.502	44.73	0.3568	PowerPlex 16, PowerPlex 18D, PowerPlex 21, PowerPlex Fusion
5q	D5S818 − CSF1PO (in 13 CODIS core)	26.345	27.76	0.2522	Identifiler, PowerPlex 16, PowerPlex 18D, IDplex, PowerPlex 21, GlobalFiler, PowerPlex Fusion, Profiler, SinoFiler
1q	F13B − D1S1656	33.897	41.69	0.3412	*None currently*
2p	TPOX − D2S441	66.746	88.81	0.4721	GlobalFiler, PowerPlex Fusion

Chromosomal position is listed by the short arm (p) or long arm (q). The physical distance in megabases (Mb), genetic distance in centimorgans (cM), and recombination fraction are from Phillips et al. 2012. Adapted from Butler et al. (2012) and Bright et al. (2014).

unrelated individuals have shown no LD issues (Budowle et al. 2011, Phillips et al. 2011, Gill et al. 2012, O'Connor et al. 2011). Jo-Anne Bright and colleagues have prepared a nice guide to calculations that can be used with linked loci (Bright et al. 2014).

Population Substructure

Genetic mixing of alleles is not completely random because parents often share some common ancestry. The consequence of this non-random mating is that there is usually a decrease in heterozygotes and an increase in homozygotes. Adjustments for the population substructure can be made with the use of a correction factor referred to as theta (θ), which is essentially the same value as F_{ST} commonly used by population geneticists to describe the level of inbreeding in a set of sample results (Hamilton 2009). Thus, theta accounts for allele sharing by common descent.

Inbreeding is a term used to describe a situation where related people have offspring. All humans are related at some level. Inbreeding reduces genetic diversity because related people are more likely to have alleles in common than unrelated people. Taken to the extreme, inbreeding results in more homozygote genotypes in a population because both parents are passing on the same allele to their offspring. "*Inbreeding* means mating of two persons who are more closely related than if they were chosen at random" (NRC 1996, p. 98). The term *co-ancestry coefficient* is typically applied to the sub-population correction *θ* rather than "inbreeding" coefficient.

D.N.A. BOX 10.5

F_{ST} AND Θ SUBPOPULATION CORRECTION TERMS

The fixation index (F) was initially defined by Sewall Wright in 1951 as a means of reflecting variation between subpopulations and total populations (Wright 1951). F_{ST}, which associates the average expected heterozygosity for a subpopulation (H_S) and the expected heterozygosity for the total population (H_T), is calculated as:

$$F_{ST} = \frac{H_T - H_S}{H_T}$$

There are multiple fixation indices, including F_{IS}, F_{ST}, and F_{IT}, where I stands for individuals, S for subpopulations, and T for total population in the subscript abbreviations. Each fixation index expresses the degree to which random mating expectations for the frequency of heterozygous genotypes is not met (Hamilton 2009). These three fixation indices are interconnected as follows:

$$1 - F_{IT} = (1 - F_{ST})(1 - F_{IS})$$

Note that if mating within subpopulations is random ($F_{IS} = 0$), then F_{IT} is equivalent to F_{ST}. A high F_{ST} value means that there is a great deal of difference in allele frequencies among subpopulation groups. When there is a low F_{ST}, then allele frequencies among subpopulation groups are very similar.

The terms θ (NRC 1996), F (Balding & Nichols 1994), and F_{ST} (Wright 1951) are typically used in an equivalent manner to reflect subpopulation structure in genetic data. Thus, Balding & Nichols (1994) match probability for a heterozygote is the same as the NRC II (1996) 4.10b equation:

$$2 \frac{\left(F + (1 - F)p_A\right)\left(F + (1 - F)p_B\right)}{(1 + F)(1 + 2F)}$$

$$\equiv \frac{2\left[\theta + (1 - \theta)p_i\right]\left[\theta + (1 - \theta)p_j\right]}{(1 + \theta)(1 + 2\theta)}$$

Sources: Hamilton, M.B. (2009). Population Genetics. Hoboken, New Jersey: Wiley-Blackwell; Wright, S. (1951). The genetic structure of populations. Annals of Eugenics, 15, 323–354; Balding, D.J., & Nichols, R.A. (1994). DNA profile match probability calculation: how to allow for population stratification, relatedness, database selection and single bands. Forensic Science International, 64, 125–140; National Research Council (NRCII) Committee on DNA Forensic Science. (1996). The Evaluation of Forensic DNA Evidence. Washington, DC: National Academy Press.

The fixation index (F) measures deviation from Hardy–Weinberg expected heterozygote frequencies (D.N.A. Box 10.5). Sewall Wright defined F as an inbreeding coefficient to compute any degree of relationship between parents (Wright 1951). The kinship coefficient is also designated by F and used to measure relationship between two people (NRC 1996, p. 99). F_{ST} is Wright's measure of population subdivision and is the same as theta (θ) when mating within subpopulations is random. F-statistics can be thought of as a measure of the correlation of alleles within individuals, and are related to inbreeding coefficients (NRC 1996, p. 102).

F-statistics describe the amount of inbreeding-like effects within subpopulations (F_{ST} or θ), among populations (F_{IS} or f), and within the entire population (F_{IT} or F). Bruce Weir and colleagues have written extensively on using and calculating θ and the theory of population substructure (Weir & Cockerham 1984, Weir & Hill 2002). Bruce Weir describes four different meanings of theta: (1) identity by descent — "the probability that two alleles, one taken at random from each of two individuals are identical by descent," (2) variance among populations, (3) F_{ST}, and (4) a measure of genetic distances (Weir 1998).

Matthew Hamilton in his 2009 *Population Genetics* text describes F_{ST} as "the reduction in heterozygosity due to subpopulation divergence in allele frequency; the difference between the average expected heterozygosity of subpopulations and the expected heterozygosity of the total population; alternatively, the probability that two alleles sampled at random from a single subpopulation are identical given the probability that two alleles sampled from the total population are identical" (Hamilton 2009, p. 121).

The 1996 National Research Council report entitled *The Evaluation of Forensic DNA Evidence* discusses issues that surround population structure. The NRC II report makes several recommendations for taking population substructure into account. Recommendation 4.1 (see Appendix 2) substructure adjustments replace p^2 for homozygote calculations with $p^2 + p(1 - p)\theta$, where θ is an empirically determined measure of population subdivision or substructure. The value for θ is inversely rated to mutation rate and although not treated that way, every STR locus can have a slightly different θ value.

A conservative value for θ is 0.01 for typical at-large populations and 0.03 with smaller, isolated, and more inbred groups of people (NRC 1996). A number of studies have demonstrated that $\theta = 0.01$ is a reliable and conservative estimate of population substructure with extensive population data (Budowle & Chakraborty 2001, Budowle et al. 2001).

A theta correction adjusts for population stratification. "Without suitable adjustment, there is concern that allele frequencies in broad population groups might be unrepresentative of smaller, often isolated, subpopulation groups from which a defendant might originate — underestimating those in subpopulations and artificially exaggerating the rarity estimate of the culprit's profile" (Lareu 2013). These values of theta may be used to compensate for the potential to underestimate allele frequencies in subpopulations, due to what is known as the Wahlund effect (D.N.A. Box 10.6).

While global databases with theta (F_{ST}) corrections can be used to estimate the STR profile frequency from a crime scene stain, it is typically better to have local population databases if they are available. These local allele frequencies should more accurately reflect the weight-of-evidence when a Q-to-K comparison is performed, as the local allele information will be a better fit to the model. A theta correction is a theoretical construct and we can never know exactly how high or low F_{ST} really is for a specific evidentiary STR profile.

D.N.A. BOX 10.6

THE WAHLUND EFFECT

Sten Gösta William Wahlund (1901−1976), a Swedish geneticist, first described the phenomenon that bears his name in 1928. The Wahlund effect is that subpopulations, which may themselves be in Hardy−Weinberg equilibrium (HWE), will exhibit a reduction in the number of heterozygotes (heterozygosity) when combined. One impact of the Wahlund effect is that F_{ST} will always be positive since the numerator in the expression for F_{ST} is ($H_T - H_S$) and H_S is always smaller than H_T. The underlying causes of this population subdivision could be geographic barriers to gene flow followed by genetic drift in the subpopulations.

Sources: Hamilton, M.B. (2009). Population Genetics. Hoboken, New Jersey: Wiley-Blackwell; http://en.wikipedia.org/wiki/Wahlund_effect

PRACTICAL CONSIDERATIONS

Forensic Journal Publication Policies Regarding Population Data

Around the turn of the century, the *Journal of Forensic Science* (*JFS*) (Gaensslen 1999) and *Forensic Science International* (*FSI*) (Lincoln & Carracedo 2000) decided to reduce the amount of space taken up by published DNA population data information since STR typing has become fairly routine with the use of commercial STR kits. *JFS* population data was reported in "For the Record" articles while *FSI* population information was recorded in "Announcements of Population Data." The goal of these policies was to enable researchers and forensic scientists to report population genetic data for common loci in an efficient manner and to encourage formation of web-based repositories of population data.

After 2005, *JFS* decided to stop publishing "For the Record" population data sets. The number of population data publications has declined in recent years but still makes up a significant portion of overall articles in various forensic journals. *Forensic Science International: Genetics*, which spun off of *FSI* in 2007, has the highest overall percentage of articles related to STR population data (Table 10.7). These articles are mostly written as letters to the editor, and many of them are published only in electronic form. Several guidance documents describe changing requirements for population data in *Forensic Science International: Genetics* (Carracedo et al. 2010, Carracedo et al. 2013, Carracedo et al. 2014) and *International Journal of Legal Medicine* (Pfeiffer & Bajanowski 2010). Specific guidance has also been provided for publication of lineage marker data from Y-chromosome and mitochondrial DNA (Parson & Roewer 2010).

Understanding the Numbers used in Population Data Publications

A list of values that can be used to evaluate the relative usefulness of each STR marker that has been typed is usually at the end of allele frequency tables in forensic population data publications. These measures of the evaluated DNA markers include the power of discrimination (PD), the power of exclusion (PE), the *a priori* chance of exclusion (CE), the polymorphism information content (PIC), and a marker's heterozygosity (H).

Unfortunately, authors publishing such data fail to describe what the various measures of DNA markers mean or how the values are related to one another either because of lack of space or lack

TABLE 10.7 Numbers of STR Population Papers Published in Various Journals from 1995 to 2013

Journal	# Articles on STR Population Data (1995 to 2013)
Forensic Science International: Genetics	251 of 841 (29.8%)
International Journal of Legal Medicine	258 of 1811 (14.2%)
Legal Medicine	117 of 1146 (10.2%)
Forensic Science International	434 of 5387 (8.1%)
Journal of Forensic Sciences	309 of 4709 (6.6%)
Croatian Medical Journal	35 of 1728 (2.0%)

Results from PubMed.org searches conducted March 2014 using journal name with and without "STR population" along with publication years.

TABLE 10.8 Summary of Formulas and Calculations Used to Compute Various Parameters for Population Data Analyses

Genetic Function and Formula

Homozygosity(h) $= \sum_{i=1}^{n} p_i^2$

Heterozygosity(H) $= 1 -$ Homozygosity $= 1 - \sum_{i=1}^{n} p_i^2$

Effective number of alleles(n_e) $= \frac{1}{Homozygosity} = \frac{1}{\sum_{i=1}^{n} p_i^2}$

PIC $= 1 - \sum_{i=1}^{n} p_i^2 - (\sum_{i=1}^{n} p_i^2)^2 + \sum_{i=1}^{n} p_i^4$

PD $= 1 - 2(\sum_{i=1}^{n} p_i^2)^2 + \sum_{i=1}^{n} p_i^4$

PE $= 1 - 2\sum_{i=1}^{n} p^2 - 2[\sum_{i=1}^{n} p_i^2]^2 + 2\sum_{i=1}^{n} p_i^4 - \sum_{i=1}^{n} p_i^3 + 3\sum_{i=1}^{n} p_i^3 + 3\sum_{i=1}^{n} p_i^2 \sum_{i=1}^{n} p_i^3$

Probability of Identity (Matching Probability) $= P_I = \sum_{i=1}^{n} x_i^2$

Paternity Index(PI) $= \frac{H+h}{2h} = \frac{(1-h)+h}{2h} = \frac{1}{2h} = \frac{1}{2\sum_{i=1}^{n} p_i^2}$

The symbols above are according to the following key: p_i is frequency of ith allele in a population of n samples; x_i is frequency of ith genotype; h = homozygosity; H = heterozygosity.

of understanding. Typically the numbers for each of these statistical measures are generated by a computer program, and therefore the user does not need to think about what the values indicate. Table 10.8 attempts to put a number of calculated genetic functions into context with one another.

The number of homozygotes (h) plus the number of heterozygotes (H) equals 100% of the samples tested. Thus, since h + H = 1, then H = 1 − h and h = 1 − H.

Heterozygosity (H) is simply the proportion of heterozygous individuals in the population. It is calculated by dividing the number of samples containing heterozygous alleles into the total number of samples (Weir 1996, pp. 141−150). A higher heterozygosity means that more allele diversity exists, and therefore there is less chance of a random sample matching. Edwards et al. (1992) described the following formula for calculating an unbiased estimate of the expected heterozygosity:

$$H \frac{n}{(n-1)} \left[1 - \sum_{j=1}^{k} \left(n_j / n \right)^2 \right] = \frac{n}{(n-1)} \left[1 - \sum_{j=1}^{k} \left(p_j \right)^2 \right]$$

where $n_1, n_2, ..., n_k$ are the allele counts of K alleles at a locus in a sample of n genes drawn from the population and p_j is the allele frequency.

Gene Diversity, often referred to as expected heterozygosity, is defined as the probability that two randomly chosen alleles from the population are different (Weir 1996, pp. 150−156).

Power of Discrimination (PD), or probability of discrimination, was first described by Fisher (1951). PD is equal to 1 minus the sum of the square of the genotype frequencies. PD is equal to $1 - P_I$ (see below).

Power of Exclusion (PE), or probability of exclusion, was first described by Fisher (1951) and may be determined by the formula: PE $= H^2(1 - 2H(1 - H)^2)$, where H = observed heterozygosity (Brenner & Morris 1990).

Probability of Identity (P$_I$) is the probability that two individuals selected at random will have an identical genotype at the tested locus (Jones 1972, Sensabaugh 1982). It is calculated by summing the square of the genotype frequencies. The probability of discrimination (PD) is equal to $1 - P_I$.

Matching probability (*pM*) as defined by Jones (1972) is the same as Sensabaugh's probability of identity (Sensabaugh 1982):

$$pM = \sum_{k=1}^{m} p_k^2$$

where p_k is the frequency of each distinct phenotype (genotype) k, and m is the number of distinct types. Effectively this is a pair-wise comparison where every type is compared against itself.

Polymorphism Information Content or Power of Information Content (PIC) reflects the probability that a given offspring of a parent carrying a rare allele at a locus will allow deduction of the parental genotype at the locus and is determined by summing the mating frequencies multiplied by the probability that an offspring will be informative (Botstein et al. 1980).

Probability of a Match (PM or pM) is sometimes referred to as the probability of a random match and is the inverse of the genotype frequency for a marker (or full profile).

Paternity Index (PI) is the likelihood that the genetic alleles obtained by the child support the assumption that the tested man is the true biological father rather than an untested, randomly selected, unrelated man. The *Combined Paternity Index* (CPI) is determined by multiplying the individual PIs for each locus tested.

Probability of Paternity Exclusion (PPE) is the probability, averaged over all possible mother-child pairs, that a random alleged father will be excluded from paternity (Chakraborty & Stivers 1996).

What Are the "Best" Markers for Use?

Having learned now how to judge measured parameters such as the probability of exclusion for a marker, it is perhaps worthwhile to step back and consider the STR markers used in human identity applications. Are some markers better than others, and if so, is it possible to get results from the best markers when partial profiles or mixtures arise (see Chapter 6)?

In human identity testing, a primary goal is to reliably distinguish unrelated individuals from one another (see Chapter 11) or to match related ones through kinship analysis (see Chapter 14). This is done by using polymorphic markers so that we have less of a chance of a type from another individual randomly matching when it should not. In order to have this high discrimination power we typically use approximately a dozen or more unlinked STR markers. Until a few years ago, European laboratories were largely using the SGM Plus kit that amplifies 10 STR loci, and North American laboratories were using the 13 core CODIS loci with sometimes the addition of two more loci, depending on the commercial STR kit.

As of early 2014, there are eight STR loci in common between the European and North American STR testing sets: FGA, TH01, VWA, D3S1358, D8S1179, D16S539, D18S51, and D21S11. The degree of overlap is likely to increase in the future as additional loci are adopted with DNA database growth. The U.S. plans to expand to 20 or more core STR loci (Hares 2012a, 2012b).

The probability of obtaining a match between two distinct and unrelated individuals (random match probability, RMP) provides a useful measure for evaluating the discriminating power of the DNA profiling system (Foreman & Evett 2001). The probability of identity examines the pairwise comparison of genotypes at a locus: the lower the probability of identity, the more variable the DNA markers. Table 10.9 lists the probability of identity values for the commonly used STR loci. Table 10.10 lists the various combinations that are available with the use of different commercial kits.

A higher gene diversity (heterozygosity) level will result from having more alleles at a locus and having alleles that are fairly equal in terms of their observed frequency. Examining Table 10.1, note that the heterozygosity of TPOX (0.690) is lower than D16S539 (0.776) even though they have the same number of alleles (9) because D16S539 has a better balance of allele frequencies and exhibits more heterozygotes. Likewise the probability of identity for D16S539 (0.0749) is better than TPOX (0.1358) (Table 10.9).

Estimating the Most Common and Rarest Genotypes Possible

Another measure to reflect the usefulness of a particular set of DNA markers is to examine the frequencies of the most common genotypes, which would therefore be the least powerful in terms of being able to differentiate between two unrelated individuals (Edwards et al. 1992). The theoretically most common type can be calculated by considering a sample type that is heterozygous at all loci possessing the two most common alleles at each locus (Foreman & Evett 2001).

For example, with D18S51, the two most common alleles in U.S. Caucasians are 15 (frequency of 0.170) and 16 (frequency of 0.147) (see Appendix 1). In Table 10.11 frequencies from the two most common alleles at each of the 29 autosomal STR loci are used to estimate a theoretical most common STR profile.

For the 13 CODIS STRs this value is 6.62×10^{-12}, or about 1 in 150 billion. With the 21 autosomal STRs in GlobalFiler, the most common type is 1.37×10^{-20}. With the 22 autosomal STRs in PowerPlex Fusion, the most common type is 3.05×10^{-21}. The combination of all 29 autosomal STRs would theoretically produce a most common type of 2.26×10^{-27} (Table 10.11).

The rarest theoretical STR profile can be calculated with heterozygous rare alleles using the 5/2N minimum allele frequency rule, or 0.00693 in the case of the U.S. Caucasian data in Appendix 1, raised to the power of the number of loci:

$$13 \text{ STRs} : (2pq)^{13} = [2 \times (0.00693) \times (0.00693)]^{13} = 5.92 \times 10^{-53} (1 \text{ in } 169 \times 10^{52})$$

$$21 \text{ STRs} : (2pq)^{21} = [2 \times (0.00693) \times (0.00693)]^{21} = 4.92 \times 10^{-85} (1 \text{ in } 2.33 \times 10^{84})$$

Thus, based on the allele frequencies present in a U.S. Caucasian database and independence assumptions between alleles and loci, the theoretical 13-locus STR profile estimates can range from 6.62×10^{-12} to 5.92×10^{-53}. The 21 STRs in GlobalFiler can produce a theoretical range from 1.37×10^{-20} to 4.29×10^{-85}. Specific STR profile frequency estimates should come somewhere in this range depending on genotypes present and allele frequencies used.

Internet Resources with Global Population Data

Several on-line resources enable comparison of STR population data across population groups. Some sites or programs can perform profile frequency estimates against various population data sets, while others provide allele frequencies for common STR loci (Table 10.12).

TABLE 10.9   Probability of Identity Values of 29 Autosomal STRs with NIST 1036 U.S. Population Samples

STR Locus	Total (N=1036)	Locus Rank	Caucasians (N=361)	Locus Rank	Black (N=342)	Locus Rank	Hispanics (N=236)	Locus Rank	Asians (N=97)	Locus Rank
SE33	0.0066	(1)	0.0079	(1)	0.0108	(1)	0.0099	(1)	0.0190	(1)
Penta E	0.0147	(2)	0.0243	(4)	0.0200	(2)	0.0184	(2)	0.0194	(2)
D2S1338	0.0220	(3)	0.0276	(5)	0.0229	(3)	0.0297	(5)	0.0428	(4)
D1S1656	0.0224	(4)	0.0211	(2)	0.0338	(8)	0.0284	(4)	0.0481	(6)
D18S51	0.0258	(5)	0.0305	(6)	0.0280	(5)	0.0303	(6)	0.0507	(8)
D12S391	0.0271	(6)	0.0237	(3)	0.0373	(9)	0.0332	(7)	0.0473	(5)
FGA	0.0308	(7)	0.0399	(7)	0.0318	(7)	0.0278	(3)	0.0528	(9)
D6S1043	0.0321	(8)	0.0517	(9)	0.0295	(6)	0.0334	(8)	0.0324	(3)
Penta D	0.0382	(9)	0.0588	(10)	0.0268	(4)	0.0506	(10)	0.0766	(13)
D21S11	0.0403	(10)	0.0512	(8)	0.0435	(11)	0.0468	(9)	0.0566	(10)
D8S1179	0.0558	(11)	0.0617	(11)	0.0660	(16)	0.0621	(12)	0.0492	(7)
D19S433	0.0559	(12)	0.0838	(16)	0.0401	(10)	0.0677	(13)	0.0724	(11)
vWA	0.0611	(13)	0.0660	(13)	0.0623	(13)	0.0730	(14)	0.0885	(15)
F13A01	0.0678	(14)	0.1164	(22)	0.0637	(14)	0.0783	(16)	0.1935	(26)
D7S820	0.0726	(15)	0.0628	(12)	0.0889	(22)	0.0867	(19)	0.1006	(18)
D16S539	0.0749	(16)	0.0983	(19)	0.0733	(18)	0.0762	(15)	0.0928	(17)
D13S317	0.0765	(17)	0.0777	(15)	0.1342	(29)	0.0526	(11)	0.0766	(12)
TH01	0.0766	(18)	0.0931	(18)	0.1050	(26)	0.0848	(18)	0.1361	(23)
Penta_C	0.0769	(19)	0.1031	(21)	0.0652	(15)	0.0787	(17)	0.1017	(19)
D2S441	0.0841	(20)	0.0884	(17)	0.1051	(27)	0.1098	(22)	0.1187	(22)
D10S1248	0.0845	(21)	0.0989	(20)	0.0693	(17)	0.1050	(21)	0.0919	(16)
D3S1358	0.0915	(22)	0.0758	(14)	0.1090	(28)	0.0904	(20)	0.1485	(25)
D22S1045	0.0921	(23)	0.1239	(23)	0.0552	(12)	0.1743	(29)	0.1030	(20)
F13B	0.0973	(24)	0.1294	(25)	0.0968	(23)	0.1370	(24)	0.3880	(29)
CSF1PO	0.1054	(25)	0.1285	(24)	0.0827	(19)	0.1255	(23)	0.1040	(21)
D5S818	0.1104	(26)	0.1486	(27)	0.0983	(24)	0.1457	(26)	0.0788	(14)
FESFPS	0.1128	(27)	0.1444	(26)	0.0847	(20)	0.1405	(25)	0.1474	(24)
LPL	0.1336	(28)	0.1516	(28)	0.1028	(25)	0.1549	(27)	0.2854	(28)
TPOX	0.1358	(29)	0.1811	(29)	0.0879	(21)	0.1554	(28)	0.2188	(27)

The CODIS 13 loci are in bold font. Genotypes are available at http://www.cstl.nist.gov/strbase/NISTpop.htm. See also Butler et al. (2012).

II. STATISTICAL INTERPRETATION

TABLE 10.10   Probability of Identity for Various Sets of STR Loci, which Illustrates the Resolving Power of Different STR Typing Kits on the Same DNA Samples

STR Kit or Core Set of Loci	Total N = 1036	361 Caucasians	342 Blacks	236 Hispanics	97 Asians
CODIS 13	5.02×10^{-16}	2.97×10^{-15}	1.14×10^{-15}	1.36×10^{-15}	1.71×10^{-14}
Identifiler	6.18×10^{-19}	6.87×10^{-18}	1.04×10^{-18}	2.73×10^{-18}	5.31×10^{-17}
PowerPlex 16	2.82×10^{-19}	4.24×10^{-18}	6.09×10^{-19}	1.26×10^{-18}	2.55×10^{-17}
PowerPlex 18D	3.47×10^{-22}	9.82×10^{-21}	5.60×10^{-22}	2.54×10^{-21}	7.92×10^{-20}
ESS 12	3.04×10^{-16}	9.66×10^{-16}	9.25×10^{-16}	2.60×10^{-15}	3.42×10^{-14}
ESI 16 / ESX 16 / NGM	2.80×10^{-20}	$2.20 v 10^{-19}$	6.23×10^{-20}	4.03×10^{-19}	9.83×10^{-18}
ESI 17 / ESX 17 / NGM SElect	1.85×10^{-22}	1.74×10^{-21}	6.71×10^{-22}	3.97×10^{-21}	1.87×10^{-19}
CODIS 20	9.35×10^{-24}	7.32×10^{-23}	6.12×10^{-23}	8.43×10^{-23}	4.22×10^{-21}
GlobalFiler	7.73×10^{-28}	1.30×10^{-26}	$3.20 v 10^{-27}$	2.27×10^{-26}	1.81×10^{-24}
PowerPlex Fusion	6.58×10^{-29}	2.35×10^{-27}	1.59×10^{-28}	2.12×10^{-27}	1.42×10^{-25}
All 29 autosomal STRs	2.24×10^{-37}	7.36×10^{-35}	3.16×10^{-37}	2.93×10^{-35}	4.02×10^{-32}

Table 10.9 has individual probability of identity values used to produce the kit-specific probability of identity based on combinations of STR loci present in each kit (see Table 1.2). Adapted from Butler et al. (2012).

TABLE 10.11   Calculations for Theoretically Most Common Genotype Frequencies and Profile Frequency Based on Two Most Common Alleles Found in a U.S. Caucasian Allele Frequency Database (Appendix 1)

STR Locus	Two most common alleles		Allele 1 Freq (p)	Allele 2 Freq (q)	Model	Most Common Genotype Frequency
	Allele 1	Allele 2				
CSF1PO	12	11	0.360	0.309	2pq	0.222
FGA	22	21	0.205	0.179	2pq	0.073
TH01	9.3	6	0.345	0.235	2pq	0.162
TPOX	8	11	0.525	0.252	2pq	0.265
vWA	17	18	0.284	0.202	2pq	0.115
D1S1656	15	16	0.150	0.136	2pq	0.041
D2S441	11	14	0.343	0.241	2pq	0.165
D2S1338	17	20	0.186	0.157	2pq	0.058
D3S1358	15	16	0.273	0.238	2pq	0.130
D5S818	12	11	0.388	0.356	2pq	0.276
D6S1043	11	12	0.296	0.237	2pq	0.140

TABLE 10.11 Calculations for Theoretically Most Common Genotype Frequencies and Profile Frequency Based on Two Most Common Alleles Found in a U.S. Caucasian Allele Frequency Database (Appendix 1) (*cont'd*)

STR Locus	Two most common alleles		Allele 1 Freq (*p*)	Allele 2 Freq (*q*)	Model	Most Common Genotype Frequency
	Allele 1	Allele 2				
D7S820	10	11	0.256	0.205	2pq	0.105
D8S1179	13	12	0.330	0.168	2pq	0.111
D10S1248	13	14	0.307	0.298	2pq	0.183
D12S391	18	21	0.172	0.129	2pq	0.044
D13S317	11	12	0.325	0.269	2pq	0.175
D16S539	11	12	0.314	0.314	2pq	0.197
D18S51	15	16	0.170	0.147	2pq	0.050
D19S433	14	13	0.361	0.255	2pq	0.184
D21S11	30	29	0.283	0.202	2pq	0.114
D22S1045	16	15	0.382	0.321	2pq	0.245
Penta D	12	13	0.233	0.197	2pq	0.092
Penta E	12	11	0.199	0.0873	2pq	0.035
SE33	27.2	28.2	0.0942	0.0762	2pq	0.014
F13A01	6	7	0.350	0.316	2pq	0.221
F13B	10	9	0.392	0.247	2pq	0.194
FESFPS	11	10	0.411	0.281	2pq	0.231
LPL	10	11	0.425	0.262	2pq	0.223
Penta C	11	12	0.396	0.211	2pq	0.167
					13 CODIS	6.62×10^{-12}
					Identifiler	7.11×10^{-14}
					GlobalFiler	1.37×10^{-20}
				PowerPlex Fusion		3.05×10^{-21}
				All 29 STRs		2.26×10^{-27}

TABLE 10.12   Description of Available Online Population Databases

Name	Brief Description	Website
OmniPop	Can calculate STR profile frequency against up to 202 published population studies.	http://www.cstl.nist.gov/strbase/population/OmniPop200.1.xls (can download Excel macro developed by Brian Burritt)
ALLST*R	A database of literature studies compiled by Qualitype GmbH; new data can be inputted.	http://allstr.de/
popSTR	Open-access online frequency browser; enables searching on >3,800 population samples with >30 STR loci.	http://spsmart.cesga.es/popstr.php (Amigo et al. 2009)
str-base	Can calculate profile frequency estimate using 5,700 SGM Plus profiles collected by ENFSI.	http://strbase.org/index.php (Gill et al. 2003)

SUMMARY

In order to determine the probability of a random match between the DNA profile obtained from a crime scene and that of a suspect, a reliable estimation of allele and genotype frequencies in relevant population(s) are needed. Hence, population data have been gathered in numerous studies and examined for HWE and linkage equilibrium. Once a specific database has been deemed "reliable" following allele and locus independence tests, the allele frequencies are then used to estimate a specific DNA profile's frequency, as will be described in Chapter 11. Corrections for subpopulation structure and possible involvement of relatives reduce the match probability and typically provide a more conservative estimate for the defendant.

Reading List and Internet Resources

Introductory Genetic Principles

Barbujani, G., et al. (1997). An apportionment of human DNA diversity. *Proceedings of the National Academy of Sciences of the United States of America, 94,* 4516–4519.

Burgess, D. J. (2011). Comparative genomics: mammalian alignments reveal human functional elements. *Nature Review Genetics, 12,* 806–807.

Butler, J. M. (2012). *Advanced Topics in Forensic DNA Typing: Methodology.* San Diego: Elsevier Academic Press.

Butler, J. M., et al. (2012). Variability of new STR loci and kits in U.S. population groups. *Profiles in DNA.* Available at http://www.promega.com/resources/articles/profiles-in-dna/2012/variability-of-new-str-loci-and-kits-in-us-population-groups/. Accessed April 1, 2014.

Castle, W. E. (1903). Mendel's law of heredity. *Proceedings of the American Academy of Arts and Sciences, 38,* 535–548.

Cavalli-Sforza, L. L., & Bodmer, W. F. (1971). *The Genetics of Human Populations.* Mineola, New York: Dover Publications.

Crow, J. F. (1999). Hardy, Weinberg and language impediments. *Genetics, 152,* 821–825.

Freeman, J. L., et al. (2006). Copy number variation: new insights in genome diversity. *Genome Research, 16,* 949–961.

Gonick, L., & Wheelis, M. (1983). *The Cartoon Guide to Genetics, Updated Edition.* New York: HarperCollins Publishers.

Hardy, G. H. (1908). Mendelian proportions in a mixed population. *Science, 17,* 49–50.

Hartl, D. L., & Orel, V. (1992). What did Gregor Mendel think he discovered? *Genetics, 131,* 245–253.

Hartl, D. L., & Jones, E. W. (1998) (4th ed.). *Genetics: Principles and Analysis*. Sudbury, Massachusetts: Jones and Bartlett Publishers.

Lewontin, R. C. (1972). The apportionment of human diversity. *Evolutionary Biology, 6*, 381–398.

Sandler, I. (2000). Development: Mendel's legacy to genetics. *Genetics, 154*, 7–11.

Weinberg, W. (1908). Uber den Nachwels der Vererbung beim Menschen. *Jahresh. Wuertt. Ver. Vaterl. Natkd., 64*, 369–382 [English translation: "On the demonstration of heredity in man," *Papers on Human Genetics*, Prentice-Hall (1963) translation by S.H. Boyer].

Allele Nomenclature Examples

Balding, D. J. (2005). *Weight-of-Evidence for Forensic DNA Profiles*. Hoboken, New Jersey: John Wiley & Sons.

Brenner, C. H. (1997). Symbolic kinship program. *Genetics, 145*, 535–542.

Buckleton, J., Triggs, C. M., & Walsh, S. J. (2005). *Forensic DNA Evidence Interpretation*. London: CRC Press.

Buckleton, J. S., et al. (2011). The interpretation of lineage markers in forensic DNA testing. *Forensic Science International: Genetics, 5*, 78–83.

Evett, I. W. (1992). Evaluating DNA profiles in a case where the defence is "it was my brother. *Journal of Forensic Science Society, 32*, 5–14.

Evett, I. W., & Weir, B. S. (1998). *Interpreting DNA Evidence: Statistical Genetics for Forensic Scientists*. Sunderland, MA: Sinauer Associates.

Fung, W. K., & Hu, Y.-Q. (2008). *Statistical DNA Forensics: Theory, Methods and Computation*. Hoboken, NJ: Wiley.

Lucy, D. (2005). *Introduction to Statistics for Forensic Scientists*. Hoboken, New Jersey: John Wiley & Sons.

National Research Council (NRC) Committee on DNA Forensic Science. (1992). *DNA Technology in Forensic Science*. Washington, DC: National Academy Press.

National Research Council (NRC) Committee on DNA Forensic Science. (1996). *The Evaluation of Forensic DNA Evidence*. Washington, DC: National Academy Press.

SWGDAM. (2010). *SWGDAM Interpretation Guidelines for Autosomal STR Typing by Forensic DNA Testing Laboratories*. Available at http://www.fbi.gov/about-us/lab/codis/swgdam-interpretation-guidelines. Accessed April 3, 2014.

Weir, B. S. (2007). Forensics. In D. J. Balding, M. Bishop, & C. Cannings (Eds.), *Handbook of Statistical Genetics* (3rd ed.) (pp. 1368–1392). Hoboken: John Wiley & Sons.

Population Genetics & Data

Chakraborty, R. (1992). Sample size requirements for addressing the population genetic issues of forensic use of DNA typing. *Human Biology, 64*, 141–159.

Devlin, B. (1993). Forensic inference from genetic markers. *Statistical Methods in Medical Research, 2*, 241–262.

Emigh, T. H. (1980). A comparison of tests for Hardy–Weinberg equilibrium. *Biometrics, 36*(4), 627–642.

Evett, I. W., & Gill, P. (1991). A discussion of the robustness of methods for assessing the evidential value of DNA single locus profiles in crime investigations. *Electrophoresis, 12*, 226–230.

Fung, W. K. (1996a). Statistical issues in comparing random DNA samples. *Forensic Science International, 78*, 231–232.

Fung, W. K. (1996b). Are convenience DNA samples significantly different? *Forensic Science International, 82*, 233–241.

Fung, W. K., & Hu, Y.-Q. (2008). Population genetics. In *Statistical DNA Forensics: Theory, Methods and Computation*. Hoboken, New Jersey: John Wiley & Sons Inc.

Guo, S.-W., & Thompson, E. A. (1992). Performing the exact test of Hardy-Weinberg proportion for multiple alleles. *Biometrics, 48*, 361–372.

Hamilton, M. B. (2009). *Population Genetics*. Hoboken, New Jersey: Wiley-Blackwell.

Hartl, D. L., & Clark, A. G. (2007) (4th ed.). *Principles of Population Genetics*. Sunderland, Massachusetts: Sinauer Associates.

Lander, E. (1989). Population genetic considerations in the forensic use of DNA typing. In *Banbury Report 32: DNA Technology and Forensic Science* (pp. 143–156). Cold Spring Harbor, NY: Cold Spring Harbor Laboratory Press.

STRBase. (2014). http://www.cstl.nist.gov/biotech/strbase. Accessed April 1, 2014.

Taylor, D. (2013). Hardy Weinberg equilibrium, allele frequencies, genotype probabilities, confidence intervals, databases, linkage. Available at http://www.cstl.nist.gov/strbase/pub_pres/ISFG2013basic-Taylor.pdf *International Society for Forensic Genetics (ISFG) workshop on Basic Principles in Forensic DNA Interpretation*. Accessed April 1, 2014.

Triggs, C., et al. (2000). The calculation of DNA match probabilities in mixed race populations. *Science & Justice, 40*, 33–38.

Triggs, C. M., & Buckleton, J. S. (2002). Logical implications of applying the principles of population genetics to the interpretation of DNA profiling evidence. *Forensic Science International, 128,* 108–114.

Weir, B. S. (1996). *Genetic Data Analysis II: Methods for Discrete Population Genetic Data.* Sunderland, Massachusetts: Sinauer Associates.

The Product Rule

Buckleton, J. S., et al. (2001). The fallacy of independence testing and the use of the product rule. *Science & Justice, 41,* 81–84.

Curran, J. M., et al. (2002). Assessing uncertainty in DNA evidence caused by sampling effects. *Science & Justice, 42,* 29–37.

Curran, J. M., et al. (2007). Empirical testing of estimated DNA frequencies. *Forensic Science International: Genetics, 1,* 267–272.

Law, B., et al. (2003). Effects of population structure and admixture on exact tests for association between loci. *Genetics, 164,* 381–387.

Autosomal STR Population Studies

Aguiar, V. R., et al. (2012). Updated Brazilian STR allele frequency data using over 100,000 individuals: an analysis of CSF1PO, D3S1358, D5S818, D7S820, D8S1179, D13S317, D16S539, D18S51, D21S11, FGA, Penta D, Penta E, TH01, TPOX and vWA loci. *Forensic Science International: Genetics, 6,* 504–509.

Al-Obaidli, A., et al. (2009). Present day inbreeding does not forbid the forensic utility of commonly explored STR loci: a case study of native Qataris. *Forensic Science International: Genetics, 4,* e11–e13.

Ali, I., et al. (2012). Allele frequencies of 15 STR loci using AmpFlSTR Identifiler kit in the Maldivian population. *Forensic Science International: Genetics, 6,* e136.

Alvarez, M., et al. (2008). Genetic population data of 15 autosomal loci from the Central Region of Venezuela. *Forensic Science International: Genetics Supplement Series, 1,* 303–305.

Amorim, A., et al. (2012). Genetic portrait of Brazilian immigrant population living in Lisboa. *Forensic Science International: Genetics, 6,* e121–e124.

Amorim, A., et al. (2012). Genetic portrait of a native population of Cabo Verde living in Lisboa. *Forensic Science International: Genetics, 6,* e166–e169.

Aranda, X. G., et al. (2010). Genetic data for D1S1677, D2S441, D4S2364, D10S1248, D14S1434 and D22S1045 miniSTR loci from Libya. *Forensic Science International: Genetics, 4,* 267–268.

Barbaro, A., et al. (2012). Allele frequencies of the new European Standard Set (ESS) loci in a population of Southern Italy (Calabria). *Forensic Science International: Genetics, 6,* e37–e38.

Barbaro, A., et al. (2012). Distribution of allele frequencies of 20 STRs loci in a population sample from Calabria, Southern Italy. *Forensic Science International: Genetics, 6,* e137–e138.

Berti, A., et al. (2011). Allele frequencies of the new European Standard Set (ESS) loci in the Italian population. *Forensic Science International: Genetics, 5,* 548–549.

Borosky, A., et al. (2009). Analysis of 17 STR loci in different provinces of Argentina. *Forensic Science International: Genetics, 3,* e93–e95.

Bouabdellah, M., et al. (2008). STR data for the 15 AmpFlSTR Identifiler loci in the Moroccan population. *Forensic Science International: Genetics Supplement Series, 1,* 306–308.

Branco, C. C., et al. (2008). Study of the genetic relationship and diversity patterns in the Azores based on 15 STR markers. *Forensic Science International: Genetics Supplement Series, 1,* 312–314.

Branham, A., et al. (2012). Allele frequencies of fifteen STR loci in U.S. immigrants from Haiti compared with African Americans and Afro-Caribbeans. *Forensic Science International: Genetics, 6,* e3–e4.

Bright, J. A., et al. (2010). Allele frequencies for the four major sub-populations of New Zealand for the 15 Identifiler loci. *Forensic Science International: Genetics, 4,* e65–e66.

Brisighelli, F., et al. (2009). Allele frequencies of fifteen STRs in a representative sample of the Italian population. *Forensic Science International: Genetics, 3,* e29–e30.

Budowle, B., et al. (2001). CODIS STR loci data from 41 sample populations. *Journal of Forensic Sciences, 46,* 453–489.

Butler, J. M., et al. (2003). Allele frequencies for 15 autosomal STR loci on U.S. Caucasian, African American, and Hispanic populations. *Journal of Forensic Sciences, 48,* 908–911.

Carboni, I., et al. (2007). Genetic STRs variation in a large population from Tuscany (Italy). *Forensic Science International: Genetics, 1,* e10–e11.

Chen, J. G., et al. (2012). Population genetic data of 15 autosomal STR loci in Uygur ethnic group of China. *Forensic Science International: Genetics, 6,* e178–e179.

Cho, E. H., et al. (2011). Variant alleles detected in a large Korean population using AmpFlSTR Profiler Plus. *Forensic Science International: Genetics, 5,* 552—554.

Chula, F. G., et al. (2009). 15 STR loci frequencies with mutation rates in the population from Rio Grande do Sul, Southern Brazil. *Forensic Science International: Genetics, 3,* e35—e38.

Cortellini, V., et al. (2011). Population data on 5 non-CODIS STR loci (D10S1248, D22S1045, D2S441, D1S1656, D12S391) in a population sample from Brescia county (Northern Italy). *Forensic Science International: Genetics, 5,* e97—e98.

de Assis, P. L., et al. (2010). Allele frequencies of 15 STRs in a representative sample of the Brazilian population. *Forensic Science International: Genetics, 4,* e61—e63.

Di, C. J., et al. (2012). Genetic data of 15 STR loci in five populations from Afghanistan. *Forensic Science International: Genetics, 6,* e44—e45.

Diaz-Lacava, A., et al. (2011). Spatial assessment of Argentinean genetic admixture with geographical information systems. *Forensic Science International: Genetics, 5,* 297—302.

Dognaux, S., et al. (2012). Allele frequencies for the new European Standard Set (ESS) loci and D1S1677 in the Belgian population. *Forensic Science International: Genetics, 6,* e75—e77.

Einum, D. D., & Scarpetta, M. A. (2004). Genetic analysis of large data sets of North American Black, Caucasian, and Hispanic populations at 13 CODIS STR loci. *Journal of Forensic Sciences, 49,* 1381—1385.

Elmrghni, S., et al. (2012). Genetic data provided by 15 autosomal STR loci in the Libyan population living in Benghazi. *Forensic Science International: Genetics, 6,* e93—e94.

Fernandez-Formoso, L., et al. (2012). Allele frequencies of 20 STRs from Northwest Spain (Galicia). *Forensic Science International: Genetics, 6,* e149—e150.

Fridman, C., et al. (2008). Brazilian population profile of 15 STR markers. *Forensic Science International: Genetics, 2,* e1—e4.

Garcia, O., et al. (2012). Population genetic data and concordance study for the kits Identifiler, NGM, PowerPlex ESX 17 System and Investigator ESSplex in Spain. *Forensic Science International: Genetics, 6,* e78—e79.

Gazi, N. N., et al. (2010). Genetic polymorphisms of 15 autosomal STR loci in three isolated tribal populations of Bangladesh. *Forensic Science International: Genetics, 4,* 265—266.

Ghosh, T., et al. (2011). Genetic diversity of autosomal STRs in eleven populations of India. *Forensic Science International: Genetics, 5,* 259—261.

Gomes, V., et al. (2009). Population data defined by 15 autosomal STR loci in Karamoja population (Uganda) using AmpF/STR Identifiler kit. *Forensic Science International: Genetics, 3,* e55—e58.

Graydon, M., et al. (2009). Inferring ethnicity using 15 autosomal STR loci—comparisons among populations of similar and distinctly different physical traits. *Forensic Science International: Genetics, 3,* 251—254.

Gutierrez, C. C., et al. (2011). Population genetic data for 15 STR loci (PowerPlex 16 kit) in Nicaragua. *Forensic Science International: Genetics, 5,* 563—564.

Haliti, N., et al. (2009). Evaluation of population variation at 17 autosomal STR and 16 Y-STR haplotype loci in Croatians. *Forensic Science International: Genetics, 3,* e137—e138.

Hatzer-Grubwieser, P., et al. (2012). Allele frequencies and concordance study of 16 STR loci—including the new European Standard Set (ESS) loci—in an Austrian population sample. *Forensic Science International: Genetics, 6,* e50—e51.

Herrera-Paz, E. F., et al. (2008). Allele frequencies distributions for 13 autosomal STR loci in 3 Black Carib (Garifuna) populations of the Honduran Caribbean coasts. *Forensic Science International: Genetics, 3,* e5—e10.

Hill, C. R., et al. (2013). U.S. population data for 29 autosomal STR loci. *Forensic Science International: Genetics, 7,* e82—e83.

Huang, Q., et al. (2013). Genetic polymorphism of 15 STR loci in Chinese Han population from Shanghai municipality in East China. *Forensic Science International: Genetics, 7,* e31—e34.

Illeperuma, R. J., et al. (2009). Genetic profile of 11 autosomal STR loci among the four major ethnic groups in Sri Lanka. *Forensic Science International: Genetics, 3,* e105—e106.

Illeperuma, R. J., et al. (2010). Genetic variation at 11 autosomal STR loci in the aboriginal people, the Veddahs of Sri Lanka. *Forensic Science International: Genetics, 4,* 142.

Jacewicz, R., et al. (2008). Population database on 15 autosomal STR loci in 1000 unrelated individuals from the Lodz region of Poland. *Forensic Science International: Genetics, 2,* e1—e3.

Jakovski, Z., et al. (2012). Allele frequencies of the new European Standard Set (ESS) loci plus SE33 locus in a population from the Republic of Macedonia. *Forensic Science International: Genetics, 6,* e90—e92.

Jedrzejczyk, M., et al. (2012). Genetic population studies on 15 NGM STR loci in central Poland population. *Forensic Science International: Genetics, 6,* e119—e120.

II. STATISTICAL INTERPRETATION

Juarez-Cedillo, T., et al. (2008). Genetic admixture and diversity estimations in the Mexican Mestizo population from Mexico City using 15 STR polymorphic markers. *Forensic Science International: Genetics, 2*, e37–e39.

Kalpana, D., et al. (2012). Pentaplex typing of new European Standard Set (ESS) STR loci in Indian population. *Forensic Science International: Genetics, 6*, e86–e89.

Konarzewska, M., et al. (2010). Population data and sequence analysis of a 'new' microsatellite locus HumHUU (D16S3433). *Forensic Science International: Genetics, 4*, e143–e144.

Kraaijenbrink, T., et al. (2008). Allele frequency distribution of 21 forensic autosomal STRs in 7 populations from Yunnan, China. *Forensic Science International: Genetics, 3*, e11–e12.

Lagoa, A. M., et al. (2008). Allele frequencies of six miniSTR loci in the population of Northern Portugal. *Forensic Science International: Genetics, 2*, 379–381.

Lane, A. B. (2008). The nature of tri-allelic TPOX genotypes in African populations. *Forensic Science International: Genetics, 2*, 134–137.

Lao, O., et al. (2010). Evaluating self-declared ancestry of U.S. Americans with autosomal, Y-chromosomal and mitochondrial DNA. *Human Mutation, 31*, E1875–E1893.

Lauc, G., et al. (2008). Empirical support for the reliability of DNA interpretation in Croatia. *Forensic Science International: Genetics, 3*, 50–53.

Li, S., et al. (2012). Allele frequencies of nine non-CODIS STR loci in Chinese Uyghur ethnic minority group. *Forensic Science International: Genetics, 6*, e11–e12.

Lohmueller, K. E. (2010). Graydon et al. provide no new evidence that forensic STR loci are functional. *Forensic Science International: Genetics, 4*, 273–274.

Lopes, V., et al. (2009). Allelic frequency distribution of 17 STRs from Identifiler and PowerPlex-16 in Central Portugal area and the Azores archipelago. *Forensic Science International: Genetics, 4*, e1–e7.

Marques dos, S. R., et al. (2012). Genetic portrait of an immigrant population from Angola living in Lisboa. *Forensic Science International: Genetics, 6*, e170–e173.

Melo, M. M., et al. (2010). Genetic study of 15 STRs loci of Identifiler system in Angola population. *Forensic Science International: Genetics, 4*, e153–e157.

Mertens, G., et al. (2011). Population genetic analysis of Moroccans residing in Belgium using 16 autosomal STRs of the PowerPlex ESI 17 multiplex. *Forensic Science International: Genetics, 5*, 352–353.

Molnar, A., et al. (2011). Allele distribution of the new European Standard Set (ESS) loci in the Hungarian population. *Forensic Science International: Genetics, 5*, 555–556.

Montelius, K., et al. (2008). STR data for the AmpFlSTR Identifiler loci from Swedish population in comparison to European, as well as with non-European population. *Forensic Science International: Genetics, 2*, e49–e52.

Monterrosa, J. C., et al. (2012). Population genetic data for 16 STR loci (PowerPlex ESX-17 kit) in El Salvador. *Forensic Science International: Genetics, 6*, e134.

Montinaro, F., et al. (2012). Using forensic microsatellites to decipher the genetic structure of linguistic and geographic isolates: A survey in the eastern Italian Alps. *Forensic Science International: Genetics, 6*, 827–833.

Munoz, A., et al. (2012). Allele frequencies of 15 STRs in the Calchaqui Valleys population (North-Western Argentina). *Forensic Science International: Genetics, 6*, e58–e60.

Nascimento, E., et al. (2011). Population database defined by 13 autosomal STR loci in a representative sample from Bahia, Northeast Brazil. *Forensic Science International: Genetics, 5*, e38–e40.

Nie, S., et al. (2008). Genetic data of 15 STR loci in Chinese Yunnan Han population. *Forensic Science International: Genetics, 3*, e1–e3.

Noor, S., et al. (2011). An autosomal STR database of Muslims: the largest minority community, Uttar Pradesh, India. *Forensic Science International: Genetics, 5*, e117–e118.

Novkovic, T., et al. (2010). Genetic polymorphisms of 15 AmpFlSTR Identifiler loci in a Serbian population. *Forensic Science International: Genetics, 4*, e149–e150.

Ocampos, M., et al. (2009). 15 STR loci frequencies in the population from Santa Catarina, Southern Brazil. *Forensic Science International: Genetics, 3*, e129–e131.

Omran, G. A., et al. (2009). Genetic variation of 15 autosomal STR loci in Upper (Southern) Egyptians. *Forensic Science International: Genetics, 3*, e39–e44.

Park, H., et al. (2012). Detection of very large off-ladder alleles at the PentaE locus in a 15 locus autosomal STR database of 199 Korean individuals. *Forensic Science International: Genetics, 6*, e189–e191.

Pepinski, W., et al. (2011). Polymorphism of 11 non-CODIS STRs in a population sample of Lithuanian minority residing in northeastern Poland. *Forensic Science International: Genetics, 5,* e37.

Petric, G., et al. (2012). Genetic variation at 15 autosomal STR loci in the Hungarian population of Vojvodina Province, Republic of Serbia. *Forensic Science International: Genetics, 6,* e163–e165.

Phillips, C., et al. (2008). D9S1120, a simple STR with a common Native American-specific allele: forensic optimization, locus characterization and allele frequency studies. *Forensic Science International: Genetics, 3,* 7–13.

Phillips, C., et al. (2011). Analysis of global variability in 15 established and 5 new European Standard Set (ESS) STRs using the CEPH human genome diversity panel. *Forensic Science International: Genetics, 5,* 155–169.

Piatek, J., et al. (2008). Population genetics of 15 autosomal STR loci in the population of Pomorze Zachodnie (NW Poland). *Forensic Science International: Genetics, 2,* e41–e43.

Piglionica, M., et al. (2013). Allele frequencies of the new European Standard Set (ESS) loci in a population of Apulia (Southern Italy). *Forensic Science International: Genetics, 7,* e35–e36.

Poiares, L. A., et al. (2009). 15 STR loci frequencies in the population from Parana, Southern Brazil. *Forensic Science International: Genetics, 4,* e23–e24.

Pontes, M. L., & Pinheiro, M. F. (2012). Population data of the AmpFlSTR® NGM STR loci in a North of Portugal sample. *Forensic Science International: Genetics, 6,* e127–e128.

Porras, L., et al. (2008). Genetic polymorphism of 15 STR loci in central western Colombia. *Forensic Science International: Genetics, 2,* e7–e8.

Powell, G. T., et al. (2007). The population history of the Xibe in northern China: a comparison of autosomal, mtDNA and Y-chromosomal analyses of migration and gene flow. *Forensic Science International: Genetics, 1,* 115–119.

Previdere, C., et al. (2013). The 2011 GeFI collaborative exercise. Concordance study, proficiency testing and Italian population data on the new ENFSI/EDNAP loci D1S1656, D2S441, D10S1248, D12S391, D22S1045. *Forensic Science International: Genetics, 7,* e15–e18.

Raimann, P. E., et al. (2012). Genetic data for D1S1677, D2S441, D4S2364, D10S1248, D14S1434 and D22S1045 miniSTR loci from the state of Rio Grande do Sul, Southern Brazil. *Forensic Science International: Genetics, 6,* e42–e43.

Rak, S. A., et al. (2011). Population genetic data on 15 STR loci in the Hungarian population. *Forensic Science International: Genetics, 5,* 543–544.

Rangel-Villalobos, H., et al. (2010). Admixture estimates and statistical parameters of forensic importance based on PowerPlex 16 system in Mexican-Mestizos from the States of Guanajuato (Center) and Veracruz (East). *Forensic Science International: Genetics, 4,* 271–272.

Ribeiro, T., et al. (2013). Population data of the AmpFlSTR® NGM loci in South Portuguese population. *Forensic Science International: Genetics, 7,* e37–e39.

Roby, R. K., et al. (2009). Autosomal STR allele frequencies and Y-STR and mtDNA haplotypes in Chilean sample populations. *Forensic Science International: Genetics Supplement Series, 2,* 532–533.

Rocchi, A., et al. (2012). Italian data of 23 STR loci amplified in a single multiplex reaction. *Forensic Science International: Genetics, 6,* e157–e158.

Rodenbusch, R., et al. (2012). Allele frequencies of the five new generation forensic STR (D1S1656, D2S441, D10S1248, D12S391 and D22S1045) in the population from Rio Grande do Sul, Southern Brazil. *Forensic Science International: Genetics, 6,* e55–e57.

Rodrigues, E. L., et al. (2009). Genetic data on 15 STR autosomal loci for a sample population of the Northern Region of the State of Rio de Janeiro, Brazil. *Forensic Science International: Genetics, 4,* e25–e26.

Rubi-Castellanos, R., et al. (2009). Genetic data of 15 autosomal STRs (Identifiler kit) of three Mexican Mestizo population samples from the States of Jalisco (West), Puebla (Center), and Yucatan (Southeast). *Forensic Science International: Genetics, 3,* e71–e76.

Sanchez-Diz, P., et al. (2008). 16 STR data of a Greek population. *Forensic Science International: Genetics, 2,* e71–e72.

Sanchez-Diz, P., et al. (2009). Population data on 15 autosomal STRs in a sample from Colombia. *Forensic Science International: Genetics, 3,* e81–e82.

Schlebusch, C. M., et al. (2012). Genetic variation of 15 autosomal STR loci in various populations from southern Africa. *Forensic Science International: Genetics, 6,* e20–e21.

Seider, T., et al. (2010). Allele frequencies of the five miniSTR loci D1S1656, D2S441, D10S1248, D12S391 and D22S1045 in a German population sample. *Forensic Science International: Genetics, 4,* e159–e160.

Shotivaranon, J., et al. (2009). DNA database of populations from different parts in the Kingdom of Thailand. *Forensic Science International: Genetics, 4,* e37–e38.

II. STATISTICAL INTERPRETATION

Silva, M. B., et al. (2010). Allele frequencies of fifteen STR loci in a population from Central Brazil. *Forensic Science International: Genetics, 4,* e151–e152.

Simms, T. M., et al. (2008). The genetic legacy of the Transatlantic Slave Trade in the island of New Providence. *Forensic Science International: Genetics, 2,* 310–317.

Simms, T. M., et al. (2012). Divergent genetic strata in five Bahamian islands. *Forensic Science International: Genetics, 6,* 81–90.

Soltyszewski, I., et al. (2008). Analysis of forensically used autosomal short tandem repeat markers in Polish and neighboring populations. *Forensic Science International: Genetics, 2,* 205–211.

Song, X. B., et al. (2011). Genetic polymorphisms of 9 non-combined of DNA index system short tandem repeat loci of Chinese Tibetan ethnic minority group in Tibet. *Forensic Science International: Genetics, 5,* 356–357.

Sotak, M., et al. (2008). Genetic variation analysis of 15 autosomal STR loci in Eastern Slovak Caucasian and Romany (Gypsy) population. *Forensic Science International: Genetics, 3,* e21–e25.

Stanciu, F., et al. (2009). STR data for the AmpFlSTR Identifiler from Dobruja region (SE Romania). *Forensic Science International: Genetics, 3,* 146–147.

Stanciu, F., et al. (2009). Allele frequencies of 15 STR loci in Moldavia region (NE Romania). *Forensic Science International: Genetics, 4,* e39–e40.

Talledo, M., et al. (2010). Comparative allele distribution at 16 STR loci between the Andean and coastal population from Peru. *Forensic Science International: Genetics, 4,* e109–e117.

Taylor, D. A., et al. (2008). South Australian Aboriginal sub-population data for the nine AMPFlSTR Profiler Plus short tandem repeat (STR) loci. *Forensic Science International: Genetics, 2,* e27–e30.

Tillmar, A. O., et al. (2009). Genetic variation of 15 autosomal STR loci in a Somali population. *Forensic Science International: Genetics, 4,* e19–e20.

Tillmar, A. O., et al. (2013). Analysis of Investigator HDplex markers in Swedish and Somali populations. *Forensic Science International: Genetics, 7,* e21–e22.

Tong, D., et al. (2009). Polymorphism analysis of 15 STR loci in a large sample of the Han population in southern China. *Forensic Science International: Genetics, 4,* e27–e29.

Tucker, V. C., et al. (2012). UK population data generated with the PowerPlex® ESI 16 system. *Forensic Science International: Genetics, 6,* e112–e118.

Venables, S. J., et al. (2011). An in-depth population genetic analysis of forensic short tandem repeat loci in Indonesia. *Forensic Science International: Genetics Supplement Series, 3,* e157–e158.

Vergara, I. A., et al. (2012). Autosomal STR allele frequencies for the CODIS system from a large random population sample in Chile. *Forensic Science International: Genetics, 6,* e83–e85.

Vullo, C., et al. (2010). Frequency data for 12 mini STR loci in Argentina. *Forensic Science International: Genetics, 4,* e79–e81.

Walsh, S. J., et al. (2007). Use of subpopulation data in Australian forensic DNA casework. *Forensic Science International: Genetics, 1,* 238–246.

Wang, R., et al. (2008). Genetic distribution on 15 STR loci from a population of Southern Liaoning in northeast of China. *Forensic Science International: Genetics, 2,* e25–e26.

Wolfgramm, E. V., et al. (2011). Genetic analysis of 15 autosomal and 12 Y-STR loci in the Espirito Santo State population. Brazil. *Forensic Science International: Genetics, 5,* e41–e43.

Wu, Y. M., et al. (2008). Genetic polymorphisms of 15 STR loci in Chinese Han population living in Xi'an city of Shaanxi Province. *Forensic Science International: Genetics, 2,* e15–e18.

Xing, J., et al. (2011). Genetic polymorphism of 15 STR loci in a Manchu population in Northeast China. *Forensic Science International: Genetics, 5,* e93–e95.

Yang, L., et al. (2013). Allele frequencies of 15 STRs in five ethnic groups (Han, Gelao, Jing, Shui and Zhuang) in South China. *Forensic Science International: Genetics, 7,* e9–e14.

Yurrebaso, I., et al. (2011). Allele frequencies and concordance study between the Identifiler and the PowerPlex ESX17 systems in the Basque Country population. *Forensic Science International: Genetics, 5,* e79–e80.

Zhivotovsky, L. A., et al. (2009). An STR database on the Volga-Ural population. *Forensic Science International: Genetics, 3,* e133–e136.

Zhivotovsky, L. A., et al. (2009). Developing STR databases on structured populations: the native South Siberian population versus the Russian population. *Forensic Science International: Genetics, 3,* e111–e116.

Zhivotovsky, L. A., et al. (2009). A reference data base on STR allele frequencies in the Belarus population developed from paternity cases. *Forensic Science International: Genetics, 3,* e107–e109.

Zhu, Y., et al. (2009). Genetic analysis of 15 STR loci in the population of Zhejiang Province (Southeast China). *Forensic Science International: Genetics, 3*, e139—e140.

Linkage and Linked Loci

Bright, J.-A., et al. (2013). Relatedness calculations for linked loci incorporating subpopulation effects. *Forensic Science International: Genetics, 7*, 380—383.

Buckleton, J., & Triggs, C. (2006). The effect of linkage on the calculation of DNA match probabilities for siblings and half siblings. *Forensic Science International, 160*, 193—199.

Haldane, J. B. S. (1919). A combination of linkage values and the calculation of distances between loci of linked factors. *Journal of Genetics, 8*, 299—309.

Kling, D., et al. (2012). FamLink — a user friendly software for linkage calculations in family genetics. *Forensic Science International: Genetics, 6*, 616—620.

Kosambi, D. D. (1944). The estimation of map distance from recombination values. *Annals of Eugenics, 12*, 172—175.

Tillmar, A. O., et al. (2008). Analysis of linkage and linkage disequilibrium for eight X-STR markers. *Forensic Science International: Genetics, 3*, 37—41.

Ott, J. (1999) (3rd ed.). *Analysis of Human Genetic Linkage*. Baltimore: The Johns Hopkins University Press.

Closely Spaced Loci: D12S391 and vWA

Bright, J.-A., et al. (2014). A guide to forensic DNA interpretation and linkage. Available from *Profiles in DNA* http://www.promega.com/resources/profiles-in-dna/2014/a-guide-to-forensic-dna-interpretation-and-linkage/. Accessed April 1, 2014.

Budowle, B., et al. (2011). Population genetic analyses of the NGM STR loci. *International Journal of Legal Medicine, 125*, 101—109.

Gill, P., et al. (2012). An evaluation of potential allelic association between the STRs vWA and D12S391: implications in criminal casework and applications to short pedigrees. *Forensic Science International: Genetics, 6*, 477—486.

O'Connor, K. L., et al. (2011). Linkage disequilibrium analysis of D12S391 and vWA in U.S. population and paternity samples. *Forensic Science International: Genetics, 5*, 538—540 (Corrigendum erratum, pp. 541—542).

O'Connor, K. L., & Tillmar, A. O. (2012). Effect of linkage between vWA and D12S391 in kinship analysis. *Forensic Science International: Genetics, 6*, 840—844.

Phillips, C., et al. (2011). Analysis of global variability in 15 established and 5 new European Standard Set (ESS) STRs using the CEPH human genome diversity panel. *Forensic Science International: Genetics, 5*, 155—169.

Phillips, C., et al. (2012). The recombination landscape around forensic STRs: Accurate measurement of genetic distances between syntenic STR pairs using HapMap high density SNP data. *Forensic Science International: Genetics, 6*, 354—365.

Population Structure

Al-Obaidli, A., et al. (2009). Present day inbreeding does not forbid the forensic utility of commonly explored STR loci: a case study of native Qataris. *Forensic Science International: Genetics, 4*, e11—e13.

Anderson, A. D., & Weir, B. S. (2006). An assessment of the behavior of the population structure parameter, θ, at the CODIS loci. *Progress in Forensic Genetics 11, ICS, 1288*, 495—497.

Balding, D. J., & Nichols, R. A. (1994). DNA profile match probability calculation: how to allow for population stratification, relatedness, database selection and single bands. *Forensic Science International, 64*, 125—140.

Buckleton, J. S., et al. (2006). How reliable is the sub-population model in DNA testimony? *Forensic Science International, 157*, 144—148.

Budowle, B., & Chakraborty, R. (2001). Population variation at the CODIS core short tandem repeat loci in Europeans. *Legal Medicine, 3*, 29—33.

Curran, J. M., et al. (2003). What is the magnitude of the subpopulation effect? *Forensic Science International, 135*, 1—8.

Curran, J. M., & Buckleton, J. (2007). The appropriate use of subpopulation corrections for differences in endogamous communities. *Forensic Science International, 168*, 106—111.

Ewens, W. J. (1972). The sampling theory of selectively neutral alleles. *Theoretical Population Biology, 3*, 87—112.

Harbison, S. A., & Buckleton, J. S. (1998). Applications and extensions of subpopulation theory: a caseworkers guide. *Science & Justice, 38*, 249—254.

Holsinger, K. E., & Weir, B. S. (2009). Genetics in geographically structured populations: defining, estimating and interpreting F_{ST}. *Nature Reviews Genetics, 10*, 639—650.

Lareu, M. (2013) (2nd ed.). *Short tandem repeats. Encyclopedia of Forensic Sciences*. San Diego: Elsevier Academic Press. pp. 219–226.

Lauc, G., et al. (2008). Empirical support for the reliability of DNA interpretation in Croatia. *Forensic Science International: Genetics, 3*, 50–53.

McDonald, D. B. (2013). Worked example of calculating *F-statistics* from genotypic data. Available at http://www.uwyo.edu/dbmcd/popecol/maylects/fst.html. Accessed April 3, 2014.

Rowold, D. J., & Herrera, R. J. (2005). On human STR sub-population structure. *Forensic Science International, 151*, 59–69.

Tvedebrink, T. (2009). Overdispersion in allelic counts and θ-correction in forensic genetics. *Forensic Science International: Genetics Supplement Series, 2*, 455–457.

Tvedebrink, T. (2010). Overdispersion in allelic counts and θ-correction in forensic genetics. *Theoretical Population Biology, 78*, 200–210.

Walsh, S. J., et al. (2003). Evidence in support of self-declaration as a sampling method for the formation of sub-population DNA databases. *Journal of Forensic Sciences, 48*, 1091–1093.

Weir, B. S. (1994). The effects of inbreeding on forensic calculations. *Annual Review of Genetics, 28*, 597–621.

Weir, B. S. (1998). The coancestry coefficient in forensic science. *Proceedings from the Eighth International Symposium on Human Identification 1997 (Promega Corporation)*, 87–91.

Weir, B. S. (2013) (2nd ed.). *DNA — statistical probability. Encyclopedia of Forensic Sciences*. San Diego: Elsevier Academic Press. pp. 282–286.

Weir, B. S., & Cockerham, C. C. (1984). Estimating F-statistics for the analysis of population structure. *Evolution, 38*, 1358–1370.

Weir, B. S., & Hill, W. G. (2002). Estimating F-statistics. *Annual Review of Genetics, 36*, 721–750.

Wright, S. (1951). The genetic structure of populations. *Annals of Eugenics, 15*, 323–354.

Impact of Relatives

Buckleton, J., & Triggs, C. M. (2005). Relatedness and DNA: are we taking it seriously enough? *Forensic Science International, 152*, 115–119.

Software Programs

Excoffier, L., & Lischer, H. E. L. (2010). Arlequin suite ver 3.5: A new series of programs to perform population genetics analyses under Linux and Windows. *Molecular Ecology Resources, 10*, 564–567.

Lange, K., et al. (2013). Mendel: The Swiss army knife of genetic analysis programs. *Bioinformatics, 29*, 1568–1570.

Raymond, M., & Rousset, F. (1995). GENEPOP (version 1.2): population genetics software for exact tests and ecumenicism. *Journal of Heredity, 86*, 248–249.

Rousset, F. (2008). Genepop'007: a complete re-implementation of the genepop software for Windows and Linux. *Molecular Ecology Resources, 8*(1), 103–106.

Tereba, A. (1999). Tools for analysis of population statistics. *Profiles in DNA, 2*(3), 14–16.

Database Size

Aguiar, V. R., et al. (2012). Updated Brazilian STR allele frequency data using over 100,000 individuals: an analysis of CSF1PO, D3S1358, D5S818, D7S820, D8S1179, D13S317, D16S539, D18S51, D21S11, FGA, Penta D, Penta E, TH01, TPOX and vWA loci. *Forensic Science International: Genetics, 6*, 504–509.

Einum, D. D., & Scarpetta, M. A. (2004). Genetic analysis of large data sets of North American Black, Caucasian, and Hispanic populations at 13 CODIS STR loci. *Journal of Forensic Sciences, 49*(6), 1381–1385.

Restrepo, T., et al. (2011). Database sample size effect on minimum allele frequency estimation: database comparison analysis of samples of 4652 and 560 individuals for 22 microsatellites in Columbian population. *Forensic Science International: Genetics Supplement Series, 3*, e13–e14.

Guidance on Publication of Population Data

Carracedo, A., et al. (2010). Publication of population data for forensic purposes. *Forensic Science International: Genetics, 4*, 145–147.

Carracedo, A., et al. (2013). New guidelines for the publication of genetic population data. *Forensic Science International: Genetics, 7*, 217–220.

Carracedo, A., et al. (2014). Update of the guidelines for the publication of genetic population data. *Forensic Science International: Genetics, 10,* A1−A2.

Fisher, R. A. (1951). Standard calculations for evaluating a blood-group system. *Heredity, 5,* 95−102.

Gaensslen, R. E. (1999). Editorial communication: journal policy on the publication of DNA population genetic data. *Journal of Forensic Science, 44*(4), 671−674 [same article was repeated in *44(5),* 1096−1099 and 44(6), 1336−1339].

Lincoln, P., & Carracedo, A. (2000). Publication of population data of human polymorphisms. *Forensic Science International, 110,* 3−5.

Parson, W., & Roewer, L. (2010). Publication of population data of linearly inherited DNA markers in the International Journal of Legal Medicine. *International Journal of Legal Medicine, 124,* 505−509.

Pfeiffer, H., & Bajanowski, T. (2010). Editorial. *International Journal of Legal Medicine, 124,* 351.

Genetic Marker Informativeness

Botstein, D., et al. (1980). Construction of a genetic linkage map in man using restriction fragment length polymorphisms. *American Journal of Human Genetics, 32,* 314−331.

Brenner, C., & Morris, J. W. (1990). Paternity index calculations in single locus hypervariable DNA probes: validation and other studies. *Proceedings of the International Symposium on Human Identification.* Madison, Wisconsin: Promega Corporation. pp. 21−53.

Chakraborty, R., & Stivers, D. N. (1996). Paternity exclusion by DNA markers: effects of paternal mutations. *Journal of Forensic Sciences, 41,* 671−677.

Edwards, A., et al. (1992). Genetic variation at five trimeric and tetrameric tandem repeat loci in four human population groups. *Genomics, 12,* 241−253.

Foreman, L. A., & Evett, I. W. (2001). Statistical analyses to support forensic interpretation for a new 10-locus STR profiling system. *International Journal of Legal Medicine, 114,* 147−155.

Gill, P., et al. (2006a). The evolution of DNA databases-Recommendations for new European STR loci. *Forensic Science International, 156,* 242−244.

Gill, P., et al. (2006b). New multiplexes for Europe-amendments and clarification of strategic development. *Forensic Science International, 163,* 155−157.

Hares, D. R. (2012a). Expanding the CODIS core loci in the United States. *Forensic Science International: Genetics, 6*(1), e52−e54.

Hares, D. R. (2012b). Addendum to expanding the CODIS core loci in the United States. *Forensic Science International: Genetics, 6*(5), e135.

Jones, D. A. (1972). Blood samples: probability of discrimination. *Journal of Forensic Science Society, 12,* 355−359.

Lauritzen, S. L., & Mazumder, A. (2008). Informativeness of genetic markers for forensic inference − an information theoretic approach. *Forensic Science International: Genetics Supplement Series, 1,* 652−653.

Sensabaugh, G. (1982). Biochemical markers of individuality. In R. Saferstein (Ed.), *Forensic Science Handbook* (pp. 338−415). New York: Prentice-Hall.

On-Line Global Population Data

AllST*R Autosomal Database for Short Tandem Repeats: http://allstr.de/allstr/home.seam. Accessed April 3, 2014.

Amigo, J., et al. (2009). *pop.STR*—an online population frequency browser for established and new forensic STRs. *Forensic Science International: Genetics Supplement Series, 2,* 361−362.

Autosomal STR DNA Database: http://www.strdna-db.org/. Accessed April 3, 2014.

Gill, P., et al. (2003). Analysis of DNA databases across Europe compiled by the ENFSI group. *Forensic Science International, 131,* 184−196.

OmniPop: http://www.cstl.nist.gov/strbase/population/OmniPop200.1.xls. Accessed April 3, 2014.

Pereira, L., et al. (2011). PopAffiliator: online calculator for individual affiliation to a major population group based on 17 autosomal short tandem repeat genotype profile. *International Journal of Legal Medicine, 125,* 629−636.

PopAffiliator: Available at http://cracs.fc.up.pt/popaffiliator/. Accessed April 3, 2014.

PopAffiliator 2. Available at http://cracs.fc.up.pt/∼nf/popaffiliator2/. Accessed April 3, 2014.

popSTR: http://spsmart.cesga.es/popstr.php. Accessed April 3, 2014.

STRBase Population Data Listing: Available at http://www.cstl.nist.gov/strbase/populationdata.htm. Accessed April 3, 2014.

11

DNA Profile Frequency Estimates and Match Probabilities

"Without the probability assessment, the jury does not know what to make of the fact that the [DNA] patterns match: the jury does not know whether the patterns are as common as pictures with two eyes, or as unique as the Mona Lisa."

US v Yee, 1991

INTRODUCTION

When equivalent genotypes are observed between an evidence sample (the "unknown" or question sample, Q) and a reference sample (the "known," K), then statistical methods are typically invoked to provide information regarding the relevance of this "match" (see Figure 1.3). The prosecution argues that the Q and K DNA profiles have a common source (i.e. came from the same person), while the defense typically contends that the samples happen to match by chance. The possibility of another unrelated individual pulled at random from the population and possessing an identical genotype can be determined by calculating the frequency with which the observed genotype occurs in a representative population database. When a DNA profile is fairly common, then it is easier to imagine that the suspect might not be connected to the crime scene. If on the other hand, the genotype is found to be extremely rare, then the weight of the evidence is stronger that the suspect contributed to the crime scene sample in question.

The National Research Council 1996 (NRC II) report entitled *The Evaluation of Forensic DNA Evidence* states: "It would not be scientifically justifiable to speak of a match as proof of identity in the absence of underlying data that permit some reasonable estimate of how rare the matching characteristics actually are" (NRC, 1996, p. 192). Allele frequency information from population databases (see Chapter 10) is used to assess relative rarity of DNA profiles. As illustrated in Figure 9.1, the DNA profile, population allele frequencies, and genetic formulas all play a role in determining the DNA profile rarity estimate, which can be expressed as a random match probability (RMP) or a likelihood ratio (LR).

A number of population databases have been generated in recent years to which a DNA profile may be compared. Some basic U.S. population allele frequencies, which are listed in Appendix 1, will be used to illustrate how profile frequencies are determined. For calculations performed in one's own laboratory, a relevant population database, usually specific to possible populations in one's local area, could be used instead.

Professor Bruce Weir notes in a recent encyclopedia entry on DNA statistical probability: "The very genetic nature of DNA evidence that makes it of such value to forensic science also brings particular problems in interpretation. One problem is that as more and more genetic loci are used for DNA profiles, the proportion of a population who might be expected to share a particular profile becomes less and less. There comes a point where any attempt to quantify the probability of seeing a profile strains credulity. Certainly numbers such as one in several trillion fall into that range. Another problem is that the genetic constitution of a population is dependent on previous generations. Immediate family members are likely to have similar DNA profiles, but even apparently unrelated members of a population have a shared evolutionary history. Conveying the evidentiary strength of matching DNA profiles therefore requires the use of both probability and genetics" (Weir 2013).

It is important to keep in mind that methods for reporting DNA evidence vary between laboratories. Some laboratories present RMPs that are based on genotype frequency estimates. Another approach is to report LRs to convey relative support for the weight of DNA evidence under the hypothesis that the suspect is the source of the DNA profile versus an unrelated individual from the population at large. The FBI Laboratory has opted for a source attribution approach when RMPs are sufficiently rare (Budowle et al. 2000). In this chapter, we will discuss the issues surrounding each approach and go through the statistical calculations performed with each method.

PROFILE FREQUENCY ESTIMATE CALCULATIONS

DNA profile frequency estimates are calculated by first considering the genotype frequency for each locus and then multiplying the frequencies across all loci using what is referred to as the *product rule*. The most effective method to understand how the probability of a random match is calculated is to work through an example. Here an RMP is equated with a DNA profile frequency estimate. This RMP is different from a "match probability" that will be discussed later in the chapter.

The frequency for any DNA profile can be calculated with knowledge of the alleles from the DNA profile, allele frequencies seen in a population database, and appropriate correction factors based on genetic models. A different size database or one with different allele frequencies can result in a different expected genotype frequency for each tested locus, and hence a different DNA profile frequency. It is therefore important that the database used is large enough and representative of the population of the suspect(s).

The probability of observing any particular genotype is based on the number of ways this genotype may occur and the frequencies of the alleles. For example, with a heterozygous genotype of 11,12 for the short tandem repeat (STR) locus CSF1PO, there are two possible combinations: 11,12 and 12,11. An individual may have an 11 allele on his/her paternally received chromosome and a 12 allele on his/her maternally received chromosome, or he/she may have the 12 allele on the paternal chromosome and the 11 on the maternal chromosome. Therefore, the probability of observing this genotype is $2 \times p \times q$, where p and q are the allele frequencies of 11 and 12, respectively, in this case (see Figure 10.2). With a homozygous genotype, such as D18S51 17,17, the individual inherited a 17 from his/her mother and a 17 from his/her father. The probability of observing this homozygous 17,17 genotype is $1 \times p \times p$ or p^2.

Underlying Assumptions

There are four primary underlying assumptions to DNA profile RMP calculations:

First, that the two alleles inherited at a locus from an individual's parents are independent. In other words, the locus is in *Hardy—Weinberg equilibrium* (HWE), which permits use of p^2 and $2pq$ (see Chapter 10).

Second, that alleles at different loci are independent of one another. In other words, the loci are in *linkage equilibrium* (LE), which permits use of the product rule where genotype frequencies can be multiplied across independent loci to arrive at a profile frequency estimate.

Third, that the true perpetrator is not a relative of the suspect. An important assumption implicit in an RMP is that the calculation reflects the possibility of matching an *unrelated* individual. Relatives are expected to have DNA profiles that are more similar than a DNA profile randomly drawn from the general population. As will be discussed later in the chapter, if there is a need to account for the possibility of a particular relative, theoretical calculations may be performed, but it is preferable to obtain a DNA profile from any potential relative early in an investigation in order to effectively eliminate them as a possible contributor to the evidence profile. Depending on the particular relationship, evaluation of relatives can decrease a DNA profile rarity estimate by many orders of magnitude (see Table 11.5).

Fourth, that appropriate population data are used for genotype frequency estimates and that there are no significant subpopulation differences in allele frequencies used to compute a profile frequency estimate. A population substructure correction factor (θ) is commonly used to account for potential coancestry of alleles (see Chapter 10). Multiple RMP statistics can also be providied in a written report based on calculations from multiple population groups in order to provide a level of confidence in the true rarity of the DNA profile.

Uncertainty about Estimated Frequencies

The 1996 NRC II report discusses the fact that there are several aspects to the uncertainty about the estimated frequency values when match probabilities are estimated from a population database of allele frequencies. The report notes that accuracy of an RMP estimate depends on the genetic model, the actual allele frequencies, and the size of the population database (NRC 1996, pp. 33–34). Uncertainty in the specific allele frequency values exists because of the possibility that the population database is not representative of the population of interest. This factor in the uncertainty probably has a larger impact than the relatively small sample size typically used to estimate allele frequencies (see Chapter 10). Additionally, the mathematical and genetic models may not be fully appropriate in all situations.

The NRC II report used a practical, empirical approach to determine the extent of error if an incorrect population database was used. The report recommends that the correct ethnic/racial database for the suspect be used if that can be ascertained or that "calculations should be made for all relevant racial groups, i.e. those to which possible suspects belong" (NRC 1996). This is the reason that written reports typically contain RMP information from multiple population groups (e.g. Caucasian, African American, and Hispanic for U.S. laboratories).

The NRC II committee concluded that "it is reasonable to regard calculated multilocus match probabiltiies as accurate within a factor of 10 either way" (NRC 1996). Thus, if the calculated probability of a random match between the suspect and evidence DNA profile is 1 in 100 million, then the correct value is likely between 1 in 10 million and 1 in 1 billion.

Example Calculations

Before we begin a review of RMP calculations, a brief discussion of significant figures is in order. Reporting results to numerous decimal places is unwise as it conveys a level of accuracy and precision that simply is not present with allele frequency, genotype frequency, and profile frequency estimates. Many software programs carry a large number of decimal places through the calculations and round them down to two or three significant figures for the final report.

For the purposes of the examples in this book, allele frequencies in Appendix 1 are only reported to three significant figures and all calculations are performed with only three significant figures. Seemingly minor differences in rounding during these calculations can lead to final results that may be an order of magnitude or more different. The important thing is to be consistent and know what your software tool is doing if you hope that someone else will be able to reproduce your exact statistical calculations.

Table 11.1 compares the statistical treatment of homozygotes and heterozygotes under several different assumptions. If HWE is assumed, then p^2 and $2pq$ are appropriate. NRC II recommendation 4.1 adds an adjustment factor to homozygotes to account for some population substructure. NRC II recommendation 4.10a and 4.10b incorporate full population substructure adjustments with the Balding—Nichols matching probability formulas (Balding & Nichols 1994). The amount of difference observed between these various statistical methods depends on the allele frequencies and whether or not the genotype is homozygous or heterzygous. In general, incorporating the θ population substructure adjustments will make the overall RMP value more conservative (i.e. less rare) and therefore more favorable to the suspect.

In Table 11.2 and Table 11.3, the example DNA profile frequencies for 13 STR loci are determined using allele frequencies from two of the population groups in Appendix 1. One population group contains allele frequencies from DNA profiles generated from 361 U.S. Caucasians or 722 measured alleles (Table 11.2). The other set of allele frequencies used comes from 342 African Americans, or 684 measured alleles (Table 11.3).

The example DNA profile contains data from 13 STR loci and the sex-typing marker amelogenin (AMEL). Results with the first few loci are discussed below to illustrate statistical calculations performed, and to contrast results obtained. We will consider a homozygous locus (D18S51), a heterozygous locus (CSF1PO), and a heterozygous locus containing a rare allele (FGA).

In a population sample of 722 alleles (361 U.S. Caucasian individuals), allele 17 for D18S51 was observed 100 times, which is 0.139 or approximately 14% of the time (see D.N.A. Box 10.2 and Appendix 1). Based on this information we can assume that there is a 14% chance that any particular D18S51 allele selected at random from an unrelated U.S. Caucasian individual will be a 17.

Plugging the frequency value of $p = 0.139$ into the formula p^2 (0.139×0.139) results in an estimated genotype frequency of 0.0193. In other words, approximately 1.9% of people from a U.S. Caucasian population are expected to have a 17,17 genotype at the D18S51 locus (Table 11.2). Conducting the same analysis with an African American population database results in a similar genotype frequency of 0.0231, or 2.3% (Table 11.3).

With the CSF1PO locus, a heterozygous 11,12 genotype is observed (Table 11.2). The same comparison of the profile's observed alleles to a measured allele frequency in a population database is performed with CSF1PO, but in this case the combined probability of inheriting allele 11 and allele

TABLE 11.1 Comparison of Statistical Treatment for Homozygotes and Heterozygotes under Different Assumptions

		Under HWE	Unconditional (NRC II recommendation 4.1)	Conditional with substructure adjustment (NRC II recommendation 4.10a) (NRC II recommendation 4.10b)
Homozygote	Formula	p^2	$p^2 + p(1 - p)\theta$	$\Pr(PP\|PP) = \dfrac{[p(1 - \theta) + 2\theta]\,[p(1 - \theta) + 3\theta]}{(1 + \theta)(1 + 2\theta)}$
D18S51 17,17 $p = 0.139$ $\theta = 0.01$	Calculation	$(0.139)^2$	$(0.139)^2 + (0.139) \times$ $(1-0.139) \times (0.01)$ $= 0.0193 + 0.00120$	$= \dfrac{[0.139(1 - 0.01) + 2(0.01)]\,[0.139(1 - 0.01) + 3(0.01)]}{(1 + 0.01)(1 + 2(0.01))}$
	Result	$= 0.0193$	$= 0.0205$	$= 0.0256$
Heterozygote	Formula	$2pq$	$2pq$	$\Pr(PQ\|PQ) = \dfrac{2[p(1 - \theta) + \theta]\,[q(1 - \theta) + \theta]}{(1 + \theta)(1 + 2\theta)}$
CSF1PO 11,12 $p = 0.309$ $q = 0.360$ $\theta = 0.01$	Calculation	$2(0.309)(0.360)$	$2(0.309)(0.360)$	$= \dfrac{2[0.309(1 - 0.01) + 0.01]\,[0.360(1 - 0.01) + 0.01]}{(1 + 0.01)(1 + 2(0.01))}$
	Result	$= 0.222$	$= 0.222$	$= 0.225$

Allele frequency values (p, q) for the D18S51 and CSF1PO example data are from Appendix 1 (U.S. Caucasians). Note that if θ is zero then unconditional and conditional formulas collapse to their Hardy–Weinberg equilibrium (HWE) functions as described in D.N.A. Box 11.2.

TABLE 11.2   Random Match Probability for a 13-Locus STR Profile Using the U.S. Caucasian Allele Frequencies Found in Appendix 1

STR Locus	Allele 1	Allele 2	Allele 1 Frequency (p)	Allele 2 Frequency (q)	Formula	Expected Genotype Frequency
D18S51	17	17	0.139		p^2	0.0193
CSF1PO	11	12	0.309	0.360	$2pq$	0.222
FGA	21.2	22	0.00693	0.205	$2pq$	0.00284
TH01	8	8	0.0956		p^2	0.00914
TPOX	11	11	0.252		p^2	0.0635
VWA	17	18	0.284	0.202	$2pq$	0.115
D3S1358	16	16	0.238		p^2	0.0566
D5S818	11	12	0.356	0.388	$2pq$	0.276
D7S820	11	13	0.205	0.0346	$2pq$	0.0142
D8S1179	13	15	0.330	0.166	$2pq$	0.110
D13S317	9	10	0.0776	0.0471	$2pq$	0.00731
D16S539	11	13	0.314	0.163	$2pq$	0.102
D21S11	28	32.2	0.159	0.0900	$2pq$	0.0286
AMEL	X	Y				
						4.24×10^{-19}
						1 in 2.36×10^{18}

Since FGA 21.2 is a rare allele, the minimum allele frequency was used (shown in red font).

12 is $2pq$. Since allele 11 was observed 223 times out of 722 allele measurements in U.S. Caucasians, and allele 12 was observed 260 times out of 722 allele measurements, $p = 0.309$, $q = 0.360$, and $2pq$ is 0.222. Thus, the 11,12 genotype is expected to occur about 22% of the time in U.S. Caucasians (Table 11.2). Using the African American allele frequency for CSF1PO, $p = 0.249$, $q = 0.295$, and $2pq$ is 0.147, or about 15% (Table 11.3). Therefore, the 11,12 CSF1PO heterozygous genotype is slightly more rare in African Americans than in U.S. Caucasians.

Since these two STR loci are on separate chromosomes (e.g. chromosome 18 for D18S51 and chromosome 5 for CSF1PO), they will segregate independently during meiosis, allowing the genotype frequencies to be multiplied. In the case of a U.S. Caucasian population, the chance of a person having the combined genotype of 17,17 at D18S51 and 11,12 at CSF1PO is 22.2% of 1.93% (i.e. 0.0193×0.222) or 0.428%.

At the next STR locus in the example profile, FGA exhibits a rare allele 21.2, which was only seen four times in 2,072 alleles measured across all four population groups reported in Appendix 1. All four of these observations were in the U.S. Caucasian sample set. There were no FGA 21.2 alleles seen in the U.S. African American, Hispanic, or Asian population samples (Appendix 1). Since this allele has less than five observations, a minimum allele frequency of 5/2N (see Chapter 10) is applied. With N = 361 for the U.S. Caucasian sample set, this minimum allele frequency value

TABLE 11.3 Random Match Probability Calculations for the Same 13-Locus STR Profile Shown in Table 11.2 but Using the African American Allele Frequencies Found in Appendix 1

STR Locus	Allele 1	Allele 2	Allele 1 Frequency (p)	Allele 2 Frequency (q)	Formula	Expected Genotype Frequency
D18S51	17	17	0.152		p^2	0.0231
CSF1PO	11	12	0.249	0.295	$2pq$	0.147
FGA	21.2	22	0.00731	0.199	$2pq$	0.00291
TH01	8	8	0.196		p^2	0.0384
TPOX	11	11	0.216	0.149	p^2	0.0467
VWA	17	18	0.235		$2pq$	0.0700
D3S1358	16	16	0.319	0.370	p^2	0.102
D5S818	11	12	0.234		$2pq$	0.173
D7S820	11	13	0.203	0.0146	$2pq$	0.00593
D8S1179	13	15	0.219	0.190	$2pq$	0.0832
D13S317	9	10	0.0336	0.0307	$2pq$	0.00206
D16S539	11	13	0.314	0.123	$2pq$	0.0772
D21S11	28	32.2	0.246	0.0614	$2pq$	0.0302
AMEL	X	Y				
						5.19×10^{-20}
						1 in 1.93×10^{19}

Since FGA 21.2 is a rare allele, the minimum allele frequency was used (shown in red font).

is 0.00693 (5/(2 × 361)). For the African American sample set, the minimum allele frequency is 0.00731 (5/(2 × 342)), which is slightly higher because there were fewer chromosomes sampled. The $2pq$ formula is applied using the appropriate minimum allele frequency (p) for FGA allele 21.2, and the population-specific allele frequency (q) for FGA allele 22.

Often the rarity of a full DNA profile frequency estimate goes beyond one in billions (10^9) or trillions (10^{12}) to numbers that are not frequently used because they are so large. Working through the rest of the STR loci in Table 11.2 and Table 11.3, the final combined frequency estimate for the DNA profile in question is about 1 in 2.36 quintillion (2.36×10^{18}) using Caucasian allele frequencies (Table 11.2) and about 1 in 19.3 quintillion (1.93×10^{19}) using African American allele frequencies (Table 11.3). These values can also be reported as the profile frequency 4.24×10^{-19} (Table 11.2) or 5.19×10^{-20} (Table 11.3). Because the alleles observed in the specific STR profile under consideration are more rare in an African American population, the profile has a rarer frequency estimate in Table 11.3 than in Table 11.2.

As more and more STR loci match during a Q and K sample comparison, it becomes less and less likely that an *unrelated*, random person in the population contributed the crime scene sample. Thus, either the suspect contributed the evidence or a very unlikely coincidence occurred.

Impact of Various Population Databases

From the combined STR profile frequencies calculated in Table 11.2 and Table 11.3 it is apparent that different populations can yield different frequency estimates due to variations in allele frequencies in these populations. Calculations from another STR profile against 202 published population databases found that the cumulative profile frequency ranged from 1 in 3.43×10^{14} to 1 in 2.65×10^{21} (D.N.A. Box 11.1). Using a tool like OmniPop can be helpful to see the range of STR profile frequencies that may be obtained with different sets of allele frequencies. Table 10.12 lists several online population databases that may be used to estimate DNA profile frequencies in various population groups.

Impact of Population Substructure

As discussed earlier, the NRC II report discusses issues that surround population substructure. Their report made several recommendations for taking population structure into account (see Appendix 2). The NRC II recommendation 4.1 substructure adjustments replace p^2 for homozygote calculations with $p^2 + p(1 - p)\theta$, where θ is an estimate of coancestry that reflects population substructure (see Chapter 10). A conservative value for θ is 0.01 for typical at-large populations and 0.03 with smaller, isolated, and more inbred groups of people. Extensive population data have demonstrated that $\theta = 0.01$ is a reliable and conservative estimate of population substructure in the United States (Budowle et al. 2001).

The impact of these recommendations on homozygote and heterozygote frequency calculations was illustrated in Table 11.1. Table 11.4 contains analysis of the example DNA profile discussed previously, worked with NRC II recommendations 4.1 and 4.10 with θ values of 0.01 and 0.03. Note that while recommendation 4.1 produces only minor differences in the overall profile frequency estimate, the use of recommendation 4.10 with a 3% coancestry adjustment can reduce the RMP by about three orders of magnitude.

David Balding and Richard Nichols regard the theta correction in NRC II 4.10a and 4.10b as a measure of the degree of uncertainty about each allele frequency used to estimate the match probability for the allele (Balding & Nichols 1995, p. 5). When $\theta = 0$, which corresponds to complete certainty in the allele frequency estimate, then the single-locus match probabilities for these equations collapse to p^2 and $2pq$ that are used in the "product rule" (D.N.A. Box 11.2).

Impact of Relatives on STR Profile Frequency Estimates

If the suspect and the true perpetrator of a crime are related, then their genotype frequencies may not be independent, and a different calculation is required. Since STR profiles from relatives are expected to be more similar to the individual in question than that of a random, unrelated individual would be, NRC II recommendation 4.4 (Appendix 2) covers probability calculations from various scenarios of individuals related to the suspect.

Table 11.5 works through the example DNA profile according to NRC II recommendation 4.4 and equations 4.8a and 4.8b (see Appendix 2). More recently Bruce Weir has developed match probability formulas to calculate the effects of family relatedness that incorporate population substructure functions into them (Weir 2007).

The NRC II report emphasizes that these types of calculations should be used as a last resort, as obtaining DNA profiles of suspected relatives for elimination purposes is preferred

D.N.A. BOX 11.1

OMNIPOP: CALCULATING STR PROFILE FREQUENCIES AGAINST MULTIPLE POPULATION DATABASES

The ability to determine simultaneously the frequency for a particular STR profile in multiple population databases was recently made easier with the development of a Microsoft Excel macro called OmniPop. Below, the cumulative profile frequency range is calculated for the particular STR profile listed against 202 published population studies involving Profiler Plus kit loci and 120 published reports containing all 13 CODIS core loci. The cumulative profile frequency obtained with U.S. Caucasian allele frequencies (Butler et al. 2003) are listed as well.

These profile frequencies were all calculated with a theta value of 0.01. When using a theta value of 0.03 as recommended by NRC II for more inbred populations, the range for the computed profile with all 13 STR loci across the 120 published population data sets is 1.19×10^{14} to 1.27×10^{21}.

The computed profile is part of the U.S. Caucasian data set (Butler et al. 2003) used to generate the allele frequencies and thus, as demonstrated below, this population data set would be expected to provide fairly conservative values for this particular 13-locus STR profile.

Source: OmniPop 2001 was used for these calculations. Created by Brian Burritt of the San Diego Police Department and freely available at http://www.cstl.nist.gov/biotech/strbase/ populationdata.htm; Butler, J.M., et al. (2003). Allele frequencies for 15 autosomal STR loci on U.S. Caucasian, African American, and Hispanic populations. Journal of Forensic Sciences, 48(4), 908–911.

STR Locus	Profile Computed	Number of Populations Used	Cumulative Profile Frequency Range (1 in …)	Cumulative Profile Frequency against U.S. Caucasians (Butler et al. 2003)
D3S1358	**16,17**	202	4.53 to 62.6	9.19
VWA	**17,18**	202	37.6 to 1,080	81.8
FGA	**21,22**	202	737 to 119,000	1,010
D8S1179	**12,14**	202	8,980 to 5,430,000	16,400
D21S11	**28,30**	202	165,000 to 248,000,000	186,000
D18S51	**14,16**	202	3.85×10^6 to 2.68×10^{10}	4.88×10^6
D5S818	**12,13**	202	2.28×10^7 to 4.22×10^{11}	4.51×10^7
D13S317	**11,14**	202	4.32×10^8 to 1.69×10^{13}	1.38×10^9
D7S820	**9,9**	202	1.17×10^{10} to 2.98×10^{16}	4.22×10^{10}
D16S539	**9,11**	120	3.14×10^{11} to 1.11×10^{18}	5.82×10^{11}
TH01	**6,6**	120	3.53×10^{12} to 1.45×10^{19}	1.05×10^{13}
TPOX	**8,8**	120	9.13×10^{12} to 1.54×10^{20}	3.63×10^{13}
CSF1PO	**10,10**	120	1.42×10^{14} to 2.65×10^{21}	7.43×10^{14}

TABLE 11.4 Example Calculations with Corrections for Population Substructure Using the National Research Council 1996 (NRC II) Recommended Formulas (see Appendix 2)

STR Locus	Allele 1	Allele 2	Allele 1 Freq (p)	Allele 2 Freq (q)	Formula	Under HWE Calculated Frequency	Formula	NRCII Recommendation 4.1 $\theta = 0.01$	NRCII Recommendation 4.1 $\theta = 0.03$		NRCII Recommendation 4.10 $\theta = 0.01$	NRCII Recommendation 4.10 $\theta = 0.03$
D18S51	17	17	0.139		p^2	0.0193	$p^2 + p(1-p)\theta$	0.0205	0.0229	eq. 4.10a	0.0256	0.0401
CSF1PO	11	12	0.309	0.360	$2pq$	0.222	$2pq$	0.222	0.222	eq. 4.10b	0.225	0.229
FGA	21.2	22	0.00693	0.205	$2pq$	0.00284	$2pq$	0.00284	0.00284	eq. 4.10b	0.00697	0.0154
TH01	8	8	0.0956		p^2	0.00914	$p^2 + p(1-p)\theta$	0.0100	0.0117	eq. 4.10a	0.0139	0.0256
TPOX	11	11	0.252		p^2	0.0635	$p^2 + p(1-p)\theta$	0.0654	0.0692	eq. 4.10a	0.0731	0.0933
VWA	17	18	0.284	0.202	$2pq$	0.115	$2pq$	0.115	0.115	eq. 4.10b	0.119	0.126
D3S1358	16	16	0.238		p^2	0.0566	$p^2 + p(1-p)\theta$	0.0585	0.0621	eq. 4.10a	0.0659	0.0855
D5S818	11	12	0.356	0.388	$2pq$	0.276	$2pq$	0.276	0.276	eq. 4.10b	0.277	0.279
D7S820	11	13	0.205	0.0346	$2pq$	0.0142	$2pq$	0.0142	0.0142	eq. 4.10b	0.0504	0.0685
D8S1179	13	15	0.330	0.166	$2pq$	0.110	$2pq$	0.110	0.110	eq. 4.10b	0.114	0.123
D13S317	9	10	0.0776	0.0471	$2pq$	0.00731	$2pq$	0.00731	0.00731	eq. 4.10b	0.00955	0.0146
D16S539	11	13	0.314	0.163	$2pq$	0.102	$2pq$	0.102	0.102	eq. 4.10b	0.107	0.115
D21S11	28	32.2	0.159	0.0900	$2pq$	0.0286	$2pq$	0.0286	0.0286	eq. 4.10b	0.107	0.0396
AMEL	X	Y										
						4.24×10^{-19}		5.23×10^{-19}	7.70×10^{-19}		1.67×10^{-17}	5.69×10^{-16}

Allele frequencies are from the U.S. Caucasians (N = 361) in Appendix 1. Scenarios with theta equal to 0.01 and 0.03 are examined.

D.N.A. BOX 11.2

BALDING–NICHOLS MATCH PROBABILITY EQUATIONS WHEN THETA EQUALS ZERO

It can be helpful to see the relationship between more complex equations and simpler ones. The National Research Council in its 1996 report entitled *The Evaluation of Forensic DNA Evidence* (also known as NRC II) discusses several match probability equations (NRC 1996) that are based on work by David Balding and Richard Nichols (Balding & Nichols 1994). NRC II equations 4.10a (for homozygous loci) and 4.10b (for heterozygous loci) use A_iA_i and A_iA_j with p_i and q_i for allele frequencies (see Appendix 2). In the equations below, these variables have been changed (see D.N.A. Box 10.1) to PP and PQ with p and q for allele frequencies.

NRC II equation 4.10a (rewritten):

$$\Pr(PP|PP) = \frac{[2\theta + (1-\theta)p][3\theta + (1-\theta)p]}{(1+\theta)(1+2\theta)}$$

If $\theta = 0$, then:

$$\Pr(PP|PP) = \frac{[2*0 + (1-0)p][3*0 + (1-0)p]}{(1+0)(1+2*0)}$$

$$= \frac{[1*p][1*p]}{(1)(1)} = p*p = p^2$$

NRC II equation 4.10b (rewritten):

$$\Pr(PQ|PQ) = 2\frac{[\theta + (1-\theta)p][\theta + (1-\theta)q]}{(1+\theta)(1+2\theta)}$$

If $\theta = 0$, then:

$$\Pr(PQ|PQ) = 2\frac{[0 + (1-0)p][0 + (1-0)q]}{(1+0)(1+2*0)}$$

$$= 2\frac{[1*p][1*q]}{(1)(1)} = 2*p*q = 2pq$$

When theta (θ) is zero (i.e. there is no co-ancestry coefficient correction) these equations collapse to the standard Hardy–Weinberg equilibrium (HWE) model of p^2 and $2pq$. Thus, STR single-locus match probabilities approach the HWE model as theta values decrease. This observation helps make the connection that theta is effectively a genetic parameter that reflects the amount of uncertainty in a measured allele frequency compared to the true allele probability since the measured allele frequency has been skewed slightly by some degree of shared ancestry (Balding & Nichols 1995). Since absolute certainty in correlating measured allele frequency with true allele probability is unrealistic in practice, Balding and Nichols emphasize that the HWE product rule (i.e. only using p^2 and $2pq$) will consistently overstate the strength of the evidence against the defendant (Balding & Nichols 1995).

Sources: National Research Council (NRCII) Committee on DNA Forensic Science. (1996). The Evaluation of Forensic DNA Evidence. Washington, DC: National Academy Press; Balding, D.J., & Nichols, R.A. (1994). DNA profile match probability calculation: how to allow for population stratification, relatedness, database selection and single bands. Forensic Science International, 64, 125–140; Balding, D.J., & Nichols, R.A. (1995). A method for quantifying differentiation between populations at multi-allelic loci and its implications for investigating identity and paternity. In Human Identification: The Use of DNA Markers (Weir, B.S., editor). Boston: Kluwer Academic Publishers, pp. 3–12.

TABLE 11.5 Example Calculations with Corrections for Relatives Using the National Research Council 1996 (NRC II) Recommended Formulas (see Appendix 2)

STR Locus	Allele 1	Allele 2	Allele 1 Freq (p)	Allele 2 Freq (q)	Formulas	Under HWE Calculated Frequency	NRC II Equation	F = 1/4 (parent)	NRC II (1996) Recommendation 4.4 F = 1/8 (half sib)	F = 1/16 (1st cousin)	NRC II Equation	Full Sib
D18S51	17	17	0.139		p^2	0.0193	eq. 4.8a	0.1390	0.0792	0.0492	eq. 4.9a	0.3243
CSF1PO	11	12	0.309	0.360	2pq	0.222	eq. 4.8b	0.3345	0.2785	0.2505	eq. 4.9b	0.4729
FGA	21.2	22	0.00693	0.205	2pq	0.00284	eq. 4.8b	0.1060	0.0544	0.0286	eq. 4.9b	0.3037
TH01	8	8	0.0956		p^2	0.00914	eq. 4.8a	0.0956	0.0524	0.0308	eq. 4.9a	0.3001
TPOX	11	11	0.252		p^2	0.0635	eq. 4.8a	0.2520	0.1578	0.1106	eq. 4.9a	0.3919
VWA	17	18	0.284	0.202	2pq	0.115	eq. 4.8b	0.2430	0.1789	0.1468	eq. 4.9a	0.4002
D3S1358	16	16	0.238		p^2	0.0566	eq. 4.8a	0.2380	0.1473	0.1020	eq. 4.9a	0.3832
D5S818	11	12	0.356	0.388	2pq	0.276	eq. 4.8b	0.3720	0.3241	0.3002	eq. 4.9b	0.5051
D7S820	11	13	0.205	0.0346	2pq	0.0142	eq. 4.8b	0.1198	0.0670	0.0406	eq. 4.9b	0.3134
D8S1179	13	15	0.330	0.166	2pq	0.110	eq. 4.8b	0.2480	0.1788	0.1442	eq. 4.9b	0.4014
D13S317	9	10	0.0776	0.0471	2pq	0.00731	eq. 4.8b	0.0624	0.0348	0.0211	eq. 4.9b	0.2830
D16S539	11	13	0.314	0.163	2pq	0.102	eq. 4.8b	0.2385	0.1704	0.1364	eq. 4.9b	0.3948
D21S11	28	32.2	0.159	0.0900	2pq	0.0286	eq. 4.8b	0.1245	0.0766	0.0526	eq. 4.9b	0.3194
AMEL	X	Y										
						4.24×10^{-19}		1.40×10^{-10}	4.61×10^{-13}	4.77×10^{-15}		1.90×10^{-6}
												1 in 525,000

Allele frequencies are from the U.S. Caucasians (N = 361) in Appendix 1.

(NRC 1996). If the possibility exists that a close relative of the accused had access to the crime scene and may have been a contributor of the evidence, then the best course of action is usually to obtain a reference sample from the relative. For example, a scenario involving a brother as a potential evidence contributor should be sufficient probable cause for obtaining a reference sample from the brother and typing it with the same STR markers as used for the evidence. This information could then be used to resolve the question of whether the relative carries the same DNA profile as the accused.

The DNA Advisory Board commented on the issue of potential relatives in their 2000 statistics document (see Appendix 3): "The possibility of a close relative (typically a brother) of the accused being in the pool of potential contributors of crime scene evidence should be considered in case-specific context. *It is not appropriate to proffer that a close relative is a potential contributor of the evidence when there are no facts in evidence to suggest this instance is relevant.* However, if a relative had access to a crime scene and there is reason to believe he/she could have been a contributor of the evidence, then *the best action to take is to obtain a reference sample from the relative.* ... When a legitimate suspected relative cannot be typed, a probability statement can be provided. Given the accused DNA profile, the conditional probability that the relative has the same DNA profile can be calculated. Examples of methods for estimating the probability of the same DNA profile in a close relative are described in the NRC II Report (1996)" (DAB 2000, emphasis added).

General Match Probability

DNA profile probabilities can be calculated for a variety of scenarios. David Balding notes that there are five different sets of people and possible relationships to a suspect: (1) the suspect's siblings, (2) his other relatives, (3) other members of his sub-population, (4) other members of his ethnic/racial group, and (5) everyone else (Balding 1999).

Instead of having to calculate all of these case-specific match probabilities, some authors have proposed using general match probabilities that have been calculated from the theoretically most conservative method involving the two most common alleles for each locus (D.N.A. Box 11.3). The primary advantage of this approach is that repeated calculations are not required for each profile observed. Rather, the general match probability is provided in court as being a very conservative estimate on the rarity of the observed DNA profile. Another reason that this approach is advocated is that some statisticians feel that it is difficult to provide any sound statistical support for probabilities of such a small magnitude (e.g. 10^{-21}) given the limited sampling of possible genotypes that has been performed (Foreman & Evett 2001).

What a Random Match Probability Is Not

It is important to realize what a RMP is not. It is not the chance that someone else is guilty or that someone else left the biological material at the crime scene. Likewise, it is not the chance of the defendant not being guilty or the chance that someone else in reality would have that same genotype. Rather a *random match probability* is simply the estimated frequency at which a particular STR profile (given genetic inheritance models) would be expected to occur in a population as determined by allele frequencies from that population group. This RMP may also be thought of as the theoretical chance that if you sample one person at random from the population, they will have the particular DNA profile in question.

D.N.A. BOX 11.3

GENERAL MATCH PROBABILITY VALUES

In a paper describing statistical analyses to support forensic interpretation of the 10 loci present in the SGM Plus kit, Lindsey Foreman and Ian Evett advocate the use of general probability values when reporting full-matching STR profiles. With the 10 STR loci present in the SGM Plus kit used in the UK and Europe, the probabilities are as follows (see Foreman & Evett 2001, Table 4):

Relationship with Suspect	Match Probability
Sibling	1 in 10 000
Parent/child	1 in 1 million
Half-sibling or uncle/nephew	1 in 10 million
First cousin	1 in 100 million
Unrelated	1 in 1 billion

They argue that adoption of such figures would eliminate the need to perform case-specific match probabilities, making it much easier to present information to the court. The match probabilities for specific STR profiles are typically several orders of magnitude smaller than those given above, which were calculated from the theoretically most common SGM Plus profile (see example calculation in Table 10.11). Thus, these probabilities should provide a fair and reasonable assessment of the weight of DNA evidence for each category and in the end would probably be favorable to the suspect (defendant).

A similar calculation for a full match with the 13 CODIS loci using the most common alleles observed in U.S. population databases, such as Appendix 1, would result in even higher general match probability values since more STR loci are being examined. New general match probability values have been updated with 15-locus STR profiles that are part of the expanded European Standard Set of STR loci (Hopwood et al. 2012).

Sources: Foreman, L.A., & Evett, I.W. (2001). Statistical analyses to support forensic interpretation for a new 10-locus STR profiling system. International Journal of Legal Medicine, *114, 147—155; Balding, D.J. (1999). When can a DNA profile be regarded as unique?* Science & Justice, *39, 257—260; Hopwood, A.J., et al. (2012). Consideration of the probative value of single donor 15-plex STR profiles in UK populations and its presentation in UK courts.* Science & Justice, *52, 185—190.*

Switching the language and meaning of an RMP is sometimes referred to as the *prosecutor's fallacy* or the fallacy of the transposed conditional (Thompson & Schumann 1987, Balding & Donnelly 1994). Statements such as "there is only a 1 in 15,000 chance that the DNA profile came from someone else" or "there is only a 1 in 15,000 chance that the defendant is not guilty" are examples of the prosecutor's fallacy. A correct statement would be "the probability of selecting the observed profile from a population of random unrelated individuals is expected to be 1 in 15,000 based on the alleles present in this sample…" Note that with a 13 STR locus-match the RMPs are in the range of trillions, quadrillions, and beyond in some situations.

The *defense attorney's fallacy* is equally problematic where the assumption is made that everyone else with the same genotype has an equal chance of being guilty or that every possible genotype in a mixture has an equal chance of having committed the crime. Access to the crime scene, motive, and legitimate alibis all play a role in an investigation suggesting that it is unwise to consider DNA evidence and corresponding frequency estimates in a vacuum devoid of other information. A suspect is usually under suspicion and investigation prior to his/her DNA profile being known, and thus the DNA results are most often used to corroborate and connect a criminal perpetrator to his/her crime scene rather than as the sole evidentiary material.

LIKELIHOOD RATIO

When matching STR profiles are obtained between a suspect (known sample, K) and the crime scene evidence (question sample, Q), it is necessary to quantify the evidentiary value of this match. Another approach in assessing the weight of the Q-K comparison besides the RMP or profile frequency estimate just described is the use of a LR.

LRs involve a comparison of the probabilities of the evidence under two alternative propositions. These mutually exclusive hypotheses represent the position of the prosecution — namely that the DNA from the crime scene originated from the suspect — and the position of the defense — that the DNA just happens to coincidently match that of the defendant and is instead from an unknown person out in the population at large.

Typically the first hypothesis (and that championed by the prosecution) is placed in the numerator of the LR while the second hypothesis — that someone other than the defendant committed the crime (which is of course the defense's position) — is placed in the denominator.

Thus, in mathematical terms:

$$LR = \frac{Pr(E|H_1)}{Pr(E|H_2)} = \frac{Pr(STR\ profile|the\ DNA\ comes\ from\ the\ suspect)}{Pr(STR\ profile|the\ DNA\ comes\ from\ a\ random\ person)}$$

i.e. the LR equals the probability of the evidence given the hypothesis of the prosecution (H_1 or H_p) divided by the probability of the evidence given the hypothesis of the defense (H_2 or H_d). A random person is defined as someone in the same population who is not related to the suspect. In some publications the suspect may be referred to as the "person of interest" (Weir 1992, Taylor et al. 2013).

Since the hypothesis of the prosecution is that the defendant committed the crime, then $H_p = 1$ (assumes 100% probability) with simple single-source profile matches. On the other hand, the hypothesis of the defense that the profile originated from someone else can be calculated from the genotype frequency of the particular STR profile. If the STR typing result is heterozygous, then this probability for a specific locus would be $2pq$, where p is the frequency of allele 1 and q is the frequency of allele 2 in the relevant population for the locus in question. Alternatively, for a homozygous STR type the H_d would be p^2.

Therefore,

$$LR = \frac{Pr(E|H_p)}{Pr(E|H_d)} = \frac{1}{2pq}.$$

If the STR type in question was D18S51 alleles 14 and 16, then p is 0.134 and q is 0.147 for the Caucasian population (Appendix 1). The LR for the D18S51 genotype match then becomes

$$LR = \frac{Pr(E|H_p)}{Pr(E|H_d)} = \frac{1}{2pq} = \frac{1}{2(0.134)(0.147)} = \frac{1}{0.0394} = 25.4.$$

If the value for an LR is greater than one, then it provides support to the prosecution's case. If, on the other hand, the LR is less than one, then the defense's case is supported. In the example shown here, if there is a match between a crime stain possessing a D18S51 genotype of 14,16 and a suspect who also possesses a D18S51 genotype of 14,16, then the evidence is 25.4 times more likely if the suspect left the evidence than if it came from some unknown person out of the general Caucasian population who is unrelated to the suspect.

If the D18S51 genotype was 17,17, then

$$LR = \frac{Pr(E|H_p)}{Pr(E|H_d)} = \frac{1}{p^2} = \frac{1}{(0.139)^2} = \frac{1}{0.0193} = 51.8.$$

Note that the rarer the particular STR genotype is, the higher the LR will be since there is a reciprocal relationship. In its simplest form, an LR is the inverse of the estimated genotype frequency for each locus. If discrete alleles and independent marker systems are utilized, then the LR is simply the inverse of the relative frequency of the observed genotype in the relevant population. Of course, LRs can become much more complicated if mixtures or alternative scenarios for the evidence are possible (see Chapter 12). The product of all locus-specific LRs results in the full profile LR, which in the example of the Caucasian data shown in Table 11.2 comes to 2.36×10^{18} (the inverse of 4.24×10^{-19}).

When considering the strength of an LR in terms of supporting the prosecution's position, the following guidelines have been suggested (Evett & Weir 1998, see also Buckleton et al. 2005):

If likelihood ratio is...	Then the evidence provides...
1 to 10	limited support
10 to 100	moderate support
100 to 1000	moderately strong support
1000 to 10,000	strong support
10,000 or greater	very strong support.

With a 13-locus STR match LR of 2.36×10^{18} based on a full profile with unambiguous results (e.g. no mixture present), the evidence has extremely strong support for the proposition that the suspect supplied the evidentiary sample.

Note that LR values are always in the range of zero to infinity. There are no negative LRs. Since LR numbers can be rather large, it is often preferable to report them in terms of their logarithm (log) value. An LR of 1 produces a base-10 log(LR) of zero. Values of LRs that are greater than one, where the evidence is better explained by the prosecution's hypothesis, have a positive log(LR). LR values that are less than one, where the evidence is better explained by the hypothesis in the denominator of the LR, have a negative log(LR).

An appropriate LR statement would be: "The DNA evidence is **LR times** more likely _if_ the defendant is the source of the crime sample (event _H_) than _if_ some other person is the source of the crime sample (event *H*)" (Weir 2013). An inappropriate wording for an LR result could be "The evidence shows that the defendant is **LR times** more likely to be the source of the crime sample than not."

The LR method is an example of the scientific method in action. Experimental data inform the hypotheses under consideration. The questions being posed are clearly laid out in the formulation of the LR equation. The weight of evidence can be effectively evaluated with LRs.

SOURCE ATTRIBUTION

With average RMPs for unrelated individuals of less than one in a trillion using the 13-core STR loci (Chakraborty et al. 1999), there comes within the context of a particular case and Q-K comparison a high degree of confidence that an individual is the source of an evidentiary DNA sample with reasonable degree of scientific certainty. When the rarity of a specific DNA profile (based on frequency estimates) exceeds a predefined threshold, such as an RMP that is more rare than a thousand times the size of the United States population (e.g. 1 in 300 billion), laboratories have set policies to declare that the Q sample can be attributed to the K reference sample. Such a declaration is known as *source attribution.*

Given that DNA evidence can provide strong LRs and RMPs from forensic samples that exceed the world population many fold, the Federal Bureau of Investigation (FBI) Laboratory decided to adopt a source attribution policy around the beginning of the 21st century (Holden 1997, Budowle et al. 2000, DAB 2000). A number of laboratories in the United States have also adopted use of a source attribution statement when a DNA profile frequency estimate exceeds a predefined threshold. These thresholds can vary by laboratory. The FBI Laboratory policy in their initial publication was that when a specific profile's probability was less than a thousand times the U.S. population size, the sample's questioned source (Q sample) was attributed to the reference known (K sample) (Budowle et al. 2000).

As with any threshold (see Chapter 2), there are assumptions underlying use of this value and limitations that are important to understand. The SWGDAM 2010 Guideline 4.7 states: "If a laboratory uses source attribution statements, then it must establish guidelines for the criteria on which such a declaration is based" (SWGDAM 2010).

The reasoning behind a source attribution approach was originally described by Bruce Budowle of the FBI Laboratory in a publication released in the FBI's online journal at the time, *Forensic Science Communications* (Budowle et al. 2000). The DNA Advisory Board's endorsement of source attribution is very similar (DAB 2000, see Appendix 3). There have been no other publications supporting source attribution since then.

If p_x is the RMP for a given evidentiary profile X, then $(1 - p_x)^N$ is the probability of not observing the particular profile in a sample of N *unrelated* individuals. When this probability is greater than or equal to a $1 - \alpha$ confidence level (with α being 0.01 for 99%), then $(1 - p_x)^N \geq 1 - \alpha$ or $p_x \leq 1 - (1 - \alpha)^{1/N}$, which enables the calculation that if N is approximately the size of the U.S. population (N = 317,000,000), then an RMP of less than 3.17×10^{-11} will confer at least 99% confidence that the evidentiary profile is "unique" in the population (Table 11.6). Use of a source attribution statement comes with the assumption that identical twins or close relatives are not possible suspects since the underlying calculations involve *unrelated* individuals.

A statement provided with a report involving a source attribution might include the following words: "In the absence of identical twins or close relatives, it can be concluded to a reasonable

TABLE 11.6   Random Match Probability Thresholds for Source Attribution at Various Population Sizes and Confidence Levels

	Sample Size (N)	Confidence Levels (1-α)			
		0.90	0.95	0.99	0.999
	2	5.13×10^{-2}	2.53×10^{-2}	5.01×10^{-3}	5.00×10^{-4}
	5	2.09×10^{-2}	1.02×10^{-2}	2.01×10^{-3}	2.00×10^{-4}
	10	1.05×10^{-2}	5.12×10^{-3}	1.00×10^{-3}	1.00×10^{-4}
	25	4.21×10^{-3}	2.05×10^{-3}	4.02×10^{-4}	4.00×10^{-5}
	50	2.10×10^{-3}	1.03×10^{-3}	2.01×10^{-4}	2.00×10^{-5}
	100	1.05×10^{-3}	5.13×10^{-4}	1.00×10^{-4}	1.00×10^{-5}
	1000	1.05×10^{-4}	5.13×10^{-5}	1.01×10^{-5}	1.00×10^{-6}
	100,000	1.05×10^{-6}	5.13×10^{-7}	1.01×10^{-7}	1.00×10^{-8}
	1,000,000	1.05×10^{-7}	5.13×10^{-8}	1.01×10^{-8}	1.00×10^{-9}
	10,000,000	1.05×10^{-8}	5.13×10^{-9}	1.01×10^{-9}	1.00×10^{-10}
	50,000,000	2.11×10^{-9}	1.03×10^{-9}	2.01×10^{-10}	2.00×10^{-11}
U.S. (1999)	260,000,000	4.05×10^{-10}	1.97×10^{-10}	3.87×10^{-11}	3.85×10^{-12}
U.S. (2014)	317,000,000	3.32×10^{-10}	1.62×10^{-10}	$\mathbf{3.17 \times 10^{-11}}$	3.16×10^{-12}
	1,000,000,000	1.05×10^{-10}	5.13×10^{-11}	1.01×10^{-11}	1.00×10^{-12}
World population	7,100,000,000	1.48×10^{-11}	7.22×10^{-12}	1.42×10^{-12}	1.41×10^{-13}

With a random match probability of 4.24×10^{-19} in U.S. Caucasians (see Table 11.2), the example STR profile would be considered "unique." Adapted from Budowle et al. (2000).

scientific certainty that the DNA from (Q) and from (K) came from the same individual" or "Reasonable scientific certainty means that you are (x%) certain that you would not see this profile in a sample of (y) unrelated individuals."

A problem with source attribution or an identity statement is that identical twins or other close relatives are not accounted for in a sweeping statement that has "unrelated" individuals in mind with the statistical result. Not everyone reading a lab report may appreciate the caveats that exist in a reporting statement involving source attribution.

Even with very small probabilities, it is important to keep in mind that absolute certainty is outside the realm of scientific inquiry. Yet a high degree of confidence in individualization of a DNA profile can be obtained when the rarity of a profile exceeds the world population many fold.

Criticism of Source Attribution

Critics of the source attribution approach have had a lot to say on the topic. In a 2002 article, Christopher Triggs and John Buckleton of New Zealand express concerns over prior probabilities being ignored when source attribution is within the posterior probability domain (Triggs & Buckleton 2002). They predict that multiple sets of persons (brothers) will eventually be found to match at the 13 CODIS STRs. Triggs and Buckleton conclude that "the predictions [of independence testing] are largely beyond experimental verification" (Triggs & Buckleton 2002). In some situations, estimations of DNA profile frequencies should consider close relatives (see Table 11.5) and members of the subpopulation (see Table 11.4).

David Balding writes in a 1999 article entitled "When can a DNA profile be regarded as unique?": "Perhaps the most problematic assumption underlying the calculation of a probability of uniqueness is the assumption that there is no evidence in favor of [the suspect]. In some cases there is evidence favoring the defendant. More generally, it is usually not appropriate for the forensic scientist to pre-empt the jurors' assessment of the non-scientific evidence.... Focusing on the directly relevant issue, whether or not the defendant is the source of the crime stain, rather than uniqueness, makes more efficient use of the evidence and, properly presented and explained to the court, can suffice as a basis for satisfactory prosecutions" (Balding 1999). In his 2005 *Weight-of-Evidence for Forensic DNA Profiles*, Balding offers additional commentary on why declaring uniqueness is unwise (Balding 2005).

Bruce Weir, speaking on the topic "Are DNA profiles unique?" at the 1998 International Symposium on Human Identification, concluded: "It is very difficult to arrive at a satisfactory probabilistic or statistical genetic theory which will give the probability that a second person in a population has the same DNA profile as the one featuring in a criminal trial. The difficulties stem from possible dependencies between loci and between individuals. This … led the 1996 NRC report to state: 'The definition of uniqueness is outside our province. It is for the courts to decide …' Uniqueness is not an issue that can be addressed with statistics" (Weir 1998).

Addressing the topic of individualization even more directly, Ian Evett and Bruce Weir wrote in their 1998 book (pp. 243–244) after discussing the use of a profile rarity threshold of greater than a thousand times the population size: "This might be viewed as implying a 99.9% probability that nobody else in the population has the profile. An immediate problem with this formulation is the assumption of independence between all the genotypes in the population, which cannot be true. Furthermore, this apparent objectivity of the calculation is an illusion. … whether it has any real provenance is a matter of opinion" (Evett & Weir 1998).

In some ways, it is hard to imagine how any DNA profiles could be claimed to be "unique" without a survey of all the world's profiles. Millions of STR profiles have been run in forensic DNA laboratories around the world – and some interesting results have been seen. The closest published "near-miss" with very similar STR profiles from two different individuals came recently with two brothers found in the Israel DNA database (D.N.A. Box 11.4). This rather rare observation is a reminder that declaration of source attribution is based on models that only apply for unrelated individuals and specific assumptions related to the populations from which the DNA profile could have come.

It may be worth noting that there are a growing number of twins in the general population – more than 137,000 were born in 2009, amounting to 1 in 30 births, according to a January 4, 2012 report (Beasley 2012). The number of twins born in the United States has doubled in the last three decades largely as a result of fertility treatments (Beasley 2012). Thus, a substantial number of fraternal and identical twins may exist in the general population. Half-siblings, unknown to each other, can also exist from the use of sperm bank donations. Understanding this dynamic is important in the way

D.N.A. BOX 11.4

DNA PROFILES THAT MATCH AT 31 OF 32 ALLELES: ISRAELI BROTHERS

In 2013, the Israel Police DNA laboratory published a report that they had two DNA profiles from different people that were almost identical. The two profiles had been run with PowerPlex ESI 16, which examines 15 STR loci. With the exception of D18S51, the two DNA profiles were a perfect match at these 14 STRs: FGA, TH01, vWA, D1S1656, D2S441, D2S1338, D3S1358, D8S1179, D10S1248, D12S391, D16S539, D19S433, D21S11, and D22S1045. One profile had a 12,15 genotype at D18S51 and the other was a 12,12. Since these results were from reference DNA samples, peak heights were outside of the range where stochastic effects might make it possible for the allele 15 to have dropped out.

Follow-up study by the Israel Police found: "Demographic data verified that *the samples belong to brothers*, one of them was born in January 1973 and his brother in November 1974, therefore the possibility of identical twins with a mutation in one of them was rejected. The demographic data also indicated that *the brothers belong to a*

small ethno-religious community, numbering 130,000 persons in Israel" (Zaken et al. 2013, emphasis added). The authors of this study go on to comment: "A partial match, in 14 out of 15 STR genotypes, is expected to occur in one out of 137 thousand same-sex pairs (the maximum is 1 in 22 thousand pairs). A partial match of 29 out of 30 alleles at the 15 STR loci (as the one observed in our particular case) is expected to occur in one out of 283 thousand pairs of full, same-sex siblings (the maximum is 1 in 48 thousand pairs). *All these are calculated under the assumption of a randomly mated population.* The markedly uncommon occurrence of the match described here can probably be attributed to the genetic isolation and the strong endogamy of this particular community" (Zaken et al. 2013, emphasis added).

Source: Zaken, N., et al. (2013). Can brothers share the same STR profile? Forensic Science International: Genetics, 7, 494–498.

that DNA statistical data are presented. Using assumptions that only consider "unrelated" people may be shortsighted in some situations and case scenarios.

ISSUES WITH DNA PROFILE FREQUENCY ESTIMATES

The previous sections have all focused on different approaches to providing statistical interpretation on single-source autosomal STR data. There are a number of other scenarios that may exist and that may be confronted by a forensic scientist needing to provide statistical support for a DNA result. Several of these other scenarios are briefly discussed below. Greater detail on these topics may be found by consulting the articles or texts cited in the reference list for this chapter as well as the next two chapters.

Cases with pristine single-source DNA profiles do not always occur. The following topics are covered in more detail in other chapters in this book:

- Mixtures (see Chapter 12).
- Allele drop-out due to degradation or stochastic efforts from attempting to amplify low amounts of DNA from single-source samples or mixtures (see Chapter 13).
- Relatives (see Chapter 14).
- Lineage markers (see Chapters 15).

Concepts of Probability vs. Frequency

We have been discussing DNA profile frequency and RMP interchangeably throughout this chapter. Such is the convention used by the community. However, perhaps we should be a little more precise in our future discussions. Regarding the difference between probability and frequency, forensic mathematician Charles Brenner commented recently (Brenner 2010):

"Traditionally the forensic community answers the matching probability question by consulting a population sample, typically of several hundred or thousand people. The sample frequency is then taken as an estimate for population frequency which in turn is used as a surrogate for probability. As a result it has become habit in the forensic community to conflate frequency and probability. There is an institutionalized misconception that population frequency is matching probability. For common traits such as an allele at an STR locus the frequency approximation is simple and is reasonable enough. But frequency isn't the goal, probability is, and if matching probability can be decided without the distraction and detour of considering population frequency, so much the better—especially for rare traits for which population frequency cannot be accurately estimated."

In a follow-up article Brenner concludes: "Distinguishing probability from frequency doesn't matter so much for autosomal forensic work. The product rule covers up a lot of sins. The right astronomical number and the wrong astronomical number are not usually different in their practical evidential impact" (Brenner 2014).

Match Probability vs. Profile Probability (Frequency)

While the forensic DNA community tends to refer to a match probability, what is typically being determined is a *profile probability* based on an estimate of a DNA profile frequency and assumptions such as independence of alleles and loci, etc. (see above). However, a true *match probability* as it was originally envisioned (Balding & Nichols 1994) is taking a position of the defendant when establishing the hypotheses used in an LR calculation — namely that the suspect and the perpetrator may be different individuals. Given that a DNA profile has been observed in the evidence and in the suspect, what is the chance that this profile exists in another unknown individual? In other words, can you condition on the known person to look for an unknown person?

Bruce Weir makes a key point in a recent article: "The interpretation of matching DNA profiles often relies on some statements of probability. These statements refer to the chance of an unknown person having the profile given that a known person has been seen to have the profile. *A simple approach is to ignore the conditioning on the known person and use an estimate of the population frequency of the profile. However, this ignores the possibility that the known and unknown persons are related either by being in the same family or by being in the same population*" (Weir 2013).

Back in 2001, Bruce Weir made the point about "profile probability" being different from "match probability" in a *Forensic Science Communications* article. He wrote (Weir 2001):

> *It is very helpful to use the term "profile probability" for the chance of a single individual having a particular profile, in distinction to "match probability" for the chance of a person having the profile when it is known that another person has the profile. The match probability, therefore, explicitly requires statements about two profiles. Profile probabilities are of some interest but are unlikely to be relevant in forensic calculations. If an evidentiary profile is known to be that of the perpetrator of a crime and a person found to have that profile becomes the defendant in a trial, then the numerical values given in court are derived under the proposition that the defendant is not the perpetrator. It is of little consequence that the profile is rare in the population — what is relevant is the rarity of the profile, given that one person (e.g. the perpetrator) has the profile. In other words, what is the probability that the defendant would have the profile given that the perpetrator has the profile and these are different people? This number is the match probability, and it is seen to be a conditional probability.*

> The distinction between profile and match probabilities is rarely made by practicing forensic scientists, and this is most likely because the two quantities have the same value in the simple case when "product rule" calculations are valid. *If there is no relatedness in a large population, due to either immediate family membership or common evolutionary history, and there is completely random mating and population homogeneity, and an absence of linkage, selection, mutation, and migration, then all the alleles in a DNA profile are independent. The profile probability and the match probability are both just the product of the allele probabilities, together with factors of two for each heterozygous locus (Weir 2001, emphasis added).*

Thus, match probability is not necessarily the same as RMP as a regular RMP calculation assumes no relatives and no subpopulation structure. Perhaps we sometimes make things too simple by just using frequency of a profile in the population based on HWE and LE (the so-called "product rule" approach).

Some of these topics may not seem like a big deal from a practical point of view. Aren't DNA profiles pretty rare? And are there any real serious flaws in the statistical approaches being used today?

Triggs and Buckleton write: "Our belief in the validity of [statistical DNA interpretation] is based largely on how strong or weak are our beliefs in the underlying models. ... We accept that the lack of strong practical implications may be a disincentive to invest any large amount of effort in this area. Nonetheless, we would urge readers to critically examine the basis of their forensic testimony and to try to set the highest standards in logic and rigor" (Triggs & Buckleton 2002).

What Question Are You Trying to Answer?

David Balding comments: "Inappropriate ideas from classical statistics [have] caused much confusion about the interpretation of DNA profile evidence...The key principle [turns] out to be astonishingly simple: Focus on the relevant question. Many misleading statistical approaches [turn] out to be providing valid answers to the wrong questions" (Balding 2000). Table 11.7 considers some of the statistical approaches and what question they answer. A statistic can be "right" but not "appropriate" depending on the question that is trying to be addressed.

TABLE 11.7 Different Calculations Answer Different Questions

What Are the Questions?	Which Method Is Used?	How Is the Answer Estimated?
What is the rarity of a specific DNA profile given the alleles observed? What is the chance that a particular profile exists in a population based on allele frequencies?	**Profile probability** (random match probability)	Product rule with $2pq$ and p^2
Given that a particular profile has been seen (in the crime scene evidence and in the suspect), what is the chance of it occuring again?	**Match probability**	Balding & Nichols 1994 NRC 1996 recommendation 4.10 equations
How often would a DNA profile match the relevant forensic sample in a database of size N?	**Database match probability**	NRC 1996 Chakraborty & Ge 2009 RMP × database size (N)

Thoughts on Seeking to Be "Conservative"

Aren't we fine if our method is "conservative"? In other words, what do we have to worry about if the DNA statistical results given in a report are the most favorable for the defendant (i.e. match probability that is least rare)?

Almost 20 years ago, Ian Evett shared an interesting perspective on being "conservative" to forensic evidence results: "There is a wide-spread view that the expert must quote an assessment of the evidence which is conservative in the sense of erring so as to favor the defendant. This idea seems partly based on the view that, by understating the evidence, the scientist will give himself a more comfortable time in the witness box. On the contrary, once we concede the principle that it is necessary to be conservative we put ourselves in the situation which invites the defense to show that there is another method which is still more conservative than ours. And there always is — unless we opt out completely and say the evidence has no value" (Evett 1996, modified to U.S. spelling).

Error Rates and Probability Calculations

Occasionally the topic of incorporating laboratory error rates into DNA match probabilities is discussed or revisited (e.g. Koehler et al. 1995; Thompson et al. 2003). My typical response to questions on this topic is "Yes, errors do occasionally occur in forensic DNA testing. However, how can measuring some overall laboratory error rate provide any kind of meaningful value that can reflect performance on a specific case? And how would it be possible to combine this general error rate with the rare match statistic that is produced with a DNA match?"

The 1996 National Research Council (NRC II) discussed the topic of whether or not an error rate should be included in statistical calculations that accompany a DNA match (NRC 1996, pp. 85–87). Attempting to pool results of proficiency tests across laboratories has been suggested as a possible way to estimate an "industry-wide" error rate (Koehler et al. 1995). The NRC II committee points out that this approach would penalize the better laboratories. Furthermore, under the quality assurance systems in place in modern forensic DNA laboratories, when errors are discovered, then root cause(s) of these errors are supposed to be investigated and corrective action taken (see section 14 of the FBI Quality Assurance Standards).

Thus, a laboratory and a specific analyst would not likely make the same error again if effective corrective action has been taken. The NRC II panel members conclude: "We believe that a calculation that combines error rates with match probabilities is inappropriate. The *risk of error is properly considered case by case*, taking into account the record of the laboratory performing the tests, the extent of redundancy, and the overall quality of the results" (NRC 1996, emphasis added). The NRC II report goes on to encourage retesting if there is a concern with a DNA result: "A wrongly accused person's best insurance against the possibility of being falsely incriminated is the opportunity to have the testing repeated" (NRC 1996).

The 1997 summer issue of *Jurimetrics Journal* contained several articles debating this topic. Bill Thompson, professor of criminology at University of California-Irvine, suggested that DNA evidence should be excluded as "unacceptable scientifically if the probability of an erroneous match cannot be quantified" (Thompson 1997). Newton Morton, professor of human genetics, countered: "Coincidental identity and laboratory error are different phenomena, so the two cannot and should not be combined in a single estimate" (Morton 1997).

Database Match Probability

The development of national DNA databases filled with profiles from both convicted offenders and unsolved casework samples permits searches for matches between evidentiary and database profiles. In order to calculate what might be termed a *database match probability*, the NRC II report recommendation 5.1 advocates that the RMP be multiplied by N, the number of persons in the database (NRC 1996, see Appendix 2). The FBI's DNA Advisory Board in their February 2000 recommendations on statistical approaches endorsed this NRC II report recommendation (DAB 2000). It is important to remember that the database match probability answers a different question than an RMP question does (Budowle et al. 2009).

DNA databases searched for intelligence purposes, such as the National DNA Index System (NDIS) in the United States, consist of DNA profiles of previous offenders. Thus, admitting during court proceedings that the suspect (defendant) was apprehended due to a DNA database search is equivalent to admitting that the defendant was a previous offender. This revelation is of course not advantageous to the defendant! And more importantly, it may be viewed as inappropriate in a court system where a defendant is considered innocent until proven guilty. In fact, a mistrial could result from bringing up a defendant's prior record. Therefore, DNA database matches are not typically part of any U.S. court proceedings.

SUMMARY

Matching DNA results must be provided with statistical interpretation to help determine their rarity and relevance. The frequency of alleles and genotypes are assessed by gathering a sampling of a particular population. Provided that the alleles and their loci are independent from one another, results can be combined using what is commonly referred to as "the product rule." The RMP for a particular DNA profile represents the chance of drawing this combination of alleles at random from a population of unrelated individuals and is not the probability of guilt — a philosophical mistake known as the "prosecutor's fallacy." Corrections for subpopulation structure and possible involvement of relatives reduce the match probability and typically provide a more conservative estimate for the defendant.

Reading List and Internet Resources

General Information

Brenner, C. H. (2003). *Forensic genetics: mathematics*. In D. N. Cooper (Ed.), *Nature Encyclopedia of the Human Genome (Vol. 2)*; (pp. 513–519). New York: Macmillan Publishers Ltd., Nature Publishing Group.

DAB — DNA Advisory Board. (2000). Statistical and population genetic issues affecting the evaluation of the frequency of occurrence of DNA profiles calculated from pertinent population database(s). *Forensic Science Communications, 2*(3). Available at http://www.fbi.gov/about-us/lab/forensic-science-communications/fsc/july2000/dnastat.htm. Accessed April 3, 2014.

Evett, I. W., & Weir, B. S. (1998). *Interpreting DNA Evidence: Statistical Genetics for Forensic Scientists*. Sunderland, MA: Sinauer Associates.

Fung, W. K., & Hu, Y.-Q. (2008). *Statistical DNA Forensics: Theory, Methods and Computation*. Hoboken, New Jersey: John Wiley & Sons.

National Research Council (NRCII) Committee on DNA Forensic Science. (1996). *The Evaluation of Forensic DNA Evidence*. Washington, DC: National Academy Press.

Zaken, N., et al. (2013). Can brothers share the same STR profile? *Forensic Science International: Genetics, 7*, 494–498.

Profile Frequency Estimate Calculations

Balding, D. J., & Nichols, R. A. (1994). DNA profile match probability calculation: how to allow for population stratification, relatedness, database selection and single bands. *Forensic Science International, 64*, 125–140.

Balding, D. J., & Nichols, R. A. (1995). A method for quantifying differentiation between populations at multi-allelic loci and its implications for investigating identity and paternity. In B. S. Weir (Ed.), *Human Identification: The Use of DNA Markers* (pp. 3–12). Boston: Kluwer Academic Publishers.

Balding, D. J. (2000). Interpreting DNA evidence: can probability theory help? Chapter 3. In J. L. Gastwirth (Ed.), *Statistical Science in the Courtroom* (pp. 51–70). New York: Springer.

Beecham, G. W., & Weir, B. S. (2011). Confidence intervals for DNA evidence likelihood ratios. *Journal Forensic Sciences, S1*, S166–S171.

Budowle, B., et al. (2001). CODIS STR loci data from 41 sample populations. *Journal Forensic Sciences, 46*, 453–489.

Butler, J. M., et al. (2003). Allele frequencies for 15 autosomal STR loci on U.S. Caucasian, African American, and Hispanic populations. *Journal Forensic Sciences, 48*(4), 908–911.

Chakraborty, R., et al. (1999). The utility of short tandem repeat loci beyond human identification: implications for development of new DNA typing systems. *Electrophoresis, 20*, 1682–1696.

Curran, J. M., et al. (2007). Empirical testing of estimated DNA frequencies. *Forensic Science International Genetics, 1*, 267–272.

Steele, C. D., & Balding, D. J. (2014). Statistical evaluation of forensic DNA profile evidence. *Annual Review Statistics Application, 1*, 20.1–20.24.

Tracey, M. (2001). Short tandem repeat-based identification of individuals and parents. *Croatian Medical Journal, 42*, 233–238.

Weir, B. S. (2003). *DNA evidence: inferring identity*. In D. N. Cooper (Ed.), *Nature Encyclopedia of the Human Genome (Vol. 2)*; (pp. 85–88). New York City: Macmillan Publishers Ltd., Nature Publishing Group.

Weir, B. S., et al. (2006). Genetic relatedness analysis: modern data and new challenges. *Nature Reviews Genetics, 7*, 771–780.

Weir, B. S. (2007). Forensics. In D. J. Balding, M. Bishop, & C. Cannings (Eds.), *Handbook of Statistical Genetics, 3rd Edition* (pp. 1368–1392). Hoboken, New Jersey: John Wiley & Sons.

Weir, B. S. (2007). The rarity of DNA profiles. *Annals Applied Statistics, 1*, 358–370.

Weir, B. S. (2013). *DNA — statistical probability. Encyclopedia of Forensic Sciences* (2nd ed.). San Diego: Elsevier Academic Press. pp. 282–286.

Population Substructure Correction

Buckleton, J., Triggs, C. M., & Walsh, S. J. (Eds.). (2005). *Forensic DNA Evidence Interpretation*. Boca Raton: CRC Press [Chapter 3: Population genetic models, pp. 65–122].

Buckleton, J. S., et al. (2006). How reliable is the sub-population model in DNA testimony? *Forensic Science International, 157*, 144–148.

Curran, J. M., et al. (2003). What is the magnitude of the subpopulation effect? *Forensic Science International, 135*, 1–8.

Impact of Relatives

Belin, T. R., et al. (1997). Summarizing DNA evidence when relatives are possible suspects. *Journal American Statistical Association, 92*, 706–716.

Bright, J.-A., et al. (2013). Relatedness calculations for linked loci incorporating subpopulation effects. *Forensic Science International: Genetics, 7*, 380–383.

Brookfield, J. F. Y. (1994). The effect of relatives on the likelihood ratio associated with DNA profile evidence. *Science Justice, 34*, 193–197.

Buckleton, J., & Triggs, C. M. (2005). Relatedness and DNA: are we taking it seriously enough? *Forensic Science International, 152*, 115–119.

Nordgaard, A., et al. (2012). Assessment of forensic findings when alternative explanations have different likelihoods — "Blame-the-brother" syndrome. *Science Justice, 52*, 226–236.

Slooten, K. (2012). Match probabilities for multiple siblings. *Forensic Science International Genetics, 6*, 466–468.

General Match Probability

Bright, J.-A., et al. (2013). Considerations of the probative value of single donor 15-plex STR profiles in UK populations and its presentation in UK courts II. *Science Justice, 53*, 371.

Foreman, L. A., & Evett, I. W. (2001). Statistical analyses to support forensic interpretation for a new 10-locus STR profiling system. *International Journal Legal Medicine, 114*, 147–155.

Hopwood, A. J., et al. (2012). Consideration of the probative value of single donor 15-plex STR profiles in UK populations and its presentation in UK courts. *Science Justice, 52*, 185–190.

Prosecutor's Fallacy

Balding, D. J., & Donnelly, P. (1994). The prosecutor's fallacy and DNA evidence. *Criminal Law Review Oct, 1994*, 711–721.

Leung, W. C. (2002). The prosecutor's fallacy — a pitfall in interpreting probabilities in forensic evidence. *Medicine Science Law, 42*, 44–50.

Thompson, W. C., & Schumann, E. L. (1987). Interpretation of statistical evidence in criminal trials: the prosecutor's fallacy and the defense attorney's fallacy. *Law Human Behavior, 11*, 167–187.

Likelihood Ratios

Buckleton, J. S., et al. (2006). An extended likelihood ratio framework for interpreting evidence. *Science Justice, 46*, 69–78.

Evett, I. W., & Weir, B. S. (1998). *Interpreting DNA Evidence: Statistical Genetics for Forensic Scientists*. Sunderland, MA: Sinauer Associates.

Evett, I. W. (2000). The impact of the principles of evidence interpretation on the structure and content of statements. *Science Justice, 40*, 233–239.

Goos, L. M., et al. (2002). The influence of probabilistic statements on the evaluation of the significance of a DNA match. *Canadian Society Forensic Sciences Journal, 35*, 77–90.

Mullen, C., et al. (2014). Perception problems of the verbal scale. *Science Justice, 54*, 154–158.

Stockmarr, A. (2000). The choice of hypotheses in the evaluation of DNA profile evidence. In J. L. Gastwirth (Ed.), *Statistical Science in the Courtroom* (pp. 143–159). New York: Springer.

Taylor, D., et al. (2013). The interpretation of single source and mixed DNA profiles. *Forensic Science International Genetics, 7*(5), 516–528.

Weir, B. S. (1992). Population genetics in the forensic DNA debate. *Proceedings National Academy Sciences United States America, 89*, 11654–11659.

Source Attribution

Balding, D. J. (1999). When can a DNA profile be regarded as unique? *Science & Justice, 39*, 257–260.

Balding, D. J. (2005). *Weight-of-Evidence for Forensic DNA Profiles*. Hoboken, New Jersey: John Wiley & Sons [p. 148 discusses the uniqueness fallacy].

Beasley, D. (2012). *U.S. twin births have doubled in three decades: study. Reuters January 4, 2012 article*. Available at http://www.reuters.com/article/2012/01/04/us-usa-twins-idUSTRE80321S20120104. Accessed April 3, 2014.

Biedermann, A., et al. (2013). The subjectivist interpretation of probability and the problem of individualization in forensic science. *Science & Justice, 53*, 192–200.

Budowle, B., et al. (2000). Source attribution of a forensic DNA profile. *Forensic Science Communications, 2*(3). Available at http://www.fbi.gov/about-us/lab/forensic-science-communications/fsc/july2000/source.htm. Accessed April 3, 2014.

Evett, I. W., & Weir, B. S. (1998). *Interpreting DNA Evidence: Statistical Genetics for Forensic Scientists*. Sunderland, MA: Sinauer Associates [pp. 243–244 discuss statistical basis for individualization].

Holden, C. (1997). DNA fingerprinting comes of age. *Science, 278*, 1407.

Stoney, D. A. (1991). What made us ever think we could individualize using statistics? *Journal Forensic Science Society, 31*, 197–199.

SWGDAM. (2010). *SWGDAM Interpretation Guidelines for Autosomal STR Typing by Forensic DNA Testing Laboratories*. Available at http://www.fbi.gov/about-us/lab/biometric-analysis/codis/swgdam-interpretation-guidelines. Accessed April 3, 2014.

Triggs, C. M., & Buckleton, J. S. (2002). Logical implications of applying the principles of population genetics to the interpretation of DNA profiling evidence. *Forensic Science International, 128*, 108–114.

Weir, B. S. (1998). *Are DNA profiles unique? Proceedings of the Ninth International Symposium on Human Identification*. Available at http://www.promega.com/products/pm/genetic-identity/ishi-conference-proceedings/9th-ishi-oral-presentations/. Accessed March 4, 2014.

Other Issues

Evett, I. W. (1996). Expert evidence and forensic misconceptions of the nature of exact science. *Science Justice, 36*, 118–122.

Match Probability vs. Profile Frequency

Balding, D. J. (2000). Interpreting DNA evidence: can probability theory help? In J. L. Gastwirth (Ed.), *Statistical Science in the Courtroom* (pp. 51–70) New York: Springer.

Balding, D. J. (2005). *Weight-of-evidence for Forensic DNA Profiles*. Hoboken, New Jersey: John Wiley & Sons.

Brenner, C. H. (2010). Fundamental problem of forensic mathematics — the evidential value of a rare haplotype. *Forensic Science International: Genetics, 4*, 281–291.

Brenner, C. H. (2012). *(Matching) probability isn't (population) frequency*. Available at http://dna-view.com/ProbIsNotFreq.htm. Accessed April 3, 2014.

Brenner, C. H. (2014). Understanding Y haplotype matching probability. *Forensic Science International: Genetics, 8*, 233–243.

Weir, B. S. (2001). DNA match and profile probabilities: comment on Budowle et al. (2000) and Fung and Hu (2000). *Forensic Science Communications, 3*(1). Available at http://www.fbi.gov/about-us/lab/forensic-science-communications/fsc/jan2001/weir.htm. Accessed April 3, 2014.

Database Match Probability

Balding, D. J. (1997). Errors and misunderstandings in the second NRC report. *Jurimetrics, 37*, 603–607.

Balding, D. J., & Donnelly, P. (1996). Evaluating DNA profile evidence when the suspect is identified through a database search. *Journal Forensic Sciences, 41*, 603–607.

Balding, D. J. (2002). The DNA database search controversy. *Biometrics, 58*, 214–244.

Biedermann, A., et al. (2011). Recent misconceptions about the "database search problem": a probabilistic analysis using Bayesian networks. *Forensic Science International, 212*, 51–60.

Budowle, B., et al. (2006). Clarification of statistical issues related to the operation of CODIS. *Proceedings Seventeenth International Symposium Human Identification*. Promega Corporation. Available at http://www.promega.com/geneticidproc/ussymp17proc/. Accessed April 3, 2014.

Budowle, B., et al. (2009). Partial matches in heterogeneous offender databases do not call into question the validity of random match probability calculations. *International Journal Legal Medicine, 123*, 59–63.

Chakraborty, R., & Ge, J. (2009). Statistical weight of a DNA match in cold-hit cases. *Forensic Science Communications, 11*(3). Available at http://www.fbi.gov/about-us/lab/forensic-science-communications/fsc/july2009. Accessed April 3, 2014.

Devlin, B. (2000). The evidentiary value of a DNA database search. *Biometrics, 56*, 1276−1277.

Evett, I. W., Foreman, L. A., & Weir, B. S. (2000). Letter to the editor of Biometrics. *Biometrics, 56*(4), 1274−1275.

Gittelson, S., et al. (2012). The database search problem: a question of rational decision making. *Forensic Science International, 222*, 186−199.

Kaye, D. H. (2008). People v. Nelson: a tale of two statistics. *Law, Probability, and Risk, 7*(4), 249−257.

Meester, R., & Sjerps, M. (2003). The evidentiary value in the DNA database search controversy and the two-stain problem. *Biometrics, 59*, 727−732.

Mueller, L. D. (2008). Can simple population genetic models reconcile partial match frequencies observed in large forensic databases? *Journal of Genetics, 87*, 101−108.

Nordgaard, A., et al. (2012). Comments on "The database search problem" with respect to a recent publication in Forensic Science International. *Forensic Science International, 217*, e32−e33.

Rudin, N., & Inman, K. (2007). *A frosty debate: the chilling effect of a "cold hit." CAC News 1st Quarter 2007.* pp. 31−35. Available at http://www.cacnews.org/. or http://www.forensicdna.com/Articles.html. Accessed April 3, 2014.

Stockmarr, A. (1999). Likelihood ratios for evaluating DNA evidence when the suspect is found through a database search. *Biometrics, 55*, 671−677.

Storvik, G., & Egeland, T. (2007). The DNA database search controversy revisited: bridging the Bayesian−frequentist gap. *Biometrics, 63*, 922−925.

Taylor, C., & Colman, P. (2010). Forensics: experts disagree on statistics from DNA trawls. *Nature, 464*, 1266−1267.

Tvedebrink, T., et al. (2012). Analysis of matches and partial-matches in a Danish STR data set. *Forensic Science International Genetics, 6*, 387−392.

Weir, B. S. (2004). Matching and partially-matching DNA profiles. *Journal Forensic Sciences, 49*, 1009−1014.

Incorporating Error Rates

Koehler, J. J., et al. (1995). The random match probability (RMP) in DNA evidence: irrelevant and prejudicial? *Jurimetrics Journal, 35*, 201−219.

Morton, N. E. (1997). The forensic DNA endgame. *Jurimetrics Journal, 37*, 477−494.

National Research Council (NRCII) Committee on DNA Forensic Science. (1996). *The Evaluation of Forensic DNA Evidence.* Washington, DC: National Academy Press [see discussion of error rates on pp. 85−87].

Thompson, W. C. (1997). Accepting lower standards: the National Research Council's second report on forensic DNA evidence. *Jurimetrics Journal, 37*, 405−423.

Thompson, W. C., et al. (2003). How the probability of a false positive affects the value of DNA evidence. *Journal Forensic Science, 48*, 47−54.

Scurich, N., & John, R. S. (2013). Mock jurors' use of error rates in DNA database trawls. *Law Human Behavior, 37*, 424−431.

DNA Mixture Statistics

"There is a considerable aura to DNA evidence. Because of this aura it is vital that weak evidence is correctly represented as weak or not presented at all."

Buckleton & Curran (2008)

INTRODUCTION

The points that have been addressed in the previous chapter involve obtaining a "clean" full DNA profile from a single-source. However, crime scene evidence can produce mixed DNA profiles from more than one individual (see Chapters 6 and 7). These mixtures can be challenging to interpret and may never be unambiguously separated depending on the short tandem repeat (STR) alleles present in the profile of the individual components. An indistinguishable mixture is a DNA profile where major and minor(s) components cannot be ascertained with confidence. In addition, partial profiles where entire loci have dropped out sometimes occur due to the presence of degraded DNA or polymerase chain reaction (PCR) inhibitors.

Many forensic cases involve multiple pieces of DNA evidence, and not all of these will be mixtures. Thus, if additional samples can be tested that are easier to interpret, they should be sought after versus complicated mixtures. Reference samples from individuals (e.g. victims or suspects) may unexpectedly exhibit a mixed STR profile. Natural DNA mixtures can exist in some people from birth or temporarily following a bone marrow transplant (D.N.A. Box 12.1).

At the turn of the 21st century, mixtures did not represent a majority of cases in forensic DNA laboratories, especially if a good differential extraction was performed in a sexual assault case where the sperm fraction could be fully separated from the victim's DNA (see Butler 2012). As an example, over a four-year period from 1997 to 2000, one forensic laboratory in Spain worked 1,547 criminal cases that involved a total of 2,424 samples, yet only 163 showed a mixed profile or 6.7% (Torres et al. 2003). In more recent years, however, crimes in which touch DNA evidence is present, such as burglaries, are investigated, and therefore an increasing number of mixtures are being observed (Roman et al. 2008).

The statistical methods described in this chapter will focus on two-person mixtures that contain a relatively high amount of DNA such that allele drop-out is not expected. Sexual assault evidence with a mixture of DNA from a victim and a perpetrator is an example of a sample in this category (Figure 12.1). Chapter 13 will cover situations where allele drop-out is a possibility, such as exists in complex mixtures with three or more contributors or compromised DNA samples.

D.N.A. BOX 12.1

NATURAL MIXTURES AND CHIMERIC INDIVIDUALS

In May 2002, the *New England Journal of Medicine* published a report of the genetic analysis of a phenotypically normal chimeric individual who was unexpectedly identified because histocompatibility testing of family members suggested that she was not the biological mother of two of her three children (Yu et al. 2002). The doctors examining this chimeric individual proposed that her condition had arisen because two fertilized eggs, destined originally to be fraternal twins, had fused to form a zygote that possessed DNA of two different types. Thus, from a genetic perspective she was both her children's mother and their aunt.

Among the various genetic tests performed on this chimeric individual was analysis of 22 STR loci. All of the 13 U.S. core loci except CSF1PO were examined in this study. This unusual patient possessed some differences in her STR profiles among various tissues tested. While the buccal and blood samples that were tested matched exactly, a mixture containing another type was present as the minor component in her thyroid, hair, and skin cells.

While chimeric individuals such as the one described above are most likely extremely rare in the general population, it is possible in theory for DNA testing from different tissues of a chimeric individual to not match one another and thus lead to a false exclusion. This situation may increase in

frequency with the rise of in vitro fertilization since multiple eggs are sometimes fertilized in order to increase the success rate of the procedure.

STR profiles from chimeric individuals have been seen in forensic cases and observed in single-source reference samples. An individual may exhibit chimeric characteristics, where some body tissues have a natural mixture of DNA from the donor and the recipient, following a bone marrow transplant. A study of DNA from buccal swabs of 77 recipients of allogeneic hematopoietic cell transplantation found relative donor chimerism levels between 0% and 100%, although blood always exhibited the donor's STR genotypes and hair samples always provided the recipient's genotypes (Berger et al. 2013). This study points out that if blood stem cell transplantation has occurred between a donor and a recipient then plucked hair samples (with roots) should be collected in addition to standard buccal swabs to obtain the recipient's true DNA profile.

Sources: Yu et al. (2002) New England Journal of Medicine, 346, 1545–1552; David Baron, "DNA tests shed light on hybrid human," National Public Radio-Morning Edition, August 11, 2003 (http://www.npr.org); Berger, B., et al. (2013). Chimerism in DNA of buccal swabs from recipients after allogeneic hematopoietic stem cell transplantations: implications for forensic DNA testing. International Journal of Legal Medicine, 127, 49–54.

Genotypes — Not Alleles — Matter in Profiles!

Since humans are diploid and typically possess two alleles at each locus, it is important to keep in mind that it is the genotype, or specific combination of alleles (the allele pair) found at each locus in an individual, that matters in both interpretation and statistical analysis. Simply describing and determining the statistical rarity of alleles present at a locus and in the entire DNA profile does not reflect the true nature of the sample contributor(s). Thus, a fundamental tenet of mixture interpretation involves effort to decipher possible *genotype* combinations of contributors, not simply the evaluation of whether or not *alleles* are present.

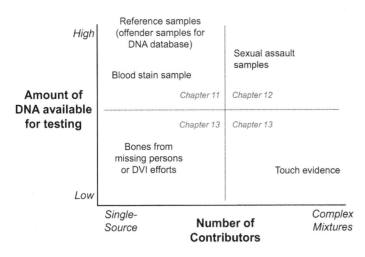

FIGURE 12.1 Comparison of sample types and challenges in terms of the amount of DNA available for testing and the potential number of contributors. Sexual assault samples typically involve DNA mixtures from people who are not related, whereas touch evidence (e.g. an item from a home) may very well have DNA from related people in a complex mixture. Statistical interpretation information in Chapter 11 focused on single-source samples with high amounts of DNA, and information in Chapter 12 is directed primarily to two-person mixtures with high amounts of DNA. Principles explained in Chapter 13 deal with low amounts of DNA that may be seen in complex mixtures or compromised samples from disaster victim identification (DVI) efforts.

D.N.A. Box 12.2 provides a simple test to see whether a person is thinking in terms of genotypes or alleles when it comes to mixture interpretration and evaluation. Specific assumptions as to the number of potential contributors in a mixture informs the interpretation process. These decisions are made in the context of examining a DNA profile as a whole and not focusing on a single locus.

An essential part of any DNA interpretation effort involves assuming the number of contributors. Making a specific assumption is sometimes referred to as *conditioning*. Quantitative information in the form of peak heights can aid efforts to reduce the number of genotype combinations that are reasonable in a mixture. While *unrestricted* approaches permit all possible combinations of genotypes with the alleles observed at a locus, *restricted* approaches limit the number of genotypes under consideration. As discussed in Chapter 6, use of peak height ratios (PHRs) and examination of mixture ratios across the profile are important elements in forming the assumptions regarding what can be restricted (Clayton et al. 1998). Appropriate statistical methods should be applied that correspond to the interpretation an analyst has made of the evidence.

Examples help improve understanding of concepts. A few simple illustrations are provided in this chapter to introduce concepts, and a more detailed worked example is contained in Appendix 4 at the back of the book.

Figure 12.2 illustrates some potential mixture data from a single STR locus. Since alleles P and Q are much taller than alleles R and S, they may be grouped into a major genotype of PQ and a minor genotype of RS. With this example, the major component is a 14,16 genotype and the minor component is an 18,19 genotype. This mixture deconvolution used to create these inferred allele pairs is conditioned on an assumption of two contributors.

If more than two contributors are assumed, then the other peaks labeled "stutter?" could be from additional contributors to the original biological sample. The decision as to the number of potential contributors comes from examining the STR profile as a whole, not just this single locus (see Chapter 5). The process of considering restricting potential genotype combinations by using relative peak height information and mixture proportions is reviewed in the example found in Appendix 4.

D.N.A. BOX 12.2

ARE YOU THINKING IN TERMS OF ALLELES RATHER THAN GENOTYPES?

This profile can be used as a simple test to see if an analyst is thinking in terms of alleles or genotypes. **Would you include or exclude a reference sample that is 13,14 and 28,30 at these two loci?** The alleles 13 and 14 and 28 and 30 are present, but, are allele pairs (genotypes) of 13,14 and 28,30 reasonable for contributors to this mixture result? Of course the answer depends on information from additional loci and careful consideration of locus peak height ratios (PHRs) and mixture proportions (M_x).

If (because of information from the entire profile) it can be assumed that there are only two contributors, then the reasonable major contributor for the locus on the left would be 13,16 (PHR = 0.92) and the reasonable minor contributor would be 14,15 (PHR = 0.76), although this value may be slightly skewed due to some stutter contribution in the allele 15 position from allele 16. Thus, the genotype 13,14, which has an unreasonable PHR of 0.22, would be <u>excluded</u> from this two-person mixture. Likewise, for the locus on the right, a 28,30 genotype possesses an unreasonable PHR of 0.15. It would be more reasonable to assume that the major contributor is a 28,28 genotype and the minor contributor is a 30,32.2 genotype.

Assessment of the number of contributors and likely genotypes present in this mixture should be completed *prior to comparison to a reference sample*. The important point to note here is that under a specific assumption of two contributors the genotypes of 13,14 and 28,30 are not reasonable, and therefore these genotypes should be <u>excluded</u> as possibilities even though the alleles are present!

If, instead, an analyst is thinking only in terms of alleles without conditioning on the number of contributors, which is often done when approaching a mixture interpretation scenario with a combined probability of inclusion (CPI) viewpoint, then the presence of alleles 13 and 14 for the locus on the left and alleles 28 and 30 for the locus on the right can lead to <u>inclusion</u> of unreasonable genotypes.

Genotypes of possible contributors matter — not simply the presence of corresponding alleles between reference samples and the evidentiary mixture profile. Likewise, assumptions as to the number of contributors are crucial to effective mixture interpretation. If more than two contributors can be reasonably assumed based on review of the profile as a whole, then some low-level allele information may be missing in this situation. For example, a possible pairing allele may not be amplified and detected to complete the true genotype with the 95 RFU allele 14 in the left locus or with the 74 RFU allele 32.2 in the right locus. If all alleles and genotypes are not represented at a locus, then an inconclusive result may need to be reported at least for the minor component(s) due to insufficient data being available to render a reliable conclusion on the evidentiary result.

Source: Charlotte Word presentation at the 2012 International Symposium on Human Identification mixture workshop; see http://www.cstl.nist.gov/strbase/training/ISHI2012-Mixture Workshop-DifferentAssumptions.pdf (slide 16).

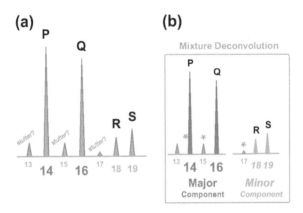

FIGURE 12.2 Hypothetical example of STR mixture data at the D18S51 locus. (a) The crime scene evidence data possesses alleles 14, 16, 18, and 19. Additional peaks at allele positions 13, 15, and 17 could be stutter products of the observed alleles or potentially alleles from other contributor(s), depending on the number of contributors present in the mixture. The suspect is 14,16 and the victim is 18,19. (b) Assuming two contributors, the mixture profile from (a) can be divided (deconvoluted) into major and minor components using relative peak height ratios to determine genotype combinations. Assuming this result is from a two-person mixture, the best explanation for peaks labeled with asterisks (*) is that they are stutter products.

Importance of Quantitative Assessments for Mixture Results

In the past, laboratory reports have provided qualitative assessment of mixture results with statements such as "the profile of the suspect cannot be excluded as being a possible contributor to the crime scene DNA mixture." Qualitative statements, such as "cannot be excluded" without a numerical qualifier, can be dangerous because an investigator or the court may assume that this situation with "failure to exclude" is equivalent to a DNA "match" with astronomical numbers like those described in Chapter 11 for single-source evidence and reference sample associations.

Presenting a simple qualitative statement of inclusion or exclusion rather than performing any calculations is often not satisfactory in a court of law where a judge typically requires some kind of numerical estimate to give statistical weight to the evidence. As pointed out in *The Evaluation of Forensic DNA Evidence*, "to make appropriate use of DNA technology in the courtroom, the trier of fact must give the DNA evidence appropriate weight" (NRC 1996, p. 203).

As John Buckleton and James Curran have observed: "There is a considerable aura to DNA evidence. Because of this aura it is vital that weak evidence is correctly represented as weak or not presented at all" (Buckleton & Curran 2008). With some mixtures where "failure to exclude" a particular suspect is the conclusion reached, a very large percentage of the population could also be part of the mixture evidence. In such a situation, the inclusionary statement may be weak, such as 1 in 10 or 1 in 100 randomly selected, unrelated individuals could also be part of the mixture result.

For this reason, the Scientific Working Group on DNA Analysis Methods (SWGDAM) in their 2010 interpretation guidelines clearly state in section 4.1: "The laboratory must perform statistical analysis in support of any inclusion that is determined to be relevant in the context of a case, irrespective of the number of alleles detected and the quantitative value of the statistical analysis" (SWGDAM 2010). Furthermore, the SWGDAM 2010 guidelines state that "the genetic loci and assumptions used for statistical calculations must be documented, at a minimum, in the case notes." Approaches to providing a statistic to the DNA mixture are provided below.

DIFFERENT STATISTICAL APPROACHES TO MIXTURE INTERPRETATION

As stated in earlier chapters, there is no one universal formula that fits all situations when interpreting DNA evidence. This reality certainly applies for mixture interpretation and reporting. Various laboratories have adopted different approaches to these challenging situations. There are three primary approaches to interpretating two-person DNA mixtures (Ladd et al. 2001).

First, if major and minor components can be separated into individual profiles due to sufficient differences in peak heights (see Chapter 6), then it may be possible to compute the random match probability (RMP) for the individual profiles as if each component was from a single source. However, since RMP technically refers to single-source samples, use of this statistic for deduced profiles is typically referred to as a modified RMP (mRMP) (see SWGDAM 2010). Genotypes are restricted to specific combinations using allele peak heights and mixture proportions, as described in Chapter 6 (see D.N.A. Box 6.4).

With the mRMP approach, it is sometimes only possible to interpret the major profile confidently as ambiguity may prevent complete deciphering of the minor component genotype(s) due to potential allele masking by the major alleles or potential allele drop-out with low-level minor components. Example calculations for two-person and three-person mixtures with mRMP have been published (Bille et al. 2013). This approach requires specific assumptions as to the number of contributors in the mixture.

Second, for indistinguishable mixtures, where allele peak heights and mixture proportions are similar, exclusion (or inclusion) probabilities may be calculated from the evidence profile. The random man not excluded (RMNE) approach utilizes combined probability of inclusion (CPI) statistics where all possible genotype combinations are given equal weight. A probability of inclusion (PI) calculation involves summing all of the observed alleles at a locus and then squaring this value to obtain the combination of all possible genotypes.

Individual locus PI values are multiplied to obtain an overall profile CPI. A CPI calculation is performed on the evidence and is therefore independent of any suspect's STR profile genotypes. A CPI statistic does not need any assumptions as to the number of contributors because it is calculating all possible combinations of genotypes based on the evidence profile results. A combined probability of exclusion (CPE) can also be determined, which is $1 - CPI$ (SWGDAM 2010).

Because each possible genotype is given an equal weight, this approach wastes information and is not very efficient when genotypes are in fact distinguishable.

Third, likelihood ratios (LRs) can be calculated where the weight of evidence is ascertained by examining the probability of observing the mixture data under one hypothesis compared to the probability of observing the mixture data under a second, mutually exclusive hypothesis. LRs can be unrestricted (if based on allele calls only) or restricted (if peak height information is used to limit the number of possible genotype combinations). When applied to two-person mixtures, a restricted LR is equivalent to the inverse of the mRMP except when there is no known contributor (Bille et al. 2013). LR calculations require an assumption as to the number of contributors in the mixture.

Table 12.1 compares these three methods in terms of the questions addressed, how a statistical answer is estimated, and specific requirements. More detail will be provided on these approaches later in the chapter.

TABLE 12.1 Comparison of Methods Used to Statistically Evaluate DNA Mixtures

Method	What Question Is Asked?	How Is the Answer Estimated?	Specific Requirements
Modified random match probability (mRMP)	Having inferred a specific major component (and possibly a minor component), what is the probability of the inferred profile occurring in a specific population based on population genetic models and STR allele frequencies? *Note*: This approach is dependent on the ability to reliably infer specific genotypes based on peak height information and will generally not work well with low-level data where stochastic effects occur.	Following mixture deconvolution where major and minor components are deduced using peak height information, the random match probability is calculated for deduced genotypes as if they originated from a single-source sample	Typically an assumption of two contributors; usually a 4:1 or greater major-to-minor component ratio to provide confidence that a clean separation can be obtained between the major and minor components so that specific genotypes can be inferred
Random man not excluded (RMNE)	What fraction of the population would not be excluded (i.e. would be included) as a potential contributor to the crime scene evidence mixture? *Note*: This statistic, which is calculated from the evidence result (Q profile), does not directly answer whether or not a specific suspect (known K profile) can be included in the mixture result. The Q-to-K profile comparison can be somewhat subjective with more complex mixtures.	Combined probability of inclusion (CPI) which involves giving equal weight to all potential genotypes based on alleles observed; is easily calculated by squaring the sum of frequencies of observed alleles	Alleles are all present (i.e. no allele drop-out), contributors are not related
Likelihood ratio (LR)	What is the weight of evidence for or against a specific suspect being in the crime scene evidence mixture? *Note*: LRs can be challenging to formulate with mixtures containing more than two contributors	Formulating a ratio of probabilities for the evidence under two different hypotheses with specific genotype combinations	An assumption as to the number of contributors and specification of a hypothesis for the prosecution (H_p) and a hypothesis for the defense (H_d)

See also Buckleton & Curran (2008), Bille et al. (2013).

NRC I and NRC II on DNA Mixtures

As described in Appendix 2, there have been two National Research Council (NRC) reports written on forensic DNA analysis: (NRC I) "DNA Technology in Forensic Science" published in 1992 and (NRC II) "The Evaluation of Forensic DNA Evidence" released in 1996. An examination of their discussions on DNA mixture interpretation is instructive. Some of these topics are still not fully appreciated by forensic DNA scientists almost two decades later.

On page 59 of NRC I (NRC 1992): "If the samples are mixtures from more than one person, one should see additional bands for all or most polymorphic probes, but not for a single-copy monomorphic probe. Mixed samples can be very difficult to interpret because the components can be present in different quantities and states of degradation. It is important to examine the results of multiple RFLPs, as a consistency check. Typically, it will be impossible to distinguish the individual genotypes of each contributor. If a suspect's pattern is found within the mixed pattern, the appropriate frequency to assign such a 'match' is *the sum of the frequencies of all genotypes that are contained within (i.e. that are a subset of) the mixed pattern.*" Emphasis has been added here to show what is a description of the combined probability of inclusion (CPI) statistic.

In NRC II (NRC 1996) the discussion of mixed samples is found on pages 129 and 130: "Mixed samples are sometimes found in crime situations — for instance, blood from two or more persons at the scene of a crime, victim and assailant samples on a vaginal swab, and material from multiple sexual assailants. … when the contributors to a mixture are not known or cannot otherwise be distinguished, *a likelihood ratio approach offers a clear advantage and is particularly suitable*" (emphasis added). The NRC II text continues by quoting the 1992 report page 59 statement (shown above) and an example CPI calculation is illustrated.

The top of page 130 begins (NRC 1996): "That [CPI] calculation is hard to justify, because it does not make use of some of the information available, namely, the genotype of the suspect. The correct procedure [i.e. the likelihood ratio approach], we believe, was described by Evett et al. (1991)." A simple example is then illustrated for the likelihood ratio approach. The text continues: "This LR [likelihood ratio], compared with that derived from the recommendation of the 1992 NRC report [i.e. CPI], is larger when the suspect bands are relatively rare and smaller when the suspect bands are relatively common. The reason is that *we have taken account of the information in the genotype of the suspect rather than averaging over the set of possible genotypes* consistent with the four-band evidence-sample profile" (emphasis added).

The text then notes (NRC 1996): "We have considered only simple cases. With VNTRs [variable number of tandem repeats], it is possible, though very unlikely, that the four bands were contributed by more than two persons, who were either homozygous or shared rare alleles. With multiple loci, it will usually be evident if the sample was contributed by more than two persons. Calculations taking those possibilities into account could be made if there were reason to believe that more than two persons contributed to the sample. …The problem is complex, and some forensic experts follow the practice of making several reasonable assumptions and then using the calculation that is most conservative. For a fuller treatment of mixed samples, see Weir et al. (1997)."

The final section of NRC II that deals with mixtures is found on pages 162 and 163 (NRC 1996): "Mixed stains introduce a number of complexities. We limit our consideration to cases in which the stain comes from two persons, but only one suspect is identified." …[In the case of potential allele drop-out], "the 2p rule may be needed." A table (NRC II, Table 5.1) provides some likelihood ratio formulas for each potential combination of crime scene and suspect genotypes in which there is either

TABLE 12.2   Likelihood Ratios for Mixed Stains Using p^2 Rule for True Homozygotes Assuming No Allele Drop-Out or $2p$ Rule for a False Homozygote Where Allele Drop-Out Has Occurred

Crime Scene (question genotype)	Suspect (known genotype)	Likelihood Ratio (assuming no drop-out, p^2)	Likelihood Ratio (assuming drop-out, $2p$)
PQRS	PQ	$\dfrac{1}{12pq}$	$\dfrac{1}{12pq}$
PQR	QR	$\dfrac{p + 2q + 2r}{12qr(p + q + r)}$	$\dfrac{1 + q + r}{12qr(p + q + r)}$
PQR	P	$\dfrac{1}{6p(p + q + r)}$	$\dfrac{1}{4p(3 + p + q + r)}$
PQ	PQ	$\dfrac{(p + q)^2}{2pq(3pq + 2p^2 + 2q^2)}$	$\dfrac{p + q + pq}{2pq(2 + 2p + 2q + pq)}$
PQ	P	$\dfrac{2p + q}{2p(3pq + 2p^2 + 2q^2)}$	$\dfrac{1 + p}{2p(2 + 2p + 2q + pq)}$

Allele frequencies (p, q, r, s) for observed alleles (P, Q, R, S) can be obtained from population databases, such as Appendix 1. Adapted from (NRC 1996, p. 163).

a false homozygote ($2p$) or a true homozygote (p^2). The information in this table has been reorganized and included in Table 12.2.

DNA Advisory Board 2000 Statement on Mixtures

The DNA Advisory Board (DAB) was a 13-member, congressionally mandated entity created and funded by the United States Congress DNA Identification Act of 1994. During its 1995–2000 tenure, the DAB discussed challenges facing forensic DNA and issued guidance to the community. Bruce Budowle (FBI Laboratory), Fred Bieber (Harvard Medical School, Boston), Ranajit Chakraborty (University of Texas Health Science Center, Houston), and George Carmody (Carleton University, Ottawa) formed the statistical subcommittee of the DAB and thus were involved in writing the February 2000 statistical issues statement that was published later in *Forensic Science Communications* (see Appendix 3).

A few excerpts from the DAB statistical issues document regarding mixtures are included below:

> "...*When intensity differences are sufficient to identify the major contributor in the mixed profile, it can be treated statistically as a single-source sample. At times, when alleles are not masked, a minor contributor to the mixed profile may be elucidated. Almost always in a mixture interpretation, certain possible genotypes can be excluded.* **It may be difficult to be confident regarding the number of contributors in some complex mixtures of more than two individuals**; *however, the number of contributors often can be inferred by reviewing the data at all loci in a profile.*

"...*When the contributors of a DNA mixture profile cannot be distinguished, two calculations convey the probative value of the evidence... The PE [probability of exclusion] provides an estimate of the portion of the population that has a genotype composed of at least one allele not observed in the mixed profile. Knowledge of the accused and/or victim profiles is not used (or needed) in the calculation. The calculation is particularly useful in analyses involving complex mixtures because it requires no assumptions about the identity or number of contributors to a mixture. The probabilities derived are valid and for all practical purposes are conservative. However, the PE does not make use of all of the available genetic data.*

"*Calculation of an LR considers the identity and actual number of contributors to the observed DNA mixture.* Certainly, LR makes better use of the available genetic data than does the PE. ... The DAB finds either one or both PE or LR calculations acceptable *and strongly recommends that one or both calculations be carried out whenever feasible and a mixture is indicated*" (DAB 2000, see Appendix 3, emphasis added).

When this statement was made in 2000 by the DAB, the types of mixtures being encountered in laboratories were mostly simple two-person mixtures primarily from sexual assault evidence (Clayton et al. 1998, Torres et al. 2003). Complex mixtures with three or more contributors were not routinely encountered by forensic DNA laboratories at that time. Therefore trying to extrapolate the DAB statement to the challenges faced with touch evidence today, in which allele drop-out is common, (see Chapter 13) is probably not appropriate.

ISFG 2006 Recommendations and SWGDAM 2010 Interpretation Guidelines

Chapter 6 introduces the July 2006 International Society for Forensic Genetics (ISFG) nine recommendations covering mixture interpretation principles and the SWGDAM 2010 interpretation guidelines (see Table 6.4).

The ISFG DNA Commission that issued the July 2006 mixture recommendations was chaired by Peter Gill (UK Forensic Science Service) and had as co-authors mathematicians and statisticians Charles Brenner (DNA View, Berkeley, California), John Buckleton (ESR, New Zealand), Michael Krawczak (Institute of Medical Informatics and Statistics, Kiel, Germany), and Bruce Weir (University of Washington, Seattle) in addition to the ISFG Board members Angel Carracedo (Spain), Wolfgang Mayr (Austria), Niels Morling (Denmark), Mecki Prinz (USA), and Peter Schneider (Germany).

A primary emphasis of the ISFG recommendations was the value of using the likelihood ratio as a preferred approach to mixture interpretation (Gill et al. 2006). Recommendation 1 notes that RMNE may not be conservative with low-level profiles (see Buckleton & Triggs 2006). Recommendation 2 encourages scientists to be trained in the likelihood ratio methodology and reminds the scientific community that it "has a responsibility to support improvement of standards of scientific reasoning in the court-room" (Gill et al. 2006).

As noted in Chapter 6, published support for the principles underlying the ISFG recommendations has come from the European DNA Profiling Group (EDNAP) and the European Network of Forensic Science Institutes (ENFSI) DNA working group (Morling et al. 2007), the UK DNA working group (Gill et al. 2008), an FBI-led mixture committee (Budowle et al. 2009), Australian and New Zealand forensic leadership (Stringer et al. 2009), and the German Stain Commission (Schneider et al. 2009).

Further guidance on the use of probabilistic genotyping for statistical analysis of DNA mixtures having the potential of allele drop-out and drop-in was published by the ISFG DNA Commission in December 2012 (Gill et al. 2012). This material will be discussed in Chapter 13.

SWGDAM approved interpretation guidelines in January 2010 that address mixture interpretation and statistical analysis. As reviewed earlier in this chapter, these SWGDAM guidelines require statistical analysis in support of any inclusion and documentation for assumptions and data used in generating numerical support for a conclusion. The SWGDAM guidelines review statistical principles and formulas for mRMP, CPI, and LR (SWGDAM 2010).

The "frequently asked questions" section of the SWGDAM website (SWGDAM FAQs 2014) states that the 2010 guidelines were "written with single-source samples and two-person mixtures in mind," and that while "the *basic concepts* outlined in the 2010 SWGDAM Mixture Interpretation Guidelines hold true as they relate to DNA mixtures of three or more contributors, low-level DNA samples, and mixtures containing biologically related individuals…there are nuances and limitations to the interpretation of these more complex mixtures, which are not fully explored in the 2010 guidelines" (emphasis in the original). This statement by SWGDAM also encourages laboratories to "perform additional validation studies of complex mixtures to further their understanding of the issues related to these challenging samples."

Allele Masking and Handling Alleles in the Stutter Position

Two primary challenges with interpreting DNA mixtures involve allele masking and handling potential minor contributor alleles in the stutter position of major contributor alleles. Allele masking results when two STR alleles from different contributors are indistinguishable in terms of size. Since these same-size alleles comigrate through the capillary electrophoresis separation process, their individual signals stack on top of each other. This is known as *allele sharing* or *allele stacking*. The outcome for a minor allele is *allele masking* by a major allele. In other words, the smaller height minor allele is hidden within the taller peak height of the major allele.

Sometimes multiple minor alleles can add up to produce the appearance of a false apparent major allele (see Figure 6.6). Allele masking and stacking present a problem for mixture interpretation because it is impossible to know exactly how much of the peak-height signal arises from one mixture component versus another. Assumptions can be made to partition part of a potential shared allele peak height to different potential contributor genotypes through assuming a certain peak height ratio with a potential sister allele peak (see example in Appendix 4 and Figure A4.4).

In the Figure 12.2 example, the "stutter?" labeled peaks can be categorized as *indistinguishable from stutter* (Heidebrecht 2013). When minor alleles have peak heights that are similar in amount to stutters of major alleles, then these stutter peaks and minor alleles are indistinguishable and may need to be accounted for in the interpretation of the profile (Gill et al. 2006, SWGDAM 2010). Depending on the assumed number of contributors in the STR profile, those indistinguishable from stutter peaks could be part of a minor component.

In the case of Figure 12.2, if we assume two contributors, then the PQ (major) and RS (minor) account for all of the possible genotypes and the peaks at allele positions 13, 15, and 17 can be assumed to be only stutter peaks of alleles 14, 16, and 18. However, if the number of contributors is not assumed (as with a CPI calculation) or if the number of potential contributors can reasonably be assumed to be greater than two, then these peaks have to be considered as alleles that could: (1) potentially pair with alleles masked by the major allele peaks (P and Q) or (2) potentially form genotypes with the minor allele peaks (R and S) or alleles masked by these minor peaks. Ambiguity increases as the potential number of contributors increases.

REPORTING MATCH PROBABILITIES ON DEDUCED COMPONENTS

In some cases it may be possible to confidently pull apart the alleles from individual contributors to a mixture. In cases of sexual assault, the victim's DNA profile is typically compared to the mixed profile and this comparison may be helpful in identifying the STR alleles present in the perpetrator's DNA profile.

The DNA Advisory Board recommendations on statistics issued in February 2000 state that "when intensity differences are sufficient to identify the major contributor in the mixed profile, it can be treated statistically as a single source sample" (DAB 2000; see Appendix 3). In such a situation, after deciphering the individual components for the major and minor contributors, the statistical treatment of their profiles could be conducted as described in Chapter 11 for single-source samples.

Interpretation of genotypes present in a mixture is much more complicated when the contributions of the donors are approximately equal and thus a major contributor cannot be definitively determined, or when true alleles for a contributor are masked by stutter products (see Chapter 6) or other alleles in the mixture. It is not always possible to unambiguously determine all of the alleles present in a mixture, especially with a partial profile from a degraded DNA sample. Likewise, it is not always possible to infer the complete genotypes of all contributors with a high degree of confidence because the mixture combination may be too complex to easily decipher.

Computer programs using probabilistic genotyping approaches (see Chapter 13) have been developed to help interpret DNA mixtures that are too complex to easily solve by manually considering all potential combinations (Perlin et al. 2013, Balding 2013, Taylor et al. 2013).

RANDOM MAN NOT EXCLUDED (RMNE)

A statistical significance can be placed on a DNA mixture following the interpretation process using the combined probability of inclusion (CPI) method (DAB 2000, Ladd et al. 2001). The random man not excluded (RMNE) concept, which utilizes the CPI calculation, was originally developed for paternity testing (Devlin 1993). This probability-of-inclusion statistic provides an estimate of the portion of the population that has a genotype composed of at least one allele observed in the mixed profile. Alternatively, results can be reported from the other perspective with the combined probability of exclusion (CPE). CPE and CPI add up to 1, so as mentioned earlier, CPE = 1 − CPI.

In the example data illustrated in Figure 12.2, determination of CPI would involve calculation of the frequency of genotypes that possess the alleles 14, 16, 18, and 19 present in the evidentiary mixed profile. Depending on the peak heights of the "stutter?" peaks in Figure 12.2, they may need to also be considered in the CPI calculation.

The CPI approach avoids the potential pitfalls associated with attempting to decipher specific genotype combinations of mixture contributors (e.g. overlooking a true allele because it is in a stutter position). No prior knowledge or assumptions regarding the number of possible contributors to the mixture are needed and results can still be reported without knowledge of a known profile, such as the victim's profile. Problems can arise when trying to associate the mixture profile to a specific suspect. Determining whether a suspect is included or excluded from the mixture is a separate step (Buckleton & Curran 2008) that can sometimes be subjective.

While calculating the CPI is not as powerful a technique as the likelihood ratio method that is discussed in the next section, a supposed advantage with the CPI approach is that the number of contributors to the crime scene DNA profile does not need to be taken into account. Simply all alleles observed in the stain are considered in the CPI statistic. In principle, this approach is considered conservative because an individual can be excluded if he/she has any allele at any locus that is not detected in the stain. However, as will be seen in the next chapter, things are not always quite so simple when allele drop-out is a possibility, and attempts are being made to interpret low-level DNA results.

The inclusion probability reflects the combined frequency of all genotypes that can be included in a mixture, assuming Hardy—Weinberg equilibrium for the genotype frequencies (see Chapter 10). CPI is based on the evidence only. Selecting different loci for comparison purposes, something often referred to as "suspect-driven CPI" is inappropriate since decisions on which loci are suitable for comparison should be made prior to doing a comparison to reference sample(s).

What often makes CPI a subjective process with some DNA mixtures is that decisions about whether a reference sample is appropriately included in the mixture are made outside of the statistical framework. LR methods, on the other hand, actually address the question of the suspect's profile, locus-by-locus, genotype-by-genotype.

Example CPI Calculation

For the locus on the left in D.N.A. Box 12.2 with alleles 13, 14, 15, and 16, a CPI calculation accounts for genotypes 13,13 and 14,14 and 15,15 and 16,16 (four homozygotes) as well as 13,14 and 13,15 and 13,16 and 14,15 and 14,16 and 15,16 (six heterozygotes). Under a CPI approach, no consideration is given to the relative peak heights present in the four alleles. Alleles 13, 14, 15, and 16 for this locus are effectively being viewed as equal in intensity.

All possible genotypes are considered with equal probabilities in RMNE (Table 12.3). Thus, with a CPI calculation, a homozygote (such as r^2) is given the same weight as a heterozygote (e.g. $2pr$) that may fit the mixture pattern better. In the D.N.A. Box 12.2 (left locus) example, only two genotypes are reasonable due to relative peak height ratios when assuming two contributors: 13,16 and 14,15. The

TABLE 12.3 Possible Genotypes Considered with Equal Probabilities for Random Man Not Excluded (RMNE) Approach using Combined Probability of Inclusion (CPI) Calculations

Alleles Observed in Mixture	Possible Genotypes	Genotype Frequencies for RMNE = (sum of allele frequencies)^2
1 allele: P	PP	$p^2 = p^2$
2 alleles: P, Q	PP, QQ, PQ	$p^2 + q^2 + 2pq = (p + q)^2$
3 alleles: P, Q, R	PP, QQ, RR, PQ, PR, QR	$p^2 + q^2 + r^2 + 2pq + 2pr + 2qr$ $= (p + q + r)^2$
4 alleles: P, Q, R, S	PP, QQ, RR, SS, PQ, PR, PS, QR, QS, RS	$p^2 + q^2 + r^2 + s^2 + 2pq + 2pr + 2ps + 2qr + 2qs + 2rs = (p + q + r + s)^2$
5 alleles: P, Q, R, S, T	PP, QQ, RR, SS, TT, PQ, PR, PS, PT, QR, QS, QT, RS, RT, ST	$p^2 + q^2 + r^2 + s^2 + t^2 + 2pq + 2pr + 2ps + 2pt + 2qr + 2qs + 2qt + 2rs + 2rt + 2st$ $= (p + q + r + s + t)^2$
6 alleles: P, Q, R, S, T, U	PP, QQ, RR, SS, TT, UU, PQ, PR, PS, PT, PU, QR, QS, QT, QU, RS, RT, RU, ST, SU, TU	$p^2 + q^2 + r^2 + s^2 + t^2 + u^2 + 2pq + 2pr + 2ps + 2pt + 2pu + 2qr + 2qs + 2qt + 2qu + 2rs + 2rt + 2ru + 2st + 2su + 2tu$ $= (p + q + r + s + t + u)^2$

use of additional genotypes in the statistical calculation effectively dilutes the overall statistic and robs it of its potential probative power. Note that the more observed alleles there are, the more unreasonable genotypes there are.

The CPE wastes a lot of information from the evidentiary sample because not all of these possibilities are equally probable. Likelihood ratios, on the other hand, are specific to the case scenario of interest. With LR calculations, data are evaluated to see how well they address a proposition that the mixture is composed of specific combinations of genotypes that happen to match the individuals of interest in the case.

Limitations of CPI/CPE

Since all possible genotype combinations need to be considered with CPI, all observed alleles need to be included in the calculation. SWGDAM 2010 Guideline 4.6.3 states: "When using CPE/CPI (with no assumptions of number of contributors) to calculate the probability that a randomly selected person would be excluded/included as a contributor to the mixture, loci with alleles below the stochastic threshold may not be used for statistical purposes to support an inclusion. In these instances, *the potential for allelic drop-out raises the possibility of contributors having genotypes not encompassed by the interpreted alleles*" (SWGDAM 2010, emphasis added).

CPI Is Not an Interpretation Tool!

CPI is a statistical calculation and should not be used as an interpretation tool. Analysts should interpret their evidentiary profiles by examining potential genotype combinations considering relative peak heights, potential minor alleles in stutter positions of major contributors, etc. Unfortunately, through simply looking at the presence of alleles and blindly applying a stochastic threshold (see Chapter 4) to decide when loci should be dropped from statistical calculations, some analysts have inappropriately used CPI as an *interpretation* tool.

One of the most significant deficiencies of the CPI calculation is that this approach does not take into account an alternative hypothesis. How can you make an informed opinion on a topic if you consider only a single point of view? This is why likelihood ratios are essential in mixture interpretation and why they have been strongly recommended by the ISFG DNA Commission (Gill et al. 2006) — because two different possibilities are compared in developing an opinion. In the words of Professor Max Baur of Bonn University in Germany: "RMNE is a deficient method and we should not use it!" (Author notes from ISFG 2009 conference).

LIKELIHOOD RATIOS

The likelihood ratio (LR) is the ratio of possibilities under alternative propositions and provides a reliable method that is able to make full use of available genetic data (Evett & Weir 1998, Buckleton & Curran 2008). Two competing hypotheses are set up: the hypothesis of the prosecution (H_p), which is that the defendant committed the crime, and the hypothesis of the defense (H_d), that some unknown individual committed the crime. Thus, the LR involves a ratio describing the probability of the evidence given the prosecution's hypothesis over the probability of the evidence given the defense's hypothesis:

$$LR = \frac{Pr(E|H_p)}{Pr(E|H_d)}$$

Unfortunately, determination of which hypotheses to consider is not necessarily straightforward. Interpretation of a mixture depends on the circumstances of the case and involves assumptions about the identity and number of contributors to the mixture in question. LR calculations are more widely used in Europe than in the United States for forensic applications. Paternity testing routinely uses LR calculations (see Chapter 14). The LR method makes better use of the available genetic data than does the CPI method discussed previously (Buckleton & Curran 2008).

If evidence contains four alleles at a locus (P, Q, R, and S) and the victim possesses R and S while the suspect exhibits P and Q, then the prosecution's hypothesis would be that the DNA evidence is from the victim and the suspect. On the other hand, the defense's hypothesis would be that the DNA evidence is from the victim and an unknown person. The probability of the prosecution's hypothesis is one because their position is that they are 100% confident (probability = 1) that the defendant committed the crime, which is why the trial is occurring in the first place.

The defense's hypothesis can vary depending on the circumstances of the case, such as the number of other possible contributors under consideration and the alleles present in the evidentiary DNA profile. The H_d considers that the suspect is truly innocent and the DNA profile came from an unknown, unrelated individual. The likelihood ratio describes the relative chance of observing a specific mixture and combination of STR alleles. Some LR examples for various scenarios are listed in Table 12.2. Hypothesis statements for three general categories of two-person mixtures are provided in Table 12.4.

TABLE 12.4   Three General Categories of Two-Person Mixture Likelihood Ratio (LR) Calculations

Category	Hypothesis Statements for Prosecution (H_p) and Defense (H_d)	Likelihood Ratio
1	H_p: mixture contains the DNA of the victim and the suspect H_d: mixture contains the DNA of the victim and an unknown, unrelated person	$LR = \dfrac{V + S}{V + U}$
	H_p: mixture contains the DNA of the suspect and the victim H_d: mixture contains the DNA of the suspect and an unknown, unrelated person	$LR = \dfrac{V + S}{S + U}$
2	H_p: mixture contains the DNA of suspect 1 and suspect 2 H_d: mixture contains the DNA of two unknown, unrelated people	$LR = \dfrac{S1 + S2}{U1 + U2}$
	H_p: mixture contains the DNA of victim 1 and victim 2 H_d: mixture contains the DNA of two unknown, unrelated people	$LR = \dfrac{V1 + V2}{U1 + U2}$
3	H_p: mixture contains the DNA of the suspect and an unknown, unrelated person H_d: mixture contains the DNA of two unknown, unrelated people	$LR = \dfrac{S + U}{U1 + U2}$
	H_p: mixture contains the DNA of the victim and an unknown, unrelated person H_d: mixture contains the DNA of two unknown, unrelated people	$LR = \dfrac{V + U}{U1 + U2}$

LRs are formulated from possible genotype combinations of match probabilities for victim (V), suspect (S), and unknown, unrelated person (U). Adapted from Buckleton et al. (2005), p. 226.

TABLE 12.5   Various Likelihood Ratio (LR) Formats

LR Formats	Verbal Description of Equation Involved
Hypothesis form	$$\text{information gain in hypothesis} = \frac{\text{Odds}(hypothesis|data)}{\text{Odds}(hypothesis)}$$
Likelihood form	$$\text{information gain in likelihood} = \frac{\Pr(data|identification\ hypothesis)}{\Pr(data|alternative\ hypothesis)}$$
Genotype form	$$\text{information gain in genotype} = \frac{\Pr(evidence\ genotype)}{\Pr(coincidental\ genotype)}$$
Match form	$$\text{information gain in match} = \frac{\Pr(evidence\ match)}{\Pr(coincidental\ match)}$$

The likelihood form is what is commonly used in forensic DNA literature. TrueAllele software uses the match form. Adapted from Perlin (2010).

As introduced previously in Chapter 9 and Chapter 11, likelihood ratios evaluate "what if" scenarios by comparing two opinions or hypotheses against one another. These two hypotheses (H_p and H_d) must be mutually exclusive, which means that their proposed ideas do not overlap. All LR calculations make assumptions about the number of contributors. These calculations are all "conditional" — that is, they make specific assumptions. If peak height information is utilized to confidently pair alleles into genotypes, then "restricted" sets of genotypes are deduced. If the mixture does not contain a discernible major and minor contributor, then an "unrestricted" approach is typically used where all possible genotype combinations are permitted for the detected alleles (see D.N.A. Box 6.4).

There are multiple formats whereby likelihood ratios can be reported (Table 12.5). The most commonly used form in forensic DNA publications is the likelihood form. The TrueAllele software developed by Cybergenetics (Pittsburgh, PA) uses the match form in which the LR is calculated by evaluating the probability of the evidence match (i.e. between the mixture and the suspect) against the probability of a coincidental match (i.e. between the mixture and an unknown, unrelated individual) (Perlin et al. 2009, Perlin 2010).

Example LR Calculation

Table 12.6 contains a simple worked example using the illustrated data from Figure 12.2. Readers are referred to a more detailed example that is provided in Appendix 4.

Rather than reporting very large LR values, many computer programs, such as TrueAllele (Perlin et al. 2013) or likeLTD (Balding 2013) prefer to report their weight of evidence values on a logarithmic

TABLE 12.6 Example of mRMP, CPI, and LR Calculations Using Data Illustrated in Figure 12.2

Method	Peak Height Ratios Used	Genotype Combinations Considered	Calculations Suspect = 14,16 Victim = 18,19
mRMP	Yes	Major: PQ (2pq) = 14,16 Minor: RS (2rs) = 18,19	Inferred genotype 14,16 matches suspect genotype 14,16 2pq = 2(0.134)(0.147) = 0.0394 **1 in 25.4**
RMNE (CPI)	No	Depending on peak heights: P, Q, R, S plus peaks in stutter positions (13, 15, 17) allele frequencies to be used in CPI calculations = 13, 14, 15, 16, 17, 18, 19	*Inconclusive if any peaks in stutter position are below stochastic threshold (and assuming potential contributor alleles are a portion of these peak heights)* If CPI calculation is performed: $(0.123 + 0.134 + 0.170 + 0.147 + 0.139 + 0.0776 + 0.0402)^2 = (0.831)^2 = 0.691$ = 69.1% of population could be included **1 in 1.45**
LR (restricted)	Yes	PQ with RS	$$LR = \frac{V + S}{V + U} = \frac{1}{2pq} = \frac{1}{2(0.134)(0.147)}$$ LR = **25.4**
LR (unrestricted)	No	When conditioning on the victim's genotype, in this case the unrestricted LR is the same as the restricted LR because victim and suspect are fully represented without any ambiguity in possible genotype combinations	$$LR = \frac{V + S}{V + U} = \frac{1}{2pq} = \frac{1}{2(0.134)(0.147)}$$ LR = **25.4**

D18S51 allele frequencies were from U.S. Caucasians in Appendix 1.

scale to compress the data and make it a little easier to compare among sample results. The log(LR) is sometimes referred to as a "ban" (D.N.A. Box 12.3).

ADDITIONAL TOPICS

Interpretation of mixtures can be quite complicated, such as in the case of *People of the State of California versus Orenthal James Simpson* (Weir & Buckleton 1996). However, interpretations in that particular case would probably have been simplified if STR testing had been available at the time; STRs have more possible alleles than the dot blot methods used to recover DNA evidence in the O.J. Simpson trial.

Evett and Weir (1998) note that the essence of mixture interpretation is to first identify the alleles in the crime scene evidence sample and alleles carried by the known contributor(s) to the sample, such as the victim. Then any alleles present in the evidence sample that are not provided by the known

---

D.N.A. BOX 12.3

THE "BAN" AS A WAY TO REPRESENT LARGE NUMBERS

In 1940, while working to crack the communication code used by the German navy with their Enigma cipher machine, British mathematician Alan Turing and his colleague Irving John (I.J.) "Jack" Good proposed a unit of measure to simplify weight-of-evidence (WoE) descriptions. Their method involved condensing numerical information reflecting the WoE towards a particular hypothesis (i.e. a likelihood ratio) through applying base 10 logarithms, where $\log_{10}$(number) = x ban. (Computers store information in "bits" (binary digits) based on powers of 2 and base 2 logarithms). Thus, instead of having to record the number one million (1,000,000) with seven digits, it can be reduced to 10^6 or simply 6 ban. Because the long sheets of paper used to work on code breaking came from Banbury, England, the cryptanalysis process was referred to as Banburismus. Thus, Turing's logarithmic unit of measurement for the WoE became the "**ban.**" This unit of measurement has also been referred to as a **hartley** (named for Ralph Hartley who proposed it in 1928) or a **dit** (decimal digit).

A few examples are worked below to show the relationship between a number and its ban value.

Number	Number in powers of 10	Ban
10	10^1	1
100	10^2	2
1,000,000	10^6	6
1,547,623	1.547623×10^6	6.189665

TrueAllele software (Cybergenetics, Pittsburgh, PA) utilizes the ban in its mixture match statistics (Perlin 2010), as does David Balding with his likeLTD program (Balding 2013). Thus, a likelihood ratio (LR) of 10^{12} is reported by its $\log_{10}$(LR) value, which is 12.

Sources: Good, I.J. (1985). Weight-of-evidence: a brief survey. Bayesian Statistics, 2, 249–270; http://en.wikipedia.org/wiki/ Ban_(information); http://en.wikipedia.org/wiki/Banburismus; Perlin, M.W. (2010). Explaining the likelihood ratio in DNA mixture interpretation. Proceedings of the 21st International Symposium on Human Identification *(Promega Corporation). Available at http://www.cybgen.com/ information/publication/page.shtml.; Balding, D.J. (2013). Evaluation of mixed-source, low-template DNA profiles in forensic science. Proceedings of the National Academy of Sciences of the United States of America, 110(30), 12241–12246.*

---

contributor(s) must be carried by one or more unknown contributors, which may or may not include the suspect.

The DNA Advisory Board recommends that either or both CPE and LR calculations be performed whenever feasible when a mixture exists (DAB 2000). However, there will be mixture results for which no interpretation of the profile can be made due to low-copy number stochastic limits, DNA template degradation or PCR inhibition. In the end, the interpretation of results in forensic casework, whether arising from single-source samples or mixtures, is a matter of professional judgment and expertise.

Mixtures will be complicated by the fact that some loci will possess intensity differences that permit contributors to be deciphered, while other loci may not be fully interpretable due to overlapping allele combinations. With STRs and peak intensity differences, some loci may be interpretable so that contributors can be statistically treated as single sources, while other loci may be too complex to confidently attribute alleles to their sources. Thus, when performing mixture interpretation, analysts should do everything possible to first eliminate artifacts such as stutter products from consideration and then interpret remaining alleles to determine how many contributors are present.

Partial DNA Profiles

Interpretation of a DNA profile can only be performed on loci for which there are results. Unfortunately, with degraded DNA specimens or low-copy number samples (see Chapter 7) the PCR amplification may fail to generate signals above the detection threshold of the instrument, and individual alleles and entire loci may be lost from the final DNA profile. Foreman and Evett (2001) note that partial profiles occur in approximately 20% of cases seen by the Forensic Science Service. Given that it is often not possible to know what alleles would have been present had the sample not been degraded, the standard practice is to interpret only the detected alleles.

Obtaining matching alleles between a full-profile suspect and a partial-profile evidentiary sample is not as powerful as a full-profile to full-profile match. However, any data is better than none. Even if results are obtained from only a few STR loci, this information may provide ample assistance to either include or exclude the suspect and therefore aid in resolving the case.

Occasionally results from additional loci may be recovered from degraded DNA samples through the use of miniSTR primer sets or other genetic systems such as single nucleotide polymorphisms that amplify smaller regions of the DNA template (see Butler 2012). Finally, in most cases, the forensic sample has been divided into two or more parts so that unused portions are retained to permit additional tests as desired by the court according to NRC II recommendation 3.3 (see Appendix 2). These retained samples can be tested as occasion warrants in order to verify previous test results.

Software

GeneMapper*ID-X* has a mixture interpretation function that can be used for calculating two-person LRs and CPI with more than two-person mixtures (Hansson & Gill 2011). However, laboratories often create their own spreadsheet programs to perform LR or CPI calculations. Validation can be tedious as manual calculations are often performed to evaluate formulas used and mathematical operations performed by the software.

A number of software programs have been developed recently to perform probabilistic genotyping and to cope with potential allele drop-out (see Table 13.1). ISFG supports an open-source software resource page on forensic statistics packages (ISFG 2014). A list of available programs is available on the NIST STRBase website mixture section (NIST 2014).

Historical Perspectives on Approaches Used for Mixture Statistics

Historical perspectives are often valuable to provide an understanding of where we as a forensic DNA community have come over the past several decades. Hopefully we can learn from the past as we try to move forward into the future in a productive manner. Table 12.7 reviews the use of LR and CPI approaches with some key events in each area. Publications cited in the table can be found in the reference list at the back of the chapter.

TABLE 12.7 Brief Historical Timeline Comparison of Likelihood Ratio (LR) and Combined Probability of Inclusion (CPI)/Random Man Not Excluded (RMNE) Approaches to DNA Mixture Interpretation

LR

1977	Dennis Lindley describes value of LRs in forensic science interpretation
1991	Ian Evett et al. publish first work with LRs for DNA mixtures
1995	Bruce Weir uses LRs in OJ Simpson case
1996	NRC II (p. 130) endorses Evett et al. 1991 LR approach
1997	Bruce Weir et al. describe LRs for mixtures
1998	Ian Evett & Bruce Weir publish their book *Interpreting DNA Evidence*
2005	John Buckleton et al. publish book *Forensic DNA Evidence Interpretation*
2005	David Balding publishes book *Weight-of-evidence for Forensic DNA Profiles*
2006	ISFG DNA Commission recommends LR over CPI
2009	Mark Perlin describes his match likelihood ratio approach used in TrueAllele
2009	ISFG session in Buenos Aires debates LR and CPI
2010	SWGDAM guidelines provide RMP, CPI, and LR as possibilities
2012	ISFG DNA Commission discusses LR with drop-out
2013	Articles are published describing probabilistic genotyping software approaches (TrueAllele and STRmix)

RMNE (CPI)

1982	RMNE (CPI) used for paternity testing
1992	NRC I (p. 59) mentions CPI calculation for mixtures
1993	Bernie Devlin article discusses CPI for paternity testing
2000	DAB Stats document (see Appendix 3) states that either CPI or LR can be used with DNA mixtures and uses Devlin 1993 article as support for CPI; simple two-person mixtures are implied as this was what all laboratories were doing at the time
2001	Carl Ladd et al. publish review article that promotes use of CPI
2008	John Buckleton & James Curran discuss CPI and LR pros and cons
2009	Bruce Budowle et al. defend CPI in *Journal of Forensic Sciences* article on mixtures
2009	Max Baur mentions deficiencies of CPI at ISFG session
2010	Buckleton & Curran publish article on possibility of false inclusion with CPI
2010	SWGDAM guidelines provide RMP, CPI, and LR as possibilities
2011	Charles Brenner attacks CPI deficiencies at AAFS meeting
2013	Problems with CPI are reviewed at DNA Technical Leader Summit

As DNA testing has shown its value to the criminal justice community, more samples and more mixtures have been added to the docket of DNA analysts. As has been stated multiple times in this book, increased detection sensitivity means more challenges for interpretation. Complex mixtures containing more than two contributors add to the challenge of determining if a suspect should be included or excluded, especially if allele drop-out is possible. This is the subject of the next chapter.

Reading List and Internet Resources

General Information

Balding, D. J. (2005). *Weight-of-evidence for Forensic DNA Profiles*. John Wiley & Sons. see mixture section on pp. 101−110.

Butler, J. M. (2012). *DNA extraction methods. Chapter 2 in* Advanced Topics in Forensic DNA Typing: Methodology. San Diego: Elsevier Academic Press. pp. 29−47.

Clayton, T. M., et al. (1998). Analysis and interpretation of mixed forensic stains using DNA STR profiling. *Forensic Science International, 91*, 55−70.

Clayton, T., & Buckleton, J. (2005). *Mixtures. Chapter 7 in* Forensic DNA Evidence Interpretation, J. Buckleton, C. M. Triggs, & S. J. Walsh (Eds.) (pp. 217−274). Boca Raton, Florida: CRC Press.

Crespillo, M., et al. (2014). GHEP-ISFG collaborative exercise on mixture profiles of autosomal STRs (GHEP-MIX01, GHEP-MIX02 and GHEP-MIX03): results and evaluation. *Forensic Science International: Genetics, 10*, 64−72.

DNA Advisory Board. (2000). Statistical and population genetics issues affecting the evaluation of the frequency of occurrence of DNA profiles calculated from pertinent population database(s). *Forensic Science Communications, 2*(3). Available at http://www.fbi.gov/about-us/lab/forensic-science-communications/fsc/july2000/dnastat.htm/. Accessed April 2, 2014.

Gill, P., et al. (2006). DNA commission of the International Society of Forensic Genetics: Recommendations on the interpretation of mixtures. *Forensic Science International, 160*, 90−101.

Gill, P., et al. (2008). National recommendations of the technical UK DNA working group on mixture interpretation for the NDNAD and for court going purposes. *Forensic Science International: Genetics, 2*, 76−82.

Gill, P., et al. (2012). DNA Commission of the International Society of Forensic Genetics: Recommendations on the evaluation of STR typing results that may include drop-out and/or drop-in using probabilistic methods. *Forensic Science International: Genetics, 6*(6), 679−688.

Hansson, O., & Gill, P. (2011). Evaluation of GeneMapperID-X mixture analysis tool. *Forensic Science International: Genetics Supplement Series, 3*, e11−e12.

Heidebrecht, B. J. (2013). *Mixture interpretation (interpretation of mixed DNA profiles with STRs only). Encyclopedia of Forensic Sciences, Second Edition*. San Diego: Elsevier Academic Press. pp. 243−251.

International Society for Forensic Genetics (ISFG). (2014). *Forensic Software Resources*. http://www.isfg.org/software. Accessed April 2, 2014.

Ladd, C., et al. (2001). Interpretation of complex forensic DNA mixtures. *Croatian Medical Journal, 42*, 244−246.

National Research Council. (1992). *DNA Technology in Forensic Science*. Washington, DC: National Academy Press.

National Research Council (NRCII) Committee on DNA Forensic Science. (1996). *The Evaluation of Forensic DNA Evidence*. Washington, DC: National Academy Press.

NIST. (2014). DNA Mixture Interpretation. http://www.cstl.nist.gov/strbase/mixture.htm. Accessed April 2, 2014.

Puch-Solis, R., et al. (2012). *Assessing the probative value of DNA evidence: guidance for judges, lawyers, forensic scientists and expert witnesses. Practitioner Guide No. 2. Prepared under the auspices of the Royal Statistical Society's Working Group on Statistics and the Law (Chairman: Colin Aitken)*. Available at http://www.rss.org.uk/uploadedfiles/userfiles/files/Practitioner-Guide-2-WEB.pdf. Accessed April 2, 2014.

Robertson, B., & Vignaux, G. A. (1995). *DNA evidence: wrong answers or wrong questions?* Human Identification: The Use of DNA Markers. In B. S. Weir (Ed.) (pp. 145−152). The Netherlands: Kluwer Academic Publishers.

Roman, J. K., et al. (2008). *The DNA field experiment: cost-effectiveness analysis of the use of DNA in the investigation of high-volume crimes*. Washington, DC: Urban Institute Justice Policy Center. Available at https://www.ncjrs.gov/pdffiles1/nij/grants/222318.pdf. Accessed April 2, 2014.

Schneider, P. M., et al. (2009). The German Stain Commission: recommendations for the interpretation of mixed stains. *International Journal of Legal Medicine, 123*, 1−5 (originally published in German in 2006 − Rechtsmedizin 16:401−404).

Stringer, P., et al. (2009). Interpretation of DNA mixtures — Australian and New Zealand consensus on principles. *Forensic Science International: Genetics, 3*, 144–145.

SWGDAM. (2014). *Frequently Asked Questions (FAQs)*. http://swgdam.org/faq.html. Accessed April 2, 2014.

SWGDAM. (2010). *SWGDAM Interpretation Guidelines for Autosomal STR Typing by Forensic DNA Testing Laboratories*. Available at http://swgdam.org/Interpretation_Guidelines_January_2010.pdf. Accessed April 2, 2014.

Torres, Y., et al. (2003). DNA mixtures in forensic casework: a 4-year retrospective study. *Forensic Science International, 134*, 180–186.

Yu, N., et al. (2002). Disputed maternity leading to identification of tetragametic chimerism. *New England Journal of Medicine, 346*, 1545–1552.

Random Match Probability

Bille, T., et al. (2013). Application of random match probability calculations to mixed STR profiles. *Journal of Forensic Sciences, 58*(2), 474–485.

Buckleton, J., & Triggs, C. (2006). Is the 2p rule always conservative? *Forensic Science International, 159*, 206–209.

Random Man Not Excluded

Buckleton, J. S., & Curran, J. M. (2008). A discussion of the merits of random man not excluded and likelihood ratios. *Forensic Science International: Genetics, 2*, 343–348.

Buckleton, J., Triggs, C. M., & Walsh, S. J. (2005). *Forensic DNA Evidence Interpretation*. Boca Raton, Florida: CRC Press.

Budowle, B., et al. (2009). Mixture interpretation: defining the relevant features for guidelines for the assessment of mixed DNA profiles in forensic casework. *Journal of Forensic Sciences, 54*, 810–821.

Curran, J. M., & Buckleton, J. (2010). Inclusion probabilities and dropout. *Journal of Forensic Science, 55*, 1171–1173.

Devlin, B. (1993). Forensic inference from genetic markers. *Statistical Methods in Medical Research, 2*, 241–262.

Morling, N., et al. (2007). Interpretation of DNA mixtures — European consensus on principles. *Forensic Science International: Genetics, 1*, 291–292.

Van Nieuwerburgh, F., et al. (2009a). Impact of allelic dropout on evidential value of forensic DNA profiles using RMNE. *Bioinformatics, 25*, 225–229.

Van Nieuwerburgh, F., et al. (2009b). RMNE probability of forensic DNA profiles with allelic drop-out. *Forensic Science International: Genetics Supplement Series, 2*, 462–463.

Likelihood Ratios

Brenner, C. H. (1997). Proof of a mixed stain formula of Weir. *Journal of Forensic Sciences, 42*, 221–222.

Curran, J. M., et al. (1999). Interpreting DNA mixtures in structured populations. *Journal of Forensic Sciences, 44*, 987–995.

Curran, J. M., et al. (2005). Interpretation of repeat measurement DNA evidence allowing for multiple contributors and population substructure. *Forensic Science International, 148*, 47–53.

Cybergenetics publications: http://www.cybgen.com/information/publication/page.shtml. Accessed April 2, 2014.

Dørum, G., et al. (2014). Exact computation of the distribution of likelihood ratios with forensic applications. *Forensic Science International: Genetics, 9*, 93–101.

Evett, I. W., et al. (1991). A guide to interpreting single locus profiles of DNA mixtures in forensic cases. *Journal of Forensic Science Society, 31*(1), 41–47.

Evett, I. W., & Weir, B. S. (1998). *Interpreting DNA Evidence: Statistical Genetics for Forensic Scientists*. Sunderland, MA: Sinauer Associates.

Fung, W. K., & Hu, Y.-Q. (2008). *Statistical DNA Forensics: Theory, Methods and Computation*. Hoboken, NJ: Wiley.

Fung, W. K., & Hu, Y.-Q. (2001). The evaluation of mixed stains from different ethnic origins: general result and common cases. *International Journal of Legal Medicine, 115*, 48–53.

Fung, W. K., & Hu, Y.-Q. (2002). Evaluating mixed stains with contributors of different ethnic groups under the NRC-II Recommendation 4.1. *Statistics in Medicine, 21*, 3583–3593.

Fung, W. K., & Hu, Y.-Q. (2002). The statistical evaluation of DNA mixtures with contributors from different ethnic groups. *International Journal of Legal Medicine, 116*, 79–86.

Fung, W. K., et al. (2006). On statistical analysis of forensic DNA: theory, methods and computer programs. *Forensic Science International, 162*, 17–23.

Hu, Y.-Q., & Fung, W. K. (2003). Evaluating forensic DNA mixtures with contributors of different structured ethnic origins: a computer software. *International Journal of Legal Medicine, 117*, 248–249.

Lindley, D. V. (1977). A problem in forensic science. *Biometrika, 64*, 207–213.

Pascali, V. L., & Merigioli, S. (2012). Joint Bayesian analysis of forensic mixtures. *Forensic Science International: Genetics, 6*, 735–748.

Perlin, M. W. (2006). Scientific validation of mixture interpretation methods. *Proceedings of Promega's Seventeenth International Symposium on Human Identification.* Available at http://www.promega.com/products/pm/genetic-identity/ishi-conference-proceedings/17th-ishi-oral-presentations/. Accessed April 2, 2014.

Perlin, M. W., et al. (2009). Match likelihood ratio for uncertain genotypes. *Law, Probability and Risk, 8*, 289–302.

Perlin, M. W., & Sinelnikov, A. (2009). An information gap in DNA evidence interpretation. *PLoS ONE, 4*(12), e8327.

Perlin, M. W. (2010). *Explaining the likelihood ratio in DNA mixture interpretation.* Proceedings of the 21st International Symposium on Human Identification (Promega Corporation). Available at http://www.cybgen.com/information/publication/page.shtml. Accessed April 2, 2014.

Perlin, M. W., et al. (2011). Validating TrueAllele® DNA mixture interpretation. *Journal of Forensic Sciences, 56*, 1430–1447.

Perlin, M. W., et al. (2013). New York State TrueAllele® Casework validation study. *Journal of Forensic Sciences, 58*, 1458–1466.

Perlin, M. W., et al. (2014). TrueAllele Casework on Virginia DNA mixture evidence: computer and manual interpretation in 72 reported criminal cases. *PLoS ONE, 9*(3), e92837.

Weir, B. S., et al. (1997). Interpreting DNA mixtures. *Journal of Forensic Sciences, 42*, 213–222.

Additional Topics

Foreman, L. A., & Evett, I. W. (2001). Statistical analyses to support forensic interpretation for a new ten-locus STR profiling system. *International Journal of Legal Medicine, 114*, 147–155.

Kelly, H., et al. (2014). A comparison of statistical models for the analysis of complex forensic DNA profiles. *Science & Justice, 54*, 66–70.

Weir, B. S., & Buckleton, J. S. (1996). *Statistical issues in DNA profiling.* In A. Carracedo, B. Brinkmann, & W. Bar (Eds.), *Advances in Forensic Haemogenetics, 6*; (pp. 457–464). New York: Springer-Verlag.

Estimating the Number of Contributors

Biedermann, A., et al. (2012). Inference about the number of contributors to a DNA mixture: comparative analyses of a Bayesian network approach and the maximum allele count method. *Forensic Science International: Genetics, 6*, 689–696.

Brenner, C. H., et al. (1996). Likelihood ratios for mixed stains when the number of donors cannot be agreed. *International Journal of Legal Medicine, 109*, 218–219.

Buckleton, J. S., et al. (1998). Setting bounds for the likelihood ratio when multiple hypotheses are postulated. *Science & Justice, 38*, 23–26.

Buckleton, J. S., et al. (2007). Towards understanding the effect of uncertainty in the number of contributors to DNA stains. *Forensic Science International: Genetics, 1*, 20–28.

Egeland, T., et al. (2003). Estimating the number of contributors to a DNA profile. *International Journal of Legal Medicine, 117*, 271–275.

Haned, H., et al. (2011). The predictive value of the maximum likelihood estimator of the number of contributors to a DNA mixture. *Forensic Science International: Genetics, 5*, 281–284.

Haned, H., et al. (2011b). Estimating the number of contributors to forensic DNA mixtures: does maximum likelihood perform better than maximum allele count? *Journal of Forensic Sciences, 56*, 23–28.

Lauritzen, S. L., & Mortera, J. (2002). Bounding the number of contributors to mixed DNA stains. *Forensic Science International, 130*, 125–126.

Manabe, S., et al. (2013). Simulated approach to estimate the number and combination of known/unknown contributors in mixed DNA samples using 15 short tandem repeat loci. *Forensic Science International: Genetics Supplement Series, 4*, e154–e155.

Paoletti, D. R., et al. (2005). Empirical analysis of the STR profiles resulting from conceptual mixtures. *Journal of Forensic Sciences, 50*, 1361–1366.

Paoletti, D. R., et al. (2012). Inferring the number of contributors to mixed DNA profiles. *IEEE/ACM Transactions on Computational Biology and Bioinformatics, 9*, 113–122.

Perez, J., et al. (2011). Estimating the number of contributors to two-, three-, and four-person mixtures containing DNA in high template and low template amounts. *Croatian Medical Journal, 52*(3), 314—326.

Presciuttini, S., et al. (2003). Allele sharing in first-degree and unrelated pairs of individuals in the Ge.F.I. AmpFlSTR Profiler Plus database. *Forensic Science International, 131*, 85—89.

Dealing with Potential Relatives

Egeland, T., et al. (2014). Mixtures with relatives: a pedigree perspective. *Forensic Science International: Genetics, 10*, 49—54.

Hu, Y.-Q., & Fung, W. K. (2003). Interpreting DNA mixtures with the presence of relatives. *International Journal of Legal Medicine, 117*, 39—45.

Hu, Y.-Q., & Fung, W. K. (2005). Evaluation of DNA mixtures involving two pairs of relatives. *International Journal of Legal Medicine, 119*, 251—259.

Puch-Solis, R., et al. (2010). Calculating likelihood ratios for a mixed DNA profile when a contribution from a genetic relative of a suspect is proposed. *Science & Justice, 50*, 205—209.

Dealing with Low-Level DNA Mixtures

Balding, D. J. (2013). Evaluation of mixed-source, low-template DNA profiles in forensic science. *Proceedings of the National Academy of Sciences of the United States of America, 110*(30), 12241—12246.

Taylor, D., et al. (2013). The interpretation of single source and mixed DNA profiles. *Forensic Science International: Genetics, 7*(5), 516—528.

13

Coping with Potential Missing Alleles

"Uncertainty is present throughout any scientific procedure…it is now recognized that the only tool for handling uncertainty is probability."

Dennis Lindley (Foreword to Aitken & Taroni 2004 text "Statistics and the Evaluation of Evidence for Forensic Scientists")

INTRODUCTION TO THE PROBLEM

A consequence of improving DNA test sensitivity in recent years is the generation of more complicated DNA profiles for interpretation. When attempting to use the polymerase chain reaction (PCR) to amplify biological samples with low quantities of DNA, stochastic effects often result in loss of information. Allele drop-out occurs when the PCR process fails to amplify and thus to not fully represent all of the alleles present in a DNA sample (e.g. Figure 4.3). In addition, with highly sensitive detection methods that can be used to try to recover more information from low-level DNA samples, allele drop-in from contamination may occur.

Stochastic effects during PCR amplification may decouple short tandem repeat (STR) genotypes. In other words, with a low amount of DNA template, allele pairs may not be fully amplified. The possibility of allele drop-out makes low-level DNA samples difficult to interpret when comparisons are made between evidence question (Q) profiles and known reference (K) profiles. If some of the Q profile alleles are missing due to stochastic effects that occurred during the PCR amplification process, then the Q-to-K comparison is not a perfect match even when the samples come from the same biological source (Figure 13.1).

STR alleles can be considered in one of three categories: (1) unmistakable alleles, which contribute to clear and complete DNA profile results; (2) alleles masked by artifacts like stutter, which add a degree of uncertainty in the interpretation of the results; and (3) alleles that have dropped out and are not detected and therefore complicate Q-K comparisons (Gill et al. 2006, Balding 2013). The information in the previous chapters has focused on what to do with unmistakable alleles or how to statistically account for alleles in the stutter position.

This chapter will address approaches to handling alleles that have dropped out and therefore are unable to be detected. Is it appropriate to include or exclude a suspect as a potential contributor to a DNA mixture when there is not a complete correspondence of genotypes between the Q and K

Advanced Topics in Forensic DNA Typing: Interpretation
http://dx.doi.org/10.1016/B978-0-12-405213-0.00013-0

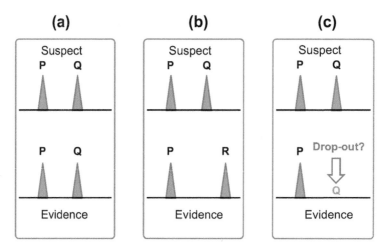

FIGURE 13.1 Potential evidence-to-suspect comparisons with a hypothetical heterozygous locus. (a) Evidence PQ genotype matches suspect PQ genotype. (b) Evidence PR genotype fails to match suspect PQ genotype and would be excluded. (c) Evidence P- does not match suspect PQ possibly because the Q allele dropped out due to a stochastic failure to amplify a low-level allele.

profiles? False exclusions, which may permit the guilty to go free, can have a negative impact on the justice system, just as false inclusions can when an innocent person is inappropriately associated with a crime sample.

An allele drop-out situation may occur when only a few copies of the DNA target are available for amplification due to poor-quality DNA, which may contain PCR inhibitors or possess broken DNA template strands. Stochastic (random) amplification effects occur with low amounts of DNA template. And when many contributors are present in a DNA sample, some of those contributors are likely present at a low template amount, resulting in stochastic effects.

Meeting in Rome in April 2012

Recognizing the need to address the difficult challenges with complex DNA profiles, an international conference was held on April 27 and 28, 2012 in Rome, Italy. A summary of this meeting, which was titled "The hidden side of DNA profiles: artifacts, errors and uncertain evidence," was published in a special issue of *Forensic Science International: Genetics* (Pascali & Prinz 2012). The conference was organized by Vincent Pascali from the Institute of Legal Medicine of the Catholic University in Rome. A total of 332 participants from 26 countries and 80 different institutes attended. Panel discussions covered topics such as protocols for low-template DNA (LTDNA) analysis, probabilistic models for mixture interpretation, and use of Bayesian networks.

There were a number of insightful statements made at the conference, and recognition that there was room for improvement with interpretation of complex DNA cases. For example, David Balding stated, "Low-template DNA [LTDNA] cases are coming to court with limited abilities for sound interpretation…There are dangers with LTDNA but we know how to handle and manage them. Unfortunately, proper management is not a universal practice" (Rome 2012). Limitations exist with any method, and these limitations need to be recognized in order to use the method appropriately.

Limitations of CPI

The combined probability of inclusion (CPI) has been used for many years by U.S. laboratories (e.g. Ladd et al. 2001; Budowle et al. 2009). While CPI is intended as a statistical method to represent all possible genotype combinations that may occur with a particular set of alleles (see Chapter 12), for some analysts the method has evolved into an interpretation approach in which they are no longer thinking about genotype possibilities of contributors, but are instead looking only at the alleles present in an evidentiary profile.

CPI can be a valid *statistical* representation of DNA mixture data provided that there are no missing alleles. The calculation also assumes that the mixture contributors are not close biological relatives and that they are from the same ethnic/racial group so that allele frequency information from a specific population can be used.

A number of common misconceptions have crept into the community regarding CPI. In a presentation given in November 2013 at the DNA Technical Leaders Summit, I termed these misunderstandings "urban legends of CPI" (D.N.A. Box 13.1). Each of these concepts is discussed briefly below:

Urban Legend #1: The number of contributors to a mixture does not matter. The number of contributors *always matters during the interpretation* of mixture evidence. Sometimes there will be greater uncertainty in the ability to make confident assumptions as to the number of contributors. It is true that the statistical CPI calculation does not rely on the number of contributors as CPI calculates all possible genotype combinations given a set of alleles. However, some of these genotype combinations may not fit a reasonable interpretation of the data. Keep in mind also that a higher number of contributors dilutes out the amount of DNA for each contributor, which leads to more stochastic effects and the possibility of allele dropout and therefore less certainty in the overall interpretation.

Urban Legend #2: It is okay to report "conservative" numbers like 1 in 10. When the numerical statistic is low, it is important to keep in mind that there is a reduced ability to exclude innocent people when loci are dropped from consideration in the evidence-to-known comparison due to the possibility of allele drop-out (see Figure 13.2). Thus, low-value "conservative" statistics are only conservative for guilty suspects (Brenner 2011).

Urban Legend #3: CPI provides a true and relevant statement to aid investigators and the court. As discussed in Table 12.1, CPI does not directly answer whether or not a specific suspect can be included in the mixture result. The profile of the suspect under investigation is not explicitly considered with CPI.

Urban Legend #4: CPI is easy to understand for non-DNA users of information. Investigators and lawyers may be accustomed to seeing single-source match statistics and find a CPI result that reflects the fraction of the population that could be included as a potential contributor a little confusing. Speaking at the American Academy of Forensic Sciences meeting in February 2011, Charles Brenner expressed his opinion that "the supposed ease of understanding [of CPI values] by judge or jury is really an illusion" (Brenner 2011).

Urban Legend #5: It is okay to apply CPI statistics without worrying about relative peak heights for alleles. With many mixtures, information existing in the relative peak heights can be used to restrict possible genotypes from consideration (e.g. D.N.A. Box 12.2).

D.N.A. BOX 13.1

URBAN LEGENDS OF CPI

Urban legends are funny (or sometimes horrifying) stories that spread quickly, often via email. While they are seldom based in reality, urban legends often reflect the paranoia of the population that perpetuates them. In recent years a number of misconceptions have arisen within the forensic DNA community surrounding the purpose and practice of the combined probability of inclusion (CPI) statistic in DNA mixture analysis.

In trying to describe problems with the application of CPI to complex mixtures, I have come up with several urban legends that can be associated with this approach to DNA mixture analysis.

1. The number of contributors to a mixture does not matter.
2. It is okay to report "conservative" numbers like 1 in 10.
3. CPI provides a true and relevant statement to aid investigators and the court.
4. CPI is easy to understand for non-DNA users of information.
5. It is okay to apply CPI stats without worrying about relative peak heights for alleles.
6. If all peaks at a locus are above the established stochastic threshold, then the locus is safe to use.
7. It is okay to apply CPI without thinking about the mixture because you assume nothing.
8. Suspect-driven CPI (where the comparison of each suspect results in a different statistical result) is fine.
9. CPI works fine even if potential relatives are in the mixture.
10. It is okay to just consider the presence of potential donor alleles.

Brief explanations of each are provided in the chapter.

Source: Author's presentation at the DNA Technical Leaders Summit held in Norman, Oklahoma on November 20, 2013. For more on the concept of urban legends, see http://en.wikipedia.org/wiki/Urban_legend and http://www.snopes.com/.

Urban Legend #6: If all peaks at a locus are above the established stochastic threshold, then the locus is safe to use. Allele stacking is a possibility (see Figure 6.6), especially with less polymorphic STR loci, such as TPOX and D5S818. Therefore, having for example TPOX alleles 8 and 11 above an established stochastic threshold (a situation that could occur due to allele stacking) does not mean that allele drop-out did not occur with one of the contributors to this mixture. This urban legend relates to Urban Legend #1 regarding the number of potential contributors.

Urban Legend #7: It is okay to apply CPI without thinking about the mixture because you assume nothing. Assumptions are always being made even though some may be implicit and not necessarily documented in case notes.

Urban Legend #8: Suspect-driven CPI (where the comparison of each suspect results in a different statistical result) is fine. The CPI statistic is calculated from the evidence profile and should not vary based on the reference profile. See discussion in the next section based on work by Curran and Buckleton (Curran & Buckleton 2010).

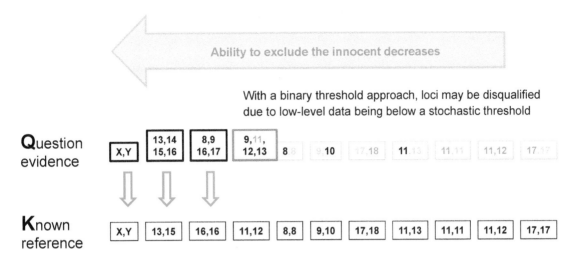

FIGURE 13.2 Representation of a question (Q) to known (K) profile comparison where loci in the Q profile were disqualified from consideration due to alleles being observed below a stochastic threshold. By reducing the points of comparison on the Q profile through disqualifying and eliminating loci with low-level data, a partial profile may be artificially created. This reduction in the possible points of comparison between the Q and K profile reduces the ability to exclude innocent suspects.

Urban Legend #9: CPI works fine even if potential relatives are in the mixture. The CPI statistic is based on a model using unrelated people — hence the name "random man not excluded." It is expected that close relatives will share alleles, and therefore the model of relating observed alleles to possible genotype combinations may not hold up with related individuals in the mixture. **Urban Legend #10: It is okay to just consider the presence of potential donor alleles.** Interpretation should always consider genotypes, not simply the observation of alleles (see D.N.A. Box 12.2).

Problem of Dropping Loci

Speaking of the practice of dropping loci from consideration in mixture calculations, John Buckleton and James Curran noted in 2008: "Most labs leave out any locus that may have drop-out and where the suspect has an allele that is not present in the mixture, irrespective of whether they use RMNE or LR. This practice is conservative only if the evidence at that locus has no exclusionary potential" (Buckleton & Curran 2008).

To test the impact of dropping loci where a non-concordance may exist, Curran and Buckleton performed simulations with 1,000 two-person mixtures that were probed with 10,000 unrelated third profiles (Curran & Buckleton 2010). A CPI statistic was calculated for the loci where the third profile was completely represented. Loci with non-concordance when compared to the third profile were ignored. This study found that "in 87% of the simulated cases, evidence was produced that had some tendency to inculpate the random third profile that was in fact not in any way a contributor to the mixture." They conclude "the risk of producing apparently strong evidence against an innocent suspect by this approach was not negligible" (Curran & Buckleton 2010).

Thus, performing suspect-driven CPI or dropping loci that have a different allele compared to the suspect reduces the power of the "interpretable" evidentiary DNA profile to exclude potentially innocent suspects (Figure 13.2).

A challenge that many U.S. forensic laboratories have faced in recent years is protocol changes where a mixture result that might have previously led to an inclusion now is deemed "inconclusive" after adoption of new protocols, such as the use of a stochastic threshold (SWGDAM 2010). Clearly laboratories need a modern solution to the complex DNA mixture problems they face.

Challenges with Allele Drop-Out

Allele drop-out may result in a situation where the suspect reference sample displays non-concordance with the evidence profile (see Figure 13.1(c)). Should this suspect be excluded with even a single mismatch? It all depends on the strength of the evidence profile. If the allele peak height of the surviving allele is low, then there may be a strong possibility for the missing allele to have been present in the original evidence sample but to have failed to be successfully copied during the PCR process.

The International Society for Forensic Genetics (ISFG) 2006 DNA Commission recognized this and their recommendation #7 states: "If drop-out of an allele is required to explain the evidence under [the prosecution's hypothesis], then the [surviving potential sister] allele should be small enough [in terms of its height] to justify this. Conversely, if a full crime stain profile is obtained where alleles are well above the background level, and the probability of drop-out approaches $Pr(D) \approx 0$, then [the prosecution's hypothesis that the suspect's genotype is in the evidence sample] is not supported" (Gill et al. 2006).

The "2p" rule has been used to statistically account for zygosity ambiguity — i.e. is this single peak below the stochastic threshold the result of a homozygous genotype or the result of a heterozygous genotype with allele drop-out of the sister allele? However, the "2p" approach has been shown to be non-conservative in some situations (Buckleton & Triggs 2006). Thus, probabilistic approaches have been advocated in recent years (Gill et al. 2012).

Estimating and Using the Probability of Drop-Out

The probability of drop-out, often shortened to Pr(D), is an estimate of how often alleles are expected to fail to amplify under certain PCR amplification conditions typically involving low-template DNA amounts. The initial theory and concepts of modeling Pr(D) were described in 2000 by the Forensic Science Service with their low-copy-number DNA work (Gill et al. 2000). Peter Gill, John Buckleton, and David Balding have been developing theoretical interpretation models involving allele drop-out over the past few years (Gill et al. 2009, Balding 2013, Buckleton et al. 2014). There have been a number of articles published on methods for calculating Pr(D), many of them from Torben Tvedebrink, a Danish mathematician (Tvedebrink et al. 2009, 2012a, 2012b, 2013).

As discussed previously in Chapter 4 (Figure 4.4), probability of allele drop-out is a function of the surviving sister allele peak height (Gill et al. 2009). D.N.A. Box 13.2 shows how a logistic regression can be used to calculate Pr(D) (Gill et al. 2012).

The ISFG DNA Commission published recommendations in December 2012 for how to statistically handle the probability of drop-out [Pr(D)] and the probability of drop-in [Pr(C)] (Gill et al. 2012). As noted below, software programs have been developed to incorporate these ideas of Pr(D) and Pr(C) to

D.N.A. BOX 13.2

LOGISTIC REGRESSION MODELING TO DETERMINE THE PROBABILITY OF DROP-OUT

Linear regression models involve the formula:

$$y = a + bx$$

where y is the dependent variable, in this case the level of drop-out of the allele of interest, and x is the explanatory variable, in this situation the height of the sister allele in relative fluorescence units (RFUs). The variable y has a linear relationship with x. In other words, with lower peak heights of a sister allele (variable x), there is an increase in the probability of drop-out (variable y). The "a" and "b" values of the equation above are linear model parameters that can be estimated via linear regression.

The odds of drop-out can be determined by comparing the probability of an allele dropping out [Pr(D)] over the probability of the allele not dropping out [1-Pr(D)]. Applying a natural logarithm to this odds calculation enables improved symmetry in the results.

$$ln\left[\frac{Pr(D)}{1 - Pr(D)}\right] = a + bx$$

Through algebraic rearrangement, the Pr(D) can be calculated as

$$\frac{Pr(D)}{1 - Pr(D)} = e^{(a+bx)}$$

$$Pr(D) = e^{(a+bx)}[1 - Pr(D)]$$
$$= e^{(a+bx)} - Pr(D)\, e^{(a+bx)}$$

$$Pr(D) + Pr(D)e^{(a+bx)} = e^{(a+bx)}$$

$$Pr(D)\left(1 + e^{(a+bx)}\right) = e^{(a+bx)}$$

$$Pr(D) = \frac{e^{(a+bx)}}{1 + e^{(a+bx)}} = \frac{e^{(a+bx)}/e^{(a+bx)}}{1/e^{(a+bx)} + e^{(a+bx)}/e^{(a+bx)}}$$
$$= \frac{1}{e^{-(a+bx)} + 1}$$

Sources: Gill, P., et al. (2012). DNA Commission of the International Society of Forensic Genetics: Recommendations on the evaluation of STR typing results that may include drop-out and/or drop-in using probabilistic methods. Forensic Science International: Genetics, 6, 679–688.

enable calculations that reflect the lack of certainty in interpretation that exists when suspect reference profiles show non-concordance with poor-quality, complex evidentiary DNA profiles.

PROBABILISTIC GENOTYPING — A WAY FORWARD

A nice review article comparing statistical models for the analysis of complex forensic DNA profiles was published in the January 2014 issue of *Science & Justice* (Kelly et al. 2014). Interpretation methods that use thresholds to make decisions are referred to as *binary* because either the genotype is included (probability = 1) or it is excluded (probability = 0). Binary models cannot cope with a locus exhibiting non-concordance due to allele drop-out, such as shown in Figure 13.1(c).

When allele drop-out is possible, probabilitistic genotyping methods represent a way forward. These methods are referred to as *semi-continuous* or *fully continuous* (Kelly et al. 2014).

Discrete (Semi-Continuous) versus Fully Continuous Methods

Probabilistic genotyping approaches for DNA mixture interpretation can be divided into two general areas: (1) the so-called discrete or "semi-continuous" approaches that focus on information available from the alleles present in an evidentiary sample without consideration of peak heights, and (2) "fully continuous" approaches that incorporate biological parameters such as peak height ratios, mixture ratios, and stutter percentages (Kelly et al. 2014). Fully continuous approaches involve numerous calculations and simulations to model observed data with expected behavior of DNA profiles based on previous validation studies. Both semi-continuous and fully continuous approaches utilize a likelihood ratio framework where two hypotheses are compared (e.g. the suspect was a contributor to the evidence sample or he was not).

By using only the alleles present in the result, semi-continuous approaches do not make full use of the data. However, they are much simpler programs and can analyze mixture results much faster because only the presence or absence of alleles is being considered.

Fully continuous methods utilize simulations to try to fit the observed data with the best set of potential genotype combinations. These simulations are performed with Markov-chain Monte Carlo (MCMC) methods (Curran 2008, Perlin et al. 2014). Paul Lewis, a population geneticist at the University of Connecticut, has created a Windows software program and an iPad app to teach how MCMC works (MCMC Robot 2014).

Software Programs

Table 13.1 summarizes features of the various software programs developed to aid DNA mixture interpretation through probabilistic genotyping. More details on each program can be obtained by visiting the websites included in the reference list (see also Steele & Balding 2014).

The only program in Table 13.1 that currently cannot be downloaded from an open-source website or be purchased is FST (Forensic Statistical Tool), which was developed by Adele Mitchell at the New York City Office of Chief Medical Examiner (OCME) Forensic Biology Laboratory. Their validation work has been published and subjected to court admissibility hearings in New York City. DNA quantity levels are used to estimate and inform the FST program with Pr(D) levels based on validation data developed with serial dilutions of DNA template under specific PCR conditions (Mitchell et al. 2012).

Table A4.5 in Appendix 4 provides an example of genotype probability distributions that can be obtained with the probabilistic genotyping software STRmix.

European Forensic Genetics Network of Excellence

European forensic DNA scientists have been leaders in improving forensic DNA methodology and interpretation since the development of the field in the mid-1980s. The next generation of improvements is expected to come from a new initiative lead by Professor Peter Schneider of Cologne, Germany. The European Forensic Genetics Network of Excellence (EuroForGen-NoE) began in January 2012 with funding from the European Union to improve forensic DNA evidence

TABLE 13.1 Available Software Programs for DNA Mixture Interpretation that Use Probabilistic Genotyping as of March 2014

Program Name	Type	Creator(s)	Availability
LRmix	Discrete (semi-continuous)	Hinda Haned & Peter Gill	Open-source https://sites.google.com/site/forensicdnastatistics/PCR-simulation/lrmix
Lab Retriever	Discrete (semi-continuous)	Developed by David Balding and maintained by Norah Rudin and colleagues	Open-source http://www.scieg.org/lab_retriever.html
likeLTD	Discrete (semi-continuous)	David Balding	Open-source https://sites.google.com/site/baldingstatisticalgenetics/software/likeltd-r-forensic-dna-r-code
FST	Discrete (semi-continuous)	Adele Mitchell	Proprietary to the NYC OCME Forensic Biology Laboratory
Armed Xpert	Discrete (semi-continuous)	Developed by USACIL and maintained and improved by NicheVision	Commercial product http://www.armedxpert.com/
TrueAllele	Fully-continuous	Mark Perlin	Commercial product http://www.cybgen.com/
STRmix	Fully-continuous	Duncan Taylor, Jo-Anne Bright, John Buckleton	Commercial product http://strmix.esr.cri.nz/
DNA View Mixture Solution	Fully-continuous	Charles Brenner	Commercial product http://dna-view.com/

Discrete (semi-continuous) methods use only the allele information in conjunction with probabilities of drop-out and drop-in. Fully-continuous methods use peak height data and other parameters in addition to the allele information.

interpretation (D.N.A. Box 13.3). Not only does this work fund research, but also training so that new research methods can be implemented into forensic DNA laboratories. Much of the new DNA interpretation work coming out of Europe is being funded by EuroForGen-NoE.

Following a 2012 training session held in Madrid, Spain on the LRmix software, analysts from 18 laboratories participated in an interlaboratory study involving two DNA mixture exercises (Prieto et al. 2014). A high degree of uniformity was obtained in the statistical results from these complex mixtures. Thus, appropriate training and effective use of probabilistic genotyping software can produce standardized and uniform results from complex mixtures.

Summary and Concluding Thoughts

David Lucy notes in his 2005 *Introduction to Statistics for Forensic Scientists*: "Statistical science has been undergoing a fundamental change since the early 1990s from frequentist implementations and interpretations, to more and more Bayesian approaches. This change has been enabled by statisticians' increased ability to make complex calculations in highly multivariate spaces, and driven by data and

---

D.N.A. BOX 13.3

EUROFORGEN-NoE PROJECT TO DEVELOP NEXT GENERATION DNA INTERPRETATION TOOLS

The European Forensic Genetics Network of Excellence (EuroForGen-NoE) is an important effort working to improve forensic DNA interpretation methods. This five-year project, which was begun in January 2012, is being coordinated by Professor Peter Schneider of the Institute of Legal Medicine at the University Hospital of Cologne, Germany. Five work packages define the project: (1) management; (2) research and networking; (3) exemplar projects; (4) ethical, legal, and social aspects; and (5) education, training, and career development. A primary objective of this project involves the creation of a European Virtual Centre of Forensic Genetic Research that can be sustained after the specific project funds are exhausted.

EuroForGen-NoE involves 12 partners from 8 countries throughout Europe. Participating partner laboratories include the University of Cologne, Epiontis GmbH and GABO:milliarium (Germany), the University of Santiago de Compostela (Spain), the Norwegian Institute of Public Health and University of Life Sciences (Norway), King's College-London and Northumbria University (UK), the University of Copenhagen (Denmark), the Netherlands Forensic Institute (Holland), Innsbruck Medical University (Austria), and Jagiellonian University-Krakow (Poland).

One of the stated EuroForGen-NoE tasks is to develop methods for interpretation and deconvolution of STR and SNP mixtures that incorporate concepts of allele drop-out and drop-in. One way this is being done is through adopting open-source software (e.g. LRmix and euroMix) and carrying out comparative studies with existing methods and new software solutions. Designing validation exercises and conducting training workshops will then help facilitate the understanding and adoption of these new DNA interpretation approaches.

EuroForGen-NoE has a goal of establishing common European-wide standards for generating and interpreting genetic data related to biological evidence and to help train "trainers" that can assist in education within each country. This training has directly benefited the ability to obtain consistent results with complex mixtures in a recent interlaboratory study (Prieto et al. 2014). A March 2013 survey on the current status of education and training in Europe conducted through national contact persons in 28 European countries found that the most urgently needed courses included interpretation of results and weight of evidence in crime cases (74% of respondents) and interpretation of result in complex relationship cases (65% of respondents).

Source: http://www.euroforgen.eu; http://www.euroforgen.eu/fileadmin/websites/euroforgen/images/Training/White_book_final.pdf; Prieto, L., et al. (2014). Euroforgen-NoE collaborative exercise on LRmix to demonstrate standardization of the interpretation of complex DNA profiles. Forensic Science International: Genetics, 9, 47–54.

---

propositions of greater complexity. It should not be thought that classical type hypothesis tests are in some sense wrong. They are not. They have exactly the same firm grounding in probability theory that later approaches have. *It all depends on where and how the classical tests are applied and the interpretation one expects to be able to place upon their results"* (Lucy 2005; emphasis added).

This idea applies to the use of CPI for complex mixture interpretation. The CPI method works well enough with mixtures in which allele drop-out has not occurred. For analysis of the increasingly complex DNA evidence being encountered by laboratories, new tools and approaches are needed. Unfortunately, some analysts have attempted to extrapolate the CPI statistic beyond its limited capabilities.

Probabilistic genotyping methods enable a way forward with low-level DNA samples. The worked example in Appendix 4 demonstrates the ability of a probabilistic genotyping approach to recover substantial information from a profile that would be rendered "inconclusive" with the commonly used CPI method.

David Balding writes at the end of his *Weight-of-Evidence for Forensic DNA Profiles* book (Balding 2005, p. 154): "Uncertainty [in interpretation] prevails for all forms of evidence, and the attempt to quantify should be seen as a sign of the strength of DNA evidence, not as a weakness." Methods are evolving for DNA interpretation in an attempt to better address the needs of the more complex data that laboratories are facing in the 21st century.

As the forensic DNA community moves forward in seeking solutions to complex mixtures and low-level DNA results with probabilistic genotyping, it may be worth keep in mind some thoughts from U.S. President John F. Kennedy spoken more than 50 years ago. Delivering the Yale University commencement address on June 11, 1962, President Kennedy offered this advice as part of his remarks to the graduating class: "For the greatest enemy of truth is very often not the lie — deliberate, contrived and dishonest — but the myth — persistent, persuasive, and unrealistic. Too often we hold fast to the clichés of our forebears. We subject all facts to a prefabricated set of interpretations. *We enjoy the comfort of opinion without the discomfort of thought*" (Kennedy 1962, emphasis added).

Moving forward with probabilistic genotyping will require some discomfort of thought — and perhaps giving up comforts of current protocols that are inadequate at handling complex DNA profiles being processed now and those that will be processed in the future (see also Rudin & Inman, 2012).

Reading List and Internet Resources

General Information

Aitken, C., & Taroni, F. (2014). *Statistics and the Evaluation of Evidence for Forensic Scientists (2nd Edition)*. Chichester, England: John Wiley & Sons.

Rudin, N., & Inman, K. (2012). *The discomfort of thought: a discussion with John Butler*. The CAC News, 1st Quarter. 2012, pp. 8—11. Available at http://www.cacnews.org/news/1stq12.pdf. Accessed April 3, 2014.

Schneider, P. M., et al. (2009). The German Stain Commission: recommendations for the interpretation of mixed stains. *International Journal of Legal Medicine, 123*, 1—5 (originally published in German in 2006 — Rechtsmedizin 16:401—404).

STRBase mixture information: http://www.cstl.nist.gov/strbase/mixture.htm. Accessed April 3, 2014.

SWGDAM. (2010). *SWGDAM Interpretation Guidelines for Autosomal STR Typing by Forensic DNA Testing Laboratories*. Available at http://www.fbi.gov/about-us/lab/biometric-analysis/codis/swgdam-interpretation-guidelines. Accessed April 3, 2014.

Stochastic Effects & Allele Drop-out

Balding, D. J., & Buckleton, J. (2009). Interpreting low template DNA profiles. *Forensic Science International: Genetics, 4*, 1—10.

Benschop, C. C. G., et al. (2011). Low template STR typing: effect of replicate number and consensus method on genotyping reliability and DNA database search results. *Forensic Science International: Genetics, 5*, 316—328.

Bright, J.-A., et al. (2012). A comparison of stochastic variation in mixed and unmixed casework and synthetic samples. *Forensic Science International: Genetics, 6*(2), 180—184.

Bright, J.-A., et al. (2012). Composite profiles in DNA analysis. *Forensic Science International: Genetics, 6*(3), 317–321.

Gill, P., et al. (2005). A graphical simulation model of the entire DNA process associated with the analysis of short tandem repeat loci. *Nucleic Acids Research, 33*, 632–643.

Gill, P., et al. (2008). Interpretation of complex DNA profiles using empirical models and a method to measure their robustness. *Forensic Science International: Genetics, 2*, 91–103.

Gill, P., et al. (2008). Interpretation of complex DNA profiles using Tippett plots. *Forensic Science International: Genetics Supplement Series, 1*, 646–648.

Gill, P., & Haned, H. (2013). A new methodological framework to interpret complex DNA profiles using likelihood ratios. *Forensic Science International: Genetics, 7*, 251–263.

Kelly, H., et al. (2012). The interpretation of low level DNA mixtures. *Forensic Science International: Genetics, 6*(2), 191–197.

Kennedy, J. F. (1962). *Commencement Address at Yale University*. New Haven, Connecticut, 11 June 1962 http://www.jfklibrary. org/Asset-Viewer/Archives/JFKWHA-104.aspx. Accessed April 3, 2014.

Puch-Solis, R., et al. (2009). Assigning weight of DNA evidence using a continuous model that takes into account stutter and dropout. *Forensic Science International: Genetics Supplement Series, 2*, 460–461.

Puch-Solis, R., et al. (2013). Evaluating forensic DNA profiles using peak heights, allowing for multiple donors, allelic dropout and stutters. *Forensic Science International: Genetics, 7*, 555–563.

Stenman, J., & Orpana, A. (2001). Accuracy in amplification. *Nature Biotechnology, 19*, 1011–1012.

Taberlet, P., et al. (1996). Reliable genotyping of samples with very low DNA quantities using PCR. *Nucleic Acids Research, 24*, 3189–3194.

Tvedebrink, T., et al. (2008). Amplification of DNA mixtures — missing data approach. *Forensic Science International: Genetics Supplement Series, 1*, 664–666.

Tvedebrink, T., et al. (2009). Estimating the probability of allelic drop-out of STR alleles in forensic genetics. *Forensic Science International: Genetics, 3*, 222–226.

Tvedebrink, T., et al. (2012a). Statistical model for degraded DNA samples and adjusted probabilities for allelic drop-out. *Forensic Science International: Genetics, 6*(1), 97–101.

Tvedebrink, T., et al. (2012b). Allelic drop-out probabilities estimated by logistic regression — further considerations and practical implementation. *Forensic Science International: Genetics, 6*(2), 263–267.

Walsh, P. S., et al. (1992). Preferential PCR amplification of alleles: Mechanisms and solutions. *PCR Methods and Applications, 1*, 241–250.

Weiler, N. E. C., et al. (2012). Extending PCR conditions to reduce drop-out frequencies in low template STR typing including unequal mixtures. *Forensic Science International: Genetics, 6*(1), 102–107.

Rome Meeting April 2012

Budowle, B., et al. (2009). Mixture interpretation: defining the relevant features for guidelines for the assessment of mixed DNA profiles in forensic casework. *Journal of Forensic Sciences, 54*, 810–821.

Ladd, C., et al. (2001). Interpretation of complex forensic DNA mixtures. *Croatian Medical Journal, 42*, 244–246.

Pascali, V., & Prinz, M. (2012). Highlights of the conference "The hidden side of DNA profiles: artifacts, errors and uncertain evidence." *Forensic Science International: Genetics, 6*, 775–777.

Rome meeting. (2012). *Video of conference entitled "The hidden side of DNA profiles: artifacts, errors and uncertain evidence."* kindly provided by Vince Pascali to Author following the April 27–28, 2012 meeting.

Limitations of CPI and Problems with Dropping Loci

Brenner, C. H. (2011). *The mythical "exclusion" method for analyzing DNA mixtures — does it make any sense at all?* (Vol. 17). Proceedings of the American Academy of Forensic Sciences, Feb 2011. p. 79.

Buckleton, J. S., & Curran, J. M. (2008). A discussion of the merits of random man not excluded and likelihood ratios. *Forensic Science International: Genetics, 2*, 343–348.

Curran, J. M., & Buckleton, J. (2010). Inclusion probabilities and dropout. *Journal of Forensic Sciences, 55*, 1171–1173.

Van Nieuwerburgh, F., et al. (2009). Impact of allelic dropout on evidential value of forensic DNA profiles using RMNE. *Bioinformatics, 25*, 225–229.

Van Nieuwerburgh, F., et al. (2009). RMNE probability of forensic DNA profiles with allelic drop-out. *Forensic Science International: Genetics Supplement Series, 2*, 462–463.

Modified RMP and 2p

Bille, T., et al. (2013). Application of random match probability calculations to mixed STR profiles. *Journal of Forensic Sciences,* *58,* 474—485.

Buckleton, J., & Triggs, C. (2006). Is the 2p rule always conservative? *Forensic Science International, 159,* 206—209.

Probability of Drop-Out

Buckleton, J., et al. (2014). Utilising allelic dropout probabilities estimated by logistic regression in casework. *Forensic Science International: Genetics, 9,* 9—11.

Gill, P., et al. (2000). An investigation of the rigor of interpretation rules for STRs derived from less than 100 pg of DNA. *Forensic Science International, 112,* 17—40.

Gill, P., et al. (2008). Interpretation of complex DNA profiles using Tippett plots. *Forensic Science International: Genetics Supplement Series, 1,* 646—648.

Gill, P., et al. (2009). The low-template-DNA (stochastic) threshold — its determination relative to risk analysis for national DNA databases. *Forensic Science International: Genetics, 3,* 104—111.

Haned, H., et al. (2011). Estimating drop-out probabilities in forensic DNA samples: a simulation approach to evaluate different models. *Forensic Science International: Genetics, 5,* 525—531.

Mitchell, A. A., et al. (2011). Likelihood ratio statistics for DNA mixtures allowing for drop-out and drop-in. *Forensic Science International: Genetics Supplement Series, 3,* e240—e241.

Pfeifer, C., et al. (2012). Comparison of different interpretation strategies for low template DNA mixtures. *Forensic Science International: Genetics, 6(6),* 716—722.

Puch-Solis, R., et al. (2009). Assigning weight of DNA evidence using a continuous model that takes into account stutter and dropout. *Forensic Science International: Genetics Supplement Series, 2,* 460—461.

Tvedebrink, T., et al. (2008). Amplification of DNA mixtures — missing data approach. *Forensic Science International: Genetics Supplement Series, 1,* 664—666.

Tvedebrink, T., et al. (2009). Estimating the probability of allelic drop-out of STR alleles in forensic genetics. *Forensic Science International: Genetics, 3,* 222—226.

Tvedebrink, T., et al. (2012a). Statistical model for degraded DNA samples and adjusted probabilities for allelic drop-out. *Forensic Science International: Genetics, 6,* 97—101.

Tvedebrink, T., et al. (2012b). Allelic drop-out probabilities estimated by logistic regression — further considerations and practical implementation. *Forensic Science International: Genetics, 6,* 263—267.

Tvedebrink, T., et al. (2013). Estimating drop-out probabilities of STR alleles accounting for stutters, detection threshold truncation and degradation. *Forensic Science International: Genetics Supplement Series, 4,* e51—e52.

Information on Solutions with Probabilistic Genotyping

Aitken, C., Roberts, P., & Jackson, G. (2010). *Fundamentals of Probability and Statistical Evidence in Criminal Proceedings: Guidance for Judges, Lawyers, Forensic Scientists and Expert Witnesses. Practitioner Guide No. 1.* London: Royal Statistical Society's Working Group on Statistics and the Law. Available at http://www.maths.ed.ac.uk/~cgga/Guide-1-WEB.pdf. Accessed April 3, 2014.

Balding, D. J. (2013). Evaluation of mixed-source, low-template DNA profiles in forensic science. *Proceedings of the National Academy of Sciences of the United States of America, 110(30),* 12241—12246.

Carracedo, A., et al. (2012). Focus issue — analysis and biostatistical interpretation of complex and low template DNA samples. *Forensic Science International: Genetics, 6,* 677—678.

Gill, P., & Buckleton, J. (2010). A universal strategy to interpret DNA profiles that does not require a definition of low-copy-number. *Forensic Science International: Genetics, 4,* 221—227.

Gill, P., & Haned, H. (2013). A new methodological framework to interpret complex DNA profiles using likelihood ratios. *Forensic Science International: Genetics, 7,* 251—263.

Haned, H. (2011). Forensim: an open-source initiative for the evaluation of statistical methods in forensic genetics. *Forensic Science International: Genetics, 5,* 265—268.

Kelly, H., et al. (2014). A comparison of statistical models for the analysis of complex forensic DNA profiles. *Science & Justice, 54,* 66—70.

Lohmueller, K. E., & Rudin, N. (2013). Calculating the weight of evidence in low-template forensic DNA casework. *Journal of Forensic Science, 58(Suppl. 1),* S243—249.

Lucy, D. (2005). *Introduction to Statistics for Forensic Scientists*. Hoboken, New Jersey: John Wiley & Sons.

Taroni, F., et al. (2002). Evaluation and presentation of forensic DNA evidence in European laboratories. *Science & Justice, 42*, 21–28.

ISFG DNA Commission Recommendations

Gill, P., et al. (2006). DNA commission of the International Society of Forensic Genetics: Recommendations on the interpretation of mixtures. *Forensic Science International, 160*, 90–101.

Gill, P., et al. (2012a). DNA Commission of the International Society of Forensic Genetics: Recommendations on the evaluation of STR typing results that may include drop-out and/or drop-in using probabilistic methods. *Forensic Science International: Genetics, 6*(6), 679–688.

Gill, P., et al. (2012b). The interpretation of DNA evidence (including low-template DNA). Available at http://www.homeoffice.gov.uk/publications/agencies-public-bodies/fsr/interpretation-of-dna-evidence. Accessed April 3, 2014.

Probabilistic Genotyping

Balding, D. J. (2005). *Weight-of-Evidence for Forensic DNA Profiles*. Hoboken, New Jersey: John Wiley & Sons.

Ballantyne, J., et al. (2013). DNA mixture genotyping by probabilistic computer interpretation of binomially-sampled laser captured cell populations: combining quantitative data for greater identification information. *Science & Justice, 53*, 103–114.

Bright, J. A., et al. (2013). Developing allelic and stutter peak height models for a continuous method of DNA interpretation. *Forensic Science International: Genetics, 7*, 296–304.

Bright, J. A., et al. (2014). Searching mixed DNA profiles directly against profile databases. *Forensic Science International: Genetics, 9*, 102–110.

Cowell, R. G., et al. (2008). Probabilistic modeling for DNA mixture analysis. *Forensic Science International: Genetics Supplement Series, 1*, 640–642.

Cowell, R. G., et al. (2011). Probabilistic expert systems for handling artifacts in complex DNA mixtures. *Forensic Science International: Genetics, 5*(3), 202–209.

Cybergenetics education information: http://www.cybgen.com/information/courses/page.shtml. Accessed April 3, 2014.

Gill, P., & Buckleton, J. (2010). Commentary on: Budowle B, Onorato AJ, Callaghan TF, Della Manna A, Gross AM, Guerrieri RA, Luttman JC, McClure DL. Mixture interpretation: defining the relevant features for guidelines for the assessment of mixed DNA profiles in forensic casework. *J Forensic Sci 2009, 54*(4), 810–821. Journal of Forensic Sciences, 55(1), 265-268.

Goos, L. M., et al. (2013). The influence of probabilistic statements on the evaluation of the significance of a DNA match. *Canadian Society of Forensic Science Journal, 35*(2), 77–90.

Graversen, T., & Lauritzen, S. (2013). Estimation of parameters in DNA mixture analysis. *Journal of Applied Statistics, 40*, 2423–2436.

Graversen, T., & Lauritzen, S. (2014). Computational aspects of DNA mixture analysis. *Statistics and Computing* [In Press].

Haned, H., & Gill, P. (2011). Analysis of complex DNA mixtures using the Forensim package. *Forensic Science International: Genetics Supplement Series, 3*, e79–e80.

Haned, H., et al. (2012). Exploratory data analysis for the interpretation of low template DNA mixtures. *Forensic Science International: Genetics, 6*, 762–774.

Kokshoorn, B. (2013). *Implementation of probabilistic models in casework: A case study*. Presentation at ISFG 2013 meeting. Available at http://isfg2013.org/wp-content/uploads/2013/09/Fri-P3-1145-B-Kokshoorn-Y.pdf. Accessed April 3, 2014.

Mitchell, A. A., et al. (2012). Validation of a DNA mixture statistics tool incorporating allelic drop-out and drop-in. *Forensic Science International: Genetics, 6*(6), 749–761.

Perlin, M. W. (2006). *Scientific validation of mixture interpretation methods*. Proceedings of the 17th International Symposium on Human Identification (Promega Corporation). Available at http://www.cybgen.com/information/publication/page.shtml. Accessed April 3, 2014.

Perlin, M. W., & Sinelnikov, A. (2009). An information gap in DNA evidence interpretation. *PloS ONE, 4*(12). e8327.

Perlin, M. W., et al. (2009). Match likelihood ratio for uncertain genotypes. *Law, Probability and Risk, 8*, 289–302.

Perlin, M. W., et al. (2011). Validating TrueAllele DNA mixture interpretation. *Journal of Forensic Sciences, 56*(6), 1430–1447.

Perlin, M. W. (2012). Easy reporting of hard DNA: computer comfort in the courtroom. *Forensic Magazine, 9*(4), 32–37. Available at http://www.cybgen.com/information/publication/page.shtml. Accessed April 3, 2014.

Perlin, M. W., et al. (2013). New York State TrueAllele® casework validation study. *Journal of Forensic Sciences, 58*(6), 1458–1466.

Perlin, M. W., et al. (2014). TrueAllele Casework on Virginia DNA mixture evidence: *computer and manual interpretation in 72 reported criminal cases. PLoS ONE, 9*(3), e92837.

Puch-Solis, R., et al. (2013). Evaluating forensic DNA profiles using peak heights, allowing for multiple donors, allelic dropout and stutters. *Forensic Science International: Genetics, 7,* 555–563.

Steele, C. D., & Balding, D. J. (2014). Statistical evaluation of forensic DNA profile evidence. *Annual Review of Statistics and Its Application, 1*(20), 1–20, 24.

Taylor, D., et al. (2013). The interpretation of single source and mixed DNA profiles. *Forensic Science International: Genetics, 7*(5), 516–528.

Taylor, D. (2013). *Going totally Bayesian: Lab experiences when moving to a continuous DNA interpretation model.* Presentation given at ISFG 2013 meeting. Available at http://isfg2013.org/wp-content/uploads/2013/09/Fri-P3-1000-D-Taylor-Y.pdf. Accessed April 3, 2014.

Software for DNA Analysis and Interpretation

Armed Xpert (NicheVision): http://www.armedxpert.com. Accessed April 3, 2014.

BatchExtract: ftp://ftp.ncbi.nih.gov/pub/forensics/BATCHEXTRACT. Accessed April 3, 2014.

DNAMIX (Bruce Weir): http://www.biostat.washington.edu/~bsweir/DNAMIX3/webpage/. Accessed April 3, 2014.

DNA Mixture Separator (Torben Tvedebrink): http://people.math.aau.dk/~tvede/mixsep/. Accessed April 3, 2014.

EPG Maker program (Steven Myers): http://www.cstl.nist.gov/strbase/tools/EPG-Maker(SPMv.3,Dec2–2011).xlt (13 Mb Excel file). Accessed April 3, 2014.

EuroMix (Thore Egeland): http://euromix.r-forge.r-project.org/. Accessed April 3, 2014.

Forensic DNA Statistics (Peter Gill): https://sites.google.com/site/forensicdnastatistics/. Accessed April 3, 2014.

Forensim (Hinda Haned): http://forensim.r-forge.r-project.org/. Accessed April 3, 2014.

GeneMapper*ID-X* (from Applied Biosystems): http://www.lifetechnologies.com/us/en/home/technical-resources/software-downloads/genemapper-id-x-software.html. Accessed April 3, 2014.

GeneMarker HID (from Soft Genetics): http://www.softgenetics.com/GeneMarkerHID.html. Accessed April 3, 2014.

GenoProof Mixture (Qualitype): http://www.qualitype.de/en/qualitype/genoproof-mixture. Accessed April 3, 2014.

ISFG Software Resources Page: http://www.isfg.org/software. Accessed April 3, 2014.

Lab Retriever (Scientific Collaboration, Innovation & Education Group): http://www.scieg.org/lab_retriever.html. Accessed April 3, 2014.

likeLTD (David Balding): https://sites.google.com/site/baldingstatisticalgenetics/software/likeltd-r-forensic-dna-r-code. Accessed April 3, 2014.

LRmix (Hinda Haned): https://sites.google.com/site/forensicdnastatistics/PCR-simulation/lrmix. Accessed April 3, 2014.

OSIRIS (Open Source Independent Review and Interpretation System): http://www.ncbi.nlm.nih.gov/projects/SNP/osiris/. Accessed April 3, 2014.

STRmix™ (Duncan Taylor, 2014 STRmix™ (Duncan Taylor, Jo-Anne Bright, John Buckleton): http://strmix.com/. Accessed April 3, 2014.

TrueAllele Casework (Cybergenetics): http://www.cybgen.com/systems/casework.shtml. Accessed April 3, 2014.

Markov Chain Monte Carlo (MCMC)

Andrieu, C., et al. (2003). An introduction to MCMC for machine learning. *Machine Learning, 50,* 5–43.

Curran, J. M. (2008). A MCMC method for resolving two person mixtures. *Science & Justice, 48,* 168–177.

Gelfand, A. E., & Smith, A. F. M. (1990). Sampling-based approaches to calculating marginal densities. *Journal of the American Statistical Association, 85*(410), 398–409.

Markov Chain Monte Carlo: http://en.wikipedia.org/wiki/Markov_chain_Monte_Carlo. Accessed April 3, 2014.

Markov Chain Monte Carlo (MCMC) Robot: http://www.mcmcrobot.org/. Accessed April 3, 2014.

EUROFORGEN-NoE Efforts

European Forensic Genetics Network of Excellence EUROFORGEN-NoE): http://www.euroforgen.eu/. Accessed April 3, 2014.

Prieto, L., et al. (2014). Euroforgen-NoE collaborative exercise on LRmix to demonstrate standardization of the interpretation of complex DNA profiles. *Forensic Science International: Genetics, 9,* 47–54.

Bayesian Networks

Biedermann, A., & Taroni, F. (2012). Bayesian networks for evaluating forensic DNA profiling evidence: a review and guide to literature. *Forensic Science International: Genetics, 6,* 147—157.

Dawid, A. P., et al. (2007). Object-oriented Bayesian networks for complex forensic DNA profiling problems. *Forensic Science International, 169,* 195—205.

Gittelson, S., et al. (2014). Decision analysis for the genotype designation in *low-template-DNA* profiles. *Forensic Science International: Genetics, 9,* 118—133.

Pascali, V. L., & Merigioli, S. (2012). Joint Bayesian analysis of forensic mixtures. *Forensic Science International: Genetics, 6,* 735—748.

Taroni, F., et al. (2006). *Bayesian Networks and Probabilistic Inference in Forensic Science.* Hoboken: John Wiley & Sons.

Taroni, F., & Biedermann, A. (2013). *Bayesian networks. Encyclopedia of Forensic Sciences, Second Edition.* San Diego: Elsevier Academic Press.

Relationship Testing: Kinship Statistics

"The whole of science is nothing more than a refinement of everyday thinking."

Albert Einstein

INTRODUCTION

Besides its use in criminal investigations, DNA data plays an important role in other applications such as parentage and kinship testing where DNA results from potential relatives are compared. Different questions are usually being asked in parentage testing than in criminal casework. While criminal casework involves looking for direct matches between evidence and suspect DNA profiles, relationship testing relies on additional assumptions that involve genetic inheritance patterns and the possibility of mutation.

A direct DNA match, where all alleles are expected to be comparable between the question (Q) and known (K) profiles, will always provide a stronger weight-of-evidence than kinship associations made with biological relatives, where only some of the alleles are being shared. There is a greater level of interpretation uncertainty with results from kinship analysis due to inheritance patterns that vary depending on the relationship being considered and the possibility of an unrelated person sharing common alleles.

While most kinship analysis is performed in relationship testing laboratories, which have traditionally focused on paternity testing, there are situations were a crime lab may need to turn to kinship to answer a question. Calculations for criminal paternity or maternity are needed with allegations of incest, products of conception from sexual assault, and child abandonment cases. Many forensic DNA scientists are not familiar with kinship analysis — in part because articles regarding parentage or kinship testing are often published in the American Association of Blood Banks (AABB) journal "Transfusion" and thus may be less accessible and less known to the forensic community.

For missing persons investigations and disaster victim identification, there may not be a preexisting primary reference sample available for a direct comparison. In these situations, DNA information is needed from close biological relatives to help identify recovered remains through kinship analysis. Genetic pedigrees are used to reflect these family relationships (D.N.A. Box 14.1).

This chapter will explore the calculations and challenges involved with several applications of DNA evidence from related individuals. These include traditional parentage testing that usually involves addressing questions of paternity (i.e. Who is the father?) and missing persons and mass

D.N.A. BOX 14.1

GENETIC PEDIGREES: A METHOD TO REPRESENT INHERITANCE IN FAMILIES

Inheritance patterns are typically represented with pedigrees that are drawn to reflect family relationships. The figure below shows a three-generation pedigree with results from a single genetic marker. The oldest generation, in this case the grandparents, is shown at the top of a genetic pedigree. Males are represented as squares and females as circles. A horizontal line connects two biological parents. A vertical line connects offspring to their parents. A diagonal line through a square or circle indicates that the individual depicted is deceased or unavailable for testing.

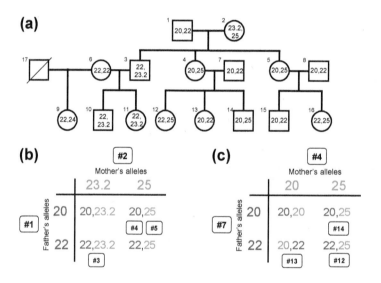

Figure caption: (a) A three-generation family pedigree with results from a single genetic locus (STR marker FGA). Squares represent males and circles females. (b) A Punnett square showing the possible allele combinations for offspring of individuals #1 and #2 in the pedigree. Individual #3 is 22,23.2 and inherited the 22 allele from his father and the 23.2 allele from his mother. (c) A Punnett square for one of the families in the second generation showing possible allele combinations for offspring of individuals #4 and #7.

The genotypes from a single genetic marker — in this case, the STR locus FGA — are shown within the squares and circles representing the family members in this pedigree [section (a)]. People represented on this pedigree are labeled from #1 through #17 with the small number to the upper left-hand corner of each square or circle. Individual #2 (the grandmother) has a genotype of "23.2,25." The "23.2" is a variant allele that typically occurs in less than 0.3% of the population. Note that this 23.2 allele is transmitted to her son (individual #3) but not to her two daughters (individuals #4 and #5). They get her other allele — the "25," which typically occurs around 7% of the time in Caucasian individuals. Children will get either one or the other of their parent's two alleles at every locus [see section (b)]. Note also that the grandmother's "23.2" allele was passed on to her grandson (individual #10) and her granddaughter (individual #11). However, her other grandchildren (individuals #12 through #16) did not receive the 23.2 because neither of their parents had that particular allele.

In section (c), inheritance patterns for the three children of individuals #4 and #7 can be seen. In this situation, all three children (#12, #13, and #14) have different genotype combinations. As illustrated in this example, if enough of the children's genotypes are known, then it is possible to determine the parents' alleles and genotypes with a high degree of confidence.

disaster investigations that involve reverse parentage analysis (i.e. Could these sets of remains have come from a child of these biological reference samples?). Immigration cases also involve kinship testing to determine whether an individual could have a proposed relationship to reference samples. Figure 14.1 illustrates the questions posed with parentage and reverse parentage analysis.

In the case of people who are close relatives, such as parents and offspring, full siblings, or half siblings, and even with more distant relatives such as cousins, we can use the model of Mendelian segregation to estimate the amount of shared genetic information. Table 14.1 shows how many identical-by-descent (IBD) alleles are expected to be in common at each genetic locus. For example, identical twins are expected to share two alleles at each locus, or in other words, to have an identical DNA profile.

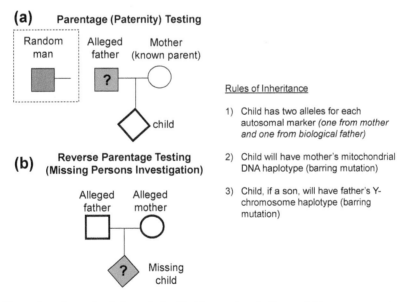

FIGURE 14.1 Illustration of question being asked with (a) parentage testing and (b) reverse parentage testing. The most common form of parentage testing, paternity testing, uses results from a mother and a child to answer the question of whether the alleged father could have fathered the child versus the child being fathered by a random man. With a reverse parentage test, DNA types from one or both parents are used to determine if an observed type could have resulted from a child of the alleged father and mother.

TABLE 14.1   Degrees of Relatedness and Probability of Sharing an Allele that Is Identical by Descent (IBD) at a Genetic Marker with a Common Ancestor

Relationship	Level	0 alleles (k_0)	1 allele (k_1)	2 alleles (k_2)
Self or identical twin	Same DNA	0	0	1
Parent–child	1st degree	0	1	0
Full siblings	1st degree	1/4	1/2	1/4
Half siblings*	2nd degree	1/2	1/2	0
Uncle–nephew* or Aunt–niece*	2nd degree	1/2	1/2	0
Grandparent–grandchild*	2nd degree	1/2	1/2	0
First cousins	3rd degree	3/4	1/4	0
Double first cousins	3rd degree	9/16	3/8	1/16
Second cousins	4th degree	15/16	1/16	0
Unrelated[†]	–	1	0	0

* Half siblings, uncle- or aunt- nephew or niece, and grandparent–grandchild relationships are genetically identical with autosomal loci.

[†] Unrelated individuals can share alleles that are identical by coincidence (IBS) rather than IBD.

k is the kinship coefficient where k_0 is the probability that neither allele of one relative is inherited by the second relative, k_1 is the probability that one allele of one relative is inherited by the second relative, and k_2 is the probability that both alleles of one relative are inherited by the second relative. The level of confidence in a calculated relationship decreases with the degree of separation between them. Adapted from Wenk et al. (1996) and Weir (2007).

Each parent should (barring mutation) have a single allele in common with each of their offspring. Full siblings should share one IBD allele approximately 50% of the time, two alleles 25% of the time, and no alleles 25% of the time (Table 14.1). First-degree relatives include parent–child and full sibling relationships. Half-siblings, uncle- or aunt- nephew or niece, and grandparent–grandchild relationships are genetically equivalent from an autosomal marker perspective and are second-degree relatives. With each degree of separation between two tested relatives, there is a greater chance of allele segregation or mutation confounding the ability to confirm a specific relationship.

Once expected conditional probabilities between two potential relatives have been established, DNA profiles can be obtained and statistical calculations performed. Results are provided in the form of a likelihood ratio (LR) expressing how much more likely it is that the DNA evidence would be observed under a hypothesis that the evidence came from people with a specific relationship as opposed to seeing the DNA evidence given a hypothesis that the observed data came from two presumably unrelated people:

$$LR = \frac{Pr(E|H_1)}{Pr(E|H_2)}$$

For example, in this LR equation, E involves the DNA profiles for the tested individuals, and H_1 is the hypothesis that an alleged father is the biological father of the tested child and H_2 is the hypothesis that a random, unrelated man is the biological father of the tested child. When testing hypotheses involving a father—child relationship, this LR is called the *paternity index* (PI). When testing hypotheses involving a mother—child relationship, this LR is called the *maternity index*.

This approach has a long-standing precedent in the calculations for paternity determination where an exclusion probability can be calculated to express how rare it would be to find a random man who could not be excluded as the biological father of a child. The first publication appeared in 1938 that developed the theoretical framework for calculating what we now refer to as the PI (Essen-Möller 1938). Since that time, it has become common to calculate an LR that quantifies the DNA evidence under two competing hypotheses.

It is important to keep in mind that kinship testing does not seek to answer a general question of "are these two tested people related to one another?" Instead, given a specific scenario such as "is one tested individual a potential biological father to another tested individual?" does the observed data support the stated hypothesis — and if so, how strongly? The LR calculation is set up based on how the kinship question is framed.

PARENTAGE TESTING

On January 4, 1975, President Gerald Ford signed into law the Social Security Amendments of 1974, which, among its other provisions, created a state—federal child support enforcement program with a mission of "enforcing the support obligations owed by absent parents to their children and the spouse (or former spouse) with whom such children are living, locating absent parents, *establishing paternity*, obtaining child and spousal support, and assuring that assistance in obtaining support will be available ... to all children (whether or not eligible for aid under [the "Assistance to Families with Dependent Children" program]), for whom such assistance is requested (Morgan 2002, emphasis added).

Every year in the United States more than 400,000 paternity cases are performed where the identity of the father of a child is in dispute (AABB 2008, 2010). It has been noted that over 99% of current paternity testing laboratory casework is resolved without trial, and therefore "disputed paternity has become essentially a scientific matter" (Faigman et al. 2002, p. 798).

Paternity cases typically involve the mother, the child, and one or more alleged fathers. Although roughly 30% of individuals tested are excluded from being the father of the tested child, this does not mean that these individuals all falsely assumed that they were the father (D.N.A. Box 14.2).

For example, in 2008, almost one million samples were analyzed for this purpose in the United States alone (AABB 2008). Several dozen DNA laboratories have been accredited by the American Association of Blood Banks (AABB) to perform parentage testing (AABB 2014). AABB-accredited labs abide by standards similar to the FBI Quality Assurance Standards followed by U.S. forensic DNA laboratories. In January 2014, the AABB Standards for Relationship Testing Laboratories implemented the 11th edition of the standards (D.N.A. Box 14.3).

The determination of parentage is based on whether or not alleles are shared between the child and the alleged father or mother when a number of genetic markers are examined. Thus, the outcome of parentage testing is simply inclusion or exclusion with the weight of an inclusion assessed using an LR known as the paternity or maternity index. Parentage testing laboratories often utilize the same short tandem repeat (STR) multiplexes and commercial kits used by forensic testing laboratories. However, rather than looking for a complete one-to-one match in a DNA profile, the source of the non-maternal or "obligate paternal allele" at each genetic locus is under investigation.

D.N.A. BOX 14.2

NON-PATERNITY RATES VERSUS PATERNITY TESTING EXCLUSION RATES

Non-paternity can be defined as an alleged father learning that he cannot be the biological father of a child based on genetic test results. Paternity testing exclusion rates, however, are not strictly the same as non-paternity rates because not all tested alleged fathers think that they are the biological father of a child.

Although non-paternity rates of 10% have been widely cited in the past, the reliability of these numbers has been challenged (Macintyre & Sooman 1991). For example, a study of 1,607 Swiss children and their parents conducted about 20 years ago found only 11 exclusions or <1% non-paternity (Sasse et al. 1994). A 2006 examination of 67 published studies found non-paternity was typically around 1.9% (Anderson 2006). Of course, rates may vary depending on cultures and changing social norms. Regardless of the actual rate, it is important to keep in mind when gathering family reference samples in disaster victim identification and family reconstruction cases that non-paternity is a possibility.

An analysis of the 2000 U.S. paternity testing results found that paternity inclusions occurred in 72% of cases (Bishai et al. 2006). In other words, there was a 28% exclusion rate for alleged fathers that were DNA tested. The AABB 2010 annual report comments: "AABB has seen the exclusion rate misused by several organizations trying to claim that 30% of men are misled into believing they are biological fathers of children when the mother knows this not to be true. This view is incorrect. The exclusion rate includes a number of factors. One is a woman may allege

several men as possible fathers because she was sexually active with these individuals. These are not men who were misled into believing they were fathers and then later discover they are not. The testing merely sorts out which man is the biological father and excludes the others. Another factor is that the unexcluded alleged father, as part of his defense, will allege the mother had multiple sexual partners during the time of conception. These men are subsequently tested. Sometimes testing of a man is required because of a legal presumption. This is when the mother properly names the correct biological father, but because the child is the product of a marriage (she is (was) married to someone other than the biological father), there is a legal presumption the husband is the father. The husband is tested to rebut the legal presumption even though no one believes he is the biological father of the child. There is no evidence that a large number of the men excluded in the testing were misled into believing they are the biological father of a given child" (AABB 2010 annual report, pp. 3–4).

Sources: AABB 2010 annual report available at http://www.aabb. org/sa/facilities/Documents/rtannrpt10.pdf; Anderson, K.G. (2006). How well does paternity confidence match actual paternity? Evidence from worldwide nonpaternity rates. Current Anthropology, 47, 513–520; Bishai, D., et al. (2006). A national sample of US paternity tests: do demographics predict test outcomes? Transfusion, 46, 849–853; Macintyre, S., & Sooman, A. (1991). Non-paternity and prenatal genetic screening. Lancet, 338, 869–871; Sasse, G., et al. (1994). Estimating the frequency of nonpaternity in Switzerland. Human Heredity, 44(6), 337-343; http://en.wikipedia.org/wiki/Non-paternity_event.

D.N.A. BOX 14.3

AABB AND RELATIONSHIP TESTING STANDARDS

AABB (originally known as the American Association of Blood Banks) has accredited relationship testing laboratories since 1984. Similar to the FBI's Quality Assurance Standards (QAS), relationship testing laboratories are audited against the AABB *Standards for Relationship Testing Laboratories*, which as of January 2014 is in its 11th edition. The first six editions were titled *Standards for Parentage Testing Laboratories*. The name was changed in more recent editions to reflect the broadened scope of identity testing, which has moved beyond traditional parentage testing into more complex relationship testing, including analysis to resolve immigration issues.

A committee comprised of about a dozen members prepares the AABB standards, which are then approved by the AABB Board of Directors and the Standards Program Committee following usually a 60-day time period for public comment and input. The AABB *Standards for Relationship Testing Laboratories* covers ten primary topics: (1) organization; (2) resources; (3) equipment; (4) supplier and customer issues; (5) process control; (6) documents and records; (7) deviations and nonconforming products and services; (8) internal and external assessments; (9) process improvement through corrective and preventive action; and (10) facilities, work environment, and safety. A glossary defines terms and a crosswalk traces each standard in the current edition to the previous one to help laboratories update their procedures. A detailed guidance document is provided as a compact disc in the back of each edition of the standards. This guidance document contains a number of helpful appendices with worked paternity testing examples.

A listing of more than two dozen AABB accredited labs is available (AABB 2014). The AABB website also contains annual reports of relationship testing laboratories and a newsletter.

Sources: AABB (2013). Standards for Relationship Testing Laboratories (11th edition). Bethesda, Maryland: AABB; http://www.aabb.org/sa/facilities/Pages/relationshipreports.aspx; http://www.aabb.org/sa/facilities/newsletter/Pages/default.aspx; http://www.aabb.org/sa/facilities/Pages/RTestAccrFac.aspx.

The basis of parentage testing comes down to the fact that, in the absence of mutation, a child receives one allele matching each parent at every genetic locus examined (Figure 14.2). Thus, parents with genotypes 28,30 (father) and 31,32.2 (mother) may produce offspring with the following types: 28,31; 28,32.2; 30,31; and 30,32.2. Conversely, if the mother's genotype is known to be 31,32.2 and the children possess alleles 28, 30, 31, and 32.2, then we may deduce that their father contributed alleles 28 and 30 — provided of course that the same individual fathered all the children.

The obligate paternal allele for each child in this example is shown in Figure 14.2(b). In this particular example, the parents had non-overlapping alleles. Parentage testing becomes more complicated when mother and father happen to share alleles, but the logic remains the same in calculating exclusion probability and the PI LR described below.

Statistical Calculations

Although the concepts are the same with maternity testing, the remainder of this section will focus on paternity testing since most parentage testing efforts focus on identifying the father of a child. If

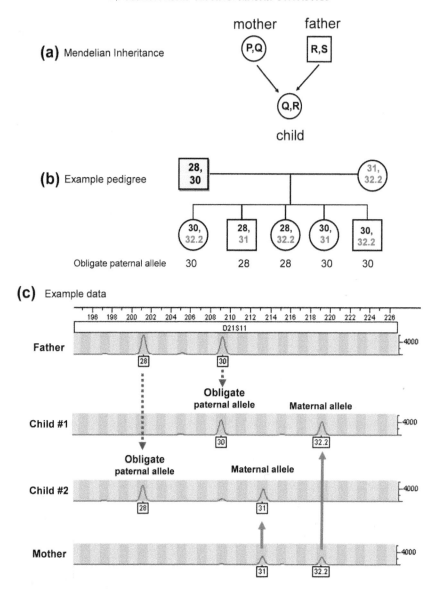

FIGURE 14.2   (a) Mendelian inheritance patterns with a mother possessing alleles P and Q contributing one of them to the child while the father who possesses alleles R and S also contributes one of his alleles to the child. (b) An example pedigree for a family where the parents possess different alleles enabling identification of the obligate paternal allele in each of the children. This scenario can become more complicated to interpret if mutations occur or maternal and paternal alleles are shared. (c) Example data showing family inheritance at the STR locus D21S11 and identification of the obligate paternal allele once the mother's alleles are compared to the tested children (shown with red arrows).

the man tested cannot be excluded as the biological father of the child in question (due to allele sharing), then statistical calculations are performed to aid in understanding the strength of the association. The most commonly applied test in this regard is the paternity index (PI). The PI can also be called an RI or *relationship index*.

The PI is the ratio of two conditional probabilities where the numerator assumes paternity and the denominator assumes a random man of similar ethnic background as the father. The selection of an appropriate population database is important as different populations have different allele frequencies (see Chapter 10). The numerator is the probability of observed genotypes, given the tested man is the father, while the denominator is the probability of the observed genotypes, given that a random man is the father. The PI is generally represented in the formula X/Y, where X is the chance that the alleged father (AF) could transmit the obligate allele and Y is the chance that some other man of the same race/ethnicity could have transmitted the allele.

$$PI = \frac{X}{Y} = \frac{\text{Pr(types observed|hypothesis that the tested man is the father)}}{\text{Pr(types observed|hypothesis that a random man is the father)}}$$

The PI LR for each genetic marker (locus) is calculated separately and then combined using the product rule to provide an overall PI value. Using mathematical symbols, this is written (Gjertson et al. 2007):

$$PI_N = \prod_{i=1}^{N} PI_i = PI_1 \times PI_2 \times PI_3 \times ... \times PI_N$$

where $i = 1$ to N are the individual independently inherited genetic systems (e.g. STR loci).

Typically, the numerator of the PI (or X in the formula above) is assigned the value of 1 if the alleged father is homozygous for the allele of interest and 0.5 if the AF is heterozygous at the locus. A population database containing frequency distributions for the various alleles at the tested genetic markers, such as Appendix 1, is used to calculate the potential of a randomly selected man passing the obligate allele to the child.

The PI LR reflects how many times more likely it is to see the evidence (e.g. a particular set of alleles) under the first hypothesis compared to the second hypothesis. The probability that the untested alternative father will transmit a specific allele to his child is equal to the allele frequency of the specific allele under consideration.

As noted above, the PI is calculated for each locus and then individual PI values are multiplied together to obtain the combined paternity index (CPI) for the entire set of genetic loci examined. This CPI abbreviation should not be confused with the combined probability of inclusion CPI discussed in Chapter 12 and Chapter 13. To avoid this confusion, this book uses PI to describe either a single-locus PI or a combined PI from multiple loci.

The generally accepted minimum standard for an inclusion of paternity is a PI of 100 or greater (Coleman & Swenson 2000). A PI of 100 correlates to the probability that the alleged father has a 99 to 1 chance of being the father compared to a random man.

Another statistical test performed in paternity testing is the *exclusion probability* (PE), which is the combined frequency of all genotypes that would be excluded if the pedigree relationships were true assuming Hardy−Weinberg equilibrium (see Chapter 10). Alternatively, the inclusion probability can be calculated, which is referred to as *Random Man Not Excluded* (RMNE), where RMNE $= 1 -$ PE. The RMNE is effectively a weighted average of inverse LRs (Slooten & Egeland 2014).

Besides the PI, there are several other methods of stating information regarding the strength of evidence for or against paternity. A brief historical perspective on paternity calculations is provided in the International Society for Forensic Genetics (ISFG) 2007 recommendations on paternity biostatistics (Gjertson et al. 2007).

Probability of paternity was originally described in 1938 (Essen-Möller 1938) and is often abbreviated as W for *Wahrscheinlichkeit*, which is German for likelihood or probability. It is described by the formula:

$$W = \frac{X}{(X + Y)}$$

where X is the probability of the hypothesis of paternity and Y is the probability of the hypothesis of non-paternity as discussed earlier. Note that this probability of paternity is an application of Bayes' theorem (see Chapter 9). By multiplying the PI LR with a prior probability, the posterior probability can be obtained. Typically a prior probability of 0.5 is used where it is just as likely for paternity versus non-paternity. The impacts of different prior probabilities are shown in D.N.A. Box 14.4.

Parentage Testing Equations

Depending on the genotypes of the parents, different allele combinations exist at each locus in their offspring. For example, both parents may have indistinguishable heterozygous genotypes (e.g. mother with 8,9 and father with 8,9), which reduces the number of possible combinations that their offspring can have (e.g. 8,8; 8,9; or 9,9). Parents could both be homozygous with the same alleles (e.g. 8,8 and 8,8) in which case all of their children would be homozygous (8,8 in this example). Alternatively, parents may have non-overlapping heterozygous alleles (e.g. 28,30 and 31,32.2) in which case their offspring could potentially have different genotypes from one another (e.g. 28,31; 28,32.2; 30,31; or 30,32.2 as in Figure 14.2).

Ideally parentage cases involve a full trio where a child's DNA profile is compared to his mother's DNA profile and the DNA profile of an alleged father. However, in some situations the DNA profile of one parent is not available and the child's DNA profile is compared with a DNA profile from only an alleged father (in the case of a paternity examination) or an alleged mother (in a maternity case). As will be described later in the chapter, these *deficient cases* are more challenging without the anchoring alleles of a known parent to help decipher obligate alleles from the parent in question.

A total of 21 possible scenarios exist in a paternity trio involving a mother, child, and alleged father (Table 14.2). The various allele combinations give rise to different PI calculations. In Table 14.2, example calculations are worked with D18S51 Caucasian allele frequencies from Appendix 1. With a D18S51 genotype of the child being either 14,14 (PP) or 14,15 (PQ), then the allele 14 frequency (*p*) of 0.134 and the allele 15 frequency (*q*) of 0.170 are used.

Note that based on the allele inheritance pattern being examined, many of the allele combination scenarios produce the same PI value. For example, if the child has a genotype PP and the alleged father is also a PP (scenarios #1 and #4), then it does not matter if the mother's genotype is PP or PQ. The transmission of allele P with frequency *p* is what matters in the determination of a $1/p$ PI value (Table 14.2).

D.N.A. BOX 14.4

IMPACT OF DIFFERENT PRIOR PROBABILITIES OR PRIOR ODDS ON PI RESULTS

Probability of paternity (*W*) is a posterior probability and therefore according to Bayes' theorem is calculated by multiplying a prior probability with the likelihood ratio (LR; paternity index) that considers two mutually exclusive hypotheses. Typically a prior probability of 0.5 is used — in other words, a 50—50 chance that the alleged father (tested man) is the biological father. If the alleged father has a 50% prior probability, then the prior odds are 1 as shown below:

$$odds = \frac{\text{Pr}(H)}{\text{Pr}(\bar{H})} = \frac{0.5}{1 - 0.5} = \frac{0.5}{0.5} = 1$$

If Bayes' theorem is formulated in terms of odds instead of probability, then posterior odds = LR × prior odds or LR × 1 (when a prior probability of 0.5 is used) (see Brenner 2006). Therefore, in this situation the posterior odds will equal the LR (i.e. the paternity index in the case of paternity testing).

If a prior probability of 0.25 was used instead, then the odds would be $(0.25)/(1 - 0.25) = 0.33$. Or if a prior probability was 0.9, then the odds would be $(0.9)/(1 - 0.9) = 9$.

The ISFG biostatistical recommendations encourage listing the prior probability in summary statements made in paternity case reports. For example, PI = 200 and *W* = 99.5% (assuming a prior probability of 0.5). While confidence intervals of PI or *W* are irrelevant in probability estimates, multiple prior probabilities can be assumed to test the sensitivity and range of posterior probabilities and thus provide context in the interpretation of a specific case (Gjertson et al. 2007).

Sources: Gjertson, D.W., et al. (2007). ISFG: recommendations on biostatistics in paternity testing. Forensic Science International: Genetics, 1, 223—231. Brenner, C.H. (2006). Some mathematical problems in the DNA identification of victims in the 2004 tsunami and similar mass fatalities. Forensic Science International, 157, 172—180.

Paternity index LRs are conventionally calculated without any theta correction (i.e. $\theta = 0$), and are thus ignoring any potential coancestry or subpopulation structure. Equations involving theta corrections have been published by Karen Ayres (Ayres 2000), David Balding (Balding 2005, p. 116), John Buckleton (Buckleton et al. 2005, Buckleton et al. 2007), and Bruce Weir (Weir 2007). When theta is not equal to zero and potential coancestry is involved, then the genotype of the mother plays a role as well as that of the alleged father (Weir 2007).

The Paternity Testing Commission (PTC) of the International Society for Forensic Genetics (ISFG) recommendations on biostatistics in paternity testing state that "if a significant degree of substructuring is known to be present in a population, algorithms that take substructure into consideration shall be used" (Gjertson et al. 2007). However, the PTC comments that "in many populations the degree of substructuring is so small that, for practical purposes, it does not affect the biostatistical evidence to any significant degree in paternity testing. If no significant substructuring exists in a population, the biostatistical calculations can be performed without correcting for substructuring" (Gjertson et al. 2007).

When performing kinship analysis such as paternity testing, three sets of information are needed: (1) the genotypes at multiple genetic loci for each of the individuals tested, (2) relevant allele

TABLE 14.2   Single-Locus Paternity Testing Calculations and Formulas for 21 Different Full-Trio Combinations of Genotypes

#	G_C	G_M	G_{TM}	Numerator (X)	Denominator (Y)	Paternity Index (PI)	PI if p=0.134, q=0.170	Random Man Not Excluded (RMNE)	RMNE if p=0.134, q=0.170	#
1	PP	PP	PP	1	p	1/p	7.46	p(2-p)	0.250	1
2			PQ	1/2	p	1/2p	3.73	p(2-p)	0.250	2
3			QR	0	p	0	0	0	0	3
4		PQ	PP	1/2	p/2	1/p	7.46	p(2-p)	0.250	4
5			PQ	1/4	p/2	1/2p	3.73	p(2-p)	0.250	5
6			PR	1/4	p/2	1/2p	3.73	p(2-p)	0.250	6
7			QR	0	p/2	0	0	0	0	7
8	PQ	PP	QQ	1	q	1/q	5.88	q(2-q)	0.311	8
9			PQ	1/2	q	1/2q	2.94	q(2-q)	0.311	9
10			QR	1/2	q	1/2q	2.94	q(2-q)	0.311	10
11			RS	0	q	0	0	0	0	11
12		PQ	PP	1/2	(p+q)/2	1/(p+q)	3.29	(p+q)(2−p−q)	0.516	12
13			PQ	1/2	(p+q)/2	1/(p+q)	3.29	(p+q)(2−p−q)	0.516	13
14			PR	1/4	(p+q)/2	1/[2(p+q)]	0.608	(p+q)(2−p−q)	0.516	14
15			QR	1/4	(p+q)/2	1/[2(p+q)]	0.608	(p+q)(2−p−q)	0.516	15
16			RS	0	(p+q)/2	0	0	0	0	16
17		QR	QQ	0	p/2	0	0	p(2−p)	0.250	17
18			PQ	1/4	p/2	1/2p	3.73	p(2−p)	0.250	18
19			QR	0	p/2	0	0	p(2−p)	0.250	19
20			QS	0	p/2	0	0	p(2−p)	0.250	20
21			RS	0	p/2	0	0	0	0	21

Genotypes from the child (G_C), mother (G_M), and tested man (G_{TM}) possessing alleles P, Q, R, or S with frequencies p, q, r, or s. These formulas assume no null alleles or mutations. Random man not excluded (RMNE) formulas from AABB (2011). Probability of exclusion (PE) is $1 - $ RMNE. Adapted from Lucy (2005), Evett & Weir (1998), and AABB (2011).

frequencies for the genetic loci examined, and (3) a method to assess the relationship of interest based on genetic inheritance models. As part of (3), a user makes the decision whether or not to incorporate subpopulation structure theta corrections in the calculations.

In the case of paternity testing, the appropriate equation from Table 14.2 would be selected based on the allele combinations present at each STR locus in the tested individuals. These steps are illustrated in D.N.A. Box 14.5 for a worked example at a single locus from a hypothetical paternity case. Fortunately, these calculations are typically performed by computer programs.

Computer Programs and Calculation Validation

A number of computer programs have been used for statistical calculations in parentage testing including DNA View (Brenner 1997), familias (Egeland et al. 2000), and EasyDNA

D.N.A. BOX 14.5

WORKED PATERNITY EXAMPLE

A paternity trio consists of DNA samples from a child (C), a mother (M), and an alleged father (AF). Deficient paternity testing can be performed with just the C and AF samples, but will not be as statistically significant without the mother's DNA profile to help ascertain the father's obligate alleles. The probability that an alleged father is the actual biological father rather than having the required alleles by coincidence (i.e. that a random man is the true father) is represented as a likelihood ratio (LR) known as the paternity index (PI). A maternity index (MI) may be calculated in the same fashion using the allele frequencies for the observed alleles in common between the mother and the child.

In order to perform parentage analysis, three sets of information are needed: (1) the genotypes for each of the individuals being tested, (2) the relevant allele frequencies for the genetic loci examined, and (3) the appropriate equation from 1 of 21 specific scenarios (see Table 14.2) that depends on the allele combinations present in the tested individuals.

(1) Genotypes present at the STR locus D18S51:

   M: 14,15   C: 14,14   AF: 14,16

Substituting the actual alleles for alphabetical symbols starting with "P," we obtain: $14 = P$; $15 = Q$; and $16 = R$. Thus, $M = PQ$, $C = PP$, and $AF = PR$.

(2) D18S51 allele frequencies (Caucasians, N=361; see Appendix 1):
Allele 14 (p): 0.134
Allele 15 (q): 0.170
Allele 16 (r): 0.147

Note that by convention the allele frequencies are represented by the lower case letter for the corresponding allele. Thus, allele $15 = Q$ while the frequency of allele $15 = q$.

(3) Specific scenario equation (#6 in Table 14.2) to be used $(1/2p)$, where $p =$ frequency of allele 14, or 0.134:

$$\mathbf{PI} = 1/2p = 1/(2 \times 0.134) = \mathbf{3.73}$$

Because the child and the alleged father share allele 14, the frequency for this allele is used to determine the PI calculations for this STR marker. In the case illustrated here, the results of the DNA testing using a single STR locus are 3.73 times more likely <u>if</u> the tested man is the biological father of the child than <u>if</u> the biological father is another man, unrelated to the tested man.

By multiplying the various PI values for each STR marker together, the combined paternity index (CPI) might be greater than 100,000 with 13 or 15 STRs examined. The probability of parentage is calculated by using the PI values: $[PI/(PI+1)] \times 100\%$. Thus, with a combined PI of 100,000, the probability of paternity would be 99.999%.

(Fung et al. 2004). Jiri Drábek from the Czech Republic in a 2009 review article described the capabilities and cost of 13 different software programs he evaluated for calculating the LR in parentage and kinship analysis (Drábek 2009). An abbreviated summary of the information on these programs is found in Table 14.3. Some of these programs are freeware, while others have a cost associated with purchase and maintenance that can include regular software upgrades. All programs should be validated before casework use.

TABLE 14.3   Software Programs Available for Performing Parentage and Kinship Likelihood Ratio Calculations

Program Name	Source	Contact or Reference
DNA-View	Charles Brenner, USA	http://dna-view.com/index.html
Easy DNA	Wing Kam Fung, Hong Kong	http://www.hku.hk/statistics/EasyDNA/
EasyPat	Michael Krawczak, Germany	http://www.uni-kiel.de/medinfo/mitarbeiter/krawczak/download/
eDNA	eDNA Consortium	http://www.ednalims.com/
familias	Petter Mostad, Norway	http://www.familias.name/
FamLink	David Kling, Norway	http://www.famlink.se
FSS-ibd	Forensic Science Service	(Maguire & Woodward 2008); *availability today unknown*
GenoProof	Qualitype, Germany	http://www.qualitype.de/en/qualitype/genoproof
GeneMarker HID	SoftGenetics, USA	http://www.softgenetics.com/GeneMarkerHID.html
KinCalc	Steven Myers, USA	Email to request copy: Steven.Myers@doj.ca.gov

See also Drábek (2009).

In order to validate the kinship analysis calculations made by computer software programs, a laboratory has to generate and then analyze pedigrees and genotypes for individuals with known familial relationships. These genotypes are either simulated or taken from previous casework in the laboratory.

It is time-consuming to manually calculate kinship equations to verify software performance. To help standardize the validation of kinship calculations, a dataset of familial genotypes was produced several years ago by the National Institute of Standards and Technology (NIST). This standard reference family data (SRFD) is an artificial four-generation pedigree based on data collected from six different Caucasian family groups (Figure 14.3). The SRFD contains information on 46 autosomal STRs and 17 Y-STRs (O'Connor et al. 2010) that can be downloaded from the kinship section of the NIST STRBase website (STRBase Kinship 2014).

The genotypes of the SRFD pedigree reflect observed Mendelian inheritance patterns, including mutations, rare alleles, and null alleles within real families. The pedigree structure allows for kinship testing of pairwise comparisons (parent—offspring, full siblings, half siblings, first cousins, etc.), paternity trios, and motherless paternity. The SRFD can be used to verify the functionality of calculations performed within kinship analysis programs, including the handling of mutations, rare alleles, and null alleles (Azevedo et al. 2011). Illustrations of how the pedigree data can be used have been demonstrated with a commercially available program and an Excel-based freeware program (O'Connor et al. 2010).

Interlaboratory Studies of Relationship Testing Laboratories

The English Speaking Working Group (ESWG) of the ISFG has annually conducted interlaboratory studies of paternity and relationship testing laboratories since 1991 (Table 14.4). Since 2000, in addition to the laboratory tests these ESWG interlaboratory studies have involved a paper exercise

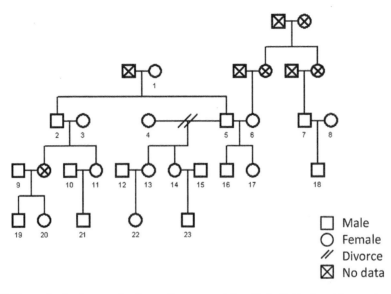

FIGURE 14.3 NIST standard reference family pedigree containing 23 individuals with genotype information at 46 autosomal STRs and 17 Y-STRs available at http://www.cstl.nist.gov/strbase/kinship.htm.

TABLE 14.4 Summary of Paternity (Relationship) Testing Workshops Coordinated by the English Speaking Working Group of the International Society for Forensic Genetics (ESWG-ISFG)

Year	# Labs	Reference	Year	# Labs	Reference
1991	12	Syndercombe-Court & Lincoln (1996)	2003	51	Thomsen et al. (2009)
1992	13	Syndercombe-Court & Lincoln (1996)	2004	55	Thomsen et al. (2009)
1993	16	Syndercombe-Court & Lincoln (1996)	2005	62	Thomsen et al. (2009)
1994	19	Syndercombe-Court & Lincoln (1996)	2006	64	Thomsen et al. (2009)
1995	18	Bjerre et al. (1997)	2007	69	Thomsen et al. (2009), Hallenberg et al. (2008)
1996	21	Bjerre et al. (1997)	2008	68	Thomsen et al. (2009)
1997	24	Hallenberg & Morling (2001)	2009	62	Friis et al. (2009), Poulsen et al. (2014)
1998	31	Hallenberg & Morling (2001)	2010	62	Poulsen et al. (2014)
1999	32	Hallenberg & Morling (2001)	2011	62	Poulsen et al. (2011), Poulsen et al. (2014)
2000	33	Hallenberg & Morling (2002)	2012	60	Not published
2001	36	Hallenberg & Morling (2002)	2013	56	Friis et al. (2013)
2002	46	Thomsen et al. (2009)			

Niels Morling, University of Copenhagen, kindly provided some of this information.

in which a specific scenario is provided, and the laboratories perform biostatistical calculations. The variation in the approaches are analyzed and reported.

In one study in 2011, for example, blood samples from a father and two children were sent from the coordinating laboratory at the University of Copenhagen in Denmark to 62 participating laboratories (Poulsen et al. 2011). Assuming that the man is the biological father of both children, the participants were asked to investigate whether the children were full siblings or half siblings. Of the 39 laboratories submitting only autosomal STR and Y-chromosome STR results, 8% concluded that the children were full siblings, 46% concluded that they were half siblings, and the remainder did not provide any results or provided an "inconclusive" finding. On the other hand, 87% of the 23 laboratories with X-chromosome STR, mitochondrial DNA, or other genetic marker capabilities concluded that the children were half siblings and none of them provided a full-sibling conclusion. This study confirmed that use of additional lineage markers can aid relationship testing.

The ESWG paper challenge exercise in 2011 consisted of STR profiles from a mother, a male child, and the brother of the alleged father (Poulsen et al. 2011). Laboratories were provided with data from 15 autosomal STRs, 16 Y-STRs, and relevant Danish database allele and haplotype frequencies. The scenario involved possible null (silent) alleles, a rare allele, and one Y-STR genetic inconsistency. Likelihood ratio calculations were performed by 44 laboratories, but a total of 16 different formulas were submitted. The LR values for Y-STR data ranged from 0.237 to 237. Of the 26 laboratories that submitted Y-STR results, 86% concluded in favor of paternity between the male child and the untested alleged father with the remaining 14% providing an "inconclusive" finding. In spite of only observing a typing result error rate of 0.08%, the ESWG study noted the large interpretation variability due to variation in formulas used for biostatistical calculations of rare events (Poulsen et al. 2011).

ISFG Recommendations

The ISFG Paternity Testing Commission (PTC) published recommendations in 2002 for augmenting the ISO 17025 guidelines with specific needs for relationship testing laboratories (Morling et al. 2002). The 2002 PTC recommendations are summarized in D.N.A. Box 14.6. Biostatistics recommendations were published in 2007 (Gjertson et al. 2007) and provide recommendations in five areas that are described in more detail below: (1) mathematics, (2) population genetics, (3) special cases, (4) handling non-paternity, and (5) documentation.

Mathematics: The significance of the DNA evidence needs to be estimated using LR principles where mutually exclusive hypotheses are clearly stated and calculated regarding the parentage of a child or another disputed genetic relationship. The possibility of mutation needs to be considered when a genetic inconsistency is observed. Methods of modifying the PI to incorporate mutation rate need to be documented. The probability of silent (null) alleles needs to be considered in biostatistical calculations.

Population Genetics: To avoid bias towards paternity, the probability of observing an allele should be estimated as $(x_i + 1)/(N + 1)$, where x_i is the number of i alleles and N is the total number of alleles in the existing population allele frequency database (e.g. Appendix 1). Laboratories may choose to use the 5/2N minimum allele frequency approach recommended by the NRC II (see Chapter 10). Y-chromosome and mitochondrial DNA results are handled as

D.N.A. BOX 14.6

PTC-ISFG PATERNITY RECOMMENDATIONS

The Paternity Testing Commission (PTC) of the International Society for Forensic Genetics (ISFG) has published two sets of recommendations (Morling et al. 2002, Gjertson et al. 2007). The 2002 recommendations review the ISO 17025 standard for general requirements for the competence of testing laboratories and adds supplemental information specific to paternity testing. Most of the ISO 17025 standard was accepted without comments. Specific ISFG recommendations are outlined here.

The 2002 PTC ISFG recommendations (Morling et al. 2002) provide specific requirements for a laboratory director to have at least a Master's degree in human genetics, at least three years of training in a competent paternity testing laboratory, and documented experience preparing or reviewing at least 100 reports. A laboratory performing PCR-based testing needs to take steps to prevent contamination with PCR products, such as separate areas and dedicated equipment for pre- and post-PCR, and have procedures for monitoring potential contamination. Test methods and genetic markers used for paternity testing need to have available proficiency testing, documented population distribution data, and documented mutation frequencies that are used appropriately.

Non-standard methods cannot be used as the only method for paternity testing unless a second laboratory uses the same method in order to provide a second opinion if necessary. Laboratories need to participate in a graded proficiency-testing program at least twice a year. Relevant population frequency data for ethnic groups need to be used. The measurement uncertainty of tests needs to be known and included in the interpretation of results. All manual calculations have to be performed in duplicate and technically reviewed. All computer-assisted calculations need to be validated. Weight-of-evidence calculations need to be based on likelihood ratio (LR) principles (i.e. the paternity index, PI). Procedures guaranteeing the identity of the individual from which the sample is taken and the traceability of the sample need to be covered by contract with clients. Any other use of samples for scientific purposes needs to be covered by contract with clients.

Sources: Morling, N., et al. (2002). Paternity Testing Commission of the International Society of Forensic Genetics: recommendations on genetic investigations in paternity cases. Forensic Science International, 129, *148–157; Gjertson, D.W., et al. (2007). ISFG: recommendations on biostatistics in paternity testing.* Forensic Science International: Genetics, 1, *223–231.*

haplotypes and may be combined with the genetic weight from independent, autosomal genetic markers by multiplication of contributions to the overall LR. If significant population substructuring is known to be present, then formulas that take substructure into consideration need to be used. However, given that the degree of substructuring is fairly small in most populations, for practical purposes biostatistical calculations can be performed without co-ancestry theta corrections.

Special Cases: The basic principles for biostatistical calculations are the same for standard paternity cases and more complicated deficiency or reconstruction cases. Deficiency cases involve not having genetic test results from pertinent individuals. Reconstruction cases involve deducing the genetic profile of the person of interest using expected inheritance patterns and genetic information from biological relatives. All biostatistical calculations in immigration cases need to be based on LR principles with clearly defined mutually exclusive hypotheses. The PTC emphasizes the need to avoid speculative hypotheses without specific knowledge about case circumstances and to be cautious about assignment of prior probabilities.

Non-paternity: Laboratories are responsible for establishing and documenting their exclusion criteria with preference given to criteria stated in terms of a PI threshold (e.g. $PI < 0.001$). Some laboratories exclude based on the number of genetic inconsistencies observed (e.g. 3 out of 13 tested STR loci).

Documentation: Biostatistical results need to be presented in sufficient detail to enable recalculation. Thus, the PTC recommends that test reports include individual PI values for each genetic system evaluated along with the combined PI and allele frequency sources used for calculations. If reporting probability of paternity (W) results, then prior probability assumptions need to be documented. If a threshold PI exists for issuing test reports, the value(s) need to be documented. Assumptions necessary to calculate and interpret PI results can be categorized as (a) fundamental, (b) empirical, (c) specific, and (d) changeable.

Fundamental assumptions are derived from basic principles and involve laws of genetics and mathematics. *Empirical assumptions* are the estimated STR genotype or Y-STR haplotype probabilities based on allele frequency or haplotype frequency databases gathered from sampling specific population groups. *Specific assumptions* involve relationships among tested individuals and quality results. For example, in paternity cases it is typically assumed that subjects to be tested have been accurately identified, maternity is undisputed, mating is random (i.e. possible fathers are not related to the mother or to each other), laboratory results were obtained without any genotyping errors, and tested genetic systems are independent so that the product rule can be used.

Changeable assumptions include an individual's race or ethnic group and prior probabilities. STR allele and Y-STR haplotype frequencies can vary from one population group to another. An alleged father's race/ethnicity is often assigned by interview when the case is opened. The untested alternative father's race/ethnicity is usually equated with that of the putative father's so that population group's allele frequencies can be used in the PI calculations. The PTC notes that "the alternative hypothesis may include an assumption of the population to which the alternative father belongs" in the case of mixed races between the mother and putative father. If defining a single specific race/ethnicity is difficult, then PI calculations can be performed under multiple assumptions. The PTC concludes that "changeable assumptions like the calculation race and prior probabilities should be noted on a test report, whereas specific assumptions are usually implicit and not noted" (Gjertson et al. 2007).

MUTATIONS AND MUTATION RATES

Mutations happen and represent apparent inconsistencies when comparing potentially related individuals to one another. Since parentage and kinship testing involve measuring genetic relationships across generations (rather than matching of direct references as in the case of forensic comparisons), mutations that may occur must be taken into account in these investigations. These mutations are *germ-line mutations* in that they occur in either the father's sperm or mother's egg cell and are passed on during zygote formation. Thus, every cell in the body will contain the mutation in its genetic code. *Somatic mutations*, on the other hand, occur within different cells or tissues coming from the same individual, such as with cancerous tumors.

As with any region of DNA, mutations can and do occur at STR loci. STR alleles can change over time by some not completely characterized mechanism (Ellegren 2004). According to the current theories, all of the alleles that exist today for a particular STR locus have resulted from only a few "founder" individuals by slowly changing over tens of thousands of years (Wiegand et al. 2000). The mutational event may be in the form of a single base change or in the length of the entire repeat. The molecular mechanisms by which STRs mutate are thought to involve replication slippage or defective DNA replication repair (Nadir et al. 1996, Ellegren 2004).

Impact of Mutation Rates on Paternity Testing

Any time parentage testing is performed or a family reference sample is used to try to associate recovered remains during a mass disaster or missing persons investigation, mutations become an important issue because an exact match between the missing person question (Q) sample cannot be confidently made to a biological known (K) reference sample when a mutation is present. Mutation rates for genetic markers are typically measured through analysis of many parent–offspring allele comparisons.

Low mutation rates are especially critical for genetic markers used in parentage testing and other forms of kinship analysis. Associations between a child and an alleged father are based on the assumption that alleles remain the same when they are passed from one generation to the next. Since relationship testing is attempting to link samples across at least one meiosis (e.g. offspring-to-parent), stable loci with little to no mutation would be preferable. A high mutation rate for an STR marker could result in a false exclusion at that locus. However, loci with very low mutation rates do not typically exhibit very many alleles − and thus any inherited characteristics would be seen in many people, limiting the power of the genetic test. Having STR markers with mutation rates in the range of 1 mutation per 1,000 meioses (0.1%) works fairly well most of the time.

Discovery of STR Allele Mutations

Estimation of mutational events at a DNA marker may be achieved by comparison of genotypes from offspring to those of their parents. Genotype data from paternity trios involving a father, a mother, and at least one child is examined. A discovery of an allele difference between the parents and the child is seen as evidence for a possible mutation (Figure 14.4). The search for mutations in STR loci involves examining many, many parent–child allele transfers because the mutation rate is rather low in most STRs.

Measuring the Mutation Rate

The majority of STR mutations involve the gain or loss of a single repeat unit, which is often referred to as a *single-step mutation*. Thus, a D18S51 allele with 14 repeats would show up as a 13 allele or a 15 allele in the next generation following a mutational event (Figure 14.4). Some studies have shown that more than 90% of the time a single-step mutation occurs such that the child inherits an allele that is either one repeat shorter or longer than the parent possesses (AABB 2008, Sun et al. 2014).

FIGURE 14.4 STR results illustrated for two different family trios where (a) normal transmission of alleles occurred versus (b) a mutation of paternal allele 14 into the child's allele 13.

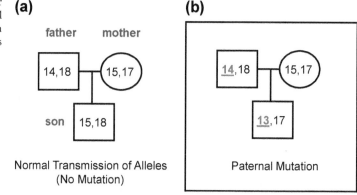

(a) Normal Transmission of Alleles (No Mutation)

(b) Paternal Mutation

Paternal mutations appear to be more frequent than maternal ones for STR loci (Sajantila et al. 1999, Henke & Henke 1999, AABB 2003). However, depending on the genotype combinations it can be difficult to ascertain from which parent the mutant allele was inherited. Several studies have constructed linked-loci haplotypes using flanking STR markers to help confirm the parental origin of a mutant allele (Klintschar et al. 2004, Müller et al. 2010).

The mutation rates for commonly used STR loci have been gathered from paternity testing laboratory results or studies reported in the literature. As can be seen in Table 14.5, mutation rates for STR loci vary by marker and are on the order of 1 to 4 per thousand meioses or 0.1% to 0.4%. The STR loci with the lowest observed mutation rates are CSF1PO, TH01, TPOX, D5S818, and D8S1179. Not surprisingly, the STR loci with the highest mutation rates — D21S11, FGA, D7S820, D16S539, and D18S51 — are among the most polymorphic and possess the highest number of observed alleles (see Appendix 1). Mutation rates for most of the autosomal STRs, Y-chromosome STRs, or X-chromosome STRs appear to fall in the same range of approximately 0.1% to 0.4%.

Since the average mutation rate is sometimes below 0.1%, approximately 1,000 parent—offspring allele transfers would have to be observed before one mutation would be seen in some STR markers (Weber & Wong 1993). Brinkman and co-workers examined 10,844 parent—child allele transfers at nine STR loci and observed 23 mutations (Brinkman et al. 1998). No mutations were observed at three of the loci (TH01, F13B, CD4). Sajantila et al. (1999) studied 29,640 parent—child allele transfers at five STRs and four minisatellites and observed only 18 mutational events (11 in three STR loci: D3S1359, VWA, and TH01). Two of the STRs, TPOX and FES/FPS, had no detectable mutations.

The correlation of higher locus heterozygosity with a higher mutation rate was made in a Chinese study of 6,441 parent—child meioses that observed 195 mutations across 22 of 24 tested STR loci (Lu et al. 2012). The two loci with no mutations were TH01 and TPOX, which also display the lowest mutation rate in Table 14.5.

A Brazilian study of 10,959 paternity cases with 284,934 allelic transfers identified 355 mutations of which 348 involved the gain or loss of a single repeat unit (Mardini et al. 2013). The paternal mutation rate was approximately five times higher than the maternal mutation rate. In-depth analysis of 98 families exhibiting 101 mutations at one of four STRs D3S1358, FGA, SE33, and vWA found a

TABLE 14.5 Mutation Rates of Common Autosomal STR Loci Observed during Paternity Testing

STR System	Maternal Meioses (%)	Paternal Meioses (%)	Number from Either	Total Number of Mutations	Mutation Rate
CSF1PO	95/304,307 (0.031)	982/643,118 (0.15)	410	1,487/947,425	0.16%
FGA	205/408,230 (0.050)	2,210/692,776 (0.32)	710	3,125/1,101,006	0.28%
TH01	31/327,172 (0.0095)	41/452,382 (0.0091)	28	100/779,554	0.013%
TPOX	18/400,061 (0.0045)	54/457,420 (0.012)	28	100/857,481	0.012%
vWA	184/564,398 (0.033)	1,482/873,547 (0.17)	814	2,480/1,437,945	0.17%
D3S1358	60/405,452 (0.015)	713/558,836 (0.13)	379	1,152/964,288	0.12%
D5S818	111/451,736 (0.025)	763/655,603 (0.12)	385	1,259/1,107,339	0.11%
D7S820	59/440,562 (0.013)	745/644,743 (0.12)	285	1,089/1,085,305	0.10%
D8S1179	96/409,869 (0.023)	779/489,968 (0.16)	364	1,239/899,837	0.14%
D13S317	192/482,136 (0.040)	881/621,146 (0.14)	485	1,558/1,103,282	0.14%
D16S539	129/467,774 (0.028)	540/494,465 (0.11)	372	1,041/962,239	0.11%
D18S51	186/296,244 (0.063)	1,094/494,098 (0.22)	466	1,746/790,342	0.22%
D21S11	464/435,388 (0.11)	772/526,708 (0.15)	580	1,816/962,096	0.19%
Penta D	12/18,701 (0.064)	21/22,501 (0.093)	24	57/41,202	0.14%
Penta E	29/44,311 (0.065)	75/55,719 (0.13)	59	163/100,030	0.16%
D2S1338	15/72,830 (0.021)	157/152,310 (0.10)	90	262/225,140	0.12%
D19S433	38/70,001 (0.054)	78/103,489 (0.075)	71	187/173,490	0.11%
SE33 (ACTBP2)	0/330 (<0.30)	330/51,610 (0.64)	None reported	330/51,940	0.64%
D1S1656 (Hill et al. 2011)	—	0/393 (<0.25)	—	0/393	<0.25%
D12S391 (Lu et al. 2012)	1/3,078 (0.032)	10/3,363 (0.30)	0	11/6,441	0.17%
D2S441 (Hill et al. 2011)	—	0/393 (<0.25)	—	0/393	<0.25%
D10S1248 (Hill et al. 2011)	—	0/393 (<0.25)	—	0/393	<0.25%
D22S1045 (Hill et al. 2011)	—	0/393 (<0.25)	—	0/393	<0.25%
D6S1043 (Lu et al. 2012)	0/3,078 (<0.032)	2/3,363 (0.060)	0	2/6,441	0.031%

See also http://www.cstl.nist.gov/strbase/mutation.htm. Information derived from AABB 2003 annual report provided from over three dozen paternity testing laboratories. The reported mutations are divided into maternal or paternal sources or from either when the source of the mutation observed in a child could not be determined. Very little mutation rate data has been published to-date on the newer STR loci. References have been included below the locus where there are data available.

100:1 ratio of one-step to two-step mutations, a 76:8 ratio of paternal to maternal mutations, and a 47:50 ratio of repeat gains to losses (Müller et al. 2010).

An examination of 45,085 trios from China and Brazil with 15 STRs found 1,587 mutations across the 1,623,378 possible allele transfers (Sun et al. 2014). Single-step mutations occurred 97% of the time (all but 48 mutations). With the 122 mutations found in 100,558 meioses measured at D18S51, there were two +2 step, five −2 step, and two −3 step mutations (Sun et al. 2014). Where mutation gender could be assigned with confidence, there were 1,066 male mutations compared to only 277 female mutations. This joint Chinese—Brazilian study points out that the AABB 2008 study may slightly overestimate the mutation rate because some of the contributing laboratories may not have submitted data upon observing no mutations (Sun et al. 2014).

Probably the largest mutation rate study performed to-date involved examining 2,477 autosomal STR loci in 24,832 father—mother—child Icelander trios (Sun et al. 2012). This study identified 1,695 mutations in 5,085,672 transmissions within the studied family trios and reported that paternal mutations were 3.3 times more common than maternal mutations (Sun et al. 2012).

Allele-Specific Mutation Rates

While mutation rates are typically reported in terms of the number of mutations over the total number of meioses examined, there have been some studies that have focused on allele-specific mutation rates (D.N.A. Box 14.7). For example, from analysis of 31,808 paternity cases conducted at a DNA lab in Colombia from 2008 to 2011, 606 mutational events were detected in 15 STRs analyzed (Paredes 2011). Of these 606 mutations, 97 (16%) were from FGA with 74% of these being paternal mutations, 11% maternal, and 15% not possible to establish the origin. Six different FGA alleles (22, 23, 24, 25, 26, and 27) were involved in 82% of the mutations with repeat expansions (e.g. 23 → 24) occurring more commonly than repeat contractions (e.g. 23 → 22). With allele 27, repeat contractions were ten times more frequent than repeat expansions (Paredes 2011).

Much like stutter percentages discussed in Chapter 3, STR mutation rates appear to be highly dependent on the number of consecutive repeat units, the purity of the repeats (i.e. whether or not a compound repeat structure exists with several different repeat motifs), and the length of the repeat unit as well as the local genomic sequence (Sun et al. 2014).

Statistical Calculations Incorporating Mutation Rate

Mutations that are encountered in parentage testing need to be incorporated into the overall statistical result. Several approaches for incorporating mutation rates in PI calculations have been described (AABB 2011, Allen 2013). Charles Brenner discusses treatment of mutations on his DNA View website (Brenner 2006).

A genetic marker's mutation rate is often abbreviated with the Greek letter mu (μ). One approach is to simply assign the mutation rate as the PI for that locus if a discrepancy is observed. With this approach, if a mutation rate was $\mu = 0.0022$ and a mismatch was observed, then a value of 0.0022 is used for the PI at that locus. This is not ideal because two hypotheses are not being compared.

A more appropriate approach in the LR framework of using two mutually exclusive hypotheses would be to consider

$$PI = \frac{Pr(\text{mismatched allele}|\text{the tested man is the father of the child and a mutation occurred})}{Pr(\text{mismatched allele}|\text{the tested man is not the father of the child})}$$

D.N.A. BOX 14.7

ALLELE-SPECIFIC MUTATION RATES

Until recently, only general information on STR mutation rates was reported—namely, how many mutations occurred relative to the number of meioses measured (see Table 14.5). The realization that certain alleles are more prone to mutation than others has prompted the American Association of Blood Banks (AABB) to carefully examine *which alleles* were mutating based on records from accredited parentage testing laboratories (AABB 2003, AABB 2008).

Appendix 5 in the AABB Annual Report Summary for Testing in 2002, prepared by the parentage testing program unit in November 2003, notes the number of paternal and maternal mutations by both locus and allele. For example, with the STR locus FGA an apparent change from allele 24 to 25 was observed 62 times (11.7%) out of 530 total paternal mutations seen in 2002, while an apparent change from allele 19 to 20 was seen only 8 times (1.5%). In general longer alleles were seen to mutate more frequently.

The directionality of the mutation as either an expansion or a contraction of the repeat array can also vary significantly. For example, with paternal D16S539 mutations observed in 2002,

there were 10 instances of allele 11 expanding to become allele 12, but only 4 examples of allele 11 contracting to allele 10. The process of expansion and contraction of the STR repeat regions probably occurs in a similar fashion, as illustrated in Figure 3.11 for stutter product formation. As this information continues to be collated in future studies, it should prove useful in refining mutation rates and aid in a better understanding of the process of STR origins and variability over human history.

The chart below collates allele-specific mutation rates from several sources and population groups (AABB 2008, Sun et al. 2014). The AABB original data are broken out by paternal or maternal mutation from trios and also whether or not the mutation was a gain or a loss of a repeat. Only the paternal data and total mutations per allele are displayed here. The AABB data may be overestimating the mutation rate because some of the contributing laboratories may not have submitted data upon observing no mutations (Sun et al. 2014). However, there definitely are population-specific differences in the allele-specific mutation rates.

D18S51 Allele	Chinese Parental Mutation Rate ($\times 10^{-5}$)	Brazilian Parental Mutation Rate ($\times 10^{-5}$)	Caucasian Paternal Mutation Rate ($\times 10^{-5}$)	Black Paternal Mutation Rate ($\times 10^{-5}$)
12	—	0.1	4.8	6.2
13	0.5	0.2	6.4	7.4
14	0.3	—	13	5.0
15	0.3	0.3	9.5	24
16	1.2	0.3	18	26
17	—	0.2	11	33
18	0.6	0.3	19	36
19	0.7	0.7	21	38

(Continued)

D.N.A. BOX 14.7   (cont'd)

D18S51 Allele	Chinese Parental Mutation Rate ($\times 10^{-5}$)	Brazilian Parental Mutation Rate ($\times 10^{-5}$)	Caucasian Paternal Mutation Rate ($\times 10^{-5}$)	Black Paternal Mutation Rate ($\times 10^{-5}$)
20	8.0	0.7	13	42
21	7.9	2.0	1.6	25
22	9.3	0.7	3.2	14
23	17	3.4	4.8	9.9
24	11	5.9	3.2	3.7
25	—	—	—	1.2
26	160	38	—	—
27	—	32	—	—
Overall	26 (0.026%)	110 (0.11%)	170 (0.17%)	350 (0.35%)
# Meioses	18,066	100,558	62,932	80,662
Source	Sun et al. 2014	Sun et al. 2014	AABB 2008	AABB 2008

Sources: AABB Annual Report Summary for Testing in 2002 (http://www.aabb.org/sa/facilities/Documents/ptannrpt02.pdf); AABB 2008 report (http://www.aabb.org/sa/facilities/Documents/rtannrpt08.pdf); Sun, H., et al. (2014). Comparison of southern Chinese Han and Brazilian Caucasian mutation rates at autosomal short tandem repeat loci used in human forensic genetics. International Journal of Legal Medicine, 128, 1—9.

This LR can be calculated as

$$PI = \frac{\mu}{PE_x}$$

where μ is the general locus mutation rate and PE_x is the average probability of exclusion for the locus, which is the probability that a random man would have a genotype inconsistent with paternity at this locus (Allen 2013).

If μ is 0.0022 and PE_x is 0.49, then PI would be 0.0045. The inverse of 0.0045 is 222. If we invert the LR formulated above, then we can conclude that the observation of a mismatched allele at this locus is 222 times more likely if the tested man is not the father of the child than if he is the father of the child and a mutation occurred. Although the PI in this case favors non-paternity at this locus (as it should with a mismatch), the overall combined PI may be in favor of paternity provided the other loci match between the alleged father and the child.

However, the approach just reviewed does not consider the transmission of a specific mutant allele from the parent to the child. D.N.A. Box 14.8 explores a more precise approach of handling mutational events involving probabilities of specific allele transmissions.

In paternity testing situations, a high mutation rate for an STR marker could result in a false exclusion at that locus. The AABB standards recognize that mutations are naturally occurring genetic

D.N.A. BOX 14.8

WORKED EXAMPLE WITH METHODS FOR INCORPORATING MUTATION

Three approaches for handling mutations (μ) in paternity testing include: (1) use of the locus mutation rate in place of the PI, (2) use of the locus mutation rate divided by the average probability of exclusion of the locus, and (3) addressing specific probabilities of mutant allele transition from parent to child (Gjertson 2011).

For D18S51, the average mutation rate is 0.0022 or 0.22% (Table 14.5). Alternatively the average D18S51 locus specific mutation rate for Caucasians could be used of 0.0017 (AABB 2008) instead of 0.0022 (Table 14.5, which originates from AABB 2003).

Approach 1: PI = μ = 0.0022
Approach 2: PI = μ/ PE$_x$ = 0.0022/0.732 = 0.0030

where the e average probability of exclusion (PE$_x$) of 0.732 is calculated from a D18S51 heterozygosity of 0.8687 (using NIST Caucasian data, Butler et al. 2012) and a formula of PE$_x$ = $H^2(1-2H(1-H)^2)$ where H is the locus heterozygosity.

Approach 3: PI = 0.00024 (see calculations and assumptions below)

Using allele-specific D18S51 alleles (14 → 13) with example shown in Figure 14.3 and Fimmers et al. 1992 approach:

$$PI = \frac{\mu_{14\to13} + \mu_{12\to13}}{2p_{13}} = \frac{0.000048 + 0.000048}{2 \times 0.123}$$
$$= 0.00024$$

where μ is the allele-specific mutation rate and p is the frequency of mutant allele (in this case allele

13). Mutation rate (in Caucasians, AABB 2008) for D18S51 14 → 13 is 0.000048 and for 12 → 13 is 0.000048. [Note that the directional mutation rate information from AABB 2008 is more specific than the information provided in D.N.A. Box 14.7 that incorporates all of the mutations seen for a particular allele].

These three approaches generate paternity indices that differ by more than an order of magnitude (0.00024 to 0.0030). Approach 3 is dependent on having allele-specific mutation information, which has only been collected recently as part of the annual AABB report (AABB 2003). Also many assumptions have to be made in terms of which mutation rate to use. With all these different mutation model and mutation rate possibilities it is no wonder that differences arise in interlaboratory studies that involve relationship testing where mutation is a possibility.

Sources: Gjertson, D.W. (2011). Appendix 9: the effect of isolated inconsistencies in the statistical evaluation of paternity: a 2005 update. In AABB Guidance for Standards for Relationship Testing Laboratories, 10th Edition. *AABB: Bethesda, Maryland; Fimmers, R., et al. (1992). How to deal with mutations in DNA-testing.* Advances in Forensic Haemogenetics, *Rittner, C., & Schneider, P.M. (eds.). Berlin: Springer-Verlag, pp. 285-287; Brenner, C.H. (2004). Multiple mutations, covert mutations and false exclusions in paternity casework.* Progress in Forensic Genetics 10 (In-ternational Congress Series), *1261, 112-114; Brenner, C.H. (2006). Mutations in paternity. Available at http://dna-view. com/mudisc.htm; American Association of Blood Banks Relationship Testing Program Unit (2003). Annual report summary for testing in 2003. Available from http://www. aabb.org/sa/facilities/Documents/ptannrpt03.pdf; American Association of Blood Banks Relationship Testing Program Unit (2008). Annual report summary for testing in 2008. Available from http://www.aabb.org/sa/facilities/Documents/ rtannrpt08.pdf.*

events and require that the mutation frequency at a tested locus be documented (AABB 2011). The AABB standards also emphasize that an opinion of non-paternity shall not be rendered on the basis of a single mismatch "exclusion" at a single DNA locus (i.e. a single inconsistency) (AABB 2011, standard 6.3.1.1). When mismatches due to mutational events occur in the alleged father vs. child comparison, a paternity testing laboratory may have to run additional STR loci in order to produce a combined PI that exceeds their threshold for calling paternity (e.g. PI $\geq$ 100).

However, it is important to keep in mind that when more genetic systems are examined there is a greater chance of a random mutation being observed. With STR analysis often examining a battery of a dozen or more loci, it is not uncommon to see two inconsistencies between a child and the true biological father (Gunn et al. 1997, Nutini et al. 2003). The "at-least-two-exclusions-before-declaring-non-paternity" rule is commonly accepted in parentage testing laboratories (Balloch et al. 2008) although instances of two or even three exclusions have been observed in mutation rate studies and paternity cases (Sun et al. 2012).

Silent (Null) Alleles

When examining test results from parentage trios it is expected that a child will have alleles in common with his/her parents. Sometimes, however, a discrepancy exists with a single STR locus that is due to a primer binding site mutation rather than a repeat mutation. These so-called silent or null alleles may be undetected in both parent and child giving rise to an apparent discrepancy in allele inheritance. As described in Chapter 4, the use of additional primer pairs (e.g. analysis of the samples with a different STR kit) can unveil the silent allele. A mutation in the Identifiler D19S433 primer binding site was discovered to occur in the Japanese population (Mizuno et al. 2008). Approaches have been published to account for null alleles (Wagner et al. 2006, Lane 2013).

OTHER TOPICS WITH PARENTAGE TESTING

Unfortunately, complete parentage trios are not always available. Sometimes the mother's DNA sample may not be included in a case or the father is not available for testing. When a potential sample is not available for testing, these cases are referred to as *deficiency cases*. The advantage of having a mother's DNA in a paternity testing case is that the obligate paternal alleles can be more easily deciphered in the child's DNA profile.

All relationship testing LR calculations are based on two mutually exclusive hypotheses. Analysts must be careful with how these hypotheses are formulated. Will the answer obtained provide the needed information? Scientists must present the evidence and not try to specifically provide support for one side or the other in a dispute. In some cases, more reference samples were needed to gain a better understanding of the potential pedigree. In other cases, additional loci may provide the needed clarity to the relationship being investigated.

While more statistical uncertainty can arise in deficient parentage cases (where one of the parents is not tested), they can still be brought to a reasonable degree of resolution, although sometimes results from additional genetic loci are needed. Analysis of genetic information from mitochondrial DNA, the Y-chromosome, or the X-chromosome can help with confirming relationships between individuals. These additional loci extend the range of informative reference samples to more distantly related relatives. A combination of samples from more than one close relative can help provide greater confidence in this kinship analysis.

Testing without the Mother (Deficient Paternity Tests)

While testing can be performed between a child and an alleged father without a mother's sample, there are a number of reasons to avoid this situation if possible. Without the mother's DNA results, determining the paternal obligate allele is more difficult, which can reduce the opportunity to obtain a sufficient PI to confidently answer the relationship question being examined (AABB 2008). Not only is the ability to detect a falsely accused man reduced, but more importantly false inclusions of close biological relatives may occur especially with difficult cases such as incest. Laboratories may also have legal and ethical issues with testing for paternity if the biological mother has not provided consent to access her genetic information (Barrot et al. 2014).

An important aspect of having the mother's DNA sample is that a quality control check is in place. If alleles are not shared between the child and mother at the tested loci, then fraud may be involved (where the father brings a child that is his but not the mother's to try and get welfare assistance) or a potential sample switch may have occurred in the laboratory. The AABB annual report emphasizes: "Testing without the mother should only be done when the mother's location is unknown or she is deceased. Every effort should be made to test the mother" (AABB 2010).

Testing without the Father (Reconstruction Cases)

If an alleged father's sample is not available, testing of other children (child's siblings) or the alleged father's parents (child's grandparents) may help ascertain the true biological father's obligate alleles. If the man in question had other children and their samples and their mother's sample are available for testing, then it may be possible to determine the precise genotype of the alleged father. These types of reconstruction cases can be challenging and may require consulting a kinship analysis expert.

Use of Highly Polymorphic Loci in Relationship Testing

Generally speaking, genetic loci that exhibit more alleles are more variable or polymorphic in a population — usually as a result of a higher mutation rate compared to less polymorphic markers. More alleles and a higher degree of variation among samples are highly beneficial locus characteristics with forensic DNA testing involving direct matching between suspect and evidence. Success in deciphering DNA mixtures also improves when there are more alleles and therefore less chance of allele sharing and stacking. However, the strength of relationship testing when looking for allele associations across one generation or more can be diminished with a highly polymorphic and rapidly mutating genetic marker.

For example, the STR marker SE33 has a mutation rate of 0.64% (Table 14.5), which is about three times higher than the average STR marker. If a mutation occurs at SE33 when only a deficient pedigree is available to test (e.g. motherless paternity test), then it may be more difficult to separate a wrongly named first-degree relative, such as a brother, of the true father when a few STR exclusions result. Thus, having loci in a relationship testing battery with lower mutation rates and hence lower powers of discrimination can be beneficial to reduce the possibility of mutation.

Benefits of Additional Genetic Markers

Having additional STR kits capable of extending the number of autosomal STR loci in a laboratory's arsenal can help address challenging relationship testing scenarios (Carboni et al. 2011, Carnevali et al. 2011). However, it is sometimes best to seek information from lineage markers to aid with specific inheritance scenarios and/or single nucleotide polymorphisms (SNPs) or insertion-deletion (InDel) markers that have lower mutation rates (Børsting et al. 2008, Børsting & Morling 2011). The reference list at the back of the chapter contains examples where SNPs or InDels have aided complex kinship analysis (Phillips et al. 2008, Phillips 2012, Pinto et al. 2013). Lineage markers including Y-chromosome and X-chromosome markers can aid kinship analysis depending on the situation, especially in deficiency cases (Aquino et al. 2009, Builes et al. 2009).

Simulations can be performed to explore the number of STR markers needed to detect specific relatives with a certain degree of probability. One study found that at least 5 independent STR markers are needed to detect first-degree relatives (e.g. parent-offspring, see Table 14.1) with 90% probability, 27 STRs to detect second-degree relatives with the same level of certainty, 123 STRs to detect third-degree relatives, and 525 STRs to detect fourth-degree relatives (e.g. second cousins) with a 90% probability (Wilkening et al. 2006).

Chromosomally closely spaced loci can aid kinship analysis in some cases (Egeland & Sheehan 2008, Du et al. 2013). FamLink is a new program designed to enable linked markers to be used in relationship testing (Kling et al. 2012).

MISSING PERSONS & DISASTER VICTIM IDENTIFICATION

When direct reference samples are not available, biological reference samples are sought to aid missing persons and disaster victim identification (DVI) efforts. For more on issues faced with DVI, see Chapter 9 in *Advanced Topics in Forensic DNA Typing: Methodology* (Butler 2012).

Reference Samples

Several studies have attempted to determine a rank order of which biological relatives are most helpful in kinship analysis for DVI or missing persons investigations (Brenner 2006b, Prinz et al. 2007, Ge et al. 2011). Preferred family reference samples in order of preference include: (1) both parents; (2) one parent, spouse, and children; (3) children and spouse; (4) one parent and sibling; (5) two or more siblings; and (6) known identical twin (Prinz et al. 2007). Kinship index simulations with various combinations of relatives found that one full sibling provided a probability of identity of 92.1% (with a 10% prior probability), while a sibling plus a parent increased the probability of identity to 99.996% (Brenner 2006b). In examining 37 common reference scenarios, three children plus spouse provided the highest average LR (2.63×10^{12}) with a single first cousin as a reference sample providing the lowest average LR (1.77) (Ge et al. 2011).

The following recommendations were made based on results from simulating various reference relatives and seeing what combinations yielded the highest LRs for true pedigree relationships and the best probability of excluding false relationships (Ge et al. 2011). Parents are the preferred relatives, and when possible both parents of the missing person should be typed. Children are the second preferred relatives, and as many children as possible should be examined in an effort to reconstruct the missing person's genotype at each locus. If the missing person is male, then Y-chromosome analysis of sons can be effective. The spouse of a missing person (if he/she is the father/mother of the children) in combination with the children can help identify the obligate alleles in reconstructing the missing persons' genotype at each locus. Full siblings of the missing person are the next best reference samples. All other distant relatives only provide limited capability with auto-somal markers, but their Y-chromosome or mitochondrial DNA can help filter out false relationships. Finally, when limited numbers of relatives are available, examine as many markers as possible (Ge et al. 2011).

Reverse Parentage Testing

In identification of remains as part of missing persons investigations or mass disaster victim iden-tification work, the question under consideration may be whether or not a child belongs to the mother and father tested or other biological references available (see Figure 14.1). This is essentially the oppo-site question as that asked in parentage testing, namely, given a child's genotype, who are the par-ents? The samples examined may be the same family trio as studied in parentage testing: alleged mother, alleged father, and child, and the reverse PI may be formulated as follows:

$$\text{Reverse Paternity Index} = \frac{\text{Pr(Child}|AP_1 \text{ and } AP_2 \text{ are the parents of Child)}}{\text{Pr(Child}|\text{two randomly selected people are the parents of Child)}}$$

Unfortunately, it is normally a luxury to have samples from both parents available in some disaster victim identification situations. In addition, sometimes the submitted "father" sample is not the true biological father. Typically, only a single parent or sibling samples are available, which makes the reverse parentage analysis more challenging.

Likelihood Ratio Distributions to Assess Risk of False Inclusion or Exclusion

There is a probabilistic nature to relationship inference. True relatives may appear unrelated and unrelated people may appear related due to alleles being identical by coincidence (this is known as "identical by state" and abbreviated as "IBS"). Simulations of many genotype combinations can be performed in order to understand the LR distributions of related versus unrelated individuals (Figure 14.5). The genotype combinations in these simulations are informed with empirical allele frequencies for a specific population group (e.g. U.S. Caucasians). The shape and position of the LR distributions are also influenced by the relationship under investigation, such as parent—offspring or full siblings.

By definition, when LR = 1, then the two hypotheses under consideration are equally probable. If a pairwise comparison of two unrelated people produces an LR > 1, then this can be considered a false positive. In other words, the statistical calculation suggests that the genetic data are in favor of the two individuals being related when in fact they are not. Alternatively, if true relatives exhibit an LR < 1, then this is a false negative because the LR is in favor of the compared individuals being unrelated when in fact they are related.

The overlap in related and unrelated LR distributions can be reduced for some scenarios by adding additional STR markers (O'Connor 2010). Ideally there would be no overlap in these distributions. In other words, we would like to avoid or minimize false negatives and false positives as much as

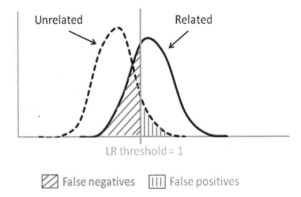

FIGURE 14.5   Illustration of the overlap in likelihood ratio (LR) distributions between related and unrelated individuals showing where false positives (unrelated individuals that have an LR > 1) and false negatives (related individuals that have a LR <1) can arise. Figure courtesy of Kristen O'Connor, former NIST postdoc. Adapted from O'Connor (2010).

possible to avoid the possibility of false inclusions or false exclusions. These types of LR distribution simulations can be helpful in exploring the capabilities or limitations of familial searching (Bieder et al. 2006, Ge et al. 2011, Myers et al. 2011), which involves searching a DNA offender database for potential relatives to make an extended association to an unsolved crime scene profile (Maguire et al. 2014, D.N.A. Box 14.9).

D.N.A. BOX 14.9

FAMILIAL SEARCHING

Familial searching is "a deliberate search of a DNA database conducted for the intended purpose of potentially identifying close biological relatives of the source of the unknown forensic profile obtained from crime scene evidence" (SWGDAM 2014). Using familial search capabilities in the UK, the Forensic Science Service (FSS) worked on 188 police investigations that led to the identification of 41 perpetrators between 2002 and 2011 (Maguire et al. 2014). Largely due to the July 2010 familial search success with the Grim Sleeper case in California (see Butler 2012), other states in the U.S. have initiated use of familial searching programs as a tool to attempt to identify suspects when other investigative efforts have failed. Familial searching experiences low success rates due to a lack of close relatives of the perpetrator in the database or from false

negatives where true relatives in the database are missed due to the search strategy used. Once a ranked candidate list of potential relatives is developed from an initial familial search of a database, Y-STR testing on male samples helps filter false positives. The most significant problem with familial searching is the production of false positives due to the crime scene profile having common alleles that are shared by unrelated individuals, potentially producing likelihood ratio (LR) values indicative of a putative relationship. Even with relatively low LRs for individual loci, the combination of LRs across 13 or 15 STR loci can produce fairly large LRs that appear high in a ranked list. Familial searches, as presently conducted, can produce many false negative results with true siblings and work best with father–son situations, where alleles are shared across an entire profile. However, the majority of convicted offenders with DNA profiles in the database probably do not have children old enough to be committing crimes (Butler 2012).

The Scientific Working Group on DNA Analysis Methods (SWGDAM) recently released recommendations on familial searching (SWGDAM 2014). Three questions were posed to SWGDAM and some research simulations were performed to address them. These questions were:

(1) Is kinship matching (producing a ranked list of candidates based upon kinship statistics) more efficient at detecting relatives than counting the number of alleles shared?

(2) If the number of false positives generated prior to finding a true match is inversely related to the likelihood of sibship, does this suggest that many true siblings would not be found in large databases? If so, is there an optimal database size range for performing familial searching?

(3) Can we establish the number of ranked candidates (kinship matching) that would require investigation in order to ascertain a "true" relative when searching a database with over 10 million DNA profiles? If so, what is that number?

The SWGDAM working group endorsed the use of kinship LRs as the preferred method for familial searching because this approach takes into account the allele frequencies as well as the number of alleles that match, and is therefore more effective in identifying the true relative than

a method that only counts the number of shared alleles. For purposes of studying the potential impact of database size on the familial search success, three different-size state databases were explored: Wyoming (19,300), Virginia (356,000), and California (1,780,000), as well as a combined database (2,130,000). Additionally, a mock national database with 10 million profiles was created for testing purposes. A true relative was seeded into the databases prior to the simulated familial searches.

With a parent–child relationship, the "relative" ranked #1 on the various candidate lists in declining percentages depending on the size of the database. For Wyoming a #1 ranking on the candidate list occurred 73% of the time while with the much larger California database a #1 ranking was achieved about 19% of the time. With the 10 million-profile database, the true relative only made it into the top 100 candidates on the ranked list about 56% of the time. Thus, efforts to follow up on long candidate lists with familial searching of large DNA databases would likely be a big burden with potentially little success, and therefore familial searching at the national level was not recommended.

Sources: Butler, J.M. (2012). Familial DNA searches: potential, pitfalls, and privacy concerns. Appendix 2 in Advanced Topics in Forensic DNA Typing: Methodology. *Elsevier Academic Press: San Diego, pp. 603–610; SWGDAM (2014). Recommendations from the SWGDAM Ad Hoc Working Group on Familial Searching. Available at www.SWGDAM.org; Maguire, C.N., et al. (2014). Familial searching: a specialist forensic profiling service utilizing the National DNA Database to identify unknown offenders via their relatives — the UK experience.* Forensic Science International: Genetics, 8, 1–9.

COMPLEX KINSHIP ANALYSIS

Kinship analysis can become complex depending on specific scenarios, questions being asked, and reference samples available. In the final section of this chapter, some challenges and issues are reviewed regarding sibling analysis, testing extended family relationships for immigration purposes, attempting to connect distant relatives, and trying to separate close relatives. Improvements can be seen in these scenarios either by collecting data from more genetic markers in the DNA samples being compared or by increasing the pool of reference samples. In terms of the Q-to-K comparison discussed throughout this book, either (1) more data points (different markers) are collected on the Q and the K samples or (2) more K samples (different relatives) are gathered. Either approach improves the number of points of comparison.

Sibling Testing

Since siblings do not necessarily have an obligate allele between them like parent–offspring relationships do, sibling analyses may be more problematic and challenging. As seen in Table 14.1, there is a 25% chance that one full sibling will inherit both alleles of the other sibling IBD (identical by descent) from common parents, a 50% chance that a sibling will inherit IBD one parent allele of the other, and a 25% chance that a sibling will inherit IBD no parental alleles of the other sibling.

One of the first studies examining the specificity of sibship determination looked at 50 full sibling and 50 non-sibling sample pairs with the 15 STR loci in the Identifiler kit (Reid et al. 2004). This study found that the combined sibship indices ranged from 4.6 to >1 billion in the full siblings and from 4.5 $\times 10^{-8}$ to 0.12 in the non-sibling controls. Thus, no overlap between the true sibling pairs and the non-sibling pairs were observed in this limited sample set. All true siblings had an LR > 1 and all non-siblings had an LR < 1.

However, larger sample sets may exhibit some false positives and false negatives. A simulation of 5,000 full sibling pairs using 13 STRs with U.S. Caucasian allele frequencies (Butler et al. 2003) found that 2.7% of the time non-siblings have a sibship index LR > 1 (i.e. a false positive) (O'Connor 2010). Conversely, 3.3% of the time true-siblings had a sibship index LR < 1 (i.e. a false negative). Figure 14.6 displays simulation data with related versus unrelated LR distributions for parent–offspring, full siblings, and half siblings.

Typically studies in the literature are performed with simulations of pairwise comparisons involving single sets of parent–child or sibling–sibling LR calculations. An examination of the variation seen in paternity indices and sibship indices within a single family can be instructive as well (D.N.A. Box 14.10).

The combined paternity index results from the six children discussed in D.N.A. Box 14.10 varied three orders of magnitude from 223,000,000 in Child-1 down to 22,000 in Child-3 with the 15 STR loci examined. This variability in PI values illustrates the probabilistic nature of genetic inheritance. When a rare allele is transmitted to an individual in a pedigree, the PI is higher for this locus. Likewise, when homozygous alleles are inherited from both parents, the locus PI values are higher than with heterozygous genotypes.

For sibling comparisons, parental genotypes influence the possible allelic combinations. The sibship indices range from 14,100 to 0.727 (D.N.A. Box 14.10). When non-overlapping heterozygous alleles occur in the parents, then full siblings may have completely different genotypes (see Figure 14.2), which lowers the statistical assessment of potential relatedness. In some cases, such as Sibling-5 and Sibling-6 in D.N.A. Box 14.10, the resulting sibship index LR is less than one, which means the evidence favors the hypothesis of these siblings not being related to the individual in question.

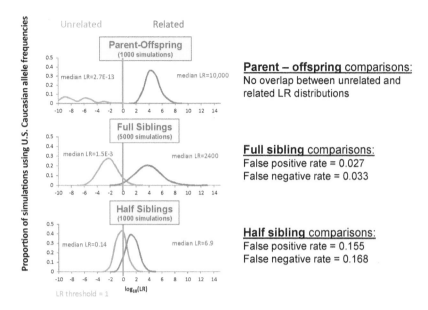

FIGURE 14.6 Likelihood ratio (LR) distributions calculated through simulating pairwise comparisons of related and unrelated individuals using 13 STR loci and U.S. Caucasian allele frequencies. The degree of overlap in the LR distributions corresponds with possible false positive or false negative results (see Figure 14.5). Full siblings and half siblings may have true relatives with LR < 1 because these individuals may not share any alleles at a locus. Adding more STR loci can shift the related distribution to the right. Figure courtesy of Kristen O'Connor, former NIST postdoc. Adapted from O'Connor (2010).

Here the probabilistic nature of allele inheritance creates a situation where a report may be issued that the evidence (combined sibship index = 0.771) does not favor two true brothers (individual #3 and individual #12) from being siblings. Yet there are no mutations, and when both parent profiles (individual #1 and individual #2 in the D.N.A. Box 14.10 pedigree) are factored in, the separate paternity indices for both individual #3 and individual #12 strongly favor both of these individuals being members of the same family. As a point of reference, the sibship index with an unrelated individual was also explored. A pairwise comparison of individual #3 and individual #14 (a brother-in-law) resulted in a sibship index of 0.00135 using 15 STR loci.

Immigration Testing

Immigration testing faces many of the same challenges discussed in the sibling section. True biological relatives may not exhibit high LRs depending on the reference samples available for testing or the number of genetic markers examined. Immigration impacts families. Immigration testing is performed to try to prevent fraud such as a situation where an unrelated person or a more distant relative tries to falsely represent him- or herself as a close relative. Genetic testing results can factor into a family being inappropriately separated or someone falsely qualifying to immigrate.

Unfortunately, with such high stakes involved, fraud does occur with U.S. immigration petitioners (D.N.A. Box 14.11). The substitution of a biological sample from a close blood relative in place of one from a more distant relative or an unrelated person has occurred (Wenk 2011).

D.N.A. BOX 14.10

VARIATION IN PATERNITY AND SIBSHIP INDICES WITHIN A FAMILY

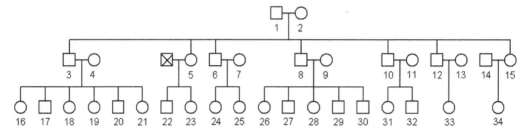

Examining genetic data from individual #3 in the above pedigree compared to his six children as well as his six siblings is instructive regarding the variation that can exist in paternity index (PI) and sibship index (SI) values, respectively, across members of the same family based on inherited alleles present in each individual. These calculations were performed with GeneMarkerHID v1.95 (SoftGenetics, State College, PA) using the 15 STR loci present in the Identifiler kit and U.S. Caucasian allele frequencies (Butler et al. 2003). The observed numerical range shown below occurs due to the rarity of specific alleles present in the parents and which alleles happen to be individually inherited from each parent.

Combined Paternity Index		Combined Sibship Index	
Child-1 (#16)	**223,000,000**	Sibling-1 (#5)	**14,100**
Child-2 (#17)	28,100,000	Sibling-2 (#6)	250
Child-3 (#18)	**22,200**	Sibling-3 (#8)	6,980
Child-4 (#19)	6,980,000	Sibling-4 (#10)	242
Child-5 (#20)	4,840,000	Sibling-5 (#12)	0.771
Child-6 (#21)	121,000	Sibling-6 (#15)	**0.727**

The four orders of magnitude difference between Child-1 (223,000,000) and Child-3 (22,000) is a product of multiple causes. Child-1 inherited rare alleles more often by chance and was also homozygous at CSF1PO, D5S818, FGA, TH01, and D2S1338 where a p^2 calculation can elevate locus PI values compared to a $2pq$ heterozygous calculation when alleles with lower frequencies are inherited. The biggest single locus difference between Child-1 and Child-3 (PI = 10.4 vs 1.47) came at D13S317 where Child-1 inherited a rare 14 allele (frequency = 0.048) from the father while Child-3 received a more common allele 11 (frequency = 0.339) from the father. Both children were heterozygous (12,14 and 11,12) at D13S317 having received allele 12 from their mother.

For the siblings, a detailed comparison of genotypes present in Sibling-1 (14,100) versus Sibling-6 (0.727) found that Sibling-1 shared two alleles (i.e. matching genotypes) with the "alleged sibling" (her brother) at four loci while Sibling-6 only matched her brother's genotype at a single locus. Due to non-overlapping heterozygous alleles present at D8S1179, D18S51, and D2S1338 in their parents, Sibling-6 shared no alleles with her brother at these loci, which helps explain why the combined sibship index is less than one when in fact they are true siblings. For example, the "alleged sibling" possesses alleles 14 and 16 at D18S51 while Sibling-6 received alleles 13 and 18 from their parents who have genotypes 13,14 and 16,18.

In this example, DNA profiles were available from both parents for paternity calculations and sibship comparisons, and there were no mutations observed at the tested STR loci. Specific casework situations faced by relationship testing laboratories may not always be so straightforward.

Sources: Calculations were performed by Kristen Lewis O'Connor (while a NIST postdoc). Butler, J.M., et al. (2003). Allele frequencies for 15 autosomal STR loci on U.S. Caucasian, African American, and Hispanic populations. Journal of Forensic Sciences, 48, 908–911.

D.N.A. BOX 14.11

GENOTYPE RECYCLING FRAUD WITH U.S. IMMIGRATION APPLICANTS AND THE PROBABILITY OF IDENTICAL GENOTYPES

As part of the immigration process, relationship testing laboratories are often called upon to test DNA samples from immigrant applicants and compare these STR profiles to results derived from U.S. citizen petitioners to support or refute claims of kinship. Sometimes immigration fraud occurs and DNA deception is attempted through substituting the biological sample of a close relative on behalf of the applicant who is really a more distant relative or even an unrelated individual. Robert Wenk, who for many years was associated with the BRT Laboratories in Baltimore, Maryland when it did extensive immigration testing, uncovered what he termed "genotype recycling." Dr. Wenk began exploring this form of immigration fraud when he found a 15-locus STR profile for a female applicant that had a male amelogenin type — and the STR profile perfectly matched a previously tested alleged brother. It turned out that the applicant's alleged father had petitioned to have 15 children emigrate to the U.S. from Ghana.

In reviewing laboratory records, Dr. Wenk found that among 555 alleged pedigrees from Ghana, there were 17 in which two or more putative relatives possessed identical 15-locus STR profiles (data from PowerPlex 16). Usually these identical profiles were tested on different dates such that direct comparison of fully matching genotypes would not be possible within the confines of a single immigration case comparison (Wenk 2011). The author of this case report comments: "When a relationship analyst finds identical 15-locus genotypes in two purportedly different people, the best explanation is a duplication of results following inadvertent or intentional testing of two samples from the same biologic source" (Wenk 2011). The following table provides the probability that one individual will possess the identical single-locus genotype of the other. The individual locus probabilities can be combined to determine the probability of the full 15-locus STR profile.

Genotype	Parent–Child	Two Full Siblings	Two Half Siblings	Two Unrelated People
Heterozygous (PQ)	$0.5p + 0.5q$	$0.25 + 0.25p + 0.25q + 0.5pq$	$0.25p + 0.25q + pq$	$2pq$
Homozygous (PP)	p	$0.25 + 0.5p + 0.25p^2$	$0.5p + 0.5p^2$	p^2

(Continued)

D.N.A. BOX 14.11 (cont'd)

Worked example with D18S51 (14,16); $p = 0.134$, $q = 0.147$

With a D18S51 14,16 genotype, it is about 10 times more probable for two full siblings

Genotype	Parent–Child	Two Full Siblings	Two Half Siblings	Two Unrelated People
Heterozygous (PQ)	0.5(0.134) + 0.5(0.147) = **0.141**	0.25 + 0.25(0.134) +0.25(0.147) +0.5(0.134)(0.147) = **0.330**	0.25(0.134) + 0.25(0.147) + (0.134)(0.147) = **0.090**	2(0.134)(0.147) = **0.039**
Homozygous (PP)	(0.134) = **0.134**	0.25 + 0.5(0.134) + 0.25(0.134)^2 = **0.321**	0.5(0.134) + 0.5(0.134)^2 = **0.076**	(0.134)^2 = **0.018**

(probability = 0.330) to share this genotype than two unrelated people (probability = 0.039). Furthermore, full siblings (0.330) are more than twice as likely to share this genotype compared to a parent–child relationship (probability = 0.141). Fraudulent specimen handling at overseas collection sites enabled the systematic genotype recycling that occurred for a time. This collection process has since been changed and improved (Wenk 2011). Nevertheless what was described in Dr. Wenk's article illustrates the importance of vigilance on the part of immigration laboratories in looking for discrepancies in gender between amelogenin tests and the stated sex on sample submission forms. Being suspicious of high parentage index results within a case and looking across cases for potentially identical profiles can help maintain the integrity of DNA immigration testing.

Source: Wenk, R.E. (2011). Detection of genotype recycling fraud in U.S. immigrants. Journal of Forensic Sciences, 56 (Suppl 1), S243–S246.

Studies have shown that even a fairly large number of examined STR loci can fail to reveal even one genetic inconsistency if two siblings are posed as parent and child (Wenk et al. 2005). Approximately 25 STR loci appear necessary to achieve a 95% confidence of detecting at least one genetic inconsistency that would suggest non-parentage (Karlsson et al. 2007). Of course as more loci are examined, the chance of mutation increases. Nevertheless, published studies show the value of additional STR loci in assessing whether or not a single alleged parent could be related to tested children (Poetsch et al. 2011).

However, genetic testing ambiguity can result in siblings falsely presenting themselves as having a parent–child relationship (for the purposes of immigration). One study found that "when 11 to 25 independent loci were tested per two-sibling case to verify or refute parentage, tests failed to demonstrate any genetic inconsistencies in 9%, and PI was greater than SI in seven of ten of these cases" (Wenk & Shao 2014). It has been noted that adding reference relatives to create reference pedigrees is "a far more powerful analytical strategy than adding test loci" (Wenk & Shao 2012). The possibility of fraud and issues of kinship analysis ambiguity (Fimmers et al. 2008) make immigration testing much more challenging than routine paternity testing.

Connecting Distant Relatives with Use of High-Density SNP Arrays

Using the 15 STR loci from the Identifiler kit, several National Institutes of Health (NIH) researchers worked to infer family relationships within households in order to help address gaps in household-interview records (Katki et al. 2010). They noted that their STR genetic data was useful for verifying reported relationships and identifying data quality issues, but found that 15 STRs alone were insufficient to distinguish second-degree relationships and cousins from being unrelated. These NIH researchers concluded that "relationship inference could be improved by using large numbers of single nucleotide polymorphisms (SNPs) instead of STRs" (Katki et al. 2010).

Due to the fairly high mutation rate of STRs ($\approx 10^{-3}$), their value for demonstrating that alleles are identical by inheritance (IBD) rather than by coincidence (IBS) weakens across multiple generations. SNPs, which have mutation rates of $\approx 10^{-8}$ (about 100,000 times lower than that of STRs), exhibit more stable IBD alleles across generations. However, SNPs do not exhibit as much variation as STRs, and therefore more SNP markers are needed to achieve similar matching probabilities. The recent availability of large batteries of SNP markers in the form of microarrays provides the opportunity to answer new questions such as how far out on a family tree can DNA reliably evaluate a putative relationship?

Faced with two females claiming to be second cousins who shared common great grandparents with no other pedigree reference points, the Forensic Genetics Unit at the University of Santiago de Compostela (Spain) attempted typing with all available human identity loci, including 32 STRs and 52 SNPs (Lareu et al. 2012, Phillips et al. 2012). The absence of other pedigree members created a significant challenge. Even after analysis of all of these genetic loci, theoretical LR probability distributions for second-cousin relationships gave almost identical LR probability distributions to random pairwise comparisons from the same population.

The Santiago scientists then turned to high-density SNP genotyping with an Affymetrix genome-wide array capable of typing more than 900,000 SNP markers (Lareu et al. 2012). Each reference sample test required 500 ng of high-quality DNA, so this approach is not something that would work routinely with forensic casework samples. The SNP data set was reduced by applying filters related to the chromosomal distance between SNP markers and their minimum allele frequency. With less than 7,000 SNPs it was possible to obtain a small degree of separation in the probability distributions between second-cousin pairs and random pairs. Comparisons to 10 unrelated control samples and simulation studies modeling different potential degrees of relatedness aided this investigation (Phillips et al. 2012).

After exploring a number of possible distant relatives, a Swedish and Norwegian team concluded that "a second-cousin relationship appears to be the limitation to what can be determined with current methods, or by any means presently available" (Kling et al. 2012). This group notes that genetic material is diluted as it is passed to each generation, and they hypothesize that the average background relatedness shared by all individuals of the same race/ethnicity is probably not far from the third-cousin relationship. They further comment that simulations and modeling are limited to some extent due to the challenge of accounting for linkage disequilibrium when so many genetic markers are being examined (Kling et al. 2012).

Separating Close Relatives and Resolving Twins

Just as trying to establish a connection between distant relatives such as cousins can be accomplished with additional genetic markers, efforts to separate very close relatives like identical twins or a father from a son have also been explored. Incest cases can be especially challenging to resolve genetically as they may involve trying to determine whether a brother impregnated his sister or a father is both the father and the grandfather of a child born. These situations often require use of additional autosomal STR markers (Tamura et al. 2000, Macan et al. 2003) or lineage markers such as the X-chromosome (Pinto et al. 2013).

Perhaps the ultimate challenge in kinship analysis is attempting to separate monozygotic (MZ) twins that have identical or nearly identical DNA (D.N.A. Box 14.12). Full-scale genome DNA sequencing has been utilized to locate subtle differences in MZ twins that could be exploited to determine which twin was the father of a child (Weber-Lehmann et al. 2014).

D.N.A. BOX 14.12

GENETICALLY DISTINGUISHING A POTENTIAL FATHER FROM A TWIN BROTHER

Monozygotic (MZ) twins arise from a single fertilized ovum, develop from one zygote, and have long been thought to be genetically "identical." STR profiles from MZ twins are identical. This fact can provide a challenge when either twin could be a participant in a crime or the father of a child in a paternity dispute. Thus, in paternity or forensic cases where a sufficient alibi is not available to exclude one of the twin brothers, traditional genetic testing cannot provide an answer. However, scientists at Eurofins Genomics in Ebersberg, Germany recently demonstrated that MZ twins could be differentiated through use of extremely rare mutations (Weber-Lehmann et al. 2014). Finding these rare mutations is a challenge, but one that can be addressed with ultra-deep next generation sequencing. After producing hundreds of billions of bases of DNA sequence information from two MZ twins and a child and carefully sifting through the data for differences, five single nucleotide polymorphisms (SNPs) were identified as being present in the twin father and child but not the twin uncle. With these particular MZ twins, the five differentiating SNPs were located on chromosomes 4, 6, 11, 14, and 15. Follow-up assays targeting these specific SNPs were performed to confirm results with the child and the child's mother and to test various tissues including sperm, buccal mucosa, and blood from the twins. The ability to genetically resolve MZ twins had been predicted in a thought experiment by Michael Krawczak and colleagues (Krawczak et al. 2012) more than a year before it was demonstrated (Weber-Lehmann et al. 2014).

Sources: *Krawczak, M., et al. (2012). How to distinguish genetically between an alleged father and his monozygotic twin: a thought experiment. Forensic Science International: Genetics, 6, e129–e130; Weber-Lehmann, J., et al. (2014). Finding the needle in the haystack: differentiating "identical" twins in paternity testing and forensics by ultra-deep next generation sequencing. Forensic Science International: Genetics, 9, 42–46.*

This whole-genome sequencing approach is far from routine, but it does demonstrate how advancing technologies can expand the future of kinship analysis. Nevertheless, there will be situations in complex kinship analysis where conclusive results cannot be obtained.

Reading List and Internet Resources

General Information

Alford, R. L., et al. (1994). Rapid and efficient resolution of parentage by amplification of short tandem repeats. *American Journal of Human Genetics, 55*, 190–195.

Allen, R. W. (2013). *Parentage testing and kinship analysis. Encyclopedia of Forensic Sciences* (2nd ed.). San Diego: Elsevier Academic Press, 287–294.

Chakraborty, R., & Jin, L. (1993). Determination of relatedness between individuals using DNA fingerprinting. *Human Biology, 65*, 875–895.

Evett, I. W., & Weir, B. S. (1998). *Interpreting DNA Evidence: Statistical Genetics for Forensic Scientists.* Sunderland, MA: Sinauer Associates.

Gonick, L., & Wheelis, M. (1983). *The Cartoon Guide to Genetics, Updated Edition.* New York: HarperCollins Publishers.

Lucy, D. (2005). *Introduction to Statistics for Forensic Scientists.* Hoboken, New Jersey: Wiley.

Orrego, C., & King, M.-C. (1990). Determination of familial relationships. In M. A. Innis, D. H. Gelfand, J. J. Sminsky, & T. J. White (Eds.), *PCR Protocols* (pp. 416–426). San Diego: Academic Press.

Pena, S. D. J., & Chakraborty, R. (1994). Paternity testing in the DNA era. *Trends in Genetics, 10*, 204–209.

Schneider, P. M. (2007). Scientific standards for studies in forensic genetics. *Forensic Science International, 165*, 238–243.

Weir, B. S., et al. (2006). Genetic relatedness analysis: modern data and new challenges. *Nature Reviews Genetics, 7*, 771–780.

Wenk, R. E. (2004). Testing for parentage and kinship. *Current Opinions in Hematology, 11*, 357–361.

Parentage Testing

AABB Relationship Testing Annual Reports: http://www.aabb.org/sa/facilities/Pages/relationshipreports.aspx. Accessed April 3, 2014.

AABB. (2003). *Annual Report Summary for Testing in 2003: Prepared by the Relationship Testing Program Unit.* Available at http://www.aabb.org/sa/facilities/Documents/ptannrpt03.pdf. Accessed April 7, 2014.

AABB. (2008). *Annual Report Summary for Testing in 2008: Prepared by the Relationship Testing Program Unit.* Available at http://www.aabb.org/sa/facilities/Documents/rtannrpt08.pdf. Accessed April 3, 2014.

AABB. (2010). *Annual Report Summary for Testing in 2010: Prepared by the Relationship Testing Program Unit.* Available at http://www.aabb.org/sa/facilities/Documents/rtannrpt10.pdf. Accessed April 3, 2014.

AABB. (2011). *Guidance for standards for relationship testing laboratories* (10th ed.). Bethesda, MD: AABB.

AABB. (2014). *Accredited labs.* Available at http://www.aabb.org/sa/facilities/Pages/RTestAccrFac.aspx. Accessed April 4, 2014.

Allen, R. W. (1998). Parentage testing in the United States: the role of the American Association of Blood Banks. *Profiles in DNA, 2*(2), 7–8. Available at http://www.promega.com/profiles/issues.html. Accessed April 3, 2014.

Anderson, K. G. (2006). How well does paternity confidence match actual paternity? Evidence from worldwide nonpaternity rates. *Current Anthropology, 47*, 513–520.

Arroyo-Pardo, E., et al. (2002). Predictive pedigree analysis in a case of a sample of four brothers. *Canadian Society of Forensic Sciences Journal, 35*, 67–75.

Ayres, K. L. (2000). Relatedness testing in subdivided populations. *Forensic Science International, 114*, 107–115.

Ayres, K. L. (2002). Paternal exclusion in the presence of substructure. *Forensic Science International, 129*, 142–144.

Ayres, K. L., et al. (2005). Paternity index calculations when some individuals share common ancestry. *Forensic Science International, 151*, 101–103.

Ayres, K. L. (2005). The expected performance of single nucleotide polymorphism loci in paternity testing. *Forensic Science International, 154*, 167–172.

Balding, D. J. (2005). *Weight-of-Evidence for Forensic DNA Profiles.* Hoboken, New Jersey: John Wiley & Sons.

Bellis, M. A., et al. (2005). Measuring paternal discrepancy and its public health consequences. *Journal of Epidemiology and Community Health, 59*, 749–754.

Bishai, D., et al. (2006). A national sample of US paternity tests: do demographics predict test outcomes? *Transfusion, 46,* 849–853.

Brenner, C. H., & Morris, J. (1989). Paternity index calculations in single locus hypervariable DNA probes: validation and other studies. *Proceedings of the First International Symposium on Human Identification, 21–53.*

Brinkmann, B., et al. (2001). The evidential value of STRs: an analysis of exclusion cases. *International Journal of Legal Medicine, 114,* 173–177.

Buckleton, J., et al. (2005). Parentage testing. In Triggs Buckleton, & Walsh (Eds.), *Forensic DNA Evidence Interpretation* (pp. 341–394). Boca Raton: CRC Press. Chapter 10.

Buckleton, J., et al. (2007). Parentage analysis and other applications of human identity testing. In I. Freckelton, & H. Selby (Eds.), *Expert Evidence.* Thomson Lawbook Co. Chapter 82.

Cifuentes, L. O., et al. (2006). Probability of exclusion in paternity testing: time to reassess. *Journal of Forensic Sciences, 51,* 349–350.

Coleman, H., & Swenson, E. (2000). *DNA in parentage testing. Chapter 4 in* DNA in the Courtroom: A Trial Watcher's Guide.

Csete, K., et al. (2005). Prenatal and newborn paternity testing with DNA analysis. *Forensic Science International, 147 Supplemental,* S57–S60.

Dario, P., et al. (2009). SNP in paternity investigation: the simple future. *Forensic Science International: Genetics Supplement Series, 2,* 127–128.

Essen-Möller, E. (1938). Die Beweiskraft der Aehnlichkeit im Vaterschaftsnachweis; theoretische Grundlagen. *Mitt. Anthropol. Gesellschaft, 68,* 9–53. [Rough English translation: The probative value of paternity calculations: theoretical foundations].

Evett, I. W., et al. (1989). Paternity calculations from DNA multilocus profiles. *Journal of Forensic Science Society, 29,* 249–254.

Faigman, D. L., et al. (2002). *Science in the Law: Forensic Science Issues.* St. Paul, MN: West Group. Chapter 12 "Parentage Testing," pp. 762–798.

Fung, W. K., et al. (2004). EasyDNA: user-friendly paternity and kinship testing programs. *Progress in Forensic Genetics 10, ICS, 1261,* 628–630.

Fung, W. K., et al. (2002). Power of exclusion revisited: probability of excluding relatives of the true father from paternity. *International Journal of Legal Medicine, 116,* 64–67.

Gjertson, D. W. (2002). Parentage testing. In T. L. Simon, et al. (Eds.), *Rossi's Principles of Transfusion Medicine* (3rd ed.) (pp. 898–911). Philadelphia: Lippincott, Williams & Wilkins. Chapter 63.

Henke, L., et al. (1999). Usefulness of conventional blood groups, DNA-minisatellites, and short tandem repeat polymorphisms in paternity testing: a comparison. *Forensic Science International, 103,* 133–142.

Hepler, A. B., & Weir, B. S. (2008). Object-oriented Bayesian networks for paternity cases with allelic dependancies. *Forensic Science International: Genetics, 2,* 166–175.

Hu, Y.-Q., & Fung, W. K. (2005). Power of excluding an elder brother of a child from paternity. *Forensic Science International, 152,* 321–322.

Junge, A., et al. (2006). Mutations or exclusion: an unusual case in paternity testing. *International Journal of Legal Medicine, 120,* 360–363.

Lee, H.-S., et al. (2000). Motherless case in paternity testing. *Forensic Science International, 114,* 57–65.

Macintyre, S., & Sooman, A. (1991). Non-paternity and prenatal genetic screening. *Lancet, 338,* 869–871.

Morgan, L. W. (2002). *Child support enforcement in the United States and the role of the private bar.* Available at http://www.childsupportguidelines.com/articles/art200009.html. What the law looks like today can be found at http://www.ssa.gov/OP_Home/ssact/title04/0451.htm. Accessed April 3, 2014.

Narkuti, V., et al. (2007). Mother-child double incompatibility at vWA and D5S818 loci in paternity testing. *Clinical Chemistry Laboratory Medicine, 45,* 1288–1291.

Pena, S. D. J. (1995). Letter to the editor: Pitfalls of paternity testing based solely on PCR typing of minisatellites and microsatellites. *American Journal of Human Genetics, 56,* 1503–1504. response by Maha, G.C., et al. on pp. 1505–1506.

Rittner, C. K., et al. (2003). Expert witness in paternity testing in Germany. *Legal Medicine, 5,* 65–67.

Sasse, G., et al. (1994). Estimating the frequency of nonpaternity in Switzerland. *Human Heredity, 44*(6), 337–343.

Schlenk, J., et al. (2004). Development of a 13-locus PCR multiplex system for paternity testing. *International Journal of Legal Medicine, 118,* 55–61.

Silver, H. (1989). Paternity testing. *Critical Reviews in Clinical Laboratory Science, 27,* 391–408.

Thacker, C. R., et al. (2009). Prenatal testing in paternity testing: a positive perspective. *Forensic Science International: Genetics Supplement Series, 2,* 232–233.

Thomson, J. A., et al. (1999). Validation of short tandem repeat analysis for the investigation of cases of disputed paternity. *Forensic Science International, 100*, 1−16.

Wegener, R., et al. (2006). Mother-child exclusion due to paternal uniparental disomy 6. *International Journal of Legal Medicine, 120*, 282−285.

Weir, B. S. (2007). Forensics. In D. J. Balding, M. Bishop, & C. Cannings (Eds.), *Handbook of Statistical Genetics* (3rd ed.) (pp. 1368−1392). Hoboken, NJ: Wiley. Chapter 43.

Zehethofer, K., & Rolf, B. (2011). A molecular analysis of three amelogenin negative males in two routine paternity tests. *Forensic Science International: Genetics, 5*, 550−551.

Zhao, G., et al. (2005). Study on the application of parent-of-origin specific DNA methylation markers to forensic genetics. *Forensic Science International, 154*, 122−127.

Calculations and Software

Azevedo, D. A., et al. (2011). Genetic kinship analysis: a concordance study between calculations performed with the software Familias and algebraic formulas of the American Association of Blood Banks. *Forensic Science International: Genetics Supplement Series, 3*, e186−e187.

Baur, M. P., & Rittner, C. (1976). Program for the computation of plausibilities of paternity. I. Description of program. *Zeitschrift für Rechtsmedizin (Journal of Legal Medicine), 78*(3), 227−242.

Baur, M. P., et al. (1986). No fallacies in the formulation of the paternity index. *American Journal of Human Genetics, 39*, 528−536.

Brenner, C. H. (1997). Symbolic kinship program. *Genetics, 145*, 535−542.

Dawid, A. P., et al. (2001). Non-fatherhood or mutation? A probabilistic approach to parental exclusion in paternity testing. *Forensic Science International, 124*, 55−61.

DNA-View: http://dna-view.com. Accessed April 3, 2014.

Donnelly, P. (1995). Non-independence of matches at different loci in DNA profiles: quantifying the effect of close relatives on the match probability. *Heredity, 75*, 26−34.

Drábek, J. (2009). Validation of software for calculating the likelihood ratio for parentage and kinship. *Forensic Science International: Genetics, 3*, 112−118.

Drábek, J. (2009). Use of animal/plant freeware for calculating likelihood ratio for paternity and kinship in complicated human pedigrees. *Forensic Science International: Genetics Supplement Series, 2*, 469−471.

EasyDNA: http://www.hku.hk/statistics/EasyDNA/. Accessed April 3, 2014.

Egeland, T., et al. (2000). Beyond traditional paternity and identification cases: selecting the most probable pedigree. *Forensic Science International, 110*, 47−59.

Egeland, T., & Mostad, P. F. (2002). Statistical genetics and genetical statistics: A forensic prespective. *Scandinavian Journal of Statistics, 29*, 1−11.

Eisenberg, A. (2003). *Popstats Relatedness Statistics*. Workshop presented at 14th International Symposium on Human Identification. Available at http://www.promega.com/products/pm/genetic-identity/ishi-conference-proceedings/14th-ishi-statistics-workshop/. Accessed April 3, 2014.

Familias software program: http://www.math.chalmers.se/~mostad/familias/. Accessed April 3, 2014.

FamLink: http://www.famlink.se/. Accessed April 3, 2014.

Fung, W. K. (2003). User-friendly programs for easy calculations in paternity testing and kinship determinations. *Forensic Science International, 136*, 22−34.

Fung, W. K., et al. (2004). EasyDNA: user-friendly paternity and kinship testing programs. *Progress in Forensic Genetics 10, ICS, 1261*, 628−630.

Fung, W. K., & Hu, Y.-Q. (2008). *Statistical DNA Forensics: Theory, Methods and Computation*. Hoboken, NJ: Wiley.

Gilliam, K. L., & Wang, T. W. (2010). Sign mistake in allele sharing probability formulae of Curran et al. *Forensic Science International: Genetics, 4*, 213−214.

Hepler, A. B., & Weir, B. S. (2008). Object-oriented Bayesian networks for paternity cases with allelic dependencies. *Forensic Science International: Genetics, 2*, 166−175.

Kling, D., et al. (2012). FamLink − a user friendly software for linkage calculations in family genetics. *Forensic Science International: Genetics, 6*, 616−620.

Maguire, C., & Woodward, M. (2008). DNA-based kinship analysis. *Profiles in DNA (March 2008)*, pp. 3−6. Available at http://www.promega.com/profiles. Accessed April 3, 2014.

II. STATISTICAL INTERPRETATION

Morris, J. W., et al. (1989). Biostatistical evaluation of evidence from continuous allele frequency distribution deoxyribonucleic acid (DNA) probes in reference to disputed paternity and identity. *Journal of Forensic Sciences, 34*, 1311–1317.

O'Connor, K. L. (2010). *Effect of additional loci on likelihood ratio values from complex kinship analysis.* San Antonio, TX: Presentation at the 21st International Symposium on Human Identification. October 12, 2010, Available at http://www.cstl.nist.gov/strbase/pub_pres/OConnor-Promega2010-Additional-Loci-Kinship.pdf. Accessed April 3, 2014.

O'Connor, K. L., et al. (2010). *Candidate reference family data: a tool for validating kinship analysis software.* San Antonio, TX: Poster presentation at the 21st International Symposium on Human Identification. Available at http://www.cstl.nist.gov/strbase/pub_pres/Promega2010_OConnor.pdf. Accessed April 3, 2014.

Riancho, J. A., & Zarrabeitia, M. T. (2003). A Windows-based software for common paternity and sibling analyses. *Forensic Science international, 135*, 232–234.

Slooten, K. (2011). Validation of DNA-based identification software by computation of pedigree likelihood ratios. *Forensic Science International: Genetics, 5*, 308–315.

Slooten, K.-J., & Egeland, T. (2014). Exclusion probabilities and likelihood ratios with applications to kinship problems. *International Journal of Legal Medicine.* (in press). [last checked 3/3/2014].

STRBase, Kinship (2014). http://www.cstl.nist.gov/strbase/kinship.htm. Accessed April 3, 2014.

Tracey, M. (2001). Short tandem repeat-based identification of individuals and parents. *Croatian Medical Journal, 42*, 233–238.

Proficiency/Interlaboratory Studies

Bjerre, A., et al. (1997). A report of the 1995 and 1996 Paternity Testing Workshops of the English Speaking Working Group of the International Society for Forensic Haemogenetics. *Forensic Science International, 90*, 41–55.

Builes, J. J., et al. (2009). Results of the 2008 Colombian paternity testing quality control exercise. *Forensic Science International: Genetics Supplement Series, 2*, 93–94.

Friis, S. L., et al. (2009). Results of the 2009 Paternity Testing Workshop of the English Speaking Working Group of the International Society for Forensic Genetics. *Forensic Science International: Genetics Supplement Series, 2*, 91–92.

Friis, S. L., et al. (2013). Results of the 2013 Relationship Testing Workshop of the English Speaking Working Group. *Forensic Science International: Genetics Supplement Series, 4*, e282–e283.

Hallenberg, C., & Morling, N. (2001). A report of the 1997, 1998 and 1999 Paternity Testing Workshops of the English Speaking Working Group of the International Society for Forensic Genetics. *Forensic Science International, 116*, 23–33.

Hallenberg, C., & Morling, N. (2002). A report of the 2000 and 2001 Paternity Testing Workshops of the English Speaking Working Group of the International Society for Forensic Genetics. *Forensic Science International, 129*, 43–50.

Hallenberg, C., et al. (2008). Results of the 2007 Paternity Testing Workshop of the English Speaking Working Group of the International Society for Forensic Genetics. *Forensic Science International: Genetics Supplement Series, 1*, 680–681.

Poulsen, L., et al. (2011). Results of the 2011 Relationship Testing Workshop of the English Speaking Working Group. *Forensic Science International: Genetics Supplement Series, 3*, e512–e513.

Poulsen, L., et al. (2014). A report of the 2009-2011 Paternity and Relationship Testing Workshops of the English Speaking Working Group of the International Society for Forensic Genetics. *Forensic Science International: Genetics, 9*, e1–e2.

Syndercombe-Court, D., & Lincoln, P. (1996). A review of the 1991-1994 Paternity Testing Workshops of the English-Speaking Working Group. In A. Carracedo, B. Brinkmann, & W. Bar (Eds.), *Advances in Forensic Haemogenetics 6* (pp. 683–685). Berlin: Springer-Verlag.

Thomsen, A. R., et al. (2009). A report of the 2002-2008 Paternity Testing Workshops of the English Speaking Working Group of the International Society for Forensic Genetics. *Forensic Science International: Genetics, 3*, 214–221.

Recommendations

Allen, R. W., et al. (2008). The importance of peer review in maintaining the quality of accreditation for the evolving field of family relatedness testing. *Transfusion, 48*, 1517–1519.

Gjertson, D. W., et al. (2007). ISFG: recommendations on biostatistics in paternity testing. *Forensic Science International: Genetics, 1*, 223–231.

Morling, N., et al. (2002). Paternity Testing Commission of the International Society of Forensic Genetics: recommendations on genetic investigations in paternity cases. *Forensic Science International, 129*, 148–157.

Mutations and Mutation Rates

American Association of Blood Banks Relationship Testing Program Unit (2003). Annual report summary for testing in 2003. Available from http://www.aabb.org/sa/facilities/Documents/ptannrpt03.pdf. Accessed April 3, 2014.

American Association of Blood Banks Relationship Testing Program Unit (2008). Annual report summary for testing in 2008. Available from http://www.aabb.org/sa/facilities/Documents/rtannrpt08.pdf. Accessed April 3, 2014.

Arnheim, N., & Calabrese, P. (2009). Understanding what determines the frequency and pattern of human germline mutations. *Nature Reviews Genetics, 10,* 478–488.

Amos, W., et al. (2008). Heterozygosity increases microsatellite mutation rate, linking it to demographic history. *BMC Genetics, 9,* 72.

Balloch, K. J. D., et al. (2008). Reporting paternity testing results when 2 exclusions are encountered. *Forensic Science International: Genetics Supplement Series, 1,* 492–493.

Banchs, I., et al. (1994). New alleles at microsatellite loci in CEPH families mainly arise from somatic mutations in the lymphoblastoid cell lines. *Human Mutation, 3,* 365–372.

Becker, D., et al. (2007). New alleles and mutational events at 14 STR loci from different German populations. *Forensic Science International: Genetics, 1,* 232–237.

Brenner, C. H. (2004). Multiple mutations, covert mutations and false exclusions in paternity casework. *Progress in Forensic Genetics 10 (International Congress Series), 1261,* 112–114.

Brenner, C. H. (2006). *Mutations in paternity.* Available at http://dna-view.com/mudisc.htm. Accessed April 3, 2014.

Brinkmann, B., et al. (1995). Structure of new mutations in 2 STR systems. *International Journal of Legal Medicine, 107,* 201–203.

Brinkmann, B., et al. (1996). Complex mutational events at the HumD21S11 locus. *Human Genetics, 98,* 60–64.

Brinkmann, B., et al. (1998). Mutation rate in human microsatellites: influence of the structure and length of the tandem repeat. *American Journal of Human Genetics, 62,* 1408–1415.

Caplinskiene, M., et al. (2008). Autosomal and Y-STR mutations in Lithuanian population. *Forensic Science International: Genetics Supplement Series, 1,* 237–238.

Chakraborty, R., et al. (1996). Estimation of mutation rates from parentage exclusion data: applications to STR and VNTR loci. *Mutation Research, 354,* 41–48.

Conrad, D. F., et al. (2011). Variation in genome-wide mutation rates within and between human families. *Nature Genetics, 43(7),* 712–714.

Crow, J. F. (2000). The origins, patterns and implications of human spontaneous mutation. *Nature Reviews Genetics, 1,* 40–47.

Dauber, E. M., et al. (2012). Germline mutations of STR-alleles include multi-step mutations as defined by sequencing of repeat and flanking regions. *Forensic Science International: Genetics, 6,* 381–386.

Dawid, A. P., et al. (2001). Non-fatherhood or mutation? A probabilistic approach to paternal exclusion in paternity testing. *Forensic Science International, 124,* 55–61.

De Andrade, E. S., et al. (2009). Mutation rates at 14 STR loci in the population from Pernambuco, Northeast Brazil. *Forensic Science International: Genetics, 3,* e141–e143.

Dieringer, D., & Schlötterer, C. (2003). Two distinct modes of microsatellite mutation processes: evidence from the complete genomic sequences of nine species. *Genome Research, 13,* 2242–2251.

Eckert, K. A., & Hile, S. E. (2009). Every microsatellite is different: intrinsic DNA features dictate mutagenesis of common microsatellites present in the human genome. *Molecular Carcinogenesis, 48,* 379–388.

Edwards, M., & Allen, R. W. (2004). Characteristics of mutations at the D5S818 locus studied using a tightly linked marker. *Transfusion, 44,* 83–90.

Ellegren, H. (2000). Heterogeneous mutation processes in human microsatellite DNA sequences. *Nature Genetics, 24,* 400–402.

Ellegren, H. (2000). Microsatellite mutations in the germline: implications for evolutionary inference. *Trends in Genetics, 16,* 551–558.

Ellegren, H. (2004). Microsatellites: simple sequences with complex evolution. *Nature Reviews Genetics, 5,* 435–445.

Fan, H., & Chu, J.-Y. (2007). A brief review of short tandem repeat mutation. *Genomics, Proteomics, & Bioinformatics, 5,* 7–14.

Fimmers, R., et al. (1992). How to deal with mutations in DNA-testing. In C. Rittner, & P. M. Schneider (Eds.), *Advances in Forensic Haemogenetics 4* (pp. 285–287). Berlin: Springer-Verlag.

Geada, H., et al. (2001). A STR mutation in a heteropaternal twin case. *Forensic Science International, 123,* 239–242.

Gjertson, D. W. (2011). Appendix 9: the effect of isolated inconsistencies in the statistical evaluation of paternity: a 2005 update. In *AABB Guidance for Standards for Relationship Testing Laboratories* (10th ed.). Bethesda, Maryland: AABB.

Gunn, P. R., et al. (1997). DNA analysis in disputed parentage: the occurrence of two apparently false exclusions of paternity, both at short tandem repeat (STR) loci, in the one child. *Electrophoresis, 18*, 1650–1652.

Haldane, J. B. S. (1947). The mutation rate of the gene for haemophilia, and its segregation ratios in males and females. *Annals of Eugenics, 13*(4), 262–271.

Henke, L., & Henke, J. (1999). Mutation rate in human microsatellites. *American Journal of Human Genetics, 64*, 1473. (with reply by B. Rolf and B. Brinkmann, 1473–1474).

Henke, L., & Henke, J. (2006). Supplemented data on mutation rates in 33 autosomal short tandem repeat polymorphisms. *Journal of Forensic Sciences, 51*, 446–447.

Hill, C. R., et al. (2011). Concordance and population studies along with stutter and peak height ratio analysis for the PowerPlex® ESX 17 and ESI 17 systems. *Forensic Science International: Genetics, 5*, 269–275.

Hohoff, C., et al. (2006). Meiosis study in a population sample from Afghanistan: allele frequencies and mutation rates of 16 STR loci. *International Journal of Legal Medicine, 120*, 300–302.

Hohoff, C., et al. (2009). Meiosis study in a population sample from Nigeria: allele frequencies and mutation rates of 16 STR loci. *International Journal of Legal Medicine, 123*, 259–261.

Jiang, W., et al. (2011). Identification of dual false indirect exclusions on the D5S818 and FGA loci. *Legal Medicine, 13*, 30–34.

Kayser, M., et al. (2000). Characteristics and frequency of germline mutations at microsatellite loci from the human Y chromosome, as revealed by direct observation in father/son pairs. *American Journal of Human Genetics, 66*, 1580–1588.

Kelkar, Y. D., et al. (2008). The genome-wide determinants of human and chimpanzee microsatellite evolution. *Genome Research, 18*, 30–38.

Kong, A., et al. (2012). Rate of de novo mutations and the importance of father's age to disease risk. *Nature, 488*, 471–475.

Klintschar, M., et al. (2004). Haplotype studies support slippage as the mechanism of germline mutations in short tandem repeats. *Electrophoresis, 25*, 3344–3348.

Lai, Y., & Sun, F. (2003). The relationship between microsatellite slippage mutation rate and the number of repeat units. *Molecular Biology and Evolution, 20*, 2123–2131.

Li, H. X., et al. (2011). Mutation analysis of 24 autosomal STR loci using in paternity testing. *Forensic Science International: Genetics Supplement Series, 3*, e159–e160.

Leopoldine, A. M., & Pena, S. D. J. (2003). The mutational spectrum of human autosomal tetranucleotide microsatellites. *Human Mutation, 21*, 71–79.

Levinson, G., & Gutman, G. A. (1987). Slipped-strand mispairing: a major mechanism for DNA sequence evolution. *Molecular Biology and Evolution, 4*, 203–221.

Lu, D., et al. (2012). Mutation analysis of 24 short tandem repeats in Chinese Han population. *International Journal of Legal Medicine, 126*, 331–335.

Mansuet-Lupo, A., et al. (2009). A paternity case with three genetic incompatibilities between father and child due to maternal uniparental disomy 21 and a mutation at the Y chromosome. *Forensic Science International: Genetics, 3*, 141–143.

Mardini, A. C., et al. (2013). Mutation rate estimates for 13 STR loci in a large population from Rio Grande do Sul, Southern Brazil. *International Journal of Legal Medicine, 127*, 45–47.

Mertens, G., et al. (2009). Non-exclusion maternity case with two genetic incompatibilties, a mutation and a null allele. *Forensic Science International: Genetics Supplement Series, 2*, 224–225.

Müller, M., et al. (2010). Haplotype-assisted characterization of germline mutations at short tandem repeat loci. *International Journal of Legal Medicine, 124*, 177–182.

Nadir, E., et al. (1996). Microsatellite spreading in the human genome: evolutionary mechanisms and structural implications. *Proceedings of the National Academy of Sciences of the United States of America, 93*, 6470–6475.

Narkuti, V., et al. (2007). Microsatellite mutation in the maternally/paternally transmitted D18S51 locus: two cases of allele mismatch in the child. *Clinical Chimica Acta, 381*, 171–175.

Narkuti, V., et al. (2008). Single and double incompatibility at vWA and D8S1179/D21S11 loci between mother and child: implications in kinship analysis. *Clinical Chimica Acta, 395*, 162–165.

Nutini, A. L., et al. (2003). Double incompatibility at human alpha fibrinogen and penta E loci in paternity testing. *Croatian Medical Journal, 44*, 342–346.

Ohta, T., & Kimura, M. (1973). A model of mutation appropriate to estimate the number of electrophoretically detectable alleles in a finite population. *Genetic Research, 22*, 201–204.

Paredes, L. (2011). Mutational dynamics of STRs: analysis of FGA-FIBRA locus. *Forensic Science International: Genetics Supplement Series, 3*, e261–e262.

Pemberton, T. J. (2009). Sequence determinants of human microsatellite variability. *BMC Genomics, 10*(612), 1–19.

Pumpernik, D., et al. (2008). Replication slippage versus point mutation rates in short tandem repeats of the human genome. *Molecular Genetics and Genomics, 279*, 53–61.

Sajantila, A., et al. (1999). Experimentally observed germline mutations at human micro- and minisatellite loci. *European Journal of Human Genetics, 7*, 263–266.

Singh, N. D., et al. (2006). Multistep microsatellite mutation in the maternally transmitted locus D13S317: a case of maternal allele mismatch in the child. *International Journal of Legal Medicine, 120*, 286–292.

Slooten, K., & Ricciardi, F. (2013). Estimation of mutation probabilities for autosomal STR markers. *Forensic Science International: Genetics, 7*, 337–344.

STRBase Mutation Rates for Common Loci: http://www.cstl.nist.gov/biotech/strbase/mutation.htm. Accessed April 3, 2014.

Sun, H., et al. (2014). Comparison of southern Chinese Han and Brazilian Caucasian mutation rates at autosomal short tandem repeat loci used in human forensic genetics. *International Journal of Legal Medicine, 128*, 1–9.

Sun, H.-Y., et al. (2012). A paternity case with mutations at three CODIS core STR loci. *Forensic Science International: Genetics, 6*(1), e61–e62.

Sun, J. X., et al. (2012). A direct characterization of human mutation based on microsatellites. *Nature Genetics, 44*, 1161–1165.

Thacker, C. R., et al. (2009). A paternal mutation in the Penta D STR locus. *Forensic Science International: Genetics Supplement Series, 2*, 221–223.

Valdes, A. M., et al. (1993). Allele frequencies at microsatellite loci: the stepwise mutation model revisited. *Genetics, 133*, 737–749.

Vicard, P., & Dawid, A. P. (2004). A statistical treatment of biases affecting the estimation of mutation rates. *Mutation Research, 547*, 19–33.

Vicard, P., et al. (2008). Estimating mutation rates from paternity casework. *Forensic Science International: Genetics, 2*, 9–18.

Weber, J. L., & Wong, C. (1993). Mutation of human short tandem repeats. *Human Molecular Genetics, 2*, 1123–1128.

Wiegand, P., et al. (2000). Microsatellite structures in the context of human evolution. *Electrophoresis, 21*, 889–895.

Wojtas, M., et al. (2013). Mutations of microsatellite autosomal loci in paternity investigations of the Southern Poland population. *Forensic Science International: Genetics, 7*(3), 389–391.

Xu, X., et al. (2000). The direction of microsatellite mutations is dependent upon allele length. *Nature Genetics, 24*, 396–399.

Yan, J., et al. (2006). Mutations at 17 STR loci in Chinese population. *Forensic Science International, 162*, 53–54.

Other Topics with Parentage Testing
Deficient Paternity Testing

Asano, M., et al. (1980). General formulas of the estimated likelihood ratio Y/X in the diagnosis of paternity of a deceased putative father. *Zeitschrift für Rechtsmedizin (Journal of Legal Medicine), 84*, 125–133.

Asano, M., et al. (1980). Diagnosis of paternity for cases without mother and without both mother and putative father bases on blood group findings from the relatives. *Zeitschrift für Rechtsmedizin (Journal of Legal Medicine), 84*, 135–144.

Babol-Pokora, K., et al. (2006). Identifiler system as an inadequate tool for judging motherless paternity cases. *Progress in Forensic Genetics 10, ICS, 1288*, 462–464.

Barash, M., et al. (2012). A search for obligatory paternal alleles in a DNA database to find an alleged rapist in a fatherless paternity case. *Journal of Forensic Sciences, 57*(4), 1098–1101.

Barrot, C., et al. (2014). DNA paternity tests in Spain without the mother's consent: the legal responsibilities of the laboratories. *Forensic Science International: Genetics, 8*, 33–35.

Brenner, C. H. (1993). A note on paternity computation in cases lacking a mother. *Transfusion, 33*, 51–54.

Cerri, N., & Caenazzo, L. (2011). Investigation of paternity loss: is statistical evaluation reliable? A case report. *Forensic Science International: Genetics Supplement Series, 3*, e49–e50.

Clayton, T. M., et al. (2002). Motherless case in paternity testing by Lee, et al. *Forensic Science International, 125*, 284.

González-Andrade, F., et al. (2009). Two fathers for the same child: a deficient paternity case of false inclusion with autosomic STRs. *Forensic Science International: Genetics, 3*, 138–140.

Ihm, P., & Hummel, A. (1975). A method to calculate the plausibly of paternity using blood group results of any relatives. *Zeitschrift für Immunitätsforschung, experimentelle und klinische Immunologie, 149*, 405–416.

Lee, H.-S., et al. (2000). Motherless case in paternity testing. *Forensic Science International, 114*, 57–65.

Lee, J. W., et al. (2001). Paternity determination when the alleged father's genotypes are unavailable. *Forensic Science International, 123*, 202–210.

Mixich, F., et al. (2004). Paternity analysis in special fatherless cases without direct testing of alleged father. *Forensic Science International, 146S*, S159–S161.

Poetsch, M., et al. (2006). The problem of single parent/child paternity analysis — Practical results involving 336 children and 348 unrelated men. *Forensic Science International, 159*, 98–103.

Poetsch, M., et al. (2013). The new guidelines for paternity analysis in Germany — how many STR loci are necessary when investigating duo cases? *International Journal of Legal Medicine, 127*, 731–734.

Pretty, I. A., & Hildebrand, D. P. (2005). The forensic and investigative significance of reverse paternity testing with absent maternal sample. *American Journal of Forensic Medicine and Pathology, 26*, 340–342.

Thomson, J. A., et al. (2001). Analysis of disputed single-parent/child and sibling relationships using 16 STR loci. *International Journal of Legal Medicine, 115*, 128–134.

Valentin, J. (1979). Bayesian probability of paternity when mother or putative father are not tested: formulas for manual computation. *Hereditas, 91*, 163–167.

Vicard, P., & Dawid, A. P. (2006). Remarks on: "Paternity analysis in special fatherless cases without direct testing of alleged father." *Forensic Science International, 146S*(2004), S159–S161. Forensic Science International, 163, 158–160.

Wenk, R. E., et al. (2006). Maternal typing and test sufficiency in parentage analyses. *Transfusion, 46*(2), 199–203.

Wurmb-Schwark, N., et al. (2006). Possible pitfalls in motherless paternity analysis with related putative fathers. *Forensic Science international, 159*, 92–97.

Impact of Null Alleles

Dakin, E. E., & Avise, J. C. (2004). Microsatellite null alleles in parentage analysis. *Heredity, 93*, 504–509.

Lane, A. B. (2013). STR null alleles complicate parentage testing in South Africa. *South African Medical Journal, 103*, 1004–1008.

Mizuno, N., et al. (2008). A D19S433 primer binding site mutation and the frequency in Japanese of the silent allele it causes. *Journal of Forensic Sciences, 53*, 1068–1073.

Wagner, A. P., et al. (2006). Estimating relatedness and relationships using microsatellite loci with null alleles. *Heredity, 97*, 336–345.

Use of Additional Autosomal STR Markers

Betz, T., et al. (2007). "Paterniplex," a highly discriminative decaplex STR multiplex tailored for investigating special problems in paternity testing. *Electrophoresis, 28*, 3868–3874.

Calafell, F. (2000). The probability distribution of the number of loci indicating exclusion in a core set of STR markers. *International Journal of Legal Medicine, 114*, 61–65.

Carboni, I., et al. (2011). 87 DNA markers for a paternity testing: are they sufficient? *Forensic Science International: Genetics Supplement Series, 3*, e552–e553.

Carnevali, E., et al. (2011). Is it always possible to avoid exhumation in particular defective paternity cases by increasing autosomal STRs number? *Forensic Science International: Genetics Supplement Series, 3*, e363–e364.

Grubwieser, P., et al. (2007). Evaluation of an extended set of 15 candidate STR loci for paternity and kinship analysis in an Austrian population sample. *International Journal of Legal Medicine, 121*, 85–89.

Henke, J., & Henke, L. (2005). Which short tandem repeat polymorphisms are required for identification? Lessons from complicated kinship cases. *Croatian Medical Journal, 46*, 593–597.

Li, L., et al. (2012). Maternity exclusion with a very high autosomal STRs kinship index. *International Journal of Legal Medicine, 126*, 645–648.

Use of Lineage Markers, SNPs, or INDELs

Acar, E., et al. (2009). Optimization and validation studies of the Mentype Argus X-8 kit for paternity cases. *Forensic Science International: Genetics Supplement Series, 2*, 47–48.

Amorim, A., & Pereira, L. (2005). Pros and cons in the use of SNPs in forensic kinship investigation: a comparative analysis with STRs. *Forensic Science International, 150*, 17–21.

Aquino, J., et al. (2009). A X-chromosome STR hexaplex as a powerful tool in deficiency paternity cases. *Forensic Science International: Genetics Supplement Series, 2*, 45–46.

Borsting, C., & Morling, N. (2011). Mutations and/or close relatives? Six case work examples where 49 autosomal SNPs were used as supplementary markers. *Forensic Science International: Genetics, 5*, 236–241.

Børsting, C., et al. (2008). Performance of the SNPforID 52 SNP-plex assay in paternity testing. *Forensic Science International: Genetics, 2,* 292–300.

Borsting, C., et al. (2009). Validation of a single nucleotide polymorphism (SNP) typing assay with 49 SNPs for forensic genetic testing in a laboratory accredited according to the ISO 17025 standard. *Forensic Science International: Genetics, 4,* 34–42.

Børsting, C., et al. (2011). SNP typing of the reference materials SRM 2391b 1-10, K562, XY1, XX74, and 007 with the SNPforID multiplex. *Forensic Science International: Genetics, 5,* e81–e82.

Børsting, C., et al. (2012). *Typing of 49 autosomal SNPs by single base extension and capillary electrophoresis for forensic genetic testing.* DNA Electrophoresis Protocols for Forensic Genetics. In A. Alonso (Ed.), *Methods in Molecular Biology, 830;* (pp. 87–107).

Builes, J. J., et al. (2009). Utility of Y- and X-STRs in the research of complex biological relationship. *Forensic Science International: Genetics Supplement Series, 2,* 236–237.

Dario, P., et al. (2009). SNPs in paternity investigation: the simple future. *Forensic Science International: Genetics Supplement Series, 2,* 127–128.

Dario, P., et al. (2011). Complex casework using single nucleotide polymorphisms. *Forensic Science International: Genetics Supplement Series, 3,* e379–e380.

Dario, P., et al. (2011). 20 SNPs as supplementary markers in kinship testing. *Forensic Science International: Genetics Supplement Series, 3,* e508–e509.

Gusmao, L., et al. (2012). *Capillary electrophoresis of an X-chromosome STR decaplex for kinship deficiency cases.* DNA Electrophoresis Protocols for Forensic Genetics. In A. Alonso (Ed.), *Methods in Molecular Biology, 830;* (pp. 57–71).

Ibarra, A., et al. (2013). Using STR, miniSTR and SNP markers to solve complex cases of kinship analysis. *Forensic Science International: Genetics Supplement Series, 4,* e91–e92.

Jobling, M. A., et al. (1997). The Y chromosome in forensic analysis and paternity testing. *International Journal of Legal Medicine, 110,* 118–124.

Krawczak, M. (2007). Kinship testing with X-chromosomal markers: mathematical and statistical issues. *Forensic Science International: Genetics, 1,* 111–114.

Magalhaes, M., et al. (2011). When the alleged father is a close relative of the real father: the utility of insertion/deletion polymorphisms. *Forensic Science International: Genetics Supplement Series, 3,* e9–e10.

Miozzo, C., et al. (2009). A case of chimerism in a paternity study. *Forensic Science International: Genetics Supplement Series, 2,* 228–229.

Phillips, C., et al. (2008). Resolving relationship tests that show ambiguous STR results using autosomal SNPs as supplementary markers. *Forensic Science International: Genetics, 2,* 198–204.

Phillips, C. (2012). Applications of autosomal SNPs and Indels in forensic analysis. *Forensic Science Review, 24*(1), 43–62.

Pinto, N., et al. (2011). X-chromosome markers in kinship testing: a generalisation of the IBD approach identifying situations where their contribution is crucial. *Forensic Science International: Genetics, 5,* 27–32.

Pinto, N., et al. (2012). A general method to assess the utility of the X-chromosomal markers in kinship testing. *Forensic Science International: Genetics, 6,* 198–207.

Pinto, N., et al. (2013). Assessing paternities with inconclusive STR results: The suitability of bi-allelic markers. *Forensic Science International: Genetics, 7,* 16–21.

Ryan, A., et al. (2013). Informatics-based, highly accurate, noninvasive prenatal paternity testing. *Genetics in Medicine, 15*(6), 473–477.

Serra, A., et al. (2008). X-chromosome STR typing in deficiency paternity cases. *Forensic Science International: Genetics Supplement Series, 1,* 162–163.

Tomas, C., et al. (2012). *A 48-plex autosomal SNP GenPlex assay for human individualization and relationship testing.* DNA Electrophoresis Protocols for Forensic Genetics. In A. Alonso (Ed.), *Methods in Molecular Biology, 830;* (pp. 73–85).

Whittle, M. R., et al. (2009). Paternity investigation experience with a 40 autosomal SNP panel. *Forensic Science International: Genetics Supplement Series, 2,* 149–150.

Ye, Y., et al. (2014). A case study of SNPSTR efficiency in paternity testing with locus incompatibility. *Forensic Science International: Genetics, 9,* 72–75.

Use of Linked Markers in Kinship Testing

Brenner, C. H. (2014). *Paternity calculation with 3-banded pattern.* Available at http://www.dna-view.com/3band.htm. Accessed April 3, 2014.

Buckleton, J., & Triggs, C. (2006). The effect of linkage on the calculation of DNA match probabilities for siblings and half siblings. *Forensic Science International, 160,* 193–199.

II. STATISTICAL INTERPRETATION

Budowle, B., et al. (2012). Population genetic analyses of the NGM STR loci. *International Journal of Legal Medicine, 125,* 538—540.

Du, J.-P., et al. (2013). Potential forensic application of closely linked autosomal STR haplotype in complex kinship testing. *Forensic Science International: Genetics Supplement Series, 4,* e137—e139.

Egeland, T., & Sheehan, N. (2008). On identification problems requiring linked autosomal markers. *Forensic Science International: Genetics, 2,* 219—225.

Gill, P., et al. (2012). An evaluation of potential allelic association between the STRs vWA and D12S391: implications in criminal casework and applications to short pedigrees. *Forensic Science International: Genetics, 6(4),* 477—486.

Haldane, J. B. S. (1919). A combination of linkage values and the calculation of distances between loci of linked factors. *Journal of Genetics, 8,* 299—309.

Haseman, J. K., & Elston, R. C. (1972). The investigation of linkage between a quantitative trait and a marker locus. *Behavioral Genetics, 2,* 3—19.

O'Connor, K. L., et al. (2011). Linkage disequilibrium analysis of D12S391 and vWA in U.S. population and paternity samples. *Forensic Science International: Genetics, 5,* 538—540.

O'Connor, K. L., & Tillmar, A. O. (2012). Effect of linkage between vWA and D12S391 in kinship analysis. *Forensic Science International: Genetics, 6(6),* 840—844.

Suarez, B. K., et al. (1978). The generalized sib pair IBD distribution: its use in the detection of linkage. *Annals of Human Genetics London, 42,* 87.

Products of Conception

Johnson, D. J., et al. (2010). Isolation and individualization of conceptus and maternal tissues from abortions and placentas for parentage testing in cases of rape and abandoned newborns. *Journal of Forensic Sciences, 55,* 1430—1436.

Missing Persons, DVI, & Family Reconstruction Cases

Biedermann, A., et al. (2007). Equal prior probabilities: can one do any better? *Forensic Science International, 172,* 85—93.

Biedermann, A., et al. (2012). Reply to Budowle, Ge, Chakraborty and Gill-King: use of prior odds for missing persons identifications. *Investigative Genetics, 3(1),* 2.

Brenner, C. H. (2006). Some mathematical problems in the DNA identification of victims in the 2004 tsunami and similar mass fatalities. *Forensic Science International, 157,* 172—180.

Brenner, C. H. (2006b). *Reuniting El Salvador families.* Available at http://dna-view.com/ProBusqueda.htm. Accessed April 3, 2014.

Bruigning-van Dongen, C. J., et al. (2009). Bayesian networks for victim identification on the basis of DNA profiles. *Forensic Science International: Genetics Supplement Series, 2,* 466—468.

Budowle, B., et al. (2011). Use of prior odds for missing persons identifications. *Investigative Genetics, 2(1),* 15.

Budowle, B., et al. (2012). Response to: Use of prior odds for missing persons identifications — authors' reply. *Investigative Genetics, 3(1),* 3.

Butler, J. M. (2012). Missing persons and disaster victim identification efforts. *Chapter 9 in Advanced Topics in Forensic DNA Typing: Methodology.* San Diego: Elsevier Academic Press, pp. 271—292.

Chakraborty, R., et al. (2011). Response to: DNA identification by pedigree likelihood ratio accommodating population substructure and mutations — authors' reply. *Investigative Genetics, 2(1),* 8.

Da Silva, L. A. F., et al. (2009). Missing and unidentified persons database. *Forensic Science International: Genetics Supplement Series, 2,* 255—257.

Donker voort, S., et al. (2008). Enhancing accurate data collection in mass fatality kinship identifications: lessons learned from Hurricane Katrina. *Forensic Science International: Genetics, 2,* 354—362.

Garcia, M., et al. (2009). Analysis of complex kinship cases for human identification of civil war victims in Guatemala using M-FISys software. *Forensic Science International: Genetics Supplement Series, 2,* 250—252.

Ge, J., et al. (2010). DNA identification by pedigree likelihood ratio accommodating population substructure and mutations. *Investigative Genetics, 1(1),* 8.

Ge, J., et al. (2011). Choosing relatives for DNA identification of missing persons. *Journal of Forensic Sciences, 56 Supplemental, 1,* S23—S28.

Hartman, D., et al. (2011). The contribution of DNA to the disaster victim identification (DVI) effort. *Forensic Science International, 205,* 52—58.

Hartman, D., et al. (2011). Examples of kinship analysis where Profiler Plus™ was not discriminatory enough for the identification of victims using DNA identification. *Forensic Science International, 205*, 64–68.

Lalueza-Fox, C., et al. (2011). Genetic analysis of the presumptive blood from Louis XVI, King of France. *Forensic Science International: Genetics, 5*, 459–463.

Matsumura, S., et al. (2011). Kinship analysis using DNA typing from five skeletal remains with an unusual postmortem course. *Medicine, Science, and the Law, 51*(4), 240–243.

National Institute of Justice. (2006). *Lessons learned from 9/11: DNA identifications in mass fatality incidents.* Available at http://massfatality.dna.gov/. Chapter 12 covers statistical issues. Accessed April 3, 2014.

Neuhuber, F., et al. (2012). An unusual case of identification by DNA analysis of siblings. *Forensic Science International: Genetics, 6*, 121–123.

Ntwari, A., et al. (2011). DNAc: a clustering method for identifying kinship relationship between DNA profiles using a novel similarity measure. *Journal of Forensic Sciences, 56 Supplemental, 1*, S17–S22.

Prinz, M., et al. (2007). DNA Commission of the International Society for Forensic Genetics (ISFG): recommendations regarding the role of forensic genetics for disaster victim identification (DVI). *Forensic Science International: Genetics, 1*, 3–12.

Sozer, A. C. (2014). *DNA Analysis for Missing Person Identification in Mass Fatalities.* Boca Raton: CRC Press.

Thompson, W. C., et al. (2013). The role of prior probability in forensic assessments. *Frontiers in Genetics, 4*, 1–3.

Van Dongen, C. J., et al. (2011). Bonaparte: application of new software for missing persons program. *Forensic Science International: Genetics Supplement Series, 3*, e119–e120.

Yoshida, K., et al. (2011). Efficacy of extended kinship analyses utilizing commercial STR kit in establishing personal identification. *Legal Medicine, 13*, 12–15.

Reverse Paternity Testing

Gornik, I., et al. (2002). The identification of war victims by reverse paternity is associated with significant risks of false inclusion. *International Journal of Legal Medicine, 116*, 255–257.

Pretty, I. A., & Hildebrand, D. P. (2005). The forensic and investigative significance of reverse paternity testing with absent maternal sample. *American Journal of Forensic Medicine and Pathology, 26*, 340–342.

Familial Searching

Balding, D. J., et al. (2012). Decision-making in familial database searching: KI alone or not alone? *Forensic Science International: Genetics, 7*, 52–54.

Bieder, F. R., et al. (2006). Finding criminals through DNA of their relatives. *Science, 312*, 1315–1316.

Budowle, B. (2010). Familial searching: extending the investigative lead potential of DNA typing. *Profiles in DNA, 13*(2). Available at http://www.promega.com/resources/profiles-in-dna/familial-searching-extending-the-investigative-lead-potential-of-dna-typing/. Accessed April 3, 2014.

Butler, J. M. (2012). Familial DNA searches: potential, pitfalls, and privacy concerns. *Appendix 2 in Advanced Topics in Forensic DNA Typing: Methodology.* San Diego: Elsevier Academic Press. pp. 603–610.

Chung, Y.-K., et al. (2010). Familial database search on two-person mixture. *Computational Statistics and Data Analysis, 54*, 2046–2051.

Cowen, S., & Thompson, J. (2008). A likelihood ratio approach to familial searching of large DNA databases. *Forensic Science International: Genetics Supplement Series, 1*, 643–645.

Curran, J. M., & Buckleton, J. S. (2008). Effectiveness of familial searches. *Science & Justice, 48*, 164–167.

Garrison, N., et al. (2013). Forensic familial searching: scientific and social implications. *Nature Reviews Genetics, 14*(7), 445.

Ge, J., et al. (2011). Comparisons of familial DNA database searching strategies. *Journal of Forensic Sciences, 56*(6), 1448–1456.

Ge, J., & Budowle, B. (2012). Kinship index variations among populations and thresholds for familial searching. *PLoS ONE, 7*(5), e37474.

Gershaw, C. J., et al. (2011). Forensic utilization of familial searches in DNA databases. *Forensic Science International: Genetics, 5*, 16–20.

Maguire, C. N., et al. (2014). Familial searching: a specialist forensic profiling service utilizing the National DNA Database to identify unknown offenders via their relatives — the UK experience. *Forensic Science International: Genetics, 8*, 1–9.

Miller, G. (2010). Familial DNA testing scores a win in serial killer case. *Science, 329*, 262.

II. STATISTICAL INTERPRETATION

Myers, S. P., et al. (2011). Searching for first-degree familial relationships in California's offender DNA database: validation of a likelihood ratio-based approach. *Forensic Science International: Genetics, 5*(5), 493–500.

O'Connor, K. L. (2011). *Introduction to familial searching*. Washington, DC: Presentation given at International Symposium on Human Identification. Available at http://www.cstl.nist.gov/strbase/pub_pres/OConnor_Promega2011.pdf. Accessed April 3, 2014.

Ram, N. (2011). Fortuity and forensic familial identification. *Stanford Law Review, 63*, 751–812.

Reid, T. M., et al. (2008). Use of sibling pairs to determine the familial searching efficiency of forensic databases. *Forensic Science International: Genetics, 2*(4), 340–342.

Rohlfs, R., et al. (2012). Familial identification: Population structure and relationship distinguishability. *PLoS Genetics, 8.* e1002469.

Rohlfs, R. V., et al. (2013). The influence of relatives on the efficiency and error rate of familial searching. *PLoS ONE, 8*(8). e70495.

Sjerps, M., & Kloostermann, A. D. (1999). On the consequences of DNA profile mismatches for close relatives of an excluded suspect. *International Journal of Legal Medicine, 112*, 176–180.

Slooten, K., & Meester, R. (2011). Statistical aspects of familial searching. *Forensic Science International: Genetics Supplement Series, 3*, e167–e169.

SWGDAM. (2009). SWGDAM recommendations to the FBI Director on the "Interim plan for the release of information in the event of a 'partial match' at NDIS." *Forensic Science Communications, 11*(4). Available at http://www.fbi.gov/about-us/lab/forensic-science-communications/fsc/oct2009/index.htm/standard_guidlines/swgdam.html. Accessed April 3, 2014.

SWGDAM. (2014). *Recommendations from the SWGDAM Ad Hoc Working Group on Familial Searching*. Available at http://swgdam.org/SWGDAM%20Recs%20on%20Familial%20Searching%20APPROVED%2010072013.pdf. Accessed April 3, 2014.

Complex Kinship Analysis

Brenner, C. H., & Staub, R. W. (2003). *Can DNA solve this? Poster at 14th International Symposium on Human Identification (Phoenix, Arizona, October 2003).*

Butler, J. M., et al. (2003). Allele frequencies for 15 autosomal STR loci on U.S. Caucasian, African American, and Hispanic populations. *Journal of Forensic Sciences, 48*, 908–911.

Caine, L., et al. (2011). Interest of X chromosome (Argus X-12 kit) in complex kinship analysis. *Forensic Science International: Genetics Supplement Series, 3*, e206–e207.

Fimmers, R., et al. (2008). STR-profiling for the differentiation between related and unrelated individuals in cases of citizen rights. *Forensic Science International: Genetics Supplement Series, 1*, 510–513.

Fung, W. K., et al. (2003). Testing for kinship in a subdivided population. *Forensic Science International, 135*, 105–109.

Gomes, C., et al. (2011). How useful is your X in discerning pedigrees? *Forensic Science International: Genetics Supplement Series, 3*, e161–e162.

Hubig, M., et al. (2013). Setting the boundaries of prior influence on kinship relation testing: the case of many hypotheses. *International Journal of Legal Medicine, 127*(6), 1055–1063.

Inturri, S., et al. (2011). An Italian Jean Jacques Rousseau: a complex kinship case. *Forensic Science International: Genetics Supplement Series, 3*, e520–e521.

Katki, H. A., et al. (2010). Using DNA fingerprints to infer familial relationships within NHANES III households. *Journal of the American Statistical Association, 105*, 552–563.

Morris, J. W., et al. (1988). The avuncular index and the incest index. In W. R. Mayr (Ed.), *Advances in Forensic Haemogenetics 2* (pp. 607–611). Berlin: Springer-Verlag.

Nothnagel, M., et al. (2010). Potentials and limits of pairwise kinship analysis using autosomal short tandem repeat loci. *International Journal of Legal Medicine, 124*, 205–215.

Pinto, N., et al. (2009). Distinguishing kinship from genealogical likelihoods. *Forensic Science International: Genetics Supplement Series, 2*, 453–454.

Pinto, N., et al. (2010). Likelihood ratios in kinship analysis: contrasting kinship classes, not genealogies. *Forensic Science International: Genetics, 4*, 218–219.

Tamura, T., et al. (2012). Evaluation of the allele-sharing approach, known as the IBS method, in kinship analysis. *Journal of Forensic and Legal Medicine, 20*(2), 112–116.

Wenk, R. E., et al. (2003). Better tools are needed for parentage and kinship studies. *Transfusion, 43*(7), 979–981.

Wilkening, S., et al. (2006). STR markers for kinship analysis. *Human Biology, 78*, 1–8.

Sibship Testing

Allen, R. W., et al. (2007). Considerations for the interpretation of STR results in cases of questioned half-sibship. *Transfusion, 47*, 515–519.

Brenner, C. H. (2011). *Thinking clearly about likelihood ratios and siblingship.* Available at http://www.dna-view.com/LRconfusion.htm. Accessed April 3, 2014.

Gaytmenn, R., et al. (2002). Determination of the sensitivity and specificity of sibship calculations using AmpFlSTR Profiler Plus. *International Journal of Legal Medicine, 116*, 161–164.

Giroti, R. I., et al. (2007). A grey zone approach for evaluation of 15 short tandem repeat loci in sibship analysis: a pilot study in Indian subjects. *Journal of Forensic and Legal Medicine, 14*(5), 261–265.

Gorlin, J. B., & Polesky, H. F. (2000). Letter to editor: the use and abuse of the full-sibling and half-sibling indices. *Transfusion, 40*, 1148.

Immel, U. D., et al. (2011). Determination of siblings: a special case report from Halle. *Forensic Science International: Genetics Supplement Series, 3*, e463–e464.

Mályusz, V., et al. (2006). Problems of assessing sibship probabilities by means of genetic analysis. *Archives of Kriminology, 218*, 44–54. [Article in German].

Mayor, L. R., & Balding, D. J. (2006). Discrimination of half-siblings when maternal genotypes are known. *Forensic Science International, 159*, 141–147.

Neuhuber, F., et al. (2012). An unusual case of identification by DNA analysis of siblings. *Forensic Science International: Genetics, 6*, 121–123.

Presciuttini, S., et al. (2002). Inferring relationships between pairs of individuals from locus heterozygosities. *BMC Genetics, 3*, 23.

Presciuttini, S., et al. (2003). Allele sharing in the first-degree and unrelated pairs of individuals in the GeFI AmpFlSTR Profiler Plus database. *Forensic Science International, 131*, 85–89.

Pu, C. E., & Linacre, A. (2008). Systematic evaluation of sensitivity and specificity of sibship determination by using 15 STR loci. *Journal of Forensic and Legal Medicine, 15*, 329–334.

Pu, C. E., & Linacre, A. (2008). Increasing the confidence in half-sibship determination based upon 15 STR loci. *Journal of Forensic and Legal Medicine, 15*, 373–377.

Reid, T. M., et al. (2004). Specificity of sibship determination using the ABI Identifiler multiplex system. *Journal of Forensic Sciences, 49*, 1262–1264.

Sulzer, A., et al. (2011). Reliability of results in sibship cases. *Forensic Science International: Genetics Supplement Series, 3*, e95–e96.

Wenk, R. E., et al. (1996). Determination of sibship in any two persons. *Transfusion, 36*, 259–262.

Wenk, R. E., & Chiafari, F. A. (2000). Distinguishing full siblings from half-siblings in limited pedigrees. *Transfusion, 40*, 44–47.

Wenk, R. E., & Shao, A. (2012). Empowering sibship analyses with reference pedigrees. *Transfusion, 52*(12), 2614–2619.

Zhao, S., et al. (2011). Comparison study in determination of full sibling with Identifiler multiplex system between ITO method and identity by state scoring method. *Forensic Science International: Genetics Supplement Series, 3*, e335–e336.

Immigration Testing

Ballard, D. J., et al. (2009). Supplementary markers for deficient immigration cases: additional STRs or SNPs? *Forensic Science International: Genetics Supplement Series, 2*, 153–154.

Cowell, R. G. (2013). A simple greedy algorithm for reconstructing pedigrees. *Theoretical Population Biology, 83*, 55–63.

Fung, W. K., et al. (2002). Power of exclusion revisited: probability of excluding relatives of the true father from paternity. *International Journal of Legal Medicine, 116*, 64–67.

Fung, W. K., et al. (2003). How well do serial tandem repeat loci perform in excluding paternity in relatives of the biologic father among immigration cases? *Transfusion, 43*, 982–983.

Fung, W. K., et al. (2004). Full siblings impersonating parent/child prove most difficult to discredit with DNA profiling alone. *Transfusion, 44*, 1513–1515.

Hu, Y. Q., & Fung, W. K. (2005). Power of excluding an elder brother of a child from paternity. *Forensic Science International, 152*, 321–322.

Jeffreys, A. J., et al. (1985). Positive identification of an immigration test-case using human DNA fingerprints. *Nature, 317*, 818–819.

Karlsson, A. O., et al. (2007). DNA-testing for immigration cases: the risk of erroneous conclusions. *Forensic Science International, 172*, 144–149.

Lancia, M., et al. (2009). Analysis of complex family cases with probabilistic expert systems. *Forensic Science International: Genetics Supplement Series, 2*, 472–474.

Lee, J. W., et al. (1999). Paternity probability when a relative of the father is an alleged father. *Science & Justice, 39*, 223–230.

Pena, M. A., et al. (2009). DNA profile evidence in complex disputed paternity cases: the analysis of 300 real cases. *Forensic Science International: Genetics Supplement Series, 2*, 151–152.

Poetsch, M., et al. (2011). The new PowerPlex ESX 17 and ESI 17 kits in paternity and maternity analyses involving people from Africa — including allele frequencies for three African populations. *International Journal of Legal Medicine, 125*, 149–154.

Sheehan, N. A., & Egeland, T. (2007). Structured incorporation of prior information in relationship identification problems. *Annals of Human Genetics, 71*, 501–518.

Silva, D. A., et al. (2009). Paternity testing involving human remains identification and putative half sister: usefulness of an X-hexaplex STR markers. *Forensic Science International: Genetics Supplement Series, 2*, 230–231.

Wenk, R. E., et al. (2005). The specific power of parentage exclusion in a child's blood relatives. *Transfusion, 45*, 440–444.

Wenk, R. E. (2010). Sporadic genotype recycling fraud in relationship testing of immigrants. *Transfusion, 50*(8), 1852–1853.

Wenk, R. E. (2011). Detection of genotype recycling fraud in U.S. immigrants. *Journal of Forensic Sciences, 56*(Suppl. 1), S243–S246.

Wenk, R. E., & Shao, A. (2014). Pretense of parentage by siblings in immigration: Polesky's paradox reconsidered. *Transfusion, 54*(2), 456–460.

Incest Cases

Macan, M., et al. (2003). Paternity testing in case of brother–sister incest. *Croatian Medical Journal, 44*, 347–349.

Pinto, N., et al. (2013). Paternity exclusion power: comparative behavior of autosomal and X-chromosomal markers in standard and deficient cases with inbreeding. *Forensic Science International: Genetics, 7*(2), 290–295.

Tamura, A., et al. (2000). Sibling incest and formulation of paternity probability: case report. *Legal Medicine, 2*, 189–196.

Toscanini, U., et al. (2009). X-STRs analysis in paternity testing when the alleged father is related to the biological father. *Forensic Science International: Genetics Supplement Series, 2*, 234–235.

Wenk, R. E. (2008). Incest indices from microsatellite genotypes of mother–child pairs. *Transfusion, 48*(2), 341–348.

Extended Relatives with High-Density SNP Arrays

Inaoka, Y., et al. (2011). Kinship analysis based on SNP data from microarray assay. *Forensic Science International: Genetics Supplement Series, 3*, e275–e276.

Kling, D., et al. (2012). DNA microarray as a tool in establishing genetic relatedness — Current status and future prospects. *Forensic Science International: Genetics, 6*, 322–329.

Lareu, M. V., et al. (2012). Analysis of a claimed distant relationship in a deficient pedigree using high density SNP data. *Forensic Science International: Genetics, 6*, 350–353.

Phillips, C., et al. (2012). SNPs as supplements in simple kinship analysis or as core markers in distant pairwise relationship tests: when do SNPs add value or replace well-established and powerful STR tests? *Transfusion Medicine and Hemotherapy, 39*, 202–210.

Roberson, E., & Pevsner, J. (2009). Visualization of shared genomic regions and meiotic recombination in high-density SNP data. *PLoS ONE, 4*(8), e6711.

Seo, S. B., et al. (2013). Single nucleotide polymorphism typing with massively parallel sequencing for human identification. *International Journal of Legal Medicine, 127*, 1079–1086.

Skare, Ø., et al. (2009). Identification of distant family relationships. *Bioinformatics, 25*, 2376–2382.

Resolving Twins

Bruder, C. E., et al. (2008). Phenotypically concordant and discordant monozygotic twins display different DNA copy-number-variation profiles. *American Journal of Human Genetics, 82*, 763–771.

Fraga, M. F., et al. (2005). Epigenetic differences arise during the lifetime of monozygotic twins. *Proceedings of the National Academy of Sciences of the United States of America, 102*, 10604–10609.

Kaminsky, Z. A., et al. (2009). DNA methylation profiles in monozygotic and dizygotic twins. *Nature Genetics, 41*, 240–245.

Krawczak, M., et al. (2012). How to distinguish genetically between an alleged father and his monozygotic twin: a thought experiment. *Forensic Science International: Genetics, 6*, e129–e130.

Li, C., et al. (2011). Identical but not the same: the value of DNA methylation profiling in forensic discrimination within monozygotic twins. *Forensic Science International: Genetics Supplement Series, 3*, e337–e338.

Weber-Lehmann, J., et al. (2014). Finding the needle in the haystack: differentiating "identical" twins in paternity testing and forensics by ultra-deep next generation sequencing. *Forensic Science International: Genetics, 9*, 42–46.

II. STATISTICAL INTERPRETATION

15

Lineage Marker Statistics

Until recently, the Y chromosome seemed to fulfill the role of juvenile delinquent among human chromosomes — rich in junk, poor in useful attributes, reluctant to socialize with its neighbors and with an inescapable tendency to degenerate...

Mark Jobling & Chris Tyler-Smith (2003)

LINEAGE MARKER INHERITANCE PATTERNS

Lineage markers include mitochondrial DNA (mtDNA) and Y-chromosome short tandem repeat (Y-STR) haplotypes that are transferred directly from generation to generation either from mother to child in the case of mtDNA, or from father to son in the case of the Y-chromosome (Figure 15.1(a)). X-chromosome markers are another tool that can be used for genetic identity testing. Lineage markers can be helpful in missing persons investigations, disaster victim identification, forensic case-work where other evidence is limited, and some complex kinship situations. X-chromosome analysis is especially helpful in assessing some kinship scenarios (see Butler 2012).

Normal males possess one X-chromosome and one Y-chromosome while females possess two X-chromosomes. Both males and females receive their mitochondrial DNA from their mothers. Specific patterns of inheritance across two generations are illustrated in Figure 15.2 for a son and a daughter.

Due to the inheritance patterns, Y-STR haplotypes and mtDNA sequence information are treated as linked markers with the entire profile inherited as a block (Figure 15.1(b)). Thus, Y-STR haplotypes can be effectively considered a single genetic locus with many different alleles. Since the inheritance of individual alleles is not independent, the product rule that is used in autosomal STR analysis cannot be employed with lineage markers. Barring mutation, sons will have the same Y-STR profile as their fathers, and children will possess the same mtDNA sequence as their mothers.

However, there is some recombination that occurs along the X-chromosome so that the entire X-chromosome is not passed along unchanged from generation to generation. Typically X-STR markers are divided into four linkage groups so that depending on chromosomal proximity, statistical weight of evidence calculations can be combined and multiplied for some X-STR loci in a similar fashion as is done with autosomal STRs (Szibor 2007). This chapter will focus primarily on Y-STR information, although many of the principles are applicable to mtDNA and X-STR interpretation.

Advanced Topics in Forensic DNA Typing: Interpretation
http://dx.doi.org/10.1016/B978-0-12-405213-0.00015-4

2015 Published by Elsevier Inc.

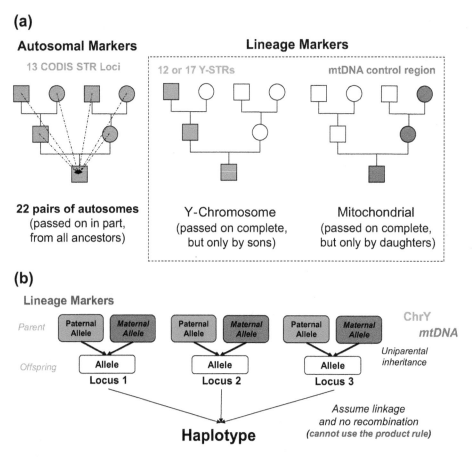

FIGURE 15.1   (a) Illustration of inheritance patterns from recombining autosomal genetic markers and the lineage markers from the Y-chromosome (ChrY) and mitochondrial DNA (mtDNA). (b) Lineage markers involve uniparental inheritance and assume linkage so that the product rule cannot be used. Essentially Y-STRs and mtDNA can each be treated as a single genetic locus with many alleles (haplotypes).

Compared to mtDNA, Y-STRs are easier to analyze and interpret because commercial kits enable the polymerase chain reaction (PCR) amplification of 12, 17, 23, or more Y-STR loci (e.g. see Figure 1.8). Far fewer laboratories are conducting mtDNA analysis in part due to extra precautions that are needed to avoid contamination with mtDNA that occurs in a higher number of copies per cell (see Butler 2012).

Y-STRs offer finer resolution than mtDNA in terms of distinguishing among genetic lineages. The higher mutation rate of STRs ($\approx 10^{-3}$) compared to DNA sequence changes ($\approx 10^{-8}$) leads to more variation in haplotypes with Y-STRs compared to mtDNA. Unrelated individuals, and even related people in some cases, can be genetically resolved with Y-STR loci by exploiting this higher mutation rate.

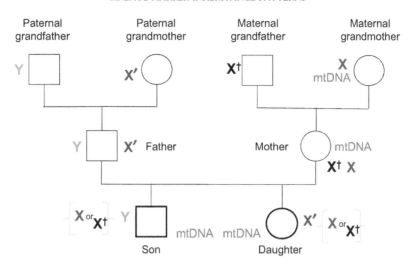

FIGURE 15.2 Possible genetic contributors of mtDNA, X- or Y-chromosome information to a son and a daughter. Specific alleles with autosomal loci can be contributed by any or none of the grandparents. Different symbols and colors are used to track passage of genetic information across generations. The X and X′ in the grandparent generation are actually {X1,X2} and {X′1,X′2} so that siblings at parent generation (and 1st cousins at son/daughter level) may not share the same grand maternal X chromosome. Note that depending on the parentage question being asked, different markers from particular reference samples may be more or less useful. Adapted from Buckleton et al. 2007.

Estimating Rarity of a Haplotype

If the evidence question (Q) profile matches a reference known (K) profile for a lineage marker, then it is important to provide an estimate of the rarity of this Q-to-K match. This is commonly done through examining a population database that contains previously tested DNA samples with coverage of the relevant lineage marker. The number of times the specific haplotype is observed is counted, hence the term *counting method*. Sampling correction factors such as an upper bound confidence interval have been used as well in an effort to reflect uncertainty around the point estimate provided by the counting method.

As with autosomal markers (see Figure 9.1), there are three aspects of estimating a haplotype frequency: (1) generating the Y-STR haplotype or mtDNA sequence information, (2) querying a population database, and (3) reporting the frequency estimate or match probability using genetic and statistical models (Figure 15.3).

Population databases (see below) are relied upon in attempting to understand the real-world rarity of a haplotype Q-to-K match. An important difference with lineage markers is that associations made in a Q-to-K comparison are to a paternal lineage (in the case of Y-STRs) or maternal lineage (in the case or mtDNA) rather than to a specific individual. Thus, report wording needs to emphasize that a Y-STR "match" between an evidentiary sample and a suspect's profile can also include the reference sample's father, brother, or other relatives in the same paternal lineage. Likewise, mtDNA Q-to-K matches are to individuals in a particular maternal lineage, not to a specific individual. While this fact inhibits interpretation specificity, it enables a wider range of reference samples, which can be helpful in disaster victim identification or missing persons investigations.

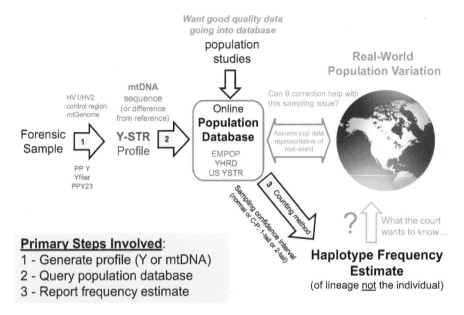

FIGURE 15.3 Summary of issues faced with lineage markers. A Y-STR profile or mtDNA sequence haplotype is generated from a forensic evidence sample. An online population database is queried (EMPOP for mtDNA or YHRD/US Y-STR for Y-STRs). The number of matching haplotypes is counted and a haplotype frequency estimate provided, often with a sampling confidence interval and/or a subpopulation theta correction. This approach assumes that the population database reliably represents the real-world variation for the haplotype lineage being measured.

GUIDANCE ON INTERPRETATION

The Scientific Working Group on DNA Analysis Methods (SWGDAM) has provided interpretation guidelines for Y-STRs (SWGDAM 2009, SWGDAM 2014) and mitochondrial DNA (SWGDAM 2003, SWGDAM 2013). The DNA Commission of the International Society for Forensic Genetics (ISFG) has also published some general recommendations on mtDNA (Carracedo et al. 2000) and Y-STR analysis (Gill et al. 2001, Gusmão et al. 2006). Thus far, neither SWGDAM or the ISFG has issued specific guidance for X-chromosome markers, which are not used as often in the forensic community.

In terms of example laboratory protocols, Manuel Crespillo Marquez from the National Institute of Toxicology and Forensic Science in Barcelona, Spain provides some detailed guidance on mtDNA control region sequence evaluation and interpretation (Marquez 2012). Lutz Roewer and Maria Geppert from the Institute of Legal Medicine in Berlin, Germany review interpretation guidelines for Yfiler testing (Roewer & Geppert 2012). The use of an X-chromosome decaplex for kinship deficiency cases is covered by Leonor Gusmão and colleagues at the Institute of Pathology and Molecular Immunology of the University of Porto in Portugal (Gusmão et al. 2012).

Y-STR data sharing has benefited from a number of standardization efforts over the past few years. These include selection of a core set of Y-STR loci, availability of commercial kits, consistent allele nomenclature, online searchable population databases, and interpretation guidelines (Table 15.1). Mitochondrial DNA and X-STR analysis are not as widely used as Y-STRs and do not have all of these same standardization advantages. For example, there are no commercial kits for mtDNA analysis.

TABLE 15.1 Standardization Efforts to Aid Data Sharing with Y-STR Markers

Needs	How/When Accomplished
Core Y-STR loci	European 9-locus minimal haplotype (MH) selected in 1997; SWGDAM Y-STR Committee selected 11-locus core (MH + DYS438, DYS439) in January 2003
Consistent allele nomenclature	NIST Standard Reference Material 2395 Human Y-Chromosome DNA Profiling Standard (2003); kit allelic ladders; ISFG (2006) and NIST (2008) publications
Commercially available Y-STR kits	Early ReliaGene kits (2001–2003); **PowerPlex Y** (2003), **Yfiler** (2004), **PowerPlex Y23** (2012), **Yfiler Plus** (2014)
Accessible, searchable population databases for haplotype frequency estimations	**YHRD** (99,823 11-locus haplotypes from >850 worldwide populations) **US Y-STR** (32,972 11-locus haplotypes from primarily U.S. population groups)
Interpretation guidelines	SWGDAM Y-STR Interpretation Guidelines published in January 2009 (*revisions made in January 2014*)

The one commercial kit for X-STR testing, Investigator Argus X-12 from Qiagen (Hilden, Germany), is not sold in the United States.

SWGDAM Y-STR Interpretation Guidelines

In January 2009 SWGDAM Y-STR Interpretation Guidelines were published in the FBI online journal *Forensic Science Communications* (SWGDAM 2009). The first four sections discuss evaluation of data, designation of alleles, interpretation of results, and conclusions and reporting — all of which are very similar to autosomal STR interpretation guidelines. Section 5 briefly touches on statistical interpretation and addresses haplotype database searches, the counting method, use of a 95% confidence limit, and a recognition that Y-STR mixtures can be performed with probability of exclusion and likelihood ratios, that autosomal and Y-STR haplotype frequencies can be combined, and that population substructure exists for Y-STR haplotypes but is small for most populations.

A consolidated U.S. Y-STR population database (U.S. Y-STR, 2014) is also endorsed. A revision and update to these guidelines was made in 2014 with further information on many of these topics, especially population substructure issues (SWGDAM 2014).

SWGDAM Mitochondrial DNA Interpretation Guidelines

Over the past two decades, the U.S. mitochondrial DNA community has had several sets of guidelines to aid mtDNA interpretation (Wilson et al. 1993, SWGDAM 2003, SWGDAM 2013). The SWGDAM 2013 guidelines cover the following topics: (1) evaluation of controls, (2) sequence analysis and nomenclature, (3) sequence comparisons and reporting results, (4) weight of evidence, and (5) references and literature.

One of the major challenges with mtDNA interpretation is converting DNA sequence information uniformly into standard sequence shorthand for database storage and searching. Designating the same DNA sequence two different ways in two different laboratories could mean that a database search would not appropriately hit on what should be a matching sequence. The SWGDAM 2013 guidelines supply an accompanying examples document that reviews 20 difficult sequences to demonstrate how new nomenclature rules blend application of rule-based and phylogenetic approaches (SWGDAM 2013) These guidelines advocate for alignment-free nucleotide sequence string searches where possible as described previously (Röck et al. 2011). Also, the European DNA Profiling Group mtDNA Population Database (EMPOP) is recommended for population frequency searches (EMPOP 2014).

SWGDAM nomenclature rules are as follows (SWGDAM 2013):

Rule 1: maintain known patterns of polymorphisms — most violations to known positions of polymorphisms involve insertions and deletions

Rule 2: use nomenclature with the least number of differences unless it violates known patterns of polymorphisms

Rule 3a: homopolymeric C-stretches in hypervariable region I (HV1) should be interpreted with a 16189 C when the otherwise anchored T at position 16189 is not present

Rule 3b: homopolymeric C-stretches in HV2 should be interpreted with a 310 C when the otherwise anchored T at position 310 is not present

Rule 4: maintain the AC repeat motif in HV3 region from nucleotide positions 515 to 525

Rule 5: prefer substitutions to insertions/deletions (InDels)

Rule 6: prefer transitions to transversions unless this is in conflict with Rule 1

Rule 7: place InDels contiguously when possible

Rule 8: place InDels on the 3′-end of the light strand.

As with other forms of forensic evidence, mtDNA sequence comparisons can result in findings of exclusions, inconclusive, or cannot exclude (SWGDAM 2013). If samples differ at two or more nucleotide positions (excluding length heteroplasmy), they can be excluded as coming from the same source or maternal lineage (guideline 3.1.1). For further information on issues impacting mtDNA interpretation, such as heteroplasmy, mixtures, and nuclear pseudogenes, see Chapter 14 in *Advanced Topics in Forensic DNA Typing: Methodology* (Butler 2012).

GENERATING LINEAGE MARKER HAPLOTYPES

Y-STR or X-STR haplotypes are created with multiplex PCR amplification of Y-STR or X-STR loci using laboratory-developed assays or commercial kits. The process for interpretation of alleles versus artifacts such as stutter products is the same with Y-STRs and X-STRs as with the autosomal STR information discussed in Chapter 3. Generating mtDNA sequence information is very labor-intensive and challenging since hundreds of nucleotides need to be reviewed in both the forward and reverse directions with traditional Sanger sequencing methods (see Chapter 14 in Butler 2012).

Impact of Additional Information on Increasing Profile Rarity

The rarity of an autosomal DNA profile increases as additional information is included (see Table 10.10). This same principle is true with lineage markers. For mtDNA, specificity in identifying a particular mtDNA lineage improves with more data from sequence analysis of a single hypervariable region (HV1) (≈ 300 bases) to HV1 and HV2 (≈ 600 bases) to the full control region ($\approx 1,200$ bases) to the control region plus coding region single nucleotide polymorphisms ($\approx 1,300$ bases) to sequencing the whole mitochondrial DNA genome ($\approx 16,500$ bases). In the progression of mtDNA information just described, each set of sequence data encompasses the previous one.

With Y-STR loci, a set of nine minimal haplotype loci were originally chosen when Y-STR population databases began to be created in the late 1990s in Europe. These minimal haplotype loci are single-copy markers DYS19, DYS389I, DYS389II, DYS390, DYS391, DYS392, and DYS393 and the multi-copy marker DYS385 a/b, which typically generates two amplicons with a single primer set.

When SWGDAM selected U.S. core Y-STR loci in 2003, two new loci DYS438 and DYS439 were added to the nine European minimal haplotype loci. PowerPlex Y, the first commercial Y-STR kit from Promega Corporation, added DYS437 to the SWGDAM core set (Krenke et al. 2005). Yfiler from Applied Biosystems added five additional loci to the twelve used in PowerPlex Y: DYS448, DYS456, DYS458, DYS635, and Y-GATA-H4 (Mulero et al. 2006). PowerPlex Y23, which was released in 2012, encompasses the 17 Yfiler loci and adds 6 more: DYS481, DYS533, DYS549, DYS570, DYS576, and DYS643 (Thompson et al. 2013). The Yfiler Plus kit, which is scheduled for release in 2014, plans to add a few more markers, including some rapidly mutating Y-STR loci (see Figure 1.8).

Each of these Y-STR loci has different characteristics and variability. Table 15.2 ranks 23 Y-STRs according to their variability in the National Institute of Standards and Technology (NIST) 1,036 U.S. population data set (see D.N.A. Box 1.4). The degree of variability in this case is measured using probability of identity (see Chapter 10), which involves a pairwise comparison of data from each locus. Note that loci can exhibit different degrees of polymorphism depending on the population group. For example, DYS481 is the second best marker in terms of polymorphism in African American samples, but only the sixth best in Caucasians.

The increasing number of loci in commerical kits is driven by the desire to make Y-STR profiling more discriminatory since haplotypes do not benefit from the independent inheritance and product rule of autosomal markers. Table 15.3 illustrates the benefits of going from 12 to 17 to 23 Y-STRs in terms of an increased resolution of haplotypes.

In this NIST data set of 1,032 males, there were 70 sets of samples that contained two or more matching samples when examined with the 12 Y-STRs present in PowerPlex Y (Table 15.3). Increasing the number of loci to 17 with the Yfiler loci reduced the number of sample sets to 15 that could not be subdivided. Finally, when all 23 Y-STRs were applied to the data set, only three sets of sample pairs remained that could not be subdivided into individual sample haplotypes.

There are 1,026 23-locus Y-STR haplotypes occurring once in the NIST dataset and three separate unresolved pairs. By comparison, the 17 Yfiler loci produce 998 singletons, 12 pairs, 2 triplicates, and 1 quadruplicate. Thus, in the NIST dataset, PowerPlex Y23 has a discrimination capacity of 99.7% (1,029 types/1,032 samples) compared to 98.2% (1,013 types/1,032 samples) with Yfiler and 86.3% (891 types/1,032 samples) with the 12-locus PowerPlex Y (Butler et al. 2012).

Y-STR Locus Duplication or Deletion

Sections of the Y-chromosome can be deleted or duplicated in normal human males (Jobling & Tyler-Smith 2003). Y-STR assays are impacted when these duplications or deletions occur (D.N.A. Box 15.1). It is important to be aware that this variation does occur and could potentially impact interpretation of Y-STR data (Butler et al. 2005). Studies with father and son samples have shown that duplications, triplications, and deletions are inheritable traits as they are present in both the father and the son (Decker et al. 2008). Deletions in flanking regions of a Y-STR marker, such as DYS448, can

TABLE 15.2   Y-STR Locus Variability across 1032 Male Samples in the NIST 1036 Data Set (see D.N.A. Box 1.4) using the Powerplex Y23 Kit

Y-STR Locus	Alleles Observed	P_I (total)	P_I (Cauc)	Rank	P_I (AfAm)	Rank	P_I (Hisp)	Rank	P_I (Asian)	Rank
DYS385 a/b	17 (69 types)	0.0700	0.1482	(1)	0.0608	(1)	0.0815	(1)	0.0549	(1)
DYS481	16	0.1670	0.2653	(6)	0.1401	(2)	0.2033	(4)	0.1765	(2)
DYS576	9	0.1922	0.2292	(2)	0.1917	(3)	0.2020	(3)	0.2392	(7)
DYS570	12	0.2161	0.2575	(4)	0.2085	(4)	0.2008	(2)	0.1895	(4)
DYS458	15	0.2166	0.2352	(3)	0.2410	(6)	0.2144	(5)	0.1825	(3)
DYS390	8	0.2242	0.2966	(7)	0.3233	(11)	0.3605	(16)	0.2480	(8)
DYS643	10	0.2373	0.3790	(12)	0.2130	(5)	0.3292	(13)	0.2639	(9)
DYS635	11	0.2421	0.3313	(9)	0.2778	(9)	0.2604	(6)	0.2769	(11)
DYS389II	12	0.2541	0.3157	(8)	0.2623	(7)	0.2711	(7)	0.2054	(5)
DYS448	16	0.2650	0.3904	(13)	0.2789	(10)	0.2982	(8)	0.2739	(10)
DYS438	7	0.2861	0.3942	(14)	0.4311	(18)	0.3046	(9)	0.4201	(16)
DYS19	10	0.2996	0.4860	(21)	0.2746	(8)	0.3308	(14)	0.2384	(6)
DYS549	7	0.3095	0.3656	(11)	0.3325	(12)	0.3354	(15)	0.3540	(14)
DYS456	8	0.3098	0.2629	(5)	0.3571	(14)	0.3072	(10)	0.4322	(20)
DYS439	11	0.3460	0.3627	(10)	0.3502	(13)	0.3124	(11)	0.4004	(15)
DYS533	7	0.3654	0.4119	(16)	0.3775	(15)	0.3857	(19)	0.4220	(18)
DYS392	11	0.3752	0.4024	(15)	0.5546	(21)	0.3170	(12)	0.3445	(13)
DYS437	8	0.3800	0.4289	(18)	0.4950	(20)	0.3778	(17)	0.6248	(21)
Y-GATA-H4	6	0.3957	0.4286	(17)	0.3842	(16)	0.3983	(20)	0.4203	(17)
DYS389I	8	0.4203	0.4546	(20)	0.4808	(19)	0.3805	(18)	0.3232	(12)
DYS391	7	0.4758	0.4430	(19)	0.5603	(22)	0.4411	(21)	0.6992	(22)
DYS393	6	0.5018	0.6020	(22)	0.4169	(17)	0.5582	(22)	0.4231	(19)

The six additional loci beyond those in Yfiler. Loci are ranked by the total probability of identity (P_I) values across the entire data set with the P_I rank for each population included next to the individual P_I value. There are 17 different alleles seen for DYS385 in 69 combinations of the "a" and "b" amplicons. Numbers highlighted in red include a deletion null allele (see D.N.A. Box 15.1). Adapted from Butler et al. (2012).

cause these PCR amplicons to shift into another STR detection region and potentially confuse interpretation (Budowle et al. 2008).

As discussed in Chapter 5, the deletion of the amelogenin Y region can impact interpretation of this sex-typing assay so that a male sample may only exhibit an amelogenin X allele. In this situation, the autosomal STR profile may be incorrectly classified as coming from a female individual. If such a sample is studied with Y-STR loci, it is possible that loci that are close to the amelogenin Y region, such as DYS458, can also be deleted (see Table 1.3). Thus, knowing the relative position of loci on

TABLE 15.3 Number of Unique and Shared Haplotypes Observed with Various Combinations of Y-STR Loci across 1032 Unrelated U.S. Population Samples

N = 1032 males	PowerPlex Y (12 loci)	Yfiler (17 loci)	PowerPlex Y23 (23 loci)
# haplotypes	891	1013	1029
discrimination capacity	0.863	0.982	0.997
# times haplotype observed			
1	821	998	1026
2	41	12	3
3	16	2	.
4	6	1	.
5	2	.	.
6	2	.	.
7	1	.	.
8	.	.	.
9	1	.	.
10	.	.	.
11	.	.	.
12	.	.	.
13	.	.	.
14	.	.	.
15	.	.	.
16	.	.	.
17	.	.	.
18	.	.	.
19	1	.	.

As expected, the discrimination capacity increases with additional Y-STR loci. With 23 Y-STRs, there were 1,029 haplotypes observed in 1,032 samples for a discrimination capacity of 99.7%. Of the 1,029 haplotypes, 1,026 were seen only once (i.e. singletons) and three different haplotypes were observed twice (i.e. three sets of duplicate haplotypes). Adapted from Butler et al. (2012).

the Y-chromosome can be helpful. Sometimes deletions from the Y-chromosome can be greater than one megabase in size (Takayama et al. 2009).

Allelic drop-out may occur at specific Y-STR loci due to molecular reasons, such as chromosomal rearrangements or deletions or primer binding site mutations, or stochastic effects caused by low amounts of DNA template or DNA degradation. Since there is only a single allele with single-copy Y-STR alleles, determining if an allele is missing from a profile due to low-level stochastic effects or deletion can sometimes be challenging (Andersen et al. 2013).

II. STATISTICAL INTERPRETATION

Mutation Rates

The mutation rates for most Y-STRs are in the same range as autosomal STRs, namely around one to four per thousand (0.1% to 0.4%) generational events (Table 15.4). Of the first 17 Y-STR loci in use, only DYS458 and DYS439 mutate faster than 0.5%. However, some of the more recently added loci such as DYS481 (0.955%), DYS570 (2.23%) and DYS576 (1.91%) exhibit a higher rate of mutation.

As with autosomal STRs, single-repeat changes are typically favored over multiple-repeat jumps. Whether the mutation is a repeat loss or a repeat gain depends on the size of the allele. Mutations occur not only with locus-specific, but also allele-specific, differences in mutation rate (Dupuy et al. 2004). Mutations typically only occur when 11 or more homogeneous repeats are immediately adjacent to one another (Kayser et al. 2000).

D.N.A. BOX 15.1

Y-STR DUPLICATION OR DELETION

Usually single-copy Y-chromosome short tandem repeat (Y-STR) loci produce a single amplicon in single-source samples. Thus, the observation of multiple peaks at such a locus could suggest to an analyst that a mixture of more than one male contributor is present in the tested sample. However, many regions of the Y-chromosome are duplicated or even triplicated in some individuals and this fact can thus complicate potential mixture interpretation. Some samples have been observed with multiple Y-STR locus duplication (see below). Duplicated loci typically possess alleles that differ by only a single repeat unit and possess similar peak heights (Butler et al. 2005). Studies with father-son sample pairs have demonstrated paternal inheritance of Y-STR locus duplication, triplication, and deletion (Decker et al. 2008).

Y-STR marker duplication likely arises due to a Y-chromosome region duplication followed by a single-step mutation in the Y-STR repeat region for either the original marker or the copy. If a large section of the Y-chromosome containing multiple Y-STR markers was duplicated, then it may be possible for these sets of Y-STR alleles to diverge through mutation over multiple generations. Early population data studies may have underestimated the frequency of these duplication or deletion events because laboratories suspected contamination (in the case of locus duplication) or allele drop-out due to stochastic effects (in the case of locus deletion).

It is important to remember that if an evidentiary sample contains a single-source sample that exhibits locus duplication, then the true perpetrator should also display this same duplication. Therefore, duplication events should not be cause for concern in forensic investigations when using Y-STR assays. Multiple duplications are possible in the same single-source sample and thus analysts should not draw premature conclusions regarding the number of contributors when more than one equal intensity allele is observed at a "single-copy" locus (Butler et al. 2005). True male–male mixtures commonly exhibit more than one locus-specific PCR product across multiple Y-STR loci that are not adjacent to one another on the Y-chromosome.

Sources: Butler, J.M., et al. (2005). Chromosomal duplications along the Y-chromosome and their potential impact on Y-STR interpretation. Journal of Forensic Sciences, 50, 853–859; Decker, A.E., et al. (2008) Analysis of mutations in father-son pairs with 17 Y-STR loci. Forensic Science International: Genetics, 2, e31–e35.

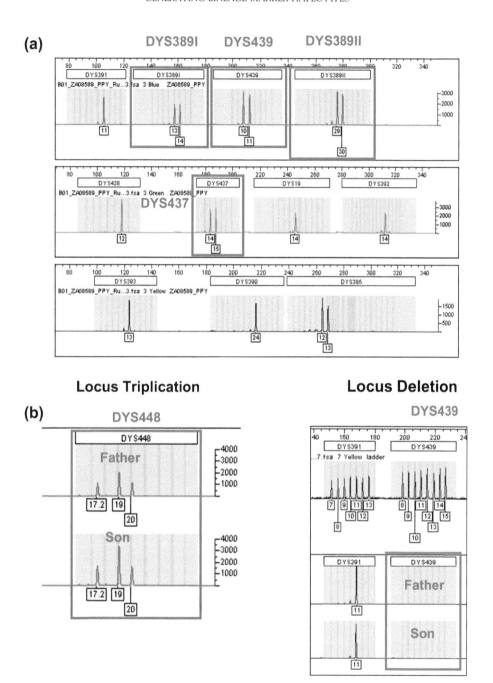

(a) Multiple Y-STR loci, which are closely spaced on the Y-chromosome, can be duplicated in a single-source male sample (Butler et al. 2005).
(b) Paternal inheritance demonstrated for a triplication at DYS448 and a deletion at DYS439 (Decker et al. 2008).

II. STATISTICAL INTERPRETATION

TABLE 15.4   Mutation Rates for Y-STR Markers

Y-STR locus	Mutations	Meioses	Mutation Rate
DYS19	36	15,539	0.232%
DYS389I	37	13,788	0.268%
DYS389II	52	13,759	0.378%
DYS390	31	15,061	0.206%
DYS391	38	14,935	0.254%
DYS392	6	14,867	0.040%
DYS393	15	13,713	0.109%
DYS385 a/b	59	25,620	0.230%
DYS438	3	10,122	0.030%
DYS439	54	10,096	0.535%
DYS437	12	10,101	0.119%
DYS448	11	6,678	0.165%
DYS456	28	6,678	0.419%
DYS458	45	6,677	0.674%
DYS635	28	7,525	0.372%
Y-GATA-H4	19	7,709	0.246%
DYS481	3	314	0.955%
DYS533	0	314	<0.318%
DYS549	1	314	0.318%
DYS570	7	314	2.23%
DYS576	6	314	1.91%
DYS643	1	314	0.318%
TOTAL	492	194,752	0.253%

Note that DYS570 and DYS576 are rapidly mutating Y-STRs with significantly higher mutation rates, which differ here slightly from the information in Table 15.5 (Ballantyne et al. 2012). Information collected from the Y-Chromosome Haplotype Database (see http://www.yhrd.org/Research/Loci).

Kayser and Sajantila (2001) discuss the implications of mutations for paternity testing and forensic analysis. They observed mutations at two Y-STRs within the same father—son pair, suggesting that differences at three or more Y-STRs are needed before an "exclusion" can be declared with paternity testing or kinship analysis, which is typically the same criteria used for paternity testing with autosomal loci. However, a more recent study found a single instance of three mutations out of 17 Y-STRs tested in a confirmed father—son pair (Goedbloed et al. 2009).

Rapidly Mutating Y-STR Loci

For some applications of Y-STR testing it is helpful to have haplotypes that remain consistent from generation to generation to enable paternal relatives to serve as reference samples. These applications include missing persons investigations and familial searching. However, it can be advantageous to resolve close paternal relatives in forensic cases to determine for example which brother left a crime stain.

A theoretical study noted that with analysis of 40 Y-STRs there was a 10% chance of finding a single mutation in two Y-STR haplotypes that were only a generation apart (e.g. father and son) if these markers all had an average mutation rate of about 0.28% (Gusmão et al. 2006). Manfred Kayser's group at Erasmus University in Rotterdam, Holland began a search to find Y-STRs with a higher mutation rate to improve the capability of separating close paternal relatives.

An analysis of 186 Y-STR markers in nearly 2,000 DNA-confirmed father–son pairs, which provided coverage of over 350,000 meiotic transfers, resulted in the discovery of a set of Y-STR loci that mutated more frequently than the others (Ballantyne et al. 2010). These loci were dubbed "rapidly mutating" or RM Y-STRs. Many of these RM Y-STRs are multi-copy loci, which can be challenging to interpret (Table 15.5). A follow-on study found that nearly 50% of fathers and sons and 60% of brothers could be distinguished with 13 RM Y-STRs, while among the same samples only 7.7% fathers and sons and 8% of brothers could be resolved with 17 Y-STRs in Yfiler (Ballantyne et al. 2012). Several of these RM Y-STRs have been included in the newer Y-STR kits PowerPlex Y23 and Yfiler Plus (Table 15.5).

POPULATION DATABASES FOR LINEAGE MARKERS

The forensic population databases contain collections of anonymous individuals and can be used to estimate the frequency of specified Y-STR (or mtDNA) haplotypes. Genetic genealogy databases, such as Ysearch, contain Y-STR haplotype information gathered by genetic genealogy companies with different sets of loci from males trying to make genealogical connections. Thus, the haplotypes in these genealogy databases are associated with specific individuals and family names.

Genetic genealogy databases are typically not used for Y-STR forensic haplotype frequency estimates, but could be helpful in trying to associate a family surname with a particular haplotype if this information was desired in an investigation. Ysearch.org, for example, contains Y-STR haplotypes on over 135,000 males. These genetic genealogy databases contain information from the minimal haplotype loci, a subset of the minimal haplotype loci, or additional Y-STRs, and therefore cannot always be searched across all loci of interest.

The discussion here will focus on the online haplotype reference databases for Y-STRs and mtDNA sequences used for forensic purposes.

YHRD

The largest and most widely used forensic and general population genetics Y-STR database, known as the Y-STR Haplotype Reference Database (YHRD), was created by Lutz Roewer and colleagues at Humbolt University in Berlin, Germany, and has been available on-line since 2000 (Roewer 2003, Willuweit & Roewer 2007). YHRD is Internet-accessible (YHRD 2014). As of March

TABLE 15.5   Information on Rapidly Mutating (RM) Single-Copy and Multi-Copy Y-STR Loci

#	RM Y-STR locus	Chromosome position (Mb)	STR repeat motif	Allele range	Mutation rate
	single-copy				
1	DYS449	8.28	$(TTCT)_nN_{50}(TTCT)_o$	24 to 37	1.22%
2	DYS518	17.32	$(AAAG)_3(GAAG)_1(AAAG)_n(GGAG)_1$ $(AAAG)_4N_6(AAAG)_o$	23 to 35	1.84%
3	DYS547	18.87	$(CCTT)_nT(CTTC)_oN_{56}(TTTC)_pN_{10}$ $(CCTT)_4(TCTC)_1(TTTC)_q$	36 to 48	2.36%
4	DYS570	6.86	$(TTTC)_n$	10 to 21	1.24%
5	DYS576	7.05	$(AAAG)_n$	13 to 23	1.43%
6	DYS612	15.75	$(CCT)_5(CTT)_1(TCT)_4(CCT)_1(TCT)_n$	14 to 31	1.45%
7	DYS626	24.41	$(GAAA)_nN_{24}(GAAA)_3N_6(GAAA)_5(AAA)_1$ $(GAAA)_o(GAAG)_1(GAAA)_3$	11 to 23	1.22%
8	DYS627	8.65	$(AGAG)_3(AAAG)_n$	10 to 24	1.20%
	multi-copy				
9	DYF387S1 a/b	28.0, 25.9	$(AAAG)_3(GTAG)_1(GAAG)_4N_{20}$ $(GAAG)_n(AAAG)_o$	28 to 38	1.59%
10	DYS399S1	25.1, 26.77, 27.2	$(GAAA)_3N_{7-8}(GAAA)_n$	10 to 23	7.73%
11	DYSF403S1 a	6.2, 9.65, 9.52	$(TTCT)_nN_o(TTCT)_p$	12 to 39	3.10%
12	DYSF403S1b	6.3	$(TTCT)_nN_2(TTCT)_o(TTCC)_p(TTCT)_q$	40 to 59	1.19%
13	DYF404S1	25.95, 28.0	$(TTTC)_n$	10 to 20	1.25%
14	DYS526 a	3.64	$(CCTT)_n$	10 to 17	1.25%
15	DYS526 b	3.64	$(CTTT)_o(CCTT)_pN_{113}(CCTT)_n$	29 to 42	1.25%

Loci in blue font are part of the Yfiler Plus kit and those in red are part of both Yfiler Plus and PowerPlex Y23 (see Figure 1.8). The variable portions of the STR repeat motif are shown in bold font with "n," "o," "p," and "q" repeats. Adapted from Ballantyne et al. (2012).

2014, YHRD contains results from more than 125,000 samples with minimal haplotype loci results representing 876 different groups of sample submissions from various populations and over 100 countries around the world. Searches on YHRD may be conducted by population group or geographic location.

US Y-STR

A U.S. population-specific Y-STR Database (US Y-STR) was launched in December 2007 to enable haplotype frequency estimates on five different U.S. groups using the 11 SWGDAM recommended loci (Fatolitis & Ballantyne 2008). The original version of US Y-STR contained 4,796 African American profiles, 820 Asian, 5,047 Caucasians, 2,260 Hispanics, and 983 Native Americans. In some cases,

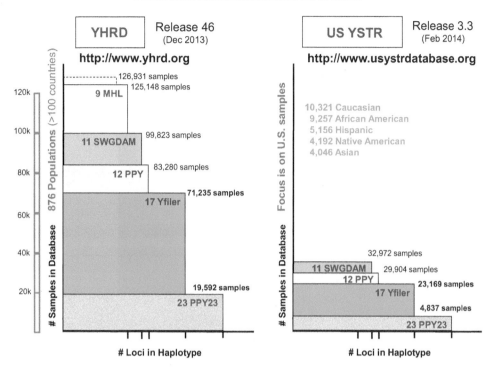

FIGURE 15.4 Comparison of YHRD and US Y-STR database relative sample sizes and data content as of March 2014.

further subdivision of these five primary groups can be examined if desired. An analysis of a version of the US Y-STR Database containing 7,812 samples with full 17-locus Yfiler results found that 93.7% were distinct and 92.9% of these haplotypes were population-specific (Ge et al. 2010).

As of March 2014, US Y-STR had expanded to 32,972 SWGDAM profiles of which 23,169 contained information at the 17-Yfiler loci. Where possible, US Y-STR has attempted to ensure that no duplicates are present through examining autosomal STR typing results on any samples possessing the same Y-STR profile. Having both autosomal and Y-STR data can be helpful in trying to sort out cases of common Y-STR haplotypes.

Figure 15.4 compares the relative sizes of YHRD and US Y-STR as of March 2014 along with the number of samples containing various sets of typed Y-STR loci. When performing a search it is important to keep in mind that the denominator will change based on the loci selected in the search (see D.N.A. Box 15.2).

EMPOP

The European DNA Profiling Group mitochondrial DNA population database is commonly referred to by its abbreviation of EMPOP and can be accessed online (EMPOP 2014). EMPOP applies phylogenetic analysis of the mtDNA data for quality control purposes (Brandstätter et al. 2004, Parson et al. 2004, Parson & Dür 2007). Over its first seven years of existence, EMPOP grew from 5,173 to 34,617 mtDNA haplotypes over 11 releases (Table 15.6).

D.N.A. BOX 15.2

A Y-STR PROFILE SEARCHED AGAINST SEVERAL HAPLOTYPE FREQUENCY DATABASES

The following profile was searched on 19 March 2014 against several Y-STR haplotype databases:

DYS19 (14), DYS389I (13), DYS398II (29), DYS390 (24), DYS391 (11), DYS392 (13), DYS393 (13), DYS385 a/b (11,15), DYS438 (12), DYS439 (13), DYS437 (15), DYS448 (19), DYS456 (17), DYS458 (18), DYS635 (23), GATA-H4 (12), DYS481 (25), DYS533 (12), DYS549 (11), DYS570 (17), DYS576 (15), and DYS643 (10).

The count and frequency of each of these searches is listed below:

The results shown here represent the counting method. Note that by adding loci the numerator goes down as the haplotype becomes more rare. Depending on the database and the type of haplotypes present (see Figure 15.4), the denominator can also become smaller as fewer profiles containing the requested information are being searched. As can be seen in the Yfiler column, there were no observations of the searched profile in the YHRD and Yfiler databases. The frequencies listed in this column are based on <1 observation in the size of the database.

Database	Minimal Haplotype (9 loci)	SWGDAM (11 loci)	PowerPlex Y (12 loci)	Yfiler (17 loci)	PowerPlex Y23 (23 loci)	3/N for Zero Observations
YHRD	634/125148 = 0.51%	69/99823 = 0.069%	52/83280 = 0.062%	0/71234 = <0.0014%	0/19592 = <0.0051%	3/71234 = 0.0042%
US Y-STR	275/32972 = 0.83%	42/32972 = 0.13%	24/29904 = 0.080%	2/23169 = 0.0086%	0/4837 = <0.021%	3/4837 = 0.062%
Yfiler database	64/11393 = 0.56%	4/11393 = 0.035%	4/11393 = 0.035%	0/11393 = <0.0088%	–	3/11393 = 0.026%

The final column illustrates an upper bound 95% confidence interval for the frequency estimate when no observations are observed, which can be approximated by 3/N, where N is the size of the database. The application of a 95% upper bound confidence interval on those results with

at least one observation is covered in D.N.A. Box 15.3.

Sources: http://www.yhrd.org; http://usystrdatabase.org/; http://www6.appliedbiosystems.com/yfilerdatabase/

The initial FBI mtDNA population database with 4,839 mtDNA haplotypes (Monson et al. 2002) was used for about a decade by many U.S. forensic laboratories. This database has now been superceded by EMPOP, although CODIS (Combined DNA Index System) software users have access to the SWGDAM Mitochondrial DNA Population Database that contains over 10,000 sequences created in collaboration with the Armed Forces DNA Identification Laboratory (AFDIL), EMPOP, and the FBI Laboratory (SWGDAM 2013). The 2013 SWGDAM mtDNA interpretation guidelines invite the use of EMPOP for mtDNA haplotype frequency assessments (SWGDAM 2013).

TABLE 15.6 European DNA Profiling Group Mitochondrial DNA Population Database Project (EMPOP) Growth over First 11 Releases

Release	Date	Number of mtDNA Sequences
1	16 October 2006	5,173
2	16 April 2010	10,970
3	27 December 2010	12,247
4	24 March 2011	12,785
5	5 July 2011	14,847
6	22 December 2011	16,121
7	25 April 2012	17,321
8	5 September 2012	26,073
9	17 January 2013	29,444
10	18 July 2013	33,195
11	16 October 2013	34,617

Release 8 added 8,945 mtDNA haplotypes from 26 U.S. states based on work performed by the Armed Forces DNA Identification Laboratory. For up-to-date information, see http://empop.org.

A group in Korea maintains the mtDNAmanager database (Lee et al. 2008) that is available online (mtDNAmanager 2014). As of March 2014, mtDNAmanager contained 9,294 mtDNA control region sequences grouped in the following five subsets: African (1496), West Eurasian (3673), East Asian (2326), Oceanian (114), and Admixed (1685).

Population Data

It is important to have the best-quality data present in population databases. Reliable estimates of haplotype frequency can be compromised with poor-quality data in a population database. While many concerns with mtDNA data quality were raised in the scientific literature in the early 2000s, use of stringent quality control measures including phylogenetic analysis have significantly improved mtDNA data quality (Parson & Dür 2007). Since it is easier to generate high-quality Y-STR data, especially with the availability of commercial kits, Y-STR population databases are larger (e.g. >125,000 profiles in YHRD) compared with mtDNA (e.g. ≈35,000 profiles in EMPOP).

An extensive reference list is provided at the end of this chapter to illustrate the range of population data collection studies that have been conducted on mtDNA, Y-STR, and X-STR genetic markers. Population data that are published on Y-STRs and mtDNA in the top forensic journals *Forensic Science International: Genetics* (Carracedo et al. 2010, 2013, 2014) and the *International Journal of Legal Medicine* (Parson & Roewer, 2010) require submission of the data to YHRD and EMPOP for quality control verification prior to article acceptance. The latest requirements from *Forensic Science International: Genetics* (Carracedo et al. 2014) request submissions of data sets from at least a minimum of 500 samples for X-STR data (with a minimum of 12 loci), 200 samples for Y-STRs (with a minimum of 17 loci), and 200 samples for mtDNA (with a minimum of the entire control region sequence, Carracedo et al. 2013).

GENETIC MODELS AND REPORTING

Since the Y-chromosome is passed down unchanged (except for mutations) from father to son and mtDNA is transmitted from a mother to her children, the observation of a match with these lineage markers does not carry the same power of discrimination and weight in court as an autosomal STR match would. The lack of recombination between lineage markers means that Y-STR or mtDNA results have to be combined into a haplotype for searching available databases as well as estimating the rarity of a particular haplotype.

Estimates for a random match with Y-STR haplotypes (and mtDNA sequence information) are done by the *counting method*, where the number of times the haplotype of interest is observed is divided by the total number of haplotypes in the database used. The size of the database used for the counting method makes a difference when trying to estimate the rarity of a Y-STR profile or an mtDNA sequence. The larger the number of unrelated individuals in the database (i.e. the denominator in the counting method calculation), the better the statistics will be for a random match frequency estimate.

D.N.A. Box 15.2 works through some example calculations with searches using 9, 11, 12, 17, and 23 Y-STR loci. This example explores the ability of different marker sets to resolve the Y-STR profile from unrelated lineages. When the full 17-locus profile was searched, it was not found in 71,234 17-locus haplotypes found in YHRD, but matched two haplotypes in 23,169 17-locus haplotypes located in US Y-STR.

David Balding in his 2005 *Weight-of-evidence for Forensic DNA Profiles* textbook emphasizes that a simple "pseudo-count" estimation method works fairly well to produce a useful and conservative estimate of lineage marker haplotype rarity (Balding 2005). Balding's pseudo-count equation is

$$\hat{p} = \frac{x + 2}{N + 2}$$

where $\hat{p}$ is determined by adding the two haplotype observations (i.e. the evidence and the suspect results) to the haplotype count (x) in the population database and to the population database itself to effectively increase its size (N) by the number of observations made for the haplotype outside of the previously observed information in the population database.

For the US Y-STR Yfiler search example in D.N.A. Box 15.2, Balding's pseudo-count method would provide a result of

$$\hat{p} = \frac{x + 2}{N + 2} = \frac{2 + 2}{23,169 + 2} = \frac{4}{23,171} = 0.0173 \, \%$$

which is more conservative than the 0.0086% provided by the straight counting method. As will be seen in the next two sections, other corrections for sampling and subpopulation structure have been advocated.

Sampling Correction with Confidence Intervals

Confidence intervals may be used to reflect the reliability of a statistical estimate and are based on observed data. Provided that the statistical model is correct, confidence intervals are intended to offer assurance that all data obtained with a procedure, or that might be obtained in the future, should include the true value of the data with a given level of confidence. A 95% confidence interval is most commonly calculated.

The upper bound 95% "normal" approximation confidence interval for a binomial distribution (see Chapter 9) has been widely used for many years for mtDNA (Holland & Parsons 1999, Tully et al. 2001). This approach was also endorsed by the 2009 SWGDAM Y-STR Interpretation Guidelines (SWGDAM 2009). However, normal confidence intervals are known to be problematic in situations with small sample sizes or very few observations (Buckleton et al. 2011), such as 2 out of 23,169 17-locus Y-STR haplotypes.

The Clopper–Pearson formula provides a more conservative value when very low counts are observed (D.N.A. Box 15.3). The Clopper-Pearson approach is now advocated in the 2013 SWGDAM mtDNA (SWGDAM 2013) and 2014 SWGDAM Y-STR guidelines (SWGDAM 2014).

Not everyone feels that confidence intervals are helpful. In a recent analysis of Y haplotype matching probability, Charles Brenner points out that forensic matching calculations should be based on a model and that any error in results comes from error in the model and its inability to approximate reality (Brenner 2014). Thus, he feels that trying to account for sampling variation with a confidence interval is not helpful.

Accounting for Potential Population Substructure

When a match is observed between an evidentiary sample profile and a reference sample profile, a haplotype frequency estimate for Y-STR or mtDNA lineage markers is commonly provided using the count of the observed haplotype in a population database such as YHRD or EMPOP. It has been noted that while this count is a factual statement it does not take into account any potential subpopulation effects that may be acting on the data (Cockerton et al. 2012).

For lineage markers, a match probability (p') that accounts for subpopulation effects can be calculated with:

$$p' = \theta + p(1 - \theta)$$

or with rearrangement

$$p' = p + \theta(1 - p)$$

where p is the true but unknown frequency of a particular haplotype in the population that is estimated using a count of the number of times the haplotype occurs in a population database such as YHRD or EMPOP and theta (θ) is a co-ancestry correction factor for subpopulation effects. This equation is derived from the initial Balding–Nichols DNA profile match probability theory (Balding & Nichols 1994).

The likelihood ratio for a simple Y-STR or mtDNA match would be the inverse of the equation listed above. Note that for $p < \theta$, θ bounds the equation. Thus, the practical impact of a subpopulation theta correction is different in lineage markers than when applied to autosomal loci such as described in Chapter 10 and Chapter 11.

D.N.A. BOX 15.3

95% UPPER BOUND CONFIDENCE INTERVALS USING NORMAL AND CLOPPER–PEARSON APPROACHES

When a Y-STR haplotype (or mtDNA sequence) has not been observed in a database of size N, the 95% confidence interval is $1 - (0.05)^{1/N}$. This value is very close to 3/N, which was used in the D.N.A. Box 15.2 example calculations. An upper bound 95% confidence interval can be placed on a profile's frequency using:

$$p + 1.96\sqrt{\frac{(p)(1-p)}{N}}$$

where the frequency (p) is determined from the number of observations (x) in a database containing N profiles. This "normal" approximation interval is the simplest formula to calculate and has been widely used (see Holland & Parsons, 1999; Tully et al. 2001), but is known to be problematic in situations with small sample sizes or very few observations.

The Clopper–Pearson formula, named after the authors of the paper describing it in 1934, provides a more conservative value for confidence intervals when very low counts are observed from a haplotype database. The formula for the upper 95% confidence limit using Clopper-Pearson is

$$\sum_{k=0}^{x}\binom{N}{k}p_0^k(1-p_0)^{N-k} = 0.05$$

where N = the database size, x = the number of observations of the haplotype in the database, k = 0, 1, 2, 3 … x observations, and p = the haplotype frequency at which x or fewer observations are expected to occur 5% of the time. This cumulative binomial distribution formula is solved for p through serial literations and therefore requires the use of a computer program. In the examples below, an Excel spreadsheet from Steven Myers (California Department of Justice) was utilized.

Count Values	Frequency	Normal	Clopper-Pearson
(see D.N.A. Box 15.2)	$p = x/N$	95% confidence interval	95% confidence interval
YHRD 9 loci: **634**/125148	0.507%	0.540%	0.541%
YHRD 12 loci: **52**/83280	0.0624%	0.0767%	0.0787%
US Y-STR 17 loci: **2**/23169	0.00863%	0.0187%	0.0272%

Note that with a large number of observations, such as 634 out of a database of 125,148, there is almost no difference between the normal and Clopper–Pearson approaches. However, the normal method is less conservative (i.e. provides a more rare frequency) when the haplotype frequency is low, such as 2 out of 23,169 (0.0187% vs 0.0272%). Although there are differences in these calculations, re-evaluation by the Clopper–Pearson method will not suddenly change a reported result by orders of magnitude or likely change the outcome of a report significantly.

In March 2010 the US Y-STR database changed its 95% confidence interval calculations to the Clopper–Pearson method. The YHRD also calculates confidence intervals using the Clopper-Pearson method. EMPOP uses the Wilson approach (Wilson 1927), which produces a result similar to the Clopper–Pearson method, to calculate its 95% confidence intervals.

Sources: Clopper, C.J., & Pearson, E.S. (1934). The use of confidence or fiducial limits illustrated in the case of the binomial. Biometrika, 26, 404–413; Holland, M.M., & Parsons, T.J. (1999). Mitochondrial DNA sequence analysis — validation and use for forensic casework. Forensic Science Review, 11, 21–50; Wilson, E.B. (1927). Probable inference, the law of succession, and statistical inference. Journal of the American Statistical Association, 22, 209–212; *HaploCALc_1.0 Excel spreadsheet kindly provided by Steven P. Myers, California Department of Justice; http://en.wikipedia.org/wiki/Binomial_proportion_confidence_interval and http://en.wikipedia.org/wiki/Confidence_interval.*

An examination of 56 previously published Y-STR population studies (typically with either 12 or 17 Y-STR haplotypes) derived θ values ranging from 0.0000 to 0.0731 (Cockerton et al. 2012). Since there appears to be a real effect across populations as well as with different numbers of loci in the observed haplotype, the choice of an appropriate and relevant θ value may be challenging if subpopulation corrections are used in a laboratory's lineage marker match statistic.

Just as haplotype frequency is impacted by the number of loci included in the haplotype (see Table 15.3), calculated subpopulation effects vary on a sliding scale with the number of Y-STR markers. More markers lead to a lower θ value, fewer markers result in a higher θ value. In reporting this observation, researchers at the University of North Texas noted: "Partial profile evidence may require a correction for the effects of population substructure. As the number of Y-STR markers that comprise a haplotype decreased, the number of shared haplotypes within and between sample populations increased. Thus, the F_{ST} [i.e. θ] value was expected to increase for partial profiles from evidence samples. At some point, an F_{ST} correction will not be overwhelmed by the upper bound of the count proportion, and then a θ correction should be invoked in a statistical calculation" (Budowle et al. 2009).

From a practical point-of-view, partial Y-STR profiles typically exhibit an increase in counts in the population database such that $p > \theta$. Therefore, applying a θ correction with Y-STR haplotypes, while perhaps significant to some on a theoretical basis, may not be truly impactful on a practical basis.

In his 2013 International Society for Forensic Genetics (ISFG) meeting presentation, Bruce Weir echoed the need for a theta correction with Y-STR matching statistics (Weir 2013). It is important to keep in mind that since male and female migration patterns throughout history have differed, Y-STR and mtDNA subpopulation effects are not expected to be the same (Cockerton et al. 2012).

SWGDAM 2013 mtDNA interpretation guideline 4.3 states: "It is recognized that population substructure exists for mtDNA haplotypes. However, determination of an appropriate theta (θ) value is complicated by the variety of primer sets, covering different portions of HV1 and/or HV2, which may be applied to forensic casework. *SWGDAM has not yet reached consensus on the appropriate statistical approach to estimating θ for mtDNA comparisons*" (SWGDAM 2013, emphasis added).

Approaches to Handling Rare Haplotypes

In the D.N.A. Box 15.2 example, a YHRD search found no matches to the given 17-locus haplotype when compared against 71,234 samples. Likewise, no matches were observed with 19,592 23-locus haplotypes. With the capability to discriminate more effectively with larger numbers of Y-STR loci (see Table 15.3), the vast majority of searches can result in no matches.

Charles Brenner, a forensic mathematician, has proposed the use of a probability estimate rather than a frequency estimate to judge the evidentiary value of a rare haplotype (Brenner 2010, Brenner 2014). Under his "kappa model," the fraction of singletons, or once-observed haplotypes, in a dataset become important to predict the rarity of future haplotypes that might be observed.

In the 1,032 males examined with Table 15.3, there are 998 singleton 17-locus haplotypes. In other words, over 96% (998/1,032) of Yfiler haplotypes only occur once in this data set, which is close to the 95% singletons found in a world-wide survey of available literature data several years ago (Butler et al. 2007). Thus, if 95% of 17-locus Y-STR profiles have never been observed before in a data set, then a new 17-locus Y-STR profile being compared against this data set would likely not be observed 95% of the time.

The kappa model involves a likelihood ratio (LR) as follows:

$$LR = \frac{N}{1 - \kappa}$$

where N is the number of samples in the database and kappa (κ) is the fraction of the database that are singletons. Thus, if 95% of 17-locus haplotypes are singletons, then $\kappa = 0.95$.

$$LR = \frac{N}{1 - \kappa} = \frac{N}{1 - 0.95} = \frac{N}{0.05} = 20 \times N$$

In this case with a κ value of 0.95, the kappa model inflates the LR by 20 times the size of the database. In other words, the evidence is much stronger when a rare Y-STR haplotype that has never been seen in the database before matches between evidence and suspect.

While this kappa method is not yet widely used, it has potential to help provide greater strength to rare haplotypes that are not present in current databases, such as the example shown in D.N.A. Box 15.2 with 17-loci. Research studies from Denmark have confirmed that the kappa method is reasonably accurate (Andersen et al. 2013b).

Statistically Combining Lineage Markers with Autosomal Loci

Bruce Walsh and colleagues at the University of Arizona published an article in 2008 expressing support for combining autosomal STR and Y-STR data (Walsh et al. 2008). This article was followed by a reminder that the approach should not be used with relatives (Amorim 2008). More recently John Buckleton and colleagues can provided some further thoughts and guidance on combining autosomal and Y-chromosome match probabilities (Buckleton et al. 2011, Buckleton & Myers 2014).

SWGDAM, 2013 mtDNA interpretation guideline 4.4 discusses combining statistics for mtDNA and autosomal results: "The frequency estimates for autosomal and mtDNA typing results obtained for a given sample may be combined. There are examples of dependencies between autosomal and mtDNA profiles, the extent of which has been demonstrated to be small" (SWGDAM 2013).

In terms of combining mtDNA, Y-STR, and autosomal STR statistics, SWGDAM, 2013 mtDNA interpretation guideline 4.5 states: "The CODIS software generates a combined likelihood ratio for autosomal, mtDNA, and Y-STR results for missing person searches to rank potential candidates."

Two references to non-peer reviewed work are then listed that "provide evidence of statistical independence between mtDNA and Y-STR profiles in U.S. and Chilean populations." The guideline continues: "Prior to reporting combined statistics for mtDNA and Y-STR results, the laboratory issuing the report should determine that each population used demonstrates independence between the mtDNA and Y-STR results. *If independence cannot be determined between the mtDNA and Y-STR results for the referenced population(s), combining these systems is not recommended*" (SWGDAM 2013, emphasis added).

Analysis of Mixtures with Lineage Markers

The US Y-STR Database contains a page with mixture analysis tools (US Y-STR 2014). As of March 2014, spreadsheet programs had been developed by scientists from the California Department of Justice; Harris County Institute of Forensic Sciences, Denver; Connecticut Forensic Laboratory; and Massachusetts State Police. These programs can be downloaded and used free of charge. The YHRD also has a mixture tool (2014) that is based on a German publication (Wolf et al. 2005).

In regards to mtDNA and mixtures, mixture interpretation is not presently attempted in forensic laboratories performing routine casework.

X-STR Analysis

Inheritance patterns of the X-chromosome (ChrX) enable application of ChrX markers in specific human identity testing situations, including complex kinship cases involving at least one female. Over 40 X-STR markers have been characterized and a number of assays developed for their analysis. Dozens of population studies have been published describing X-STR allele frequencies from groups around the world. The Investigator Argus X-12 kit amplifies the sex-typing marker amelogenin along with 12 X-STR loci from four linkage groups: *Group 1* (DXS10148, DXS10135, DXS8378), *Group 2* (DXS7132, DXS10079, DX10074), *Group 3* (DXS10103, HPRTB, DXS10101), and *Group 4* (DXS10146, DXS10134, DXS7423). D.N.A. Box 15.3 in *Advanced Topics in Forensic DNA Typing: Methodology* (Butler 2012) discusses statistical equations involved in analysis of X-STR data.

SUMMARY THOUGHTS

Lineage markers have important roles in human identity testing, but are not as widely used on a routine basis as autosomal STR markers. Y-STR and mtDNA haplotype databases are growing in size, enabling greater statistical power with the counting method. Research efforts are underway to better model potential population substructure and to account for rare haplotypes.

Commercial kits are now available and beginning to be used in greater numbers to aid forensic cases. In addition to benefiting forensic casework, Y-chromosome testing has aided familial searching efforts in screening out adventitious matches due to autosomal allele sharing (see D.N.A. Box 14.9). Y-STR markers can be helpful in some cases with predicting biogeographical ancestry and even surnames when genetic genealogy information is used. The future may involve more interaction between the application of genetic genealogy and forensic science to help bring cases to closure without prior suspects.

Reading List and Internet Resources

General Information

Balding, D. J. (2005). *Weight-of-evidence for Forensic DNA Profiles*. Hoboken, New Jersey: John Wiley & Sons.

Buckleton, J., Triggs, C. M., & Walsh, S. J. (Eds.). (2005). *Forensic DNA Evidence Interpretation*. Boca Raton: CRC Press [Chapter 9, Nonautosomal forensic markers, pp. 299–340].

Buckleton, J., et al. (2007). Parentage analysis and other applications of human identity testing. In I. Freckelton, & H. Selby (Eds.), *Expert Evidence*. Thomson Lawbook Co.

Butler, J. M. (2012). *Advanced Topics in Forensic DNA Typing: Methodology*. San Diego: Elsevier Academic Press [see Chapter 13 on Y-chromosome DNA testing, Chapter 14 on mtDNA, and Chapter 15 on X-chromosome analysis].

Jobling, M., & Tyler-Smith, C. (2003). The human Y chromosome: an evolutionary marker comes of age. *Nature Reviews Genetics, 4*, 598–612.

Roewer, L. (2009). Y chromosome STR typing in crime casework. *Forensic Science, Medicine, and Pathology, 5*, 77–84.

Interpretation

Andersen, M. M., et al. (2013). Estimating Y-STR allelic drop-out rates and adjusting for interlocus balances. *Forensic Science International: Genetics, 7*, 327–336.

Brenner, C. H. (2014). Understanding Y haplotype matching probability. *Forensic Science International: Genetics, 8*, 233–243.

Buckleton, J. S., et al. (2011). The interpretation of lineage markers in forensic DNA testing. *Forensic Science International: Genetics, 5*, 78–83.

Butler, J. M., et al. (2008). Y-chromosome short tandem repeat (Y-STR) allele nomenclature. *Journal of Genetic Genealogy, 4*(2), 125–148.

Carracedo, A., et al. (2000). DNA Commission of the International Society for Forensic Genetics: guidelines for mitochondrial DNA typing. *Forensic Science International, 110*, 79–85.

Gill, P., et al. (2001). DNA Commission of the International Society of Forensic Genetics (ISFG): recommendations on forensic analysis using Y-chromosome STRs. *Forensic Science International, 124*, 5–10.

Gusmão, L., et al. (2006). DNA Commission of the International Society of Forensic Genetics (ISFG): an update of the recommendations on the use of Y-STRs in forensic analysis. *Forensic Science International, 157*, 187–197.

Gusmão, L., et al. (2012). Capillary electrophoresis of an X-chromosome STR decaplex for kinship deficiency cases. *Chapter 5 in DNA Electrophoresis Protocols for Forensic Genetics*. In A. Alonso (Ed.), *Methods in Molecular Biology, 830*; (pp. 57–71).

Holland, M. M., & Parsons, T. J. (1999). Mitochondrial DNA sequence analysis – validation and use for forensic casework. *Forensic Science Review, 11*, 21–50.

Krawczak, M. (2007). Kinship testing with X-chromosomal markers: mathematical and statistical issues. *Forensic Science International: Genetics, 1*, 111–114.

Marquez, M. C. (2012). Interpretation guidelines of mtDNA control region sequence electropherograms in forensic genetics. *Chapter 21 in DNA Electrophoresis Protocols for Forensic Genetics*. In A. Alonso (Ed.), *Methods in Molecular Biology, 830*; (pp. 301–319).

Parson, W., & Bandelt, H.-J. (2007). Extended guidelines for mtDNA typing of population data in forensic science. *Forensic Science International: Genetics, 1*, 13–19.

Roewer, L., & Geppert, M. (2012). Interpretation guidelines of a standard Y-chromosome STR 17-plex PCR-CE assay for crime casework. *Chapter 4 in DNA Electrophoresis Protocols for Forensic Genetics*. In A. Alonso (Ed.), *Methods in Molecular Biology, 830*; (pp. 43–56).

SWGDAM. (2003). Guidelines for mitochondrial DNA (mtDNA) nucleotide sequence interpretation. *Forensic Science Communications, 5*(2). Available at http://www.fbi.gov/about-us/lab/forensic-science-communications/fsc/april2003/index.htm/swgdammitodna.htm. Accessed April 4, 2014.

SWGDAM. (2009). Y-STR interpretation guidelines. *Forensic Science Communications, 11*(1). Available at http://www.fbi.gov/about-us/lab/forensic-science-communications/fsc/jan2009/index.htm/standards/2009_01_standards01.htm. Accessed April 4, 2014.

SWGDAM. (2013). *Interpretation guidelines for mitochondrial DNA analysis by forensic DNA testing laboratories*. Available at http://swgdam.org/SWGDAM%20mtDNA_Interpretation_Guidelines_APPROVED_073013.pdf. Accessed April 4, 2014.

SWGDAM. (2014). *Interpretation guidelines for Y-chromosome STR typing by forensic DNA testing laboratories*. Available at http://swgdam.org. Accessed April 4, 2014.

Trindade-Filho, A., et al. (2013). Impact of a chromosome X STR decaplex in deficiency paternity cases. *Genetics and Molecular Biology, 36*, 507–510.

Tully, G., et al. (2001). Considerations by the European DNA profiling (EDNAP) group on the working practices, nomenclature and interpretation of mitochondrial DNA profiles. *Forensic Science International, 124*, 83–91.

Wilson, I. J., et al. (2003). Inferences from DNA data: population histories, evolutionary processes, and forensic match probabilities. *Journal of Royal Statistical Society A, 166*(2), 155–187.

Wilson, M. R., et al. (1993). Guidelines for the use of mitochondrial DNA sequencing in forensic science. *Crime Laboratory Digest, 20*, 68–77.

Wilson, M. R., et al. (2002a). Recommendations for consistent treatment of length variants in the human mitochondrial DNA control region. *Forensic Science International, 129*, 35–42.

Wilson, M. R., et al. (2002b). Further discussion of the consistent treatment of length variants in the human mitochondrial DNA control region. *Forensic Science Communications, 4*(4). Available at http://www.fbi.gov/about-us/lab/forensic-science-communications/fsc/oct2002/index.htm/wilson.htm. Accessed April 4, 2014.

Y-STR Kit Validation

Davis, C., et al. (2013). Prototype PowerPlex® Y23 System: a concordance study. *Forensic Science International: Genetics, 7*, 204–208.

Gross, A. M., et al. (2008). Internal validation of the AmpFlSTR Yfiler amplification kit for use in forensic casework. *Journal of Forensic Sciences, 53*, 125–134.

Krenke, B. E., et al. (2005). Validation of male-specific, 12-locus fluorescent short tandem repeat (STR) multiplex. *Forensic Science International, 151*, 111–124.

Mayntz-Press, K. A., & Ballantyne, J. (2007). Performance characteristics of commercial Y-STR multiplex systems. *Journal of Forensic Sciences, 52*, 1025–1034.

Mulero, J. J., et al. (2006). Development and validation of the AmpFlSTR Yfiler PCR amplification kit: a male specific, single amplification 17 Y-STR multiplex system. *Journal of Forensic Sciences, 51*, 64–75.

Shewale, J. G., et al. (2004). Y-chromosome STR system, Y-PLEX 12, for forensic casework: development and validation. *Journal of Forensic Sciences, 49*, 1278–1290.

Thompson, J. M., et al. (2013). Developmental validation of the PowerPlex Y23 System: a single multiplex Y-STR analysis system for casework and database samples. *Forensic Science International: Genetics, 7*, 240–250.

Impact of Additional Y-STR Loci

Alves, C., et al. (2003). Evaluating the informative power of Y-STRs: a comparative study using European and new African haplotype data. *Forensic Science International, 134*, 126–133.

Beleza, S., et al. (2003). Extending STR markers in Y chromosome haplotypes. *International Journal of Legal Medicine, 117*, 27–33.

Butler, J. M., et al. (2007). New autosomal and Y-chromosome STR loci: characterization and potential uses. *Proceedings of the Eighteenth International Symposium on Human Identification*. Available at http://www.promega.com/geneticidproc/. Accessed April 4, 2014.

Butler, J. M., et al. (2012). Variability of new STR loci and kits in U.S. population groups. *Profiles in DNA*. Available at http://www.promega.com/resources/articles/profiles-in-dna/2012/variability-of-new-str-loci-and-kits-in-us-population-groups/. Accessed April 4, 2014.

D'Amato, M. E., et al. (2010). Characterization of highly discriminatory loci DYS449, DS481, DYS518, DYS612, DYS626, DYS644, and DYS710. *Forensic Science International: Genetics, 4*, 104–110.

Decker, A. E., et al. (2007). The impact of additional Y-STR loci on resolving common haplotypes and closely related individuals. *Forensic Science International: Genetics, 1*, 215–217.

Hanson, E. K., & Ballantyne, J. (2007). An ultra-high discrimination Y chromosome short tandem repeat multiplex DNA typing system. *PLoS ONE, 2*, e688.

Leat, N., et al. (2007). Properties of novel and widely studies Y-STR loci in three South African populations. *Forensic Science International, 168*, 154–161.

Maybruck, J. L., et al. (2009). A comparative analysis of two different sets of Y-chromosome short tandem repeats (Y-STRs) on a common population panel. *Forensic Science International: Genetics, 4*, 11–20.

II. STATISTICAL INTERPRETATION

Redd, A. J., et al. (2002). Forensic value of 14 novel STRs on the human Y chromosome. *Forensic Science International, 130,* 97–111.

Rodig, H., et al. (2007). Population study and evaluation of 20 Y-chromosome STR loci in Germans. *International Journal of Legal Medicine, 121,* 24–27.

Rodig, H., et al. (2008). Evaluation of haplotype discrimination capacity of 35 Y-chromosomal short tandem repeat loci. *Forensic Science International, 174,* 182–188.

Vermeulen, M., et al. (2009). Improving global and regional resolution of male lineage differentiation by simple single-copy Y-chromosomal short tandem repeat polymorphisms. *Forensic Science International: Genetics, 3,* 205–213.

Insertions/Deletions/Null Alleles

Balaresque, P., et al. (2008). Dynamic nature of the proximal AZFc region of the human Y chromosome: multiple independent deletion and duplication events revealed by microsatellite analysis. *Human Mutation, 29,* 1171–1180.

Balaresque, P., et al. (2009). Genomic complexity of the Y-STR DYS19: inversions, deletions and founder lineages carrying duplications. *International Journal of Legal Medicine, 123,* 15–23.

Budowle, B., et al. (2008). Null allele sequence structure at the DYS448 locus and implications for profile interpretation. *International Journal of Legal Medicine, 122,* 421–427.

Butler, J. M., & Schoske, R. (2004). Duplication of DYS19 flanking regions in other parts of the Y chromosome. *International Journal of Legal Medicine, 118,* 178–183.

Butler, J. M., et al. (2005). Chromosomal duplications along the Y-chromosome and their potential impact on Y-STR interpretation. *Journal of Forensic Sciences, 50,* 853–859.

Carboni, I., & Ricci, U. (2009). Unexpected patterns in Y-STR analyses and implications for profile identification. *Forensic Science International: Genetics Supplement Series, 2,* 55–56.

Chang, Y. M., et al. (2007). A distinct Y-STR haplotype for Amelogenin negative males characterized by a large Yp11.2 (DYS458-MSY1-AMEL-Y) deletion. *Forensic Science International, 166,* 115–120.

Diederiche, M., et al. (2005). A case of double alleles at three Y-STR loci: forensic implications. *International Journal of Legal Medicine, 119,* 223–225.

Glock, B., et al. (2008). A DYS438 null allele observed in two generations of a large family. *Forensic Science International: Genetics Supplement Series, 1,* 206–207.

Takayama, T., et al. (2009). Determination of deletion regions from Yp11.2 of an amelogenin negative male. *Legal Medicine, 11,* S578–S580.

Turrina, S., et al. (2011). Two additional reports of deletion on the short arm of the Y chromosome. *Forensic Science International: Genetics, 5,* 242–246.

Rapidly Mutating Y-STR Loci

Ballantyne, K. N., et al. (2010). Mutability of Y-chromosomal microsatellites: rates, characteristics, molecular bases, and forensic implications. *American Journal of Human Genetics, 87,* 341–353.

Ballantyne, K. N., et al. (2012). A new future of forensic Y-chromosome analysis: rapidly mutating Y-STRs for differentiating male relatives and paternal lineages. *Forensic Science International: Genetics, 6,* 208–218.

Y-STR Mutations

Ballard, D. J., et al. (2005). A study of mutation rates and the characterisation of intermediate, null and duplicated alleles for 13 Y chromosome STRs. *Forensic Science International, 155,* 65–70.

Bonne-Tamir, B., et al. (2003). Maternal and paternal lineages of the Samaritan isolate: mutation rates and time to most recent common male ancestor. *Annals of Human Genetics, 67,* 153–164.

Burgarella, C., & Navascués, M. (2011). Mutation rate estimates for 110 Y-chromosome STRs combining population and father–son pair data. *European Journal of Human Genetics, 19,* 70–75.

Decker, A. E., et al. (2008). Analysis of mutations in father–son pairs with 17 Y-STR loci. *Forensic Science International: Genetics, 2,* e31–e35.

Donbak, L., et al. (2006). Y-STR haplotypes in populations from the Eastern Mediterranean region of Turkey. *International Journal of Legal Medicine, 120,* 395–396.

Dupuy, B. M., et al. (2004). Y-chromosomal microsatellite mutation rates: differences in mutation rate between and within loci. *Human Mutation, 23,* 117–124.

Farfan, M. J., & Prieto, V. (2009). Mutations at 17 Y-STR loci in father–son pairs from Southern Spain. *Forensic Science International: Genetics Supplement Series, 2,* 425–426.

Ge, J., et al. (2009). Mutation rates at Y chromosome short tandem repeats in Texas populations. *Forensic Science International: Genetics, 3,* 179–184.

Goedbloed, M., et al. (2009). Comprehensive mutation analysis of 17 Y-chromosomal short tandem repeat polymorphisms included in the AmpFlSTR Yfiler PCR amplification kit. *International Journal of Legal Medicine, 123,* 471–482.

Gusmão, L., et al. (2005). Mutation rates at Y chromosome specific microsatellites. *Human Mutation, 26,* 520–528.

Heyer, E., et al. (1997). Estimating Y chromosome specific microsatellite mutation frequencies using deep rooting pedigrees. *Human Molecular Genetics, 6,* 799–803.

Hohoff, C., et al. (2007). Y-chromosomal microsatellite mutation rates in a population sample from northwestern Germany. *International Journal of Legal Medicine, 121,* 359–363.

Kayser, M., et al. (2000). Characteristics and frequency of germline mutations at microsatellite loci from the human Y chromosome, as revealed by direct observation in father/son pairs. *American Journal of Human Genetics, 66,* 1580–1588.

Kayser, M., & Sajantila, A. (2001). Mutations at Y-STR loci: implications for paternity testing and forensic analysis. *Forensic Science International, 118,* 116–121.

Laouina, A., et al. (2013). Mutation rate at 17 Y-STR loci in "father/son" pairs from Moroccan population. *Legal Medicine, 15,* 269–271.

Lee, H. Y., et al. (2007). Haplotypes and mutation analysis of 22 Y-chromosomal STRs in Korean father–son pairs. *International Journal of Legal Medicine, 121,* 128–135.

Marino, M., & Furfuro, S. (2011). Haplotype frequencies and mutation rates for 17 Y-STRs in a sample from Mendoza province (Argentina). *Forensic Science International: Genetics Supplement Series, 3,* e65–e66.

Onofri, V., et al. (2009). Evaluating Y-chromosome STRs mutation rates: a collaborative study of the Ge.F.I.-ISFG Italian Group. *Forensic Science International: Genetics Supplement Series, 2,* 419–420.

Pinto, N., et al. (2014). Mutation and mutation rates at Y chromosome specific short tandem repeat polymorphisms (STRs): a reappraisal. *Forensic Science International: Genetics, 9,* 20–24.

Pollin, T. I., et al. (2008). Investigations of the Y chromosome male founder structure and YSTR mutation rates in the Old Order Amish. *Human Heredity, 65,* 91–104.

Sánchez-Diz, P., et al. (2008). Population and segregation data on 17 Y-STRs: results of a GEP-ISFG collaborative study. *International Journal of Legal Medicine, 122,* 529–533.

Soares, P. A., et al. (2006). Relative Y-STR mutation rates estimated from variance inside SNP defined lineages. *International Congress Series (Progress in Forensic Genetics 11), 1288,* 82–84.

Tamura, A., et al. (2008). Sequence analysis of two de novo mutation alleles at the Y-STR locus. *Forensic Science International: Genetics Supplement Series, 1,* 250–251.

Toscanini, U., et al. (2008). Y chromosome microsatellite genetic variation in two Native American populations from Argentina: Population stratification and mutation data. *Forensic Science International: Genetics, 2,* 274–280.

Turrina, S., et al. (2006). Y-chromosomal STR haplotypes in a Northeast Italian population sample using 17plex loci PCR assay. *International Journal of Legal Medicine, 120,* 56–59.

Vieira-Silva, C., et al. (2009). Y-STR mutational rates determination in South Portugal Caucasian population. *Forensic Science International: Genetics Supplement Series, 2,* 60–61.

Weng, W., et al. (2013). Mutation rates at 16 Y-chromosome STRs in the South China Han population. *International Journal of Legal Medicine, 127,* 369–372.

Yoshida, Y., et al. (2005). Population study of Y-chromosome STR haplotypes in Japanese from the Tokushima. *International Journal of Legal Medicine, 119,* 172–176.

Zhivotovsky, L. A., et al. (2004). The effective mutation rate at Y chromosome short tandem repeats, with application to human population-divergence time. *American Journal of Human Genetics, 74,* 50–61.

mtDNA Mutations

Bandelt, H.-J., et al. (2006). Estimation of mutation rates and coalescence times: some caveats. In H.-J. Bandelt, V. Macaulay, & M. Richards (Eds.), *Mitochondrial DNA and the Evolution of Homo sapiens* (pp. 47–90). Berlin: Springer-Verlag.

Freitas, F., & Pereira, L. (2008). Heterogeneity in coding mtDNA mutation rates: implications in forensic genetics. *Forensic Science International: Genetics Supplement Series, 1,* 274–276.

Parsons, T. J., et al. (1997). A high observed substitution rate in the human mitochondrial DNA control region. *Nature Genetics, 15,* 363–368.

X-STR Mutations

Fracasso, T., et al. (2008). An X-STR meiosis study in Kurds and Germans: allele frequencies and mutation rates. *International Journal of Legal Medicine, 122,* 353–356.

Hering, S., et al. (2010). X chromosomal recombination — a family study analysing 39 STR markers in German three-generation pedigrees. *International Journal of Legal Medicine, 124,* 483–491.

Tamura, A., et al. (2003). Sequence analysis of two de novo mutation alleles at the DXS10011 locus. *Legal Medicine, 5,* 161–164.

Population Data and Databases for Lineage Markers
mtDNA Population Databases

Brandstätter, A., et al. (2004). Mitochondrial DNA control region sequences from Nairobi (Kenya): inferring phylogenetic parameters for the establishment of a forensic database. *International Journal of Legal Medicine, 118,* 294–306.

EMPOP Mitochondrial DNA Control Region Database. (2014). http://www.empop.org. Accessed April 4, 2014.

Lee, H. Y., et al. (2008). mtDNAmanager: a web-based tool for the management and quality analysis of mitochondrial DNA control-region sequences. *BMC Bioinformatics, 9,* 483. Available at http://www.biomedcentral.com. Accessed April 4, 2014.

Monson, K. L., et al. (2002). The mtDNA population database: an integrated software and database resource. *Forensic Science Communications, 4*(2). Available at http://www.fbi.gov/about-us/lab/forensic-science-communications/fsc/april2002/index.htm/miller1.htm. Accessed April 4, 2014.

mtDNAmanager. (2014). http://mtmanager.yonsei.ac.kr/. Accessed April 4, 2014.

Parson, W., et al. (2004). The EDNAP mitochondrial DNA population database (EMPOP) collaborative exercises: organization, results and perspectives. *Forensic Science International, 139,* 215–226.

Parson, W., & Dür, A. (2007). EMPOP — a forensic mtDNA database. *Forensic Science International: Genetics, 1*(2), 88–92.

Y-STR Haplotype Databases

Ballantyne, J., et al. (2006). Creating and managing effective Y-STR databases. *Profiles in DNA, 9*(2), 10–13.

Egeland, T., & Salas, A. (2008). Estimating haplotype frequency and coverage of databases. *PLoS ONE, 3*(12). e3988.

Fatolitis, L., & Ballantyne, J. (2008). The US Y-STR database. *Profiles in DNA, 11*(1), 13–14.

Ge, J., et al. (2010). US forensic Y-chromosome short tandem repeats database. *Legal Medicine, 12,* 289–295.

Kayser, M., et al. (2002). Online Y-chromosomal short tandem repeat haplotype reference database (YHRD) for U.S. populations. *Journal of Forensic Sciences, 47,* 513–519.

Lessig, R., et al. (2003). Asian online Y-STR haplotype reference database. *Legal Medicine, 5*(Suppl. 1), S160–S163.

Roewer, L., et al. (2001). Online reference database of European Y-chromosomal short tandem repeat (STR) haplotypes. *Forensic Science International, 118,* 106–113.

Roewer, L. (2003). The Y-short tandem repeat haplotype reference database (YHRD) and male population stratification in Europe — impact on forensic genetics. *Forensic Science Review, 15,* 163–170.

STRBase Listing of Y-STR Databases: http://www.cstl.nist.gov/strbase/y_strs.htm. Accessed April 4, 2014.

U.S. Y-STR Database: http://www.usystrdatabase.org/. Accessed April 4, 2014.

Willuweit, S., & Roewer, L. (2007). Y chromosome haplotype reference database (YHRD): Update. *Forensic Science International: Genetics, 1,* 83–87.

Y-Chromosome Haplotype Reference Database (YHRD, 2014): http://www.yhrd.org. Accessed April 4, 2014.

Yfiler Haplotype Database: http://www6.appliedbiosystems.com/yfilerdatabase/. Accessed April 4, 2014.

Ysearch (Genetic Genealogy): http://www.ysearch.org/. Accessed April 4, 2014.

X-STR Databases

ChrX-STR.org 2.0: http://xdb.qualitype.de/xdb/index.jsf. Accessed April 4, 2014.

Szibor, R., et al. (2006). A new web site compiling forensic chromosome X research is now online. *International Journal of Legal Medicine, 120,* 252–254.

Requirements for Publication of Lineage Marker Data

Carracedo, A., et al. (2010). Publication of population data for forensic purposes. *Forensic Science International: Genetics, 4,* 145–147.

Carracedo, A., et al. (2013). New guidelines for the publication of genetic population data. *Forensic Science International: Genetics, 7,* 217–220.

Carracedo, A., et al. (2014). Update of the guidelines for the publication of genetic population data. *Forensic Science International: Genetics. 10,* A1–A2.

Parson, W., & Roewer, L. (2010). Publication of population data of linearly inherited DNA markers in the International Journal of Legal Medicine. *International Journal of Legal Medicine, 124,* 505–509.

mtDNA Population Studies

Afonso, C., et al. (2008). mtDNA diversity in Sudan (East Africa). *Forensic Science International: Genetics Supplement Series, 1,* 257–258.

Afonso Costa, H., et al. (2008). Mitochondrial DNA sequence analysis of native Bolivians population. *Forensic Science International: Genetics Supplement Series, 1,* 259–261.

Alshamali, F., et al. (2008). Mitochondrial DNA control region variation in Dubai, United Arab Emirates. *Forensic Science International: Genetics, 2,* e9–10.

Alvarez-Iglesias, V., et al. (2007). Coding region mitochondrial DNA SNPs: targeting East Asian and Native American haplogroups. *Forensic Science International: Genetics, 1,* 44–55.

Ballantyne, K. N., et al. (2012). MtDNA SNP multiplexes for efficient inference of matrilineal genetic ancestry within Oceania. *Forensic Science International: Genetics, 6,* 425–436.

Bandelt, H. J., & Salas, A. (2012). Current next generation sequencing technology may not meet forensic standards. *Forensic Science International: Genetics, 6,* 143–145.

Bini, C., et al. (2008). Polymorphism of mitochondrial DNA D-loop in Rimini and Valmarecchia areas in the North of Italy. *Forensic Science International: Genetics Supplement Series, 1,* 262–263.

Bodner, M., et al. (2011). Inspecting close maternal relatedness: towards better mtDNA population samples in forensic databases. *Forensic Science International: Genetics, 5,* 138–141.

Brandstatter, A., et al. (2008). Mitochondrial DNA control region variation in Ashkenazi Jews from Hungary. *Forensic Science International: Genetics, 2,* e4–e6.

Brisighelli, F., et al. (2008). Exploring mitochondrial DNA variation in the Italian Peninsula. *Forensic Science International: Genetics Supplement Series, 1,* 264–265.

Budowle, B., et al. (1999). Mitochondrial DNA regions HVI and HVII population data. *Forensic Science International, 103,* 23–35.

Cardoso, S., et al. (2012). Mitochondrial DNA control region variation in an autochthonous Basque population sample from the Basque Country. *Forensic Science International: Genetics, 6,* e106–e108.

Castro de, G. D., et al. (2012). Sequence variation of mitochondrial DNA control region in North Central Venezuela. *Forensic Science International: Genetics, 6,* e131–e133.

Chen, F., et al. (2008). Analysis of mitochondrial DNA polymorphisms in Guangdong Han Chinese. *Forensic Science International: Genetics, 2,* 150–153.

Desmyter, S., & Hoste, B. (2007). Influence of the electrophoresis-resequencing method on the forensic mtDNA profiling quality. *Forensic Science International: Genetics, 1,* 199–200.

Diegoli, T. M., et al. (2009). Mitochondrial control region sequences from an African American population sample. *Forensic Science International: Genetics, 4,* e45–e52.

Egyed, B., et al. (2007). Mitochondrial control region sequence variations in the Hungarian population: analysis of population samples from Hungary and from Transylvania (Romania). *Forensic Science International: Genetics, 1,* 158–162.

Fendt, L., et al. (2012). Mitochondrial DNA control region data from indigenous Angolan Khoe-San lineages. *Forensic Science International: Genetics, 6,* 662–663.

Fendt, L., et al. (2012). MtDNA diversity of Ghana: a forensic and phylogeographic view. *Forensic Science International: Genetics, 6,* 244–249.

Fridman, C., et al. (2008). Mitochondrial HVI and HVII polymorphisms and heteroplasmies inheritance in Brazilian pairs of mother/child. *Forensic Science International: Genetics Supplement Series, 1,* 277–278.

Grignani, P., et al. (2009). Multiplex mtDNA coding region SNP assays for molecular dissection of haplogroups U/K and J/T. *Forensic Science International: Genetics, 4,* 21–25.

Grzybowski, T., et al. (2007). Complex interactions of the Eastern and Western Slavic populations with other European groups as revealed by mitochondrial DNA analysis. *Forensic Science International: Genetics, 1,* 141–147.

Irwin, J. A., et al. (2007). Development and expansion of high-quality control region databases to improve forensic mtDNA evidence interpretation. *Forensic Science International: Genetics, 1*, 154–157.

Irwin, J. A., et al. (2009). Mitochondrial DNA control region variation in a population sample from Hong Kong, China. *Forensic Science International: Genetics, 3*, e119–e125.

Irwin, J. A., et al. (2011). mtGenome reference population databases and the future of forensic mtDNA analysis. *Forensic Science International: Genetics, 5*, 222–225.

Just, R. S., et al. (2008). Complete mitochondrial genome sequences for 265 African American and U.S. "Hispanic" individuals. *Forensic Science International: Genetics, 2*, e45–e48.

Just, R. S., et al. (2011). Titanic's unknown child: the critical role of the mitochondrial DNA coding region in a re-identification effort. *Forensic Science International: Genetics, 5*, 231–235.

Kohnemann, S., & Pfeiffer, H. (2011). Application of mtDNA SNP analysis in forensic casework. *Forensic Science International: Genetics, 5*, 216–221.

Lander, N., et al. (2008). Haplotype diversity in human mitochondrial DNA hypervariable regions I–III in the city of Caracas (Venezuela). *Forensic Science International: Genetics, 2*, e61–e64.

Lehocky, I., et al. (2008). A database of mitochondrial DNA hypervariable regions I and II sequences of individuals from Slovakia. *Forensic Science International: Genetics, 2*, e53–e59.

Liu, C., et al. (2011). Mitochondrial DNA polymorphisms in Gelao ethnic group residing in Southwest China. *Forensic Science International: Genetics, 5*, e4–e10.

Lopez-Parra, A. M., et al. (2011). Preliminary results of mitochondrial DNA sequence variation in Jujuy population (Argentina). *Forensic Science International: Genetics Supplement Series, 3*, e7–e8.

Mikkelsen, M., et al. (2010). Mitochondrial DNA HV1 and HV2 variation in Danes. *Forensic Science International: Genetics, 4*, e87–e88.

Mikkelsen, M., et al. (2011). Frequencies of 33 coding region mitochondrial SNPs in a Danish and a Turkish population. *Forensic Science International: Genetics, 5*, 559–560.

Mosquera-Miguel, A., et al. (2009). Testing the performance of mtSNP minisequencing in forensic samples. *Forensic Science International: Genetics, 3*, 261–264.

Nagai, A., & Bunai, Y. (2008). Analysis of mtDNA HVIII length heteroplasmy. *Forensic Science International: Genetics Supplement Series, 1*, 290–291.

Nakamura, S., et al. (2008). Analysis of mtDNA control region using mitoSEQr™ resequencing system and its forensic application. *Forensic Science International: Genetics Supplement Series, 1*, 292–294.

Nilsson, M., et al. (2008). Evaluation of mitochondrial DNA coding region assays for increased discrimination in forensic analysis. *Forensic Science International: Genetics, 2*, 1–8.

Parson, W., & Dür, A. (2007). EMPOP – a forensic mtDNA database. *Forensic Science International: Genetics, 1*, 88–92.

Parson, W., & Bandelt, H. J. (2007). Extended guidelines for mtDNA typing of population data in forensic science. *Forensic Science International: Genetics, 1*, 13–19.

Prieto, L., et al. (2008). 2006 GEP-ISFG collaborative exercise on mtDNA: reflections about interpretation, artefacts, and DNA mixtures. *Forensic Science International: Genetics, 2*, 126–133.

Prieto, L., et al. (2011). The GHEP-EMPOP collaboration on mtDNA population data – A new resource for forensic casework. *Forensic Science International: Genetics, 5*, 146–151.

Prieto, L., et al. (2013). GHEP-ISFG proficiency test 2011: Paper challenge on evaluation of mitochondrial DNA results. *Forensic Science International: Genetics, 7*, 10–15.

Röck, A., et al. (2011). SAM: String-based sequence search algorithm for mitochondrial DNA database queries. *Forensic Science International: Genetics, 5*, 126–132.

Salas, A., et al. (2012). A cautionary note on switching mitochondrial DNA reference sequences in forensic genetics. *Forensic Science International: Genetics, 6*, e182–e184.

Saunier, J. L., et al. (2008). Mitochondrial control region sequences from a U.S. "Hispanic" population sample. *Forensic Science International: Genetics, 2*, e19–e23.

Saunier, J. L., et al. (2009). Mitochondrial control region sequences from an Egyptian population sample. *Forensic Science International: Genetics, 3*, e97–103.

Scheible, M., et al. (2011). Mitochondrial DNA control region variation in a Kuwaiti population sample. *Forensic Science International: Genetics, 5*, e112–e113.

Tang, H., et al. (2008). Haplotypes of mtDNA control region in Yao ethnic from China. *Forensic Science International: Genetics Supplement Series, 1*, 298–300.

II. STATISTICAL INTERPRETATION

Turchi, C., et al. (2009). Polymorphisms of mtDNA control region in Tunisian and Moroccan populations: an enrichment of forensic mtDNA databases with Northern Africa data. *Forensic Science International: Genetics, 3*, 166–172.

Zimmermann, B., et al. (2007). Mitochondrial DNA control region population data from Macedonia. *Forensic Science International: Genetics, 1*, e4–e9.

Zimmermann, B., et al. (2011). Application of a west Eurasian-specific filter for quasi-median network analysis: sharpening the blade for mtDNA error detection. *Forensic Science International: Genetics, 5*, 133–137.

Y-STR Population Studies

Aboukhalid, R., et al. (2010). Haplotype frequencies for 17 Y-STR loci (AmpFlSTR Yfiler) in a Moroccan population sample. *Forensic Science International: Genetics, 4*, e73–e74.

Achakzai, N. M., et al. (2012). Y-chromosomal STR analysis in the Pashtun population of Southern Afghanistan. *Forensic Science International: Genetics, 6*, e103–e105.

Acosta, M. A., et al. (2009). The genetic male component of two South-Western Colombian populations. *Forensic Science International: Genetics, 3*, e59–e61.

Alakoc, Y. D., et al. (2010). Y-chromosome and autosomal STR diversity in four proximate settlements in Central Anatolia. *Forensic Science International: Genetics, 4*, e135–e137.

Alam, S., et al. (2010). Haplotype diversity of 17 Y-chromosomal STR loci in the Bangladeshi population. *Forensic Science International: Genetics, 4*, e59–e60.

Alvarez, M., et al. (2009). Y-chromosome haplotype database in Venezuelan central region and its comparison with other Venezuelan populations. *Forensic Science International: Genetics Supplement Series, 2*, 407–408.

Ambrosio, B., et al. (2012). Y-STR genetic diversity in autochthonous Andalusians from Huelva and Granada provinces (Spain). *Forensic Science International: Genetics, 6*, e66–e71.

Andreassen, R., et al. (2010). Icelandic population data for the STR loci in the AMPFlSTR SGM Plus system and the PowerPlex Y-system. *Forensic Science International: Genetics, 4*, e101–e103.

Bai, R., et al. (2008). Y-chromosomal STRs haplotypes in Chinese Manchu ethnic group. *Forensic Science International: Genetics, 3*, e13–e15.

Bai, R., et al. (2008). Y-chromosomal STRs haplotypes in Chinese Hui ethnic group samples. *Forensic Science International: Genetics, 3*, e17–e19.

Bai, R., et al. (2013). Haplotype diversity of 17 Y-STR loci in a Chinese Han population sample from Shanxi Province, Northern China. *Forensic Science International: Genetics, 7*, 214–216.

Bembea, M., et al. (2011). Y-chromosome STR haplotype diversity in three ethnically isolated population from North-Western Romania. *Forensic Science International: Genetics, 5*, e99–100.

Bento, A. M., et al. (2008). Population data for Y-chromosome haplotypes defined by 17 STRs (AmpFlSTR Yfiler) in Central Portugal. *Forensic Science International: Genetics Supplement Series, 1*, 179–180.

Bento, A. M., et al. (2009). Distribution of Y-chromosomal haplotypes in the Central Portuguese population using 17-STRs. *Forensic Science International: Genetics, 4*, e35–e36.

Blanco-Verea, A., et al. (2010). Y-chromosome lineages in native South American population. *Forensic Science International: Genetics, 4*, 187–193.

Brisighelli, F., et al. (2012). Patterns of Y-STR variation in Italy. *Forensic Science International: Genetics, 6*, 834–839.

Builes, J. J., et al. (2008). Analysis of 16 Y-chromosomal STRs in an African descent sample population of Chocó (Colombia). *Forensic Science International: Genetics Supplement Series, 1*, 184–186.

Builes, J. J., et al. (2008). Analysis of 17 Y-STRs in a sample of Colombian males. *Forensic Science International: Genetics Supplement Series, 1*, 187–189.

Capelli, C., et al. (2007). Phylogenetic evidence for multiple independent duplication events at the DYS19 locus. *Forensic Science International: Genetics, 1*, 287–290.

Carvalho, M., et al. (2011). Paternal and maternal lineages in Guinea-Bissau population. *Forensic Science International: Genetics, 5*, 114–116.

Catanesi, C. I., et al. (2009). Y-STR haplotype variation in a sample from Buenos Aires (Argentina). *Forensic Science International: Genetics Supplement Series, 2*, 437–438.

Chang, Y. F., et al. (2012). Genetic polymorphism of 17 STR loci in Chinese population from Hunan province in Central South China. *Forensic Science International: Genetics, 6*, e151–e153.

Chang, Y. M., et al. (2009). Haplotype diversity of 17 Y-chromosomal STRs in three native Sarawak populations (Iban, Bidayuh and Melanau) in East Malaysia. *Forensic Science International: Genetics, 3*, e77–e80.

D'Amato, M. E., et al. (2009). Evaluation of 21 Y-STRs for population and forensic studies. *Forensic Science International: Genetics Supplement Series, 2,* 446–447.

Diaz, V., & Carracedo, A. (2008). The distribution of Y-chromosome STRs in Dominican population. *Forensic Science International: Genetics Supplement Series, 1,* 195–197.

Diaz-Lacava, A., et al. (2011). Geostatistical inference of main Y-STR-haplotype groups in Europe. *Forensic Science International: Genetics, 5,* 91–94.

Djelloul, S., & Sarafian, V. (2008). Validation of a 17-locus Y-STR multiplex system. *Forensic Science International: Genetics Supplement Series, 1,* 198–199.

Elmrghni, S., et al. (2012). Population genetic data for 17 Y STR markers from Benghazi (East Libya). *Forensic Science International: Genetics, 6,* 224–227.

Fan, S. L., et al. (2012). Population genetics polymorphisms on 17 autosomal STRs from Chinese Bai ethnic minority group. *Forensic Science International: Genetics, 6,* e22–e23.

Fernandes, A. T., et al. (2008). Y-chromosome haplotype mismatch in different haplogroups: coincidence or evidence of SNP mutation? *Forensic Science International: Genetics Supplement Series, 1,* 200–202.

Fernandes, A. T., et al. (2011). Y-chromosomal STRs in two populations from Israel and the Palestinian Authority Area: Christian and Muslim Arabs. *Forensic Science International: Genetics, 5,* 561–562.

Ferri, G., et al. (2008). Molecular characterization and population genetics of the DYS458 .2 allelic variant. *Forensic Science International: Genetics Supplement Series, 1,* 203–205.

Ferri, G., et al. (2009). Slow and fast evolving markers typing in Modena males (North Italy). *Forensic Science International: Genetics, 3,* e31–e33.

Fujihara, J., et al. (2009). Allele frequencies and haplotypes for five Y-STRs (DYS441, DYS442, DYS443, DYS444, and DYS445) in Ovambo and Turks populations using multiplex PCR system. *Forensic Science International: Genetics, 3,* 268–269.

Gayden, T., et al. (2012). Y-chromosomal microsatellite diversity in three culturally defined regions of historical Tibet. *Forensic Science International: Genetics, 6,* 437–446.

Ghosh, T., et al. (2011). Genetic diversity of 17 Y-short tandem repeats in Indian population. *Forensic Science International: Genetics, 5,* 363–367.

Gomes, V., et al. (2008). Refining the analysis of Y-chromosomal diversity in Alentejo (Portugal). *Forensic Science International: Genetics Supplement Series, 1,* 208–209.

Gomes, V., et al. (2010). Nilotes from Karamoja, Uganda: haplotype data defined by 17 Y-chromosome STRs. *Forensic Science International: Genetics, 4,* e83–e86.

Gonzalez-Andrade, F., et al. (2009). Y-STR variation among ethnic groups from Ecuador: Mestizos, Kichwas, Afro-Ecuadorians and Waoranis. *Forensic Science International: Genetics, 3,* e83–e91.

Goundar, A. A., et al. (2009). Investigation of population structure in the Victorian Italian and Greek population using Y chromosome STR haplotype analysis. *Forensic Science International: Genetics Supplement Series, 2,* 423–434.

Gusmão, A., et al. (2008). Y-chromosomal STR haplotypes in a Gypsy population from Portugal. *Forensic Science International: Genetics Supplement Series, 1,* 212–213.

Haliti, N., et al. (2009). Evaluation of population variation at 17 autosomal STR and 16 Y-STR haplotype loci in Croatians. *Forensic Science International: Genetics, 3,* e137–e138.

Hallenberg, C., et al. (2009). Y-chromosome STR haplotypes in males from Greenland. *Forensic Science International: Genetics, 3,* e145–e146.

Hashiyada, M., et al. (2008). Population genetics of 17 Y-chromosomal STR loci in Japanese. *Forensic Science International: Genetics, 2,* e69–e70.

Hedman, M., et al. (2011). Dissecting the Finnish male uniformity: the value of additional Y-STR loci. *Forensic Science International: Genetics, 5,* 199–201.

Illeperuma, R. J., et al. (2010). Haplotype data for 12 Y-chromosome STR loci of Sri Lankans. *Forensic Science International: Genetics, 4,* e119–e120.

Immel, U. D., & Kleiber, M. (2009). Y-chromosomal STR haplotypes in an Arab population from Somalia. *Forensic Science International: Genetics Supplement Series, 2,* 409–410.

Jacewicz, R., et al. (2008). Applying the 16 Y-chromosome STRs in the population of central Poland. *Forensic Science International: Genetics Supplement Series, 1,* 214–216.

Jakovski, Z., et al. (2011). Genetic data for 17 Y-chromosomal STR loci in Macedonians in the Republic of Macedonia. *Forensic Science International: Genetics, 5,* e108–e111.

II. STATISTICAL INTERPRETATION

Jiménez, S., et al. (2008). Analysis of 8 Y-chromosome STR loci in population from Alicante (Spain). *Forensic Science International: Genetics Supplement Series, 1,* 217–218.

Kayser, M., et al. (2007). Relating two deep-rooted pedigrees from Central Germany by high-resolution Y-STR haplotyping. *Forensic Science International: Genetics, 1,* 125–128.

Kim, S. H., et al. (2008). Genetic polymorphisms of 16 Y chromosomal STR loci in Korean population. *Forensic Science International: Genetics, 2,* e9–e10.

Kim, S. H., et al. (2009). Population genetics and mutational events at 6 Y-STRs in Korean population. *Forensic Science International: Genetics, 3,* e53–e54.

Kim, S. H., et al. (2012). Forensic genetic data of 6 Y-STR loci: an expanded Korean population database. *Forensic Science International: Genetics, 6,* e35–e36.

Kovatsi, L., et al. (2009). Population genetics of Y-chromosome STRs in a population of Northern Greeks. *Forensic Science International: Genetics, 4,* e21–e22.

Laouina, A., et al. (2011). Allele frequencies and population data for 17 Y-STR loci (The AmpFlSTR® Yfiler) in Casablanca resident population. *Forensic Science International: Genetics, 5,* e1–e3.

Larmuseau, M. H., et al. (2011). Micro-geographic distribution of Y-chromosomal variation in the central-western European region Brabant. *Forensic Science International: Genetics, 5,* 95–99.

Lessig, R., et al. (2009). Haplotyping of Y-chromosomal short tandem repeats DYS481, DYS570, DYS576 and DYS643 in three Baltic populations. *Forensic Science International: Genetics Supplement Series, 2,* 429–430.

Li, C., et al. (2009). Genetic polymorphism of 17 STR loci for forensic use in Chinese population from Shanghai in East China. *Forensic Science International: Genetics, 3,* e117–e118.

Luna-Vazquez, A., et al. (2008). Haplotype frequencies of the PowerPlex Y system in a Mexican-Mestizo population sample from Mexico City. *Forensic Science International: Genetics, 2,* e11–e13.

Marino, M., et al. (2007). Genetic attributes of the YHRD minimal haplotype in 10 provinces of Argentina. *Forensic Science International: Genetics, 1,* 129–133.

Marino, M., & Furfuro, S. (2010). Genetic population data of 12 Y-chromosome STRs loci in Mendoza population (Argentina). *Forensic Science International: Genetics, 4,* e89–e93.

Martinez-Gonzalez, L. J., et al. (2012). Distribution of Y chromosomal STRs loci in Mayan and Mestizo populations from Guatemala. *Forensic Science International: Genetics, 6,* 136–142.

Martins, T., & Pinheiro, M. F. (2008). Y-miniSTR: new application for compromised samples (population data). *Forensic Science International: Genetics Supplement Series, 1,* 222–223.

Maybruck, J. L., et al. (2009). A comparative analysis of two different sets of Y-chromosome short tandem repeats (Y-STRs) on a common population panel. *Forensic Science International: Genetics, 4,* 11–20.

Melo, M. M., et al. (2011). Y-STR haplotypes in three ethnic linguistic groups of Angola population. *Forensic Science International: Genetics, 5,* e83–e88.

Mielnik-Sikorska, M., et al. (2013). Genetic data from Y chromosome STR and SNP loci in Ukrainian population. *Forensic Science International: Genetics, 7,* 200–203.

Nunez, C., et al. (2012). Y chromosome haplogroup diversity in a Mestizo population of Nicaragua. *Forensic Science International: Genetics, 6,* e192–e195.

Oliveira, A. M., et al. (2009). Analysis of Y chromosome lineages in a sample from Sub-Saharan Africa descendants in Rio de Janeiro. *Forensic Science International: Genetics Supplement Series, 2,* 442–443.

Omran, G. A., et al. (2008). Diversity of 17-locus Y-STR haplotypes in Upper (Southern) Egyptians. *Forensic Science International: Genetics Supplement Series, 1,* 230–232.

Onofri, V., et al. (2008). Y-chromosome markers distribution in Northern Africa: high-resolution SNP and STR analysis in Tunisia and Morocco populations. *Forensic Science International: Genetics Supplement Series, 1,* 235–236.

Palet, L., et al. (2010). Y-STR genetic diversity in Moroccans from the Figuig oasis. *Forensic Science International: Genetics, 4,* e139–e141.

Palha, T., et al. (2012). Fourteen short tandem repeat loci Y chromosome haplotypes: Genetic analysis in populations from northern Brazil. *Forensic Science International: Genetics, 6,* 413–418.

Palha, T. J., et al. (2010). Y-STR haplotypes of Native American populations from the Brazilian Amazon region. *Forensic Science International: Genetics, 4,* e121–e123.

Palo, J. U., et al. (2007). High degree of Y-chromosomal divergence within Finland – forensic aspects. *Forensic Science International: Genetics, 1,* 120–124.

II. STATISTICAL INTERPRETATION

Parson, W., et al. (2008). Y-STR analysis on DNA mixture samples — results of a collaborative project of the ENFSI DNA Working Group. *Forensic Science International: Genetics, 2*, 238—242.

Pelotti, S., et al. (2008). Microgeographic variation of Y-chromosome haplotypes in Italy. *Forensic Science International: Genetics Supplement Series, 1*, 239—241.

Pelotti, S., et al. (2008). Microgeographic genetic variation of Y chromosome in a population sample of Ravenna's area in the Emilia—Romagna region (North of Italy). *Forensic Science International: Genetics Supplement Series, 1*, 242—243.

Petrejcikova, E., et al. (2011). Allele frequencies and population data for 11 Y-chromosome STRs in samples from Eastern Slovakia. *Forensic Science International: Genetics, 5*, e53—e62.

Piatek, J., et al. (2012). Y-chromosomal haplotypes for the AmpFlSTR Yfiler PCR amplification kit in a population sample of Bedouins residing in the area of the Fourth Nile Cataract. *Forensic Science International: Genetics, 6*, e176—e177.

Piglionica, M., et al. (2013). Population data for 17 Y-chromosome STRs in a sample from Apulia (Southern Italy). *Forensic Science International: Genetics, 7*, e3—e4.

Pokupcic, K., et al. (2008). Y-STR genetic diversity of Croatian (Bayash) Roma. *Forensic Science International: Genetics, 2*, e11—e13.

Ramallo, V., et al. (2009). Comparison of Y-chromosome haplogroup frequencies in eight Provinces of Argentina. *Forensic Science International: Genetics Supplement Series, 2*, 431—432.

Ramos-Luis, E., et al. (2009). Phylogeography of French male lineages. *Forensic Science International: Genetics Supplement Series, 2*, 439—441.

Rangel-Villalobos, H., et al. (2009). South to North increasing gradient of paternal European ancestry throughout the Mexican territory: evidence of Y-linked short tandem repeats. *Forensic Science International: Genetics Supplement Series, 2*, 448—450.

Rebala, K., et al. (2011). Forensic analysis of polymorphism and regional stratification of Y-chromosomal microsatellites in Belarus. *Forensic Science International: Genetics, 5*, e17—e20.

Rodriguez, V., et al. (2008). Evaluation of 12 Y-chromosome STR loci in Western Mediterranean populations. *Forensic Science International: Genetics Supplement Series, 1*, 244—245.

Roewer, L., et al. (2009). A Y-STR database of Iranian and Azerbaijanian minority populations. *Forensic Science International: Genetics, 4*, e53—e55.

Romero, R. E., et al. (2008). A Colombian Caribbean population study of 16 Y-chromosome STR loci. *Forensic Science International: Genetics, 2*, e5—e8.

Roy, S., et al. (2012). Genetic analysis of 17 Y-chromosomal STRs haplotypes of three ethnic groups residing in West Bengal, India. *Forensic Science International: Genetics, 6*, e5—e7.

Schwengber, S. P., et al. (2009). Population data of 17 Y-STR loci from Rio Grande do Sul state (South Brazil). *Forensic Science International: Genetics, 4*, e31—e33.

Seong, K. M., et al. (2011). Population genetic polymorphisms of 17 Y-chromosomal STR loci in South Koreans. *Forensic Science International: Genetics, 5*, e122—e123.

Shi, M., et al. (2008). Population genetics for Y-chromosomal STRs haplotypes of Chinese Tujia ethnic group. *Forensic Science International: Genetics, 2*, e65—e68.

Shi, M., et al. (2009). Haplotype diversity of 22 Y-chromosomal STRs in a southeast China population sample (Chaoshan area). *Forensic Science International: Genetics, 3*, e45—e47.

Shi, M., et al. (2011). Population genetics for Y-chromosomal STRs haplotypes of Chinese Xibe ethnic group. *Forensic Science International: Genetics, 5*, e119—e121.

Simkova, H., et al. (2009). Allele frequency data for 17 short tandem repeats in a Czech population sample. *Forensic Science International: Genetics, 4*, e15—e17.

Siriboonpiputtana, T., et al. (2010). Y-chromosomal STR haplotypes in Central Thai population. *Forensic Science International: Genetics, 4*, e71—e72.

Soares-Vieira, J. A., et al. (2008). Y-chromosomal STR haplotypes in a sample from São Paulo (Brazil). *Forensic Science International: Genetics Supplement Series, 1*, 248—249.

Sotak, M., et al. (2011). Population database of 17 autosomal STR loci from the four predominant Eastern Slovakia regions. *Forensic Science International: Genetics, 5*, 262—263.

Taylor, D., et al. (2009). Knowing your DNA database: issues with determining ancestral Y haplotypes in a Y-Filer database. *Forensic Science International: Genetics Supplement Series, 2*, 411—412.

Taylor, D., et al. (2012). An investigation of admixture in an Australian Aboriginal Y-chromosome STR database. *Forensic Science International: Genetics, 6*, 532—538.

Taylor, D. A., & Henry, J. M. (2012). Haplotype data for 16 Y-chromosome STR loci in Aboriginal and Caucasian populations in South Australia. *Forensic Science International: Genetics, 6*, e187–e188.

Theves, C., et al. (2010). Population genetics of 17 Y-chromosomal STR loci in Yakutia. *Forensic Science International: Genetics, 4*, e129–e130.

Tillmar, A. O., et al. (2009). Population data of 12 Y-STR loci from a Somali population. *Forensic Science International: Genetics Supplement Series, 2*, 413–415.

Tillmar, A. O., et al. (2011). Y-STR diversity in the Swedish population and its implication on forensic casework. *Forensic Science International: Genetics Supplement Series, 3*, e405–e406.

Toscanini, U., et al. (2008). Y chromosome microsatellite genetic variation in two Native American populations from Argentina: population stratification and mutation data. *Forensic Science International: Genetics, 2*, 274–280.

Trynova, E. G., et al. (2011). Presentation of 17 Y-chromosomal STRs in the population of the Sverdlovsk region. *Forensic Science International: Genetics, 5*, e101–e104.

Valverde, L., et al. (2012). 17 Y-STR haplotype data for a population sample of residents in the Basque Country. *Forensic Science International: Genetics, 6*, e109–e111.

Vermeulen, M., et al. (2009). Improving global and regional resolution of male lineage differentiation by simple single-copy Y-chromosomal short tandem repeat polymorphisms. *Forensic Science International: Genetics, 3*, 205–213.

Villalta, M., et al. (2008). Haplotype data for 12 Y-chromosome STR loci from Costa Rica. *Forensic Science International: Genetics Supplement Series, 1*, 252–254.

Volgyi, A., et al. (2009). Hungarian population data for 11 Y-STR and 49 Y-SNP markers. *Forensic Science International: Genetics, 3*, e27–e28.

Wolanska-Nowak, P., et al. (2009). A population data for 17 Y-chromosome STR loci in South Poland population sample — some DYS458.2 variants uncovered and sequenced. *Forensic Science International: Genetics, 4*, e43–e44.

Wolfgramm, E. V., et al. (2011). Genetic analysis of 15 autosomal and 12 Y-STR loci in the Espirito Santo State population. Brazil. *Forensic Science International: Genetics, 5*, e41–e43.

Wozniak, M., et al. (2007). Continuity of Y chromosome haplotypes in the population of Southern Poland before and after the Second World War. *Forensic Science International: Genetics, 1*, 134–140.

Wu, W., et al. (2011). Population genetics of 17 Y-STR loci in a large Chinese Han population from Zhejiang Province, Eastern China. *Forensic Science International: Genetics, 5*, e11–e13.

Yadav, B., et al. (2011). Haplotype diversity of 17 Y-chromosomal STRs in Saraswat Brahmin Community of North India. *Forensic Science International: Genetics, 5*, e63–e70.

Yanmei, Y., et al. (2010). Genetic polymorphism of 11 Y-chromosomal STR loci in Yunnan Han Chinese. *Forensic Science International: Genetics, 4*, e67–e69.

Zahra, N., et al. (2008). The analysis of UAE populations using AmpFlSTR® Y Filer™: identification of novel and null alleles. *Forensic Science International: Genetics Supplement Series, 1*, 255–256.

Zalan, A., et al. (2011). Paternal genetic history of the Vlax Roma. *Forensic Science International: Genetics, 5*, 109–113.

Zastera, J., et al. (2010). Assembly of a large Y-STR haplotype database for the Czech population and investigation of its substructure. *Forensic Science International: Genetics, 4*, e75–e78.

Zhang, D., et al. (2009). Haplotypes of six miniY-STR loci in the Han population from Sichuan province and the Zhuang population in Guangxi Zhuang autonomous region. *Forensic Science International: Genetics, 3*, e49–e51.

Zhang, Y., et al. (2013). Allele frequencies of 12 Y-chromosomal STRs in Chinese Tuvans in the Altay region. *Forensic Science International: Genetics, 7*, e7–e8.

X-STR Population Studies

Aler, M., et al. (2007). Genetic data of 10 X-STRs in a Spanish population sample. *Forensic Science International, 173*, 193–196.

Asamura, H., et al. (2006). Japanese population data for eight X-STR loci using two new quadruplex systems. *International Journal of Legal Medicine, 120*, 303–309.

Asmundo, A., et al. (2006). Allele distribution of two X-chromosomal STR loci in a population from Sicily (Southern Italy). *Progress in Forensic Genetics 11, ICS, 1288*, 346–348.

Baeta, M., et al. (2013). Analysis of 10 X-STRs in three population groups from Ecuador. *Forensic Science International: Genetics, 7*, e19–e20.

Barbaro, A., et al. (2008). Population data of 8 X-STRs in South Italy (Calabria) using the Mentype® Argus X-8 PCR Amplification Kit (Biotype). *Forensic Science International: Genetics Supplement Series, 1*, 135–139.

Barbaro, A., et al. (2012). Distribution of 8 X-chromosomal STR loci in an Italian population sample (Calabria). *Forensic Science International: Genetics, 6*, e174–e175.

Becker, D., et al. (2008). Population genetic evaluation of eight X-chromosomal short tandem repeat loci using Mentype Argus X-8 PCR amplification kit. *Forensic Science International: Genetics, 2*, 69–74.

Bekada, A., et al. (2009). Analysis of 12 X-chromosomal STRs in an Algerian population sample. *Forensic Science International: Genetics Supplement Series, 2*, 400–401.

Bentayebi, K., et al. (2012). Genetic diversity of 12 X-chromosomal short tandem repeats in the Moroccan population. *Forensic Science International: Genetics, 6*, e48–e49.

Bobillo, C., et al. (2011). Genetic analysis of 10 X-STRs in Argentinian population. *Forensic Science International: Genetics, 5*, e14–e16.

Builes, J. J., et al. (2008). Allele distribution of three X-chromosome STR loci in an antioquian population sample. *Forensic Science International: Genetics Supplement Series, 1*, 140–141.

Cainé, L. M., et al. (2010). Genetic data of a Brazilian population sample (Santa Catarina) using an X-STR decaplex. *Journal of Forensic and Legal Medicine, 17*, 272–274.

Carvalho, R., et al. (2008). Study of 16 X-STRs in a prostate cancer population sample (preliminary results). *Forensic Science International: Genetics Supplement Series, 1*, 142–144.

Castaneda, M., et al. (2011). Study of two X-linked microsatellite blocks: allelic frequencies in mixed and isolated population groups. *Forensic Science International: Genetics Supplement Series, 3*, e248–e250.

Cerri, N., et al. (2006). Population data for four X-chromosomal STR loci in a population sample from Brescia (northern Italy). Progress in Forensic Genetics 11. *ICS, 1288*, 286–288.

Cerri, N., et al. (2008). Population data for 8 X-chromosome STR loci in a population sample from Northern Italy and from the Sardinia island. *Forensic Science International: Genetics Supplement Series, 1*, 173–175.

Chen, M. Y., et al. (2002). Population data on X chromosome short tandem repeat loci HPRTB and AR in Taiwan. *Forensic Science International, 126*, 171–172.

Chen, M. Y., & Pu, C. E. (2004). Population data on the X chromosome short tandem repeat loci DXS10011, DXS101, DXS6789, DXS7132, DXS8377, and DXS9895 in Taiwan. *Forensic Science International, 146*, 65–67.

Chen, M. Y., et al. (2014). Genetic polymorphisms of twelve X-chromosomal STR loci in Taiwanese individuals and likelihood ratio calculations applied to case studies of blood relationships. *Electrophoresis* (in press).

Cybulska, L., et al. (2008). Polymorphism of four X-chromosomal STR loci in Belarusians and Slovaks. *Forensic Science International: Genetics Supplement Series, 1*, 145–146.

Deng, J. Q., et al. (2003). Two X-chromosome STR loci DXS6804 and DXS9896 frequency data in Chinese population. *Journal of Forensic Sciences, 48*, 886–886.

Deng, J. Q., et al. (2004). Population data of two X-chromosome STR loci GATA186D06 and GATA198A10 in China. *Journal of Forensic Sciences, 49*, 173.

Diegoli, T. M., et al. (2011). Population study of fourteen X chromosomal short tandem repeat loci in a population from Bosnia and Herzegovina. *Forensic Science International: Genetics, 5*, 350–351.

Diegoli, T. M., & Coble, M. D. (2011). Development and characterization of two mini-X chromosomal short tandem repeat multiplexes. *Forensic Science International: Genetics, 5*, 415–421.

Diegoli, T. M., et al. (2011). Allele frequency distribution of twelve X-chromosomal short tandem repeat markers in four U.S. population groups. *Forensic Science International: Genetics Supplement Series, 3*, e481–e483.

Diegoli, T. M., et al. (2014). Population genetic data for 15 X chromosomal short tandem repeat markers in three U.S. populations. *Forensic Science International: Genetics, 8*, 64–67.

Edelmann, J., et al. (2001). 16 X-chromosome STR loci frequency data from a German population. *Forensic Science International, 124*, 215–218.

Edelmann, J., et al. (2004). Allele frequencies for X-chromosomal microsatellites in different populations. *Progress in Forensic Genetics 10, ICS, 1261*, 263–265.

Edelmann, J., et al. (2008). Characterisation of the STR markers DXS10146, DXS10134 and DXS10147 located within a 79.1 kb region at Xq28. *Forensic Science International: Genetics, 2*, 41–46.

Edelmann, J., et al. (2009). Chromosome X centromere region—haplotype frequencies for different populations. *Forensic Science International: Genetics Supplement Series, 2*, 398–399.

Edelmann, J., et al. (2011). Haplotype frequency data of the chromosome X centromere region. *Forensic Science International: Genetics Supplement Series, 3*, e170–e171.

Edelmann, J., et al. (2012). X-chromosomal haplotype frequencies of four linkage groups using the Investigator Argus X-12 Kit. *Forensic Science International: Genetics, 6,* e24—e34.

Edwards, A., et al. (1992). Genetic variation at five trimeric and tetrameric tandem repeat loci in four human population groups. *Genomics, 12,* 241—253.

Elakkary, S., et al. (2014). Genetic polymorphisms of twelve X-STRs of the Investigator Argus X-12 kit and additional six X-STR centromere region loci in an Egyptian population sample. *Forensic Science International.* Genetics, (in press).

Ferreira da Silva, I. H., et al. (2010). An X-chromosome pentaplex in two linkage groups: haplotype data in Alagoas and Rio de Janeiro populations from Brazil. *Forensic Science International: Genetics, 4,* e95—e100.

Gao, S., et al. (2007). Allele frequencies for 10 X-STR loci in Nu population of Yunnan, China. *Legal Medicine, 9,* 284—286.

Garcia, B., et al. (2012). Population data for 10 X-chromosome STRs from north-east of Spain. *Forensic Science International: Genetics, 6,* e13—e15.

Gelabert-Besada, M., et al. (2012). Genetic characterization of Western Iberia using Mentype(R) Argus X-8 kit. *Forensic Science International: Genetics, 6,* e39—e41.

Gomes, I., et al. (2007). Analysis of 10 X-STRs in three African populations. *Forensic Science International: Genetics, 1,* 208—211.

Gomes, I., et al. (2007). Genetic analysis of 3 US population groups using an X-chromosomal STR decaplex. *International Journal of Legal Medicine, 121,* 198—203.

Gomes, I., et al. (2008). Sequence variation at three X chromosomal short tandem repeats in Caucasian and African populations. *Forensic Science International: Genetics Supplement Series, 1,* 147—149.

Gomes, I., et al. (2009). The Karimojong from Uganda: genetic characterization using an X-STR decaplex system. *Forensic Science International: Genetics, 3,* e127—e128.

Gomes, I., et al. (2009). Genetic patterns of 10 X chromosome short tandem repeats in an Asian population from Macau. *Forensic Science International: Genetics Supplement Series, 2,* 402—404.

Gusmão, L., et al. (2009). A GEP-ISFG collaborative study on the optimization of an X-STR decaplex: data on 15 Iberian and Latin American populations. *International Journal of Legal Medicine, 123,* 227—234.

Gu, S., & Li, S. (2006). X-chromosome STRs analysis of Ewenke ethnic population. *Forensic Science International, 158,* 72—75.

Hashiyada, M., et al. (2008). Polymorphism of eight X-chromosomal STRs in a Japanese population. *Forensic Science International: Genetics Supplement Series, 1,* 150—152.

Hedman, M., et al. (2009). X-STR diversity patterns in the Finnish and the Somali population. *Forensic Science International: Genetics, 3,* 173—178.

Hering, S., et al. (2011). Chromosome X markers DXS6795, DXS9907 and GATA144D04: repeat structure and allele distribution in a German population. *Forensic Science International: Genetics Supplement Series, 3,* e321—e322.

Horvath, G., et al. (2012). A genetic study of 12 X-STR loci in the Hungarian population. *Forensic Science International: Genetics, 6,* e46—e47.

Hou, Q. F., et al. (2007). Genetic polymorphisms of nine X-STR loci in four population groups from Inner Mongolia, China. Genomics Proteomics. *Bioinformatics, 5,* 59—65.

Hwa, H. L., et al. (2009). Thirteen X-chromosomal short tandem repeat loci multiplex data from Taiwanese. *International Journal of Legal Medicine, 123,* 263—269.

Illescas, M. J., et al. (2011). Genetic diversity of 10 X-STR markers in a sample population from the region of Murcia in Spain. *Forensic Science International: Genetics Supplement Series, 3,* e437—e438.

Illescas, M. J., et al. (2011). X-STR admixture analysis of two populations of the Basque Diaspora in America. *Forensic Science International: Genetics Supplement Series, 3,* e441—e442.

Illescas, M. J., et al. (2012). Population genetic data for 10 X-STR loci in autochthonous Basques from Navarre (Spain). *Forensic Science International: Genetics, 6,* e146—e148.

Illescas, M. J., et al. (2012). Genetic characterization of ten X-STRs in a population from the Spanish Levant. *Forensic Science International: Genetics, 6,* e180—e181.

Inturri, S., et al. (2011). Linkage and linkage disequilibrium analysis of X-STRs in Italian families. *Forensic Science International: Genetics, 5,* 152—154.

Jedrzejczyk, M., et al. (2008). Polymorphism of X-chromosome STR loci: DXS8378, DXS7132, HPRTB, DXS7423 in a population of Central Poland. *Problems of Forensic Sciences, 73,* 65—69.

Jia, Y., et al. (2004). Two X-chromosome STR loci DXS6803 and XS6793 frequency data in Chinese population. *Journal of Forensic Sciences, 49,* 845—846.

Kang, L., & Li, S. (2006). X-chromosome STR polymorphism of Luoba Ethnic Group living in Tibet (SW China). *Forensic Science International, 156,* 88—90.

II. STATISTICAL INTERPRETATION

Koyama, H., et al. (2002). Y-STR haplotype data and allele frequency of the DXS10011 locus in a Japanese population sample. *Forensic Science International, 125,* 273–276.

Lee, H. Y., et al. (2004). Genetic characteristics and population study of 4 X-chromosomal STRs in Koreans: evidence for a null allele at DXS9898. *International Journal of Legal Medicine, 118,* 355–360.

Lee, S., et al. (2003). X-chromosome polymorphism in Koreans on DXS7132 and DXS6800. *Forensic Science International, 126,* 88–89.

Leite, F. P., et al. (2009). Linkage disequilibrium patterns and genetic structure of Amerindian and non-Amerindian Brazilian populations revealed by long-range X-STR markers. *American Journal of Physical Anthropology, 139,* 404–412.

Li, C., et al. (2011). Genetic analysis of the 11 X-STR loci in Uigur and Northern Han populations from China. *Forensic Science International: Genetics Supplement Series, 3,* e423–e424.

Li, C., et al. (2012). Genetic analysis of the 11 X-STR loci in Uigur population from China. *Forensic Science International: Genetics, 6,* e139–e140.

Li, H., et al. (2009). A multiplex PCR for 4 X chromosome STR markers and population data from Beijing Han ethnic group. *Legal Medicine, 11,* 248–250.

Lim, E. J., et al. (2009). Genetic polymorphism and haplotype analysis of 4 tightly linked X-STR duos in Koreans. *Croatian Medical Journal, 50,* 305–312.

Liu, Q., & Li, S. (2006). Patterns of genetic polymorphism at the 10 X-chromosome STR loci in Mongol population. *Forensic Science International, 158,* 76–79.

Luczak, S., et al. (2011). Diversity of 15 human X chromosome microsatellite loci in Polish population. *Forensic Science International: Genetics, 5,* e71–e77.

Luo, H. B., et al. (2011). Characteristics of eight X-STR loci for forensic purposes in the Chinese population. *International Journal of Legal Medicine, 125,* 127–131.

Lv, M., et al. (2004). Allele frequency distribution of two X-chromosomal STR loci in Han population in China. *Journal of Forensic Sciences, 49,* 418–419.

Machado, F. B., & Medina-Acosta, E. (2009). Genetic map of human X-linked microsatellites used in forensic practice. *Forensic Science International: Genetics, 3,* 202–204.

Martínez, B., et al. (2011). Genetic data of 10 X-STR in a Columbian population of Bolivar Department. *Forensic Science International: Genetics Supplement Series, 3,* e59–e60.

Martinez, R. E., et al. (2008). Genetic polymorphisms of four X-STR loci: DXS6797, DXS6800, HPRTB and GATA172D05 in a Peruvian population sample. *Forensic Science International: Genetics Supplement Series, 1,* 153–154.

Martins, J. A., et al. (2008). Population genetic data of five X-chromosomal loci in Bauru (São Paulo, Brazil). *Forensic Science International: Genetics Supplement Series, 1,* 155–156.

Martins, J. A., et al. (2009). Genetic data of 10 X-chromosomal loci in Vitoria population (Espirito Santo State, Brazil). *Forensic Science International: Genetics Supplement Series, 2,* 394–395.

Martins, J. A., et al. (2010). X-chromosome genetic variation in São Paulo State (Brazil) population. *Annals of Human Biology, 37,* 598–603.

Martins, J. A., et al. (2010). Genetic profile characterization of 10 X-STRs in four populations of the southeastern region of Brazil. *International Journal of Legal Medicine, 124,* 427–432.

Massetti, S., et al. (2008). Analysis of 8 STR of the X-chromosome in two Italian regions (Umbria and Sardinia). *Forensic Science International: Genetics Supplement Series, 1,* 157–159.

Medina-Acosta, E. (2011). Evidence of partial and weak gametic disequilibrium across clusters of pericentromeric short tandem repeats loci on human X chromosome: proceed with caution in forensic genetics. *Forensic Science International: Genetics, 5,* 545–547.

Nadeem, A., et al. (2009). Development of pentaplex PCR and genetic analysis of X chromosomal STRs in Punjabi population of Pakistan. *Molecular Biology Reports, 36,* 1671–1675.

Nagai, A., & Bunai, Y. (2011). Structural polymorphisms at the X-chromosomal short tandem repeat loci DXS10134, DXS10135, DXS10146 and DXS10148. *Forensic Science International: Genetics Supplement Series, 3,* e343–e344.

Nothnagel, M., et al. (2012). Collaborative genetic mapping of 12 forensic short tandem repeat (STR) loci on the human X chromosome. *Forensic Science International: Genetics, 6,* 778–784.

Oguzturun, C., et al. (2006). Population study of four X-chromosomal STR loci in the UK and Irish population. *Progress in Forensic Genetics 11, ICS, 1288,* 283–285.

Pamjav, H., et al. (2012). X chromosomal recombination study in three-generation families in Hungary. *Forensic Science International: Genetics, 6,* e95–e96.

Peloso, G., et al. (2004). Allele distribution of five X-chromosome STR loci in an Italian population sample. *Progress in Forensic Genetics 10, ICS, 1261*, 260—262.

Pepinski, W., et al. (2005). Polymorphism of four X-chromosomal STRs in a Polish population sample. *Forensic Science International, 151*, 93—95.

Pepinski, W., et al. (2007). X-chromosomal polymorphism data for the ethnic minority of Polish Tatars and the religious minority of Old Believers residing in northeastern Poland. *Forensic Science International: Genetics, 1*, 212—214.

Pereira, R., et al. (2007). Genetic diversity of 10 X-chromosome STRs in northern Portugal. *International Journal of Legal Medicine, 121*, 192—197.

Pico, A., et al. (2008). Genetic profile characterization and segregation analysis of 10 X-STRs in a sample from Santander, Columbia. *International Journal of Legal Medicine, 122*, 347—351.

Picornell, A., et al. (2011). X-chromosomal haplotype frequencies of four linkage groups in a North African population. *Forensic Science International: Genetics Supplement Series, 3*, e19—e20.

Poetsch, M., et al. (2006). Population data of 10 X-chromosomal loci in Latvia. *Forensic Science International, 157*, 206—209.

Poetsch, M., et al. (2009). Allele frequencies of 11 X-chromosomal loci in a population sample from Ghana. *International Journal of Legal Medicine, 123*, 81—83.

Presciuttini, S., et al. (2011). X-chromosome in Italy: a database of 29 STR markers. *Forensic Science International: Genetics Supplement Series, 3*, e37—e38.

Ribeiro Rodrigues, E. M., et al. (2008). A multiplex PCR for 11 X chromosome STR markers and population data from a Brazilian Amazon Region. *Forensic Science International: Genetics, 2*, 154—158.

Robino, C., et al. (2006). Development of two multiplex PCR systems for the analysis of 12 X-chromosomal STR loci in a northwestern Italian population sample. *International Journal of Legal Medicine, 120*, 315—318.

Rodig, H., et al. (2010). Evaluation of seven X-chromosomal short tandem repeat loci located within the Xq26 region. *Forensic Science International: Genetics, 4*, 194—199.

Rodrigues, E. M., et al. (2010). Genetic data of twelve X-STRs in a Japanese immigrant population resident in Brazil. *Forensic Science International: Genetics, 4*, e57—e58.

Shi, M. S., et al. (2003). Two X-chromosome STR loci DXS6807 and DXS7133 frequency data in Chinese population. *Journal of Forensic Sciences, 48*, 689—689.

Shin, K. J., et al. (2004). Five highly informative X-chromosomal STRs in Koreans. *International Journal of Legal Medicine, 118*, 37—40.

Shin, S. H., et al. (2005). Genetic analysis of 18 X-linked short tandem repeat markers in Korean population. *Forensic Science International, 147*, 35—41.

Silva, F., et al. (2010). Genetic profiling of the Azores Islands (Portugal): Data from 10 X-chromosome STRs. *American Journal of Human Biology, 22*, 221—223.

Sim, J. E., et al. (2010). Population genetic study of four closely-linked X-STR trios in Koreans. *Molecular Biology Reports, 37*, 333—337.

Son, J. Y., et al. (2002). Polymorphism of nine X chromosomal STR loci in Koreans. *International Journal of Legal Medicine, 116*, 317—321.

Szibor, R., et al. (2000). Population data on the X chromosome short tandem repeat locus HumHPRTB in two regions of Germany. *Journal of Forensic Sciences, 45*, 231—233.

Szibor, R. (2007). X-chromosomal markers: past, present and future. *Forensic Science International: Genetics, 1*, 93—99.

Tabbada, K. A., et al. (2005). Development of a pentaplex X-chromosomal short tandem repeat typing system and population genetic studies. *Forensic Science International, 154*, 173—180.

Tariq, M. A., et al. (2008). Allele frequency distribution of 13 X-chromosomal STR loci in Pakistani population. *International Journal of Legal Medicine, 122*, 525—528.

Tavares, C. C., et al. (2008). Population data for six X-chromosome STR loci in a Rio de Janeiro (Brazil) sample: usefulness in forensic casework. *Forensic Science International: Genetics Supplement Series, 1*, 164—166.

Tetzlaff, S., et al. (2012). Population genetic investigation of eight X-chromosomal short tandem repeat loci from a northeast German sample. *Forensic Science International: Genetics, 6*, e155—e156.

Thiele, K., et al. (2008). Population data of eight X-chromosomal STR markers in Ewe individuals from Ghana. *Forensic Science International: Genetics Supplement Series, 1*, 167—169.

Tie, J., et al. (2010). Genetic polymorphisms of eight X-chromosomal STR loci in the population of Japanese. *Forensic Science International: Genetics, 4*, e105—e108.

II. STATISTICAL INTERPRETATION

Tillmar, A. O., et al. (2008). Analysis of linkage and linkage disequilibrium for eight X-STR markers. *Forensic Science International: Genetics, 3,* 37—41.

Tillmar, A. O., et al. (2011). Using X-chromosomal markers in relationship testing: calculation of likelihood ratios taking both linkage and linkage disequilibrium into account. *Forensic Science International: Genetics, 5,* 506—511.

Tillmar, A. O. (2012). Population genetic analysis of 12 X-STRs in Swedish population. *Forensic Science International: Genetics, 6,* e80—e81.

Toscanini, U., et al. (2009). Genetic data of 10 X-STR in two Native American populations of Argentina. *Forensic Science International: Genetics Supplement Series, 2,* 405—406.

Turrina, S., & De Leo, D. (2003). Population data of three X-chromosomal STRs: DXS7132, DXS7133 and GATA172D05 in North Italy. *Journal of Forensic Sciences, 48,* 1428—1429.

Turrina, S., et al. (2007). Development and forensic validation of a new multiplex PCR assay with 12 X-chromosomal short tandem repeats. *Forensic Science International: Genetics, 1,* 201—204.

Turrina, S., et al. (2009). Genetic studies of eight X-STRs in a Northeast Italian population. *Forensic Science International: Genetics Supplement Series, 2,* 396—397.

Turrina, S., et al. (2011). Population genetic evaluation of 12 X-chromosomal short tandem repeats of Investigator Argus X-12 kit in North-East Italy. *Forensic Science International: Genetics Supplement Series, 3,* e327—e328.

Valente, C., et al. (2009). Association between STRs from the X chromosome in a sample of Portuguese Gypsies. *Forensic Science International: Genetics Supplement Series, 2,* 391—393.

Wiegand, P., et al. (2003). Population genetic comparisons of three X-chromosomal STRs. *International Journal of Legal Medicine, 117,* 62—65.

Wu, W., et al. (2009). Allele frequencies of seven X-linked STR loci in Chinese Han population from Zhejiang Province. *Forensic Science International: Genetics, 4,* e41—e42.

Ying, B. W., et al. (2003). Chinese population data on DXS6797 and GATA144D04 loci. *Journal of Forensic Sciences, 48,* 1184.

Yoo, S. Y., et al. (2011). Genetic polymorphisms of eight X-STR loci of Mentype Argus X-8 kit in Koreans. *Forensic Science International: Genetics Supplement Series, 3,* e33—e34.

Yu, B., et al. (2005). X-chromosome STRs polymorphisms of Han ethnic group from Northwest China. *Forensic Science International, 153,* 269—271.

Zarrabeitia, M. T., et al. (2004). X-linked microsatellites in two Northern Spain populations. *Forensic Science International, 145,* 57—59.

Zarrabeitia, M. T., et al. (2006). Study of six X-linked tetranucleotide microsatellites: population data from five Spanish regions. *International Journal of Legal Medicine, 120,* 147—150.

Zarrabeitia, M. T., et al. (2009). Analysis of 10 X-linked tetranucleotide markers in mixed and isolated populations. *Forensic Science International: Genetics, 3,* 63—66.

Zeng, X. P., et al. (2011). Genetic polymorphisms of twelve X-chromosomal STR loci in Chinese Han population from Guangdong Province. *Forensic Science International: Genetics, 5,* e114—e116.

Zeng, X. P., et al. (2011). Development of a 12-plex X chromosomal STR loci typing system. *Forensic Science International: Genetics Supplement Series, 3,* e365—e366.

Zhang, S. H., et al. (2011). Genetic polymorphism of eight X-linked STRs of Mentype® Argus X-8 Kit in Chinese population from Shanghai. *Forensic Science International: Genetics, 5,* e21—e24.

Genetic Models and Reporting

Ewens, W. J. (1972). The sampling theory of selectively neutral alleles. *Theoretical Population Biology, 3,* 87—112.

Sampling Correction with Confidence Intervals

Brenner, C. H. (2000). DNA frequency uncertainty — why bother?. Available at http://dna-view.com/noconfid.htm. Accessed April 4, 2014.

Clopper, C. J., & Pearson, E. S. (1934). The use of confidence or fiducial limits illustrated in the case of the binomial. *Biometrika, 26,* 404—413.

Confidence Intervals. Definitions available at http://en.wikipedia.org/wiki/Binomial_proportion_confidence_interval and http://en.wikipedia.org/wiki/Confidence_interval. Accessed April 4, 2014.

Hanley, J., & Lippman-Hand, A. (1983). If nothing goes wrong, is everything all right? Interpreting zero numerators. *Journal of the American Medical Association, 249*, 1743–1745.

Holland, M. M., & Parsons, T. J. (1999). Mitochondrial DNA sequence analysis – validation and use for forensic casework. *Forensic Science Review, 11*, 21–50.

Louis, T. (1981). Confidence intervals for a binomial parameter after observing no successes. *The American Statistician, 35*, 154–154.

Wilson, E. B. (1927). Probable inference, the law of succession, and statistical inference. *Journal of the American Statistical Association, 22*, 209–212.

Winkler, R., et al. (2002). The role of informative priors in zero-numerator problems: being conservative versus being candid. *The American Statistician, 56*, 1–4.

Willuweit, S., et al. (2011). Y-STR frequency surveying method: a critical reappraisal. *Forensic Science International: Genetics, 5*, 84–90.

Accounting for Potential Population Substructure

Ayres, K. L., & Powley, W. M. (2005). Calculating the exclusion probability and paternity index for X-chromosomal loci in the presence of substructure. *Forensic Science International, 149*, 201–203.

Balding, D. J., & Nichols, R. A. (1994). DNA profile match probability calculation: how to allow for population stratification, relatedness, database selection and single bands. *Forensic Science International, 64*, 125–140.

Brenner, C. H. (2013). *Understanding Y haplotype evidence – (forget what you know from autosomal)*. Presentation at the ISFG 2013 meeting. Available at http://isfg2013.org/wp-content/uploads/2012/06/Understanding-Y-haplotype-evidence-for-ISFG-site.pdf. Accessed April 4, 2014.

Budowle, B., et al. (2009). Texas population substructure and its impact on estimating the rarity of Y STR haplotypes from DNA evidence. *Journal of Forensic Sciences, 54*, 1016–1021.

Cockerton, S., et al. (2012). Interpreting lineage markers in view of subpopulation effects. *Forensic Science International: Genetics, 6*, 393–397.

de Knijff, P. (2003). Son, give up your gun: presenting Y-STR results in court. *Profiles in DNA, 6*(2), 3–5. Available at http://www.promega.com/resources/articles/profiles-in-dna/2003/son-give-up-your-gun-presenting-ystr-results-in-court/. Accessed April 4, 2014.

Diaz-Lacava, A., et al. (2011). Geostatistical inference of main Y-STR-haplogroups in Europe. *Forensic Science International: Genetics, 5*, 91–94.

Hammer, M. F., et al. (2006). Population structure of Y chromosome SNP haplogroups in the United States and forensic implications for constructing Y chromosome STR databases. *Forensic Science International, 164*, 45–55.

Kayser, M., et al. (2003). Y chromosome STR haplotypes and the genetic structure of U.S. populations of African, European, and Hispanic ancestry. *Genome Research, 13*, 624–634.

Lao, O., et al. (2010). Evaluation self-declared ancestry of U.S. Americans using autosomal, Y-chromosomal and mitochondrial DNA. *Human Mutation, 31*, E1875–93.

Redd, A. J., et al. (2006). Genetic structure among 38 populations from the United States based on 11 U.S. core Y chromosome STRs. *Journal of Forensic Sciences, 51*, 580–585.

Weir, B. S. (2013). *Y-STR matching: a population-genetic perspective*. Presentation at the ISFG 2013 meeting. Available at http://isfg2013.org/wp-content/uploads/2013/09/Thu-P3-1230-B-Weir-Y.pdf. Accessed April 4, 2014.

Handling Rare Haplotypes

Andersen, M. M., et al. (2013b). The discrete Laplace exponential family and estimation of Y-STR haplotype frequencies. *Journal of Theoretical Biology, 329*, 39–51.

Andersen, M. M., et al. (2013c). Estimating trace–suspect match probabilities for singleton Y-STR haplotypes using coalescent theory. *Forensic Science International: Genetics, 7*, 264–271.

Brenner, C. H. (2010). Fundamental problem of forensic mathematics – the evidential value of a rare haplotype. *Forensic Science International: Genetics, 4*, 281–291.

Budowle, B., et al. (2005). Twelve short tandem repeat loci Y chromosome haplotypes: Genetic analysis on populations residing in North America. *Forensic Science International, 150*, 1–15.

Krawczak, M. (2001). Forensic evaluation of Y-STR haplotype matches: a comment. *Forensic Science International, 118*, 114–115.

Y-STR Mixtures

Fukshansky, N., & Bär, W. (2005). DNA mixtures: biostatistics for mixed stains with haplotypic genetic markers. *International Journal of Legal Medicine, 119*, 285–290.

Ge, J., et al. (2010). Interpreting Y chromosome STR haplotype mixture. *Legal Medicine, 12*, 137–143.

US Y-STR Database Mixture Analysis Tools. (2014). http://usystrdatabase.org/ymix.aspx. Accessed April 4, 2014.

Wolf, A., et al. (2005). Forensic interpretation of Y-chromosomal DNA mixtures. *Forensic Science International, 152*, 209–213.

YHRD Mixture Tool. (2014). http://www.yhrd.org/Analyse/Mixture. Accessed April 4, 2014.

Joint Match Probabilities

Amorim, A. (2008). A cautionary note on the evaluation of genetic evidence from uniparentally transmitted markers. *Forensic Science International: Genetics, 2*(4), 376–378.

Ayadi, I., et al. (2007). Combining autosomal and Y-chromosomal short tandem repeat data in paternity testing with male child: methods and application. *Journal of Forensic Sciences, 52*, 1068–1072.

Buckleton, J., & Myers, S. (2014). Combining autosomal and Y chromosome match probabilities using coalescent theory. *Forensic Science International: Genetics, 11*, 52–55.

Walsh, B., et al. (2008). Joint match probabilities for Y chromosomal and autosomal markers. *Forensic Science International, 174*, 234–238.

Predicting Ethnicity or Surnames with Y-STRs

Graf, O. M., et al. (2010). Surname distributions and their association with Y-chromosome markers in the Aleutian Islands. *Human Biology, 82*, 745–757.

Jobling, M. A. (2001). In the name of the father: surnames and genetics. *Trends in Genetics, 17*, 353–357.

King, T. E., et al. (2006). Genetic signatures of coancestry with surnames. *Current Biology, 16*, 384–388.

King, T. E., & Jobling, M. A. (2009). What's in a name? Y chromosomes, surnames and the genetic genealogy revolution. *Trends in Genetics, 25*, 351–360.

King, T. E., & Jobling, M. A. (2009). Founders, drift, and infidelity: the relationship between Y chromosome diversity and patrilineal surnames. *Molecular Biology and Evolution, 26*, 1093–1102.

McEvoy, B., & Bradley, D. G. (2006). Y-chromosomes and the extent of patrilineal ancestry in Irish surnames. *Human Genetics, 119*, 212–219.

Mertens, G., et al. (2008). Resolution of African versus non-African origin using a likelihood based method and 11 Y-chromosomal STRs. *Forensic Science International: Genetics Supplement Series, 1*, 224–225.

Oliveira, S. F., et al. (2008). Correlation of surnames and Y-chromosome in Central-Brazil. *Forensic Science International: Genetics Supplement Series, 1*, 228–229.

Sykes, B., & Irven, C. (2000). Surnames and the Y chromosome. *American Journal of Human Genetics, 66*, 1417–1419.

Laboratory Reports: Communicating Results and Conclusions

"One could argue that the most critical aspect of forensic science is the product of a report."

Sheila Willis (Willis 2009)

"The crucial element that the scientist brings to any case is the interpretation *of those observations. This is the heart of forensic science: it is where the scientist adds value to the process."*

Ian Evett (Evett et al. 2000b)

"Science is built up of facts, as a house is built of stones; but an accumulation of facts is no more a science than a heap of stones is a house."

Henri Poincaré (Science & Hypothesis, 1905), p. 157
(http://www.gutenberg.org/files/37157/37157-pdf.pdf)

INTRODUCTION

Drawing conclusions and effectively communicating results is critical to enable others to understand what has been determined in the course of data interpretation and statistical evaluation of a forensic case. This chapter explores these issues and examines challenges with preparing laboratory reports that are clear and concise, and appropriately communicate results of forensic DNA laboratory tests conducted in the course of an investigation. It does little good to gather great data and to carefully interpret it — and then fail to effectively share this information with those who need to understand what the data mean.

Laboratory reports are the culmination of lab work performed on a specific case. These reports are typically carefully reviewed for accuracy and completeness before they leave the laboratory and are hopefully examined thoroughly by those receiving the lab reports in an effort to understand them (Table 16.1). Some laboratory reports will become evidence in courts of law and analysts may be called upon to testify as expert witnesses to the results obtained. However, with more than 90% of cases in the United States resolved through plea bargaining (Fisher 2003), most forensic lab reports will not face the scrutiny of court. It is thus imperative that reports be well-written so they can be clearly understood by those who use them. In some situations in the past where evidence and even case files were not preserved, a written report may serve as the only record of the forensic examination performed.

TABLE 16.1   Summary of Effort Surrounding a Laboratory Casework Report and Impact on the Criminal Justice System. Note that Analysts are Termed Examiners in Some Laboratories

Work Performed	Work Product or Outcome	Who Is Involved
Experimental work on evidence and reference samples	Case folder & electronic data files	Analyst and possibly technician(s)
Q–K comparisons, conclusions drawn, and report written	Casework report	Analyst
Technical review of report	Reviewer's signature	A second qualified analyst within the laboratory
Administrative review of report	Reviewer's signature	Supervisor, DNA technical leader, or another qualified analyst
Receipt of report and examination	Decisions about arresting, prosecuting, and defending a person of interest	Investigator, prosecutor, and eventually in many cases the defense attorney
Defense review of report	Review of case data & report	Defense expert
Report conclusions presented in court	Review and defense of report conclusions through court testimony, cross-examination, and weighing evidence presented	Expert witnesses, attorneys, judge and/or jury

Contributors to This Chapter

As the research laboratories of the National Institute of Standards and Technology do not perform casework, I have never had the opportunity to draw conclusions on forensic evidence or write a report representing results from the comparison of evidentiary and reference samples. Thus, in order to write this chapter, I have reached out to others who have extensive experience reading, writing, and reviewing reports. It is their perspectives that I have woven into the fabric of this material along with other published information as cited throughout the chapter. I have attempted something similar to what was done with Chapter 18 on legal aspects of DNA testing and serving as a scientific expert in court in my *Advanced Topics in Forensic DNA Typing: Methodology* book. I welcome feedback from members of the legal community, investigators, and forensic DNA scientists who read, write, or review casework reports so that I may improve and expand the content on this topic in future editions.

In addition to what I have gleaned from studying the resources listed at the back of this chapter, I have interviewed several individuals who have extensive experience writing, reviewing, and using reports in their work within the criminal justice system. In covering various topics, I will include direct quotes from these interviews (citing the individual contributions through their initials). Prior to submission of this text for publication, all those interviewed reviewed what I have written in order to confirm that I have quoted them correctly and placed their words in an appropriate context. Contributors to this chapter include:

(RA) Ricky Ansell, Ph.D., is Forensic Advisor to the Biology Unit of the Swedish National Laboratory of Forensic Science (Statens Kriminaltekniska Laboratorium, SKL) in Linköping, Sweden, where he has been since 1995. In his current advisory role, he provides internal and external training on DNA, helps with preparing laboratory standard operating procedures, and aids overall quality assurance efforts. He has written or technically reviewed several thousand biology case reports and provided DNA evidence for court more than 35 times. Ricky is a member of the European Network of Forensic Science Institutes DNA Working Group and has served as a board member and vice-president of the Swedish Forensic Society.

(CC) Cecelia Crouse, Ph.D., is the Crime Laboratory Director and Forensic Biology Unit Manager for the Palm Beach County Sheriff's Office in West Palm Beach, Florida. Cecelia began writing and reviewing DNA reports in May 1993, and over the past 20 years has analyzed thousands of DNA cases and provided court testimony numerous times.

(CD) Christopher Duby, J.D., is a defense attorney in North Haven, Connecticut. Chris has reviewed more than 65 lab reports and accompanying case notes and other documentation.

(BH) Bruce J. Heidebrecht, M.S., is the DNA Technical Leader at the Maryland State Police, Forensic Sciences Division with over 16 years of experience in forensic DNA analysis. He has analyzed over 500 biology cases and testified in more than 50 trials regarding DNA evidence. Bruce also serves on the Mixture Committee of SWGDAM and has been an invited guest speaker on the topic of DNA mixture interpretation at several professional meetings across the United States.

(TH) Ted R. Hunt, J.D., is Chief Trial Attorney at the Jackson County Prosecutor's Office in Kansas City, Missouri. He has been a prosecuting attorney for over 20 years and has tried over 100 felony cases, most of which involved the presentation of DNA evidence. He is also actively involved in training attorneys and law enforcement officials in forensic DNA-related litigation for a number of state and federal organizations.

(TM) Terry Melton, Ph.D., is president and technical leader of Mitotyping Technologies, a private forensic laboratory in State College, Pennsylvania, accredited by ASCLD/LAB. She has over 20 years of experience in forensic mitochondrial DNA analysis. She has testified in approximately 15 mitochondrial DNA admissibility hearings and in over 100 trials regarding DNA evidence. Terry also serves on the editorial board for the *Journal of Forensic Sciences* and was a member of the NFSTC panel that created the online tutorial titled "Principles of Forensic DNA for Officers of the Court" on DNA.gov. She has published a number of peer-reviewed articles, book chapters, and encyclopedia entries on forensic mitochondrial DNA analysis.

(MoCo) Author's discussion conducted in April 2012 with Montgomery County, Maryland police investigators, a prosecutor from the State's Attorney's office, and a forensic laboratory director. Participants included Captain Dave Gillespie, Michael Fergus Sugrue, Gregory Wise, John Sheridan, Brian Labatt, Craig Wittenberger, Mary Herdman, and Ray Wickenheiser.

(MP) Mechthild (Mecki) Prinz, Ph.D., is the former director of the Department of Forensic Biology at the New York City Office of Chief Medical Examiner (OCME) and now teaches at John Jay College. She started in forensic DNA testing at the Institute of Legal Medicine of the University of Cologne in 1986 and has worked on thousands of cases either as an analyst or as the technical reviewer. In her lab director position, she was responsible for the programmatic administration and oversight of the OCME's DNA testing laboratory. The Department of Forensic Biology is a local CODIS laboratory and processes and types biological evidence collected by the New York City Police Department.

(NR) Norah Rudin, Ph.D., is an active independent consultant and expert witness. She has worked for both the prosecution and the defense. Norah served for 3 years as a full-time consultant for the California Department of Justice DNA Laboratory. She has also served as a consultant technical leader for the Idaho Department of Law Enforcement DNA Laboratory, the San Francisco Crime Laboratory, and the San Diego County Sheriff's Department. She has examined hundreds of reports from laboratories in numerous states as well as the US military crime lab, both as an internal technical reviewer and as an independent reviewer, and has testified more than 45 times. Norah has co-authored two books with Keith Inman, including *An Introduction to DNA Forensic Analysis* and *Principles and Practice of Criminalistics: The Profession of Forensic Science*. Since 2002, Norah and Keith have co-authored a regular column in the quarterly California Association of Criminalists newsletter *CAC News* (CACNews 2014).

(RW) Ray Wickenheiser, BSc Hons, MBA, is the Director of the New York State Crime Laboratory System. He previously served as the laboratory director of Montgomery County (Maryland) Police Crime Laboratory and has over 28 years of forensic experience. Prior to his current position, Ray has been a consultant, director of operations for Orchid Cellmark, lab director for the Acadiana (Louisiana) Criminalistics Laboratory, and was a forensic trace evidence examiner and DNA reporting officer for more than 15 years at the Royal Canadian Mounted Police (RCMP) Forensic Laboratory in Regina, Saskatchewan. Ray has taught DNA mixture interpretation classes as well as criminalistics as an adjunct professor. He is also a lead DNA auditor and forensic DNA consultant.

(CW) Charlotte J. Word, Ph.D., is currently a private consultant with over 20 years of experience in forensic DNA analysis. She spent 15 years at Cellmark Diagnostics, in Germantown, Maryland, and was one of the Laboratory Directors there. She has testified in numerous admissibility hearings and in over 200 trials regarding DNA evidence, and has reviewed many thousands of cases. Charlotte also serves on the editorial board for the *Journal of Forensic Sciences* and was a member of the Postconviction Issues Working Group of the National Commission on the Future of DNA Evidence.

Each of the experts whose names and brief biographies are included above were given a set of 27 questions (D.N.A. Box 16.1). Written responses were provided back to the author. Their responses reflect perspectives from US state and local forensic laboratories, private laboratories, a national laboratory outside of the United States, lab directors and DNA technical leaders, prosecutors, defense attorneys, and independent consultants/reviewers. In addition, perspectives from the Innocence Project and New York state laboratory directors on the importance of standardized report writing to wrongful conviction reform were considered (Corrado et al. 2012, Neufeld et al. 2012).

The Montgomery County, Maryland group met with the author for about an hour discussion, which was recorded, on issues with understanding and using lab reports. This discussion also explored interactions between police investigators, the prosecution, and the forensic DNA laboratory and the importance of good communication during an investigation.

The discussions in this chapter presuppose the following four requirements, which have been covered in this volume or its accompanying text *Advanced Topics in Forensic DNA Typing: Methodology*. First, that DNA evidence has been properly collected and preserved in order to prevent contamination and to maintain chain-of-custody. Second, that the DNA results were collected and analyzed properly using validated PCR and capillary electrophoresis conditions so that the results reliably reflect the sample being tested. Third, that results have been correctly interpreted (i.e. genotypes inferred where possible) to appropriately reflect the data collected. And finally, that the statistical significance of the results has been computed correctly.

Assuming that all of these requirements have been met, the focus of this chapter is on making appropriate conclusions and expressing results and conclusions in written reports effectively to help others understand — and just as importantly not misunderstand — the meaning of interpretations made.

D.N.A. BOX 16.1

QUESTIONS ASKED OF CHAPTER CONTRIBUTORS

1. What is your role in the criminal justice process and how are you involved with laboratory reports describing the results of forensic DNA casework?

2. Approximately how many reports have you written or reviewed?

3. What are the most difficult challenges with drawing conclusions from the information in a forensic case either as a user of a lab report and/or as a writer or reviewer of a lab report?

4. Who in your opinion is the primary audience for a forensic lab report?

5. What are the critical elements in a lab report?

6. How long does it typically take to write a lab report? What are the factors that might make a report take longer to write?

7. What are the advantages of short versus long reports? For report writers, how is it best to strike a happy medium in a specific case? For report reviews or users, how has a report that has been too long/short (not all the information vs. too detailed) been a problem for you?

8. How should people be trained to write/review reports?

9. Should sample allele calls be included in final reports or just in the case notes? Why or why not from your perspective?

10. Could genetic privacy be impacted by including DNA profile information from known individuals (e.g. victim) in the case report?

11. Do you have a memorable report that you have written or reviewed that you can comment on (exceptionally interesting, well-written, poorly written, or poor conclusions)?

12. What are some of the biggest problems with report writing that currently exist?

13. The NAS (2009) report encouraged standardized report writing—what are some challenges that exist for creating a standardized DNA report template?

14. Is it effective from your perspective to have standard text that can be dropped into the report as needed?

15. Can report conclusions be categorized effectively (e.g. this is an xxxx type of report)?

16. How can report writing or reviewing be done more effectively?

17. Have you ever known a report to be misinterpreted by an investigator? A prosecutor? A defense attorney? The jury or judge?

18. How can reports make clear that a sample is from a mixture rather than a single source and therefore the conclusions are typically not of the same strength?

19. From your perspective, should statistical information conveying the weight-of-evidence always be included in a laboratory report?

20. Are summary tables needed or valuable in a report?

21. Where do most mistakes come when writing a report?

22. What are some of the most challenging bits of information to confirm when reviewing a report?

23. What is typically the most misunderstood part of a report?

24. How can reports be written more effectively to avoid misunderstandings?

25. Are there words that are commonly misunderstood in reports?

26. How has the *Melendez-Diaz v. Massachusetts* (2009) Supreme Court ruling impacted your work?

27. Are there other questions that I should have asked or that you would like to answer?

DRAWING CONCLUSIONS

As noted by Alex Biedermann and colleagues from the University of Lausanne in Switzerland, who offer electronic learning courses in forensic interpretation, "interpretation of raw data and communication of findings in both written and oral statements are topics where knowledge and applied skills are needed" (Biedermann et al. 2013). They point out that most forensic scientists today have degrees in traditional sciences like biology or chemistry — and few have had full courses devoted to interpretation issues. Equally important, scientists are not usually trained extensively in written communication skills.

In 2009, the Association of Forensic Science Providers (AFSP) within the UK published "standards for the formulation of evaluative forensic science expert opinion" (AFSP 2009). This group advocates that expert opinion should be based on four general principles: *balance*, *logic*, *robustness*, and *transparency*. They write in a *Science & Justice* article (AFSP 2009):

> The expert will base his opinion upon the four principles: balance, logic, robustness and transparency. The standards set out in this document describe the mechanism by which these principles will be applied in formulating such opinion.
>
> *Balance*—the expert should address at least one pair of propositions usually one based upon the prosecution issue and one based upon an alternative (defense issue). If a reasonable alternative cannot be identified, then the expert may address only the one proposition but will make it clear that he cannot evaluate the strength of the evidence.
>
> *Logic*—the expert will address the probability of the evidence given the proposition and relevant background information and not the probability of the proposition given the evidence and background information.
>
> *Robustness*—the expert will provide opinion that is capable of scrutiny by other experts and cross-examination. He will base his opinion upon sound knowledge of the evidence type(s) and use wherever possible verified databases. He will be satisfied that the results of the tests and examinations upon which he has based his opinion are themselves robust.
>
> *Transparency*—the expert will be able to demonstrate how he came to his conclusion. He will set out in the statement or report the basis of his opinion [namely]:
>
> - Propositions addressed.
> - Test or examination results.
> - The background information he has used in arriving at his conclusion.
> - He will be able, if required, to provide the data he has used and its provenance.

According to Ian Evett, former chief statistician with the UK Forensic Science Service,[1] balance involves considering multiple propositions or hypotheses: "A scientist cannot speculate about the truth of a proposition without considering at least one alternative proposition. Indeed, an interpretation is without meaning unless the scientist clearly states the alternatives he has considered" (Evett 1996).

Graham Jackson in a 2000 editorial on the scientist and the scales of justice offered his explanations for what it means to be transparent: "[We need to explain] in a clear and explicit way what we have

---

[1] The Forensic Science Service, which was considered the premier forensic science laboratory in the world during its heyday, closed its operations in March 2012.

done, why we have done it and how we have arrived at our conclusions. We need to expose the reasoning, the rationale, behind our work. In principle, our statements should guide our customers through the process of our evaluation. *We should provide them with the information that we have used in order to lead them to draw the same conclusion as we have drawn*" (Jackson 2000; emphasis added). From the perspective of a laboratory director (MP), learning to draw the right conclusions is even more important than report writing.

Q-to-K Comparisons

DNA profiles obtained from biological evidence are meaningless without comparison to reference profile(s). Thus, conclusions for a case are assembled based on comparisons of the DNA profiles produced through analysis of the evidentiary question (Q) sample(s) and the known (K) reference sample(s). The 2010 SWGDAM Guidelines section 3.6 covers comparison of DNA typing results. Guideline 3.6.1 emphasizes "that, to the extent possible, DNA typing results from evidentiary samples are interpreted BEFORE COMPARISON with any known samples, other than those of assumed contributors" (SWGDAM 2010; emphasis added). In other words, *Q is interpreted before K is compared*.

Use of Statistical Weight-of-Evidence with Inclusions

Another important point with Q–K comparisons when the K profile cannot be excluded from the Q profile is that statistics regarding the weight-of-evidence should be provided. Just stating that a reference profile cannot be excluded from evidentiary data can potentially mislead report users into imagining that there is significant strength in this "cannot exclude" statement when the corresponding characteristics may be quite common. By way of example, if the evidentiary data could include anyone with four fingers and a thumb on their right hand, then not being able to exclude a suspect that had four fingers and a thumb on his right hand is not very meaningful since almost every potential suspect would have the same characteristics (i.e. four fingers and a thumb on their right hand).

The 2010 SWGDAM Interpretation Guidelines section 4.1 states: "The laboratory must perform statistical analysis in support of any inclusion that is determined to be relevant in the context of a case, irrespective of the number of alleles detected and the quantitative value of the statistical analysis" (SWGDAM 2010). The importance of providing statistical support for DNA results is summed up nicely by John Buckleton and James Curran: "There is a considerable aura to DNA evidence. Because of this aura it is vital that weak evidence is correctly represented as weak or not presented at all" (Buckleton & Curran 2008).

Conclusion Choices and Their Meaning

The 2010 SWGDAM Short Tandem Repeat (STR) Interpretation Guidelines note: "The conclusions reached as part of the DNA interpretation process are compiled into a written draft by the DNA analyst and are subjected to technical and administrative reviews prior to issuing a final case report" (SWGDAM 2010).

This section describes aspects of making and stating conclusions. As noted in section 3.6 of the 2010 SWGDAM Guidelines, there are typically four possible determinations that can be made: (1) the known individual cannot be excluded (i.e. is included) as a possible contributor to the DNA obtained from an evidentiary item, (2) the known individual is excluded as a possible contributor, (3) the DNA typing results are inconclusive or are uninterpretable, or (4) the DNA typing results from multiple evidentiary items are consistent or inconsistent with originating from a common source(s) (SWGDAM 2010).

Vocabulary

Use of consistent nomenclature and uniform vocabulary is crucial to effectively communicating the intended meaning of results obtained and conclusions drawn in forensic DNA cases. An analyst should use the same words to convey equivalent meaning within a case report as well as across case reports. Ideally, different analysts (including those in different laboratories) would also use the same words to convey equivalent meaning so that any user of a report would be able to consistently understand the information presented. The forensic science community certainly has room for improvement in this area as noted by the National Academy of Sciences 2009 report entitled "Strengthening Forensic Science in the United States: A Path Forward" (NAS 2009).

NAS (2009) report recommendation two states:

> "The National Institute of Forensic Science (NIFS), after reviewing established standards such as ISO 17025, and in consultation with its advisory board, should establish standard terminology to be used in reporting on and testifying about the results of forensic science investigations. Similarly, it should establish model laboratory reports for different forensic science disciplines and specify the minimum information that should be included. As part of the accreditation and certification processes, laboratories and forensic scientists should be required to utilize model laboratory reports when summarizing the results of their analyses."

A glossary of terms can be appended to a report to help report users to appreciate what is intended by specific terms or phrases like "match" or "cannot be excluded from." It is important to realize that phrases such as "cannot be excluded from" are effectively equivalent to "is included in" and should be supported by sound statistical analysis to evaluate the weight-of-evidence.

Inclusion

An inclusion is when the possibility exists that a reference sample (K profile), from an individual such as the suspect in a case, could have contributed to the evidence sample (Q profile). The word "match" is often used to describe the relationship between single-source Q and K profiles when there is a full 1-to-1 correspondence of genotypes observed. Thus, a full single-source evidentiary profile *matches* to a full single-source reference sample. A high degree of certainty essentially exists with both the Q profile and the K profile in this scenario.

However, in some situations, the evidentiary profile may not be complete due to DNA fragmentation or inhibition of the PCR amplification reaction. The phrase "is consistent with" may be used when the Q sample exhibits an incomplete, partial DNA profile that is in agreement with the reference K profile. Since some of the information is missing from the Q profile, there is some uncertainty as to whether or not the entire evidence DNA profile would correspond fully to the reference K profile. Thus, "match" is an inappropriate description of the relationship of a reference sample to the evidence result when a partial or mixed Q profile is obtained.

When a DNA mixture is observed with the Q profile, it can be appropriate to state that the reference K profile from the suspect "cannot be excluded from" being part of the Q profile. However, results from a statistical analysis of the weight-of-evidence must be included to provide

Less uncertainty ↓ Greater uncertainty

(a)

	Q sample	K sample
Locus 1	12,14	12,14
Locus 2	13,13	13,13
Locus 3	8,10	8,10
Locus 4	14,15	14,15

"Match"
Complete correlation and agreement with genotypes obtained between two single-source DNA profiles

(b)

	Q sample	K sample
Locus 1	12,14	12,14
Locus 2	13,–	13,13
Locus 3	8,10	8,10
Locus 4	–	14,15

"Is consistent with"
Agreement with genotypes observed in the Q profile, which is incomplete (partial profile) due to poor quality evidentiary material

(c)

	Q sample	K sample
Locus 1	12,14,15	12,14
Locus 2	11,12,13	13,13
Locus 3	8,10,11	8,10
Locus 4	14,15,16,17	14,15

"Cannot be excluded from"
Alleles (and likely genotypes) from the K profile are present in an evidentiary Q profile mixture

FIGURE 16.1 Illustration of several categories of Q-to-K comparisons with terms or phrases that can be used to define a relationship between the Q and K profile results. Some ambiguity or uncertainty exists when the phrase "cannot be excluded from" is used with DNA mixtures, which is why it is crucial to provide a statistical weight-of-evidence to these results. An assessment of likely genotypes is typically performed through considering peak heights and peak height ratios.

perspective on the strength of the association between the Q and K profiles. For example, a two-person DNA mixture result may be reported as "consistent with" originating from a combination of DNA types from the victim and the suspect and a likelihood ratio calculation (see Chapter 12) may provide a mathematical evaluation of the strength of the evidence in the context of specific scenarios (hypotheses). Figure 16.1 provides examples of several scenarios with Q-to-K DNA comparisons.

With missing persons cases, it may be appropriate to use the phrase "is consistent with" when describing the relationship of evidentiary profile results and DNA profile results from putative biological relatives (see Chapter 14).

Exclusion

When a Q–K comparison is performed, an exclusion may be reported if the evidence DNA profile does not match potential reference sample(s). Reporting an exclusion for a single source sample is quite easy and may be reported even if there is a mismatch at a single locus. Thus, if the Q genotype at a locus is "11,14" and a K genotype at the same locus is "8,10", then it is reasonable to assume that the two samples came from different sources. In other words, they can be excluded as being from a common source. Exclusion statements can be fairly straightforward, such as: "The donor of the known sample [exhibit XYZ] is not the source of the DNA obtained from exhibit [evidence description and/or exhibit number ABC]."

The possibility of allele dropout when examining low amounts of DNA template (see Chapter 7) makes it more difficult to conclusively establish an exclusion. Likewise, excluding a specific suspect from a complex mixture (i.e. a sample containing DNA from three or more contributors), where significant allele sharing is a possibility, cannot always be done with certainty. While exclusion criteria are necessary for interpreting profiles containing complex mixtures and/or exhibiting possible stochastic effects due to the presence of low template DNA, they are often quite difficult to establish.

Inconclusive

When there is an inability to clearly include or exclude a suspect's DNA profile from an evidentiary DNA profile, the result may be described as "inconclusive." Synonyms for the word inconclusive include uncertain, questionable, and unconvincing. With some cases, circumstances may prevent being able to draw a definitive inclusion or exclusion.

There are multiple reasons that a conclusion can be inconclusive, including: (1) no or limited data were collected from the evidence sample due to DNA degradation, inhibition of amplification and/or low amount of DNA template, (2) results from the evidence sample were too complex to reliably interpret (e.g. a complex DNA mixture), or (3) a reference sample was not available to perform the Q—K comparison. If a report provides an "inconclusive" finding, then it is appropriate to provide a reason why this conclusion was reached. In the first two situations described above, (1) and (2), the evidence samples may be deemed by the laboratory to be uninterpretable; that is, they are not suitable for comparison. For situation (3), no conclusions can be drawn because a reference sample is not available. If a suitable evidence result is obtained, then this Q profile may be used for a database search in an attempt to locate a matching K profile or a future suspect sample's profile may be compared.

One chapter contributor feels that the word "inconclusive" is "used far too often to mean just about anything that the analyst doesn't want to report. If the analyst must default to an inconclusive statement, the reasons for this should be [fully explained] in the report" (NR). SWGDAM guideline 3.6.6 states: "The laboratory should establish guidelines for identifying DNA typing results for which comparisons of evidentiary and known samples are not made (at a minimum, to include inconclusive/uninterpretable results)" (SWGDAM 2010).

Comparing Multiple Evidentiary Items

If more than one evidentiary item has been examined for a case, performing comparisons between multiple evidence items may be appropriate to try and link them to a common source (i.e. a Q-to-Q comparison). This type of comparison might be performed with multiple cuttings of stains from a bed sheet or blood stains at a crime scene.

Probabilistic Statements in Conclusions

Another approach to drawing conclusions is to use a probabilistic statement, typically a likelihood ratio (LR), instead of using an inclusion/exclusion threshold-based approach. LRs are especially valuable with mixture data and are covered in more detail in Chapters 11, 12, and 13. As Norah Rudin and Keith Inman have written: "A probabilistic approach not only exposes situations for which insufficient information exists on which to base an opinion, it relieves the analyst of having to assert an opinion" (Rudin & Inman 2013b). A challenge often exists in describing LR data because as Ricky Ansell asserts "even when explained in the correct way, people will listen with a 'transposed conditional hearing' [i.e. they will hear what is being said incorrectly]" (RA).

Attempts to Simplify Reporting Statistical Assessments

An approach to providing meaningful conclusions without using large numbers is to create a proportional scale that relates to the value of the evidence following a Q–K comparison. As early as 1987, Ian Evett proposed a verbal scale for describing ranges of likelihood ratios (Evett 1987). For example, a likelihood ratio in the range of 1,000–10,000 provides "strong evidence to support" hypothesis 1 compared to hypothesis 2 (Evett et al. 2000b). More on this topic can be found in Chapter 11.

In 1998 Colin Aitken and Franco Taroni proposed a verbal scale for the interpretation of evidence and recommended using a simplified numerical scale involving base-10 logarithms (Aitken & Taroni 1998). Thus, one thousand is simplified to "3," one million to "6," and one billion to "9." These smaller values, similar to the Richter scale used for measuring the strength of earthquakes, are typically more meaningful to a statistical layperson. A $\log_{10}$ value provides the order of magnitude and is approximately equal to the number of digits to the left of the decimal point of a large number (see D.N.A. Box 12.3). The company Cybergenetics has taken the same approach in reporting log likelihood data with their TrueAllele software (Perlin et al. 2011).

The national forensic laboratory in Sweden has put information into a simple-to-understand format where the value of evidence is placed on a +4 to a −4 scale (D.N.A. Box 16.2). Ricky Ansell observes: "Frequency or LR for a DNA profile or any other forensic investigation is not reported in our statements today. We stopped reporting frequencies (and presenting the DNA profiles obtained) just a little more than a decade ago" (RA). When a "+4" is reported, the Q–K comparison provides "extremely strong support" for a particular hypothesis, such as the suspect contributed to the evidentiary sample (Nordgaard et al. 2012). Ricky Ansell comments: "The strongest conclusion given today ('Grad+4') is achieved at a likelihood ratio of a million" (RA). A "+4" value reflects a stronger statistical significance in the Q–K association compared to a "+1" value that only provides "support to some extent" that the prosecution hypothesis is more appropriate than the defense hypothesis. Negative values on this scale (i.e. −1, −2, −3, or −4) favor the alternative hypothesis that the K sample is not strongly associated with the Q sample. A "−4" value is in effect an exclusion.

Assumptions

All analysis involves assumptions. Even the interpretation of an apparent single source profile requires the assumption that the sample is from a single contributor. It is important to be clear what assumptions are being made so that those assessing the judgment rendered by the conclusions drawn and reported can understand the basis for the decisions made. Ian Evett and Bruce Weir note in their *Interpreting DNA Evidence* text, "In spite of the often elegant mathematical arguments we have presented, we stress that *the final statistical values depend wholly on the initial assumptions*. The validity of these assumptions in any given case [is] a matter for expert opinion…" (Evett & Weir 1998, emphasis added). Furthermore, they opine that the "objectivity [of a DNA statistic] is itself an illusion because it exists only within a framework of assumptions" (Evett & Weir 1998). Are the assumptions being made clear and are they documented in the interpretation and conclusions made?

D.N.A. BOX 16.2

SWEDISH SKL SCALE OF CONCLUSIONS FOR VALUE OF EVIDENCE

A unified scale of conclusions has been developed at the Swedish National Laboratory of Forensic Sciences (SKL) to try and reflect the value of evidence to investigators and prosecutors who may be using information from a casework report (Nordgaard et al. 2012). This scale ranges from +4, where there is extremely strong support for a particular hypothesis, such as the suspect contributed to the evidentiary sample, to −4, where evidence strongly supports an alternative hypothesis, such as the suspect did not contribute to the evidentiary sample.

Level	Stated Meaning "The results of the examination	Implied Meaning
+4	extremely strongly support that …"	The possibility that these results could be found if an alternative hypothesis is true can in practice be excluded
+3	strongly support that …"	The possibility that these results could be found if an alternative hypothesis is true is considered to be very unlikely
+2	support that …"	The possibility that these results could be found if an alternative hypothesis is true is considered to be unlikely

	Stated Meaning	Implied Meaning
+1	support to some extent that …"	There is somewhat more support for the advanced hypothesis (i.e. H_p) than the alternative hypothesis (i.e. H_d)
0	neither … nor …"	The results equally support the advanced hypothesis and the alternative hypothesis
−1	support to some extent that … <u>was not</u> …"	There is somewhat more support for the alternative hypothesis (i.e. H_d) than the advanced hypothesis (i.e. H_p)
−2	support that … <u>was not</u> …"	The possibility that these results could be found if the advanced hypothesis is true is considered to be unlikely
−3	strongly support that … <u>was not</u> …"	The possibility that these results could be found if the advanced hypothesis is true is considered to be very unlikely
−4	extremely strongly support that … <u>was not</u> …"	The possibility that these results could be found if the advanced hypothesis is true can in practice be excluded

Sources: Nordgaard, A., et al. (2012). Scale of conclusions for the value of evidence. Law, Probability, & Risk, 11(1), 1–24. See also Chapter 8, "Evidence evaluation" in Lucy, D. (2005). Introduction to Statistics for Forensic Scientists. Wiley.

An evaluation of the assumptions in a commonly used source attribution conclusion may be instructive. Source attribution (Budowle et al. 2000, DAB 2000) has been declared in report conclusions with wording such as: "In the absence of identical twins or close relatives, it can be concluded to a reasonable degree of scientific certainty that the DNA from [the evidence sample] and the DNA from [the known sample] came from the same individual." In this example, the "in the absence of identical twins or close relatives" preamble to the conclusion statement represents a stated assumption. In other words, this source attribution conclusion only works within a model of unrelated individuals (see Chapter 11 for further information discussing issues with source attribution in general).

Note, however, that what constitutes a "close relative" in the statement above is not defined, but most likely represents a sibling or a parent–offspring situation. Conversely, the derivation of the conclusion statement "to a reasonable degree of scientific certainty," which is typically based on observing a random match probability that exceeds some predetermined statistical threshold, is not spelled out in this conclusion statement. Some laboratories include information in footnotes to further delineate the basis for decisions being declared in the report (e.g. a reference to the population data used to estimate the profile frequency). One of the most important assumptions made in DNA mixture interpretation relates to the potential number of contributors that provided DNA to the result obtained.

Hierarchical Levels of Propositions

In the late 1990s, the Forensic Science Service developed a model for what Ian Evett and his colleagues termed "case assessment and interpretation" (Cook et al. 1998a). The forensic scientist formulates the propositions to be tested and thinks about what might be expected as the evidence is examined. In this approach, the scientist documents his or her expectations in statements such as "if such and such a proposition were true, then I would expect to find … ." Finally, the evidence is interpreted with the likelihood ratio (LR) in the form of the probability of the evidence if the prosecution proposition is true divided by the probability of the evidence if the defense proposition is true (see Chapter 11 for more on LRs).

Ian Evett and his colleagues also introduced a "hierarchy of propositions" with first three (Cook et al. 1998b) and then four (Evett et al. 2000a) levels to help segregate questions that are trying to be addressed. These levels are illustrated in Table 16.2. By convention, these levels are designated with Roman numerals I to III and listed in reverse numerical order to emphasize that going down the table reflects movement down the hierarchy (Cook et al. 1998b).

At the highest level (Level III or *offense* level), propositions address whether or not the suspect committed the offense in question. This judgment is outside the realm of what can be answered using scientific data and is therefore generally decided in a court of law. At the next level down (Level II or *activity* level), effort is made to address whether or not a suspect performed a specific action. Did the suspect break a window or have sexual intercourse with a victim? At the activity level, decisions are not being made whether a crime was committed—only that an action occurred. For example, a defendant may claim consensual sexual contact occurred rather than rape.

Scientists are more likely to be able to address questions at the *source* level (Level I). Did the suspect provide the blood or semen evidence sample based on comparing the Q and K profiles? With improvements in sensitivity for DNA testing, DNA results may be obtained

TABLE 16.2   Hierarchical Levels of Propositions Originally Developed by the UK Forensic Science Service (Cook et al. 1998a, 1998b, Evett et al. 2000a, 2000b, Gill 2001)

Hierarchy Levels		Propositions	Decision Maker	Example
Level III	Offense	Supplies the probability that a suspect has committed a criminal offense	Responsibility of the jury or judge	Rape occurred
Level II	Activity	Informs regarding the kinds of activities which may have produced the forensic evidence	Jury or possibly scientist if given adequate case circumstances	Sexual intercourse occurred
Level I	Source	Addresses the source of the sample	Scientist	Semen on vaginal swab
Sub-level I	Sub-source	With low amounts of DNA, the scientist may not be able to infer how the DNA arrived at the site where the DNA sample was collected	Scientist	DNA profile produced from swabbing a surface containing only a few cells

where it is not possible to attribute the resultant profile to a particular body fluid source. This situation, which exists with touch DNA and low-level DNA analysis, is termed a sub-level I (Evett et al. 2000b, Gill 2001). Effectively the DNA result needs to be considered in isolation without tying it to a body fluid source. Also, contamination via transfer or persistence of DNA on the swabbed surface prior to the crime event may need to be considered in sub-level I situations.

Examples of scenarios being addressed at the various hierarchies of propositions are shown below with contrasting hypotheses:

Level III (Offense):
  1. The suspect raped the victim
  2. Some other man raped the victim
Level II (Activity):
  1. The suspect had sexual intercourse with the complainant
  2. Some other man had sexual intercourse with the complainant
Level I (Source):
  1. Recovered semen came from the suspect
  2. Recovered semen came from another man
Sub-level I (DNA observed):
  1. DNA profile came from the suspect
  2. DNA profile came from another man

As sensitivity of DNA typing improves, laboratories' abilities to examine smaller samples increases. This improved sensitivity is a two-edged sword. With greater capabilities comes greater responsibilities to report meaningful results. Given the possibility of DNA contamination and secondary or even tertiary transfer in some instances (see next section), does the presence of a single cell (or even a few cells) in an evidentiary sample truly have meaning? The answer may depend on the case context. However, in a world prone to rely heavily on DNA results, the forensic DNA community needs to be concerned with how low-level DNA results might be misunderstood or even misused.

Limitations exist with how much information can be gleaned from a DNA match. As pointed out by Chris Duby: "A lab report can only tell us that a particular sample was found at a particular location. No scientist can tell us *how* it got there or for *how long* it was there. If time is a critical element of your defense, this issue must be explored" (CD).

Contamination

Whenever Q–K comparisons are made and conclusions drawn from these comparisons, other factors need to be considered such as the potential for physical contamination of the evidence or psychological contamination of the conclusions drawn from the evidence. If additional DNA material not associated with the crime is deposited after the crime event being studied, then the final interpretation and conclusions may not address the desired question. Likewise, if the data analysis and comparison are impacted by cognitive biases, the reported conclusions may be adversely affected.

Potential for DNA Contamination via Transfer

Working with the lower amounts of DNA that can now be successfully analyzed due to improved assay sensitivity is a double-edged sword when it comes to DNA interpretation. Not only are results more susceptible to contamination, results from low template DNA are more challenging to interpret and often may not be probative or lack meaning. Thus, low template DNA results especially from touch evidence situations may not be capable of producing strong conclusions. Peter Gill, a pioneer in developing low template DNA techniques, noted in a *New Scientist* interview, "I think that when we're dealing with very low levels of DNA we need to report that a DNA profile matches, but as to how and when it got there we just don't know" (Geddes 2012).

In a 2002 article, Keith Inman and Norah Rudin discuss "the origin of evidence" where they review six fundamental concepts: transfer, identification, individualization, association between source and target, reconstruction, and the idea that matter must divide before it can be transferred (Inman & Rudin 2002). Since DNA results can be successfully obtained from only a few cells thanks to improved assay sensitivity, concerns exist regarding the potential for transfer of cells between an individual and an object or another person, which is commonly referred to as *primary transfer*. When DNA that has been deposited on an item or a person is, in turn, transferred to another item or person or onto a different place on the same item or person, this is referred to as *secondary transfer* (Goray et al. 2010a). In other words, can a DNA profile be obtained from collected cells that were transferred through a second contact rather than the primary contact from the original source? As noted by Mariya Goray and colleagues, a biological sample that has been transferred multiple times, if it can even be detected, will most often appear as a component in a DNA mixture (Goray et al. 2010a).

Figure 16.2 illustrates primary, secondary, and tertiary levels of transfer. With primary transfer, a donor sheds (biological) material on an item. For example, a burglar might cut himself on a broken window and leave a blood stain. Secondary transfer can occur if trace material from a primary deposition is transferred to another surface. Continuing the example from above, if the home owner upon

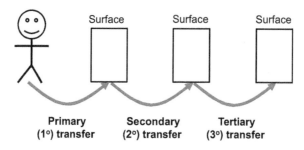

FIGURE 16.2 Illustration of transfer levels. Primary transfer is sometimes referred to as direct transfer while secondary or tertiary transfer are indirect transfer. Surfaces can also be other people. Studies have shown that the likelihood of significant DNA material being transferred decreases with each transfer and is highly dependent on the type of surface and the environmental conditions.

discovering the break-in touches the burglar's blood stain before it is fully dry and picks up some of the burglar's blood on his (the home owner's) hands, then this is secondary transfer. If the home owner then touches another surface, such as a towel, then the burglar's bloodstain may be transferred to the towel, which is now a tertiary transfer. In this example, the extent of secondary and tertiary transfer will be highly dependent on whether or not the initial bloodstain is still wet when first touched by the home owner.

A number of studies regarding the potential for DNA contamination to occur due to transfer are included in the reference list at the back of the chapter. Readers are also referred to review articles on the topic (Meakin & Jamieson 2013, van Oorschot et al. 2010, Wickenheiser 2002). The possibility of primary DNA deposits by first responders or laboratory personnel is an important reason why protective clothing and gloves are worn and staff elimination databases are used.

Research studies have shown that the amount of secondary transfer is highly dependent on the surface texture and sample moisture. Porous substances and/or dry samples provided on average less than 0.36% of the original biological material being transferred (Goray et al. 2010a). In this same study, moist samples and nonabsorbent surfaces, such as plastic, produced transfer rates of 50—95% while moist samples with absorbent surfaces, such as cotton or wool, transferred on average 2%—and only 5% when friction was applied (Goray et al. 2010a). While it has been demonstrated that secondary transfer of DNA can occur, whether or not it is plausible in a particular case will be dependent on a variety of factors including the surface texture and sample moisture (e.g. a fresh bloodstain versus an older bloodstain).

DNA transfer during autopsies was investigated in two German Institutes of Legal Medicine (Schwark et al. 2012). A DNA transfer was observed in four out of six cases investigated, showing the importance of careful cleaning between autopsies with bleach to avoid DNA contamination. This study notes that trace analysis results on homicide victims should only be reported after potential contamination in the mortuary has been ruled out (Schwark et al. 2012).

Peter Wiegand and colleagues at several Institutes of Legal Medicine in Germany examined 288 dried blood and saliva stains and showed through DNA quanititation that only small amounts of DNA were transferred. They observed 17% of 192 direct transfers produced DNA amounts in excess of 10 pg/µL. With 96 secondary transfers, only 3% had DNA quantities above 10 pg/µL (Wiegand et al. 2011). Others have proposed the development of likelihood ratio formulas that incorporate transfer probabilities (Taroni et al. 2012). For these types of calculations to be performed, additional studies with wet and dry biological materials studied on different surfaces will likely be needed (Goray et al. 2010a).

Occasionally contamination may produce results that prevent meaningful conclusions being able to be drawn from the evidentiary samples. For example, if there are results that appear to contain exogenous DNA from a staff member due to inadvertent contamination, then this observation needs to be included in the case report as an explanation for why no meaningful conclusions can be obtained from the evidence.

Dealing with Exogenous DNA Contamination

In their 2012 protocol for forensic STR analysis, the New York City Office of Chief Medical Examiner's Forensic Biology Laboratory defines exogenous DNA as the addition of DNA or biological fluid to evidence or controls subsequent to the crime (NYC OCME 2012). If during the casework evaluation it is noted that the evidentiary sample appears to contain DNA consistent with a crime scene investigator or laboratory staff, then the summary section of their report states, "The [sample] will not be used for comparison because it appears to contain DNA consistent with a {NYPD member, OCME [laboratory] member, medical responder}" (NYC OCME 2012). While names for potential sources of the exogenous DNA are not included in the report, case notes related to the event are retained in the case file for review as needed.

Having a staff elimination database against which evidence results are checked is critical to being able to detect exogenous DNA contamination from staff members. Training is crucial to reduce and even eliminate inadvertent contamination. A detective commented: "For me, training is one of the big things when you go to a crime scene because you should be worried about the potential for cross-contamination. I want to know what not to do. You do not want to put your DNA all over the place [at the crime scene]. I think hearing from the lab about the challenges that they have, knowing what their challenges are, help us understand what we need to do better [in terms of crime scene collection to avoid contamination]" (MoCo). Increased sensitivity of DNA testing procedures can make contamination detection more common. Greater vigilance on the part of everyone involved with sample collection and processing is necessary.

Psychological Contamination: Potential Contextual or Observer Bias

While concerns regarding potential physical contamination are well-known and appreciated, observer bias has been raised as another source of potentially clouding the ability to draw a correct conclusion (e.g. Saks et al. 2003). Itiel Dror, in a 2012 letter to the editor of the *Journal of Forensic Sciences*, emphasizes that steps must be taken to minimize what he called "cognitive and psychological contamination" of the interpretation process just as laboratories and forensic scientists work hard to minimize physical contamination of evidence (Dror 2012). Will a scientist run the risk of "applying tunnel vision in seeing only those signs that further support her first explanation while ignoring, or not searching for, those signs that would point away from the first explanation" (Jackson 2009)?

The February 2009 National Academy of Sciences report in recommendation #5 encouraged "research programs on human observer bias and sources of human error in forensic examinations" (NAS 2009). The NAS report specifically mentioned "studies to determine the effects of contextual bias in forensic practice (e.g. studies to determine whether and to what extent the results of forensic analyses are influenced by knowledge regarding the background of the suspect and the investigator's theory of the case)."

II. STATISTICAL INTERPRETATION

To help guarantee the Q-before-K order of conducting forensic evidence interpretation, calls have been made for what is referred to as "sequential unmasking" to prevent potential observer bias (D.N.A. Box 16.3). However, what are often good theoretical ideas may not always work well in a practical sense within a laboratory environment. Nevertheless, concern with observer bias has been expressed with fingerprint comparisons (Dror et al. 2011) as well as with DNA mixture results (Dror & Hampikian 2011). Likewise, concerns that suspect-bias can exist during DNA mixture interpretation have been raised using the Texas sharpshooter analogy where a target is painted around an arrow or a bullethole after the shot has been fired (Thompson 2009).

Efforts need to be made within a laboratory to promote good science in Q–K comparisons in order to appropriately support data obtained. Cecelia Crouse makes an important observation: "It is important that an analyst who has deemed that a profile cannot be interpreted is secure in this conclusion and does not capitulate to the potential pressures to use the profile for comparison during meetings, depositions or testimony" (CC).

Potential Impact of Technology

Advances in technology have the potential to limit the perceptions and thought processes of analysts. Itiel Dror notes, in a March 2013 letter to the editor of the *Journal of Forensic Sciences*, that global positioning systems and electronic maps available on smart phones have led to a decline in the cognitive ability to read and use physical maps to provide directions (Dror 2013). Likewise, the Automated Fingerprint Identification System (AFIS) enables rapid computer searching of numerous fingerprints but, Dror opines, at the expense of fingerprint examiners developing their expertise through experience and exposure to manual evaluation of thousands of fingerprints (Dror 2013). It is certainly possible that automation and availability of commercial kits to aid the STR typing process has dulled analysts' DNA interpretation senses in much the same way. Therefore, it is imperative that training be provided to analysts to keep up their analytical and interpretative skills so that

---

D.N.A. BOX 16.3

SEQUENTIAL UNMASKING

A letter to the editor appeared in the July 2008 issue of the *Journal of Forensic Sciences* authored by 11 (mostly academic) individuals that introduced a concept known as "sequential unmasking" (Krane et al. 2008). This letter was based on discussions held by the authors in a December 2007 gathering regarding potential ways to minimize implications of observer effects in forensic DNA testing. The primary concept of sequential unmasking is to limit case information that bench analysts have when they interpret an evidentiary DNA profile. Case information including DNA profiles from known reference samples would be sequentially made available (or unmasked) to the bench analyst from a case manager only after evidentiary samples are fully interpreted to prevent potential observer bias during the evidentiary profile interpretation. The authors suggest that laboratory documentation be performed for (1) determining the alleles associated with each sample, (2) assessing the number of contributors, and (3) assessing the likelihood that the test procedure

---

failed to detect some of the alleles of contributors prior to comparing the reference samples from potential suspects. Minus the suggested enforcement of not having access to reference profile data until the end, the three steps proposed are essentially the same steps noted by the Forensic Science Service in their January 1998 article on mixture interpretation (Clayton et al. 1998) and endorsed by the International Society of Forensic Genetics DNA Commission in their 2006 mixture interpretation recommendations (Gill et al. 2006).

The concept of performing evidence sample interpretation prior to known sample(s) comparison is not a new one and is emphasized in the 2010 SWGDAM guidelines section 3.6.1 (SWGDAM 2010). However, the sequential unmasking letter goes further and suggests formally managing the flow of information within a laboratory to minimize observer effects. Over the ensuing years, several commentaries and author responses were published in the *Journal of Forensic Sciences*.

Jeff Wells, a West Virginia University biology professor, notes in his commentary on the 2008 sequential unmasking letter to the editor: "…judging by their letter, the incidence of such bias is unknown. It appears that we do not know that there is a problem, and if Krane et al.'s recommended policies were adopted, we would not know whether or not any good had been done." Wells goes on to state that "there has been little effort to systematically survey subjective decisions by forensic DNA analysts." He concludes: "The authors are to be commended for the careful thought they have brought to this issue, but I hope that compelling theory does not distract us from the need for empirical data" (Wells 2009).

Brent Ostrum, a Canadian forensic document examiner, in a follow-up letter to the editor reviews the studies cited by Krane et al. and notes that upon review he finds them incomplete and inconclusive at best. He advocates for "well-designed research studies aimed at gaining a better understanding of the situation." Mr. Ostrum concludes: "The implementation of any solution before the 'problem' is fully understood is not a good idea. That approach may well result in new and unanticipated issues that end up being worse than the original concern. *Let us do the research and understand the situation more fully before we begin 'fixing' things that may or may not need to be fixed*" (Ostrum 2009).

One DNA analyst expressed his thoughts to me on sequential unmasking with an analogy for a visit to the doctor. He asked me, "Would you go to the doctor when you are not feeling well and say, 'Tell me what is wrong with me, doc' without providing some indication of where you may be feeling pain?" Some information will always be needed to provide context and relevance to the DNA testing being performed. John Thornton writes in a 2010 letter to the editor on this topic, "Whatever the best mechanism is for quelling contextual bias, it would not seem to reside in depriving the forensic worker of full information concerning a case, the 'working blind' approach" (Thornton 2010). While recognizing that observer effects may happen, more research in this area will certainly be beneficial as suggested by the National Academy of Sciences 2009 report recommendation #5 (NAS 2009).

It is worth noting that the entire debate in the literature so far over sequential unmasking has been conducted through letters to the editor, opinion pieces, or encyclopedia chapters without direct data from a peer-reviewed research study showing the benefit of the authors' theory in real-world application. In spite of more than 5 years passing since the "need" for sequential unmasking has been unveiled, the original 11 authors have yet to produce *any* research data supporting their initial claims that "sequential unmasking is the most efficacious means of reducing the compromising influence of observer effects on the utility of forensic DNA evidence" (Krane et al. 2008). While some observer effects and bias may exist in forensic DNA interpretation, simply repeatedly citing a 2008 letter to the editor does not make sequential unmasking an appropriate scientific solution.

Sources: see reference list in back of chapter under topic of "Sequential Unmasking."

expertise can be developed and maintained in drawing accurate and reliable scientific conclusions. Training must be in both methodology and in interpretation.

Finally, analysts need to keep in mind that using common sense and not losing track of the big picture can be just as important when drawing conclusions as paying attention to the small details. Increased sensitivity with DNA technology provides new challenges in terms of making meaningful conclusions when results are obtained. Sheila Willis, director of the Forensic Science Laboratory in Ireland, writes that forensic scientists need to "remain mindful of the thresholds of reliability and the significance of their findings in the context of the case" along with accurately "communicating their findings to a range of stakeholders" (Willis 2009).

REPORT WRITING

A laboratory report is a written communication regarding results obtained from a specific examination of submitted evidence samples. If known reference samples have been provided for comparison purposes, then report conclusions may include appropriate weight-of-evidence statistical calculations. Following completion of laboratory work and subsequent statistical calculations, the laboratory report is prepared in order to summarize and characterize the work performed (Figure 16.3).

During the course of their sample examinations, laboratories typically prepare a case folder/file containing notes describing work performed and locations of computer files with the underlying

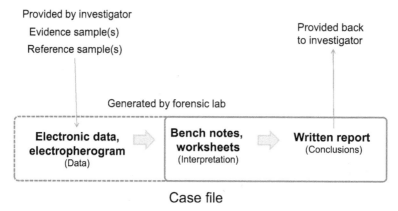

FIGURE 16.3   An investigator supplies evidence and reference samples to a forensic laboratory for testing. Following the DNA testing process, the laboratory provides the investigator with a summary of results in the form of a written report. This report is based on sample electropherogram data, bench notes, and worksheets created during data interpretation, and conclusions drawn from evaluation of the evidence results and comparisons to reference sample(s) where suitable. While the written report is the primary means of communicating results obtained, electronic data and bench notes are often requested by the defense during discovery in order to evaluate information underlying the report conclusions. As specialized software is required to view the electronic data, these data are not always requested during discovery nor can laboratories give away their licensed software to enable the review (dotted outline of box). Electropherogram print-outs can be sufficient in many cases if plots are made displaying the y-axis on a relevant scale (e.g. plotting the y-axis on a scale of 0–50 or 100 relative fluorescence units for negative controls to enable an examination of the baseline signal).

electronic data. Often printouts of electropherograms and other pertinent information are present in the case folder along with the bench notes. Assumptions and calculations performed to assess the weight-of-evidence are usually also included in the case folder. When defense discovery requests are made, the entire case file may be evaluated to assess the basis for conclusions stated in the written report. Good record keeping and organizational skills will aid in preparing an excellent case file and final report.

Communication

In reviewing his own experience at the time of more than 25 years with interpreting forensic evidence, British statistician Ian Evett states: "For too many years, forensic scientists have taken too much for granted in relation to the powers of comprehension of nonscientists. Arriving at a flawless evaluation of the evidence is not much use unless we can convey that evaluation effectively…" (Evett 1991).

Cecelia Crouse comments that "once DNA profiles have been obtained, reviewed and documented, the most significant challenge with the interpretation of the profiles generated from casework evidence is to articulate substantiated results in an intelligible report" (CC). The Palm Beach County Sheriff's Office Crime Laboratory has tried to tackle this challenge through use of some 70 automatic text templates designed to provide uniform report writing across analysts. These templates encompass evidence handling, serology, single-source samples, mixture profiles, intimate profile deduction, CODIS statements, outsourcing samples, and statistics results (CC). Because these auto text templates do not cover every possibility, "boutique" statements may sometimes be designed to clarify a DNA profile result so that the reader has a clear understanding of the results (CC).

Effective communication is crucial with case reports. A great deal of work goes into generating data underlying the information being reported and this information needs to be communicated effectively to future users of the report. Ian Evett has said this succinctly: "Good ideas are worthless if they are not presented in terms which are suitable for the recipient audience" (Evett 1991). Findings from submitted evidence and the associated uncertainty with these results are essential for report users to understand as important decisions are often made from the report conclusions.

In some situations, the conclusion statement of a report may be all that is initially read. Thus, the conclusions should be clearly conveyed to the customer(s) of a written report. A major challenge, as will be discussed below, is that there can be multiple customers or consumers of a forensic case report who are often trying to glean information for different purposes from the written report.

Since the vast majority of report users will not be scientists, reports should avoid jargon and define technical terms used. Researchers from the University of Tasmania in Australia studied the readability of 111 report conclusions from a forensic glass analysis proficiency test (Howes et al. 2013). This study found that conclusions were "written at an average grade level of 13, suggesting that some university education would be necessary to read them with ease" (Howes et al. 2013). Clearly, reports need to be accessible to nonscientists such as police investigators, lawyers, and judges — individuals who cannot be expected to be proficient with scientific terminology. Based on their study (Howes et al. 2013), the Australian researchers provide 10 suggestions to improve report readability (Table 16.3).

Clear communications make up an important section of the American Society of Crime Laboratory Directors Laboratory Accreditation Board (ASCLD/LAB) Guiding Principles (ASCLD/LAB 2014).

TABLE 16.3   Ten Suggestions to Improve the Readability of Case Report Conclusions for Nonscientific Readers

1	Keep in mind a nonscientific reader. Try to use both long and short sentences and avoid overuse of the passive voice. Aim for a Grade 7 to Grade 9 reading level.
2	Provide a sentence outlining the context or purpose at the beginning to let the reader know what was done and why.
3	To refer to the items compared, use descriptive terms followed by item numbers in parentheses.
4	Provide definitions or explanations within the text for necessary unusual or scientific terms. Avoid the use of acronyms and abbreviations.
5	Use parallel sentence structures to report positive and negative findings and inferences.
6	Write about findings and inferences in separate sentences.
7	Introduce inferences with a link to findings.
8	When making an inference about a possible common origin, state explicitly that an individual source cannot be determined (if this is the case).
9	When giving support for a proposition, state explicitly the information upon which the support is based (i.e. what are the assumptions being made?).
10	When using a conclusion scale to convey the degree of support for a proposition, provide the scale and state explicitly the basis for the scale (e.g. D.N.A. Box 16.2). If it is a subjective conclusion scale, make this clear.

Source: Adapted from Howes et al. (2013).

These guiding principles principles emphasize that ethical and professionally responsible forensic scientists will (among other things) "present accurate and complete data in reports, testimony, publications and oral presentations" (¶14), prepare reports "in which facts, opinions and interpretations are clearly distinguishable, and which clearly describe limitations on the methods, interpretations and opinions presented" (¶15), and "not alter reports or other records, or withhold information from reports for strategic or tactical litigation advantage" (¶16).

In a National Forensic Science Technology Center (NFSTC) training module on communication skills, Professor Ronald Hill shares that "most professionals (other than writers) believe that writing is a means to an end rather than a skill to be developed and perfected over time. As a result, we only engage in technical writing when necessary" (Hill 2005). Professor Hill advises that report writers should "begin with the takeaway — what is it that you want your audience to remember when they finish your report?" (Hill 2005). He emphasizes that "apart from the formatting restraints of the Quality Assurance Standards and laboratory procedures, the written report is the only communication method that is entirely under your control" (Hill 2005).

Regular meetings regarding case investigations benefit communication between those preparing reports and those using them. Formal, regular investigative case meetings was a primary conclusion of an Australian study (Kelty et al. 2013). This study, which involved interviews with 103 police, forensic scientists, lawyers, judges, coroners, pathologists, and forensic physicians, noted that practitioners benefited from understanding the bigger picture in a case and seeing where their analyses fit or conflicted with the investigation's direction. Of course, having more case details can potentially lead to contextual bias (Kassin et al. 2013). Thus, the Australian study made five recommendations for improving interagency communication, including becoming more knowledgeable of contextual bias, social influence, conformity, and groupthink (Kelty et al. 2013).

II. STATISTICAL INTERPRETATION

Reports need to communicate results clearly and effectively when they are written and even long into the future. Charlotte Word summarizes: "There should be no bias in the reporting of scientific data. DNA test reports may have a very broad audience and may be read over many, many years by a number of different individuals asking many different questions. The report should be thorough with all information regarding the testing being presented accurately whether it seems relevant to the question at hand or not. It may be valuable for the analyst and technical reviewer to 'take a step back' and evaluate the case and report from a different perspective (e.g. as a consultant to a judge, or reviewing the case for the defendant vs. the prosecution) and determine if there is information that is not being reported that could be beneficial to that perspective" (CW).

Defining the audience and writing the report to the appropriate level can be challenging because as will be discussed in the next section there is often more than a single user of a lab report.

The Primary Audience for a Lab Report

Whenever information is shared through written communication, understanding who will be reading the written material is crucial to writing well. A report writer needs to consider questions such as: *What is the education and understanding level of the intended reader? Should more detail be included or will the reader have access to original case notes, laboratory standard operating procedures, etc.? Will specific terms and phrases be understood?*

Handling the competing interests of different consumers of a laboratory report can be challenging. Below is part of the conversation held with a prosecutor and a detective (MoCo):

Author: What are you looking for in a DNA report? How do you dissect it? How do you start looking at it?

Prosecutor: From [the prosecutor's] stand point, the first thing that we always do is look for the conclusions and the charts in telling us whether it's a mixture, whether it is single-source, how many different people are in the mixture, etc. Then after reading the conclusions we always go back and look at each individual result.

Detective: I know for me and probably [the other detectives] a lot of that stuff goes right over my head — all this code stuff and all these numbers. *Just give me who it is.*

As might be expected, responses to the question of who is the primary audience for a laboratory report vary based on one's perspective and role in the criminal justice process. Below are some of the responses received from the written interviews conducted:

"*The primary audience is easy — whoever the client is who requested the work be done. However, what makes report writing so difficult is that there are a number of equally important individuals who may read the forensic report. Unlike the client who requested the testing, these individuals may not have access to the laboratory staff to get help with interpreting the report and understanding what work was performed in a case. However, the jobs they have to do may well rely on them understanding and interpreting the report correctly. These individuals include detectives and investigators, prosecuting attorney(s), the victim and/or the victim's family, the defense attorney, the defendant and family, expert witnesses consulting for either the prosecutor or defense attorney, members of the jury, staff from a laboratory asked to do additional testing in a case, judges, appellate attorneys, post-conviction attorneys — and the list goes on. The reports may be read close in time to their reporting or may be read many years later." (CW)*

II. STATISTICAL INTERPRETATION

A lab director (MP) comments: "In cases with no arrest, the primary audience is the investigating agency. After an arrest has been made, both the prosecutor and the defense attorney are the most important recipients." A defense attorney (CD) notes: "An overwhelming number of criminal cases resolve by way of a defendant agreeing to plead guilty. However, that possibility only exists against the backdrop of what could happen at trial. So all matters of evidence are looked at through that prism. I believe a jury is the primary audience for all evidence."

From the technical leader of a private lab (TM): "The report will end up in the hands of many people, so it is difficult to say who the primary audience is. Ideally, the perfect report is understandable to the individual responsible for presenting results to the trier of fact (the jury) such that with additional consultation and education from the lab it can be looked at multiple times and serve as a reference as well as a learning tool (for that case and future cases). A second audience for the report is the laboratory that produces the report. We regard the report as the complete 'diary' of how a case was handled and all reports are archived in one location for retrospective reviews of all cases and trends."

From an independent consultant (NR): "A forensic lab report must satisfy several different audiences, that is the challenge. The practice of writing highly abbreviated reports, using the justification that the prosecutor is the primary audience, is scientifically indefensible. While, because of the context in which we work, the necessity exists to provide a summary for the lay reader, that does not preclude providing more complete and more technical information in the body of the report that is aimed at a peer or colleague. Even if an attorney does not understand all of the technical information, he may understand enough to realize that he should consult an expert (either the primary analyst or an independent expert) to help clarify the meaning of the results."

Regardless of who the initial audience is for a laboratory report there can be secondary readers who need to understand the information contained in a report. Thus, it is imperative that the report be thorough in describing the testing performed and results obtained. The next section will cover essential elements that should be included in a laboratory report involving DNA testing.

Essential Elements of a Lab Report

Jules Epstein, a professor at the Widener University School of Law, notes in an entry on forensic laboratory reports for the *Encyclopedia of Forensic Sciences*: "There is no precise formula, dictated by law or science, as to what a forensic laboratory report must contain when it reports test results or analysis outcomes" (Epstein 2013). At a minimum, lab reports should contain information regarding the evidence received, what was done with the evidence, and any conclusions reached.

In one of their *CAC News* "Proceedings of Lunch" articles, Norah Rudin and Keith Inman discussed laboratory reports with Greg Matheson, who served for a number of years as the Los Angeles Crime Laboratory Director (Rudin & Inman 2013a). Matheson commented that early in his career as a criminalist he believed that a report just needed to express the final conclusion. However, with greater experience, he feels that more explanation in a report makes court testimony easier and improves the capability of the report to stand on its own if the case does not go to court. Ted Hunt concurs: "A laboratory report should be able to stand on its own to the extent that the primary consumers of the lab's product (police officers and attorneys) can both understand the report's conclusions and the process whereby those conclusions were generated in the analyst's absence" (TH).

The International Organization for Standardization (ISO) has defined requirements for what should be included in test reports in their ISO 17025 international standard entitled "General requirements for the competence of testing and calibration laboratories" (ISO 2005). ISO 17025 Standard 5.10

D.N.A. BOX 16.4

ISO 17025 REQUIREMENTS FOR REPORTING RESULTS

The International Organization for Standardization (ISO) is based in Geneva, Switzerland and is the world's largest developer of voluntary international documentary standards. Since the inception of ISO in 1947, more than 19,500 documentary standards covering all aspects of technology and business have been developed and published. These documentary standards are created by technical committees involving experts in a specific field that first create draft standards followed by review from ISO members who provide feedback and finally vote to accept a revised consensus document. The most widely used ISO document in the forensic science community is ISO 17025, which was first published in 1999 and then revised in 2005. ISO 17025 covers "general requirements for the competence of testing and calibration laboratories" and consists of five primary sections: (1) scope, (2) referenced documents, (3) terms and definitions, (4) management requirements, and (5) technical requirements.

According to Section 5.10 of ISO 17025, which covers requirements for reporting results of tests or calibrations, results need to be reported accurately, clearly, unambiguously, and objectively. These results must also be gathered in accordance with specific instructions or requirements of the specific test method being performed. Standard 5.10.2 requires that each test report include (1) a title, (2) the name and address of the laboratory where the tests were performed, (3) unique identification of the test report, (4) name and address of the customer, (5) identification of the method used, (6) a description of, condition of, and clear identification of the items tested, (7) date(s) that the tested items were received and tested, (8) reference to the sampling plan and procedures used, (9) the test results with units of measurement where appropriate, (10) the name(s), function(s) and signature(s) of person(s) authorizing the test report, and (11) where relevant, a statement to the effect that the results relate only to the items tested.

Laboratories following ISO 17025 need to document the basis (i.e. assumptions) upon which opinions and interpretations are made (Section 5.10.5). Note 3 under Section 5.10.5 suggests that it can be "appropriate to communicate opinions and interpretations by direct dialogue with the customer" and that "such dialogue should be written down." In terms of report format, Section 5.10.8 requires that the format "be designed to accommodate each type of test or calibration carried out and to minimize the possibility of misunderstanding or misuse."

In April 2004, the American Society of Crime Laboratory Directors/Laboratory Accreditation Board (ASCLD/LAB) adopted ISO 17025 standards as part of their "International" accreditation program. Another accreditation body, FQS, has accredited forensic labs to the ISO 17025 standards since 2001.

Sources: http://www.iso.org; http://www.ascld-lab.org/; http://fqsforensics.org/.

discusses how results should be reported (D.N.A. Box 16.4). During accreditation assessments, forensic DNA laboratories in the United States are also evaluated regarding compliance with the FBI Quality Assurance Standards (QAS) (QAS 2011). Section 11 of the QAS describes requirements for laboratory reports (D.N.A. Box 16.5).

D.N.A. BOX 16.5

FBI QUALITY ASSURANCE STANDARDS (QAS) FOR FORENSIC DNA TESTING LABORATORIES SECTION 11 ON REPORTS

Forensic DNA laboratories in the United States are audited against one of two sets of FBI Quality Assurance Standards (QAS) depending on whether the lab performs forensic casework or DNA databasing work. The QAS documents and audit questions, which are prepared by the Scientific Working Group on DNA Analysis Methods (SWGDAM), are available on the FBI CODIS website at http://www.fbi.gov/about-us/lab/biometric-analysis/codis. Information contained in Section 11 of the QAS for forensic DNA testing laboratories is included below as it pertains to report writing and record keeping.

11. Reports

Standard 11.1 The laboratory shall have and follow written procedures for taking and maintaining casework notes to support the conclusions drawn in laboratory reports. The laboratory shall maintain all analytical documentation generated by analysts related to case analyses. The laboratory shall retain, in hard or electronic format, sufficient documentation for each technical analysis to support the report conclusions such that another qualified individual could evaluate and interpret the data.

Standard 11.2 Casework reports shall include the following elements:

    11.2.1 Case identifier;

11.2.2 Description of evidence examined;

11.2.3 A description of the technology;

11.2.4 Locus or amplification system;

11.2.5 Results and/or conclusions;

11.2.6 A quantitative or qualitative interpretative statement;

11.2.7 Date issued;

11.2.8 Disposition of evidence; and

11.2.9 A signature and title, or equivalent identification, of the person accepting responsibility for the content of the report.

Standard 11.3 Except as otherwise provided by state or federal law, reports, case files, DNA records and databases shall be confidential.

11.3.1 The laboratory shall have and follow written procedures to ensure the privacy of the reports, case files, DNA records and databases.

11.3.2 The laboratory shall have and follow written procedures for the release of reports, case files, DNA records and databases in accordance with applicable state or federal law.

11.3.3 Personally identifiable information shall only be released in accordance with applicable state and federal law.

Source: FBI (9-1-2011). Quality assurance standards for forensic DNA testing laboratories. Available at http://www.swgdam.org/docs.html or http://www.fbi.gov/about-us/lab/biometric-analysis/codis.

Table 16.4 compares the two sets of requirements from ISO 17025 and QAS (2011). Note that the required elements for scientific reports are quite similar with regard to the basic administrative information, such as report title and lab name. QAS Standard 11 provides further guidance in terms of forensic DNA needs, such as locus or amplification system and disposition of evidence.

II. STATISTICAL INTERPRETATION

TABLE 16.4 Comparison of ISO 17025:2005 and FBI Quality Assurance Standards (QAS) 2011 Requirements for Reports

ISO 17025:2005 Standard 5.10.2 Requirements	QAS (2011) Standard 11.2 Required Elements
1. Title for test report	—
2. Name and address of lab performing work	—
3. Unique identification of the test report	11.2.1 Case identifier
4. Name and address of the customer	—
5. Identification of the method used	11.2.3 A description of the technology 11.2.4 Locus or amplification system
6. A description of, condition of, and clear identification of the items tested	11.2.2 Description of evidence examined
7. Date(s) that the tested items were received and tested	—
8. Reference to the sampling plan and procedures used	—
9. The test results with units of measurement where appropriate	11.2.5 Results and/or conclusions 11.2.6 A quantitative or qualitative interpretative statement
—	11.2.7 Date report is issued
—	11.2.8 Disposition of evidence
10. The name(s), function(s) and signature(s) of person(s) authorizing the test report	11.2.9 A signature and title, or equivalent identification, of the person accepting responsibility for the content of the report
11. Where relevant, a statement to the effect that the results relate only to the items tested	—

Norah Rudin lists the following as critical elements of lab reports: (1) a statement of purpose, (2) list and description of evidence received, (3) summary for the lay person, (4) a brief description of analytical methods used [noting that long boiler plate descriptions containing irrelevant material should be avoided], (5) complete description of results, (6) table of alleles, (7) conclusions spelling out any assumptions made and including the limitations of the test and of the evidence, and (8) printed legible names as well as signatures of the primary analyst and the technical reviewer (NR).

A few of the perspectives provided to me include: "The lab report should be a story of what happened to the evidence" (BH). "A lab report must convey what I call the 'tombstone data' which are the case related facts and identifiers, what analyses have been conducted and the results and conclusions" (RW). "I would say transparency is a critical element! The receiver of the report should hold in their hands a document that clearly shows what has been investigated (or not)" (RA).

II. STATISTICAL INTERPRETATION

Charlotte Word comments: "I frequently hear laboratory analysts say 'there is information that I will wait and explain in court' rather than include in the report. However, since such a very small proportion of the reports that get written ever make it into court with live testimony where that information can be explained, I recommend that if it is important enough to tell in court to a judge or jury, then it probably needs to be in the report initially" (CW). She adds: "[Be] sure that all readers can correctly interpret and understand the report as written now and in the future without additional consultation" (CW).

The NAS (2009) report comments: "As a general matter, laboratory reports generated as the result of a scientific analysis should be complete and thorough. They should describe, at a minimum, methods and materials, procedures, results, and conclusions, and they should identify, as appropriate, the sources of uncertainty in the procedures and conclusions along with estimates of their scale (to indicate the level of confidence in the results). Although it is not appropriate and practicable to provide as much detail as might be expected in a research paper, sufficient content should be provided to allow the nonscientist reader to understand what has been done and permit informed, unbiased scrutiny of the conclusion" (NAS 2009).

It is important for lab reports to include information on all items tested. In a review of 15,419 serology laboratory files from the North Carolina State Bureau of Investigation covering the 16-year time period of January 1987 to January 2003, a total of 230 examples (1.5%) were found where negative or inconclusive test results to confirm the presence of blood were not part of a final laboratory report (Swecker & Wolf 2010). This discovery led to some bad press for the North Carolina crime laboratory and changes to their report writing procedures.

Language of a Laboratory Report

True application of the scientific method involves precision in both measurement and meaning. In other words, how results are communicated in reports is just as important as how the results are collected. As has already been stated, to be an effective communicator, you need to know and appreciate your audience. Prosecutor Ted Hunt comments: "Analysts need to be conscious of the fact that their reports are most often read and used by cops and attorneys, not other scientists" (TH).

Reports need to be written with words and phrases that are clearly understood—and just as important, are not misunderstood. To avoid misunderstandings it is "important to make consistent use of terminology that describes evidence samples, testing results, and interpretive conclusions" (TH). Another contributor adds: "Avoid the use of 'weasel words.' Focus the report on the evidence samples, not the submitted reference samples" (NR).

Bruce Heidebrecht shares that one of the biggest problems with report writing is "striking that balance of scientific correctness, readability of the report, and impact to the investigation. Some reports don't have enough science support for their conclusions, some are near impossible for the layman to read, and some leave the reader questioning the relation of the conclusions to the advancement of the investigation" (BH).

Charlotte Word comments that "having a meaningful, simple report that is accurate, neutral and thorough, and understandable by all readers is difficult to achieve" (CW). Of course, report readers will need to possess some kind of basic understanding of what they are reading in order for it to make sense (CD). Many of the terms will be unique to DNA testing and thus attaching a glossary of commonly used terms to a report can be helpful, an approach recommended by several chapter contributors.

Norah Rudin points out that phrases such as "consistent with" can be "too vague and are used deliberately to avoid committing to a more clear result" (NR). She also notes that "…to a scientific certainty…" or "…is the source…" are phrases that are "too definitive; they fail to allow for the uncertainty inherent in even the strongest result" (NR).

Standardized Terminology and Reporting

The 2009 National Academy of Sciences report emphasized the need to standardize and improve report writing (NAS 2009):

> "The terminology used in reporting and testifying about the results of forensic science investigations must be standardized. Many terms are used by forensic scientists in scientific reports and in court testimony that describe findings, conclusions, and degrees of association between evidentiary material (e.g., hairs, fingerprints, fibers) and particular people or objects. Such terms include, but are not limited to "match," "consistent with," "identical," "similar in all respects tested," and "cannot be excluded as the source of." The use of such terms can and does have a profound effect on how the trier of fact in a criminal or civil matter perceives and evaluates scientific evidence. Although some forensic science disciplines have proposed reporting vocabulary and scales, the use of the recommended language is not standard practice among forensic science practitioners.

> "As a general matter, laboratory reports generated as the result of a scientific analysis should be complete and thorough. They should contain, at minimum, "methods and materials," "procedures," "results," "conclusions," and, as appropriate, sources and magnitudes of uncertainty in the procedures and conclusions (e.g., levels of confidence). Some forensic science laboratory reports meet this standard of reporting, but many do not. Some reports contain only identifying and agency information, a brief description of the evidence being submitted, a brief description of the types of analysis requested, and a short statement of the results (e.g., "the greenish, brown plant material in item #1 was identified as marijuana"), and they include no mention of methods or any discussion of measurement uncertainties" (NAS 2009).

Charlotte Word comments: "I think the use of different terminology by different laboratories and in the field in general either in reports and/or in conversational language leads to some confusion and possible misrepresentation of the data in some circumstances. The word 'match' is problematic for me. I think it is a carryover from the RFLP days when a single-source DNA profile was reported to 'match' the profile of a known individual, which generally implied that the individual was the source of the DNA sample due to the exclusionary power of a five to six locus RFLP 'match.' Now it seems to mean anything from a single-locus inclusion in a mixed DNA profile to a full 15 locus single-source profile inclusion and *has the risk of implying a much stronger relationship of an individual to an evidence sample than the data may warrant*. It is common to hear law enforcement personnel, attorneys and even analysts say things like 'we got DNA on him,' or 'we have a match with DNA' when the value of the evidence or the inclusion may be very limited" (CW).

In a chapter included in the 2009 *Handbook of Forensic Science*, Graham Jackson, of the former UK Forensic Science Service, cited a 1989 study where a review of 100 case files from a single laboratory found 33 different expressions used to convey evidential strength (Jackson 2009). Jackson examined 16 different phrases often used in expressing opinions in reports or in court testimony. These phrases include "…match…," "…could have come from…," "…consistent with…," "…entirely consistent with…," "…cannot exclude…," and "…supports an assertion that…."

In his analysis of the word "match," Jackson concluded "recipients of an opinion expressed as a 'match' may translate that into meaning that the two 'matching' samples share the same origin. This would be different from the meaning that the scientist would want to convey, namely that the samples share the same attributes. So, even when scientists and laypeople use the same word, the meaning to these two sets of people can be quite different" (Jackson 2009). For this reason, the Swedish National Forensic Laboratory utilizes their verbal scale (see D.N.A. Box 16.2) for all reports, not just DNA results.

Some laboratories attach a glossary as an appendix to reports to enable readers to better understand specific terminology. In addition, posting standard operating procedures (SOPs) on the Internet aids transparency and information accessibility, particularly with discovery requests. Several laboratories, including the Virginia Department of Forensic Sciences and the New York City Office of Chief Medical Examiner Forensic Biology Laboratory, have their protocols available online.

Report Wording Suggestions

Some report wording suggestions for conclusions statements were prepared in January 2013 by a group of forensic DNA scientists (SWGDAM Mixture Committee 2013) and are available on the STRBase website (STRBase 2014).

This group felt that at a minimum conclusion statements should encompass the following eight areas: (1) any statements for quality of DNA profile obtained, (2) any statements for number of contributors, (3) any statements for gender of contributors, (4) any statements for assumed known references, (5) any statements for resolution into contributor components, (6) any statements for inclusion/nonexclusion, including statistical support of probative statements, (7) any statements of exclusion, and (8) any inconclusive statements, including a reason for such. Several examples of conclusions for given scenarios are also included in this report wording suggestions document (SWGDAM Mixture Committee 2013).

Training Analysts to Write and Review Lab Reports

Learning to write and review lab reports is an essential part of a DNA analyst's training. According to the FBI QAS definitions, an analyst is an employee or contract employee, who has (1) successfully completed the laboratory's training requirements for casework sample analysis, (2) passed a competency test, and (3) has entered into a proficiency testing program. An analyst conducts and/or directs analysis of forensic samples, interprets data, and reaches conclusions (QAS 2011). Section 11 in the QAS covers the topic of reports while section 12 discusses review of reports (QAS 2011).

Becoming proficient in writing and reviewing reports requires what one contributor succinctly summarized as "exposure and practice" (BH). Prosecutor Ted Hunt notes: "DNA analysts should be trained to prepare reports with the reader/user in mind. It would certainly make no sense for a business to make a product that its customers can't use. The same is true for the authors of forensic DNA reports" (TH). Norah Rudin offers her perspective that "[analysts] should be taught to write a forensic report like a regular scientific report. It should contain all the same information. So in other words, forensic scientists should be trained to be scientists" (NR).

Most laboratories are using some kind of standard template to produce their reports. This practice saves time and prevents analysts from having to reformulate every conclusion. However, learning to write useful reports requires more than just reading a few previously written reports. The following suggestions regarding training were provided by the chapter contributors:

1. Exposure to reports from different agencies to gain a broader perspective and speaking to report users to better understand their needs

"Exposure to a variety of reports from different agencies helps with providing a broader perspective. Speaking with investigators and other users of our reports helps understanding of what information is clear and what needs improvement. Writing reports using established templates and protocols is useful, as well as obtaining practice in practical exercise and moot court discussing and defending the report and findings" (RW).

"Even with protocols and guidelines, multiple analysts from the same lab are likely to have some differences in how they write their reports. New analysts should have the opportunity to be exposed to several different experienced analysts' writing styles before writing their own reports. It is also important to have access to previously generated reports that needed unique wording since not every quirk of casework can be anticipated during training" (BH).

2. Practice with well-written reports and be mentored by experienced analysts

"Practice, practice and more practice. Having a well-structured and thorough SOP and access to well-written reports during training is important. Careful training and mentoring by experienced analysts is a must. Also, paying attention to the questions that come back via phone calls, interviews, depositions, court testimony, etc. regarding the meaning of the reports and getting feedback from clients can be very helpful for suggesting updates and modifications to the report structure and/or wording" (CW). Another contributor summed training up in three steps: "1) Review of reports done by the laboratory for all the kinds of situations that can come up, 2) Writing of mock reports based on data sets and case folders, 3) Working in tandem with an experienced analyst who co-writes with the trainee. One person can be author, and another technical reviewer" (TM).

"An experienced reporting officer, skillful also in transferring the attitudes and values framing the laboratories' work and goals, should act as a mentor during the training period and guide the trainee… [In Sweden], the training period will end with an exam for the trainee. Follow-ups will be done regularly with a formal 're-examination' every 6th year. Reporting officers [are also] trained in understanding the organization, other forensic and legal institutions and function of the actual legal system, as well as to how the report will be used and understood on different levels outside the laboratory" (RA).

3. Review past case files, write graded mock reports, and practice testifying to their reports

"The training program is a critical component of the forensic DNA process…The analyst must not only review past case files, but they must also write mock reports which are graded. Upon successful completion of the training program, the [new] analyst is paired with a senior analyst who mentors them through the report writing and quality review process. Observing an analyst testify to their report is also an important training component such that the trainee can see the merging of an analyst results within the confines of the judicial system." (CC)

"The new analyst should be given multiple data sets and be asked to practice writing their reports which reflect their interpretation and conclusions of the results. These practice sets will demonstrate to the trainer if the new analyst is preparing their reports in a scientifically correct manner which is readable, and contains the proper impact of the evidence in relation to the investigation" (BH).

II. STATISTICAL INTERPRETATION

4. Use checklists

> *"I highly recommend checklists for [report writing and report reviewing]. A checklist during report writing can help to make sure that all samples have been mentioned and all results are listed. This is an area where mistakes cannot be tolerated. A different review checklist then again checks for completeness, but also includes checks for accuracy of information and if the controls are valid"* (MP).

Charlotte Word adds: "There are different types of 'reports' that may be issued throughout the life of a case. In addition to the 'final' report that includes all of the findings on the DNA testing, other types of reports are often made, including preliminary oral or written 'reports' or letters with preliminary opinions regarding the data in a case while testing is in progress, update or status reports, and opinion reports from experts reviewing the case at the completion of testing for trial, appeals, and/or post-conviction evaluations. While training for the final reports of laboratory testing are often included in an analyst's training program with defined standard operating procedures and evaluations, these other areas of reporting also require appropriate training, review and evaluation" (CW).

Other Topics

This section addresses some of the questions asked of the chapter contributors to provide further details on the process and challenges of report writing.

How Long Does It Take to Write a Report?

Depending on the complexity of the evidentiary result and comparisons being made, reports can take a couple of hours to several days to write. Terry Melton comments: "Reports for the smallest and most uncomplicated cases (two samples, exclusions) take a couple of hours to write, followed by technical and administrative review. Obviously for cases with many samples or interpretational challenges, the writing is commensurately longer" (TM).

Swedish National Forensic Laboratory advisor Ricky Ansell notes: "A standard average statement/report including interpretation is achieved within a couple of hours. Mixtures will add more time on top, as will increased numbers of individuals to compare the results against" (RA). Mecki Prinz adds: "It makes a difference if the laboratory has a LIMS [laboratory information management software] system that can auto-populate identifying information, names of parties involved, and 'evidence received' lists. Even small cases take time if this has to be done manually" (MP).

The process workflow can impact the time needed to write a report. In one laboratory surveyed, the technical verification of data is performed prior to a report being written (CC). In addition, a case submission policy that limits the number of samples submitted for analysis has improved the turnaround time for report writing. The pretechnical review of the DNA data makes writing the report and the ultimate review of the case file a much faster process, usually an hour or two, comments their lab director (CC). Although she adds, "This depends on the number of samples and the complexity of the data, and there are instances when writing a report is a very time-consuming arduous task...due to the complexity of the DNA profile and the number of standards involved in the comparison process.... The complex DNA profile cases may take days to write" (CC).

In reviewing her experience with report writing over the past two decades, Cecelia Crouse makes another important point: "The more STRs that were added to [our laboratory's] DNA testing repertoire, the more complicated interpretation, statistical analysis and report writing have become. In turn, the amount of time necessary to interpret DNA profiles and write a report has increased concomitantly with the increase of DNA profile complexity and testing using fifteen STRs" (CC). It is sobering to think that as laboratories move to even larger multiplex STR kits in the future, interpretation time and report writing challenges will likely increase with more data to review.

Length of a Report

Ray Wickenheiser shares: "The long report has an advantage of being complete and all inclusive. The disadvantage is finding the pertinent facts potentially buried in a lot of non-forensically significant information. For that reason, I support a short format, which includes the forensically significant information, while limiting documentation of the nonsignificant information. While it is important this information is in case notes and ready if needed, it serves more to confuse if included in a lab report, in my opinion" (RW).

Ted Hunt offers: "In the short run, it may seem like writing abbreviated reports allows an analyst to be more productive at the bench, while promoting efficiency and saving time. I think that's an illusion. Time saved by writing short reports is later lost by explanations of missing content and context to detectives, lawyers, and judges. In sum, reports that are too short sometimes create more questions than they answer" (TH).

Should Standard Templates Be Used to Aid Report Writing?

Most of the chapter contributors were in favor of standard text and report templates. For example, the Palm Beach County Sheriff's Office Crime Laboratory has developed around 70 text templates designed to provide uniform report writing across analysts. Other labs may have sophisticated LIMS (laboratory information management systems) to help transfer case data, descriptions of methodology used, and other relevant details into the final report. Here are some thoughts on this topic:

> Bruce Heidebrecht remarks: *"Every single case will have nuances. We utilize a set of 'report writing guidelines' that give examples of the most commonly used conclusions in our reports. These guidelines probably have appropriate wording to cover 95% of all the reports we generate. However, there is that small percentage of cases where the evidence does not lend itself to a straightforward conclusion statement and the reporting analyst needs to modify the guidelines so that the report accurately reflects their interpretation of the evidence"* (BH). He continues: *"Having standard text that will be useful in the majority of cases will save the reporting analyst time in having to create their own wording for each and every report. The standard text also helps the reviewing analyst to ensure that the conclusions are scientifically correctly stated. And the standard text also helps the investigating officers and attorneys who can then be able to more readily understand the report since they will have seen similar wording in prior reports. This is exactly how we utilize our 'report writing guidelines.' While we know that modifications may be necessary, these standard texts can be used in the majority of reports speeding up the time needed to generate and review a report"* (BH).
>
> Ricky Ansell comments: *"Even a short statement/report will contain a lot of data of various sorts, and a lot of background lab data that are to be reviewed together with the written statement/report. Efficiency can hopefully be achieved by using standardized report templates in combination with the LIMS [laboratory information management system] integrating relevant case data directly into the statement/report"* (RA).
>
> Terry Melton adds: *"Standard text 'chunks' that can be copied and pasted are helpful and time-saving for many cases where the results are straightforward and unambiguous. However, this shortcut can be a source of*

many errors which may not be easily detectable on technical review (for example, slight differences in sample identifiers, etc.)" (TM).

     Norah Rudin shares a different viewpoint: *"Standard text is only useful in standard situations. For forensic DNA cases, instances of non-standard situations outnumber the instances of standard situations. While standard text might be useful as a starting point, it suffers from some of the same limitations as a standard report template — it discourages thinking. And that is always detrimental to a clear and complete report" (NR).*

Consistency among analysts within a laboratory will aid report users. A frequent report user remarks: "I think it is essential that once a lab approves a new report writing template, all analysts strictly adhere to that format to maintain consistency in both the form and substance of the reported data" (TH).

What Are the Most Common Mistakes Seen in Reports?

As with any written document, mistakes can sometimes arise. Chapter contributors were requested to offer their perspectives on the most common mistakes they have observed:

     "In our system, many of the mistakes are copy/paste mistakes since our criminalists are using a template report. So while adapting the template sentences, some place holder like 'his/her' may be left unmodified. Also, in cases with many items received and many stains extracted and tested, it can happen that some results are left out. This is less of a risk if a sample was compared to a reference, but it may occur for stains that did not yield enough DNA for typing" (MP).

     "From the perspective of a report reviewer, the occasional mistakes I've seen concern things like the transposition of data, mistaken evidence identifiers, and typographical errors. On rare occasions, I've seen miscalculations of a profile's statistical frequency — for example, the inclusion of one too many zeros" (TH).

     "Most frank mistakes are typographical. Many mistakes come from using a report template in which information from a previous report is accidentally included. Other mistakes result from mis-typing or mis-copying numbers. This might happen prior to actually writing the report, while inputting numbers into a statistical spreadsheet or program. It is not uncommon for results from sperm cell fractions to be transposed with results from non-sperm-cell fractions, especially if the results are not what the analyst might, a priori, expect. I have also, quite spectacularly in one memorable instance, seen conclusions transposed and attached to the wrong samples. A substantive rather than cursory review of both the results and the report can help to minimize all these types of mistakes. Of course any mistakes made prior to writing the report will simply be incorporated. Presumably these would be considered analytical errors rather than reporting errors" (NR).

     "The most common mistakes are administrative such as the misspellings of individuals' names, grammatical errors, cut and paste errors and a statistic calculation transcribed incorrectly. The second most common types of errors are when negative serology results are inadvertently left off of the report. The review process is very efficient at catching these non-DNA issues" (CC).

     "I have seen mistakes in every part of a report over the course of my career. Reports are generated by humans and all parts are therefore subject to error. The most important thing to do is to point out the error as soon as it is detected and get the report corrected as soon as possible and distributed to the appropriate individuals. SOPs should include procedures for amending reports and follow-up with corrective actions may be helpful for preventing similar errors in the future" (CW).

Should Allele Tables Be Included?

The core information from a DNA case are the STR alleles observed at the tested loci. In reviewing reports and discussing this topic with people in the community, a variety of opinions were expressed regarding the inclusion of STR allele tables in final case reports. Below are some of the contributor comments on this topic:

Ricky Ansell shares: *"There is, in my perspective, no general need for the police/prosecution/defense/court to see the DNA data. The verbal scale used in our lab [note: see D.N.A. Box 16.2] will direct the user to the strength/support of the findings made and conclusions drawn. If the prosecution, defense, or court wants or needs to see any of the laboratory documentation, these data will then be handed over. However, this rarely ever occurs. General level information for forensic biology and DNA analysis along with protocols used are referenced in our report statements and available online"* (RA).

Cecelia Crouse comments: *"The PBSO laboratory provides all casefile data through discovery and depositions so at this time we do not include allele data table when the reviewed report is submitted. There is not a compelling reason why this would be an issue however"* (CC).

Mecki Prinz notes: *"We have decided not to include allele calls in the final report. The main reason was the occurrence of typographical errors and the time needed to properly review, especially for mixed samples"* (MP). She also points out that *"allele calls of witnesses and the victim may have to be redacted if reports are distributed"* (MP).

Norah Rudin counters: *"Yes, an allele chart should requisitely be included in every report. It is simply too difficult and too fraught with peril of misunderstanding to attempt to communicate numeric results solely by prose. Further, the allele chart can immediately assist the expert to help an attorney to begin to understand the lab's conclusions. The allele chart must document not just the alleles detected, but something about their relative amounts. A chart that just lists alleles without indicating that some alleles are significantly weaker or stronger than others is, by definition, misleading"* (NR).

Bruce Heidebrecht adds: *"I do find it useful to have sample allele calls included in the final report. It is easier on the reviewer to have the interpretation of the data (single source, mixture, partial profile, etc.) and the conclusions (included, excluded, inconclusive) in a single document. I do also find that it is easier for a jury to be able to look at a results chart and come to the same conclusions that I would as the analyst. If the chart shows a 9,10 for the evidence, a 9,10 for the suspect, and 8,13 for the victim it is really easy for anyone to see how the suspect matches and the victim is excluded. As the evidence gets more complicated however, allele calls in the report could cross the line from easy to read and move into taking away from the impact of the conclusions. Even worse, complicated allele calls might also lead to the reader becoming confused and coming to their own conclusions, different from those stated in the report"* (BH).

Terry Melton comments: *"All data should be reported in the final report because cases may frequently be revisited with new samples and multiple reports. Having the data allows for cross-comparison between any samples in any report"* (TM).

Ted Hunt offers: *"I strongly prefer that allele tables be included in the reports I review... Including allelic tables in forensic DNA reports is another example of how providing more information up front may mean spending less time later explaining test results and conclusions to police officers and attorneys"* (TH).

Ray Wickenheiser provides: *"I feel that including allele calls is very helpful in reports, particularly where multiple items, suspects, or mixtures are present. Use of allele tables makes demonstration of the matches much easier and understandable and in turn permits a ready court demonstration if needed. Including an allele table in the report provides full disclosure to the defense as a matter of course through release of the report"* (RW).

Charlotte Word concludes: *"[Allele calls] are extremely helpful to me when I am asked as a consultant to review a report. ... Summary tables provide excellent documentation of the information that the report analyst and the technical reviewer relied upon for forming their conclusions. This can be especially helpful years later when the staff has changed and/or the SOPs for analysis and/or interpretation have changed in the laboratory. It also can be quite helpful to an analyst in court to recall what alleles were used in the interpretation particularly*

II. STATISTICAL INTERPRETATION

when different criteria are used for different kits, different genetic analyzers, or at different times in the laboratory. However, that being said, I have heard of some very unfortunate situations where attorneys have misused the tables to independently present inclusionary information to a jury (and presumably to a defendant as well) and without any statistical frequency calculations when the laboratory analyst and technical reviewer reported in their report and stated in court that the data could not be interpreted for legitimate scientific reasons. Some laboratories have decided not to include the table of results to avoid this unethical and unscientific evaluation of the data by less or unqualified readers of the report" (CW).

Record Confidentiality, Control, and Retention

Reports often contain detailed information regarding evidence and reference samples including the names of victim(s) and suspect(s). The FBI QAS Standard 11.3 requires US forensic DNA labs to keep reports and other records confidential as required by applicable laws (see D.N.A. Box 16.5). QAS section 11.3.3 recognizes the sensitive nature of personally identifiable information (PII) and states that PII should only be released in accordance with applicable state and federal law (QAS 2011). Likewise, ISO 17025 Standard 4.13 discusses control of records and emphasizes among other things that all records need to be held secure and in confidence (ISO 2005).

A lab report is a work product reflecting what was done on a specific case. The individual preparing a report cannot assume that case notes will always be available to the report end user. Based on the loss of physical evidence and bench notes in approximately 25% of old cases they have examined, the Innocence Project has described the importance of high-quality laboratory reports (Neufeld et al. 2012):

"At the time of forensic analysis, of course, the analyst has no way of knowing whether the piece of evidence she is testing will prove critical to a post-conviction claim. And once it has been tested, the evidence may lay dormant for years, even decades, until such a claim is brought. If the evidence, during those dormant decades, is destroyed or contaminated, the laboratory report may become the most important, and only remaining, record of the forensic results."

Modern, accredited forensic DNA labs maintain and archive lab reports, technical notes, and underlying case data so laboratory reports should not be the only source of information in the future. In fact, FBI QAS Standard 11.1 requires record retention (see D.N.A. Box 16.5) of casework notes and all analytical documentation "to support the report conclusions such that another qualified individual could evaluate and interpret the data" (QAS 2011). Even evidence has been retained as part of case files (D.N.A. Box 16.6). When laboratories are closed or moved, maintaining old reports, test results, protocols, and evidence can be crucial to enable further testing if needed during appeals, post-conviction work, and cold case review.

REPORT & CASE REVIEW

After conclusions have been decided upon based on the interpretation performed, a report is written by the analyst assigned to the case. This report is also examined by another qualified analyst for technical review and often by a supervisor for administrative review. Thus, an initial report is effectively a draft and not final until it has passed this peer-review process. One chapter contributor expressed his opinion that "with all the layers of reviews we are pretty good at limiting mistakes [in writing reports]" (RW).

D.N.A. BOX 16.6

RETAINING EVIDENCE IN CASE FILES: THE LEGACY OF MARY JANE BURTON

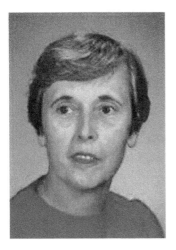

Upon beginning efforts with post-conviction DNA testing in 2001, the Virginia Department of Forensic Science discovered that a number of old casework files from the 1970s and 1980s prepared by a serologist named Mary Jane Burton had clippings of physical evidence included in them. After completing blood typing or other serological tests available at the time, Burton had the unusual practice of saving a portion of evidence that she had tested (typically a bloody cotton swab) and attaching it to a lab sheet within her case files. Standard practice in laboratories then as now is to return all of the evidence to the submitting agency for storage after testing has been completed. Depending on the type of crime, evidence samples may eventually be destroyed if there are evidence locker space issues or evidence can be lost or misplaced over time due to poor records and sample tracking processes. Thus, finding biological evidence from decades-old cases can be challenging at best.

In August 2002, Marvin Anderson was the first individual cleared (of a 1982 rape conviction) thanks to Mary Burton's evidence retention

habit. When a retrospective examination of 31 sample cases led to two exonerations, the Virginia Governor at the time, Mark Warner, ordered a full review of all available data. A comprehensive review of some 534,000 cases conducted between 1973 and 1987 identified 3,052 case files that contained evidence suitable for DNA testing. These case file serology swabs were outsourced for DNA testing and research was performed to see whether or not a named suspect had been convicted of a state violent felony offense. Only 2,204 of these cases had a named suspect, and of these 835 were state violent felony convictions.

A significant subset of these cases was deemed eligible for a National Institute of Justice (NIJ) funded study on post-conviction DNA testing based on crime type and a conviction. In June 2012, an NIJ research report from the Urban Institute analyzed the DNA results obtained from 634 sexual assault and homicide cases containing Burton's old swabs in order to understand the levels of wrongful convictions. With these 634 cases, there were 715 convictions as 62 cases had multiple suspects. In 5% of the cases (38 total), DNA testing *eliminated* the convicted offender as the source of the retained incriminating physical evidence found in the original case file. Efforts are underway to investigate the context of any exclusionary results (e.g. a "foreign" profile may come from a victim's spouse) and to locate excluded individuals to pursue post-conviction relief if appropriate to do so.

Sources: http://www.urban.org/UploadedPDF/412589-Post-Conviction-DNA-Testing-and-Wrongful-Conviction.pdf; http://www.truthinjustice.org/mjburton.htm; http://www.nbcnews.com/id/9666591/#.UaZKSdh8xK8; http://www.timesdispatch.com/news/hunt-for-the-wrongfully-convicted-continues/article_75544ee2-2b21-51e3-9eb4-c53102b824ae.html; http://richmondmagazine.com/articles/this-man-is-innocent-05-26-2011.html.

D.N.A. BOX 16.7

FBI QUALITY ASSURANCE STANDARDS (QAS) FOR FORENSIC DNA TESTING LABORATORIES SECTION 12 ON REVIEWS

Forensic DNA laboratories in the United States are audited against one of two sets of FBI Quality Assurance Standards (QAS) depending on whether the lab performs forensic casework or DNA data-basing work. The QAS documents and audit questions, which are prepared by the Scientific Working Group on DNA Analysis Methods (SWGDAM), are available on the FBI CODIS website at http://www.fbi.gov/about-us/lab/biometric-analysis/codis. Information contained in Section 12 of the QAS for forensic DNA testing laboratories is included below as it pertains to administrative and technical reviews.

12. Review

Standard 12.1 The laboratory shall conduct and document administrative and technical reviews of all case files and reports to ensure conclusions and supporting data are reasonable and within the constraints of scientific knowledge. The review of data generated external to the laboratory is governed by Standard 17.

12.1.1 An individual conducting technical reviews shall be or have been an analyst qualified in the methodology being reviewed.

Standard 12.2 Completion of the technical review shall be documented and the technical review of forensic casework shall include the following elements:

12.2.1 A review of all case notes, all worksheets, and the electronic data (or printed electropherograms or images) supporting the conclusions.

12.2.2 A review of all DNA types to verify that they are supported by the raw or analyzed data (electropherograms or images).

12.2.3 A review of all profiles to verify correct inclusions and exclusions (if applicable) as well as a review of any inconclusive result for compliance with laboratory guidelines.

12.2.4 A review of all controls, internal lane standards and allelic ladders to verify that the expected results were obtained.

12.2.5 A review of statistical analysis, if applicable.

12.2.6 A review of the final report's content to verify that the results/conclusions are supported by the data. The report shall address each tested item or its probative fraction.

12.2.7 Verification that all profiles entered into CODIS are eligible, have the correct DNA types and correct specimen category.

12.2.7.1 Prior to upload to or search of SDIS, verification of the following criteria for DNA profiles: eligibility for CODIS, correct DNA types, and appropriate specimen category.

12.2.7.2 For entry into a searchable category at SDIS, verification of the following criteria for DNA profiles by two concordant assessments by a qualified analyst or technical reviewer: eligibility for CODIS; correct DNA types; and appropriate specimen category.

Standard 12.3 The administrative review shall include the following elements, any or all of which may be included within the technical review:

12.3.1 A review of the case file and final report for clerical errors and that information specified in Standard 11.2 is present and accurate.

12.3.2 A review of chain of custody and disposition of evidence.

12.3.3 A procedure to document the completion of the administrative review.

Standard 12.4 The laboratory shall document the elements of a technical and administrative review. Case files shall be reviewed and documented according to the laboratory's procedure.

Standard 12.5 The laboratory shall have and follow a documented procedure to address unresolved discrepant conclusions between analysts and reviewer(s).

Standard 12.6 The laboratory shall have and follow a documented procedure for the verification and resolution of database matches.

Standard 12.7 The laboratory shall have and follow a program that documents the annual monitoring of the testimony of each analyst.

Source: FBI (9-1-2011). Quality assurance standards for forensic DNA testing laboratories. Available at http://www.swgdam.org/docs.html or http://www.fbi.gov/about-us/lab/biometric-analysis/codis.

Technical Review

A technical review involves the evaluation of lab reports, notes, and data by a second qualified analyst to ensure that appropriate, scientifically sound conclusions have been reached by the first analyst. If the technical reviewer does not understand why decisions were reached or does not agree with some portion of the report and work performed, then a dialogue begins between the original analyst and the technical reviewer. Before a final report is issued, some kind of understanding and agreement should occur between the two analysts. This can involve revising the original draft report. The review process and discussion sometimes can be extensive with challenging DNA cases.

As Keith Inman and Norah Rudin have written: "The reviewer's most important role is to determine if the conclusions are supported by the data" (Inman & Rudin 2001). If disagreements occur between analysts during report writing or technical review process that could impact how end users interpret the report conclusions, then it would be appropriate to disclose this disagreement. In the interest of full disclosure and transparency of the work and review performed, a statement could be included in the report referring readers to notes within the case file documenting the nature of the disagreement and its resolution. No one should sign a report where they do not agree with the conclusions being conveyed.

Some of the most challenging information to confirm when reviewing a report can occur with DNA mixtures. Cecelia Crouse comments: "When there is a complex mixture sometimes it is not always apparent why an individual is included or excluded and it takes more time to analyze and confirm the interpretation" (CC). Bruce Heidebrecht adds: "Over the last few years we've made significant advancements in how analysts document their interpretation of DNA evidence. Prior to these advancements the challenge was in understanding why the reporting analyst made decisions about such things like when to declare a major contributor is present in a mixture. There needed to be much more back-and-forth between the reviewer and the reporting analyst to ensure there was a consensus with the interpretation of the evidence. Now with better documentation it is much easier for the reviewer to 'get inside the head' of the reporting analysts and understand their interpretation" (BH).

Administrative Review

While a technical review focuses on the accuracy of data, administrative review provides an evaluation of a laboratory report and the support documentation in terms of consistency with laboratory policies. Administrative review also seeks to verify grammar and language editorial correctness. "Most errors come from copy and paste and data transcription. This is why [an administrative] review is critical" (TM).

QAS Requirements for Review

FBI QAS Standard 12 covers review of reports and casework notes (D.N.A. Box 16.7). This standard requires that an individual conducting a technical review within a forensic laboratory needs to be an analyst qualified or previously qualified in the methodology being reviewed. Case notes, worksheets, and electronic data need to be reviewed to verify that all conclusions can be supported. Administrative reviews are required to include checking for clerical errors, verifying that all of the required elements are present in the report, and reviewing chain of custody and disposition of evidence. These reviews must be documented.

REPORT RELEASE

Once a laboratory report has passed the technical and administrative review hurdles, and it has been revised as needed, the report is finalized and released to the requesting customer. It is important to keep in mind that important decisions may be made by initial users as well as later users based on the report conclusions.

Initial User/Customer

The initial user of a report is typically a police investigator and a prosecutor. Prosecutor Ted Hunt provides some excellent advice: "Report writers can be more effective by focusing on the needs of those who regularly review their reports — police officers and attorneys, not simply other scientists!" He concludes: "Better report writing is only half of the equation. The balance of the responsibility falls on report reviewers — police officers and attorneys — to take the time and put forth the effort to learn to read, speak, and understand the basic 'language' of forensic DNA analysis. This can be accomplished by self-application and interdisciplinary training. ... We're all part of one long continuum — from the crime scene to the courtroom. To a certain extent, we must all learn to live in each other's world" (TH).

Review by the Defense

If an individual is arrested and charged with a crime, then he or she becomes a defendant in legal proceedings that may culminate in a courtroom trial. Within the United States, law requires that a defendant be permitted to know what evidence is being brought against him or her. The legal process of *discovery* involves the prosecution team sharing information and materials relating to the prosecution of a defendant with defense counsel. Specific requirements for discovery are regulated by federal and state laws and, in some cases, the judge in a particular case may rule on the materials that must be provided by the forensic laboratory during the discovery process. Certainly laboratory reports and the underlying data and information that led to these conclusions, such as bench notes, are part of what the prosecution are required to share during discovery.

Defense attorney Christopher Duby shares his perspective: "The prosecution gives me lab reports during the discovery-phase of the litigation and I use my experience, secondary sources and training to get a basic understanding of what the reports contain. I also file additional discovery requests to get all lab notes, bench notes, chain of custody materials and correspondence between the lab and the prosecution. Lastly, I consult with an expert of my own choosing, ask them to review the lab reports from top to bottom and then, once they have done that, ask them for their opinion on the accuracy, thoroughness and competency of the lab reports I received. I have them prepare a written report, send me their own computer results (if applicable), and then ask them the specific questions that I have that I discovered through my own review. While it is great to consult with scientists who are experts in the science of DNA, I am the one that must present these matters to a jury of lay people in a language they understand so my client can enjoy that benefit" (CD).

REPORT COMPREHENSION AND POTENTIAL MISUSE

Ted Hunt comments: "A lab report should be able to stand on its own to the extent that the primary consumers of the lab's product (police officers and attorneys) can both understand the report's conclusions and the process whereby those conclusions were generated in the analyst's absence" (TH). Ray Wickenheiser adds: "The area with the biggest room for improvement is clarity of the report and consistency between cases and labs in reporting" (RW).

Report Comprehension

Chapter contributors provided some helpful suggestions to aid report comprehension and to avoid misunderstandings of results:

1. Call report recipients and verbally explain results

> "I have often seen report recipients need a verbal explanation over the telephone to dis-entangle the words in the report… For this reason, we precede a mailed written report in most cases with a telephone call to report the results of testing, notify the client that the report is on the way, and remind them to call if they have questions later" (TM).

2. Provide training to report users

> "Providing training to report readers without technical backgrounds and open accessibility to both prosecution and defense have been effective strategies to improve understanding" (RW). "Our laboratory has provided training on the DNA report content to NYPD investigators and is always available to discuss reports and results with the prosecution [and] defense community" (MP).

3. Provide a glossary and use appendices and website links where appropriate

"The report must be complete and scientifically accurate. This cannot be simplified too much. But a glossary with definitions is essential to explain what each conclusion means and will prevent misunderstandings. This is less a matter of writing the report, but of communicating with the stakeholders" (MP). "A smart use of relevant appendices and website links can be useful in avoiding too much explanatory text" (RA).

4. Adjust report wording based on feedback from report users

"We are constantly striving [to avoid report misunderstandings] as we frequently add to or adjust the wording in our report writing guidelines. If we receive feedback from our clients that our reports are being misunderstood we look into the wording that was used in the report to determine if something can be improved. However, if we make the wording simpler, we may lose scientific correctness and therefore could create even more misunderstanding!" (BH)

"The laboratory should routinely evaluate the clarity of report wording by conducting surveys with the laboratory staff, law enforcement and the judicial system. Recently the Biology Unit designed a survey using the auto text and requested feedback from some new prosecutors in the State Attorney's Office. It was very enlightening as the prosecutors indicated it is not uncommon that they need assistance understanding a forensic biology report. One survey recommended that we do our best to 'use basic common English,' while another asked if we would use the word 'included' or 'matches' instead of our current 'cannot be excluded.' All of these comments will be considered for discussion" (CC).

"Although we believe a statement is correct as well as simple and transparent, it may still need to be clarified and simplified further, in order to be handled and interpreted correctly downstream" (RA).

5. State statistical conclusions multiple ways

"When stating statistics I think it is often important to state them both as inclusion and exclusion. For example, a CPI of 0.01 or 1 in one 100 is also a CPE of 0.99 or 99%. While it is a different way of looking at the same statistical weight, inherently we think 1 in 100 individuals is very common while being able to eliminate 99% of the population as being a potential contributor appears very specific. Providing both statistical viewpoints in a report does a better job of conveying the weight of an inclusion. This is particularly true in the situation of an inclusion with lower weight" (RW).

No matter how well a report is written, it is of little value unless it is read and understood. "People must take time to read the report" (MP).

Potential Misuse or Misunderstanding

One area in which reports can be misunderstood is with DNA mixture results. Bruce Heidebrecht comments that "reports that don't make clear that a sample is a mixture give rise to this misunderstanding of the suspect matching the evidence when the truth is that he could be one of the several possible contributors" (BH).

The meaning of conclusions in a case can be the most misunderstood part of a report (CW). Regarding the potential of misunderstanding, Charlotte Word provides an example where there may be no indication of DNA from the suspect in a sexual assault case. She states that in such a case "it is common practice to report that the suspect is excluded as a source of the DNA obtained. However, what the results are really saying is that there was *no foreign* or *unexpected* DNA obtained from the sample; the DNA profile(s) obtained can be accounted for by the individual(s) whose DNA is expected to be present on the sample. Without this additional clarifying statement, the reader of the report may think that the suspect is excluded from being the perpetrator to the crime and release the suspect, rather than understanding that no DNA profile that may lead to identification of the perpetrator was obtained" (CW). She concludes: "In forensic cases, it may be important to clarify if there is a profile obtained that may assist with the case as opposed to a profile or sample that provides no additional useful information" (CW).

Court Testimony

An important outcome of work performed in a forensic laboratory is providing court testimony when required to do so. All that has been said in this chapter about the importance of clearly communicating results and conclusions is just as important in court as it is in preparing a written report.

US Supreme Court Decisions

In the past few years, the United States Supreme Court has delivered decisions on several cases that impact court testimony surrounding laboratory reports in the US (D.N.A. Box 16.8). These cases include *Crawford v. Washington* (2004), *Melendez-Diaz v. Massachusetts* (2009), *Bullcoming v. New Mexico* (2011), and *Williams v. Illinois* (2012).

Commenting on the *Melendez-Diaz* ruling, Chris Duby shares: "*Melendez-Diaz* and its related cases have drastically changed the way things work in court in Connecticut and in the federal courts. Now, the author of the report, the person who actually performed the scientific tests, must testify in support of his or her conclusions. This is a marked change over what occurred before when anyone qualified could testify as to the accuracy of another scientist's work" (CD).

Laboratory directors offered the following perspectives when asked how the *Melendez-Diaz* ruling has impacted their work [note these responses were received prior to the June 2012 *Williams* ruling (see D.N.A. Box 16.8)]:

> "*We are contending with subpoenas that require multiple individuals to come to court. For a large case, this might include all five staff members. I look forward to the day when attorneys determine what, exactly, they are trying to convey to the jury in a common sense way, as opposed to what they have to cover themselves for in 'confrontation.' Technicians in our lab are typically fact witnesses and have had their work thoroughly overseen and signed off on by one analyst. We state that individual cases are not even remembered by them as they 'bake the same cake' every day*" (TM).
>
> "*Our laboratory does not have this issue as there is usually one analyst per case*" (CC).
>
> "*We are prepared to have more than one analyst available for court if work on one case was performed by multiple individuals. This ruling has limited division of labor as a solution to improve lab flow, or we must be prepared to have several individuals testify on a single case*" (RW).
>
> "*…The primary purpose of a DNA report is not to be used in court. Nevertheless, this decision is being used to challenge who can testify to results; especially if the case was outsourced or if the analyst did not do all the testing her/himself. With more automation, more laboratories will be assembly-line processing, and it is important that a single person can testify to the entire work. It is important to note that, if this is not the person that originally signed the report, the new witness will be asked to only testify to his own opinions and conclusions based on the data in the file. The report itself will not be submitted into evidence. The witness will not testify to the signing analyst's conclusions or to his/her agreement with the conclusions in the report*" (MP).

D.N.A. BOX 16.8

US SUPREME COURT DECISIONS REGARDING USE OF FORENSIC LABORATORY REPORTS

Several US Supreme Court decisions in the past few years have impacted the use of forensic laboratory reports in a courtroom setting within the United States. Among other rights, the Sixth Amendment to the United States Constitution guarantees defendants the opportunity to confront witnesses against them. The US Supreme Court has interpreted this "Confrontation Clause" to mean that the prosecution is prohibited from introducing testimonial statements into court without putting a witness on the stand. Exactly who is an appropriate witness is the subject of the decisions on this topic, which include *Crawford v. Washington* (2004), *Melendez-Diaz v. Massachusetts* (2009), *Bullcoming v. New Mexico* (2011), and *Williams v. Illinois* (2012). Judge Clarence Thomas in the majority opinion for the *Williams* case concludes that DNA reports are not testimonial in nature. It is important to remember that while a DNA source may be identified in a laboratory report, no direct accusations can be made by the presence of the DNA alone (see section on hierarchy of propositions earlier in the chapter).

Jeffrey Fisher of Stanford Law School has written regarding these cases on the Supreme Court of the United States blog (http://www.scotusblog.com):

> The Confrontation Clause guarantees the accused the right "to be confronted with the *witnesses* against him." Because "witnesses" are people to give testimony, a broad coalition of Justices held in *Crawford v. Washington* (2004) that the Confrontation Clause prohibits the prosecution from introducing out-of-court "testimonial" statements without putting the declarants on the stand. In *Melendez-Diaz v. Massachusetts* (2009), the Court held that forensic reports that certify incriminating test results are testimonial. ... In *Bullcoming v. New Mexico* (2011), a five-Justice majority reaffirmed *Melendez-Diaz* and made clear that when the prosecution wishes to introduce a certified forensic report, it does not suffice to call a supervisor or other "surrogate" witness to the stand in place of the actual author of the report. The *Bullcoming* decision nonetheless left open whether the prosecution could introduce an analyst's testimonial forensic report (or transmit its substance) through an *expert* witness. ... [In *Williams*], Justice Thomas explained that "[t]here is no meaningful distinction between disclosing an out-of-court statement so that a fact finder may evaluate the expert's opinion and disclosing that statement for its truth."
>
> So where, in practical terms, does this leave us? In the realm of forensic evidence, the Confrontation Clause continues to deem *formal* forensic reports testimonial. That means that drug, blood alcohol, fingerprint, ballistics, autopsies, and related reports that typically involve testing by one person and that are incriminating on their face will continue to be inadmissible without the testimony of their authors (or some other method of satisfying the Confrontation Clause). ... By contrast, statements made as part of a lab's internal work product or in a subsidiary report used to generate a final incriminating report will generally not be testimonial. Such statements are not typically formal or solemn. Thus, in forensic testing involving multiple steps, it will often be enough for the prosecution to call to the stand the author of the final report or at least those who performed the key steps.

Sources: http://www.scotusblog.com/2012/06/the-holdings-and-implications-of-williams-v-illinois/; http://jolt.law.harvard.edu/digest/supreme-court/williams-v-illinois.

Serving as an Expert Witness

It goes without saying that court testimony for a case should match the written report. However, it can take several years for a case to get to court and therefore a progressive forensic laboratory may have new protocols. These updated protocols may result in a different interpretation of the original data. How to handle this situation is up to individual laboratories and laws impacting their work.

It is important to keep in mind that there will always be tension between science and the law because of different cultures and perspectives (see discussion regarding this topic on pp. 517–518 of Butler 2012). Science, which is always evolving and improving, should not be expected to stand still to meet legal requirements. If a new protocol would lead to a different opinion, then Dr. Robin Cotton encourages analysts to issue an amended report that reflects the new opinion (Cotton 2013). Of course, what to do in preparation for testifying in a case will depend on legal input from officers of the court or other parties involved in a specific case.

For information on preparation for court to serve as an expert witness, readers are encouraged to review Chapter 18 in the accompanying volume *Advanced Topics in Forensic DNA Typing: Methodology* (Butler 2012).

SUMMARY

When data interpretation is completed and statistical analysis is performed where warranted, conclusions are drawn from comparing evidentiary and reference samples. These results and conclusions are summarized in a laboratory report. Given that most cases in the United States and other parts of the world will not go to court due to plea bargaining, well-written, unbiased reports are needed to clearly convey results obtained and conclusions drawn. Good communication is facilitated by understanding the audience(s) who will receive and use lab reports and by providing a glossary of terms to aid report users.

This chapter discusses issues involved in drawing impartial conclusions, requirements for report writing and reviewing in the FBI Quality Assurance Standards, and concerns with report comprehension. Perspectives are provided from forensic laboratory directors, DNA technical leaders, as well as consultants, lawyers, and police investigators.

Chapter contributor Terry Melton makes an important observation: "An effective report comes from a scientist who truly understands the data and is not just mechanically following a rigid protocol" (TM). Hopefully this chapter and this book will lead to a better understanding of forensic DNA typing data and its interpretation so that laboratory case reports may be effectively communicated to all those who depend on them.

Reading List and Internet Resources

Aitken, C., & Taroni, F. (2004). *Statistics and the evaluation of evidence for forensic scientists* (2nd ed.). Chichester, England: John Wiley & Sons.

Aitken, C., et al. (2010). *Fundamentals of probability and statistical evidence in criminal proceedings: Guidance for judges, lawyers, forensic scientists and expert witnesses. Practitioner Guide No. 1. Prepared under the auspices of the Royal Statistical Society's working group on Statistics and the Law (Chairman: Colin Aitken). Communicating and interpreting statistical evidence in the administration of criminal justice.* Available at http://www.rss.org.uk/uploadedfiles/userfiles/files/Aitken-Roberts-Jackson-Practitioner-Guide-1-WEB.pdf. Accessed October 3, 2014.

Buckleton, J., Triggs, C. M., & Walsh, S. J. (2005). *Forensic DNA evidence interpretation.* London: CRC Press.

Butler, J. M. (2012). *Advanced topics in forensic DNA typing: Methodology.* New York: Elsevier Academic Press.

Evett, I. W. (1991). Interpretation: a personal odyssey. In C. G. G. Aitken, & D. A. Stoney (Eds.), *The use of statistics in forensic science* (pp. 9—22). New York: Taylor & Francis.

Fisher, G. (2003). *Plea bargaining's triumph: A history of plea bargaining in America.* Stanford, CA: Stanford University Press.

NAS — National Academy of Sciences. (2009). *Strengthening forensic science in the United States: A path forward.* Washington, DC: The National Academies Press.

Puch-Solis, R., et al. (2012). *Assessing the probative value of DNA evidence: Guidance for judges, lawyers, forensic scientists and expert witnesses. Practitioner Guide No. 2. Prepared under the auspices of the Royal Statistical Society's working group on Statistics and the Law (Chairman: Colin Aitken).* Available at http://www.rss.org.uk/uploadedfiles/userfiles/files/Practitioner-Guide-2-WEB.pdf. Accessed April 10, 2014.

Scientific Working Group on DNA Analysis Methods. (2010). *SWGDAM interpretation guidelines for autosomal STR typing by forensic DNA testing laboratories.* Available at http://www.swgdam.org/Interpretation_Guidelines_January_2010.pdf. Accessed April 10, 2014.

Willis, S. (2009). Chapter 19 — Forensic science, ethics and criminal justice. In J. Fraser, & R. Williams (Eds.), *Handbook of forensic science* (pp. 523—545). Devon, UK: Willian Publishing.

Drawing Conclusions

Aitken, C. C. G., & Taroni, F. (1998). A verbal scale for the interpretation of evidence. *Science & Justice, 38,* 279—281.

Association of Forensic Service Providers. (2009). Standards for the formulation of evaluative forensic science expert opinion. *Science & Justice, 49,* 161—164.

Biedermann, A., et al. (2013). E-learning initiatives in forensic interpretation: report on experiences from current projects and outlook. *Forensic Science International, 230,* 2—7.

Buckleton, J. (2005). A framework for interpreting evidence. In J. Buckleton, C. M. Triggs, & S. J. Walsh (Eds.), *Chapter 2: Forensic DNA evidence interpretation* (pp. 27—63). Boca Raton, Florida: CRC Press.

Buckleton, J., & Curran, J. (2008). A discussion of the merits of random man not excluded and likelihood ratios. *Forensic Science International: Genetics, 2,* 343—348.

Budowle, B., et al. (2000). Source attribution of a forensic DNA profile. *Forensic Science Communications, 2(3).* Available at http://www.fbi.gov/about-us/lab/forensic-science-communications/fsc/july2000/source.htm. Accessed April 10, 2014.

Clayton, T. M., et al. (1998). Analysis and interpretation of mixed forensic stains using DNA STR profiling. *Forensic Science International, 91,* 55—70.

Cook, R., et al. (1998a). A model for case assessment and interpretation. *Science & Justice, 38,* 151—156.

Cook, R., et al. (1998b). A hierarchy of propositions: deciding which level to address in casework. *Science & Justice, 38,* 231—239.

Cook, R., et al. (1999). Case pre-assessment and review in a two-way transfer case. *Science & Justice, 39,* 103—111.

DAB — DNA Advisory Board. (2000). Statistical and population genetic issues affecting the evaluation of the frequency of occurrence of DNA profiles calculated from pertinent population database(s). *Forensic Science Communications, 2(3).* Available at http://www.fbi.gov/about-us/lab/forensic-science-communications/fsc/july2000/dnastat.htm. Accessed April 10, 2014.

Doak, S., & Assimakopoulos, D. (2007). How do forensic scientists learn to become competent in casework reporting in practice: a theoretical and empirical approach. *Forensic Science International, 167,* 201—206.

Evett, I. W. (1993). Establishing the evidential value of a small quantity of material found at a crime scene. *Journal of Forensic Science Society, 33,* 83—86.

Evett, I. W. (1996). Expert evidence and forensic misconceptions of the nature of exact science. *Science & Justice, 36,* 118—122.

Evett, I. W., & Weir, B. S. (1998). *Interpreting DNA evidence.* Sunderland, Massachusetts: Sinauer Associates Inc.

Evett, I. W., et al. (2000a). More on the hierarchy of propositions: exploring the distinction between explanations and propositions. *Science & Justice, 40,* 3—10.

Evett, I. W., et al. (2000b). The impact of the principles of evidence interpretation on the structure and content of statements. *Science & Justice, 40,* 233—239.

Evett, I. W., et al. (2002). Interpreting small quantities of DNA: the hierarchy of propositions and the use of Bayesian networks. *Journal of Forensic Sciences, 47,* 520—530.

Gill, P. (2001). Application of low copy number DNA profiling. *Croatian Medical Journal, 42,* 229—232.

Gill, P., et al. (2006). DNA commission of the International Society of Forensic Genetics: recommendations on the interpretation of mixtures. *Forensic Science International, 160,* 90—101.

Inman, K., & Rudin, N. (2001). *Principles and practice of criminalistics: The profession of forensic science.* Boca Raton: CRC Press.

Jackson, G. (2000). The scientist and the scales of justice. *Science & Justice, 40,* 81–85.

Jackson, G. (2009). Chapter 16 – Understanding forensic science opinions. In J. Fraser, & R. Williams (Eds.), *Handbook of forensic science* (pp. 419–445). Devon, UK: Willian Publishing.

Jackson, G., et al. (2006). The nature of forensic science opinion – a possible framework to guide thinking and practice in investigations and in court proceedings. *Science & Justice, 46,* 33–44.

Perlin, M. W., et al. (2011). Validating TrueAllele® DNA mixture interpretation. *Journal of Forensic Sciences, 56*(6), 1430–1447.

Rudin, N., & Inman, K. (2013b). We're probably thinking…about probabilistic approaches to weighting evidence. *The CAC News, 2nd Quarter* 18–19. Available at http://www.cacnews.org. Accessed April 10, 2014.

Taroni, F., & Aitken, C. G. G. (1998). Probabilistic reasoning in the law, part 1: assessment of probabilities and explanation of the value of DNA evidence. *Science & Justice, 38,* 165–177.

Taroni, F., et al. (2013). Whose DNA is this? How relevant a question? (a note for forensic scientists). *Forensic Science International: Genetics, 7*(4), 467–470.

Welsh, C. (2012). A competence assessment framework for scientific support within policing in England and Wales. *Science & Justice, 52,* 119–125.

DNA Transfer Studies and Potential Contamination

Aitken, C., et al. (2003). A graphical model for recovery of cross-transfer evidence in DNA profile. *Theoretical Population Biology, 63,* 179–190.

Bright, J. A., & Petricevic, S. F. (2004). Recovery of trace DNA and its application to DNA profiling of shoe insoles. *Forensic Science International, 145,* 7–12.

Daly, D. J., et al. (2012). The transfer of touch DNA from hands to glass, fabric and wood. *Forensic Science International: Genetics, 6,* 41–46.

Farmen, R. K., et al. (2008). Assessment of individual shedder status and implication for secondary DNA transfer. *Forensic Science International: Genetics Supplement Series, 1,* 415–417.

Flanagan, N., & McAlister, C. (2011). The transfer and persistence of DNA under the fingernails following digital penetration of the vagina. *Forensic Science International: Genetics, 5,* 479–483.

Geddes, L. (Jan 14, 2012). Leaping DNA could hurt court cases. *New Scientist,* 12.

Gill, P., & Kirkham, A. (2004). Development of a simulation model to assess the impact of contamination in casework using STRs. *Journal of Forensic Sciences, 49*(3), 485–491.

Gill, P., et al. (2010). Manufacturer contamination of disposable plastic-ware and other reagents – an agreed position statement by ENFSI, SWGDAM and BSAG. *Forensic Science International: Genetics, 4,* 269–270.

Goray, M., et al. (2010a). Secondary DNA transfer of biological substances under varying test conditions. *Forensic Science International: Genetics, 4,* 62–67.

Goray, M., et al. (2010b). Investigation of secondary DNA transfer of skin cells under controlled test conditions. *Legal Medicine, 12,* 117–120.

Goray, M., et al. (2012a). Evaluation of multiple transfer of DNA using mock case scenarios. *Legal Medicine, 14,* 40–46.

Goray, M., et al. (2012b). DNA transfer within forensic exhibit packaging: potential for DNA loss and relocation. *Forensic Science International: Genetics, 6,* 158–166.

Howitt, T. (2003). Ensuring the integrity of results: a continuing challenge in forensic DNA analysis. In *Proceedings of the 14th international symposium on human identification.* Available at http://www.promega.com/products/pm/genetic-identity/ishi-conference-proceedings/14th-ishi-oral-presentations/. Accessed April 10, 2014.

Inman, K., & Rudin, N. (2002). The origin of evidence. *Forensic Science International, 126,* 11–16.

Kamphausen, D., et al. (2012). Good shedder or bad shedder – the influence of skin diseases on forensic DNA analysis from epithelial abrasions. *International Journal of Legal Medicine, 126,* 179–183.

Ladd, C., et al. (1999). A systematic analysis of secondary DNA transfer. *Journal of Forensic Sciences, 44,* 1270–1272.

Linacre, A., et al. (2010). Generation of DNA profiles from fabrics without DNA extraction. *Forensic Science International: Genetics, 4,* 137–141.

Lowe, A., et al. (2002). The propensity of individuals to deposit DNA and secondary transfer of low level DNA from individuals to inert surfaces. *Forensic Science International, 129,* 25–34.

Meakin, G., & Jamieson, A. (2013). DNA transfer: review and implications for casework. *Forensic Science International: Genetics, 7*(4), 434–443.

Petriecevic, S. F., et al. (2006). DNA profiling of trace DNA recovered from bedding. *Forensic Science International, 159,* 21–26.

II. STATISTICAL INTERPRETATION

Phipps, M., & Petricevic, S. (2007). The tendency of individuals to transfer DNA to handled items. *Forensic Science International*, *168*, 162—168.

Port, N. J., et al. (2006). How long does it take a static speaking individual to contaminate the immediate environment? *Forensic Science, Medicine, and Pathology*, *2*, 157—163.

Poy, A. L., & van Oorschot, R. A. H. (2006). Trace DNA presence, origin, and transfer within a forensic biology laboratory and its potential effect on casework. *Journal of Forensic Identification*, *56*, 558—576.

Preusse-Prange, A., et al. (2009). The problem of DNA contamination in forensic case work — how to get rid of unwanted DNA? *Forensic Science International: Genetics Supplement Series*, *2*, 185—186.

Quinones, I., & Daniel, B. (2012). Cell free DNA as a component of forensic evidence recovered from touched surfaces. *Forensic Science International: Genetics*, *6*, 26—30.

Raymond, J. J., et al. (2004). Trace DNA: an underutilised resource or Pandora's box? A review of the use of trace DNA analysis in the investigation of volume crime. *Journal of Forensic Investigation*, *54*(6), 668—686.

Raymond, J. J., et al. (2008). Assessing trace DNA evidence from a residential burglary: abundance, transfer and persistence. *Forensic Science International: Genetics Supplement Series*, *1*, 442—443.

Raymond, J. J., et al. (2009). Trace evidence characteristics of DNA: a preliminary investigation of the persistence of DNA at crime scenes. *Forensic Science International: Genetics*, *4*, 26—33.

Rudin, N., & Inman, K. (2007). The urban myths & conventional wisdom of transfer: DNA as trace evidence. *The CAC News*, 3rd Quarter 26—29. Available at http://www.cacnews.org/news/3rdq07a.pdf. Accessed April 10, 2014.

Rutty, G. N. (2002). An investigation into the transference and survivability of human DNA following simulated manual strangulation with consideration of the problem of third party contamination. *International Journal of Legal Medicine*, *116*, 170—173.

Rutty, G. N., et al. (2000). DNA contamination of mortuary instruments and work surfaces: a significant problem in forensic practice? *International Journal of Legal Medicine*, *114*, 56—60.

Rutty, G. N., et al. (2003). The effectiveness of protective clothing in the reduction of potential DNA contamination of the scene of crime. *International Journal of Legal Medicine*, *117*, 170—174.

Schmidt, T., et al. (1995). Evidence of contamination in PCR laboratory disposables. *Naturwissenschaften*, *82*, 423—431.

Schwark, T., et al. (2012). Phantoms in the mortuary — DNA transfer during autopsies. *Forensic Science International*, *216*, 121—126.

Sewell, J., et al. (2008). Recovery of DNA and fingerprints from touched documents. *Forensic Science International: Genetics*, *2*, 281—285.

Shaw, K., et al. (2008). Comparison of the effects of sterilization techniques on subsequent DNA profiling. *International Journal of Legal Medicine*, *122*, 29—33.

Taroni, F., et al. (2012). Uncertainty about the true source: a note on the likelihood ratio at the activity level. *Forensic Science International*, *220*, 173—179.

Toothman, M. H., et al. (2008). Characterization of human DNA in environmental samples. *Forensic Science International*, *178*, 7—15.

Wiegand, P., et al. (2011). Transfer of biological stains from different surfaces. *International Journal of Legal Medicine*, *125*, 727—731.

van Oorschot, R. A., & Jones, M. (1997). DNA fingerprints from fingerprints. *Nature*, *387*, 767.

van Oorschot, R. A. H., et al. (2003). Are you collecting all the available DNA from touched objects? *Progress in Forensic Genetics*, *9*. ICS 1239, 803—807.

van Oorschot, R. A. H., et al. (2009). Impact of relevant variables on the transfer of biological substances. *Forensic Science International: Genetics Supplement Series*, *2*, 547—548.

van Oorschot, R. A. H., et al. (2010). Forensic trace DNA: a review. *Investigative Genetics*, *1*, 14. Available at http://www.investigativegenetics.com/content/1/1/14. Accessed April 10, 2014.

Wickenheiser, R. A. (2002). Trace DNA: a review, discussion of theory, and application of the transfer of trace quantities of DNA through skin contact. *Journal of Forensic Sciences*, *47*, 442—450.

Confirmation and Observer Bias

Budowle, B. (2010). Authors' response [to Krane et al. (2010)]. *Journal of Forensic Sciences*, *55*(1), 275—276.

Budowle, B., et al. (2009). A perspective on errors, bias, and interpretation in the forensic sciences and direction for continuing advancement. *Journal of Forensic Sciences*, *54*(4), 798—809.

Dror, I. E. (2012). Letter to the editor — combating bias: the next steps in fighting cognitive and psychological contamination. *Journal of Forensic Sciences*, *57*(1), 276—277.

Dror, I. E. (2013). Letter to the editor — what is (or will be) happening to the cognitive abilities of forensic experts in the new technological age. *Journal of Forensic Sciences, 58*(2), 563.

Dror, I. E., & Hampikian, G. (2011). Subjectivity and bias in forensic DNA mixture interpretation. *Science & Justice, 51*(4), 204—208.

Dror, I. E., et al. (2011). Cognitive issues in fingerprint analysis: inter- and intra-expert consistency and the effect of a "target" comparison. *Forensic Science International, 208*, 10—17.

Kassin, S. M., et al. (2013). The forensic confirmation bias: problems, perspectives, and proposed solutions. *Journal of Applied Research in Memory and Cognition, 2*, 42—52.

Krane, D., et al. (2010). Commentary on: Budowle B, Bottrell MC, Bunch SG, Fram R, Harrison D, Meagher S, Oien CT, Peterson PE, Seiger DP, Smith MB, Smrz MA, Soltis GL, Stacey RB. A perspective on errors, bias, and interpretation in the forensic sciences and direction for continuing advancement. J Forensic Sci 2009;54(4):798—809. *Journal of Forensic Sciences, 55*(1), 273—274.

Saks, M. J., et al. (2003). Context effects in forensic science: a review and application of the science of science to crime laboratory practice in the United States. *Science & Justice, 43*(2), 77—90.

Thompson, W. C. (2009). Painting the target around the matching profile: the Texas sharpshooter fallacy in forensic DNA interpretation. *Law, Probability, & Risk, 8*, 257—276.

Sequential Unmasking

Inman, K., & Rudin, N. (2013). Sequential unmasking: minimizing observer effects in forensic science. In J. A. Siegel, & P. J. Saukko (Eds.), *Encyclopedia of forensic sciences* (2nd ed.). (pp. 542—548) San Diego: Elsevier Academic Press.

Krane, D. E., et al. (2008). Letter to the editor — sequential unmasking: a means of minimizing observer effects in forensic DNA interpretation. *Journal of Forensic Sciences, 53*(4), 1006—1007.

Krane, D. E., et al. (2009a). Authors' response [to Wells (2009)]. *Journal of Forensic Sciences, 54*(2), 501.

Krane, D. E., et al. (2009b). Authors' response [to Ostrum (2009)]. *Journal of Forensic Sciences, 54*(6), 1500—1501.

Ostrum, B. (2009). Letter to the editor — Commentary on: authors' response [J Forensic Sci 2009; 54(2):501] to Wells' comments [J Forensic Sci 2009; 54(2):500] regarding Krane DE, Ford S, Gilder JR, Inman K, Jamieson A, Koppl R, Kornfield IL, Risinger DM, Rudin N, Taylor MS, Thompson WC. Sequential unmasking: a means of minimizing observer effects in forensic DNA interpretation. J Forensic Sci 2008; 53(4):1006—7. *Journal of Forensic Sciences, 54*(6), 1498—1499.

Rudin, N., & Inman, K. (2011). That's not what we meant: sequential unmasking revisited. *CAC News, 1st Quarter* 9—12. Available at http://www.cacnews.org/news/1stq11.pdf. Accessed April 10, 2014.

Sequential Unmasking Frequently Asked Questions: http://www.sequentialunmasking.org/faq/ (website established on the topic by Forensic Bioinformatics, Dayton, OH). Accessed April 10, 2014.

Thompson, W. C., et al. (2011). Commentary on: Thornton JI. Letter to the editor—a rejection of "working blind" as a cure for contextual bias. J Forensic Sci 2010;55(6):1663. *Journal of Forensic Sciences, 56*(2), 562—563.

Thornton, J. I. (2010). Letter to the editor — a rejection of "working blind" as a cure for contextual bias. *Journal of Forensic Sciences, 55*(6), 1663.

Wells, J. D. (2009). Commentary on: Krane DE, Ford S, Gilder JR, Inman K, Jamieson A, Koppl R, Kornfield IL, Risinger DM, Rudin N, Taylor MS, Thompson WC. Sequential unmasking: a means of minimizing observer effects in forensic DNA interpretation. J Forensic Sci 2008;53(4):1006—7. *Journal of Forensic Sciences, 54*(2), 500.

Report Writing

Broeders, A. P. A. (1999). Some observations on the use of probability scales in forensic identification. *Forensic Linguistics: The International Journal of Speech, Language and the Law, 6*(2), 228—241.

CACNews (2014). Available at http://www.cacnews.org/news/news.shtml. Accessed April 10, 2014.

Champod, C., & Evett, I. W. (2000). Commentaries on Broeders' 'Some observations on the use of probability scales in forensic identification'. *Forensic Linguistics, 7*, 238—243.

Corrado, K., et al. (2012). Forensic laboratory perspective on standardized report writing. A memo written to the New York State Justice Task Force Subcommittee on Forensics dated February 17, 2012 in response to the Innocence Project's brief.

Epstein, J. (2013). Forensic laboratory reports. In J. A. Siegel, & P. J. Saukko (Eds.), *Encyclopedia of forensic sciences* (2nd ed.). (pp. 463—465) San Diego: Elsevier Academic Press.

ISO — International Organization for Standardization. (2005). *International Standard ISO/IEC 17025:2005(E): General requirements for the competence of testing and calibration laboratories.* Available from http://www.iso.org. Accessed April 10, 2014.

Miller, L. S., & Whitehead, J. T. (2011). *Chapter 1 — The why and how of report writing. Report writing for criminal justice professionals* (4th ed.). Boston: Elsevier. 3–38.

Neufeld, P., et al. (2012). The importance of standardized report-writing to wrongful conviction reform. A memo/brief written to the New York State Justice Task Force Subcommittee on Forensics dated January 31, 2012.

Nordgaard, A., et al. (2012). Scale of conclusions for the value of evidence. *Law, Probability, & Risk, 11*(1), 1–24.

QAS. (2011). *Quality assurance standards for forensic DNA testing laboratories effective 9-1-2011.* See http://www.fbi.gov/about-us/lab/codis/qas-standards-for-forensic-dna-testing-laboratories-effective-9-1-2011. Accessed April 10, 2014.

Rudin, N., & Inman, K. (2013a). The proceedings of lunch: journey to the red planet: curiosity meets forensic science. *The CAC News, 1st Quarter*9–12. Available at http://www.cacnews.org. Accessed April 10, 2014.

Satterthwaite, J., & Lambert, J. A. (1989). Interpreting the interpretations: a survey to assess the effectiveness of conclusions in statements written by forensic scientists. *Home Office Forensic Science Service Technical Note 714.*

STRBase, Mixture Interpretation (2014). Available at http://www.cstl.nist.gov/strbase/mixture.htm.

Swecker, C., & Wolf, M. (2010). *An independent review of the SBI forensic laboratory.* The 77 page document is available at http://dig.abclocal.go.com/wtvd/docs/081810_SBI_Lab_Review.pdf. Accessed April 10, 2014.

SWGDAM Mixture Committee. (2013). *Report wording suggestions.* Available from http://www.cstl.nist.gov/strbase/mixture/ReportWordingSuggestions2013.pdf. Accessed April 10, 2014.

Tomsey, C. S., et al. (2001). Case work guidelines and interpretation of short tandem repeat complex mixture analysis. *Croatian Medical Journal, 42*(3), 276–280.

Communication

Evett, I. W., et al. (2000). The impact of the principles of evidence interpretation and the structure and content of statements. *Science & Justice, 40,* 233–239.

Hill, R. P. (2005). *NFSTC DNA analyst training. Section 8: Communication skills.* Available at http://www.nfstc.org/pdi/Subject08/pdi_s08_m01.htm. Accessed April 10, 2014.

Inman, K., & Rudin, N. (2001). *Principles and practice of criminalistics: The profession of forensic science.* Boca Raton: CRC Press.

Kelty, S. F. (2013). Dismantling the Justice Silos: avoiding the pitfalls and reaping the benefits of information-sharing between forensic science, medicine and law. *Forensic Science International, 230,* 8–15.

Reyna, V. F., et al. (2009). How numeracy influences risk comprehension and medical decision making. *Psychological Bulletin, 135,* 943–973.

Roland, M.-C. (2009). Quality and integrity in scientific writing: prerequisites for quality in science communication. *Journal of Scientific Communication, 8*(2), A04. Available at http://jcom.sissa.it/archive/08/02/Jcom0802(2009)A04/Jcom0802(2009)A04.pdf. Accessed April 10, 2014.

Rudram, D. A. (1996). Interpretation of scientific evidence. *Science & Justice, 36,* 133–138.

Report & Case Review

Coyle, H. M. (2012). The importance of scientific evaluation of biological evidence — data from eight years of case review. *Science & Justice, 52*(4), 268–270.

Hennessey, M. (2002). World Trade Center DNA identifications: the administrative review process. In *Proceedings of the 13th international symposium on human identification.* Available at http://www.promega.com/products/pm/genetic-identity/ishi-conference-proceedings/13th-ishi-oral-presentations/. Accessed April 10, 2014.

Inman, K., & Rudin, N. (2001). *Principles and practice of criminalistics: The profession of forensic science.* Boca Raton: CRC Press.

North Carolina State Crime Laboratory. (2013). *ISO procedures.* Available at http://www.ncdoj.gov/About-DOJ/Crime-Lab/ISO-Procedures.aspx. Accessed April 10, 2014.

NYC OCME. (2012). *Protocols for forensic STR analysis.* Available at http://www.nyc.gov/html/ocme/downloads/pdf/Fbio/Protocols%20for%20Forensic%20STR%20Analysis.pdf. Accessed April 10, 2014.

Virginia Department of Forensic Sciences. (2013). *Forensic biology procedures.* Available at http://www.dfs.virginia.gov/laboratory-forensic-services/biology/manuals/. Accessed April 10, 2014.

Report Comprehension

ASCLD/LAB, Guiding Principles (2014). Available at http://www.ascld-lab.org/guiding-principles/. Accessed April 10, 2014.

Balding, D. J., & Donnelly, P. (1994). The prosecutor's fallacy and DNA evidence. *Criminal Law Review,* 711–721.

Brun, W., & Teigen, K. H. (1988). Verbal probabilities: ambiguous, context-dependent, or both? *Organizational Behavior and Human Decision Processes, 41*, 390–404.

Cashman, K., & Henning, T. (2012). Lawyers and DNA: issues in understanding and challenging the evidence. *Current Issues in Criminal Justice, 24*, 69–83.

Cotton, R. W. (2013). *Mixtures go to court. Presentation as part of NIST DNA mixture interpretation webcast*. Slides available at http://www.cstl.nist.gov/strbase/training/MixtureWebcast/10_Court-Cotton.pdf. Accessed April 10, 2014.

de Keijser, J., & Elffers, H. (2012). Understanding of forensic expert reports by judges, defense lawyers and forensic professionals. *Psychology, Crime & Law, 18*(2), 191–207.

Evett, I. W. (1987). Bayesian inference and forensic science: problems and perspectives. *The Statistician, 36*, 99–105.

Evett, I. W. (1995). Avoiding the transposed conditional. *Science & Justice, 35*, 127–131.

Evett, I. W., & Buckleton, J. S. (1989). Some aspects of the Bayesian approach to evidence evaluation. *Journal of the Forensic Science Society, 29*, 317–324.

Fenton, N., & Neil, M. (2000). The 'Jury Observation Fallacy' and the use of Bayesian networks to present probabilistic legal arguments. *Mathematics Today, 36*, 180–187.

Gatowski, S. I., et al. (2001). Asking the gatekeepers: a national survey of judges on judging expert evidence in a post-Daubert world. *Law and Human Behavior, 25*, 433–458.

Howes, L. M., et al. (2013). Forensic scientists' conclusions: how readable are they for non-scientist report-users? *Forensic Science International, 231*, 102–112.

Koehler, J. J. (1993). Error and exaggeration in the presentation of DNA evidence. *Jurimetrics Journal, 34*, 21–39.

Koehler, J. J. (2001). When are people persuaded by DNA match statistics? *Law and Human Behavior, 25*, 493–513.

Martire, K. A., et al. (2013). The psychology of interpreting expert evaluative opinions. *Australian Journal of Forensic Sciences, 45*(3), 305–314.

McQuiston-Surrett, D., & Saks, M. J. (2009). The testimony of forensic identification science: what expert witnesses say and what fact finders hear. *Law and Human Behavior, 33*(5), 436–453.

Meester, R., & Sjerps, M. (2004). Why the effect of prior odds should accompany the likelihood ratio when reporting DNA evidence. *Law & Probability, 3*, 51–62.

Meulenbroek, A. J., et al. (2011). A practical model to explain results of comparative DNA testing in court. *Forensic Science International: Genetics Supplement Series, 3*, e325–e326.

National Institute of Justice. (2012). *DNA for the defense bar* (see Chapter 2, Section 7: Forensic DNA lab report basics, pp. 17–19). Available at http://www.nij.gov/pubs-sum/237975.htm. Accessed April 10, 2014.

Olson, M. J., & Budescu, D. V. (1997). Patterns of preference for numerical and verbal probabilities. *Journal of Behavioral Decision Making, 10*, 117–131.

Peterson, J. L., et al. (2013). Effect of forensic evidence on criminal justice case processing. *Journal of Forensic Sciences, 58*(S1), S78–S90.

Robertson, B., & Vignaux, G. A. (1995). *Interpreting evidence: Evaluating forensic science in the courtroom*. Chichester, England: John Wiley & Sons.

Sjerps, M. J. (2000). Pros and cons of Bayesian reasoning in forensic science. In J. F. Nijboer, & W. J. J. M. Sprangers (Eds.), *Series criminal sciences Harmonization in forensic expertise* (pp. 557–585). Amsterdam: Thela Thesis.

Sjerps, M. J., & Biesheuvel, D. B. (1999). The interpretation of conventional and "Bayesian" verbal scales for expressing expert opinion: a small experiments among jurists. *Forensic Linguistics, 6*, 214–227.

Smith, L. L., et al. (2011). Understanding juror perceptions of forensic evidence: investigating the impact of case context on perceptions of forensic evidence strength. *Journal of Forensic Sciences, 56*, 409–414.

Taroni, F., & Aitken, C. G. G. (1998). Probabilistic reasoning and the law Part 1: assessment of probabilities and explanation of the value of DNA evidence. *Science & Justice, 38*, 165–177.

Thompson, W. C. (1989). Are juries competent to evaluate statistical evidence? *Law and Contemporary Problems, 52*, 9–40.

Thompson, W. C., & Schumann, E. L. (1987). Interpretation of statistical evidence in criminal trials: the prosecutor's fallacy and the defense attorney's fallacy. *Law and Human Behavior, 11*, 167–187.

II. STATISTICAL INTERPRETATION

STR Allele Frequencies from U.S. Population Data

The U.S. population data contained in this Appendix were compiled following collection of genetic information from 29 autosomal STR loci obtained through analysis of 1,036 DNA samples with multiple STR typing kits on an ABI 3130xl. Every attempt was made to eliminate null alleles due to primer binding site mutations. DNA samples were cross-examined with more than a dozen different STR kits including Identifiler, NGM SElect, PowerPlex 16, PowerPlex ESI 17 Pro, and PowerPlex Fusion. Potential first-order relatives (e.g. brothers) were removed from the final data set based on Y-chromosome and mitochondrial DNA data to provide a set of 1,036 *unrelated* samples of which all but four are male. Origins of the DNA samples and efforts made to characterize them are described in Butler et al. (2012). Complete genotypes of the individuals used to generate these allele tables, as well as results from 23 Y-STR loci on the 1032 males, are available on the NIST STRBase website (STRBase 2014). This NIST dataset became part of the FBI PopStats program in September 2013.

Information for each STR locus includes the observed alleles, the total number of observations for each allele, the percentage of each allele from the 2,072 chromosomes measured (2N, where N = 1,036 individuals, since each individual is diploid and will have two chromosomes to examine). In this data set, there was a single sample with a tri-allelic pattern of 9,10,11 at TPOX.

Allele frequencies from the most common allele in each population are highlighted in bold font. Allele frequencies denoted with an asterisk (*) are below the 5/2N minimum allele threshold recommended by the 1996 National Research Council report (NRCII; see Appendix 2) *The Evaluation of Forensic DNA Evidence*. The following minimum allele frequencies should be substituted into genotype frequency calculations for the designated alleles falling below the 5/2N threshold: Caucasians **0.00693** (N = 361), Blacks (African Americans) **0.00731** (N = 342), Hispanics **0.0106** (N = 236), and Asians **0.0258** (N = 97).

The allele frequencies contained in this Appendix are used throughout the book to illustrate calculations of random match probabilities (RMPs) and STR profile frequencies. Note that three significant figures are used for the allele frequency values in this book. A decision was made to use a lower number of significant figures than has been used previously to help readers appreciate that allele frequencies are rough estimates and typically should not be viewed as possessing a high level of precision given the limited sampling of populations that has been performed.

CSF1PO   9 Alleles Observed

| Allele | Total 2N=2072 | | N=361 | N=342 | N=236 | N=97 |
	#	%	Caucasian	Black	Hispanic	Asian
7	48	2.32	—	0.0556	0.0127	0.0206*
8	44	2.12	0.00554*	0.0556	0.00424*	—
9	61	2.94	0.0139	0.0395	0.0233	0.0670
10	481	23.2	0.220	0.250	0.237	0.201
11	567	27.4	0.309	0.249	0.280	0.216
12	714	34.5	**0.360**	**0.295**	**0.375**	**0.387**
13	136	6.56	0.0817	0.0468	0.0593	0.0876
14	19	0.917	0.00970	0.00877	0.00636*	0.0155*
15	2	0.0965	—	—	0.00212*	0.00515*
	Minimum allele frequency (5/2N)		**0.00693**	**0.00731**	**0.0106**	**0.0258**

FGA   27 Alleles Observed

| Allele | Total 2N=2072 | | N=361 | N=342 | N=236 | N=97 |
	#	%	Caucasian	Black	Hispanic	Asian
16.2	1	0.0483	—	0.00146*	—	—
17	3	0.145	—	—	0.00212*	0.0103*
17.2	1	0.0483	—	0.00146*	—	—
18	30	1.45	0.0249	0.00146*	0.0127	0.0258
18.2	12	0.579	—	0.0175	—	—
19	120	5.79	0.0499	0.0512	0.0805	0.0567
19.2	2	0.0965	—	0.00292*	—	—
20	183	8.83	0.123	0.0541	0.0847	0.0876
21	305	14.7	0.179	0.123	0.153	0.103
21.2	4	0.193	0.00554*	—	—	—
22	409		**0.205**	**0.199**	**0.165**	**0.242**
22.2	14	0.676	0.0125	0.00439*	0.00424*	—
22.3	1	0.0483	—	0.00146*	—	—
23	323	15.6	0.152	0.170	0.121	0.206

FGA   27 Alleles Observed (*cont'd*)

Allele	#	%	N=361 Caucasian	N=342 Black	N=236 Hispanic	N=97 Asian
23.2	5	0.241	0.00277*	0.00146*	0.00424*	—
24	284	13.7	0.134	0.133	0.142	0.149
24.2	2	0.0965	0.00139*	—	—	0.00515*
25	208	10.0	0.0789	0.118	0.119	0.0722
25.2	1	0.0483	—	0.00146*	—	—
26	102	4.92	0.0263	0.0702	0.0614	0.0309
27	41	1.98	0.00416*	0.0234	0.0445	0.00515*
28	11	0.531	—	0.0146	0.00212*	—
29	5	0.241	—	0.00585*	0.00212*	—
30	2	0.0965	—	0.00146*	0.00212*	—
30.2	1	0.0483	—	0.00146*	—	—
31.2	1	0.0483	—	0.00146*	—	—
43.2	1	0.0483	—	—	—	0.00515*
	Minimum allele frequency (5/2N)		**0.00693**	**0.00731**	**0.0106**	**0.0258**

TH01   8 Alleles Observed

Allele	#	%	N=361 Caucasian	N=342 Black	N=236 Hispanic	N=97 Asian
5	4	0.193	0.00139*	0.00439*	—	—
6	406	19.6	0.235	0.132	0.239	0.170
7	611	29.5	0.194	**0.408**	**0.297**	0.268
8	260	12.5	0.0956	0.196	0.0911	0.0722
9	350	16.9	0.119	0.159	0.146	**0.443**
9.3	426	20.6	**0.345**	0.0965	0.218	0.0412
10	14	0.676	0.00831	0.00439*	0.00847*	0.00515*
11	1	0.0483	0.00139*	—	—	—
	Minimum allele frequency (5/2N)		**0.00693**	**0.00731**	**0.0106**	**0.0258**

(*Continued*)

TPOX   9 Alleles Observed

Allele	Total 2N=2073[‡] #	%	N=361 Caucasian	N=342 Black	N=236 Hispanic	N=97 Asian
5	1	0.0482	0.00139*	–	–	–
6	66	3.18	0.00139*	0.0891	0.00847*	–
7	15	0.724	–	0.0175	0.00636*	–
8	966	46.6	**0.525**	**0.366**	**0.485**	**0.552**
9	285	13.7	0.127	0.196	0.0932	0.0773
10	124	5.98	0.0499	0.0876	0.0487	0.0258
11	508	24.5	0.252	0.216	0.254	0.299
12	106	5.11	0.0416	0.0263	0.104	0.0464
13	2	0.0965	0.00139*	0.00146*	–	–
	Minimum allele frequency (5/2N)		**0.00693**	**0.00730**	**0.0106**	**0.0258**

[‡] *The total number of alleles observed at TPOX is larger by one due to a tri-allelic pattern in one of the samples (Butler et al. 2012).*

VWA   11 Alleles Observed

Allele	Total 2N=2072 #	%	N=361 Caucasian	N=342 Black	N=236 Hispanic	N=97 Asian
11	3	0.145	–	0.00292*	0.00212*	–
12	2	0.0965	0.00139*	0.00146*	–	–
13	7	0.338	0.00139*	0.00877	–	–
14	198	9.56	0.0928	0.0804	0.0805	0.196
15	279	13.5	0.105	0.192	0.144	0.0206*
16	477	23.0	0.201	**0.250**	**0.284**	0.139
17	543	26.2	**0.284**	0.235	0.246	**0.314**
18	373	18.0	0.202	0.149	0.180	0.206
19	163	7.87	0.104	0.0629	0.0508	0.108
20	24	1.16	0.00693	0.0161	0.0106	0.0155*
21	3	0.145	0.00139*	0.00146*	0.00212*	–
	Minimum allele frequency (5/2N)		**0.00693**	**0.00731**	**0.0106**	**0.0258**

D1S1656   15 Alleles Observed

Allele	#	%	N=361 Caucasian	N=342 Black	N=236 Hispanic	N=97 Asian
		Total 2N=2072				
10	15	0.724	0.00277*	0.0146	0.00636*	—
11	106	5.12	0.0776	0.0453	0.0275	0.0309
12	179	8.64	0.116	0.0643	0.0890	0.0464
13	197	9.51	0.0665	0.101	0.114	0.134
14	300	14.5	0.0789	**0.257**	0.117	0.0619
14.3	9	0.434	0.00277*	0.00731	0.00424*	—
15	335	16.2	**0.150**	0.158	0.138	**0.278**
15.3	86	4.15	0.0582	0.0292	0.0508	—
16	295	14.2	0.136	0.110	**0.176**	0.201
16.3	141	6.81	0.0609	0.102	0.0508	0.0155*
17	87	4.20	0.0471	0.0278	0.0424	0.0722
17.3	217	10.5	0.133	0.0497	0.148	0.0876
18	12	0.579	0.00554*	0.00292*	0.00636*	0.0155*
18.3	74	3.57	0.0499	0.0234	0.0254	0.0515
19.3	19	0.917	0.0152	0.00731	0.00424*	0.00515*
	Minimum allele frequency (5/2N)		**0.00693**	**0.00731**	**0.0106**	**0.0258**

D2S441   15 Alleles Observed

Allele	#	%	N=361 Caucasian	N=342 Black	N=236 Hispanic	N=97 Asian
		Total 2N=2072				
8	1	0.0483	—	—	—	0.00515*
9	3	0.145	0.00139*	0.00292*	—	—
9.1	2	0.0965	0.00139*	—	—	0.00515*
10	421	20.3	0.211	0.0848	**0.337**	0.268
11	705	34.0	**0.343**	**0.363**	0.299	**0.351**
11.3	101	4.87	0.0609	0.0439	0.0445	0.0309

(*Continued*)

D2S441   15 Alleles Observed (cont'd)

Allele	Total 2N=2072 #	Total 2N=2072 %	N=361 Caucasian	N=342 Black	N=236 Hispanic	N=97 Asian
12	206	9.94	0.0471	0.165	0.0360	0.216
12.3	9	0.434	0.00416*	0.00585*	0.00212*	0.00515*
13	67	3.23	0.0291	0.0439	0.0233	0.0258
13.3	2	0.0965	—	0.00292*	—	—
14	470	22.7	0.241	0.268	0.206	0.0825
14.3	1	0.0483	—	0.00146*	—	—
15	81	3.91	0.0596	0.0190	0.0487	0.0103*
16	2	0.0965	0.00139*	—	0.00212*	—
17	1	0.0483	—	—	0.00212*	—
Minimum allele frequency (5/2N)			**0.00693**	**0.00731**	**0.0106**	**0.0258**

D2S1338   13 Alleles Observed

Allele	Total 2N=2072 #	Total 2N=2072 %	N=361 Caucasian	N=342 Black	N=236 Hispanic	N=97 Asian
15	2	0.0965	0.00139*	0.00146*	—	—
16	83	4.01	0.0374	0.0556	0.0297	0.0206*
17	294	14.2	**0.186**	0.101	0.169	0.0567
18	146	7.05	0.0734	0.0424	0.0805	0.134
19	308	14.9	0.120	**0.139**	**0.193**	**0.180**
20	275	13.3	0.157	0.104	0.127	0.160
21	138	6.66	0.0374	0.136	0.0318	0.0155*
22	156	7.53	0.0346	0.137	0.0572	0.0515
23	245	11.8	0.105	0.104	0.140	0.165
24	201	9.70	0.115	0.0833	0.0763	0.129
25	173	8.35	0.102	0.0775	0.0784	0.0464
26	47	2.27	0.0305	0.0146	0.0169	0.0361
27	4	0.193	—	0.00439*	—	0.00515*
Minimum allele frequency (5/2N)			**0.00693**	**0.00731**	**0.0106**	**0.0258**

D3S1358   11 Alleles Observed

Allele	Total 2N = 2072		N = 361	N = 342	N = 236	N = 97
	#	%	Caucasian	Black	Hispanic	Asian
11	1	0.0483	0.00139*	—	—	—
12	3	0.145	—	0.00439*	—	—
13	6	0.290	0.00139*	0.00292*	0.00636*	—
14	181	8.74	0.107	0.0906	0.0784	0.0258
15	631	30.5	**0.273**	0.308	**0.322**	**0.366**
15.2	1	0.0483	—	0.00146*	—	—
16	586	28.3	0.238	**0.319**	0.280	0.330
17	423	20.4	0.211	0.212	0.184	0.201
18	219	10.6	0.151	0.0570	0.123	0.0670
19	19	0.917	0.0166	0.00439*	0.00424*	0.0103*
20	2	0.0965	0.00139*	—	0.00212*	—
	Minimum allele frequency (5/2N)		**0.00693**	**0.00731**	**0.0106**	**0.0258**

D5S818   9 Alleles Observed

Allele	Total 2N = 2072		N = 361	N = 342	N = 236	N = 97
	#	%	Caucasian	Black	Hispanic	Asian
7	22	1.06	0.00277*	0.00146*	0.0339	0.0155*
8	41	1.98	0.00554*	0.0468	0.00847*	0.00515*
9	96	4.63	0.0416	0.0322	0.0530	0.0979
10	161	7.77	0.0554	0.0731	0.0572	0.227
11	653	31.5	0.356	0.234	**0.390**	**0.268**
12	733	35.4	**0.388**	**0.370**	0.339	0.206
13	339	16.4	0.143	0.224	0.108	0.165
14	23	1.11	0.00693	0.0161	0.00847*	0.0155*
15	4	0.193	0.00139*	0.00292*	0.00212*	—
	Minimum allele frequency (5/2N)		**0.00693**	**0.00731**	**0.0106**	**0.0258**

(Continued)

D6S1043   27 Alleles Observed

Allele	Total 2N=2072 #	Total 2N=2072 %	N=361 Caucasian	N=342 Black	N=236 Hispanic	N=97 Asian
8	1	0.0483	0.00139*	—	—	—
9	1	0.0483	—	0.00146*	—	—
10	24	1.16	0.0166	0.00585*	0.00424*	0.0309
11	432	20.8	**0.296**	0.154	0.178	0.149
12	445	21.5	0.237	**0.224**	**0.206**	0.124
12.3	1	0.0483	—	—	—	0.00515*
13	200	9.65	0.0859	0.0965	0.102	0.124
14	174	8.40	0.0554	0.0585	0.136	0.155
15	67	3.23	0.0125	0.0541	0.0297	0.0361
16	16	0.772	0.00416*	0.0161	0.00212*	0.00515*
17	120	5.79	0.0609	0.0570	0.0487	0.0722
18	219	10.6	0.0886	0.107	0.108	**0.160**
18.1	1	0.0483	—	—	0.00212*	—
18.3	1	0.0483	—	0.00146*	—	—
19	202	9.75	0.0983	0.113	0.0763	0.0928
19.3	2	0.0965	—	0.00146*	0.00212*	—
20	96	4.63	0.0319	0.0731	0.0318	0.0412
20.3	6	0.290	—	—	0.0127	—
21	23	1.11	0.00970	0.0175	0.00636*	0.00515*
21.3	20	0.965	—	0.00146*	0.0403	—
22	1	0.0483	0.00139*	—	—	—
22.3	6	0.290	—	—	0.0127	—
23	7	0.338	—	0.0102	—	—
23.3	1	0.0483	—	—	0.00212*	—
24	4	0.193	—	0.00585*	—	—
25	1	0.0483	—	0.00146*	—	—
26	1	0.0483	—	0.00146*	—	—
	Minimum allele frequency (5/2N)		0.00693	0.00731	0.0106	0.0258

D7S820   11 Alleles Observed

| Allele | Total 2N=2072 | | N=361 | N=342 | N=236 | N=97 |
	#	%	Caucasian	Black	Hispanic	Asian
6	1	0.0483	—	0.00146*	—	—
7	34	1.64	0.0277	0.0117	0.0106	0.00515*
8	342	16.5	0.144	0.228	0.121	0.129
8.1	1	0.0483	0.00139*	—	—	—
9	252	12.2	0.168	0.115	0.0911	0.0464
10	610	29.4	**0.256**	**0.336**	**0.307**	0.258
10.3	1	0.0483	—	—	0.00212*	—
11	488	23.6	0.205	0.203	0.278	**0.361**
12	282	13.6	0.159	0.0877	0.155	0.175
13	57	2.75	0.0346	0.0146	0.0360	0.0258
14	4	0.193	0.00416*	0.00146*	—	—
	Minimum allele frequency (5/2N)		**0.00693**	**0.00731**	**0.0106**	**0.0258**

D8S1179   11 Alleles Observed

| Allele | Total 2N=2072 | | N=361 | N=342 | N=236 | N=97 |
	#	%	Caucasian	Black	Hispanic	Asian
8	22	1.06	0.0139	0.00731	0.0148	—
9	10	0.483	0.00554*	0.00439*	0.00636*	—
10	163	7.87	0.102	0.0307	0.0932	0.124
11	139	6.71	0.0762	0.0526	0.0530	0.119
12	294	14.2	0.168	0.130	0.129	0.119
13	556	26.8	**0.330**	0.219	**0.273**	**0.201**
14	484	23.4	0.166	**0.294**	0.263	**0.201**
15	291	14.0	0.104	0.190	0.129	0.129
16	101	4.87	0.0332	0.0643	0.0318	0.0928
17	8	0.386	0.00139*	0.00439*	0.00424*	0.0103*
18	4	0.193	—	0.00292*	0.00212*	0.00515*
	Minimum allele frequency (5/2N)		**0.00693**	**0.00731**	**0.0106**	**0.0258**

(Continued)

D10S1248   12 Alleles Observed

Allele	Total 2N = 2072		N = 361	N = 342	N = 236	N = 97
	#	%	Caucasian	Black	Hispanic	Asian
8	2	0.0965	—	0.00292*	—	—
9	2	0.0965	—	0.00292*	—	—
10	6	0.290	—	0.00731	—	0.00515*
11	27	1.30	0.00139*	0.0351	0.00424*	—
12	149	7.19	0.0319	0.130	0.0424	0.0876
13	573	27.7	**0.307**	0.234	0.273	**0.320**
14	613	29.6	0.298	**0.276**	**0.339**	0.253
15	417	20.1	0.197	0.197	0.212	0.206
16	222	10.7	0.133	0.0877	0.0996	0.0979
17	55	2.65	0.0277	0.0249	0.0254	0.0309
18	3	0.145	0.00139*	0.00146*	0.00212*	—
19	3	0.145	0.00277*	—	0.00212*	—
Minimum allele frequency (5/2N)			**0.00693**	**0.00731**	**0.0106**	**0.0258**

D12S391   24 Alleles Observed

Allele	Total 2N = 2072		N = 361	N = 342	N = 236	N = 97
	#	%	Caucasian	Black	Hispanic	Asian
14	1	0.0483	—	0.00146*	—	—
15	105	5.07	0.0319	0.0775	0.0445	0.0412
16	84	4.05	0.0222	0.0673	0.0424	0.0103*
17	258	12.5	0.127	0.167	0.0763	0.0825
17.1	3	0.145	—	0.00439*	—	—
17.3	26	1.25	0.0208	0.00439*	0.0169	—
18	432	20.8	**0.172**	**0.253**	0.178	**0.263**
18.1	1	0.0483	—	0.00146*	—	—
18.3	27	1.30	0.0249	0.00439*	0.0127	—
19	314	15.2	0.125	0.148	**0.189**	0.175
19.1	7	0.338	—	0.00877	0.00212*	—

D12S391   24 Alleles Observed (*cont'd*)

Allele	Total 2N = 2072		N = 361	N = 342	N = 236	N = 97
	#	%	Caucasian	Black	Hispanic	Asian
19.3	10	0.483	0.00416*	0.00439*	0.00636*	0.00515*
20	262	12.6	0.111	0.104	0.155	0.196
20.1	2	0.0965	—	0.00292*	—	—
20.3	1	0.0483	—	—	0.00212*	—
21	209	10.1	0.129	0.0643	0.112	0.0979
22	137	6.61	0.0956	0.0365	0.0678	0.0567
22.2	1	0.0483	—	—	0.00212*	—
23	102	4.92	0.0693	0.0292	0.0572	0.0258
24	53	2.56	0.0471	0.0132	0.0169	0.0103*
24.3	1	0.0483	—	—	—	0.00515*
25	24	1.16	0.0166	0.00877	0.00636*	0.0155*
26	7	0.338	0.00277*	—	0.00636*	0.0103*
27	5	0.241	0.00139*	—	0.00636*	0.00515*
	Minimum allele frequency (5/2N)		**0.00693**	**0.00731**	**0.0106**	**0.0258**

D13S317   8 Alleles Observed

Allele	Total 2N = 2072		N = 361	N = 342	N = 236	N = 97
	#	%	Caucasian	Black	Hispanic	Asian
8	201	9.70	0.120	0.0278	0.110	0.222
9	185	8.93	0.0776	0.0336	0.165	0.144
10	122	5.89	0.0471	0.0307	0.0996	0.103
11	602	29.1	**0.325**	0.310	0.218	**0.268**
12	631	30.5	0.269	**0.418**	**0.235**	0.206
13	241	11.6	0.116	0.140	0.106	0.0567
14	87	4.20	0.0429	0.0395	0.0614	—
15	3	0.145	0.00139*	—	0.00424*	—
	Minimum allele frequency (5/2N)		**0.00693**	**0.00731**	**0.0106**	**0.0258**

(*Continued*)

D16S539   9 Alleles Observed

Allele	Total 2N=2072		N=361	N=342	N=236	N=97
	#	%	Caucasian	Black	Hispanic	Asian
5	1	0.0483	–	0.00146*	–	–
8	44	2.12	0.0180	0.0322	0.0191	–
9	337	16.3	0.107	0.183	0.140	**0.356**
10	224	10.8	0.0568	0.117	0.150	0.165
11	604	29.2	**0.314**	**0.314**	0.265	0.191
12	532	25.7	**0.314**	0.205	**0.278**	0.175
13	284	13.7	0.163	0.123	0.133	0.0979
14	45	2.17	0.0263	0.0249	0.0127	0.0155*
15	1	0.0483	–	–	0.00212*	–
	Minimum allele frequency (5/2N)		**0.00693**	**0.00731**	**0.0106**	**0.0258**

D18S51   22 Alleles Observed

Allele	Total 2N=2072		N=361	N=342	N=236	N=97
	#	%	Caucasian	Black	Hispanic	Asian
9	2	0.0965	–	0.00292*	–	–
10	10	0.483	0.00831	0.00439*	0.00212*	–
11	15	0.724	0.00970	0.00146*	0.0148	–
12	195	9.41	0.114	0.0760	0.114	0.0361
13	217	10.5	0.123	0.0409	0.123	0.216
13.2	3	0.145	–	0.00439*	–	–
14	268	12.9	0.134	0.0716	**0.161**	**0.237**
14.2	2	0.0965	0.00139*	–	0.00212*	–
15	346	16.7	**0.170**	0.165	0.159	0.180
15.2	1	0.0483	–	0.00146*	–	–
16	307	14.8	0.147	**0.171**	0.125	0.129
16.2	1	0.0483	0.00139*	–	–	–
17	276	13.3	0.139	0.152	0.125	0.0670
18	182	8.78	0.0776	0.121	0.0784	0.0309

D18S51 22 Alleles Observed (*cont'd*)

Allele	#	%	N=361 Caucasian	N=342 Black	N=236 Hispanic	N=97 Asian
		Total 2N=2072				
19	127	6.13	0.0402	0.0994	0.0466	0.0412
20	74	3.57	0.0180	0.0629	0.0275	0.0258
21	20	0.965	0.00970	0.0102	0.00847*	0.0103*
21.2	1	0.0483	—	0.00146*	—	—
22	18	0.869	0.00693	0.00731	0.0106	0.0155*
23	4	0.193	—	0.00439*	—	0.00515*
24	2	0.0965	—	0.00146*	0.00212*	—
28	1	0.0483	—	—	—	0.00515*
	Minimum allele frequency (5/2N)		**0.00693**	**0.00731**	**0.0106**	**0.0258**

D19S433 16 Alleles Observed

Allele	#	%	N=361 Caucasian	N=342 Black	N=236 Hispanic	N=97 Asian
		Total 2N=2072				
9	1	0.0483	—	—	0.00212*	—
10	9	0.434	0.00139*	0.0102	0.00212*	—
11	54	2.61	0.00554*	0.0629	0.0148	—
12	173	8.35	0.0706	0.123	0.0657	0.0361
12.2	37	1.79	0.00139*	0.0365	0.0127	0.0258
13	512	24.7	0.255	**0.246**	0.222	0.284
13.2	66	3.19	0.00693	0.0526	0.0445	0.0206*
14	630	30.4	**0.361**	0.211	**0.354**	**0.299**
14.2	106	5.12	0.0235	0.0746	0.0381	0.103
15	244	11.8	0.157	0.0804	0.136	0.0619
15.2	118	5.69	0.0360	0.0614	0.0551	0.124
16	58	2.80	0.0568	0.00439*	0.0254	0.0103*
16.2	48	2.32	0.0152	0.0263	0.0275	0.0309
17	5	0.241	0.00693	—	—	—
17.2	8	0.386	0.00139*	0.00877	—	0.00515*
18.2	3	0.145	0.00139*	0.00292*	—	—
	Minimum allele frequency (5/2N)		**0.00693**	**0.00731**	**0.0106**	**0.0258**

(Continued)

D21S11   27 Alleles Observed

Allele	Total 2N=2072 #	Total 2N=2072 %	N=361 Caucasian	N=342 Black	N=236 Hispanic	N=97 Asian
24.2	1	0.0483	—	—	0.00212*	—
25.2	1	0.0483	0.00139*	—	—	—
26	1	0.0483	—	0.00146*	—	—
26.2	1	0.0483	—	—	0.00212*	—
27	80	3.86	0.0222	0.0746	0.0275	—
28	341	16.5	0.159	**0.246**	0.0996	0.0567
28.2	1	0.0483	—	—	—	0.00515*
29	423	20.4	0.202	0.205	0.208	0.201
29.2	3	0.145	0.00277*	—	0.00212*	—
29.3	1	0.0483	—	0.00146*	—	—
30	513	24.8	**0.283**	0.170	**0.273**	**0.330**
30.2	45	2.17	0.0291	0.0175	0.0233	0.00515*
30.3	2	0.0965	—	—	—	0.0103*
31	166	8.01	0.0720	0.0789	0.0763	0.124
31.2	160	7.72	0.0983	0.0512	0.0996	0.0361
32	29	1.40	0.00554*	0.00877	0.0169	0.0567
32.2	189	9.12	0.090	0.0614	0.127	0.113
33	9	0.434	0.00139*	0.00439*	0.00424*	0.0155*
33.1	3	0.145	—	0.00292*	0.00212*	—
33.2	68	3.28	0.0263	0.0351	0.0339	0.0464
34	5	0.241	—	0.00585*	0.00212*	—
34.2	3	0.145	0.00416*	—	—	—
35	16	0.772	0.00139*	0.0219	—	—
36	7	0.338	0.00139*	0.00877	—	—
37	2	0.0965	—	0.00292*	—	—
38	1	0.0483	—	0.00146*	—	—
39	1	0.0483	—	0.00146*	—	—
	Minimum allele frequency (5/2N)		**0.00693**	**0.00731**	**0.0106**	**0.0258**

D22S1045   11 Alleles Observed

| Allele | Total 2N = 2072 | | N = 361 | N = 342 | N = 236 | N = 97 |
	#	%	Caucasian	Black	Hispanic	Asian
8	5	0.241	—	0.00731	—	—
10	35	1.69	—	0.0409	0.0148	—
11	269	13.0	0.140	0.145	0.0636	0.201
12	53	2.56	0.0125	0.0541	0.0127	0.00515*
13	11	0.531	0.00693	0.00292*	0.00847*	—
14	109	5.26	0.0568	0.0775	0.0275	0.0103*
15	665	32.1	0.321	**0.251**	**0.426**	**0.309**
16	616	29.7	**0.382**	0.192	0.350	0.227
17	283	13.7	0.0748	0.209	0.0911	0.222
18	21	1.01	0.00554*	0.0146	0.00636*	0.0206*
19	5	0.241	—	0.00585*	—	0.00515*
	Minimum allele frequency (5/2N)		**0.00693**	**0.00731**	**0.0106**	**0.0258**

PENTA D   16 Alleles Observed

| Allele | Total 2N = 2072 | | N = 361 | N = 342 | N = 236 | N = 97 |
	#	%	Caucasian	Black	Hispanic	Asian
2.2	89	4.30	0.00416*	0.114	0.0169	—
3.2	7	0.338	—	0.00877	0.00212*	—
5	33	1.59	—	0.0439	0.00636*	—
6	13	0.627	0.00416*	0.0102	0.00212*	0.0103*
7	34	1.64	0.00416*	0.0439	0.00212*	—
8	99	4.78	0.0208	0.108	0.0191	0.00515*
9	450	21.7	0.222	0.168	**0.242**	**0.314**
10	261	12.6	0.115	0.0994	0.157	0.186
11	323	15.6	0.126	**0.180**	0.157	0.180
12	354	17.1	**0.233**	0.108	0.163	0.180
13	287	13.9	0.197	0.0833	0.144	0.103
13.4	1	0.0483	—	0.00146*	—	—
14	97	4.68	0.0609	0.0249	0.0720	0.0103*
15	17	0.820	0.00970	0.00439*	0.0106	0.0103*

(Continued)

PENTA D   16 Alleles Observed (*cont'd*)

Allele	Total 2N = 2072		N = 361	N = 342	N = 236	N = 97
	#	%	Caucasian	Black	Hispanic	Asian
16	4	0.193	0.00277*	—	0.00424*	—
17	3	0.145	0.00139*	0.00146*	0.00212*	—
	Minimum allele frequency (5/2N)		**0.00693**	**0.00731**	**0.0106**	**0.0258**

PENTA E   23 Alleles Observed

Allele	Total 2N = 2072		N = 361	N = 342	N = 236	N = 97
	#	%	Caucasian	Black	Hispanic	Asian
5	151	7.29	0.0762	0.0950	0.0360	0.0722
6	1	0.0483	—	0.00146*	—	—
7	249	12.0	0.169	0.104	0.119	—
8	137	6.61	0.0139	**0.167**	0.0254	0.00515*
9	57	2.75	0.0125	0.0512	0.0169	0.0258
10	146	7.05	0.0859	0.0468	0.0847	0.0619
11	173	8.35	0.0873	0.0643	0.0742	**0.160**
12	332	16.0	**0.199**	0.129	**0.174**	0.0928
13	187	9.03	0.0859	0.104	0.0932	0.0515
14	136	6.56	0.0623	0.0687	0.0720	0.0515
15	134	6.47	0.0429	0.0556	0.0911	0.113
15.4	2	0.0965	0.00139*	—	0.00212*	—
16	105	5.07	0.0512	0.0409	0.0614	0.0567
17	107	5.16	0.0485	0.0439	0.0551	0.0825
18	66	3.19	0.0332	0.0161	0.0339	0.0773
19	34	1.64	0.0152	0.00731	0.0212	0.0412
19.4	2	0.0965	—	—	—	0.0103*
20	24	1.16	0.00970	0.00439*	0.0212	0.0206*
21	9	0.434	0.00277*	—	0.00636*	0.0206*
22	8	0.386	0.00139*	—	0.00212*	0.0309
23	7	0.338	—	—	0.00636*	0.0206*
24	1	0.0483	0.00139*	—	—	—
25	4	0.193	—	0.00146*	0.00424*	0.00515*
	Minimum allele frequency (5/2N)		**0.00693**	**0.00731**	**0.0106**	**0.0258**

SE33   52 Alleles Observed

| Allele | Total 2N=2072 | | N=361 | N=342 | N=236 | N=97 |
	#	%	Caucasian	Black	Hispanic	Asian
6.3	1	0.0483	—	—	0.00212*	—
7	1	0.0483	—	0.00146*	—	—
10.2	1	0.0483	—	0.00146*	—	—
11	1	0.0483	0.00139*	—	—	—
11.2	2	0.0965	—	0.00292*	—	—
12	9	0.434	0.00693	0.00292*	0.00424*	—
12.2	4	0.193	—	0.00292*	0.00424*	—
13	24	1.16	0.0166	0.0117	0.00847*	—
13.2	4	0.193	—	0.00585*	—	—
14	66	3.19	0.0249	0.0512	0.0275	—
14.2	7	0.338	0.00277*	0.00585*	0.00212*	—
15	78	3.76	0.0402	0.0439	0.0360	0.0103*
15.2	5	0.241	—	0.00292*	0.00636*	—
16	101	4.87	0.0402	0.0482	0.0699	0.0309
16.2	4	0.193	0.00139*	0.00439*	—	—
16.3	2	0.0965	—	—	0.00424*	—
17	152	7.34	0.0623	0.0950	0.0763	0.0309
17.2	1	0.0483	—	0.00146*	—	—
17.3	4	0.193	0.00139*	0.00146*	0.00424*	—
18	199	9.60	0.0734	0.120	**0.110**	0.0619
19	193	9.31	0.0720	**0.127**	0.0890	0.0619
19.2	6	0.290	0.00416*	—	0.00636*	—
20	150	7.24	0.0582	0.0980	0.0487	0.0928
20.2	14	0.676	0.00970	0.00292*	0.00424*	0.0155*
21	69	3.33	0.0249	0.0482	0.0169	0.0515
21.2	37	1.79	0.0235	0.0102	0.0169	0.0258
22	30	1.45	0.0139	0.0146	0.0148	0.0155*
22.2	48	2.32	0.0374	0.00439*	0.0212	0.0412
23	9	0.434	0.00277*	0.00731	—	0.0103*

(*Continued*)

SE33   52 Alleles Observed (*cont'd*)

Allele	Total 2N = 2072 #	Total 2N = 2072 %	N = 361 Caucasian	N = 342 Black	N = 236 Hispanic	N = 97 Asian
23.2	58	2.80	0.0360	0.0175	0.0233	0.0464
24	1	0.0483	0.00139*	—	—	—
24.2	48	2.32	0.0222	0.0132	0.0233	0.0619
25.2	73	3.52	0.0416	0.0307	0.0233	0.0567
26	1	0.0483	—	0.00146*	—	—
26.2	122	5.89	0.0416	0.0629	0.0742	0.0722
27	1	0.0483	—	—	0.00212*	—
27.2	153	7.38	**0.0942**	0.0424	0.0763	**0.103**
27.3	1	0.0483	—	—	0.00212*	—
28.2	133	6.42	0.0762	0.0453	0.0678	0.0773
28.3	2	0.0965	0.00139*	0.00146*	—	—
29.2	97	4.68	0.0554	0.0234	0.0614	0.0619
30	1	0.0483	—	—	0.00212*	—
30.2	78	3.76	0.0568	0.0161	0.0403	0.0361
31	3	0.145	0.00277*	0.00146*	—	—
31.2	39	1.88	0.0235	0.0161	0.0127	0.0258
32	1	0.0483	0.00139*	—	—	—
32.2	19	0.917	0.0125	0.00439*	0.0106	0.0103*
33	2	0.0965	0.00139*	—	0.00212*	—
33.2	7	0.338	0.00416*	0.00292*	0.00424*	—
34	8	0.386	0.00831	0.00292*	—	—
34.2	1	0.0483	0.00139*	—	—	—
36	1	0.0483	—	0.00146*	—	—
	Minimum allele frequency (5/2N)		**0.00693**	**0.00731**	**0.0106**	**0.0258**

F13A01   16 Alleles Observed

| Allele | Total 2N = 2072 | | N = 361 | N = 342 | N = 236 | N = 97 |
	#	%	Caucasian	Black	Hispanic	Asian
3.2	288	13.9	0.0637	0.118	0.214	0.309
4	129	6.23	0.0263	0.0687	0.0826	0.124
4.2	1	0.0483	—	0.00146*	—	—
5	475	22.9	0.193	**0.339**	0.195	0.0619
6	516	24.9	**0.350**	0.127	0.172	**0.490**
7	509	24.6	0.316	0.197	**0.303**	0.0155*
8	45	2.17	0.00416*	0.0570	0.00636*	—
9	8	0.386	—	0.00877	0.00424*	—
10	5	0.241	0.00139*	0.00585*	—	—
11	5	0.241	—	0.00731	—	—
12	6	0.290	0.00139*	0.00439*	0.00424*	—
13	27	1.30	0.00139*	0.0336	0.00636*	—
14	20	0.965	0.0111	0.0175	—	—
15	30	1.45	0.0249	0.0132	0.00636*	—
16	7	0.338	0.00693	—	0.00424*	—
17	1	0.0483	—	—	0.00212*	—
	Minimum allele frequency (5/2N)		**0.00693**	**0.00731**	**0.0106**	**0.0258**

F13B   7 Alleles Observed

| Allele | Total 2N = 2072 | | N = 361 | N = 342 | N = 236 | N = 97 |
	#	%	Caucasian	Black	Hispanic	Asian
6	375	18.1	0.0942	0.363	0.119	0.0155*
6.3	1	0.0483	—	0.00146*	—	—
7	138	6.66	0.0166	0.168	0.0212	0.00515*
8	348	16.8	0.245	0.108	0.186	0.0464
9	481	23.2	0.247	0.228	0.231	0.196
10	721	34.8	**0.392**	0.129	**0.441**	**0.732**
11	8	0.386	0.00554*	0.00292*	0.00212*	0.00515*
	Minimum allele frequency (5/2N)		**0.00693**	**0.00731**	**0.0106**	**0.0258**

(Continued)

FESFPS 12 Alleles Observed

Allele	Total 2N=2072 #	Total 2N=2072 %	N=361 Caucasian	N=342 Black	N=236 Hispanic	N=97 Asian
5	1	0.0483	0.00139*	—	—	—
6	1	0.0483	—	0.00146*	—	—
7	3	0.145	—	0.00292*	0.00212*	—
8	94	4.54	0.0249	0.0994	0.0169	—
9	26	1.25	—	0.0278	0.00847*	0.0155*
10	471	22.7	0.281	0.225	0.203	0.0928
10.3	31	1.50	—	0.0424	0.00212*	0.00515*
11	810	39.1	**0.411**	**0.327**	**0.464**	**0.361**
11.3	2	0.0965	—	0.00292*	—	—
12	487	23.5	0.237	0.227	0.214	0.309
13	136	6.56	0.0429	0.0439	0.0784	0.196
14	10	0.483	0.00139*	—	0.0106	0.0206*
	Minimum allele frequency (5/2N)		**0.00693**	**0.00731**	**0.0106**	**0.0258**

LPL 9 Alleles Observed

Allele	Total 2N=2072 #	Total 2N=2072 %	N=361 Caucasian	N=342 Black	N=236 Hispanic	N=97 Asian
7	15	0.724	0.00139*	0.0161	0.00424*	0.00515*
8	3	0.145	—	0.00439*	—	—
9	138	6.66	0.0388	0.130	0.0424	0.00515*
10	899	43.4	**0.425**	**0.348**	**0.485**	**0.644**
11	391	18.9	0.262	0.124	0.199	0.119
12	511	24.7	0.233	0.295	0.212	0.211
13	102	4.92	0.0346	0.0746	0.0487	0.0155*
14	12	0.579	0.00416*	0.00731	0.00847*	—
15	1	0.0483	0.00139*	—	—	—
	Minimum allele frequency (5/2N)		**0.00693**	**0.00731**	**0.0106**	**0.0258**

PENTA C   12 Alleles Observed

Allele	Total 2N=2072		N=361	N=342	N=236	N=97
	#	%	Caucasian	Black	Hispanic	Asian
5	36	1.74	0.00831	0.0249	0.0169	0.0258
7	17	0.820	0.00277*	0.0161	0.00636*	0.00515*
8	68	3.28	0.00554*	0.0512	0.0339	0.0670
9	399	19.3	0.148	0.173	0.222	**0.356**
10	140	6.76	0.0665	0.0702	0.0657	0.0670
10.1	1	0.0483	—	0.00146*	—	—
11	694	33.5	**0.396**	**0.278**	**0.333**	0.314
12	447	21.6	0.211	0.250	0.203	0.144
13	217	10.5	0.143	0.0877	0.108	0.0155*
14	46	2.22	0.0180	0.0395	0.0106	0.00515*
15	5	0.241	0.00139*	0.00585*	—	—
16	2	0.0965	—	0.00292*	—	—
	Minimum allele frequency (5/2N)		**0.00693**	**0.00731**	**0.0106**	**0.0258**

DYS391   7 Alleles Observed

Allele	Total 2N=2072		N=361	N=342	N=236	N=97
	#	%	Caucasian	Black	Hispanic	Asian
7	1	0.0969	—	—	0.00424*	—
8	2	0.194	0.00279*	—	—	0.0104*
9	33	3.20	0.0334	0.00587*	0.0678	0.0313*
10	607	58.8	0.451	**0.698**	**0.542**	**0.823**
11	370	35.9	**0.487**	0.273	0.377	0.135
12	18	1.74	0.0251	0.0205	0.00847*	—
13	1	0.0969	—	0.00293*	—	—
	Minimum allele frequency (5/2N)		**0.0139**	**0.0147**	**0.0212**	**0.0521**

(*Continued*)

References

Butler, et al. (2012). Variability of new STR loci and kits in U.S. population groups. *Profiles in DNA*. Available at http://www.promega.com/resources/articles/profiles-in-dna/2012/variability-of-new-str-loci-and-kits-in-us-population-groups/. Accessed April 7, 2014.

STRBase website. (2014). Available at http://www.cstl.nist.gov/strbase/NISTpop.htm. Accessed July 7, 2014.

NRC I & NRC II Recommendations

Shortly after the introduction of forensic DNA testing for criminal cases in the late 1980s, a number of vocal academic critics attacked many of the underlying assumptions and aspects of restriction fragment length polymorphism (RFLP) DNA testing, which was the primary method being used at the time. Concern had arisen from poor-quality work being performed with non-standardized interpretation guidelines as well as sub-par statistical support for assigning weight to the occurrence of a match between two DNA samples. After a lengthy pretrial hearing regarding the admissibility of DNA in the 1989 *New York v. Castro* case, the court threw out DNA evidence of a match because of concerns over data quality and claims that the private forensic laboratory had not followed generally accepted standards for testing procedures and results interpretation.

In January 1990, the National Academy of Science's National Research Council (NRC) convened a Committee on DNA Technology in Forensic Science. In April 1992, this group published their thoughts and recommendations on the issue of data quality concerns and statistical calculations needed. This 1992 NRC report entitled *DNA Technology in Forensic Science* is commonly referred to as "NRC I." An outcry arose regarding some of the conclusions (particularly the application of a so-called "ceiling principle" that was thought to be overly conservative), and a new committee was formed to revisit many of the statistical issues. Both committees received input from a number of scientists and lawyers during their deliberations. *The Evaluation of Forensic DNA Evidence* that was published in 1996 has become known as "NRC II." The NRC II recommendations for statistical calculations in handling potential sub-population structure are still used today in the United States and are often cited by other laboratories around the world as well.

NRC I (1992)

The first Committee on DNA Technology in Forensic Science was chaired by distinguished medical genetics professor **Victor McKusick** (The Johns Hopkins University Hospital, Baltimore, MD). Other members of NRC I included **Paul Ferrara** (Division of Forensic Sciences, Richmond, VA), **Haig Kazazian** (The Johns Hopkins Hospital, Baltimore, MD), **Mary-Claire King** (University of California, Berkeley, CA), **Eric Lander** (Whitehead Institute for Biomedical Research, Cambridge, MA), **Henry Lee** (Connecticut State Police, Meriden, CT), **Richard Lempert** (University of Michigan Law School, Ann Arbor, MI), **Ruth Macklin** (Albert Einstein College of Medicine, Bronx, NY), **Thomas Marr** (Cold Spring Harbor Laboratory, Cold Spring Harbor, NY),

Philip Reilly (Shriver Center for Mental Retardation, Waltham, MA), **George Sensabaugh** (University of California, Berkeley, CA), and **Jack Weinstein** (U.S. District Court, Brooklyn, NY). **Thomas Caskey** (Baylor College of Medicine, Houston, TX) and **Michael Hunkapiller** (Applied Biosystems Inc., Foster City, CA) served for a time on the committee, but resigned before the final report was completed.

A total of 46 recommendations were made in the NRC I report. These recommendations are listed below according to the chapter in which they appeared in the original 1992 report. Although these recommendations are not typically cited or specifically followed today, there are many useful ideas worthy of careful consideration. To understand these recommendations is to gain a valuable historical perspective on why things are sometimes done a certain way in the forensic DNA field [e.g. the common practice in the United States of reporting DNA profile frequencies from three racial groups, usually selected from African American (Black), Asian, Caucasian, Hispanic, or Native American classifications].

Technical Considerations (Chapter 2)

- Any new DNA typing method (or a substantial variation of an existing method) must be rigorously characterized in both research and forensic settings, to determine the circumstances under which it will yield reliable results.
- DNA analysis in forensic science should be governed by the highest standards of scientific rigor, including the following requirements:
  - Each DNA typing procedure must be completely described in a detailed, written laboratory protocol.
  - Each DNA typing procedure requires objective and quantitative rules for identifying the pattern of a sample.
  - Each DNA typing procedure requires a precise and objective matching rule for declaring whether two samples match.
  - Potential artifacts should be identified by empirical testing, and scientific controls should be designed to serve as internal checks to test for the occurrence of artifacts.
  - The limits of each DNA typing procedure should be understood, especially when the DNA sample is small, is a mixture of DNA from multiple sources, or is contaminated with interfering substances.
  - Empirical characterizations of a DNA typing procedure must be published in appropriate scientific journals.
  - Before a new DNA typing procedure can be used, it must have not only a solid scientific foundation, but also a solid base of experience.
- The committee strongly recommends the establishment of a National Committee on Forensic DNA Typing (NCFDT) under the auspices of an appropriate government agency, such as the National Institutes of Health (NIH) or the National Institute of Standards and Technology (NIST), to provide expert advice primarily on scientific and technical issues concerning forensic DNA typing.
- Novel forms of variation in the genome that have the potential for increased power of discrimination between persons are being discovered. Furthermore, new ways to demonstrate variations in the genome are being developed. The current techniques are likely to be superseded

by others that provide unambiguous individual identification and have such advantages as automatability and economy. Each new method should be evaluated by the NCFDT for use in the forensic setting, applying appropriate criteria to ensure that society derives maximal benefit from DNA typing technology.

Statistical Basis for Interpretation (Chapter 3)

- As a basis for the interpretation of the statistical significance of DNA typing results, the committee recommends that blood samples be obtained from 100 randomly selected persons in each of 15 to 20 relatively homogeneous populations; that the DNA in lymphocytes from these blood samples be used to determine the frequencies of alleles currently tested in forensic applications; and that the lymphocytes be "'immortalized" and preserved as reference standards for determination of allele frequencies in tests applied in different laboratories or developed in the future. The collection of samples and their study should be overseen by the NCFDT.

- **The ceiling principle should be used in applying the multiplication rule for estimating the frequency of particular DNA profiles. For each allele in a person's DNA pattern, the highest allele frequency found in any of the 15 to 20 populations or 5% (whichever is larger) should be used.**

- In the interval (which should be short) while the reference blood samples are being collected, the significance of the findings of multilocus DNA typing should be presented in two ways: (1) If no match is found with any sample in a total databank of N persons (as will usually be the case), that should be stated, thus indicating the rarity of a random match. (2) In applying the multiplication rule, the 95% upper confidence limit of the frequency of each allele should be calculated for separate U.S. "racial" groups and the highest of these values or 10% (whichever is the larger) should be used. Data on at least three major "races" (e.g. Caucasians, Blacks, Hispanics, Asians, and Native Americans) should be analyzed.

- Any population databank used to support DNA typing should be openly available for scientific inspection by parties to a legal case and by the scientific community.

- Laboratory error rates should be measured with appropriate proficiency tests and should play a role in the interpretation of results of forensic DNA typing.

Standards (Chapter 4)

Although standardization of forensic practice is difficult because of the nature of the samples, DNA typing is such a powerful and complex technology that some degree of standardization is necessary to ensure high standards.

- Each forensic science laboratory engaged in DNA typing must have a formal, detailed quality-assurance and quality-control program to monitor work, on both an individual and a laboratory-wide basis.

- The Technical Working Group on DNA Analysis and Methods (TWGDAM) guidelines for a quality-assurance program for DNA RFLP analysis are an excellent starting point for a quality-assurance program, which should be supplemented by the additional technical recommendations of this committee.

- The TWGDAM group should continue to function, playing a role complementary to that of the National Committee on Forensic DNA Typing (NCFDT). To increase its effectiveness, TWGDAM should include additional technical experts from outside the forensic community who are not closely tied to any forensic laboratory.
- Quality-assurance programs in individual laboratories alone are insufficient to ensure high standards. External mechanisms are needed to ensure adherence to the practices of quality assurance. Potential mechanisms include individual certification, laboratory accreditation, and state or federal regulation.
- One of the best guarantees of high quality is the presence of an active professional-organization committee that is able to enforce standards. Although professional societies in forensic science have historically not played an active role, the American Society of Crime Laboratory Directors (ASCLD) and the American Society of Crime Laboratory Directors-Laboratory Accreditation Board (ASCLD-LAB) recently have shown substantial interest in enforcing quality by expanding the ASCLD-LAB accreditation program to include mandatory proficiency testing. ASCLD-LAB must demonstrate that it will actively discharge this role.
- Because private professional organizations lack the regulatory authority to require accreditation, further means are needed to ensure compliance with appropriate standards.
- Courts should require that laboratories providing DNA typing evidence have proper accreditation for each DNA typing method used. Any laboratory that is not formally accredited and that provides evidence to the courts — e.g. a non-forensic laboratory repeating the analysis of a forensic laboratory — should be expected to demonstrate that it is operating at the same level of standards as accredited laboratories.
- Establishing mandatory accreditation should be a responsibility of the Department of Health and Human Services (DHHS), in consultation with the Department of Justice (DOJ). DHHS is the appropriate agency, because it has extensive experience in the regulation of clinical laboratories through programs under the Clinical Laboratory Improvement Act and has extensive expertise in molecular genetics through the National Institutes of Health. DOJ must be involved, because the task is important for law enforcement.
- The National Institute of Justice (NIJ) does not appear to receive adequate funds to support proper education, training, and research in the field of forensic DNA typing. The level of funding should be re-evaluated and increased appropriately.

Databanks and Privacy of Information (Chapter 5)

- In the future, if pilot studies confirm its value, a national DNA profile databank should be created that contains information on felons convicted of particular violent crimes. Among crimes with high rates of recidivism, the case is strongest for rape, because perpetrators typically leave biological evidence (semen) that could allow them to be identified. Rape is the crime for which the databank will be of primary use. The case is somewhat weaker for violent offenders who are most likely to commit homicide as a recidivist offense, because killers leave biological evidence only in a minority of cases.
- The databank should also contain DNA profiles of unidentified persons obtained from biological samples found at crime scenes. These would be samples known to be of human origin, but not matched with any known persons.

- Databanks containing DNA profiles of members of the general population (as exist for ordinary fingerprints for identification purposes) are not appropriate, for reasons of both privacy and economics.
- DNA profile databanks should be accessible only to legally authorized persons and should be stored in a secure information resource.
- Legal policy concerning access and use of both DNA samples and DNA databank information should be established before there is a widespread proliferation of repositories of DNA samples and information. Interim protection and sanctions against misuse and abuse of information derived from DNA typing should be established immediately. Policies should explicitly define authorized uses and should provide for criminal penalties for abuses.
- Although the committee endorses the concept of a limited national DNA profile databank, it doubts that existing RFLP-based technology provides an appropriate, wise, long-term foundation for such a databank. We expect current methods to be replaced soon with techniques that are simpler, easier to automate, and less expensive—but incompatible with existing DNA profiles. Accordingly, the committee does not recommend establishing a comprehensive DNA profile databank yet.
- For the short term, we recommend the establishment of pilot projects that involve prototype databanks based on RFLP technology and consisting primarily of profiles of violent sex offenders. Such pilot projects could be worthwhile for identifying problems and issues in the creation of databanks. However, in the intermediate term, more efficient methods will replace the current one, and the forensic community should not allow itself to become locked into an outdated method.
- State and federal laboratories, which have a long tradition and much experience in the management of other types of basic evidence, should be given primary responsibility, authority, and additional resources to handle forensic DNA testing and all the associated sample-handling and data-handling requirements.
- Private-sector firms should not be discouraged from continuing to prepare and analyze DNA samples for specific cases or for databank samples, but they must be held accountable for misuse and abuse to the same extent as government-funded laboratories and government authorities.
- Discovery of a match between an evidence sample and a databank entry should be used only as the basis for further testing using markers at additional loci. The initial match should be used as probable cause to obtain a blood sample from the suspect, but only the statistical frequency associated with the additional loci should be presented at trial.

DNA Information in the Legal System (Chapter 6)

- Courts should take judicial notice of three scientific underpinnings of DNA typing:
    - The study of DNA polymorphisms can, in principle, provide a reliable method for comparing samples.
    - Each person's DNA is unique (except that of identical twins), although the actual discriminatory power of any particular DNA test will depend on the sites of DNA variation examined.
    - The current laboratory procedure for detecting DNA variation (specifically, single-locus probes analyzed on Southern blots without evidence of band shifting) is fundamentally sound, although the validity of any particular implementation of the basic procedure will depend on

proper characterization of the reproducibility of the system (e.g. measurement variation) and inclusion of all necessary scientific controls.

- The adequacy of the method used to acquire and analyze samples in a given case bears on the admissibility of the evidence and should, unless stipulated by opposing parties, be adjudicated case by case. In this adjudication, the accreditation and certification status of the laboratory performing the analysis should be taken into account.
- Because of the potential power of DNA evidence, authorities should make funds available to pay for expert witnesses, and the appropriate parties must be informed of the use of DNA evidence as soon as possible.
- DNA samples (and evidence likely to contain DNA) should be preserved whenever that is possible.
- All data and laboratory records generated by analysis of DNA samples should be made freely available to all parties. Such access is essential for evaluating the analysis.
- Protective orders should be used only to protect the privacy of individuals.

DNA Typing and Society (Chapter 7)

- In the forensic context, as in the medical setting, DNA information is personal, and a person's privacy and need for confidentiality should be respected. The release of DNA information on a criminal population without the subjects' permission for purposes other than law enforcement should be considered a misuse of the information, and legal sanctions should be established to deter the unauthorized dissemination or procurement of DNA information that was obtained for forensic purposes.
- Prosecutors and defense counsel should not oversell DNA evidence. Presentations that suggest to a judge or jury that DNA typing is infallible are rarely justified and should be avoided.
- Mechanisms should be established to ensure accountability of laboratories and personnel involved in DNA typing and to make appropriate public scrutiny possible.
- Organizations that conduct accreditation or regulation of DNA technology for forensic purposes should not be subject to the influence of private companies, public laboratories, or other organizations actually engaged in laboratory work.
- Private laboratories used for testing should not be permitted to withhold information from defendants on the grounds that trade secrets are involved.
- The same standards and peer-review processes used to evaluate advances in biomedical science and technology should be used to evaluate forensic DNA methods and techniques.
- Efforts at international cooperation should be furthered in order to ensure uniform international standards and the fullest possible exchange of scientific knowledge and technical expertise.

NRC II (1996)

Renowned genetics professor **James Crow** (University of Wisconsin, Madison, WI) served as the chair of the second NRC committee. Other members of NRC II included **Margaret Berger** (Brooklyn Law School, Brooklyn, NY), **Shari Diamond** (University of Illinois-Chicago/American Bar Association, Chicago, IL), **David Kaye** (Arizona State University College of Law, Tempe, AZ), **Haig**

Kazazian (University of Pennsylvania, Philadelphia, PA — formerly of the Johns Hopkins University), **Arno Motulsky** (University of Washington, Seattle, WA), **Thomas Nagylaki** (University of Chicago, Chicago, IL), **Masatoshi Nei** (Pennsylvania State University, University Park, PA), **George Sensabaugh** (University of California, Berkeley, CA), **David Siegmund** (Stanford University, Stanford, CA), and **Stephen Stigler** (University of Chicago, Chicago, IL).

University of Pennsylvania genetics professor Haig Kazazian and University of California, Berkeley, forensic science professor George Sensabaugh were part of both the NRC I and NRC II committees.

In the introduction to the NRC II report, Chairman James Crow wrote: "We agree with some statements of the 1992 report and disagree with others. Statements that are not discussed are neither endorsed nor rejected…. The information that has accumulated since the 1992 report permits us to be more confident of our recommendations." The NRC II report included a total of 11 recommendations, which are provided below. As used here, "p" and "q" represent allele frequencies and theta (θ) corresponds to a subpopulation correction factor. For further information on these topics, see Chapters 10 and 11.

Recommendations to Improve Laboratory Performance

Recommendation 3.1. Laboratories should adhere to high-quality standards (such as those defined by TWGDAM and the DNA Advisory Board) and make every effort to be accredited for DNA work (by such organizations as ASCLD-LAB).

Recommendation 3.2. Laboratories should participate regularly in proficiency tests, and the results should be available for court proceedings.

Recommendation 3.3. Whenever feasible, forensic samples should be divided into two or more parts at the earliest practicable stage and the unused parts retained to permit additional tests. The used and saved portions should be stored and handled separately. Any additional tests should be performed independently of the first by personnel not involved in the first test, and preferably in a different laboratory.

Recommendations for Estimating Random-Match Probabilities

Recommendation 4.1. In general, the calculation of a profile frequency should be made with the product rule. If the race of the person who left the evidence-sample DNA is known, the database for the person's race should be used; if the race is not known, calculations for all the racial groups to which possible suspects belong should be made. For systems such as variable number tandem repeats (VNTRs), in which a heterozygous locus could be mistaken for a homozygous one, if an upper bound on the frequency of the genotype at an apparently homozygous locus (single band) is desired, then twice the allele (bin) frequency, $2p$, should be used instead of p^2. For systems in which exact genotypes can be determined, $p^2 + p(1 - p)\theta$ should be used for the frequency at such a locus instead of p^2. A conservative value of θ for the U.S. population is 0.01; for some small, isolated populations, a value of 0.03 may be more appropriate. For both kinds of systems, $2p_ip_j$ should be used for heterozygotes.

Recommendation 4.2. If the particular subpopulation from which the evidence sample came is known, the allele frequencies for the specific subgroup should be used as described in Recommendation 4.1. If allele frequencies for the subgroup are not available, although data for the full population are, then the calculations should use the population-structure equations 4.10 for each locus, and the resulting values should then be multiplied.

$$\text{Homozygote:} P(A_iA_i \mid A_iA_i) = \frac{[2\theta + (1-\theta)p_i][3\theta + (1-\theta)p_i]}{(1+\theta)(1+2\theta)} \tag{4.10a}$$

$$\text{Heterozygote:} P(A_iA_j \mid A_iA_j) = \frac{2[\theta + (1-\theta)p_i][\theta + (1-\theta)p_j]}{(1+\theta)(1+2\theta)} \tag{4.10b}$$

Recommendation 4.3. If the person who contributed the evidence sample is from a group or tribe for which no adequate database exists, data from several other groups or tribes thought to be closely related to it should be used. The profile frequency should be calculated as described in Recommendation 4.1 for each group or tribe.

Recommendation 4.4. If the possible contributors of the evidence sample include relatives of the suspect, DNA profiles of those relatives should be obtained. If these profiles cannot be obtained, the probability of finding the evidence profile in those relatives should be calculated with Formulae 4.8 or 4.9.

Genotype of suspect   Probability of same genotype in a relative

$$\text{Homozygote:} \quad A_iA_i \quad p_i^2 + 4p_i(1-p_i)F \tag{4.8a}$$

$$\text{Heterozygote:} \quad A_iA_j \quad 2p_ip_j + 2\left(p_i + p_j - 4p_ip_j\right)F \tag{4.8b}$$

For parent and offspring, $F = 1/4$; for half-siblings, $1/8$; for uncle and nephew, $1/8$; for first cousins, $1/16$.

Full siblings, being bilineal rather than unilineal, require different formulae (4.9):

$$A_iA_i: \left(1 + 2p_i + p_i^2\right)/4 \tag{4.9a}$$

$$A_iA_j: \left(1 + p_i + p_j + 2p_ip_j\right)/4 \tag{4.9b}$$

Recommendations on Interpreting the Results of Database Searches, on Binning, and on Establishing the Uniqueness of Profiles

Recommendation 5.1. When the suspect is found by a search of DNA databases, the random-match probability should be multiplied by N, the number of persons in the database.

Recommendation 5.2. If floating bins are used to calculate the random-match probabilities, each bin should coincide with the corresponding match window. If fixed bins are employed, then the fixed bin that has the largest frequency among those overlapped by the match window should be used.

Recommendation 5.3. Research into the identification and validation of more and better marker systems for forensic analysis should continue with a view to making each profile unique.

Recommendation for Research on Juror Comprehension

Recommendation 6.1. Behavioral research should be carried out to identify any conditions that might cause a trier of fact to misinterpret evidence on DNA profiling and to assess how well various ways of presenting expert testimony on DNA can reduce any such misunderstandings.

Reading List and Internet Resources

NRC I

Landers, E. S. (1993). DNA fingerprinting: the NRC report. *Science, 260*, 1221.

Mueller, L. D. (1993). The use of DNA typing in forensic science. *Accountability Research, 3*, 55–67.

National Research Council. (1992). *DNA Technology in Forensic Science*. Washington, D.C: National Academy Press.

Zaborsky, O. R. (1993). The NAS-NRC DNA typing report: realities and misconceptions. *Proceedings from the Fourth International Symposium on Human Identification* (pp. 101–106). Madison, WI: Promega Corporation.

Ceiling Principle Brouhaha

Budowle, B., & Monson, K. L. (1992). Perspectives on the fixed bin method and the floor approach/ceiling principle. *Proceedings from the Third International Symposium on Human Identification 1992* (pp. 391–406). Madison, Wisconsin: Promega Corporation.

Kaye, D. H. (1995). The forensic debut of the NRC's DNA report: population structure, ceiling frequencies and the need for numbers. *Genetica, 96*, 99–105.

Kobilinsky, L., & Levine, L. (1993). Commentary on the 'ceiling principle.' *Journal Forensic Sciences, 38*, 1261–1262.

Lander, E. S., & Budowle, B. (1994). DNA fingerprinting dispute laid to rest. *Nature, 371*, 735–738.

Lempert, R. (1993). DNA, science and the law: two cheers for the ceiling principle. *Jurimetrics, 34*, 41–57.

Slimowitz, J. R., & Cohen, J. E. (1993). Violations of the ceiling principle: exact conditions and statistical evidence. *American Journal Human Genetics, 53*, 314–323.

NRC II

Balding, D. J., & Nichols, R. A. (1994). DNA profile match probability calculation: how to allow for population stratification, relatedness, database selection and single bands. *Forensic Science International, 64*, 125–140.

Budowle, B., & Monson, K. L. (1996). Accepted practices by the forensic DNA community supported by NRC II report. *Proceedings from the Seventh International Symposium on Human Identification* (pp. 27–38). Madison, WI: Promega Corporation.

Crow, J. F. (1996). The 1996 NAS report. *Proceedings from the Seventh International Symposium on Human Identification* (pp. 1–11). Madison, WI: Promega Corporation.

Crow, J. F. (1998). The 1996 NRC report: another look. *Proceedings of the Ninth International Symposium on Human Identification*. Available at http://www.promega.com/products/pm/genetic-identity/ishi-conference-proceedings/9th-ishi-oral-presentations/. Accessed April 2, 2014.

Crow, J. F. (1999). DNA forensics: past, present, and future. *Proceedings of the Tenth International Symposium on Human Identification*. Available at http://www.promega.com/products/pm/genetic-identity/ishi-conference-proceedings/10th-ishi-oral-presentations/. Accessed April 2, 2014.

DNA Advisory Board. (2000). Statistical and population genetics issues affecting the evaluation of the frequency of occurrence of DNA profiles calculated from pertinent population database(s). *Forensic Science Communications, 2*(3). Available at http://www.fbi.gov/about-us/lab/forensic-science-communications/fsc/july2000/dnastat.htm. Accessed April 2, 2014.

Kaye, D. H. (1996). DNA identification in criminal cases: some lingering and emerging evidentiary issues. *Proceedings from the Seventh International Symposium on Human Identification* (pp. 12–26). Madison, WI: Promega Corporation.

Kaye, D. H. (1997). DNA, NAS, NRC, DAB, RFLP, PCR, and more: an introduction to the symposium on the 1996 NRC report on forensic DNA evidence. *Jurimetrics Journal, 37*, 395–404.

National Research Council (NRCII) Committee on DNA Forensic Science. (1996). *The Evaluation of Forensic DNA Evidence*. Washington, DC: National Academy Press.

Presley, L. A. (1996). Ensuring high standards in forensic DNA analyses: addressing quality assurance and the 1992 and 1996 National Research Council reports. *Proceedings from the Seventh International Symposium on Human Identification* (pp. 46—47). Madison, WI: Promega Corporation.

Criticisms of NRC I and NRC II

Anderson, C. (1992). Academy approves, critics still cry foul. *Nature, 356*, 552.

Balding, D. J. (1997). Errors and misunderstandings in the second NRC report. *Jurimetrics Journal, 37*, 469—476.

Balding, D. J. (2005). *Weight-of-evidence for Forensic DNA Profiles*. Hoboken, New Jersey: John Wiley & Sons (See pp. 154—155).

Chakraborty, R. (1993). NRC report on DNA typing. *Science, 260*, 1059—1060.

Chakraborty, R., et al. (1992). Effects of population subdivision and allele frequency differences on interpretation of DNA typing data for human identification. *Proceedings from the Third International Symposium on Human Identification 1992* (pp. 205—222). Madison, Wisconsin: Promega Corporation.

Devlin, B., et al. (1993). Statistical evaluation of DNA fingerprints: a critique of the NRC's report. *Science, 259*, 748—749.

Devlin, B., et al. (1993). NRC report on DNA typing. *Science, 260*, 1057—1059.

Devlin, B., et al. (1994). Comments on the statistical aspects of the NRC's report on DNA typing. *Journal Forensic Sciences, 39*, 28—40.

Federal Bureau of Investigation. (1992). The FBI's responses to recommendations by the committee on DNA Technology in Forensic Science of the National Research Council, National Academy of Sciences. *Crime Laboratory Digest, 19*, 49.

Hartl, D. L., & Lewontin, R. C. (1993). DNA fingerprinting report. *Science, 260*, 473.

Koehler, J. J. (1997). Why DNA likelihood ratios should account for error. *Jurimetrics Journal, 37*, 425—437.

Lempert, R. O. (1997). After the DNA wars: skirmishing with NRC II. *Jurimetrics Journal, 37*, 439—468.

Morton, N. E. (1995). DNA forensic science 1995. *European Journal Human Genetics, 3*, 139—144.

Morton, N. E., & Collins, A. E. (1995). Statistical and genetic aspects of quality control for DNA identification. *Electrophoresis, 16*(9), 1670—1677.

Morton, N. E. (1997). The forensic end game. *Jurimetrics Journal, 37*, 477—494.

Robertson, B., & Vignaux, G. (1992). Why the NRC report on DNA is wrong. *New Law Journal, 142*, 1619—1621.

Roeder, K. (1994). DNA fingerprinting: a review of the controversy. *Statistical Science, 9*(2), 222—247.

Thompson, W. C. (1997). The National Research Council's second report on forensic DNA evidence: a critique. *Jurimetrics Journal, 37*, 405—423.

Weir, B. S. (1992). Population genetics in the forensic DNA debate. *Proceedings of the National Academy of Sciences of the United States of America, 89*, 11654—11659.

Weir, B. S. (1993). DNA fingerprinting report. *Science, 260*, 473.

Weir, B. S. (1993). Forensic population genetics and the National Research Council (NRC). *American Journal Human Genetics, 52*(2), 437—440.

Weir, B. S. (1996). The second National Research Council report on forensic DNA evidence. *American Journal Human Genetics, 59*, 497—500.

Weir, B. S., et al. (1997). Interpreting DNA mixtures. *Journal Forensic Sciences, 42*(2), 213—222.

DAB Recommendations on Statistics

The DNA Advisory Board (DAB) was a 13-member, congressionally mandated organization created and funded by the United States Congress DNA Identification Act of 1994. During its 1995–2000 tenure, the DAB discussed challenges facing forensic DNA and issued guidance to the community. While the primary purpose of the DAB was to recommend standards for quality assurance in conducting forensic analysis of DNA, the DAB also provided guidance to forensic analysts performing those DNA analyses, including the February 2000 recommendations on statistics. *This information is included here to provide historical perspective on why many U.S. laboratories have utilized the probability-of-exclusion approach rather than likelihood ratio methods for DNA mixture interpretation.*

The following document was published in the July 2000 issue of *Forensic Science Communications*, the online FBI journal at the time. It is available at the following web site: http://www.fbi.gov/ about-us/lab/forensic-science-communications/fsc/july2000/dnastat.htm/. For convenience, the entire text is included here with some minor English usage adjustments and one reference year correction (the Devlin article publication year has been corrected to 1993 from 1992 listed in the original document). Symbols are defined and topics discussed further in Chapters 10 to 14.

DNA Advisory Board
February 23, 2000
Statistical and Population Genetics Issues Affecting the Evaluation of the Frequency of Occurrence of DNA Profiles Calculated from Pertinent Population Database(s)

INTRODUCTION

When a comparison of DNA profiles derived from evidence and reference samples fails to exclude an individual(s) as a contributor(s) of the evidence sample, statistical assessment and/or probabilistic reasoning are used to evaluate the significance of the association. Proper statistical inference requires careful formulation of the question to be answered, including, in this instance, the requirements of the legal system. Inference must take into account how and what data were collected, which, in turn, determine how the data are analyzed and interpreted.

Previously, the DNA Advisory Board (DAB; June 21, 1996, New York) endorsed the recommendations of the National Research Council's Report (1996; henceforth NRC II Report):

"The DAB congratulates Professor Crow and his NRC [National Research Council] Committee for their superb report on the statistical and population genetics issues surrounding forensic DNA profiling. We wholeheartedly endorse the findings of the report in these substantive matters."

As the NRC II Report (1996) describes, there are alternate methods for assessing the probative value of DNA evidence. Rarely is there only one statistical approach to interpret and explain the evidence. The choice of approach is affected by the philosophy and experience of the user, the legal system, the practicality of the approach, the question(s) posed, available data, and/or assumptions. For forensic applications, it is important that the statistical conclusions be conveyed meaningfully. Simplistic or less rigorous approaches are often sought. Frequently, calculations such as the random match probability and probability of exclusion convey to the trier of fact the probative value of the evidence in a straightforward fashion. Simplified approaches are appropriate, as long as the analysis is conservative or does not provide false inferences. Likelihood ratio (LR) approaches compare mutually exclusive hypotheses and can be quite useful for evaluating the data. However, some LR calculations and interpretations can be complicated, and their significance to the case may not be apparent to the practitioner and the trier of fact.

Bayesian inference, which accounts for information other than the DNA evidence, also could be applied. Bayesian approaches sometimes require knowledge of circumstances beyond the domain of the DNA scientist and have not been addressed in U.S. criminal courts for DNA analysis. The DAB believes it is for the courts to decide whether or not Bayesian statistics are solely the responsibility of the trier of fact. The DAB recognizes that these different approaches can be applied, as long as the question to be answered and the assumptions underlying the analyses are clearly conveyed to the trier of fact.

We have been charged with clarifying issues that arise for the following special cases:

- Source attribution or identity;
- Cases where relatives may be involved;
- Interpretation of mixtures; and
- The significance of a match derived through a felon database search.

SOURCE ATTRIBUTION

According to Webster's *Third New International Dictionary* (Merriam-Webster 1961; henceforth Webster's Third), the term unique can convey several meanings, including *the only one, unusual, and some [circumstance] that is the only one of its kind*. Those who question the concept of assigning source attribution for DNA evidence often dwell on the former (e.g. Balding 1999). In their argument against source attribution, some critics say that it is difficult to establish, beyond doubt, that a DNA profile is carried by only one individual in the entire world. Within that context, their argument can be compelling, especially if the profile consists of a fairly small number of loci. Their conclusion, however, is problematic because source attribution should be evaluated within the *context defined by the case*, and the world's population rarely would be the appropriate context. Because source attribution can only be meaningful within the context of the instant case, the *Webster's Third* definition of uniqueness comes closest to that required by the legal setting: a circumstance that is the only one of its kind.

By contrast to the world's population, examples of limiting, case-specific contexts are more common. Suppose, for example, the presence of a small group of individuals at the crime scene is stipulated. However, the identity of the single individual who sexually assaulted the victim is at issue. DNA evidence on the victim matches a DNA profile from only one of the named defendants. In this instance, it is simple to assign source because all other individuals are excluded. Now suppose the identities of some individuals at the crime scene are unknown, yet the DNA profile matches one of the defendants. Further suppose this defendant has no close relatives aside from parents. Source attribution is not challenging in this setting. While the answer depends on the number and kind of loci examined, in most instances the source can be assigned with a very high degree of scientific certainty. Suppose, instead, the defendant has multiple siblings, one of whom may have been the assailant and whose profile is not available for some reason. Even then source can be assigned with a high degree of scientific certainty when a sufficient number of highly polymorphic loci are typed.

Inference regarding source attribution should always be based on the facts in the case. Arguments against source attribution based on premises having nothing to do with the case at hand should not be compelling.

Another set of questions arises when commentators fail to distinguish between source attribution and guilt. Some commentators, for example, set up the following scenario: suppose inculpating DNA evidence appears to come from the defendant with high probability, yet all the non-DNA evidence is exculpatory (e.g. Balding 1999). In this instance, they say, source attribution is impossible. We do not agree. If, to a high degree of scientific certainty, the DNA evidence appears to come from the defendant, then the only reasonable conclusion is that the DNA did indeed come from the defendant. The trier of fact, however, has a different question to ponder: What value is source attribution if the preponderance of the evidence suggests the defendant cannot be the perpetrator? The trier of fact should seek other explanations for the data, some or all of which may exculpate the defendant.

As described above, the possible source of the DNA depends on the context of the case, and thus calculations for source attribution must reflect the appropriate reference population. If relatives are potential contributors, the calculations for source attribution must reflect that fact. If relatives are not potential contributors, the calculations for source attribution should be based on a defined population; that population could be as small as two unrelated individuals or an entire town, city, state, or country. The DNA analyst should take great care with evidence presentation, with two important facts in mind:

- Inference about source attribution is a probabilistic statement, and its degree of uncertainty is governed by the genetic information contained in the profile; and
- Inference about source attribution is distinct from inference regarding guilt.

One way to develop criteria to assess the question of source attribution is to let p_x equal the random match probability for a given evidentiary profile X. The random match probability is calculated using the NRC II Report (1996) Formulae 4.1b and 4.4a for general population scenarios or Formula 4.10 under the assumption that the contributor and the accused could only come from one subgroup.

The value θ is 0.01, except for estimates for isolated subgroups, where 0.03 is used. The rarity of the estimate is decreased by a factor of 10 (NRC II Report 1996).

Then $(1 - p_x)^N$ is the probability of not observing the particular profile in a population of N unrelated individuals. We require that this probability be greater than or equal to a $1 - \alpha$ confidence level $(1 - p_x)^N \geq 1 - \alpha$ or $p_x \leq (1 - \alpha)^{1/N}$. Specifying a confidence level of 0.95 or 0.99 (i.e. an α of 0.05 or 0.01) will enable determination of the random match probability threshold to assert with 95% or 99% confidence that the particular evidentiary profile is unique, given a population of N unrelated individuals.

In practice, p_x is calculated for each of the major population groups residing in the geographic area where the crime was committed (i.e. typically African-American, Caucasian, and Hispanic). When there is no reason to believe a smaller population is relevant, the FBI, for example, has set N to 260 million, the approximate size of the U.S. population. For smaller, defined populations, N should be based on census values or other appropriate values determined by the facts of the case. The source attribution formula advocated here is simple and likely to be conservative, especially when N is larger than the size of the population that would inhabit a geographic area where a crime is committed.

RELATIVES

As described previously in the Source Attribution section, the possibility of a close relative (typically a brother) of the accused being in the pool of potential contributors of crime scene evidence should be considered in case-specific context. It is not appropriate to proffer that a close relative is a potential contributor of the evidence when there are no facts in evidence to suggest this instance is relevant. However, if a relative had access to a crime scene and there is reason to believe he/she could have been a contributor of the evidence, then the best action to take is to obtain a reference sample from the relative. After all, this scenario should be sufficient probable cause for obtaining a reference sample. Typing with the same battery of short tandem repeat (STR) loci will resolve the question of whether or not the relative carries the same DNA profile as the accused.

When a legitimate suspected relative cannot be typed, a probability statement can be provided. Given the accused DNA profile, the conditional probability that the relative has the same DNA profile can be calculated. Examples of methods for estimating the probability of the same DNA profile in a close relative are described in the NRC II Report (1996) and Li and Sacks (1954).

MIXTURES

Mixtures, which for our purposes are DNA samples derived from two or more contributors, are sometimes encountered in forensic biological evidence. The presence of a mixture is evident typically by the presence of three or more peaks, bands, dots, and/or notable differences in intensities of the alleles for at least one locus in the profile.

In some situations, elucidation of a contributor profile is straightforward. An example would be the analysis of DNA from an intimate swab revealing a mixture consistent with the composition of the perpetrator and the victim. When intensity differences are sufficient to identify the major contributor in the mixed profile, it can be treated statistically as a single-source sample. At times, when alleles are not masked, a minor contributor to the mixed profile may be elucidated. Almost always in a mixture interpretation, certain possible genotypes can be excluded. It may be difficult to be confident regarding the number of contributors in some complex mixtures of more than two individuals; however, the number of contributors often can be inferred by reviewing the data at all loci in a profile.

Interpretation of genotypes is complicated when the contributions of the donors are approximately equal (i.e. when a major contributor cannot be determined unequivocally) or when alleles overlap. Also, stochastic fluctuation during polymerase chain reaction (PCR) arising from low quantity of DNA template can make typing of a minor contributor complicated. When the contributors of a DNA mixture profile cannot be distinguished, two calculations convey the probative value of the evidence.

The first calculation is the probability of exclusion (PE; Devlin (1993) and references therein). The PE provides an estimate of the portion of the population that has a genotype composed of at least one allele not observed in the mixed profile. Knowledge of the accused and/or victim profiles is not used (or needed) in the calculation. The calculation is particularly useful in complex mixtures, because it requires no assumptions about the identity or number of contributors to a mixture. The probabilities derived are valid and for all practical purposes are conservative. However, the PE does not make use of all of the available genetic data.

The LR provides the odds ratio of two competing hypotheses, given the evidence (Evett & Weir 1998). For example, consider a case of sexual assault for which the victim reported there were two assailants. A mixture of two profiles is observed in the "male fraction," and the victim is excluded as a contributor of the observed mixed profile. Two men are arrested, and their combined profiles are consistent with the mixture evidence. A likelihood calculation logically might compare the probability that the two accused individuals are the source of the DNA in the evidence versus two unknown (random men) are the source of the evidence. Various alternate hypotheses can be entertained as deemed appropriate, given the evidence. Calculation of an LR considers the identity and actual number of contributors to the observed DNA mixture. Certainly, LR makes better use of the available genetic data than does the PE.

Interpretation of DNA mixtures requires careful consideration of factors including, but not limited to, detectable alleles; variation of band, peak, or dot intensity; and the number of alleles. There are a number of references for guidance on calculating the PE or LR (Evett & Weir 1998, NRC II Report 1996, PopStats in CODIS). The DAB finds either one or both PE or LR calculations acceptable and strongly recommends that one or both calculations be carried out whenever feasible and a mixture is indicated.

DATABASE SEARCH

As felon DNA databases are developed in all 50 states, searches for matches between evidentiary and database profiles will become increasingly common. Two questions arise when a match is derived from a database search: (1) What is the rarity of the DNA profile? and (2) What is the probability of finding such a DNA profile in the database searched? These two questions address different issues. That the different questions produce different answers should be obvious. The former question addresses the random match probability, which is often of particular interest to the fact finder.

Here we address the latter question, which is especially important when a profile found in a database search matches the DNA profile of an evidence sample.

When the DNA profile from a crime scene sample matches a single profile in a felon DNA database, the NRC II Report (1996) recommended the evaluation of question number (2) be based on the size of the database. They argued for this evaluation because the probability of identifying a DNA profile by chance increases with the size of the database. Thus this chance event must be taken into account when evaluating value of the matching profile found by a database search. Those who argue against NRC II's recommended treatment (e.g. Balding & Donnelly 1996, Evett & Weir 1998, Evett, Foreman & Weir 2000) say the NRC II Report's formulation is wrong and undervalues the evidence. In fact, they argue that the weight of the evidence (defined in terms of a likelihood ratio) for a DNA database search exceeds the weight provided by the same evidence in a "probable cause" case − a case in which other evidence first implicates the suspect and then DNA evidence is developed.

When other evidence first implicates the suspect, the DNA evidence can be evaluated using the probability p_x of randomly drawing the profile X from the (appropriate) population, which expresses the degree of surprise that the suspect and evidentiary profiles match. Equivalently, we can express it as a LR for two competing hypotheses, namely the likelihood of the evidence when the data come from the same individual (H_s) versus the likelihood of the evidence when the data come from two different individuals (H_d). The LR in this instance is:

$$\text{Lik(Profile|}H_s)/\text{Lik(Profile|}H_d) = p_x/(p_x * p_x) = 1/p_x.$$

For the DNA database search, the NRC II Report recommended the calculation (defined in terms of a LR) to be evaluated as $1/(N\,p_x)$, where N is the size of the database. While justification for this calculation is given in their report, it is often misunderstood. Stockmarr (1999) re-derives this result in a way that should be more comprehensible. As a special case, assume only one profile in the database matches the evidentiary profile; we can consider that individual is a suspect. Now consider two competing hypotheses, namely the source is or is not in the database (H_{in} versus $H_{not\ in}$). These likelihood's are relevant because we wish to identify whether the suspect is likely to be the source of the sample (H_{in}) or if it is more likely he was identified merely by chance ($H_{not\ in}$). What is the LR for these hypotheses?

$$\text{Lik(Profile|}H_{in})/\text{Lik(Profile|}H_{not\ in}) = 1/(N\,p_x).$$

Stockmarr (1999) argues this formulation is the appropriate treatment of the data, as did the NRC II Report (1996) before him. Both recognize an intuitive counter example. Suppose we had a DNA database of the entire world's population (size N), except one individual ($N - 1$). A DNA profile from a crime scene is found to match one and only one profile in the database, and its frequency is $1/N$. According to critics (e.g. Balding 1997), this example demonstrates the fallacious nature of the NRC II Report's proposed evaluation of the evidence for a database search, because the value of the evidence appears to be nil (the likelihood ratio is essentially one instead of a large number). Both Stockmarr (1999) and the NRC II Report recognize this interesting result; however, by treating the problem from a Bayesian perspective and invoking prior probabilities that are a function of the size of the database, they argue the example is irrelevant. In essence, the prior probability of H_{in} rises as N rises. This approach is coherent, from the statistical perspective, but it may not be particularly helpful for the legal system. Without the use of prior probabilities, it should be apparent that the treatment of the database search recommended by the NRC II Report can be conservative when the database is extremely large.

It is important to consider the treatment proposed by Balding & Donnelly (1996) and recently endorsed by Evett, Foreman & Weir (2000). By their line of reasoning, the LR is no different whether other evidence first implicates the suspect or the suspect is identified by a database search. In fact, they argue the true weight of the evidence is actually larger for the latter, albeit the increase is small unless N is large. This argument has some intuitive appeal, especially in light of the example given above, and it is true that their LR is unaffected by sampling.

Both camps appear to present rigorous arguments to support their positions. Indeed the proper treatment superficially appears to rest in the details of arcane mathematics (Balding & Donnelly 1996, NRC II Report 1996, Stockmarr 1999). We believe, however, there is a way to see which of the two treatments is better for the legal setting without resorting to mathematical details. Consider the following scenario:

> A murder occurs, and the only evidence left at the crime scene is a cigarette butt. DNA analysis types five loci from the saliva on the cigarette butt. The probability of drawing the resulting profile X from a randomly selected individual is $p_x = 1/100,000$. A search of the DNA database, which contains $N = 100,000$ profiles, reveals a single match. No other evidence can be found to link the "suspect," whose profile matches, to the murder.

If we follow Balding & Donnelly (1996), the message for the investigators is that the evidence is 100,000 times more likely if the suspect is the source than if he is not. Alternatively, by the NRC II Report (1996) recommendations, the evidence is not compelling because the likelihood the profile, a priori, is/is not in the database is the same. In probabilistic terms, it is not surprising to find a matching profile in the database of size 100,000 when the profile probability is 1/100,000. Curiously, the mathematics underlying both approaches are correct, despite the apparently divergent answers. It is the foundations of the formulations that differ, and they differ substantially.

At present there are about 20,000 known, variable STR loci in the human genome. Of these, forensic scientists use a little more than a dozen, which is sufficient for most forensic analyses. Although not strictly accurate, let us think of the selection of STR loci as random and return to our case. The forensic scientists who worked on the cigarette butt could assay only five loci of the dozen they might type. Suppose they were to type five different loci and generate a new profile based on only these additional five loci? If our suspect were the true source of the sample, a match at those loci would be obtained; however, if he were not the source, a match would be highly unlikely. If the new (i.e. second) profile probability were again on the order of 1/100,000, someone else may have been selected. If our suspect is not the source, no one else in the database is, and yet we can easily imagine selecting a set of five loci (out of the thousands possible) to single out each individual therein. This seems like an unsatisfactory state in light of the LR espoused by Balding & Donnelly (1996).

Thus we are left with an interesting dilemma. Within a Bayesian context, the NRC II Report's LR and Balding & Donnelly's (1996) LR could be interpreted to yield a coherent evaluation of the evidence. Unfortunately, Bayesian logic has not been considered by the U.S. criminal legal system for DNA analysis. Clearly, what is required is a formulation of the LR that transparently conveys its import without resorting to Bayesian statistics. In this setting, the treatment of the database search recommended by the NRC II Report can be conservative, but only for the unlikely scenario of a very large N is it very conservative. Apparently the treatment of the database search recommended by Balding & Donnelly (1996) is not conservative when the number of loci genotyped is small and remains so until the number of loci becomes large enough to essentially ensure uniqueness. To put it another way, without the Bayesian framework, the Balding & Donnelly (1996) formulation is easily misinterpreted in a fashion unfavorable to the suspect. Stockmarr's (1999) formulation, which is a more formal exposition of what originally appeared in the NRC II Report (1996), communicates value of a database search far better, and it is always conservative. Thus, we continue to endorse the recommendation of the NRC II Report for the evaluation of DNA evidence from a database search.

CONCLUSION

Statistical analyses are sometimes thought to yield automatic rules for making a decision either to accept or reject a hypothesis. This attitude is false in any setting and should be especially avoided for forensic inference. One rarely rests his/her decisions wholly on any single statistical test or analysis. To the evidence of the test should be added data accumulated from the scientist's own past work and that of others (Snedecor & Cochran 1967). Thus, in this light, statistical analyses should be thought of as useful guides for interpreting the weight of the DNA evidence.

References

Balding, D. J. (1997). Errors and misunderstandings in the second NRC report. *Jurimetrics, 37*, 603–607.

Balding, D. J. (1999). When can a DNA profile be regarded as unique? *Science Justice, 39*, 257–260.

Balding, D. J., & Donnelly, P. (1996). Evaluating DNA profile evidence when the suspect is identified through a database search. *Journal Forensic Sciences, 41*, 603–607.

Devlin, B. (1993). Forensic inference from genetic markers. *Statistical Methods Medical Research, 2*, 241–262.

Evett, I. W., Foreman, L. A., & Weir, B. S. (2000). Letter to the editor of Biometrics. *Biometrics, 56*(4), 1274–1275.

Evett, I. W., & Weir, B. S. (1998). *Interpreting DNA Evidence*. Sunderland, MA: Sinauer.

Li, C. C., & Sacks, L. (1954). The derivation of joint distribution and correlation between relatives by the use of stochastic matrices. *Biometrics, 10*, 347–360.

Merriam-Webster, Incorporated (1961). *Webster's Third New International Dictionary*. Springfield, MA: Merriam-Webster, Incorporated.

National Research Council Committee on DNA Forensic Science. (1996). *An Update: The Evaluation of Forensic DNA Evidence*. Washington, D.C.: National Academy Press.

Snedecor, G. W., & Cochran, W. G. (1967). *Statistical Methods* (6th ed.). Ames, IA: Iowa State University Press. p.28.

Stockmarr, A. (1999). Likelihood ratios for evaluating DNA evidence when the suspect is found through a database search. *Biometrics, 55*, 671–677.

Worked Mixture Example

Dr. Michael D. Coble

NIST Applied Genetics Group

INTRODUCTION

Mixture interpretation involves *interpretation of alleles and possible genotypes* from contributors followed by an *assessment of the statistical weight-of-evidence* if an association between the evidence DNA profile and the suspect's DNA profile can be made. With some two-person mixtures involving a major and a minor profile, it may be possible to reliably decipher the genotypes of the individual contributors at each tested genetic marker through a mixture deconvolution process.

As described in Chapter 6, deconvolution of a mixture involving short tandem repeat (STR) loci should follow the steps outlined originally by the Forensic Science Service (Clayton et al. 1998) and endorsed by the International Society for Forensic Genetics (ISFG) DNA Commission on mixture interpretation (Gill et al. 2006). These steps are referred to as the "Clayton rules" after Tim Clayton, who is the first author of the 1998 publication (Clayton et al. 1998). In this example (Figure A4.1, which is the same as Figure 6.1 but is plotted differently), the process of mixture component deconvolution and assessing statistical significance will be illustrated using multiple approaches.

In casework samples where there is complexity in the DNA profile, such as multiple contributors or (as in this case) where one of the contributors is at a low level in the mixture, there is the possibility that not all alleles in the minor component are detected. This is known as *allele drop-out*. Contamination of an allele(s) from a donor who is not a true contributor to the mixture is also possible. This is known as *allele drop-in*. An ISFG DNA Commission on the interpretation of complex, low-level mixtures where drop-out and drop-in are possible recommended the use of drop-out probabilities for the statistical calculation of the weight of the evidence (Gill et al. 2012). Probabilistic modeling of this example mixture data was also performed using a continuous approach (Taylor et al. 2013).

The following parameters are used here: an analytical threshold of 50 relative fluorescence units (RFU), a stochastic threshold of 150 RFU, a heterozygote peak height ratio (PHR) of 60%, and a fixed stutter percentage of 15% for all markers. Certainly, with all data that occur on a continuous scale, using strict values such as 15% maximum stutter will not capture all of the variation present in the mixture. Exceptions will occur, and it is recognized that some loci with a large number of core repeats, such as FGA or D18S51, can present true stutter higher than 15%. The SWGDAM Autosomal

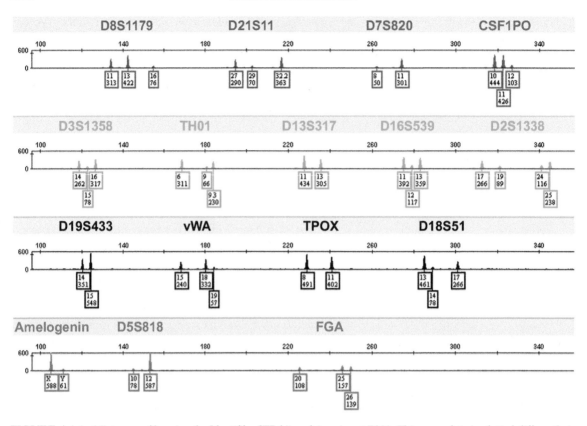

FIGURE A4.1   Mixture profile using the Identifiler STR kit and 1 ng input DNA. This same data is plotted differently in Figure 6.1. Profile courtesy of Robin Cotton and Catherine Grgicak, Boston University.

STR Interpretational Guidelines published in 2010 (referred to hereafter as SWGDAM 2010) will also be used as a guide for interpretation.

MIXTURE ASSESSMENT AND DECONVOLUTION

The first step of the Clayton rules (see Figure 6.5) is to *identify the presence of a mixture*. There is very little ambiguity that the profile in Figure A4.1 is a mixture. We can observe a distinct imbalance at amelogenin with the X allele at 588 RFU and the Y allele at 61 RFU. Severe imbalance of allelic peaks at other loci such as D7S820, D13S317, and D5S818 are also observed. Overall, we can determine from this mixture that there is a clear major female contributor with a minor male contributor (based upon the 61 RFU peak at amelogenin). It is also notable that several alleles are near the analytical threshold of 50 RFUs: the 8 allele at D7S820 (50 RFU) and the 19 allele at vWA (57 RFU), for example.

A note about nomenclature: as we deconvolve the mixture to determine the genotype of the male contributor, we will refer to this individual as the *perpetrator* and the female as the *victim*. Once we finish our inferred genotype, we will compare and refer to the *suspect*'s profile.

The second step of the Clayton rules is to *designate alleles from potential artifacts*. We can observe that most of the alleles from the minor male component are between the stochastic threshold of 150 RFU and the analytical threshold of 50 RFU. In this particular example, we don't observe any potential artifacts that may be confused for authentic alleles.

The third step of the Clayton rules is to *identify the potential number of contributors* in the mixture. This is a critical step during the interpretation process since identifying the number of contributors is necessary for deconvolution. If the profile complexity is too challenging to determine the number of contributors, then the mixture may be too difficult to interpret (designated "uninterpretable"). Looking across the entire profile, we observe no loci with more than four alleles. We observe only one marker, D2S1338, with four alleles (Figure A4.2). Nine other markers have three alleles, and five markers (excluding amelogenin) have two alleles. Based upon the number of alleles present in the mixture, it can be assumed that there are at least two individuals in the evidence.

The fourth step of the Clayton rules is to *estimate the relative ratio of contributors*. Estimation of the mixture ratio of the contributors can be useful information to determine the genotypes of each contributor in the mixture. In an assumed two-person mixture, it is easiest to start with the loci having four alleles, in this example, D2S1338 (Figure A4.2). We start by determining the PHR for each of the three pairs of genotype combinations at D2S1338 (Table A4.1).

Note that we are developing PHR information on data that falls below the stochastic threshold of 150 RFU (e.g. alleles 19 and 24). Peak height data near or below the stochastic threshold often does not exhibit the "typical" heterozygote balance of >60% PHR (see Chapter 4). In other words, two alleles that would combine to make one of the genotypes in the mixture could have a PHR of 35%.

In this example, since this is a contrived mixture and not from an actual case, the purpose here is to move through the concepts presented with an understanding that thresholds set at higher concentrations of DNA do not follow the same rules at lower template concentrations. Software programs that

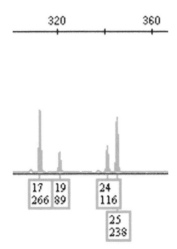

FIGURE A4.2 A portion of the electropherogram shown in Figure A4.1 displaying the four alleles observed at STR locus D2S1338. The top value in the box underneath each peak is the allele (number of STR repeats) and the bottom value is the peak height in relative fluorescence units (RFU).

TABLE A4.1   Examination of Peak Height Ratios (PHR) with Possible
Genotypes at D2S1338 Locus (see Figure A4.2)

Possible D2S1338 Genotype Combinations	Calculated PHR
17,19	89/266 = 0.335
24,25	116/238 = 0.487
17,24	116/266 = 0.436
19,25	89/238 = 0.374
17,25	**238/266 = 0.895**
19,24	**89/116 = 0.767**

avoid the use of stochastic thresholds (see below) can analyze mixture data without the "restrictions" of artificial thresholds.

An examination of Table A4.1 shows that two genotype combinations are best explained by the PHR results — the genotype 17,25 (PHR = 89.5%) and 19,24 (PHR = 76.7%). All other genotype combinations fall below our established PHR of 60% (again, we invoke the caveat that two of the alleles at this locus are below the stochastic threshold). We should also be aware that the 76.7% PHR for the 19,24 genotype is likely the *minimum* PHR observed since the 24 allele is a stutter position. That is, the 24 allele is not by itself a stutter artifact (the stutter ratio would be at 48%, well above the established maximum of 15%). However, the peak height signal at the 24 allele position may contain a portion of stutter from the 25 allele.

In Table A4.1, we considered that "all" of the 24 allele came from a contributor to the evidence (i.e. treating this peak as though it is 0% stutter). It is also possible that a portion of the 24 allele is a combination of the contributor's DNA and stutter. If we consider the *maximum* expected amount of stutter (15% of the 238 RFU from allele 25 = 36 RFU) proportion of the 24 allele, then the "contributor" portion of the 24 allele would be 116 − 36 = 80 RFU. By subtracting the maximum amount of stutter, the PHR of the 19,24 genotype combination would be 80/89 = 90%.

The purpose of this discussion is to highlight two important considerations of mixture interpretation: First, alleles in stutter positions can be challenging for mixture interpretation since these peaks may be (a) present in the profile as an allele from the perpetrator, (b) present in the profile as an artifact from the stutter process, or (c) a combination of the two. This is especially confounding when stutter peaks are about the same height as the low-level contributor.

The second concept here is that the process of stutter generation is not a consistent process — stutter may range from nearly zero to the maximum observed during kit validation studies. Establishing thresholds (for stutter, PHRs, analytical, or stochastic) essentially "draws a line in the sand" to processes that occur on a continuous scale, and therefore will lead to "exceptions" to the established threshold (Gill & Buckleton 2010, Bright et al. 2010).

Having established that the two most probable genotype combinations at D2S1338 are 17,25 (the two major peaks) and 19,24 (the two minor peaks), we can now estimate the relative mixture proportion (M_x) of contributors to the mixture at this locus. First, we sum the RFUs from all of the alleles at the locus (266 + 89 + 116 + 238 = 709 RFU). For the major contributor, we simply divide the sum of the 17,25 alleles by the overall summation at the locus ((266 + 238) / 709 = 504/709 = 0.711). The minor contributor proportion is calculated the same way ((89 + 116) / 709 = 205/709 = 0.289). The mixture ratio (M$_R$) is determined by dividing the major proportion by the minor proportion:

$$M_R \ = \ 0.711/0.289 \ = \ 2.46$$

Thus, at the D2S1338 locus the ratio of signal from major contributor to minor contributor is 2.46. One could also calculate the M$_R$ by dividing the peak heights of the major contributor alleles by peak heights of the minor contributor alleles (see D.N.A. Box 6.2).

We could also consider the contribution of stutter at the 24 allele, determined (above) to be up to 36 RFU. Subtracting this artifact from the sum of the alleles gives a total RFU of (709 − 36) = 673. For the major contributor, we divide the sum of the 17 and 25 alleles ((266 + 238) / 673 = 504/673 = 0.749). This means that the major contributor is approximately 75% of the mixture at this locus. The minor contributor proportion would be ((89 + 80) / 673 = 169/673 = 0.251, or about 25% of the mixture at D2S1338. The mixture ratio is then:

$$M_R \ = \ 0.749/0.251 \ = \ 2.98$$

We can round this to 3:1 for our discussion.

We can also use information from the amelogenin (AMEL) locus to determine the mixture ratio. We observe at amelogenin that the AMEL X allele is substantially higher in signal (588 RFU) than the AMEL Y allele (61 RFU). Since males are XY, we know that a portion of the AMEL X allele belongs to the male, and the remaining portion belongs to the female. We can also assume with high confidence that the female is the major contributor to this mixture and male is the minor contributor.

There are several approaches to determining the female-to-male ratio, including the method used for D2S1338. One quick method is to simply divide the AMEL X peak RFU value by the AMEL Y peak RFU value. In a perfect 1:1 mixture of male and female individuals, we would expect 3 AMEL X present for each AMEL Y (see Table 6.2). Dividing 588/61 gives a ratio of AMEL X to AMEL Y of 9.6-to-1. This suggests that the actual female ratio in this mixture is between 4:1 and 5:1. If we simply assume the male contribution to the X chromosome is the same as the Y chromosome, then the female-to-male ratio would be (588 − 61)/(61 + 61) = 527/122 = 4.3-to-1.

The mixture ratio at amelogenin is slightly different from the estimated ratio of 3:1 determined from D2S1338. There are several possible reasons for this difference in estimated mixture ratios. It is possible that there is some degradation in the evidence profile given the different M$_x$ from the low relative molecular mass loci compared to high relative molecular mass loci. There may be some effects of inhibition in the profile, or random stochastic effects of amplification can create variation across the profile to give differences in the M$_x$. In this particular profile, we observe alleles below the stochastic threshold at nearly every marker, so we should expect some random stochastic effects from amplifying low-level DNA. Some laboratories may consider that an M$_x$ within the range of 3:1 to 5:1 is acceptable, and note the possibility of stochastic variation in the profile. Since only one locus in the profile shows four alleles, we can only easily estimate the M$_x$ using D2S1338 and amelogenin.

We next consider the fifth step of the Clayton rules: *Consider all possible genotype combinations*. Here we go through each STR locus and try to determine the possible genotypes present in the profile. We have finished with D2S1338 − the major contributor (17,25) and the minor contributor (19,24). Depending upon the type of evidence, and the policy of the laboratory, it may be possible to use the genotype of an assumed contributor to the evidence in determining the genotype of the unknown perpetrator. For example, if the evidence tested in Figure A4.1 was an intimate sample such as a vaginal swab from a female victim of a sexual assault, we can assume that the genotype of the female would be known. We would then be able to view the profile of the female at D2S1338 and note that she has the 17,25 genotype. This would then mean that the remaining alleles, 19 and 24, would be obligate to the perpetrator. The PHR agrees with this method of subtracting the female's profile.

We will use the first locus in the blue channel — D8S1179 — to review the deconvolution process and the thoughts that go into considering possible genotypes at this locus (Figure A4.3). At the D8S1179 locus we note that there are two alleles with stronger signal, 11 and 13, both above the stochastic threshold, and one allele, 16, below the stochastic threshold (but above the analytical threshold).

In determining the optimal genotype combinations, the 11,13 genotype would give a PHR of (313/ 422 = 0.742) 74%, which is above our PHR threshold of 60% (Table A4.2a). Combinations of 11,16 or 13,16 would give PHRs of 24% and 18%, respectively, and would be outside expected PHR ranges of normal heterozygote balance. Therefore, we can rather easily determine that the major (female) contributor would be the 11,13 genotype. Using the "female" subtraction method confirms that this is in fact the genotype of the victim. The next step is to determine the perpetrator's genotype. We know that based upon PHR, the 16 allele would not optimally pair with either the 11 or 13, and this allele is considered obligate to the perpetrator. The question here is what else could pair with the 16 allele?

We can start by considering the possibility that the perpetrator's genotype is homozygous 16,16. The female genotype determined from above (11,13) is within the acceptable PHR threshold (74%). It is difficult to fully estimate the M_x for the female genotype since we know that the 16 allele is below the stochastic threshold. If we calculate the M_x for the female, it is about 91% (Table A4.2b), which is higher than the M_x determined from D2S1338 (75%). This suggests that perhaps the true genotype of the perpetrator is not 16,16.

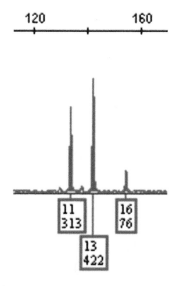

FIGURE A4.3 A portion of the electropherogram shown in Figure A4.1 displaying the three alleles observed at STR locus D8S1179.

TABLE A4.2   Examination of Peak Height Ratios (PHR) with Possible Genotypes at D8S1179 Locus (see Figure A4.3)

(a)

Genotypes	PHR
11,13	$313/422 = 0.742$
11,16	$76/313 = 0.243$
13,16	$76/422 = 0.180$

(b)

Genotypes	PHR	Mixture Proportion	M_x
11,13	$313/422 = 0.742$	$(313 + 422)/(313 + 422 + 76) = 0.906$	91%
16,16	n/a		
11*,13	$313 - 76/422 = 0.562$	$(313 - 76 + 422)/(313 + 422 + 76) = 0.813$	81%
11*,16	n/a		
11,13*	$313/422 - 76 = 0.905$	$(313 + 422 - 76)/(313 + 422 + 76) = 0.813$	81%
13*,16	n/a		

(a) Inferred genotypes for the major (female) contributor. (b) Potential genotypes for the inferred minor (male) contributor using the 11,13 genotype as an anchor genotype for the female contributor. PHRs for the male contributor were assumed to be balanced. The asterisk indicates allele sharing between the male and female contributors.

We then consider the possibility that the perpetrator shares either a portion of the 11 or 13 alleles with the female victim's genotype. If a portion of the 11 allele (we assume 76 RFU, the same as the 16 allele) is shared with the perpetrator (noted as 11* in Table A4.2b), the PHR for the female 11,13 genotype falls slightly below the 60% PHR threshold (to 56%). The M_x for the female proportion would be 81%, which is closer to the estimated 75% for D2S1338. Finally, we consider that a portion of the 13 allele from the victim is shared with the perpetrator (noted as 13* in Table A4.2b). We now observe an acceptable PHR for the victim to be 91% and the M_x is again 81% – this suggests that the most likely genotype combination (based on the results of PHR and M_x) is 11,13 for the victim and 13,16 for the perpetrator. Our conclusions here are logical, straightforward, and data driven – and possibly absolutely incorrect!

We must consider the process we just completed using both PHR and M_x as a guide to determine optimal genotypes a cautious exercise for the simple reason that we have alleles below the stochastic threshold. As discussed above, thresholds are "lines in the sand," and with a continuous process, we will eventually observe exceptions to the rule. It is possible to observe legitimate PHR at 56%. There is nothing magical about a PHR delineation of 60%. However, our analytical rules of interpretation would only favor results at 60%.

We must also consider the possibility that alleles associated with the perpetrator may have failed to be detected in the electropherogram. That is, an allele from the perpetrator may have been poorly amplified during PCR and therefore may not generate a detectable peak in the electropherogram. This failure to detect an allele (or alleles) at a locus is known as allele drop-out and is a distinct possibility when alleles fall between the analytical and stochastic thresholds. We can consider that alleles near the stochastic threshold of 150 RFU (e.g. 148 or 149 RFU) have a low probability that a sister allele has dropped-out (i.e. the correct genotype is heterozygous). Alleles near the analytical threshold of 50 RFU have a much greater probability of missing a sister allele.

For D8S1179, the obligate 16 allele is at 76 RFU, near the analytical threshold of 50 RFU. We should therefore consider the possibility that the true genotype of the perpetrator may include those we have also already considered (16,16; 11,16; and 13,16), but also 16,Q — where Q represents any other possible allele (except for 11, 13, or 16) (see Kelly et al. 2012). The uncertainty associated with data in the stochastic zone limits our ability to restrict certain genotypes using the logical process we outlined above with D8S1179. If all of the peaks in this particular profile simply had another 1,000 RFU added to their peak heights, then we would have greater confidence in our analysis and interpretation.

For the remaining three-allele loci in this profile, every allele obligate to the perpetrator is below the stochastic threshold. Therefore, we must cautiously note that allele drop-out is a possibility, which limits our effectiveness at mixture deconvolution. The issue is exacerbated at the loci having only two alleles. For example, at D7S820, there is an 11 allele above the stochastic threshold (belonging to the major contributor), and the 8 allele is equal to the analytical threshold of 50 RFU. Again, we ask the question — are all alleles present in the profile, or have some dropped out?

Loci where both alleles are above stochastic threshold should be treated just as cautiously. For example, TPOX has two alleles present in the profile: 8,11 and falls within the acceptable PHR of (402/491) 82% (and matches the female genotype using the subtraction approach). However, we have no hint at the possible obligate alleles for the perpetrator — is he also 8,11? 8,8? 11,11? or some other genotype like 9,12 — where both alleles have dropped-out. Thus, just because both detected TPOX alleles are above the established stochastic threshold does not mean that this locus is free from potential allele drop-out.

As far as the major (female) genotype — all of her alleles are above the stochastic threshold and within the acceptable PHR threshold with two exceptions — D18S51 and FGA. The PHR of the 13,17 genotype at D18S51 is slightly below the 60% PHR threshold (266/461 = 0.578 or 58%). However, if we consider that the obligate 14 allele from the perpetrator shares a portion of the 13 allele, then the PHR becomes acceptable. The female genotype at the FGA locus is 25,26, and we observe that the 26 allele is below the stochastic threshold of 150 RFU.

A mixture profile interpretation sheet is provided in Table A4.3. This sheet was developed by Dr. Charlotte Word and can be downloaded from the mixture section of the STRBase website: (Word 2014).

The worksheet has three parts: page 1 (Table A4.3(a)) allows the user to record information about the alleles above the analytical threshold, alleles below the stochastic threshold, and additional information to consider and document the mixture interpretation process. On page 2 (Table A4.3(b)) and page 3 (Table A4.3(c)), the genotypes from the major profile and minor profile can be listed as determined from the information on page 1.

This brings us to the next step of the Clayton rules: *Comparison to the reference samples*. Once the deconvolution process is completed, and all possible genotypes have been determined, it is appropriate to compare the inferred genotype of the perpetrator to the genotype of the suspect. If the genotypes match, then a statistical calculation can be performed on the inferred genotype developed from the evidence. It is important to remember that statistical calculations are never made from the reference sample, but always from the evidence profile.

TABLE A4.3 (a) An Example of a Profile Interpretation Sheet Developed by Dr. Charlotte Word
Profile Interpretation Worksheet — Page 1

IDENTIFILER

PROFILE NAME: Figure A4.1 (Figure 6.1)

ANALYST: MDC

DATE: 03/25/2014

MIXTURE: ■ yes ☐ no ☐ unsure

Analytical threshold: 50 RFU
Stutter % used: max 15%
Stochastic threshold: 150 RFU
Peak height ratio: 60% (major)
Comments: Mixture ratio calculated

Assuming 2 contributors; ~3:1 to 5:1 ratio

Allele and Locus Assessments

ID LOCUS	Alleles above Analytical Threshold	Alleles above Stochastic Threshold	Other Peaks to Consider	Minimum # of Donors	All Alleles Likely Present? Y/N	Stochastic Issues? Elevated Stutter? Missing Alleles?	Degradation Likely? Poss. Missing Alleles?	Major/Minor If Mixture, Distinguishable Profile? Y/N	Additional Comments
D8S1179	11, 13, 16	11, 13	–	2	N?	Minor allele in stochastic zone	Possible missing alleles	Major – 11,13 Minor – 16*	
D21S11	27, 29, 32.2	27, 32.2	–	2	N?	Minor allele in stochastic zone	Possible missing alleles	Major – 27,32.2 Minor – 29*	
D7S820	8, 11	11	–	2	N?	Minor allele in stochastic zone	Possible missing alleles	Major – 11,11 Minor – 8*	
CSF1PO	10, 11, 12	10, 11	–	2	N?	Minor allele in stochastic zone	Possible missing alleles	Major – 10,11 Minor – 12*	
D3S1358	14, 15, 16	14, 16	–	2	N?	Minor allele in stochastic zone	Possible missing alleles	Major – 14,16 Minor – 15*	
TH01	6, 9, 9.3	6, 9.3	–	2	N?	Minor allele in stochastic zone	Possible missing alleles	Major – 6,9,3 Minor – 9*	
D13S317	11, 13	11, 13	–	2?	N?	Missing?	Possible missing alleles	Major – 11,13 Minor – ??	2 alleles only within PHR

(Continued)

TABLE A4.3 (a) An Example of a Profile Interpretation Sheet Developed by Dr. Charlotte WordProfile Interpretation Worksheet – Page 1 (cont'd)

ID LOCUS	Alleles above Analytical Threshold	Alleles above Stochastic Threshold	Other Peaks to Consider	Minimum # of Donors	All Alleles Likely Present? Y/N	Stochastic Issues? Elevated Stutter? Missing Alleles?	Degradation Likely? Poss. Missing Alleles?	Major/Minor If Mixture, Distinguishable Profile? Y/N	Additional Comments
D16S539	11, 12, 13	11, 13	–	2	N?	Minor allele in stochastic zone	Possible missing alleles	Major – 11,13 Minor – 12*	
D2S1338	17, 19, 24, 25	17, 25	–	2	Y (assume 2)	No* (assume 2)	Possible degradation?	Major – 17,25 Minor – 19,24	
D19S433	14, 15	14, 15	–	2?	N?	Missing?	Possible missing alleles	Major – 14,15 Minor – ??	2 alleles only within PHR
vWA	15, 18, 19	15, 18	–	2	N?	Minor allele in stochastic zone	Possible missing alleles	Major – 15,18 Minor – 19*	
TPOX	8, 11	8, 11	–	2?	N?	Missing?	Possible missing alleles	Major – 8,11 Minor – ??	2 alleles only within PHR
D18S51	13, 14, 17	13, 17	–	2	N?	Minor allele in stochastic zone	Possible missing alleles	Major – 13,17 Minor – 14*	13, 17 slightly fails PHR
Amel	X, Y	X, Y	–	–	Y	Minor allele in stochastic zone	No	Major – XX Minor – XY	
D5S818	10, 12	12	–	2	N?	Minor allele in stochastic zone	Possible missing alleles	Major – 12,12 Minor – 10*	
FGA	20, 25, 26	25	–	2	N?	2 alleles in stochastic zone	Possible degradation?	Major – ?? Minor – ??	All three alleles give acceptable PHR

Available on the STRBase website: (http://www.cstl.nist.gov/strbase/training/INTERPRETATION-WORKSHEET-Example.doc). (a) An assessment of the alleles present at each locus and those above the analytical threshold and stochastic thresholds. (b) inferred genotype of the major (female) contributor, (c) inferred genotype of the minor (male) contributor.

TABLE A4.3 (b) An Example of a Profile Interpretation Sheet Developed by Dr. Charlotte Word
Profile Interpretation Worksheet — Page 2

PROFILE NAME: _____Figure A4.1 (Figure 6.1)_____

ANALYST: _____MDC_____

DATE: ___03/25/2014_____

✓ = Included	✓A# = Included with assumption
X = Excluded	XA# = Excluded with assumption
? = Inconclusive	?A# = Inconclusive with assumption
Y/A = Included with Assumptions	

Assumption 1: Number of contributors = ____2_____   Assumption 3: ___no stutter peaks_____
If distinguishable profiles, # of major contributors = ____1____
                             # of minor contributors = _____1___

Assumption 2: _____mixture ratio 3:1 to 5:1____   Assumption 4: _____

Single-source, Deduced single-source, or Mixture with Distinguishable Major and/or Minor Profile Comparison

ID LOCUS	Alleles above Analytical Threshold	Alleles above Stochastic Threshold	Single Source, Major or Minor Contributor Alleles/Genotypes	Comparison Profiles		Additional Comments
				Reference 1	Sample 2	
D8S1179			11,13	11,13	13,16	
D21S11			27,32.2	27,32.2	29,32.2	
D7S820			11,11	11,11	8,11	
CSF1PO			10,11	10,11	11,12	
D3S1358			14,16	14,16	15,16	
TH01			6,9.3	6,9.3	6,9	
D13S317			11,13	11,13	11,11	
D16S539			11,13	11,13	11,12	
D2S1338			17,25	17,25	19,24	
D19S433			14,15	14,15	15,15	
vWA			15,18	15,18	18,19	
TPOX			8,11	8,11	8,11	
D18S51			13,17	13,17	13,14	
Amel			XX	XX	XY	
D5S818			12,12	12,12	10,12	
FGA			?? (inconclusive)	25,26	20,20	

Available on the STRBase website: (http://www.cstl.nist.gov/strbase/training/INTERPRETATION-WORKSHEET-Example.doc). (a) An assessment of the alleles present at each locus and those above the analytical threshold and stochastic thresholds, (b) inferred genotype of the major (female) contributor, (c) inferred genotype of the minor (male) contributor.

(Continued)

TABLE A4.3 (c)   An Example of a Profile Interpretation Sheet Developed by Dr. Charlotte Word
Profile Interpretation Worksheet — Page 3

PROFILE NAME: _____Figure A4.1 (Figure 6.1)_____

ANALYST: _____MDC_____

DATE: ___03/25/2014_____

✓ = Included	✓A# = Included with assumption
X = Excluded	XA# = Excluded with assumption
? = Inconclusive	?A# = Inconclusive with assumption
Y/A = Included with Assumptions	

Assumption 1: Number of contributors = ____2_____   Assumption 3: ___no stutter peaks_____
If distinguishable profiles, # of major contributors = ____1____
                          # of minor contributors = _____1___

Assumption 2: _____mixture ratio 3:1 to 5:1____   Assumption 4: _____

Single-source, Deduced single-source, or Mixture with Distinguishable Major and/or Minor Profile Comparison

ID LOCUS	Alleles above Analytical Threshold	Alleles above Stochastic Threshold	Single Source, Major or Minor Contributor Alleles/Genotypes	Comparison Profiles Sample 1	Comparison Profiles Sample 2	Additional Comments
D8S1179			16,?	11,13	13,16	
D21S11			29,?	27,32.2	29,32.2	
D7S820			8,?	11,11	8,11	
CSF1PO			12,?	10,11	11,12	
D3S1358			15,?	14,16	15,16	
TH01			9,?	6,9.3	6,9	
D13S317			?? (inconclusive)	11,13	11,11	
D16S539			12,?	11,13	11,12	
D2S1338			19,24	17,25	19,24	
D19S433			?? (inconclusive)	14,15	15,15	
vWA			19,?	15,18	18,19	
TPOX			?? (inconclusive)	8,11	8,11	
D18S51			14,?	13,17	13,14	
Amel			XY	XX	XY	
D5S818			10,?	12,12	10,12	
FGA			?? (inconclusive)	25,26	20,20	

Available on the STRBase website: (http://www.cstl.nist.gov/strbase/training/INTERPRETATION-WORKSHEET-Example.doc). (a) An assessment of the alleles present at each locus and those above the analytical threshold and stochastic thresholds, (b) inferred genotype of the major (female) contributor, (c) inferred genotype of the minor (male) contributor.

STATISTICAL EVALUATION

In the profile interpretation sheets, I have listed the inferred genotypes from the major and minor profiles. We can now apply the final step of the Clayton rules: *Statistical analysis* by calculating the statistical significance of a match between the evidence and the suspect. We will evaluate the mixture data with several statistical approaches in order to contrast their capabilities and limitations.

First, we will use the Combined Probability of Inclusion (CPI) approach, followed by the modified Random Match Probability (mRMP), the binary Likelihood Ratio (LR), and finally an example of a probabilistic approach using the LR and a continuous method of interpretation. These approaches are described in more detail in Chapter 12 and Chapter 13 (see also Kelly et al. 2014).

Statistical Calculations with CPI

The Random Man Not Excluded (RMNE) approach to mixture statistics seeks to address the rarity of a match by determining the probability of finding a random person in the population who would be included in the mixture. We can calculate the RMNE of the mixture using the CPI statistic, or alternatively, the Combined Probability of Exclusion (CPE), which is mathematically: $1 - CPI$. Originally, the RMNE statistic was developed for paternity statistics (Devlin 1993) and was determined to be acceptable for simple mixtures by the National Research Council (NRC 1992) and DNA Advisory Board (DAB 2000). RMNE has been advocated as an "easy" method to both calculate and present to a jury (Buckleton & Curran 2008).

There are several requirements to consider before the RMNE approach can be appropriately used: (1) the individuals in the mixture are unrelated, (2) the individuals are from the same population group, and (3) all of the alleles in the profile are present (no drop-out), which is presumed by having all alleles at a locus possess peak heights above the stochastic threshold. Only loci where all of the alleles are present above the stochastic threshold should be used in the CPI statistical calculation. If there is any indication that data may be missing at the examined locus, perhaps due to the presence of allele peaks below the stochastic threshold that may raise the possibility of a missing sister allele, then *anyone* could technically be included in the mixture and the statistical weight of the locus would have a probability of 1.

Since the deduced profile of our perpetrator (Table A4.3(c)) violates requirement 3 above, we are limited in our ability to use CPI for determining the weight of the evidence. In Table A4.3(c), we note that eleven loci have at least one allele present in the perpetrator's profile, but which falls below the stochastic threshold. These loci are D8S1179, D21S11, D7S820, CSF1PO, D3S1358, TH01, D16S539, vWA, D18S51, D5S818, and FGA. At three of the remaining loci, two alleles are present and at least are present in the perpetrator's profile (D13S317, D19S433, and TPOX). Finally, one locus, D2S1338, unambiguously matches the genotype of the perpetrator. However, both of these alleles fall below the stochastic threshold, and according to requirement 3 listed above for using RMNE, loci with data below stochastic threshold are not to be used in the statistical calculation.

It would be tempting to simply use the three loci where two alleles are present and generate a statistic since these markers will satisfy the criteria of having data above the stochastic threshold. However, given the amount of ambiguity in the entire profile, where all of the low-level obligate alleles are below the stochastic threshold (and several alleles are at or near the analytical threshold), selecting loci above the stochastic threshold in this situation would be biased against the suspect since one cannot be absolutely certain by looking at only the evidence if all of the alleles are present. It is also tenuous to rely only on three loci for exclusionary purposes when the bulk of the data in the profile is ignored.

For this particular example, the RMNE approach is quite inefficient in providing weight to the evidence given the lack of confidence in the profile. One could conclude that the suspect cannot be excluded as a contributor to the evidence given the alleles present in the profile. Since each locus would be "inconclusive," the statistical weight would be conveyed as the probability of finding a random person in the population that could also be included in the mixture is equal to 1 in 1. Table A4.4 summaries the statistical analysis of the mixture using CPI.

There are two very important points to take away from this conclusion. First, the RMNE approach tends to waste a great deal of data that could be used, which is a severe limitation of this method. Second, note that we made our conclusions based upon the **alleles** shared between the evidence

TABLE A4.4   Summary Statistics for the Mixture Example (Figure A4.1)

STR	CPI		mRMP		STRmix
Locus	Alleles	Stat (1 in)	Alleles	Stat (1 in)	LR
D8S1179	INC	1	2p (16)	15.2	33.1
D21S11	INC	1	2p (29)	2.5	8.5
D7S820	INC	1	2p (8)	3.5	3.8
CSF1PO	INC	1	2p (12)	1.4	3.1
D3S1358	INC	1	2p (15)	1.8	3.2
TH01	INC	1	2p (9)	4.2	7.9
D13S317	INC	1	INC	1	3.7
D16S539	INC	1	2p (12)	1.6	2.3
D2S1338	INC	1	2pq (19,24)	35.7	35.7
D19S433	INC	1	INC	1	8.1
vWA	INC	1	2p (19)	4.8	11.1
TPOX	INC	1	INC	1	1.6
D18S51	INC	1	2p (14)	3.7	11.5
D5S818	INC	1	2p (10)	18.1	15.2
FGA	INC	1	INC	1	3.6
Combined Statistic:		1		2.58×10^7	2.30×10^{12}

This example uses combined probability of inclusion (CPI), modified random match probability (mRMP), and a fully continuous likelihood ratio (LR) system (STRmix). Since every locus in this mixture potentially has alleles below the stochastic threshold, the CPI approach yields "inconclusive" (INC) calls at every locus.

and person of interest. The goal of mixture interpretation is not simply to see what alleles are present in the profile, but to build a *genotype* from the evidence to compare to the person of interest's genotype. The genotype-inferred approach will be discussed below.

CPI Approach with Inflated Allele Peak Heights

As a thought experiment, we will inflate each allele in the profile by 100 RFU to remove the issues of having data below the stochastic threshold. Note that any stochastic issues in the original amplification remain in the profile, so this is a tenuous analysis at best.

By adding an extra 100 RFU, we no longer have any data below our stochastic threshold of 150 RFU, and can proceed with calculating the CPI statistic. The only issue to resolve is how to handle the two-allele loci. For the "imbalanced" two-allele loci at D7S820 and D5S818, we can be reasonably confident that all of the alleles are present at each locus. For example, at D7S820, it is unlikely that all (or a portion of) the 8 allele is entirely paired with the 11 allele given the low PHR between these loci (150/401 = 37%). If the perpetrator was for example an 8,11 genotype – sharing a portion of the 11 allele with the victim, there would still be 401 − 150 = 251 RFU remaining, making allele drop-out unlikely. We could therefore use D7S820 and D5S818 for the statistical calculation.

The issue remains for the "balanced" (or relatively balanced) two-allele loci at D13S317, D19S433, and TPOX, where ambiguity may still exist. Starting with D13S317, we note that both the 11 and 13 alleles are within the acceptable PHR (405/534 = 76%). Subtracting the remaining 11 allele from a perfect heterozygous pair – we would have (534 − 405 = 129 RFU) remaining, which would make a homozygous 11,11 perpetrator below the stochastic threshold of 150 RFU – we would need to exclude D13S317 from the statistical calculation.

We find a similar situation with the TPOX locus where the residual peak from a balanced 8,11 genotype would be (591 − 502) = 89 RFU, again, below the stochastic threshold and excluding TPOX from the statistical calculation. The issue here is that we are assuming balanced amplification between the two alleles – but we know that PCR is not a 100% efficient process, especially when low-level DNA quantities are amplified. Perhaps 200 RFU of the TPOX allele 8 belongs to the perpetrator. This would give a PHR of (591 − 200 = 391/502) 78% for the female at 8,11, which is within the acceptable PHR. Under this scenario and assumptions, TPOX would be acceptable for inclusion in the CPI statistical analysis. For D19S433, the residual peak from the 15 allele would be 648 − 351 = 297 RFU, and we would be able to use this locus in the statistical analysis.

Once again, we face the limitations of using thresholds combined with the "stacking" of shared alleles. Because of the genotype ambiguity – how much of each allele consists of victim and perpetrator – we may run the risk of failing to exclude (and thus falsely include) an innocent suspect. For now, we are resigned to designate these loci as "inconclusive" and effectively drop them from the statistical interpretation. Probabilistic genotyping methods of interpretation using a continuous approach (below) can perform simulations on all of the loci to determine optimal genotype combinations.

The statistical calculation for the probability of inclusion, or PI, at a single STR locus is very straightforward and quite simple. [Note: Do not confuse this PI with the paternity index described in Chapter 14.] We first sum the allele frequencies of all alleles above the stochastic threshold and square this value to find the probability of finding an unrelated individual in the population who would be included in the mixture. This calculation enables a statistical evaluation of all possible genotype combinations at that locus and treats each of these genotype possibilities as equally probable. Individual locus CPIs can be multiplied for independently inherited genetic markers to create the combined probability of inclusion (CPI) for the entire profile.

All calculations here use the U.S. Caucasian population data from NIST 1036 allele frequencies (see Appendix 1), which are also available on STRBase (NIST Population Data 2014).

$$PI = (f_1 + f_2 + f_3)^2$$

where $f_1 =$ the frequency of the 1st allele at the locus, and so forth.

For our modified example at the D8S1179 locus, where the peak heights were inflated above the stochastic threshold, we would sum the frequencies of alleles 11, 13, and 16:

$$PI = (f_{11} + f_{13} + f_{16})^2; f_{11} = 0.076; f_{13} = 0.330; f_{16} = 0.033$$
$$PI = (0.076 + 0.330 + 0.033)^2 = (0.439)^2 = 0.193.$$

We would expect about 19.3%, or 1 in 5.2 (1/0.193), random individuals in the Caucasian population would be included in this mixture at D8S1179. The Combined Probability of Exclusion (CPE) is simply $1 - $ CPI, so for the D8S1179 example, we could exclude $1 - 0.193 = 0.807$, or about 81% of the population.

We would then continue with the next locus, D21S11:

$$PI = (f_{27} + f_{29} + f_{32.2})^2; f_{27} = 0.022; f_{29} = 0.202; f_{32.2} = 0.090$$
$$PI = (0.022 + 0.202 + 0.090)^2 = (0.314)^2 = 0.099.$$

We would expect about 9.9% or 1 in 10.1 (1/0.099) random individuals in the Caucasian population would be included in this mixture at D21S11. The CPE for this locus would be $1 - 0.099 = 0.901$, or about 90.1% of the population.

Once we finish calculating the PI for each locus, we then multiply the individual PIs to determine the CPI:

$$CPI = PI_{(D8S1179)} \times PI_{(D21S11)} \times PI_{(D7S820)} \times etc...$$

For our two loci in this example:

$$CPI = PI_{(D8S1179)} \times PI_{(D21S11)} = 0.193 \times 0.099 = 0.0191.$$

We would therefore expect about 2%, or 1 in 52.4 (1/0.0191), random individuals in the Caucasian population to be included in this mixture if only the data at D8S1179 and D21S11 were considered. Looking at this same information from the CPE perspective, we could exclude $1 - 0.0191 = 0.9809$, or about 98.1% of the population.

One attraction of the RMNE approach is that it is easy to calculate and to explain in court. As one can see from this example, with uncertainty and complexity in the mixture profile, a "simple" approach ends up wasting much of the information in the evidence. We next focus on the genotype-inferred approach.

Statistical Calculations with mRMP

The random match probability (RMP) approach uses the same statistical formulas derived from the Hardy–Weinberg equilibrium (HWE) principles discussed in Chapter 10 for calculating the rarity of a match for a single source profile: p^2 for homozygous loci and $2pq$ for heterozygous loci, where p and q represent frequencies of alleles P and Q, respectively. The NRC II committee recommended the incorporation of a population substructure correction factor, theta (θ) for homozygous loci: $p^2 + p(1 - p)\theta$ (NRC 1996).

By definition, the RMP is calculated on a single-source profile, so for a mixture sample, where the determinations of the individual components of the mixture are made, this approach is often called a "modified" RMP (mRMP). An excellent resource on the benefits, uses, and limitations of the mRMP approach can be found in Bille et al. (2013) and SWGDAM (2010).

Since we are inferring genotypes using the mRMP approach, we must make an assumption as to the number of contributors in the mixture in order to determine all of the possible genotypes present. In this example, we assume that two individuals are in the mixture, one (major contributor) female and one (minor contributor) male.

We can start at the four-allele locus – D2S1338. Based upon our previous analysis of PHR, we determined that the minor contributor (the perpetrator) has the 19,24 genotype at D2S1338. Using CPI as a statistical tool, we were unable to use this locus since both the 19 and 24 alleles were below the stochastic threshold. For the mRMP approach, we are able to use this locus since we assume two contributors and have justified the inferred genotypes using PHRs (or through subtracting the genotype of the victim, 17,25). We would use the HWE formula for heterozygotes, $2pq$:

$$\text{mRMP}_{(minor)} = 2pq \cdots (\text{where } p = \text{frequency}(f) \text{ of the 19 allele}; q = \text{frequency}(f) \text{ of the 24 allele})$$
$$\text{mRMP}_{(minor)} = 2 \times f_{19} \times f_{24}; f_{19} = 0.120; f_{24} = 0.115$$
$$\text{mRMP}_{(minor)} = 2 \times 0.120 \times 0.115 = 0.028.$$

At the D2S1338 locus, we would expect about 2.8% (about 1 in 35.7 individuals or $1/0.028$) of the Caucasian population to match the inferred 19,24 genotype. We can clearly see the advantage of using the inferred genotype approach. Compared to CPI, where this locus was inconclusive, we are able to provide a statistical weight to the evidence.

We next examine the three-allele loci. Looking across the profile, we note that all of the three-allele loci have the minor allele below the stochastic threshold. This "zygote ambiguity" creates lack of confidence in being able to fully interpret the mixture profile. With the CPI approach, we declared all 9 of the three-allele loci inconclusive. With mRMP, we can use these loci, but are somewhat limited in the full statistical power when data are below the stochastic threshold. We first examine the D8S1179 locus.

The minor 16 allele is below the stochastic threshold, and the major genotype (11,13) gives an acceptable PHR. In considering all the possible genotypes of the perpetrator at D8S1179, we list:

11,16
13,16
16,16
16,F

where "F" could be any possible allele that failed to be detected.

To handle this ambiguity, we can use the formula "2p" (see Buckleton & Triggs (2006) for an excellent review of the 2p rule). We invoke the 2p rule at these loci as it can mathematically account for the missing sister allele. One way to think of this approach is that if a locus is heterozygous, then we would use $2pq$. If "q" is missing and could be any other allele at the locus (i.e. $q = 1$), then $2pq$ becomes $2p(1)$, or simply $2p$.

For the D8S1179 locus we would then calculate:

$$\text{mRMP}_{(\text{D8S1179})} = 2p(\text{where p} = \text{frequency}(f)\text{of the 16 allele}); f_{16} = 0.033$$
$$\text{mRMP}_{(\text{D8S1179})} = 2 \times 0.033 = 0.066.$$

At the D8S1179 locus, we would expect about 6.6% (about 1 in 15.2 individuals, or $1/0.066$) of the Caucasian population to have the obligate 16 allele observed in the mixture. Since the D8S1179 and D2S1338 are independent, we can multiply these probabilities (as we normally do with single-source samples):

$$\text{mRMP} = \text{mRMP}_{(\text{D8S1179})} \times \text{mRMP}_{(\text{D2S1338})}$$
$$\text{mRMP} = 0.066 \times 0.028 = 0.0018.$$

Based upon the two loci thus far, there is a 0.18% probability (about 1 in 556 individuals) of finding a random person in the population with the inferred genotypes at D8S1179 and D2S1338.

Hypothetically, we now imagine that the 16 allele in the profile is *above* the stochastic threshold and the perpetrator was a 16,16 homozygote (we briefly ignore the other alleles at the locus to illustrate this point). The mRMP of the perpetrator's genotype inferred from the evidence would be:

$$\text{mRMP}_{(\text{D8S1179})} = p^2(\text{where p} = \text{frequency}(f)\text{of the 16 allele}); f_{16} = 0.033$$
$$\text{mRMP}_{(\text{D8S1179})} = (0.033)^2 = 0.0011 = 0.11\% \text{ of the population or about 1 in 909 individuals.}$$

We can see that in this particular scenario, the 2p rule is very conservative compared to other genotype combinations when the non-16 alleles at D8S1179 are greater than a frequency of 0.033. There are scenarios when using the 2p rule is not conservative. Suppose the suspect has a 16,16 genotype and the evidence data only shows the 16 allele *below* the stochastic threshold — he would be included as a contributor, and a statistical calculation using 2p would be conducted. If the *real perpetrator* that truly contributed the evidence was a 12,16 genotype, and drop-out occurred at the 12 allele, then the innocent suspect (16,16) would *still* be included as a contributor (based upon the 16 allele) and a statistical weight would be given to the evidence. If both the 12 and 16 alleles were above the stochastic threshold, then the suspect (16,16) would be excluded as a contributor. Buckleton and Triggs (2006) and Balding and Buckleton (2009) provide more information on the cautious use of 2p for data in the stochastic zone.

We note that being able to subtract the female profile from the evidence (assuming the evidence is an intimate sample belonging to the female) allows an analyst to identify the low-level alleles that are obligatory to the perpetrator. For the "balanced" two-allele loci (D13S317, D19S433, and TPOX), we are once again unsure if all of the alleles from the perpetrator are in fact present in the profile. For these loci, we could determine these markers inconclusive and give a weight of "1" to the evidence.

Overall, the mRMP approach allows the analyst to use more of the information in the evidence, making this method more efficient than CPI (see Table A4.4). However, the 2p rule is less efficient than our HWE formula ($2pq$ or p^2) and may not always be conservative to an innocent suspect.

We will observe below how a continuous approach makes use of all of the data and considers the possibility of drop-out without using the 2p rule.

mRMP Approach with Inflated Allele Peak Heights

Once again, as a thought experiment, we inflate the RFU values of the alleles in the profile to serve as an example of how one would consider the data when everything is above the stochastic threshold. We will no longer need to invoke the 2p rule. We start with the modified example at the D8S1179 locus.

With the mRMP approach, our goal is to infer all possible genotypes in the mixture. The female victim has the 11,13 genotype, and this is within the acceptable PHR. We now consider all possible genotypes for the perpetrator:

"Modified" Allele (RFU)

11: 413
13: 522
16: 176

There are two approaches we can consider as we try to infer the genotypes: unrestricted mRMP or restricted mRMP. The unrestricted mRMP considers all possible genotypes without regard to PHR information. Using an unrestricted mRMP approach, we would infer the possible genotypes (using the 16 allele as an obligate allele to the perpetrator):

Unrestricted Genotypes

11,16
13,16
16,16

The restricted mRMP approach incorporates PHR (and possibly M_x) to consider the most probable genotypes and attempts to eliminate genotypes that are deemed improbable.

Restricted Genotypes

We first consider the 11,16 possible genotype of the perpetrator (Figure A4.4(a)). This would mean that the 11 allele is shared between the victim and perpetrator (noted in the illustration on the next page as 11*). If we *assume* a perfectly balanced 11,16 genotype for the perpetrator (solid blue "triangle" alleles), then 176 RFU of the 11 allele belongs to the perpetrator, leaving 413 − 176 = 237 RFU of the remaining 11 allele (white triangle allele) to match with the 13 allele from the victim.

Example 1 − the perpetrator is 11,16 and the victim is 11*,13*
Example 1 − PHR

$$\text{Victim PHR: } 237/522 = 0.454 \text{ or } 45\% \text{ (\textbf{Fails PHR of 60\%})}$$

Based upon the PHR of the victim (if there is at least balanced sharing with the proposed 11,16 perpetrator) we would determine that this combination is *likely improbable* since the PHR is less than 60%.

Next, we consider the victim 11,13 genotype (Figure A4.4(b)) and a perpetrator of 13,16 (sharing of the 13* allele). If we assume a perfectly balanced 13,16 genotype, then 176 RFU of the 13 allele belongs

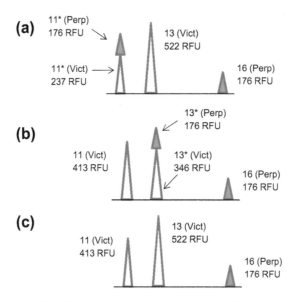

FIGURE A4.4 An illustration to show the process of restricting genotypes for the perpetrator (Perp) using PHR information from the female victim's (Victim) genotype (11,13). (a) Considering the possibility that a portion of the 11 allele (11*) is shared between the victim and the perpetrator (if we assume a balanced sharing of the 11 and 16 alleles of the perpetrator). (b) Considering the possibility that a portion of the 13 allele (13*) is shared between the victim and the perpetrator (if we assume a balanced sharing of the 13 and 16 alleles of the perpetrator). (c) Assuming that the perpetrator genotype is homozygous 16,16 since this allele is above the stochastic threshold of 150 RFU.

to the perpetrator (solid blue triangle), leaving $522 - 176 = 346$ RFU (solid white triangle) to match with the 11 allele from the female.

Example 2 — the perpetrator is 13,16 and the victim is 11,13**
Example 2 — PHR

Victim: $346/413 = 0.838$ or 84% (**Passes PHR of 60%**)

Based upon the PHR of the female, we would determine that it is probable that the perpetrator could have the 11,16 genotype.

Finally, we consider the female 11,13 genotype and a perpetrator of 16,16.

Example 3 — the perpetrator is 16,16 and the victim is 11,13
Example 3 — PHR

Victim: $413/522 = 0.791$ or 79% (**Passes PHR of 60%**)

Using the Restricted mRMP approach, we can summarize our results:

Restricted Genotypes Considered for the Perpetrator Minor Component

11,16 (improbable based upon PHR)
13,16 (possible)
16,16 (possible)

Based on the logic just reviewed, we can eliminate an 11,16 genotype for the minor-component perpetrator given the imbalance that this possibility creates in PHR for the major-component victim's genotype. The other genotype combinations of 13,16 and 16,16 produce acceptable PHRs for the victim's already-established 11,13 genotype. Again, we understand that these data are all below the stochastic threshold in reality, and inflating the RFU by 100 does not eliminate the stochastic issues.

If the suspect possesses a 13,16 genotype at D8S1179, then he cannot be excluded as a potential contributor to the evidence based upon the inferred genotypes of the perpetrator. With the unrestricted mRMP approach, we must consider *all* of the inferred genotypes in the statistical calculation:

$$\text{mRMP}_{\text{(unrestricted)}} = 11,16 \textbf{ or } 13,16 \textbf{ or } 16,16 \quad (f_{11} = 0.076; f_{13} = 0.330; f_{16} = 0.033)$$

Using the HWE formula ($2pq$ and p^2; and leaving out the theta correction here for simplicity):

$$\text{mRMP}_{\text{(unrestricted)}} = 2f_{11}f_{16} + 2f_{13}f_{16} + f_{16}{}^2$$

According to the second law of probability (see Chapter 9), we *add* the genotype frequencies since the possible combinations are mutually exclusive:

$$\text{mRMP}_{\text{(unrestricted)}} = (2 \times 0.076 \times 0.033) + (2 \times 0.330 \times 0.033) + 0.033^2 = 0.005 + 0.022 + 0.0011$$
$$= 0.0281$$

We would expect to find a randomly selected unrelated person in the population matching the inferred genotypes in this mixture about 2.8% of the time (about 1 in 35.6 individuals).

We now calculate the restricted mRMP using the same approach, but excluding the 11,16 genotype since this was determined to be improbable:

$$\text{mRMP}_{\text{(restricted)}} = 13,16 \textbf{ or } 16,16 (f_{13} = 0.330; f_{16} = 0.033)$$
$$\text{mRMP}_{\text{(restricted)}} = 2f_{13}f_{16} + f_{16}{}^2$$
$$\text{mRMP}_{\text{(restricted)}} = (2 \times 0.330 \times 0.033) + 0.033^2 = 0.022 + 0.0011 = 0.0231$$

We would expect to find a randomly selected unrelated person in the population matching the inferred genotypes in this mixture about 2.3% of the time (about 1 in 43.3 individuals).

Comparing the approaches of the unrestricted versus the restricted mRMP, we can observe that restricting particular genotypes can increase the rarity of a match (from 1 in 36 (unrestricted) to about 1 in 43 (restricted)). Looking across all of the statistical approaches we see a clear trend:

D8S1179

CPI − *inconclusive* (1 in 1)
$\text{mRMP}_{(2p)}$ − 1 in 15.2
$\text{mRMP}_{\text{(unrestricted)}}$ − 1 in 35.6
$\text{mRMP}_{\text{(restricted)}}$ − 1 in 43.3
$\text{RMP}_{(13,16)}$ − 1 in 45.5

We know from this particular mixture that the perpetrator has the 13,16 genotype and the "maximum" RMP at this locus is 1 in 45.5. We can see two trends in how we approach the analysis of the data. When data are below the stochastic threshold, using CPI is uninformative since all of the information is thrown away. The 2p rule gives a statistic substantially less than the RMP — 1 in 15.2 and could be considered a conservative approach. If the data were all *above* the stochastic threshold, the unrestricted mRMP gives a lower statistic than the restricted mRMP since additional genotype combinations are considered. The inferred genotype approach utilizes more of the data than the RMNE approach.

Statistical Calculations with LR

Another approach to inferring genotypes from a mixture is to use the binary likelihood ratio (LR). The binary LR evaluates the evidence under two propositions to explain the mixture (see Chapter 12). For the numerator (see below), evaluation of the probability of the evidence is conditioned upon a hypothesis (H_p) and any additional information (I) associated with the case. The vertical line denotes the conditioning and is read as "given." Traditionally, the numerator of the LR is called the "Prosecution's Hypothesis." For example, the Prosecution's Hypothesis of the case is that the mixture evidence in our example can be explained as a mixture of the victim and the suspect.

For the alternative proposition, in the denominator (see below), the evidence is evaluated using a different explanation of the data. This alternative hypothesis (H_d) is often called the "Defense Hypothesis." According to the Defense Hypothesis of the case, the evidence can be explained by a mixture of the victim and some unknown, random person in the population:

$$LR = \frac{\Pr(E|H_p, I)}{\Pr(E|H_d, I)}$$

We can illustrate and simplify the LR:

$$LR = \frac{\Pr(E|H_p, I) = \text{Victim \& Suspect}}{\Pr(E|H_d, I) = \text{Victim \& Unknown}}$$

where the Prosecution Hypothesis proposes the evidence is a combination of the victim and the suspect, and the Defense Hypothesis proposes the evidence is a combination of the victim and an unknown, unrelated random person in the population. Since the genotype of the victim is in both propositions, we can "cancel" this out of the calculation:

$$LR = \frac{\cancel{\text{Victim \&}} \text{Suspect}}{\cancel{\text{Victim \&}} \text{Unknown}} = \frac{\text{Suspect}}{\text{Unknown}}$$

For the Prosecution, the evidence is explained fully by the proposition that the suspect is the perpetrator and he is in the mixture, therefore, the probability that the suspect is in the mixture is equal to 1:

$$LR = \frac{1}{\text{Unknown}}$$

Since the Defense proposes that someone at random in the population was the true perpetrator, the probability of an unknown person in the population is equal to the HWE formula for either heterozygotes ($2pq$) or homozygotes (p^2). In its simplest form the LR is equal to 1/mRMP.

As an example, we will use D2S1338. For the Prosecution, the mixture is fully explained by the genotypes of the victim (17,25) and the suspect, who has a 19,24 genotype at D2S1338. Given the "certainty" of the Prosecutor's Hypothesis, the numerator is equal to 1. The Defense stipulates that the victim is in the mixture, but the 19,24 genotype is from an unknown, unrelated person in the population and not the suspect. We would therefore use the 2*pq* formula to determine the rarity of the 19,24 genotype in the population:

$$LR = \frac{1}{2pq} = \frac{1}{2f_{19}f_{24}}$$

Using $f_{19} = 0.120$ and $f_{24} = 0.115$,

$$LR = \frac{1}{2 \times 0.120 \times 0.115} = \frac{1}{0.0276} = 36.2$$

The LR would be reported using the following explanation: "The probability of the evidence is 36.2 times more likely if the stain came from Mr. Smith than if it came from an unknown, unrelated individual." It would be inappropriate to say, "The probability that Mr. Smith left the evidence is 36.2 times more likely than if the stain came from an unknown, unrelated individual." Although this statement contains much of the same wording, we have actually transposed the conditional.

In the first statement we talk about the *evidence* given the hypotheses (the "if" statements). In the second statement we are evaluating the probability that Mr. Smith committed the crime *given* the evidence, which is the proposition that is ultimately a decision of the trier of fact (Judge or Jury) and not for the forensic scientist.

For the remainder of the profile, we would use the same approach as the mRMP (i.e. using the 2p rule for loci below the stochastic threshold). The LR approach can also be used to evaluate multiple hypotheses from the Defense. For example, the Defense isn't required to stipulate that the victim is in the mixture. Perhaps the Defense would argue that the mixture came from *two* unknown individuals. Or perhaps the Defense may argue that there are actually three individuals in the mixture: the victim, and two unknown individuals. In general, it is usually more advantageous for the Defense to minimize the number of unknown contributors in the mixture. If the denominator in an LR becomes smaller because it is less probable, then the overall LR has a higher value and is stronger support for the evidence under the Prosecution's Hypothesis.

We began the discussion in this section by calling this the "binary" LR. When we evaluate the evidence to infer the genotype of the perpetrator, we compare to the suspect's profile to determine if there is an inclusion at all loci (then the Prosecution's Hypothesis is equal to "1"). Alternatively, we may observe non-concordance where genotypes do not match and the suspect cannot be a contributor of the profile (then the Prosecution's Hypothesis is equal to "0" and he is excluded from consideration as a contributor to the mixture profile). This "binary" approach is optimal when we have sufficient quantity and quality of DNA in the evidence and no allele drop-out has occurred.

If drop-out is a possibility, then the Prosecution's Hypothesis can range anywhere from 0 to 1 and is no longer binary. For now, we invoke the 2p rule when alleles fall below the stochastic threshold. As we have mentioned before, this may not be an optimal approach. The only appropriate approach to handle data when allele drop-out is a possibility is to incorporate a probabilistic approach where the probability of drop-out (and potentially allele drop-in) can be incorporated in the statistic. We will finish our example by looking at a software program that uses a probabilistic approach.

Statistical Calculations with a Probabilistic Approach

In 2012, a DNA Commission of the ISFG published recommendations for evaluating STR results where allele drop-out (or drop-in) is possible in the profile (Gill et al. 2012). We have already observed two statistical approaches for how to handle data when alleles fall below the stochastic threshold: (a) the RMNE solution is to drop the locus from consideration, and (b) the mRMP and the binary LR approaches incorporate the 2p rule. We have already discussed the limitations of both of these methods with complex low-level mixtures. Whereas the binary LR method is either 0 (excluded) or 1 (included) when allele drop-out is possible, the answer is somewhere between 0 and 1.

Including the possibility for allele drop-out allows the analyst to use all of the data in the profile and not be restricted to the limitations of a stochastic threshold. As mentioned earlier, thresholds draw a "line in the sand" to a process that is continuous, and therefore can lead to the exceptions that defy a carefully constructed validation study.

In his classic book, *Understanding Uncertainty*, Dennis Lindley remarks: "Whatever way uncertainty is approached, probability is the only sound way to think about it" (Lindley 2006). If I were a contestant on the game show *Jeopardy!* and the final category was "18th Century Opera" I would likely risk none of my winnings on the subject knowing that my uncertainty on this subject is quite high. On the other hand, if the final category was "Forensic DNA Scientists Named Butler" — I would feel my uncertainty level would be very low. A probabilistic approach to uncertainty when not all of the data is present in the electropherogram is the only logical way to handle these low-level DNA profiles. Simply ignoring the locus (or using the 2p rule) may not be conservative as discussed above.

The probabilistic methods that incorporate the probability of allele drop-out into the statistical calculation can be described as belonging to two schools of thought: the semi-continuous approach and fully continuous approach (Kelly et al. 2014). Both schools agree on one important foundation: the LR is the only appropriate method to incorporate a probability of drop-out. It is not possible to do so with RMNE or mRMP calculations.

The concept behind the semi-continuous approach is that PCR amplification of low-level samples in the stochastic range no longer follows the same convention as high-copy DNA. This "uncoupling" of the typical PHR and the standard stutter ratios normally observed above the stochastic threshold create a situation where the ability to restrict possible genotype combinations is not reliable below the stochastic threshold. The focus then for the semi-continuous approach is the *alleles present* in the mixture and the incorporation of a probability of drop-out to account for any alleles absent in the profile. Information such as peak heights, PHR, stutter ratios, M_x, and so forth are ignored for this type of analysis. There are several software programs currently available that use the semi-continuous approach (see Chapter 13).

The fully continuous approach attempts to use *all* of the data in the profile — peak heights, M_x, stutter ratio, and so forth. Recall when we were going through the steps of mixture deconvolution using the Clayton rules with the D2S1338 locus (Figure A4.2 and Table A4.1) we considered the possibility that the 24 allele was a peak that derived entirely from the perpetrator (i.e. there was 0% stutter from the victim's 25 allele), or that the 24 allele was an amalgam of the perpetrator *and* stutter from the victim's 25 allele. We looked at the extremes from 0% (minimum) to 15% (maximum).

The fully continuous approach attempts to model the variation present in the profile to take into account the possibility that stutter is not an "all or none" proposition. The fully continuous approach models the variation in PHR, M_x, stutter ratio, etc. by conducting several thousands (to hundreds of thousands) of simulations of the profile parameters. A mathematical process called Markov Chain Monte Carlo is used to conduct these simulations of the data with the goal to determine the most probable genotypes.

There are several software programs both commercially and freely available that use either the semi-continuous or fully continuous approach. We will highlight the usefulness of the probabilistic approach using our low-level mixture example. For the sake of brevity, we will survey one probabilistic software program. Otherwise, we could at least double the size of this book by devoting a chapter for each platform. I would like to state clearly that *this exercise is not meant to promote or recommend any software program*, but to stress the **usefulness** of these programs in general, and specifically for low-level complex mixtures. There are clear advantages and disadvantages for every software program, and it is highly encouraged that any laboratory interested in the probabilistic approach should do their research and "due diligence" for finding the program that fits their mixture interpretation needs.

For our example, we will examine the STRmix software program developed by a collaborative effort between the Institute of Environmental Science and Research Limited (ESR, a New Zealand Crown Research Institute) and Forensic Science South Australia (STRmix 2014). A number of publications over the past few years have described the background and mathematical underpinnings of the software (see Taylor et al. 2013 and references within).

For our example, a text file was created from the electropherogram data containing three pieces of information for each marker: the repeat number of all alleles above the analytical threshold (50 RFU), including any stutter peaks, the peak height of each allele, and the size of each allele (in base pair). For STRmix, parameters that determine the variability of peak heights within an individual laboratory are initially established by running a set of dilution samples prior to casework implementation. *Like all other probabilistic software programs, a stochastic threshold is not used.*

Text files with the reference profiles for the victim and the suspect were imported into the program and the following propositions for the H_p and H_d were submitted for analysis:

$$LR = \frac{Pr\,(E|H_p, I) = Victim\ \&\ Suspect}{Pr\,(E|H_d, I) = Victim\ \&\ Unknown}$$

The NIST 1036 allele frequencies for the Caucasian population (Appendix 1) were used and the θ correction was set to 0.

The goal of the fully continuous methods is to generate a summary of the most probable genotype(s) of the contributors to the mixture. It does this by conducting several thousands of simulations of the data while modeling certain parameters (PHR, M_x, stutter ratios, etc....) across the entire profile. Some genotypes will better explain the mixture than other genotype combinations. These genotype combinations have higher relative "weights." By normalizing the weights at a locus, we can easily infer the preferred genotype of a contributor at that locus; for example, a single unambiguous genotype combination at any locus would be assigned a weighting of one.

Table A4.5 gives the genotype distribution for our low-level mixture example. We first examine the results from the D8S1179 locus (Figure A4.3). First, notice that the female victim genotype is always 11,13. This is expected since we conditioned on the victim's profile in both the H_p and H_d propositions.

For the inferred genotype of the perpetrator (recall, our previous analyses determined that the 16 allele was obligate to the perpetrator), we observe that after the thousands of simulations, STRmix

TABLE A4.5   Genotype Probability Distribution Determined from STRmix Software

Locus	Female Victim	Inferred Genotype	Probability (weight)	Locus	Female Victim	Inferred Genotype	Probability (weight)
D8S1179	11,13	11,16	0.233	D16S539	11,13	11,12	0.302
	11,13	13,16	0.496		11,13	12,12	0.287
	11,13	16,16	0.196		11,13	Q,12	0.077
	11,13	Q,16	0.076		11,13	12,13	0.335
D21S11	27,32.2	27,29	0.237	D2S1338	17,25	19,24	1.000
	27,32.2	29,29	0.194				
	27,32.2	Q,29	0.102	D19S433	14,15	14,14	0.051
	27,32.2	29,32.2	0.466		14,15	Q,14	0.032
					14,15	14,15	0.235
D7S820	11,11	8,8	0.413		14,15	15,15	0.594
	11,11	Q,8	0.285		14,15	Q,15	0.080
	11,11	8,11	0.302		14,15	Q,Q	0.009
CSF1PO	10,11	10,12	0.271	vWA	15,18	15,19	0.193
	10,11	11,12	0.358		15,18	18,19	0.488
	10,11	12,12	0.318		15,18	19,19	0.176
	10,11	Q,12	0.053		15,18	Q,19	0.143
D3S1358	14,16	14,14	0.022	TPOX	8,11	8,8	0.351
	14,16	Q,14	0.026		8,11	Q,8	0.071
	14,16	14,15	0.187		8,11	8,11	0.363
	14,16	15,15	0.131		8,11	11,11	0.152
	14,16	Q,15	0.096		8,11	Q,11	0.051
	14,16	14,16	0.070		8,11	Q,Q	0.012
	14,16	15,16	0.324				
	14,16	16,16	0.097	D18S51	13,17	13,14	0.458
	14,16	Q,16	0.033		13,17	14,14	0.275
	14,16	Q,Q	0.012		13,17	Q,14	0.080
					13,17	14,17	0.187
TH01	6,9.3	6,9	0.418				
	6,9.3	9,9	0.243	D5S818	12,12	10,10	0.354
	6,9.3	Q,9	0.140		12,12	Q,10	0.160
	6,9.3	9,9.3	0.198		12,12	10,12	0.486

(Continued)

TABLE A4.5 Genotype Probability Distribution Determined from STRmix Software (*cont'd*)

Locus	Female Victim	Inferred Genotype	Probability (weight)	Locus	Female Victim	Inferred Genotype	Probability (weight)
D13S317	11,13	11,11	0.431	FGA	25,26	20,20	0.655
	11,13	Q,11	0.099		25,26	Q,20	0.142
	11,13	11,13	0.318		25,26	20,25	0.100
	11,13	13,13	0.079		25,26	20,26	0.103
	11,13	Q,13	0.055				
	11,13	Q,Q	0.018				

The female victim was conditioned upon in both H_p and H_d propositions. The "Q" allele represents allele drop-out of any unobserved allele at the locus. See Taylor et al. (2013).

determined that there were four possibilities for the perpetrator: 11,16 (with 23.3% of the weight); 13,16 (with 49.6% of the weight); 16,16 (with 19.6% of the weight); and Q,16 (with 7.6% of the weight). The "Q" allele represents any other possible allele except for those already observed (11, 13, and 16) and means that drop-out of some allele was possible in the profile.

We next move to D2S1338 (Figure A4.2), the only four-allele locus in the profile. Again, given the fact that we conditioned on the victim's profile, the only two obligate alleles left are 19 and 24, which STRmix assigned a probability of 1.0 as the perpetrator's genotype and represents certainty at this locus (Table A4.5).

Finally, we notice the great deal of uncertainty at the D3S1358 locus (Table A4.5). We can explain this uncertainty by observing the alleles present in the electropherogram (Figure A4.1). In our analysis of this locus for inferring the genotype using the mRMP/binary LR approach, we determined the 15 allele was an obligate allele of the perpetrator since it was well above the 15% maximum stutter ratio. During the simulations of the data, STRmix considered the possibility that the 15 allele was elevated stutter. This is not an optimal explanation of the data — for example, if the perpetrator was 14,14 (and shared the 14 allele of the victim, making the 15 allele an elevated stutter of the female's 16 allele) — this was considered likely only 2.2% of the time in all of the simulations. The most probable perpetrator genotypes were those that included the 15 allele (with 15,16 being the most probable explanation). We should also note that there was a possibility at this locus that *both* alleles of the perpetrator dropped-out: the "Q,Q" genotype (e.g. the perpetrator could be the 13,17 genotype) considered likely only 1.2% of the time from the simulations.

After taking some poetic license in explaining how we generated the distribution of inferred genotype weights from the mixture, we now apply this information to the statistical calculation of the LR. Recall that with our classic binary LR propositions, genotypes were either absent or present — an all-or-none event. The probabilistic approach allows us to extend the binary LR to now consider possibilities between 0 and 1. For STRmix, we will continue to use the propositions of the LR, but now we will provide a weight to the genotype frequencies.

Table A4.6 provides the H_p and H_d probabilities for the LR. We start with D8S1179. With the classic binary LR, the H_p in an unambiguous mixture profile where all alleles are above the stochastic

TABLE A4.6 Likelihood Ratio (LR) Calculations Determined from STRmix Software

Locus	Pr(E|H_p)	Pr(E|H_d)	LR
D8S1179	0.496	0.015	33.1
D21S11	0.466	0.055	8.5
D7S820	0.302	0.079	3.8
CSF1PO	0.358	0.114	3.1
D3S1358	0.324	0.102	3.2
TH01	0.418	0.053	7.9
D13S317	0.431	0.117	3.7
D16S539	0.302	0.132	2.3
D2S1338	1	0.028	35.7
D19S433	0.594	0.072	8.1
vWA	0.488	0.044	11.1
TPOX	0.363	0.225	1.6
D18S51	0.458	0.040	11.5
D5S818	0.486	0.031	15.2
FGA	0.142	0.039	3.6
		LR total =	2.30×10^{12}

The Pr(E\|H_p) probabilities were calculated from the genotype probability weights in Table A4.5. See Taylor et al. (2013).

threshold is equal to 1 (the mixture is fully explained by the victim and the suspect's DNA). Given the uncertainty in the profile, we can no longer say with absolute confidence the suspect (13,16) is in the mixture since allele drop-out is a possibility. We use the weights determined from the simulations of the data. In other words:

$$\Pr\left(E|H_p\right) = (\text{weight})$$

For the proposed genotype combination including the suspect (13, 16) − the weight is equal to 0.496.

$$\Pr\left(E|H_p\right) = 0.496$$

For the H_d, it is possible that any of the *four* inferred genotypes (Table A4.6) could contribute to the evidence. We also use the weighted probability to multiply by the genotype frequencies in the population:

$$\Pr\left(E|H_d\right) = \left(0.233 \times 2f_{11}f_{16}\right) + \left(0.496 \times 2f_{13}f_{16}\right) + \left(0.196 \times f_{16}^2\right) + \left(0.076 \times 2f_Q f_{16}\right) = 0.015$$

Overall, the LR for the D8S1179 locus becomes:

$$LR = \frac{Pr\,(E|H_p)}{Pr\,(E|H_d)} = \frac{0.496}{0.015} = 33.1$$

Recall that all of the weights generated by the software are made independently of the suspect's profile. If, for example, the suspect was 16,16 — then the LR would become:

$$LR = \frac{Pr\,(E|H_p)}{Pr\,(E|H_d)} = \frac{0.196}{0.015} = 13.1$$

If we multiply across the entire profile, then we observe an overall LR of 2.3×10^{12} or about 2.3 trillion (Table A4.6) — substantially greater than the 1 in 1 for CPI or 1 in 25.8 million for mRMP (Table A4.4). It would be rather simplistic to state that probabilistic approaches are "better" than the other statistical approaches since we observe larger numbers overall. Obtaining higher statistics should not be the goal of using probabilistic approaches. Instead, the goal should be to determine how well these approaches make use of all the data.

We illustrate this concept using the D3S1358 locus. In Table A4.4 we observe that for the suspect (15,16 genotype), CPI gives a statistic of 1 in 1 (inconclusive), the mRMP/binary LR using 2p gives a statistic of 1 in 1.8, and STRmix gives an LR statistic of 3.2.

Now suppose that the genotype of the suspect was 12,15 and the 12 allele has dropped-out of the electropherogram. Based upon the obligate allele at 15, we would still conclude that the CPI statistic was 1 in 1, and the mRMP/LR using 2p would still give a statistic of 1 in 1.8. For STRmix, we now adjust the probability of the H_p by using the weight of 0.096 in the numerator (i.e. 15,Q). The H_d remains the same as before:

$$LR_{15,Q} = \frac{Pr\,(E|H_p)}{Pr\,(E|H_d)} = \frac{0.096}{0.102} = 0.941$$

The evidence now favors the proposition of the Defense Hypothesis (less than 1.0) that someone other than the suspect was the source of the stain. This is an example where the 2p rule is biased against the innocent suspect as it gives weight to the evidence that favors the proposition of the Prosecution's Hypothesis.

CONCLUSIONS

In this appendix, I have tried to take the reader through the process of mixture interpretation following what I think is the best process (the Clayton rules) for mixture deconvolution. It is important to remember that one of the final steps of the Clayton procedure, and clearly stated in the SWGDAM 2010 interpretation guidelines (SWGDAM 2010), is to compare the inferred genotype to the reference profile. It is extremely important to remember our fairness and objectivity as a forensic scientist in this process.

There are multiple approaches to statistical interpretation of mixtures, and it is clear that for many of the more challenging and difficult mixtures, RMNE and the binary LR with 2p are limited in their utility and may actually be biased against an innocent suspect. Moving forward, probabilistic approaches make better use of the data in situations where drop-out may have occurred in the profile as can be clearly seen in Table A4.6. Fortunately, several software programs are now available for these complex mixtures. We must also be aware that there are limitations to these programs. Believe it or not — there are some mixtures that are just too challenging to interpret!

Acknowledgments

When Dr. Butler approached me with the idea to write an appendix for this book on the steps involved with the interpretation of a mixture — from start to stats — I started writing in a more "clinical" style better suited for a scientific paper. I eventually found myself writing as though the reader was in front of me and my goal was to try to make this process as inviting as possible, especially for new forensic scientists and those who may lack the strong scientific background of complex mixture interpretation.

I have had the extreme pleasure of discussing mixture interpretation issues with legions of forensic scientists over the past few years, especially in mixture workshops. I also appreciate all of the "mixture discussions" over the past few years with the following valued friends and colleagues who have increased my own knowledge of mixture interpretation, including: Charlotte Word, Robin Cotton, Catherine Grgicak, Peter Gill, Todd Bille, Steven Myers, Bruce Heidebrecht, Jo-Anne Bright, and John Buckleton. I also would like to thank several colleagues at NIST, especially Becky Hill, Margaret Kline, David Duewer, Kathy Sharpless, and Peter Vallone. Finally, I would like to thank John Butler for all of the scientific discussions over the years and the opportunity to make a small contribution to his book!

References

Balding, D. J., & Buckleton, J. (2009). Interpreting low template DNA profiles. *Forensic Science International Genetics, 4*, 1–10.

Bille, T., et al. (2013). Application of random match probability calculations to mixed STR profiles. *Journal Forensic Sciences, 58*, 474–485.

Bright, J. A., et al. (2010). Examination of the variability in mixed DNA profile parameters for the Identifiler multiplex. *Forensic Science International Genetics, 4*, 111–114.

Buckleton, J., & Triggs, C. (2006). Is the 2p rule always conservative? *Forensic Science International, 159*, 206–209.

Buckleton, J. S., & Curran, J. M. (2008). A discussion of the merits of random man not excluded and likelihood ratios. *Forensic Science International Genetics, 2*, 343–348.

Clayton, T. M., et al. (1998). Analysis and interpretation of mixed forensic stains using DNA STR profiling. *Forensic Science International, 91*, 55–70.

Devlin, B. (1993). Forensic inference from genetic markers. *Statistical Methods Medical Research, 2*, 241–262.

DNA Advisory Board. (2000). Statistical and population genetics issues affecting the evaluation of the frequency of occurrence of DNA profiles calculated from pertinent population database(s). *Forensic Science Communications, 2*(3). Available at http://www.fbi.gov/about-us/lab/forensic-science-communications/fsc/july2000/dnastat.htm/. Accessed April 4, 2014.

Gill, P., & Buckleton, J. (2010). A universal strategy to interpret DNA profiles that does not require a definition of low-copy-number. *Forensic Science International Genetics, 4*, 221–227.

Gill, P., et al. (2006). DNA commission of the International Society of Forensic Genetics: Recommendations on the interpretation of mixtures. *Forensic Science International, 160*, 90–101.

Gill, P., et al. (2012). DNA Commission of the International Society of Forensic Genetics: Recommendations on the evaluation of STR typing results that may include drop-out and/or drop-in using probabilistic methods. *Forensic Science International Genetics, 6*(6), 679–688.

Kelly, H., et al. (2012). The interpretation of low level DNA mixtures. *Forensic Science International Genetics, 6*(2), 191–197.

Kelly, H., et al. (2014). A comparison of statistical models for the analysis of complex forensic DNA profiles. *Science Justice, 54*, 66–70.

Lindley, D. V. (2006). *Understanding Uncertainty*. Hoboken, New Jersey: John Wiley & Sons.

National Research Council. (1992). *DNA Technology in Forensic Science*. Washington, DC: National Academy Press.

National Research Council. (1996). *The Evaluation of Forensic DNA Evidence*. Washington, DC: National Academy Press.

NIST Population Data. (2014). Available at http://www.cstl.nist.gov/strbase/NISTpop.htm. Accessed April 4, 2014.

STRmix. (2014). Available at http://strmix.esr.cri.nz/. Accessed April 4, 2014.

SWGDAM. (2010). *SWGDAM interpretation guidelines for autosomal STR typing by forensic DNA testing laboratories.* Available at http://www.swgdam.org. Accessed April 4, 2014.

Taylor, D. A., et al. (2013). The interpretation of single source and mixed DNA profiles. *Forensic Science International Genetics, 7*(5), 516–528.

Word, C. (2014). *Profile Interpretation Worksheet.* Available at http://www.cstl.nist.gov/strbase/training/INTERPRETATION-WORKSHEET-Example.doc. Accessed April 4, 2014.

Index

Note: Page numbers followed by f indicate figures; t, tables; b, boxes.